HOLY WAR

KAREN ARMSTRONG
HOLY WAR

M
MACMILLAN
LONDON

First published 1988 by
MACMILLAN LONDON LIMITED
4 Little Essex Street London WC2R 3LF
and Basingstoke

Associated companies in Auckland, Delhi, Dublin, Gaborone,
Hamburg, Harare, Hong Hong, Johannesburg, Kuala Lumpur,
Lagos, Manzini, Melbourne, Mexico City, Nairobi, New York,
Singapore and Tokyo

British Library Cataloguing in Publication Data

Armstrong, Karen
Holy war: the crusades and their impact on today's world.
1. Jihad   2. Middle East—Politics
and government
I. Title
297'.72'0956   BP182

ISBN 0–333–44544–9

Designed by Robert Updegraff
Picture research by Juliet Brightmore
Drawings by Chris Evans
Maps by Hilary Evans

Typeset by Bookworm Typesetting, Manchester
Printed in Hong Kong

Contents

For my dear friends Abdul Halim Zoabe of Nazareth, his Jewish–Israeli wife, Anat, and their sons Salah Adam and Nizar Amir, who by making me a member of their family have been a crucial influence in my developing the 'triple vision' that I have tried to articulate in this book.

Acknowledgements

Matching a filming and a publishing schedule together is not easy and I am very grateful for the patient and encouraging support I have received while I have been writing this book. First I must thank both my editors, Kyle Cathie of Macmillan and Loretta Young of Doubleday, for keeping faith so staunchly. Kyle in particular, as the editor on the spot, I thank most sincerely for her calm but absolutely unshakeable conviction that all ultimately would be well, which has been of enormous help to me. I must also thank Kate Jones for her truly excellent work on the manuscript: her inspired and brilliant suggestions made the final editing not only exciting but also a great joy. Juliet Brightmore, who did the picture research, deserves special thanks. She was working with a most inadequate early draft but cheerfully and determinedly fought her way through to an understanding of what I was trying to say, and her imaginative work has added a most important dimension to the book. Finally, I must thank Robert Updegraff for his imaginative work on the design of the book and for his constant and cheering encouragement.

Amnon Teitelbaum, the director of the television series *Holy War*, had the original germ of the idea, which has developed so much since our early discussions. We have had three extraordinary years together working on the film and I thank him for his friendship, his absolute loyalty in some very difficult circumstances and for his stimulating and challenging ideas, which have been very helpful to me in forming my own. Without his warmth, imagination and wit I doubt whether I should have got through. I also thank Erel Pardo, the production manager, for his support and calm determination in battling with ambassadors of impending destruction. I have very fond memories of the marvellous locations tour I made with him and Amnon, in which Erel, the only driver among us, had to drive thousands of miles and showed all the grit of a Crusader during this gruelling task. Finally I thank the Israeli film crew for their company, their sympathy and even their love. At exhausting moments during the shooting their unspoken support was almost a tangible force and a real charge. We also had a great deal of fun together, which I shall always remember happily. Their commitment never wavered, even when I was saying things to camera that were critical of Israel and Zionism. Indeed, some of them urged me on and I would like to think of our work together as part of the peace process.

John Ranelagh, who commissioned the series, also deserves great thanks for his support. I thank him too for his encouragement and help during his years at Channel 4.

Writing is always an isolated task, but this time the peculiarly painful nature of my subject as well as the practical pressures made the writing of this book a peculiarly lonely experience. I have not always been easy to live with and the scheduling difficulties meant that I have had to withdraw from normal social life, so I do thank those people who stood on the sidelines and cheered me on from afar: Eileen Armstrong, my mother; Sally Cockburn; R. M. Lamming; Jenny and Tom MacDonnel; Graeme Segal; Juliet Solomon; Lorraine and Robert Tollemache; Jeremy Woodhead; and the Zoabe family, to whom this book is dedicated. I thank them all for their friendship and loyalty.

Karen Armstrong

Introduction

Those of us who are not medieval historians tend, I think, to have rather vague and confused ideas about the Crusades, if indeed we give those distant holy wars any thought at all. Certainly until a few years ago, my own thoughts on the Crusades had advanced little beyond a hazy recollection of what I had learned at school. On the one hand the Crusades were linked with the age of chivalry and with heroes like Richard the Lionheart, and they seemed glamorous, exotic and rather dashing events. On the other hand, I knew that during these holy wars Christians had shed a good deal of Muslim blood and this seemed monstrous, wicked and perverse. I assumed that in our more enlightened age we had advanced beyond such cruel barbarity, although I did notice how frequently we used the word 'crusade' in a positive context. We frequently talk about crusades against poverty or injustice and praise a 'crusading journalist', who is bravely uncovering some salutary truth. Could it be that, however we might condemn the medieval holy wars, the idea of a crusade had found acceptance at some level in our minds?

In the television series that accompanies this book, we showed some of the festivals and medieval tournaments that take place every year, all over Europe, commemorating the Crusades. Hundreds of people spend a good deal of time and money rehearsing events that happened nearly a thousand years ago. There are even some men in England and Germany who have become modern knights, and have learned the difficult medieval art of jousting. They have taken great trouble to reproduce the costumes accurately and to ride their horses in exactly the same way as a Crusader would have done. Obviously the Crusades and medieval warfare are still fascinating events for all the people who take part in these festivals and for the thousands who turn out to watch them. But there is naturally a certain artificiality and a domestic quality to these depictions of medieval violence. They bear no relation at all to the grim reality of a Crusade, in which hordes of people tramped thousands of miles through alien, dangerous territory, dying like flies of starvation and disease. The modern 'knights' who tilt at the dummy model of a 'Saracen' in a festival in no way represent the murderous violence of the Crusaders when they butchered Muslims and Jews in Jerusalem in the name of God. We seem to have cut the Christian holy wars down to manageable size and to have drained them of their horror. It would probably never occur to any of the people watching those festivals to link the Crusades with the deadly conflict in the Middle East today.

My own interest in the Crusades dates back to 1983, when I spent some months in Israel researching and making another television series for Channel 4 with an Israeli film company. For the first time the Arab–Israeli conflict became an immediate reality to me. Until that time I had been shocked by Palestinian terrorism and by Israeli brutality in the Lebanon, but had felt that this tragic violence had nothing to do with me. In Israel, however, I met Israelis and Palestinians who have remained among my very closest friends. As I heard them passionately arguing their own case against the 'other side', I found myself involved, and was struck for the first time by the complexity and pain of the issues. But I also found that, even though everybody was very warm and welcoming to me personally, I was constantly having to listen to violent diatribes against 'the British' by my Arab and Israeli friends. This was very disturbing. I could see that their portrait of the British national character was a distorted stereotype, but it was implicitly believed as self-evident truth. People did not want to argue rationally with me about it. It was a strong emotional conviction that seemed necessary to their view of the world. Clearly we British had hurt Arabs and Jews at a fundamental level, and we were still somehow deeply implicated in their present dilemma. We seemed bound together in a three-sided relationship of pain.

I was also very surprised at the strength of my own reactions to the country which I had been brought up to call the 'Holy Land'. Even though I was no longer a believing and practising Christian, I found it very moving to be living and working in Jerusalem, a city which had been imaginatively and emotionally present to me since I was a small child. The film we were making was about early Christianity and that meant that I was also having to consider the Jewish roots of the Christian faith. Naturally we spent some time filming at the Wailing Wall, which is the only remaining relic of the ancient Jewish Temple. There Judaism became a reality to me for the first time. I was moved to see the passion and fervour with which Jewish pilgrims kissed the stones of the Wall and astonished to see tough young Israeli soldiers, carrying heavy submachine guns, binding their *tfillin* to their foreheads and swaying devoutly in prayer. I had been brought up to see Judaism as a superseded religion, and even though I later realised that this was a Christian distortion, I had still never really considered Judaism as anything but a prelude to Christianity. Now I saw its immense emotional power, something quite independent of my Christian vision of the world. Further, I could not quite imagine British soldiers praying so devoutly and openly, but in Jerusalem religion seemed to be in the very air and stones.

Yet there was another fact to be absorbed. When I looked up above the Wailing Wall, I saw the great mosques of the Dome of the Rock of al-Aqsa and was told that Jerusalem is the third most holy city in the Islamic world. I had, of course, realised that Islam was one of the great world religions, but I now found that to my shame I knew next to nothing about it. In my free time I went to visit the mosques and again was struck by the fervour of the Muslims praying there. I was surprised to find myself deeply drawn to the spirituality of al-Aqsa, with its great space and silences. In the Dome of the Rock I saw the rock upon which Abraham was supposed to have bound Isaac to sacrifice him to God and I was told that the Jews had deliberately built their Temple on the site of Abraham's sacrifice. Later I myself had to film in the Holy Sepulchre Church on the spot which Christians traditionally believed marked the centre of the world and which is also venerated as the site of Christ's sacrifice on the Cross. Behind me on the wall was a huge mosaic depicting Isaac's sacrifice, and I had to talk about the importance and significance of Abraham in the Christian world. I remembered the Dome of the Rock and realised for the first time how deeply related the three religions of Judaism, Christianity and Islam really were, for all their differences. I wondered why, in that case, I had never given Islam any serious consideration.

Finally there was the fact of the Holy Sepulchre Church itself, much of which had been built by the Crusaders, who had declared war upon Islam in order to liberate the tomb of Christ. Obviously Europeans had not always been so indifferent to Muslims! Further, I found that while it was quite possible to get through life in England without giving the Crusades a thought, this was simply not possible in Israel. Wherever you travel in that tiny country, which is about the size of Wales, you constantly find churches and whole cities built by the Crusaders, who had a state in the Holy Land for nearly 200 years. I was particularly intrigued by their massive castles and fortresses. It seemed that the Crusader Kingdom of Jerusalem was just as worried about national security as the State of Israel today and for much the same reasons. Like Israel it was a Western state planted in a hostile Islamic world, and it did not survive despite its powerful military defence. It is no wonder that crusading studies flourish in the Hebrew University of Jerusalem. I spent some time talking about the Crusades with Amnon Teitelbaum, my Israeli director, who was planning a new documentary series about the Crusades and the modern Middle East conflict, and I was naturally delighted when he and Channel 4 invited me to present it and to write the scripts, because it would give me a chance to go more deeply into these fascinating but important questions. I expected to find some similarities and analogies between the medieval and the modern situation but during the years that I have spent researching the series and this book I have discovered that the connections are deeper. I am now convinced that the Crusades were one of the direct causes of the conflict in the Middle East today.

I know that this is a startling statement and I welcome the opportunity presented by this book to explore it more deeply than is possible in a six-hour film. In the film, which is still far from complete at the time of writing, we have only hinted at and suggested connections between medieval and modern, in a way that suits the visual medium and which yet leaves the viewer free to draw his own conclusions. In a book, a more clearly articulated argument is necessary and I have had the time and space to explore aspects of the modern conflict in a way that was not possible in the television series. This does not mean that the book will be coldly rational. I am telling a very emotional story, in which people are continually driven to an extremity where reason and logic no longer apply. I am also aware that I sometimes argue very vehemently; I am vehement because since my first visits to Israel in 1983 I have come to feel very passionate about the relation between the Christian West and Judaism and Islam, which have been locked in a murderous triangle of hatred and intolerance ever since the Crusades.

What I am arguing for is a triple vision. Usually when we strive to be objective we say that we want to see 'both' sides of the question. In this long conflict, however, there are three. At each point I shall try to consider the position and point of view of Jews, Christians and Muslims – the three religions of Abraham. Since the Crusades, all three have been implicated in different ways in the holy wars between them. The greatest tragedies and atrocities have occurred when one tradition considers itself so pre-eminent that it seeks to eliminate the other two, or when two of the traditions have joined forces, and have completely ignored the third. In the Middle East one becomes acutely conscious of the strong connection between all three religions, and also, perhaps for that very reason, of their great alienation from one another. I realise that my argument may seem complex, but I hope that the reader will bear with me because I have found that, once you have mastered this habit of triple vision, you can never see things in quite the same way again. It has radically altered my view of the Middle East conflict and has also given me new perceptions about the mechanics of prejudice.

It is triple vision that makes this book rather different from other books about the Crusades. I am not a professional historian and I am certainly not attempting to rival the medievalists who have devoted their lives to a study of the Crusades. Quite the contrary: I am entirely dependent upon them. I acknowledge a great debt to Sir Steven Runciman, the father of crusading studies in this country, and I have also been particularly inspired by Professor Jonathan Riley-Smith's insight into the aspirations and beliefs of the Christian Crusaders, who truly saw their holy wars as a religious experience. I have also been indebted to Norman Daniel, Francesco Gabrieli and Amin Maalouf for their work on the Muslim point of view. Other writers like Schlomo Eidelberg have concentrated on the Jews' position during the Crusades. What I have attempted to do is bring the work of all these scholars together, so that we see in more detail, perhaps, than usual a three-sided picture of

Christians, Muslims and Jews engaged in a deadly conflict. In much the same way, in the modern period we have an inevitable polarisation of interest. I cannot hope to rival Amos Elon's and Amos Oz's compelling accounts of the strange history and deep dilemmas of Zionism and the State of Israel. Nor will I equal the wide-ranging scholarship of Roy Mottahedeh whose book *The Mantle of the Prophet* gives such a lucid account of the beauty of Iranian Shiism nor the passionate erudition of Edward W. Said in *Orientalism: Western Conceptions of the Orient*, in which he traces the history of Western hostility to the East. I have needed the insights of these and many other writers and scholars. Again, I have attempted to consider the Jewish case alongside the Arab and the Muslim and – most important – to include the contribution made by the Christian West in today's conflict. In order to develop a clear knowledge of any tradition, it is obviously important for scholars to isolate and examine things separately. Sometimes, however, it is important to put things back together again.

My own training has been in theology and in literature and this means that my book on the Crusades is bound to be different from the book of a professional historian, but I think that my particular disciplines are especially appropriate to the subject. Theology and literature both teach one to connect the like with the unlike and to see that this can make a new truth. Both disciplines provide an alternative to a purely rational view of the world and both are concerned with mythology: they take fiction very seriously indeed. Literature in particular teaches us the power of emotion as a force in the world and shows that our thoughts are never entirely cerebral. The Crusades, like so much of the modern conflict, were not wholly rational movements that could be explained away by purely economic or territorial ambition or by a clash of rights and interests. They were fuelled, on all sides, by myths and passion that were far more effective in getting people to act than any purely political motivation. The medieval holy wars in the Middle East could not be solved by rational treaties or neat territorial solutions. Fundamental passions were involved which touched the identity of Christians, Muslims and Jews and which were sacred to the identity of each. They have not changed very much in the holy wars of today.

I shall not be dwelling on weaponry or on the economic or military aspects of the holy wars, medieval and modern. This is a history of myths, emotions and religious passions that were tied to practical, violent policies. Because I want to develop this triple vision, I have not discussed the holy wars being fought in Northern Ireland or South America today. I am concentrating on a long struggle between Jews, Christians and Muslims that began over a thousand years ago and has led to tragic and catastrophic events in our own century.

This has been a stressful and painful book to write. It is hard to have one's old prejudices shattered and it is distressing to examine the sins of one's own culture. It is particularly difficult to enter into another culture – it might even be impossible to do so. Certainly I have tried to enter into the minds of the Crusaders, so that we can understand what they thought they were doing when they slaughtered Muslims and Jews as an act of the love of God. I have also tried to come to a greater understanding of Judaism and Islam. It has been difficult to shed my Christian-formed notions of religion and I hope that Jews and Muslims will forgive any mistakes that I have made. The journey towards understanding and peace will take all of us a long time.

Author's Note

I shall have to use rather technical terms sometimes, some of them Hebrew or Arabic words. To help the reader I have compiled a Glossary at the end of the book, but these preliminary terms might be useful at the outset.

Eretz Yisrael (Hebrew). The Land of Israel. This is a vital concept in the ideology of the Jewish holy war, which centres on the land that God promised to Abraham and to his descendants, the Jewish people. Abraham's grandson Jacob had his name changed to Israel, as a sign of God's special favour. Jacob had twelve sons, who were all born in the Promised Land, but who later emigrated to Egypt during a famine. These twelve sons of Jacob founded the twelve tribes of Israel and when Moses and Joshua led the tribes back to the Promised Land and established the children of Israel there, each tribe lived in a specially designated area in the Land of Israel. Jews regard Eretz Yisrael, therefore, as the land of their fathers, and religious Jews from the time of Joshua until the present day believe that their right to return there is authorised by God.

Crusade (from the French *croix*: cross). The term did not become common to describe the Christians who fought a holy war for the Holy Land until relatively late in the movement. As we shall see, the Crusaders usually called themselves 'pilgrims'. But from the start they were associated with the Cross. They sewed crosses on their clothes and felt that they were literally obeying Christ's command to his followers to take up their cross and follow him to death, if necessary. At the time of the First Crusade, people from England who came to France to join one of the crusading armies there but who did not know a word of French were able to show that they were Crusaders by making a cross of their fingers, and so received directions and help. The Cross and the Crucifixion were central to the movement from the beginning. The Crusaders were going to liberate the Church of the Holy Sepulchre, which they believed contained the site of Golgotha and the tomb of Christ, but which was at that time in the hands of the Muslims.

Jihad (Arabic). The word literally means 'struggle' and is used in the Koran (the sacred book of Islam) usually as a verb: Muslims are urged 'to struggle mightily in the way of God'. The idea of struggle and achievement are crucial in Islam and the word *jihad* has always retained this connotation. But most frequently the 'struggle' referred to is the war Mohammad was forced to wage against the non-Muslim Arabs of Arabia. Later, by extension, it came to mean 'holy war' and in that sense is discussed in the *Sharia* (Islamic law) in the century after Mohammad's death.

Maps

The Islamic Empire by 750

Frontiers
Routes of advance

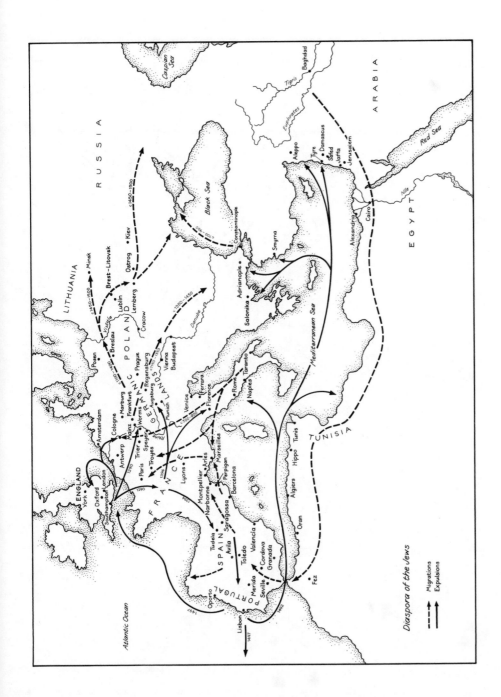

Diaspora of the Jews

Migrations
Expulsions

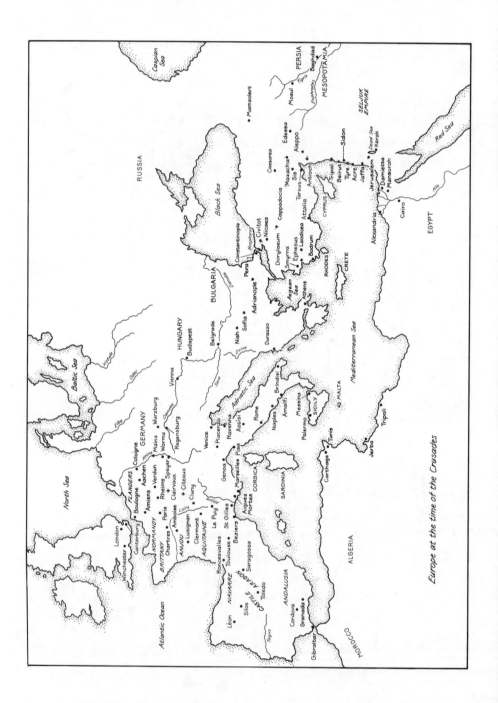

Europe at the time of the Crusades

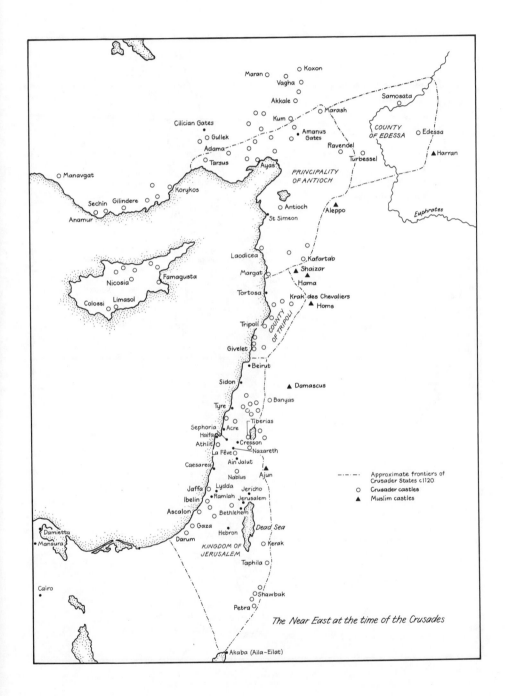

Maran ○   ○ Koxon
Vagha ○
Akkale ○   Samosata ○
Cilician Gates   ○ Marash
○ Gullek   Kum ○   COUNTY
Adama ○   Amanus   OF EDESSA   ○ Edessa
Gates   Ravendel
Tarsus ○   Ayas ○   Turbessel ▲ Harran
○ Manavgat   PRINCIPALITY
OF ANTIOCH
Sechin Gilindere   Korykos
Anamur ○   ○ Antioch   Euphrates
St Simeon   ○ Aleppo

Laodicea ○   ○ Kafartab
Margat ○   ▲ Shaizar
Nicosia   Famagusta   ▲ Hama
Tortosa ○   Krak des Chevaliers
Colossi   Limasol   ▲ Homs
Tripoli ○   COUNTY OF TRIPOLI
Givelet ○
● Beirut
Sidon ○   ▲ Damascus
Tyre ○   ○ Banyas
Sephoria ○ Acre   Tiberias
Haifa   Cresson
Athlit ○   Nazareth
La Fève
Caesarea ○   Ain Jalut   ▲ Ajun
Nablus
Jaffa ○   Lydda   Jericho   —·—· Approximate frontiers of
Ibelin   Ramlah Jerusalem   Crusader States c1120
Ascalon ○   Bethlehem   ○ Crusader castles
Gaza ○   Hebron   Dead Sea   ▲ Muslim castles
Damietta ○   Darum   Kerak ○
● Mansura   KINGDOM OF   Taphila ○
JERUSALEM
○ Cairo   ○ Shawbak
Petra ○

The Near East at the time of the Crusades

Akaba (Aila-Eilat)

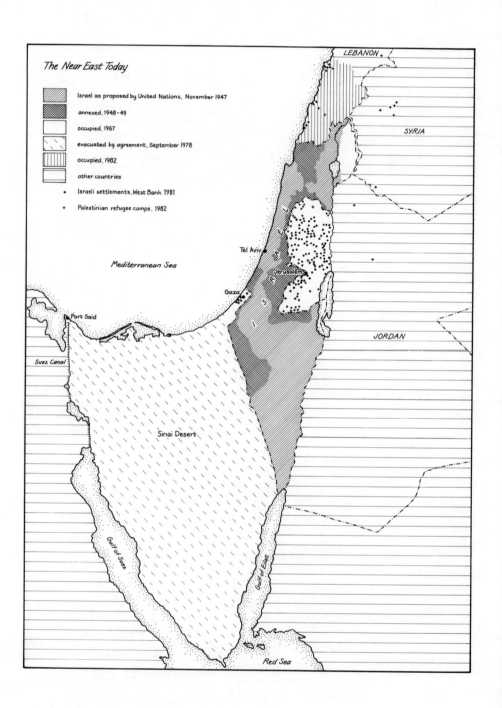

The Near East Today

- Israel as proposed by United Nations, November 1947
- annexed, 1948-49
- occupied, 1967
- evacuated by agreement, September 1978
- occupied, 1982
- other countries
- • Israeli settlements, West Bank 1981
- + Palestinian refugee camps, 1982

LEBANON

SYRIA

Mediterranean Sea

Tel Aviv

Jerusalem

Gaza

Port Said

Suez Canal

JORDAN

Sinai Desert

Gulf of Suez

Gulf of Eilat

Red Sea

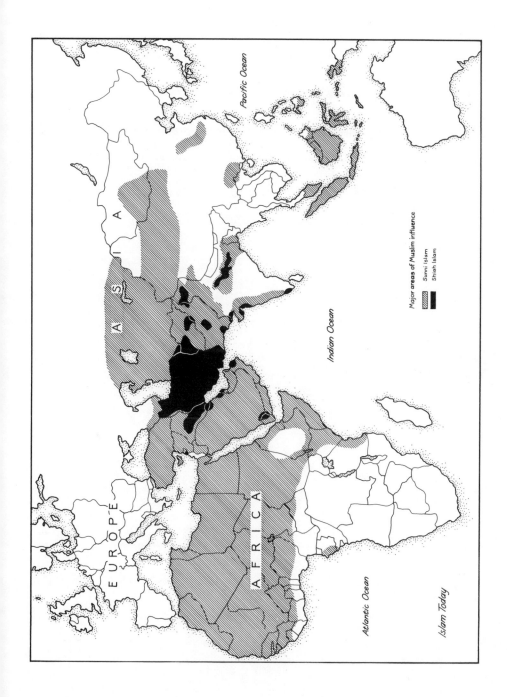

Islam Today

Major areas of Muslim influence
Sunni Islam
Shiah Islam

EUROPE

ASIA

AFRICA

Pacific Ocean

Indian Ocean

Atlantic Ocean

PART ONE

Journey to a New Self

In the Beginning

there was the Holy War. Why?

On 25 November 1095, at the Council of Clermont, Pope Urban II summoned the First Crusade. For Western Europe it was a crucial and formative event and it is having repercussions today in the Middle East. Addressing a vast crowd of priests, knights and poor people, Urban called for a holy war against Islam. The Seljuk Turks, he explained, a barbarian race from Central Asia who had recently become Muslims, had swept into Anatolia in Asia Minor (modern Turkey) and had seized these lands from the Christian empire of Byzantium. The Pope urged the knights of Europe to stop fighting each other and to make common cause against these enemies of God. The Turks, he cried, are 'an accursed race, a race utterly alienated from God, a generation, forsooth, which has neither directed its heart nor entrusted its spirit to God'.[1] Killing these Godless monsters was a holy act: it was a Christian duty to 'exterminate this vile race from our lands'.[2] Once they had purged Asia Minor of this Muslim filth, the knights would engage in a still more holy task. They would march to the Holy City of Jerusalem and liberate it from the infidel. It was shameful that the tomb of Christ should be in the hands of Islam.

There was an extraordinary response to Urban's appeal. Popular preachers like Peter the Hermit spread the news of the Crusade and in the spring of 1096 five armies of about 60,000 soldiers accompanied by a horde of non-combatant pilgrims with their wives and families set off to the East. They were followed in the autumn by five more armies of about 100,000 men and a crowd of priests and pilgrims. The numbers were astounding for this time.[3] As the first armies approached the Byzantine capital of Constantinople, it seemed to the appalled but fascinated Princess Anna Comnena as though 'the whole West, and as much of the land as lies beyond the Adriatic Sea to the Pillars of Hercules [Gibraltar] – all this, changing its seat, was bursting forth into Asia in a solid mass, with all its belongings.'[4] To the sophisticated Byzantines it looked like a great barbarian invasion, similar to those which had destroyed the Roman empire in Europe. The West was invading the East for the first time in the modern period, filled with the aggressive righteousness of a holy war, a righteousness that would characterise its future dealings with the Orient. This Crusade was the first co-operative act of the new Europe as she crawled out of the Dark Ages. It appealed to all classes of society: to popes, kings, aristocrats, priests, soldiers and peasants. People sold all they had to equip themselves for this long and dangerous expedition, and for the most part they were not inspired by lust for material gain. They were gripped by a religious passion. They sewed crosses on their clothes and marched to the land where Jesus had died to save the world. It was a devotional pilgrimage at the same time as it was a war of extermination.

Clearly crusading answered a deep need in the Christians of Europe. Yet today most of us would unhesitatingly condemn the Crusades as wicked and unChristian. After all, Jesus had told his followers to love their enemies, not to exterminate them. He was a pacifist and had more in common with Gandhi, perhaps, than with Pope Urban. Yet I would argue that the holy war is a deeply Christian act. Like Judaism and Islam, Christianity had an inherent leaning towards violence, despite the pacifism of Jesus. All three religions are historically and theologically related and all worship the same God. All three traditions are dedicated in some way to love and benevolence and yet all three have developed a pattern of holy war and violence that is remarkably similar and which seems to surface from some deep compulsion that is inherent in this tradition of monotheism, the worship of only one God. The pattern is as regular as a Jungian archetype. For over a thousand years European Christians tried to hold out against this violent tendency and to keep Christianity a religion of love and peace, yet when Pope Urban called the Crusade they responded with a sigh of relief and reproduced the pattern of holy war with an uncanny accuracy. It is as though they felt that at last they were doing what came naturally. In order to understand the Crusades, therefore, as well as the holy wars of today, we need to examine this pattern of violence and try to discover why each of the three religions felt that they needed a holy war.

In about 1850 BCE a man called Abram left his home in Ur of the Chaldees and journeyed to the land of Canaan, the modern Israel. He had been summoned to emigrate by a Divine Being who revealed that he had decided to be the special God of Abram and his offspring. Abram should change his name to Abraham as a sign of his new status, and should make a covenant agreement with God, who in return would bless him and his descendants. The children of Abraham would become a great people and God promised that he would give them the land of Canaan. This event, as it was told centuries later in the Bible,[5] changed the world. It is not only the Jews, Abraham's physical descendants, who see this as the beginning of their history – Christians and Muslims also regard themselves as children of Abraham, as we shall see later in this chapter. Christians and Muslims have persecuted or fought holy wars against Jews at different times in their history, but both claim the Jewish past as their own and see themselves as the recipients of the promises God made to the Jews. This revelation to Abraham was a revolution in the history of religion. Gradually the Jews came to realise that their God was not just one God among many. He was the *only* God and all other 'gods' were just human inventions. This was an extraordinary idea in the pagan world, where people worshipped many gods and had developed some religions of great power and beauty. The Jews themselves were often unable to believe that there truly was only one God and often lapsed naturally and easily into paganism, but eventually monotheism, the worship of only One God, was firmly established in Judaism, and later in Christianity and Islam, the two religions that derived from Judaism. These three religions are all deeply related, yet at different times they have fought each other in savage holy wars. The seed of much future strife is found in the original revelation to Abraham. Almost the first words that God spoke when he revealed himself to Abram were: 'To your descendants I will give this land' (Genesis 12:7). To make this promise good Abraham's descendants had to fight the first of many savage holy wars for this land, which many Jews today still see as essential to the integrity of Judaism. After all, God spent more time promising Abraham that he would give this land to his descendants than making any further theological revelations about himself. The Holy Land will be a key factor in our story.

Jews, Christians and Muslims all believe that God has revealed himself by intervening directly in human affairs in events that become a history of salvation. One of the most crucial of these events was the Exodus, the mythical story of the

Jews' liberation from slavery. The Israelites, Abraham's descendants, had emigrated to Egypt in about 1700 BCE. Their position there deteriorated so much that by 1250 they were mere slaves. Then God intervened. He told his prophet Moses that he had to act and save his people; he must force Pharaoh to let the Israelites go free and then lead them home to the Promised Land of Canaan. Moses was very reluctant to do this, because it seemed a hopeless task, but God promised to help him. He terrorised the Egyptians by sending cruel plagues, and when Pharaoh remained obdurate in his refusal to free the Hebrew slaves, God sent the most terrible plague of all. The Angel of Death passed over the houses of the Jews and killed the first-born son in every Egyptian family. Every year Jews celebrate this saving event in the feast of Passover, for it was a graphic demonstration of their status as the chosen people: God had drastically discriminated between themselves and the Egyptians. After this catastrophe, Pharaoh decided to let the Israelites go and Moses led his people out of Egypt. But, before they had got very far, Pharaoh changed his mind. He and his army pursued the Jews and caught up with them at the Reed Sea (usually misleadingly translated Red Sea).[6] It seemed that the Israelites would be herded back to slavery or even exterminated, but God intervened once more. He parted the waters of the sea so that his people could cross dry-shod, but drowned the whole Egyptian army when they tried to follow them. This story of violent miracles was obviously a mythical version of the Hebrews' escape from Egypt, but the myth was crucial in forming the Jews' view of themselves. It shows what is involved in their view of salvation. God's people have to act to save themselves, even though their position seems hopeless or dangerous. God will always help them in miracles that suspend the normal course of nature, and the salvation of the chosen people means the annihilation of their enemies as two sides to a single coin. Salvation is the violent separation of the just and the unjust. The next stage in the story of the Exodus reveals the archetypal paradigm that has recurred in all three of the monotheistic religions, when a holy journey or a migration becomes a holy war.

The Israelites were now an independent people, but their salvation was not yet complete. They were still only a collection of tribes who had been unused to controlling their own destiny and they had to learn how they were to live as God's chosen people. They did not journey directly to the Promised Land, but for forty years they lived as nomads in the Sinai peninsula. It was a holy journey during which the Bible tells us that they were deeply dependent upon God, who fed them with manna and guided them step by step. Most importantly, on Mount Sinai God gave Moses the Ten Commandments, the basis of the Torah or the Law.[7] This was God's greatest gift to his people, because it imposed the divine order on the world and was a revelation of God's will. By observing the 613 commandments of the Torah, which governed the smallest details of everyday life, the Jews naturally acquired a unique identity, which they believed to have been directly inspired and shaped by God. Throughout their history, Jews have revered and studied the Torah, which they believe that God gave to Moses during the forty years in the wilderness. That this formation of a new Jewish self should have begun during a journey was significant. Travelling and migration are evocative symbols of spiritual passage. The Israelites were travelling away from shame and oppression to dignity and freedom, from desolation to intimacy with God, from helplessness to self-determination. Journeys and migrations have also been crucial and formative events for Christians and Muslims.

One of the Ten Commandments given to Moses on Mount Sinai was 'Thou shalt not kill.' Indeed most of these commandments are concerned with an absolute respect for the inalienable rights of others, and this is one of the greatest legacies of Judaism to the rest of the world. But, as they prepared to enter the Promised Land,

God told his people that they would have to engage in a ruthless war of extermination. By taking his people back to Canaan, Moses was taking them back to their roots because of God's original promise to their father Abraham. They believed that the land was theirs, but there were other people living there already who had made it their home for centuries, and naturally they were not going to hand over their country without a fight. These people were in the way of the divine plan; they were also essential enemies of the new Jewish self. Because they opposed values and plans that were 'sacred' to the Jews and essential to God's plans for them, they had to be annihilated. The normal human rights that Jews were commanded to extend to other people did not apply to the Canaanites, who had become the enemies of God. This absolute hostility is a characteristic of the holy war. Because the Canaanites were obstacles to Jewish fulfilment they had to be exterminated and there was no possibility of peaceful coexistence. 'I shall exterminate these,' God told his people, 'they must not live in your country' (Exodus 23:23, 33). It was not simply a territorial matter. The Canaanites had achieved a more advanced culture than the Israelites and their lifestyle would be very attractive to the weary nomads. They could destroy this newly emerging Jewish self and the new religion of monotheism, which was still so revolutionary that it was a fragile plant. The Israelites could very easily be seduced by the Canaanites' fertility cults and idolatrous faith. Therefore God gave Moses very clear instructions, frequently repeated in the Bible, about how these new enemies and their religions were to be treated:

> When Yahweh your God has led you into the land you are entering to make your own, many nations will fall before you: Hittites, Girgashites, Amorites, Canaanites, Perizzites, Hivites and Jebusites, seven nations greater and stronger than yourselves. Yahweh your God will deliver them over to you and you will conquer them. You must lay them under a ban. You must make no covenant with them nor show them any pity. You must not marry with them: you must not give a daughter of yours to a son of theirs, nor take a daughter of theirs for a son of yours, for this would turn away your son from following me to serving other gods, and the anger of Yahweh would blaze out against you and soon destroy you. Instead, deal with them like this: tear down their altars, smash their standing stones, cut down their sacred poles and set fire to their idols. For you are a people consecrated to Yahweh your God. It is you that Yahweh our God has chosen to be his very own people out of all the peoples on the earth.
>
> (Deuteronomy 7:1–6)

In a Jewish holy war, there was no question of peaceful coexistence, mutual respect or peace treaties. The little Jewish kingdom was an island of true religion in the ocean of Middle Eastern paganism. There was a religious siege and naturally a deep insecurity. Until the Israelites felt more confident, they could only fight their enemies to the death. When God had saved his people from the Egyptians the ordinary laws of nature had been suspended; so too when the Jews had to establish themselves in the Promised Land, ordinary morality ceased to apply. This is a crucial element in the holy wars of both Jews and, later, Christians.

Moses died before reaching the Promised Land. It was Joshua who in about 1200 BCE led the Israelites into Canaan and established the twelve tribes of Israel in the Promised Land by means of a long and utterly ruthless military campaign. He fulfilled the commands of God perfectly. When a town was conquered, it was duly put 'under a ban', which meant total destruction and extermination. Men, women, children and even the animals were massacred and the cities reduced to rubble:

> When Israel finished killing all the inhabitants of Ai in the open ground and where they had followed them into the wilderness, and when all to a man had

fallen by the edge of the sword, all Israel returned to Ai and slaughtered all its people. The number of those that fell that day, men and women together, was twelve thousand, all people of Ai.... Then Joshua burned Ai, making it a ruin for evermore, a desolate place even to this day.   (Joshua 8:24, 25, 28)

Then Joshua came and wiped out the Anakim from the highlands, from Hebron, from Debir, from Anab, from all the highlands of Judah and all the inhabitants of Israel; he delivered them and their towns over to the ban. No more Anakim were left in Israelite territory except at Gaza, Gath and Ashod.   (Ibid., 11:21, 22)

The holy war continued for another 200 years, under the Judges and heroes of Israel like Gideon, Deborah and Samson. As they exterminated their foes, the Israelites also tried to build up their own faith. As the pagan towns and shrines were destroyed, temples to Yahweh were built at Shiloh, Dan, Bethel, Bethlehem and Hebron.

A turning point in the holy campaign was King David's conquest of the Jebusite city of Jerusalem in about 1000 BCE. From this point Jerusalem, the 'City of David', would be consecrated to the One God, and because of this originally Jewish occupation the city would later become holy to Christians and Muslims too. Jerusalem will be crucial in our story. But it is important to notice that it did not become 'holy' to the Jews until quite late in its own history and in the history of the chosen people, even though the Jews would later see it as essential to the integrity of Judaism. It is also true that its sanctification had certain ironies. David departed from Joshuan practice when he conquered Jerusalem. He did not massacre the Jebusites, though he had shown no squeamishness about massacring *goyim* or the non-Jews in their hundreds elsewhere. It seems that he wanted to make the Jebusites his own personal followers, whose loyalty was assured because their survival depended totally upon him. Jews were beginning to feel more confident and able to exploit the people of Canaan instead of seeing them as absolute and therefore deeply disturbing enemies. David wanted to make Jerusalem the capital of his kingdom and the centre of Judaism, so he had the Ark of the Covenant, a precious relic of the years in the wilderness, brought into the city in triumph. He then wondered whether he should build a temple for the Ark, which in some mysterious way localised the Presence of God (the *Shekinah*). But God forbade David to build a temple in Jerusalem and there are two versions of this story. In one version God said that he had always been a nomadic God who had never been associated with one particular shrine.[8] It may be that David, a passionately religious man, realised the danger of identifying the *Shekinah* with one temple, built by human hands. It could lead to an idolatry, which lifted an earthly place and a human building to the same level as God himself. In a later version, God forbade David to build the Temple because he had shed too much blood, albeit at the divine command.[9] This shows the first sign of worry about the morality of the holy war. In this version, God tells David that the building of the Temple has been assigned to his son Solomon, the man of peace. (The name Solomon comes from *shalom*, the Hebrew word for peace.) .

Solomon did indeed build a temple. This man of peace was in a very different position from his predecessors. The Kingdom of David had been torn apart internally and had modest borders, but Solomon established a strong state with significantly broader frontiers.[10] The new temple was just one aspect of a building project that was actually part of his war effort. Beside the Temple, which was a magnificent building, Solomon rebuilt the ancient towns of Hazor, Megiddo and Gezer, as military bases for his new chariot army. Thousands of labourers were conscripted into the building force as a form of national service. Like all

7

conscription it was fiercely resented, particularly as it lacked the dignity of military service and seemed to reduce the conscripts to the level of slaves. Was their position very different from the position of their fathers in Egypt, who had been forced to build Pharaoh's pyramids? There was, therefore, a rather dubious element in the building of the Temple from the very beginning. When the Temple was completed there was a further irony. When they entered this wonderful new building to pray in the Presence of the One God, the Israelites would have been inescapably reminded of the Canaanite cults that they had been told to destroy. When they entered the sanctuary, they would have seen an enormous basin called the 'molten sea' standing upon the figures of twelve brazen oxen. This was a giant bath for purification, but its imagery was identical with the Canaanite myth of Yam, the primeval waters. The tall free-standing pillars would have reminded them of the 'standing stones', the fertility symbols of Canaanite cults that they had been commanded to tear down. The whole building was designed like a typical Canaanite temple and, instead of expressing the pure monotheism of Moses, the Temple had strongly pagan elements.[11] It seems to have been part of Solomon's policy of assimilation with the surrounding culture. He had established himself as an all-powerful despot, like other Middle Eastern kings, although hitherto God and the prophets had insisted that this was an unJewish institution, for only God could command his people. Solomon also married foreign wives, which was anathema to the spirit of Judaism and directly opposed to God's specific instructions to Moses.[12] Solomon was a confident monarch and his empire was powerful and secure. He did not feel threatened by the surrounding paganism and felt that a degree of assimilation was acceptable in Yahwism. Violent and absolute rejection was unnecessary to a king who felt that the chosen people had reached a new era of security.

But such assimilation was dangerous. Solomon was a wise and religious man, but ultimately God condemned and punished him for this syncretism. How could the Jews retain their unique identity if they absorbed an alien culture? But later kings also flirted with paganism and assimilation, and the common people were fatally attracted to the pagan fertility cults of Canaan. When drought threatened their harvests, the Israelites found it natural to turn to the worship of Baal like their neighbours, who believed that they could manipulate their gods to force them to send rain. Prophets like Elias and Elijah demonstrated that this was a useless and unreligious attitude and waged a passionate war of words and violent deeds against this pervasive paganism.[13] The Temple of Solomon was not the only sanctuary in the Promised Land; the older temples continued to function and frequently the priests brought aspects of pagan worship into the rituals and liturgy of Yahwism. They were naturally influenced by the prevailing local religious climate and were not yet ready for the austere monotheism that the prophets and sages were developing. This religious strife in the Holy Land was paralleled by a political division. The northern tribes broke away from the southern kings in Jerusalem and formed their own kingdom which they called the Kingdom of Israel and which opposed the smaller Kingdom of Judah in the south. Never again would the Jews experience the unity and security they had known under Solomon. Further their independence was constantly threatened by powerful neighbours who were building mighty empires in the Middle East. Finally in the year 722 there was a catastrophe. The Kingdom of Israel was conquered by King Tiglath-Peleser III of Assyria. The ten northern tribes of Israel were deported, forced to assimilate and were, in religious terms, annihilated. These ten lost tribes disappeared from history for ever.

The Kingdom of Judah was naturally appalled by this tragedy and the kings of Jerusalem desperately sought to protect themselves from such a fate. Some of them, like Kings Ahaz and Manassah, thought that syncretism and assimilation were the answer, as many Jews have thought since. But in the year 622 King Josiah sought a religious answer to the problem of Jewish survival. While repair work was being done in the Temple, the high priest Hilkiah discovered an ancient manuscript. It may have been a manuscript of the whole of the Pentateuch or it may simply have been a manuscript of Deuteronomy that finished with the series of terrible curses that filled Josiah with horror, because they seemed already to have been partially fulfilled. The Lord had told Moses that occupation of the Holy Land depended upon a scrupulous observance of the Torah. If the Israelites disobeyed God they would lose their land:

> Just as Yahweh took delight in giving you prosperity and increase, so now he will take delight in bringing you to ruin and destruction. You will be torn from the land which you are entering to make your own. Yahweh will scatter you among all peoples, from one end of the earth to the other; there you will serve other gods of wood and stone that neither you nor your forefathers have known. Among these nations there will be no repose for you, no rest for the sole of your foot; Yahweh will give you a quaking heart, weary eyes, halting breath. Your life from the outset will be a burden to you; night and day you will go in fear, uncertain of your life. In the morning you will say, 'How I wish it were evening!' and in the evening 'How I wish it were morning!', such terror will grip your heart, such sights your eye will see. (Deuteronomy 28:63–7)

Millions of Jews in our own time have experienced the terror of exile. Josiah had already seen the ten tribes disappear and after reading this manuscript he felt that the only way for the Kingdom of Judah to survive was by a return to religion and an absolute rejection of syncretism.[14] He made the Jerusalem Temple the centre of this revival of the religion of Moses and Joshua and for the first time Jerusalem and the Temple became essential to the Jewish religious experience. Worship in the Temple now became obligatory for every Jew in Judaea. All the other shrines were destroyed and their priests were invited to serve in the Temple of Jerusalem, where they could be supervised to make sure that they were not bringing pagan practice into the pure religion of the Jews. On the great feast days all Jews were obliged to make a pilgrimage to Jerusalem and attend the sacrificial liturgy. Only in the Temple was it permissible henceforth to make a sacrifice to God. Pilgrimage, later to become an important practice in both Christianity and Islam, now became central to the Jewish faith and from the start it was linked with a new offensive against paganism, which seemed more threatening to the Jewish people than ever.

Josiah's reform can be said to be fundamentalist, because it was a return to ancient ideology, at the same time as it was innovatory. It was inspired by a fear of losing the Holy Land and saw the religion of Judaism as essentially linked to the physical occupation of the Land of Israel. This was a return to the religion of Abraham. But another view of Judaism was slowly emerging which was making the Jewish faith a religion of the heart. Prophets like Amos and Isaiah insisted that Temple sacrifice was not enough. A good Jew must take care of the poor and the needy; the Lord loved mercy and compassion more than sacrifice and pilgrimage to the Temple. In this view, external and liturgical conformity could not take the place of morality and justice.[15] The political outlook was bleak. The new Babylonian empire threatened to destroy the tiny Kingdom of Judah and the prophet Jeremiah foretold this ultimate disaster. Yet, despite his proverbial lamentations, Jeremiah also taught the Jews that the chosen people could still survive even in exile. Provided they remained faithful to the Torah and observed the covenant with Yahweh, God would still be their God as he had pledged to

Abraham.[16] In this prophetic view, Judaism did not depend upon the physical possession of the Holy Land.

The disaster struck in 589 BCE. Babylon destroyed Jerusalem and most of the inhabitants of Judaea were deported to Babylonia, leaving behind only a few peasants and poor people. The trauma of exile had entered the Jewish experience for the first time. During the exile in Babylon, Exile came to have rather the same connotations as the concept of Original Sin in Christianity.[17] Exile became a metaphor for sin, as well as a punishment. It meant a state of shameful weakness, of vulnerability unto death, apparent desertion by God and banishment from one's best self. In exile a Jew could not be what God had intended him to be: a member of a fiercely independent and autonomous people, 'set apart'[18] from all other nations in the Promised Land. Undoubtedly the exile to Babylon was traumatic, but very often trauma can lead to a new religious insight. These Jewish deportees did not disappear like the ten northern tribes. They were not forced to assimilate with the pagan population, but were permitted to live in separate Jewish communities, the first ghettos. Here they could still be 'set apart' and observe the commandments of the Torah. Some of the exiles lived in Babylon itself and others lived in a settlement on the banks of the Cheder in an area which they called Tel Aviv. In these communities Judaism came of age. When the people had been living independently in their own land, they had constantly been seduced by paganism. In exile, paganism lost its attraction for ever and the Jews learned a deeper level of religious commitment. A new individual element entered Jewish practice. Instead of renewing the covenant collectively and being herded along to the Temple for compulsory worship, the Jews of Babylon became personally responsible for their own religious life. Each Jew renewed his own covenant to Yahweh. He had to learn the Torah himself and absorb it into his heart and mind so that it became his own. Without the Temple, the Book became more important and study of the Torah and the Prophets led many of the exiles to a deeper understanding of monotheism and Judaism. Personal accountability has become a hallmark of Judaism and in exile the importance of the individual was emphasised in quite a new way.

But a minority group were unable to adapt fully to life in Babylon. All Jews certainly mourned the loss of Jerusalem, but to some Jerusalem had become more precious because of its loss. They felt quite a new hatred of the *goyim* who had made it impossible for them to live a full Jewish life:

> Beside the streams of Babylon
> we sat and wept
> at the memory of Zion
> leaving our harps
> hanging on the poplars there
>
> For we had been asked
> to sing to our captors,
> to entertain those who had carried us off:
> 'Sing,' they said
> 'some hymns of Zion.'
>
> How could we sing
> one of Yahweh's hymns
> in a pagan country?
> Jerusalem, if I forget you,
> may my right hand wither!

May I never speak again,
if I forget you!
If I do not count Jerusalem
the greatest of my joys!

Yahweh, remember
what the sons of Edom did
on the day of Jerusalem,
how they said, 'Down with her!
Raze her to the ground!'

Destructive Daughter of Babel,
A blessing on the man who treats you
as you have treated us,
a blessing on him who takes and dashes
your babies against the rock!

(Psalm 137)

This psalmist felt that the physical land of Israel was essential to his Jewish identity and because the Babylonians had destroyed Jerusalem it was as if they were destroying his Jewish self. The amoral vengeance he plans springs from a desperate insecurity.

Yet the new inner confidence felt by the majority led some Jews to wait hopefully for a return to Zion. In Babylon, the prophet Ezechiel and the anonymous prophet who is usually called the Second Isaiah promised the Jews that God would restore them to the Promised Land. They would return to Jerusalem, rebuild the Temple and build Tel Aviv again in the land of their fathers.[19] God had only wanted to punish the people for their sins, but he would reward their fidelity by a glorious return. The pre-exilic prophets had already begun to look forward to a day when the chosen people would rule the whole world in a new era of cosmic peace, when the wolf and the lamb could lie down together.[20] World dominion was a natural development of the Jews' belief in the One God and the idea has also been important in Christianity and Islam. If there is only one God, there can only be one solution for the world and this must lead to the triumph of the one true faith. The prophets in exile linked this final cosmic triumph with the return of the Jews to Jerusalem, which they often called Zion.[21] Not only would the Israelites rebuild Jerusalem, but they would also inaugurate a new era of peace and justice. All their former enemies would be forced to come to Jerusalem in a penitential pilgrimage to acknowledge Jewish sovereignty. The Second Isaiah called to Jerusalem:

Arise, shine out, for your light has come,
the glory of Yahweh is rising on you,
though night still covers the earth
and darkness the peoples.

Above you Yahweh now rises
and above you his glory appears.
The nations come to your light
and kings to your dawning brightness.

Lift up your eyes and look around:
all are assembling and coming towards you,
your sons from far away
and your daughters being tenderly carried.

And your gates will lie open continually,
shut neither by day nor by night,
for men to bring you the wealth of the nations
with their kings leading them;
for the nations and kingdom that refuses to serve you shall perish,
such nations shall be utterly ruined.
The glory of the Lebanon will come to you,
with cypress and plane and box,
to adorn the site of my sanctuary,
to glorify the resting place of my feet.

The sons of your oppressors will come to you bowing,
at your feet shall fall all who despised you.
They will call you 'City of Yahweh',
'Zion of the Holy One of Israel'.

(Isaiah 60:1–4, 11–14)

This return to Zion would result in the salvation of the whole world, because the *goyim* would be forced to worship the one God. From the very beginning there had been a universal message in Judaism. God had promised Abraham that 'all the tribes of the earth shall bless themselves in you' (Genesis 12:3). Fantasies of this Final Redemption have inspired Jews through the centuries and they are still inextricably linked to a return to the Land of Israel.

The confidence of the exilic prophets was shown to be justified just sixty years after the deportation to Babylon. The Medes and the Persians had conquered the Babylonians and in the year 538 BCE Cyrus, the King of Persia, gave the Jews permission to return to their homeland and rebuild the Temple. The Jews naturally hailed Cyrus as the anointed one of God, but Cyrus was not motivated solely by compassion for the Jews. He believed that by allowing the subject peoples of his empire religious autonomy, he would ease the burden of rule and administration. Throughout his empire he encouraged the reconstruction of ancient shrines, hoping that their gods might bless him and further his reign.[22] This suggests an essential difference between monotheism and polytheism. In general pagan rulers did not initiate religious persecution. A pagan like Cyrus believed in many gods and therefore could envisage many solutions and possibilities and this led to tolerance and to religious coexistence. The Jewish monotheists, however, had hitherto been unable to accept the presence of neighbouring shrines to gods other than their own. When Cyrus issued the edict of return, they naturally saw him as inspired by their God for their greater glory. Some 42,360 Jews left Babylon and Tel Aviv and began the long journey home.

Yet – and this is an important point – most of the Jews remained behind in exile. They no longer saw physical possession of the Holy Land as essential to the Jewish identity. Furthermore they saw certain religious problems in the return: was it likely that their brothers would create the New Jerusalem of peace and justice, foretold by the Second Isaiah? In this view, a physical return to Zion actually endangered the shining religious ideal. It was surely more religious to look forward to a divine intervention in history that would establish the full redemption than to create an imperfect Jewish state. Keeping the Return and the redemption in the future tense would ensure that a yearning for salvation did not become muddied by the squalor of politics. The year 538, therefore, marked an important parting of the ways in Judaism that still persists. There are Jews who see the Land of Israel as essential to Judaism and consider that living in the physical land is obligatory for all Jews. There are other Jews who think that secular and political hegemony in Israel is dangerous and unreligious and most Jews have remained in the diaspora.

After 538 Babylon remained an important centre of Judaism for centuries. There the Jews prayed facing Jerusalem, but kept it as a distant ideal. They were confident enough to develop a very different attitude towards the Gentiles. The scriptures composed in the diaspora sometimes show the influence of Gentile culture. The Book of Ecclesiastes, for example, has been fruitfully inspired by Hellenic Stoicism. The diaspora Book of Jonah shows real compassion to non-Jews. When Jonah warns the pagan people of Nineveh that unless they repent God will destroy their city, they do repent and the city is spared. Jonah is furious about this and goes off to sulk, but God gently teases him out of this absurdity. The Jewish prophet is to save the Gentiles as well as the chosen people: 'Am I not to feel sorry for Nineveh,' God asks, 'the great city, in which there are more than a hundred and twenty thousand people who cannot tell their right hand from their left, to say nothing of all the animals?' (4:11). The lessons of the Book of Jonah have been important to Christians and Muslims as well as Jews; the *goyim* have learned far more from this compassionate Judaism than from the scriptures written in the Land of Israel after 538, like the Books of Maccabees which speak mainly about new and violent holy wars there. In the diaspora a humanism developed in Judaism that would ultimately enter Christianity through the Jewish Jesus and St Paul and help to shape the tradition of Western humanism. In our own day, diaspora Jews like Sigmund Freud and Albert Einstein have taught Gentiles more than the Zionists who returned to the Land of Israel. As we shall see in Chapter 3, the Zionists intended to be a light unto the Gentiles by creating a model society, but in fact, like their ancestors, they have actually initiated a new cycle of violence and a revival of the holy war.

The Jews who returned to Jerusalem in 538 had originally no intention of fighting a holy war, any more than the Zionists. They had peaceful ideals, and the Return of 538 could be seen as a non-violent version of the Exodus. God had destroyed Pharaoh, but the Persian King Cyrus had co-operated with him. The journey home was intended to lead to a constructive rebuilding of the land, instead of a holy war. But sadly the Return led to new Jewish intolerance. When the exiles reached the Promised Land they discovered other people living there, as Joshua had done before them. In the north were pagans who had settled there when the ten tribes had been deported in 722. In Judaea and Samaria dwelt the descendants of the Jews who had not been deported to Babylon; they seemed very strange to the returning exiles, who rejected both sets of people, calling them the *am ha'aretz*, the people of the land. They insisted that only those who had experienced the Exile were true Jews.[23] They thus began the bitter debate about who really was a Jew, which still continues today. Naturally the People of the Land were angry. When the native Jews offered to help to rebuild Jerusalem, they were told that they had no place in the new Jewish kingdom. This led to hostility and warfare, and the building work was constantly threatened by the military attacks of the People of the Land. As Nehemiah, who led this rebuilding, explained, each builder 'did his work with one hand while gripping his weapon with the other. And as each builder worked, he wore his sword at his side' (Nehemiah 4:18). The rebuilding of Jewish Israel has led to a similar hostility from the current People of the Land. Where Jews in the diaspora were learning a new acceptance and compassion, the Jews who felt that physical occupation of the Promised Land was essential were making new enemies, who included other Jews. A religion which depends upon the physical possession of territory is necessarily more vulnerable than a religion which depends upon an interior, spiritual commitment, and will inevitably become more intolerant if threatened politically.

There had, of course, been quarrels and divisions between Jews before. From the time of King Solomon radical groups like the Rechabites and the Nazirites had made an exodus into the wilderness, in order to build communities of true Jews. This tendency marked a new level of intransigence in their relations with their fellow Jews which could lead to a holy war. At about the time of Christ, for example, the Essenes had also withdrawn from the cities into the desert to live a pure Jewish life, and they waged a holy war against the Jews of the establishment. Some confined themselves to a war of words: John the Baptist, who attacked the Jews in blistering sermons, was probably an Essene. Others believed that they should fight a physical war against their unfaithful brethren. The Essenes were also very important in the opposition to the Roman occupation of the Holy Land, which led to the Great Jewish Revolt of CE 66–73. But this tells us something very important about the holy war. The Essenes and their fellow zealots all believed that the pagan occupation of the Romans was an abomination. They believed that the integrity of Judaism depended on the political independence of the Holy Land, which must be freed of the contaminating presence of the *goyim*. They believed that they must act to save their country, however hopeless the struggle. In this they were following the great tradition of the Exodus. But for a tiny country like Israel to confront the might of the Roman empire was suicidal. God did not intervene to save his people as he had at the Red Sea and in CE 70 the Romans conquered Jerusalem and burned down the Temple. The chosen people lost their Holy Land for the second time and this time the exile would be far more traumatic and would last nearly 2000 years. The suicidal tendency of these religious zealots, who had dragged their more moderate brethren into the disaster against their will, was clearly shown at Masada in the year 73. The last remaining Jewish rebels had gathered in the mighty fortress by the Dead Sea and were finally forced to surrender to the Roman army. But when the Roman soldiers arrived, they discovered that the 960 Jewish men, women and children had preferred to take their own lives rather than submit to Rome.[24] In the history of the holy war, it would become quite common for Jews, Christians and Muslims, in their different ways, to abandon the usual policies of reason, and adopt a deliberately suicidal belligerence.

Fundamentalists like the Essenes were attracted to the Jewish apocalyptic writings that started to appear in Judaism at the end of the second century BCE and continued to be written in the Second Exile. Because terrestrial triumph seemed increasingly impossible, Jews began to look forward to a cosmic triumph at the end of time that was essentially aggressive. Scriptures like the Book of Daniel or apocryphal books like the Book of Jubilees foretold great battles in which the armies of God would defeat his monstrous enemies. All the nations of the world would gather at the Mount of Olives opposite Jerusalem and there would be a battle in which God himself would lead the Jews into the fray and cruelly exterminate all their enemies. Then the Kingdom of God would be established, the Jews would rule the conquered world and the redemption would be accomplished.[25] Many Jews began to look forward to a Messiah who would prepare for this final cosmic triumph.[26] They believed that he would be a Jew of the House of David, anointed by God for this task. When the Holy Land was occupied by the Romans, several Messiahs appeared ready to fight the occupiers as a first step to the final redemption.[27] After the loss of the Holy Land, the Jews in the Second Exile expected the Messiah to lead them back to Zion. Many radical Jews in Israel today are expecting the Messiah to come very soon.

Christianity arose from this apocalyptic Judaism. Jesus presented himself to the Jews of Palestine as the Messiah in about CE 27. He began his preaching with the announcement 'The Kingdom of God is at hand!' and urged the Jews to prepare for this great event.[28] He spent a year [29] in his native Galilee in the north of Israel, and he quickly attracted a large following. He seems to have devoted himself particularly to converting the poor and the 'sinners' of Israel, who either collaborated with the Romans or who did not observe the Torah.[30] These sinners were aggressively spurned by the establishment, but Jesus insisted that they had to be brought back into the fold and healed before the redemption. Eventually he went to Jerusalem as the Messiah. He started his triumphal procession into the city on the Mount of Olives, where the Messiah was expected to appear; he rode on an ass, as the apocalyptic prophet Zachariah had foretold, and the crowds hailed him as the Son of David, crying 'Blessings on the coming Kingdom of our father David!'[31] Then he seems to have occupied the Temple and preached of the coming Kingdom for a week.[32] It is not clear what Jesus intended to do about the Romans, but eventually he was arrested by the authorities and the Governor Pontius Pilate sentenced him to die by the Roman punishment of crucifixion, which might indicate that he was worried about Jesus' political activities. Yet it seems clear that Jesus was a strict pacifist. He told his followers to turn the other cheek when attacked and when he was arrested he refused even to defend himself verbally.[33] It has been suggested that he was expecting the Kingdom of God to arrive in a great cosmic miracle, without his having to fight the Roman occupation.[34] When this miracle failed to happen, Jesus' despair and bewilderment echo in his cry from the cross: 'My God! my God! why have you deserted me?' (Mark 15:34).

Yet even after his death, his disciples refused to despair. They had visions of him and believed that he had risen to a new kind of life. Very shortly, in their own lifetimes, he would return and establish the Kingdom of God, so they devoted themselves to preparing for the redemption. Like Jesus, they had no desire to found a new religion. They saw themselves and were seen by their fellow Jews as a perfectly legitimate Jewish sect. The only thing that distinguished them was their belief in Jesus as the Messiah and their expectation of his Second Coming. Otherwise they were fully observant Jews, worshipping daily in the Temple and living according to the Torah.[35] Certainly they had no desire to preach to the *goyim*, and when one of their number started to bring Gentiles into the Jewish sect and telling them that they had no need of the Torah, they disowned him and his converts after a very bitter dispute in about CE 50.[36]

It was the Jewish Paul who took Christianity to the Gentile world of the Roman empire and who made it a Gentile faith. He believed that Jesus had saved the whole world, not just the Jews, and that when he returned in glory to establish the Kingdom this would not just be a Jewish triumph. His death and resurrection had ended the days of the Jews' special mission, and Christianity was a universal religion. In Pauline Christianity there was no longer any possibility of a holy war, because Christians must show charity even to enemies, as Jesus had enjoined. Christianity was a spiritual religion: salvation now meant a liberation from sin and death, not an extermination of the enemies of God. Because the normal world was passing away and the Second Coming was imminent, fighting for a stake in this world was meaningless. A Christian's only duty was to prepare for the redemption.[37] Yet, although Paul rejected essential Jewish teaching, he remained deeply Jewish in spirit and stamped Christianity with the imagery and mythology of Judaism. He taught Christians that they were the fulfilment of Jewish history and that they were the New Israel. God had been preparing the world for Christ ever since he had first revealed himself to Abraham, who was therefore the father of all those who believe in Jesus, not just the father of the Jews. He taught Christians that Jesus was their 'Passover', leading them from death to a new spiritual life. They were now in 'exile', not from the Holy Land but from Christ and the imminent Kingdom of God. They already belonged to the next world. The holy men of the Jews like Abraham, David and Moses were models for the Christians too because they had been waiting for Christ without realising it.[38] Paul formed an important Christian attitude towards the Jews, which has had political consequences

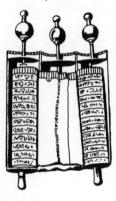

in the present conflict, as we shall see in Chapter 12. Christians were taught to appropriate Judaism for their own purposes and would ultimately find it difficult to read the Jewish scriptures except in a Pauline, and therefore distorted, way; they would find it difficult to recognise that important elements in their faith were really Jewish and would ultimately view the Jews as renegades, who had stupidly failed to recognise Jesus and had therefore lost their special vocation.

By the end of the first century, the apocalyptic Judaism that had always been important to Jesus and his first followers brought a new violence into the peaceful religion of Jesus and Paul. This is particularly clear in two of the later books of the New Testament, which were both written at least fifty years after St Paul's death. The author of Revelations was probably a Jewish convert to Christianity and when he looked forward to the Second Coming of Christ he naturally saw it in terms of the Jewish apocalyptic tradition. In his book the cosmic battles foretold by the Jewish prophets herald the final triumph of Christianity, when God would send down from heaven the New Jerusalem and a new and perfect world. The Crusaders would be deeply affected by this vision. He also spoke of God's enemies as frightening monsters. In particular he wrote of a great Beast who would crawl out of the abyss and take up residence in the Temple. This would be one of the signs of the approaching end.[39] This probably had a contemporary reference that is now completely lost to us, but later generations of Christians found their imaginations haunted by this Beast, and naturally they made their own interpretations of this strange image. The Beast was conflated with another enemy of God, whose arrival, it had been said, would herald the Last Days. The author of the Second Epistle to the Thessalonians was not St Paul, but was writing years after his death and using Paul's name as a sign of discipleship. He was struggling with a very great problem. In the First Epistle to the Thessalonians, written in about CE 52, Paul had promised that Jesus would arrive very soon, certainly within Paul's own lifetime. Why had he not appeared? The author of Second Thessalonians explained some fifty years later that Jesus could not return until the 'Great Revolt' or the 'Great Apostasy' had taken place.[40] A Rebel would appear just before the Second Coming, who would set himself up as the enemy of God and would even claim to be God himself. He would establish himself in the Temple in Jerusalem and deceive many Christians and lead many people astray. The author of Second Thessalonians implies that this was a widely held Christian belief, and again it probably had a meaning that is now lost to us. Later generations of Christians naturally identified this Rebel with the Beast, who would occupy the Temple before the Last Days. As a new Christian apocalyptic tradition grew, which had to cope with the uncomfortable fact that Jesus had not returned as quickly as had been promised, Christians developed a belief in a figure whom they called Antichrist. By the time of the Crusades, European Christians firmly believed that before the final Apocalypse, Antichrist would appear in Jerusalem, would set himself up in the Temple and fight the Christians there in the great battles foretold by Revelations. These terrible wars would herald the Last Days and the Second Coming of Christ. Some people saw Antichrist as a diabolic monster, like the Beast in Revelation; others saw him as an ordinary but absolutely evil human being like the Rebel in Second Thessalonians. Political and heretical leaders were often identified with Antichrist, and what we might call 'Antichrist-spotting' became a habit in Western Europe. Belief in Antichrist was very important in the ideology of crusading.

By the end of the first century, therefore, the peaceful religion of Jesus and Paul was being invaded by more violent and martial ideas. Alongside the pacifism of Jesus, there grew a religion of battles and horrors. Jesus had preached a Jewish humanitarian religion, which has been very formative of many Western ideals, but the more violent, apocalyptic strain of Christianity would be equally influential.

The aggression of Christianity surfaced quite early in the history of the Church in the two movements of martyrdom and monasticism which would later be very important in the ideology of the Christian holy war.

The Roman empire had destroyed the Jewish homeland and during the second and third centuries it sometimes seemed as though it would also destroy Christianity. From time to time the Roman authorities persecuted Christians who refused to sacrifice to Caesar and seemed a potential political threat. Thousands of Christians were put to death in the Roman stadiums and this trauma stamped itself on the Christian consciousness. It gave to Christians a strong sense that 'the world' was against them and would overwhelm the true religion.[41] This deep insecurity led to an aggressive cult of voluntary martyrdom, that was not very dissimilar to the spirit of the Jewish martyrs at Masada. The martyr was seen as a perfect Christian, because Christ had said that giving one's life for the beloved was the greatest act of love. The martyr was imitating Jesus perfectly in his death. But this love acquired an aggressive dimension. Christians started to denounce themselves to the authorities, in order to force the Romans to put them to death. This was not because they had a masochistic yearning for pain and for death, nor was it because they wanted to prove their love for Christ. These voluntary martyrs believed that they were taking part in a continuing cosmic battle with evil. The death of every martyr brought the final victory and the Second Coming of Christ nearer and was part of the Last Battle foretold by the prophets. The martyr seemed to be passive in that he allowed violence to be inflicted upon him, but he believed that he was a 'soldier of Christ' and that his death was a 'victory'.[42] The Church tried to stop this passion for voluntary martyrdom, but it never completely died out; it surfaced later in Europe, when Christians felt their identity threatened by the enemies of God, and the martyr impulse would be important during the Crusades.

When the persecutions stopped and Christianity became the official religion of the Roman empire, there was a gap in the Christian life. How were you to be a perfect Christian when there was no longer any possibility of martyrdom, voluntary or otherwise? The answer that some fervent Christians found was very similar to the solution of the Jewish Nazirites or Essenes. Radical Christians fled 'the world', which they felt was destructive of the Christian life, and took refuge in the wilderness. They were inspired to make this exodus in order to witness to true Christian values, and just as the Jewish sectarians saw themselves as the only true Jews, so too these monks, who had escaped from the contaminating world, persuaded other Christians to think that they were the only perfect Christians. Jesus and Paul had never envisaged this kind of asceticism but had seen Christians as living in the world and waiting for the Second Coming, but many of their sayings were reinterpreted and applied to the monastic life. Jesus had said that a disciple had to be prepared to leave his home and family, and follow him even unto death,[43] and the monks believed that they were the only Christians who did this as they struggled to 'die to themselves' in the desert. St Paul and St John had spoken disparagingly of 'the world' and now monks and their fellow Christians believed that it was impossible to preserve a truly Christian identity in the world. Monasticism began in the Middle East and did not reach Europe until the late fifth century, but once it had arrived Western Christians soon saw the monasteries as fortresses of Christianity in a Godless world. Benedict of Nursia introduced a less masochistic and more temperate version of monasticism into Europe than that which had been practised by the original Eastern Fathers of the Desert, but there was still an aggression in Western spirituality. The monks were regarded as taking part in a holy war. In the frightening world of the early Middle Ages, Europe was a very dangerous place. Christianity was threatened first by the barbarian invasions that destroyed the Roman empire in Europe and then by invasions of Norse-men, Muslims and Magyars in the ninth and tenth centuries which constantly threatened the precarious establishment. Just as the knights fought these earthly enemies of God and of Christians, the monks fought their spiritual enemies. This was written into the charters and deeds of gift to monasteries:

> The abbot is armed with spiritual weapons and supported by a troop of monks anointed with the dew of heavenly graces. They fight together in the strength of Christ with the sword of the spirit against the aery wiles of the devils. They defend the king and clergy of the realm from the onslaughts of their invisible enemies.[44]

At an early date the insecurity of Western Christians brought an aggressive element into the peaceful religion of Christianity.

Yet still Christians tried to keep this violence in check and remain pacifist. In the Greek Orthodox Church of the Byzantine empire war was always regarded as unChristian and during a campaign a soldier was denied the sacraments.[45] The Byzantines preferred to use mercenaries in their wars rather than allow Greek Christians themselves to fight. But Byzantium was less vulnerable than the Church of Western Europe, which was exposed to one invasion after another. In the West, Latin theologians developed the concept of a just war, which would enable Christians to fight and defend themselves without guilt. In the early fifth century the great St Augustine of Hippo in North Africa watched the destruction of the Western Roman empire with horror. He decided that while wars against other Christians were always sinful and unjustified, God could sometimes inspire a Christian leader to wage war against pagans as he had inspired Joshua and David to massacre their enemies in the Old Testament. What must distinguish Christian from pagan violence was that it had to be inspired by love. When he used violence, a Christian must be full of love for the enemy he is fighting, and see his violence as medicinal, used in rather the same way as a parent who chastises a child for its own good. Jesus had used this kind of violence when he drove the moneylenders out of the Temple and blinded St Paul on the road to Damascus. Sadly this medicinal Christian violence would sometimes result in the death of the enemy. Although Christians needed to defend themselves, Augustine insisted that self-defence alone could not justify violence, because self-defence could be inspired by hatred.[46] Augustine's arguments were tortuous and paradoxical and show how difficult he found it to justify a war of Christians, but, without fighting, Christianity could not survive. When the barbarian tribes sacked the great city of Rome in 410, Augustine saw this as the triumph of evil over good. Civilisation and culture had been overthrown and the existence of Christianity itself seemed in danger. Yet Augustine's church in North Africa, where there were many thriving Christian communities, was destroyed not in the sixth century by the barbarian tribes that overturned the Roman empire, but by a new religious menace that appeared in the deserts of the Hejaz in the Arabian peninsula during the seventh century. The third religion of the monotheistic tradition had been born and from the start Islam threatened the vulnerable Christians of the West.

If most Western people were asked today which of the three monotheistic religions was the most violent, they would probably unhesitatingly reply: 'Islam.' For hundreds of years, Western Christians have described Islam as 'the religion of the sword' but this is inaccurate, one of the prejudices we have inherited from the period of the Crusades. It is just one example of the distorted picture that many people in the West have of Islam, about which we are generally rather ignorant. It will therefore be important to give some account of the rise of Islam to show how Muslims see themselves as part of the divine plan for the world. It is certainly true that the holy war played its part in the establishment and spread of Islam, but it is not correct to see Islam as a bloodthirsty and essentially aggressive religion. When the first Muslims converted to Islam, the idea of the holy war was far from their minds. Like the ancient Israelites, who had responded to the trauma of slavery in Egypt by building a new identity, Islam arose from the urgent need of the Arabs of the peninsula to solve the very grave problems of the Hejaz in the early seventh century and to build a new and proud Arab self. At this time Arabia was in crisis. Trade had brought a new prosperity to the Hejaz, especially to the city of Mecca, but this meant that the old tribal values were breaking down, and people felt confused and lost. In the harsh life of the desert, where there were not enough of the necessities of life, a sharing of resources had been essential to the survival of the clan. People who were rich were expected to be generous to those who were not and a tribal leader won power by his largesse. Such generosity was prudent: a famine or a drought could easily reduce a rich man to poverty overnight and who would be generous to him if he had denied others? But in the new wealthy cities, Arabs were losing this sense of responsibility and adopting alien, elitist lifestyles. It seemed as though the old Arab way of life was being destroyed and that the rich were separating themselves from the poor. At the same time as the social order was torn apart, the Hejaz was rent by a seemingly incurable tribal warfare, where Arab fought Arab. This meant that they could not unite against their powerful neighbours, the Persians and the Byzantines, and the Arabs were frequently exploited by these great powers. If they were to make use of their new wealth and not fall into an ignoble and servile dependence on others, they had to find a way of taking their destiny into their own hands, revive the true values of Arabian society and enter history in their own right. That they were able to do this was due to Mohammad, the founder of Islam, who did for the Arabs what Moses had done for the Israelites.

As well as a social and political crisis, there was a crisis of faith, and by the seventh century the Arabs felt a strong sense of religious inferiority. There were some Jews and Christians living in the peninsula and they looked down on the Arabs as barbarians, who had received no revelation of their own and who practised a primitive pagan idolatry. In the old tribal days, life was such a struggle that there had not been much time for religion, but there had been a pantheon of Arab gods. One of these was Hubal, whose curious box-like shrine at Mecca, called the Ka'aba, was an important place of pilgrimage. From all over Arabia, people gathered in Mecca. In obscure ancient ritual, they processed round and round the Ka'aba, and also venerated the Black Stone, a meteorite set in the wall of the shrine. There were also other rites to other gods which the pilgrims performed in the desert outside Mecca, and these ceremonies were collectively known as the *Hajj*. But by the seventh century this paganism no longer satisfied all the Arabs. People were beginning to think that monotheism was a more developed faith, but most did not want to convert to Judaism or Christianity because this meant adopting yet another alien ideology. One group of Arabs, whom the pagan establishment called *hanifs* or infidels, sought an essentially Arab solution.[47]

In the old pagan pantheon, the chief God was Allah, whose name meant *the* God. Allah had not been able to exert much control over his fellow gods in the old myths, but now the *hanifs* decided to worship Allah alone and they claimed that he was the God of the Jewish–Christian tradition. They developed a belief which inserted the Arabs into God's plan from the very first days of his revelation to the world. The Jewish scriptures tell us that Abraham's wife Sarah had seemed barren, so to ensure that Abraham had descendants she encouraged him to take her Egyptian slave-girl Hagar as his concubine, a common practice at that time. Hagar bore Abraham a son called Ishmael and had a very uneasy life with Sarah, who was very jealous, despite her earlier acquiescence. But God promised Hagar that he would protect her child, whose name meant 'God has heard'. Finally when Sarah had her own son Isaac she made Abraham send Hagar and Ishmael away, which grieved Abraham very much, but God consoled him saying:

> Do not distress yourself on account of the boy and your slave girl. Grant Sarah all that she asks of you, for it is through Isaac that your name will be carried on. But the slave girl's son I will also make into a nation, for he is your child too.
>
> (Genesis 21:12)

The Bible says that God watched over Hagar and Ishmael in the desert, preserved their lives and repeated his promise that Ishmael would be the father of a mighty nation.[48] The Arab *hanifs* maintained that Ishmael had lived in the deserts of Mecca and that the Arabs were his descendants. There was a story that when Ishmael had grown up Abraham visited him in the desert and that together they had built the Ka'aba, which had been the first shrine to Allah in Arabia. Later the pagans had desecrated the shrine and given it over to idolatry.[49]

In 610 one of these *hanifs* began to have revelations which he believed came from Allah and which developed this early Arab monotheism. It also fulfilled the ancient biblical prophecy, for because of this revelation Ishmael's 'descendants' did indeed become a mighty nation. Mohammad ibn Abdullah had been born in Mecca in about 570. He was a member of the Qureish clan, which ruled the city, but was orphaned early in life and was brought up outside Mecca. Even though he was a young man of great promise, he was only a minor member of the clan and could exercise very little influence in the affairs of the city. This early impotence made him acutely aware of the new social inequality in the Hejaz, which he felt to be immoral and against the Arab spirit. He was deeply disturbed by the plight of the poor and became known for his generosity and kindness in relieving their sufferings in very practical ways. This would become an important feature of the religion he founded. Mohammad was rescued from his early poverty by marriage to a wealthy woman considerably older than himself. Khadija was probably the first person to recognise the genius of her young husband and she would become his first convert when the revelations began. It was a fortunate marriage for Mohammad but it would be a mistake to see it as wholly mercenary. He loved Khadija all his life. During her own lifetime he remained faithful to her and took no other wives; after her death he used to infuriate his later wives by constantly extolling her virtues. Managing his wife's property, Mohammad became a successful merchant, but as he approached his fortieth year he began to spend more and more time in solitary meditation. One day, without warning, he heard a voice which said, 'You are the Messenger of God,' and which then commanded him to recite these words:

> Recite in the name of thy Lord Who created: Created man from clots of blood!
>   Recite! Your Lord is the Most Bountiful One, who by the pen taught man what he did not know.
>
> (Koran 96:2–4)

These first words of the revelation told Mohammad that God had chosen him to convey his message to mankind in the name of the transcendent but beneficent God who is the creator of the Universe. The revelation stresses the original insignificance of man, but promises that this mighty God is concerned with his progress and development and will reveal himself to all mankind in a great book.

Mohammad was overwhelmed, like other prophets who have experienced a revelation. 'I was standing,' he is reported to have said, 'but I fell on my knees and dragged myself along while the upper part of my chest was trembling. I went in to Khadija and said "Cover me! Cover me!" until the terror left me.'[50] He was also very apprehensive about his ability to discharge the enormous responsibility that God had laid upon him. Khadija's words of comfort not only give us some insight into Mohammad's character, but they also tell us much about the social and moral values of Islam:

> Surely, God will never suffer thee to fail. Thou art kind and considerate toward thy kin. Thou helpest the poor and forlorn and bearest their burdens. Thou strivest to restore the high moral qualities that thy people have lost. Thou honourest the guest and goest to the assistance of those in distress.[51]

Like many of the Jewish prophets, however, Mohammad was sometimes very cautious about the Voice and the Presence that came to him more and more frequently. Was this really God or the product of his own imagination? Finally he was convinced of their divine nature. The revelations were always a painful, wrenching experience. 'Never once did I receive a revelation without thinking that my soul had been torn away from me,'[52] he said at the end of his life. His face would be covered with sweat: he lay unconscious for an hour or so afterwards, was seized with violent shudderings or heard strange noises like the sound of bells and rushing wings. 'Revelations come to me in different ways,' he said. 'Sometimes the words strike directly at my heart like the ringing of a bell, and this is physically hard on me. Sometimes I hear the words as if spoken from behind a veil. Sometimes I see a Presence that speaks the words to me.'[53] These mental experiences quite often accompany the productions of genius, when someone makes a real breakthrough to a hitherto undiscovered idea or solution to a problem. Mohammad conveyed each new revelation to his disciples, who immediately learned it by heart, and those who were educated wrote it down. Mohammad himself, like many people in the Hejaz, was illiterate. These collected revelations of God became the Koran (or the Recitation), the holy book of Islam.[54]

Mohammad insisted that his was not a new religion, but the ultimate revelation of the Jewish–Christian tradition. He called his religion 'Islam' which means 'submission' (to God) and his followers became 'Muslims', which means 'those who submit'. Abraham, he taught, had been the first 'Muslim' because he had submitted so perfectly to God: he had been neither a Jew nor a Christian because he had lived long before the Torah and the Gospels (Koran 3:66–9). Mohammad had never read the Bible, of course, but from the Jews and Christians living in the peninsula he learned some of the stories and teachings of these earlier religions and repeated these, reinterpreted according to the revelations, in the Koran. This makes them rather different from the biblical version and they probably also reflect the simple, apocryphal beliefs of the Jews and Christians of Arabia, who were so far from the main centres of their religions. The Koran, therefore, venerates Jewish figures like Abraham, Noah, Lot, Joseph and Jonah. It also venerates Jesus, whom Muslims call the Messiah. Mohammad did not believe for a moment that Jesus had been God; this seemed as blasphemous a claim to the Muslims as it had always seemed to the Jews. Jesus was a prophet, like the other Jewish prophets, not the incarnate son of God. Though Islam was the supreme revelation, the Koran taught Muslims that they must respect Jews and Christians, the People of the Book: 'Be courteous when you argue with the People of the Book, except with those who do evil. Say "We believe in that which is revealed to us and that which is revealed to you. Our God and your God is one"' (Koran 29:46). Indeed one of the greatest Islamic values is liberty of conscience and freedom of thought, to which every individual has an inalienable right.

The first Muslims learned the importance of this ideal by bitter experience. At first Mohammad had only three disciples besides Khadija: his freedman Zaid, his friend Abu Bakr and his cousin Ali ibn Talid, who was only eleven years old. But gradually the new religion attracted other converts in the city. The teaching of Islam was at first very simple. First and most important was the revelation of monotheism: there was no God but Allah and Mohammad was his Prophet. This formed the entire profession of faith. Second, Muslims must prepare for the imminent Last Judgement, and third, they had a duty to care for the poor and oppressed and work to create an equal, just society that truly reflected God's will. Like Jesus, Mohammad identified with the poor and outcast and in this respect his faith was essentially revolutionary and was protesting against the unjust rule of the Qureish in Mecca.[55] Indeed revolution and commitment to social justice is an important value in Islam, as we shall see throughout this book. The Koran taught that there could be no distinction between religion and politics but that Muslims must engage in a practical struggle (*jihad*) to create a perfect community (*umma*). Not surprisingly the first Muslim converts came from the ranks of the weak and underprivileged people of Mecca. In particular slaves, who were treated very cruelly, and women, who were considered little better than animals in pre-Islamic Arabia, both felt that in Islam they would find a means of achieving a human dignity and self-respect. But the cause of Islam made a breakthrough when Omar ibn al-Khattib, a prominent and respected citizen, unexpectedly became a Muslim. The people of Mecca began to realise that they had to take this religion seriously.

At first the Qureish had been patronising and scornful about Islam but gradually they began to see that it constituted a political threat to their regime. For how long would a man who claimed that God spoke to him and who condemned their rule as unjust and corrupt be prepared to submit to their government? Mohammad also condemned the pagan cult of Hubal and the idols in the Ka'aba and insisted that it be restored to the faith of Abraham and Ishmael. This would ruin the pilgrim trade and could even mean that trade caravans would no longer converge upon Mecca: it threatened the whole Meccan wealth and way of life. The Meccans began to persecute the Muslims. In particular those Muslims who were slaves and women were subject to torture and to inhuman treatment. At one time the Qureish confined Muslims to their houses and imposed a blockade, which cut off their food supplies, and, even though the blockade was eventually lifted, the Muslims had suffered greatly and Khadija and Abu Talid, the young Ali's father, both died. There were also frequent attempts on Mohammad's life and it became clear that the Muslims needed a new home, where they had the freedom to think and to worship as they chose.

They found this home in the year 622. Some *hanifs* of the settlement of Yathrib, which would later be called Medina (the city) and which is about 240 miles north of Mecca, invited the Muslims to settle there. Yathrib was settled by two tribes of Jews and three tribes of Arabs and there was a struggle for the leadership. The Jews had recently been expecting a prophet, who had been promised in their scriptures (Deuteronomy 18:18), to lead them to new power. When the *hanifs* heard about Mohammad during their annual pilgrimage to Mecca, they assumed that he must be this prophet and they decided to win him over to *the* Arab side. Some seventy *hanifs* converted to Islam and urged the Muslims to emigrate to Medina and to take on the leadership. This seemed a good solution, though it meant that Mohammad had to abandon his own tribe in Mecca. God, however, promised him that he would one day return to his home (Koran 28:86). Secretly, in twos and threes, the Muslims slipped out of Mecca and made the journey to Medina. Mohammad was the last to leave with Abu Bakr, and left just in time to forestall a serious attempt on his life. For two days he and Abu Bakr hid in a cave outside the city while the Meccans scoured the countryside hunting for the rebellious Prophet. Eventually the fugitives were able to escape to Medina, where they were joyfully received by the Muslim community and Mohammad eventually took over the leadership of the city. This *hijra* or migration of 622 marks the official beginning of the Muslim calendar and this journey north would be as formative for the Muslims as the Exodus had been for the Jews.

In Medina the Muslims had the chance to build the first Islamic society and, as Judaism came of age in the exile of Babylon, so did Islam come of age in Medina. The Muslims accepted five pillars of the religion. All Muslims had to make the simple profession of faith: 'There is no God but Allah and Mohammad is his Prophet.' They had to pray at stated times, facing first towards Jerusalem and later towards the Ka'aba in Mecca; they had to give alms to the poor and fast during the month of Ramadan. Finally they had to make the pilgrimage to Mecca, but in the present state of hostility between Mecca and Islam they were unable to do so. Islam was an anti-elitist religion. The prayers and requirements were the same for everybody and there was to be no hierarchy, as there was in Christianity, which made people first- and second-class Christians. Eventually a clergy emerged, who led the prayers and were expert in Islamic law, but they were never priests like Christian priests, who intervened between God and man. Almsgiving was meant to iron out material inequalities and to ensure the even distribution of wealth. Even the fast of Ramadan was a realistic fast that was within everybody's scope. Indeed we shall see that realism is a hallmark of Islam. These years in Medina were hard years. Mohammad had to struggle against the hostility of the non-Muslim Arab community in Medina, who had hoped to get the leadership, and of the Jews, who also fought against his rule. Besides the inevitable difficulties that were involved in setting up a wholly new social order in Medina, the Muslims had to worry about a possible invasion by the Meccans, who now saw Medina as an enemy because the people there had taken in the Muslims. But Mohammad urged his Muslims to take every possible practical precaution and at the same time to pray and foster their knowledge of God, in order to make this a joyful experience. What made Islam a successful and strong faith was its realism and practicality. Constantly in the Koran the Muslims are exhorted to expend every possible *human* effort in the cause. God had promised that he would help them, but he would not do so unless they had worked hard to save themselves. He would not save them by a miracle.[56] This realistic approach, established from the very beginning, is one of the distinguishing characteristics of Islam that, as I hope to show, makes it very different in spirit from both Judaism and Christianity, where the possibility of miracles is not always ruled out.

One of the precautions that Mohammad took was to establish friendly relations with neighbouring tribes. There was no attempt to force conversion upon them, for that would have meant that the Muslims were denying others the freedom of belief that they had been denied in Mecca. But more and more Arabs did convert to Islam of their own choice. The religion was very attractive. It was essentially Arab and a marvellous tonic to the Arabs' battered sense of self-esteem: as recipients of God's ultimate revelation, the Arabs were now God's new chosen people. Further, Islam had all the attractions of monotheism, without the complications of practice and belief that Jews and Christians had evolved and which were alien to the Arab way of life. Conversion to Islam was becoming an irresistible trend in the peninsula, though as with all mass movements there were people who joined for unworthy reasons. Mohammad and his most committed converts were constantly worried during these first years about a party of Medinan Arabs who had converted but were not wholly loyal. In the Koran they are called the *munafiqeen* or the hypocrites.

The Meccans were trying to spread hostility against Muslim Medina and were using their trade caravans as a means of inciting the neighbouring tribes and the Jews to fight against the city. These caravans were economically crucial to the

Meccans and were usually accompanied by an army, so they were a threat to the security of Medina. Mohammad realised that the Muslims would have to fight them if they wanted to survive. He had a revelation that justified the use of violence as a means of self-defence (22:40–2). The Meccans had persecuted the Muslims and were now pursuing them in exile. Unless right-minded people fought tyrants and oppressors, all decency and beneficence would vanish from the earth: 'Had Allah not defeated some by the might of others, the earth would have been utterly corrupted' (2:252). Muslims were forbidden to open hostilities: 'Fight for the sake of Allah those that fight against you, but do not attack them first. Allah does not love the aggressors' (2:191). The ancient Israelites had been commanded by God to attack and exterminate the Canaanites living in the Promised Land, as a holy initiative, and Christians had denied that violence could be justified by self-defence. But the concept of self-defence was central to the Islamic view of warfare from the very beginning. This was the only way the Koran could justify the military action that Muslims now undertook against the Meccans.

The practice of making a *razzia* (raid) on an enemy tribe was well established in the Hejaz and was deemed normal and acceptable. It was often a necessity in an area where there was not enough for everybody if a tribe lacked the essentials of life. The raiders usually captured cattle, animals and booty, but were careful to avoid killing people. This was not for humanitarian reasons, but because killing would mean a long and bloody vendetta. The code of the *razzia* meant that you attacked only your enemies, which was again sensible in the Hejaz, which was torn apart by tribal wars. The Muslims in Medina began to make *razzia* against the Meccan caravans. One day in 624 a small band of 313 Muslims made the hundred-mile journey to Badr in the south-west, to attack a particularly important caravan travelling to Mecca, which was accompanied by most of the Qureish leadership. They had not realised that, in order to protect them from the Medinan Muslims, the leaders of the caravan had asked for a relieving army from Mecca to come to their assistance. When the Muslims attacked the caravan, therefore, they found that they were vastly outnumbered and were fighting nearly a thousand Meccans. It was too late to withdraw, but against all the odds the Muslims won. Their victory was probably due to their tactical superiority and to the fact that they were more firmly united under their military leaders than the more undisciplined Qureish. At the end of the battle the flowers of the Qureish were dead on the battle-field and the Muslims were euphoric.[57] They had fought as hard as they could and because they had done their part God had stepped in and helped them. The success of the battle of Badr, as it was called, seemed a proof of Mohammad's divine mission. Mohammad himself called it a *furqan*, a word which means both salvation and separation.[58] He had instinctively interpreted Badr in the way that the Israelites had interpreted their victory at the Red Sea; it was a separation of the just from the unjust.

> Allah revealed his will to the angels saying 'I shall be with you. Give courage to the believers. I shall cast terror into the hearts of the infidels. Strike off all their heads, maim them in every limb.
>
> It was not you but Allah who slew them. It was not you who smote them: Allah smote them so that He might richly reward his faithful. He hears all and knows all. He will surely thwart the designs of the unbelievers.　　(8:12, 18)

During our story we shall often find that an unexpected success gives rise to a belief in God's special intervention and stronger sense of divine mission. The unexpected success of Badr meant that, although this had not been the original intention of the Prophet, the migration from Mecca to Medina had in fact been a prelude to a holy war or a *jihad*. Islam had reverted to the archetype.

Yet this still did not make Islam the religion of the sword. Indeed the word 'Islam' comes from the same Arabic root as the word 'peace'[59] and the Koran condemns war as an abnormal state of affairs opposed to God's will: when the enemies of the Muslims 'kindle a fire for war, Allah extinguishes it. They strive to create disorder in the earth, and Allah loves not those who create disorder' (Koran 28:78). Islam does not justify a total aggressive war of extermination, as the Torah does in the first five books of the Bible. A more realistic religion than Christianity, Islam recognises that war is inevitable and sometimes a positive duty in order to end oppression and suffering. The Koran teaches that war must be limited and be conducted in as humane a way as possible. Mohammad had to fight not only the Meccans but also the Jewish tribes in the area and Christian tribes in Syria who planned an offensive against him in alliance with the Jews. Yet this did not make Mohammad denounce the People of the Book. His Muslims were forced to defend themselves but they were not fighting a 'holy war' against the religion of their enemies. When Mohammad sent his freedman Zaid against the Christians at the head of a Muslim army, he told them to fight in the cause of God bravely but humanely. They must not molest priests, monks and nuns nor the weak and helpless people who were unable to fight. There must be no massacre of civilians nor should they cut down a single tree nor pull down any building.[60] This was very different from the wars of Joshua.

But though Islam does not glorify war it is still true that the paradigm of the *hijra/jihad* has been important and formative in Islam. It has constantly inspired groups of fervent Muslims to withdraw from the community when they feel that the Muslims there are no longer faithful to Islam. In this exodus they have much the same instinct as Jewish groups like the Essenes or the Christian monks. The radical Muslims have made a migration away from the main body of the Muslims into the desert and have sought to build an ideal, Islamic society dedicated to justice. Then they have fought against the establishment in a *jihad* or a holy war in order to bring about a reform and an end of corruption. They see themselves as having been persecuted by the current establishment and feel it their Muslim duty to act in order to end a period of oppression. The first group to do this, in the mid-seventh century, was the radical Kharaji sect, who have been the only Muslims who have maintained that the *jihad* is a 'pillar of Islam'. Perhaps the most recent example is the sect known as the *takfir w'al hijra* group, which withdrew from the Egypt of Anwar Sadat, built an alternative, independent community upon Muslim lines and finally waged a terrorist war against the regime. People who have had recourse to the *hijra/jihad* archetype believe that God will not help them unless they make every human effort to solve their own problems, even if this means fighting other Muslims.

The battle of Badr was not the end of Mohammad's war with Mecca. Inevitably the Meccans sent armies against Medina and for the next four years there were battles, in which Medina finally emerged as the stronger power. Many tribes of the peninsula had been delighted by the downfall of the haughty Meccans and were willing to become confederates of Medina, even if they did not wish to convert to Islam, and Medina was gradually being transformed into a powerful city-state with an exciting and dynamic new Arab ideology. It was now time for Mohammad to conquer Mecca and fulfil the prophecy of God that he would one day return home. The way he did this is instructive, especially in the terms of the archetype. Mohammad was not only a religious man, who deplored unnecessary war, but he was also a shrewd politician. He knew that the last thing Medina really needed was a long, wasteful war. Instead he decided to conquer Mecca by means of a peaceful pilgrimage.

At the traditional time for the *hajj* pilgrimage to Mecca in 628 Mohammad and a large company of Muslims with their pagan confederates set out from Medina. Accounts of this give different numbers, ranging from 700 to 1400 men. But it was an unusual army, because the soldiers were virtually unarmed and carried only swords, which Mohammad had ordered to remain sheathed. As the Meccans watched this huge army approaching they expected Mohammad to attack, but instead Mohammad halted at Hudaybiyya, just outside the Sanctuary (the twenty-square-mile area around the Ka'aba where all violence was forbidden). The Meccans sent envoys and Mohammad asked simply to be able to perform the pilgrim rites at the Ka'aba, which was the right of every Arab. At first the Meccans demurred, but eventually to ward off an attack they agreed to make a treaty with Medina that was to last ten years. Many of the Muslims thought that this treaty was one-sided and humiliating. Any Meccan who converted to Islam and migrated to Medina without the permission of his father, for example, was to be returned forthwith, yet this did not apply to a Medinan who apostasised from Islam and migrated to Mecca. But Mohammad had made an important point. The Koran insists that whenever the enemy wants to make peace, Muslims *must* enter into a treaty, provided that the terms are not dangerous to Islam. Furthermore they must observe the terms of the treaty scrupulously, however inconvenient they are.[61] Mohammad pointed out that Muslims had gained by the Treaty of Hudaybiyya. They were now permitted to make the pilgrimage to Mecca each year, as peaceful pilgrims, carrying only sheathed swords; Mecca had accepted the right of Muslims to exist and they could now concentrate on building up the *umma* without fighting unnecessary wars.

The following year, the pilgrimage journey to Mecca was repeated. In accordance with the treaty, the Meccans evacuated the city to avoid a clash with the Muslims and from the surrounding hills they watched with fascinated horror as Mohammad and his huge Muslim army solemnly circled the Ka'aba according to the ancient ritual. But instead of venerating the idols in the Ka'aba, the Muslim *muezzin* climbed on to the roof of the Ka'aba and issued the call to prayer to Allah, the only God. Thus they had returned the shrine to the religion of Abraham and Ishmael. Their devotions completed, they marched peacefully back to Medina, while the awed Meccans crept back into the city.

In the following year the Meccans foolishly broke the Treaty of Hudaybiyya just before the *hajj* and thus relieved Mohammad of his obligation to keep the peace. Mecca had attacked the tribe of Khuza'a, which was confederated to the Muslims. Yet again Mohammad and his scantily armed pilgrim army set out for the pilgrimage to Mecca, but this time they were accompanied by huge numbers of confederates. The Meccans once again sent envoys to try to make peace, in order to ward off a bloody attack. Mohammad promised that if they accepted him as their ruler there would be no bloodshed and no reprisals. No Meccan would be forced to convert to Islam. He would only smash the idols in the Ka'aba. The Meccans agreed and the Muslims honoured the conditions of the agreement. Mohammad went straight to the Ka'aba and smashed the idols himself and his army circled the shrine which was now dedicated to the religion of Islam. He was now the ruler of the city. Not a drop of blood was shed and nobody was forced to convert. Mohammad had turned his peaceful pilgrimage into a conquest. He called the event *al-Fatah*, which is a familiar term to us because it is the name of Yasir Arafat's liberation movement. *Fatah* means 'opening', 'salvation', 'conquest'.[62]

Mohammad and his Meccan Muslims had literally returned home when they entered the city, but in an important sense *fatah* was a homecoming for the Muslims of Medina also because it was a return to the origins of the Islamic faith in the One God of Abraham and Ishmael. In 632, two years after his conquest, Mohammad decided to Islamise the pagan shrines around Mecca, which made up the full pilgrimage known as the *hajj*. At each of the shrines, he and his Muslims performed and reinterpreted all the old pagan, Arab rites. They threw pebbles at the pillars of Mina, as though they were fighting evil and immorality. They ran seven times between the hills of Safa and Marwa, recalling the distress of Ishmael's mother Hagar when she had run desperately seeking water during her first days of exile in the desert. They drank from the spring that God showed to Hagar, in answer to her prayer. The Prophet also made the *ifada*, the Onrush, mounting his finest camel and charging with his Muslims in a body to Muzdalifa, the lowest point between the mountain of Arafat and Mecca. There he prayed to Allah and made an animal sacrifice to him.

Performance of the *hajj* was the fifth pillar of Islam. If he can afford it and his health and circumstances permit, each Muslim must make the *hajj* once in his lifetime. Mecca is the holiest city in the Muslim world because of its connection with Abraham, Hagar and Ishmael. The very first Muslims had followed the example of the Jews and the Christians and turned in the direction of Jerusalem when they prayed, but by returning his people to their Arab and religious roots Muslims had acquired a new centre, at the heart of their new Islamic identity. But Jerusalem was still important to Muslims, not only because it was connected with so many of the great prophets, but because of its connection with Mohammad. In 620 two years before the *hijra* Mohammad was said to have made a mystical flight to Jerusalem by night. He had alighted on the site of the old Jewish Temple and had thence ascended to heaven,[63] where he had spoken with Moses and Jesus. This vision of the Night Journey shows the Muslim connection with the two older religions and has made Jerusalem the third most holy city in Islam, after Mecca and Medina.

When Muslims make the *hajj* today, performing all the ancient rituals as Mohammad did, they feel that they are making an emotional and dynamic connection with the roots of their religion. Naturally they think about Mohammad, but they principally remember Abraham, Ishmael and Hagar. Even if Muslims are not Arabs, they are taught that Ishmael and Abraham are their ancestors, in the same way as St Paul taught Christians to see Abraham as the father of all believers. Islam began as a religion for the Arabs, but from the very first revelation it had also been a message for all mankind. When he made the *hajj* in 632 Mohammad made what has been called the Farewell Address to the *umma*, because he felt that his death was near. In addition to reminding them of the values of Islam, he is said to have looked forward to the time when Islam would have spread to other peoples and told them that all men were equal before Allah, without distinction of social class or racial origin.

> O people, your Lord is one and your ancestor is [also] one. You are all descended from Adam and Adam was [born] of the earth. *The noblest of you all in the sight of Allah is the most devout. Allah is knowing and all-wise* [Koran 49:13]. An Arab is superior to a non-Arab in nothing but devotion.[64]

When the Muslim pilgrims make the *hajj* to Mecca today they come from all over the world. All dress in the ritual white garment, so that all distinctions of race and class are obliterated. The pilgrimage is supposed to be an expression of the unity of all Muslims, the children of Adam and Abraham, and the identical clothes are an important symbol of this. Together they cry 'Here we are, O Lord,' as they approach the Ka'aba, crying to Allah with one voice. Peace and unity are the hallmark of the *hajj* and pilgrims are commanded to respect the holiness of the Ka'aba and the Sanctuary, just as Mohammad did when he conquered Mecca without bloodshed. Throughout the *hajj* the pilgrim has to abstain from the smallest hint of violence. He may not kill game (Koran 5:95) nor take part in a

quarrel (2:197). Until the late 1980s pilgrims observed these prohibitions scrupulously: they insisted that a pilgrim must not speak in a cross voice, kill even an insect or uproot a plant. While on the *hajj* a pilgrim must be at peace not only with all other Muslims but with the whole world. In Chapter 8 we will see how some radical Muslims today have turned the *hajj* into a violent declaration of war.

Shortly after making the final pilgrimage, Mohammad died and the shock of his death threatened to break the new Arab unity. In the ten years since the *hijra* of 622, Mohammad had managed to unite nearly the whole of the Hejaz under him and most of the tribes were either confederates or else they had converted to Islam. The Caliphs, Mohammad's successors, realised that if the old habits of tribal warfare were not to surface again, Muslims had to expend their aggressive instinct upon non-Muslims instead of upon one another and make sure that Islam kept expanding. There was a very similar situation in Europe at the time of the First Crusade. After the death of Mohammad, Arab armies began to invade the surrounding countries with such astounding success that just 100 years after the *hijra*, the new Islamic empire stretched from the Himalayas to Gibraltar. The soldiers were urged to fight humanely, as the Koran enjoined, but what had happened to the Koranic condemnation of aggressive warfare? To justify this apparent violation of Mohammad's principles, Muslim jurists began to develop a theology of the *jihad*. They taught that because there was only One God there should only be one state in the world that must submit to the true religion. It was the duty of the Muslim state (the House of Islam) to conquer the rest of the non-Muslim world (the House of War) so that the world could reflect the Divine Unity. Every Muslim must participate in this *jihad* and the House of Islam must never compromise with the House of War. At best a truce could be signed with a non-Muslim people, which must not exceed ten years. Until the final domination of the world was accomplished, therefore, Muslims were in a perpetual state of war.[65] It is this early doctrine of the *jihad* which has given Islam its reputation of being the religion of the sword and, had Muslims remained committed to this warlike theory, Islam would indeed have become a militaristic and imperialist religion.

But this did not happen. The theory had been developed when it looked as though Islam really *would* conquer the whole world, but by the beginning of the eighth century the *jihad* effort had burned out. The House of Islam had serious internal difficulties, which made any further wars of expansion impossible and Muslims accepted that, despite the doctrine of the *jihad*, the reality was that there would be no more 'holy wars' of conquest. Muslims now realised that the Islamic empire had frontiers that were permanent and, like the Christians and the Jews, they believed that their final world victory was to be postponed until the Last Judgement. They abandoned the doctrine of the *jihad*, which became a dead letter. Instead of seeing non-Muslim countries as enemies they developed normal trading and diplomatic contacts with them. Certainly some Muslim rulers did attack non-Muslim countries, but these were not part of the *jihad* but ordinary secular wars. The Caliphs employed a few dedicated men of war who, once in a while, would invade the House of War in a sort of token *jihad*, but in reality Muslims had learned to live side by side with other religions. This new attitude can be seen very clearly in Spain, the last of the great Islamic conquests. The Muslim land of al-Andalus was certainly an Islamic state. Almost as soon as they established their capital at Cordova they began to build the great mosque there, which, with its fortress-like exterior and contemplative interior shows the great spirituality that was possible within this apparently warlike new religion. Yet the Sultan and his amirs governed al-Andalus in a far more secular style than would have been acceptable seventy years earlier when the Muslims made their first conquests in

the Middle East. In Spain, for example, the Sultans at once recognised the existence
of the Christian Kingdom of Leon in the north and had diplomatic and trade relations with their Christian neighbours – something that directly contradicted the theology of *jihad* propounded by the jurists in the Sharia, or Holy Law of Islam. The Arab holy war had become Arab imperialism, and no longer entailed a branding of the non-Muslim world as the perpetual enemy.

Muslims may have forgotten the *jihad* but the Christians found it less easy to forget. The Christian world had watched aghast as this new religion swept through the Middle East and North Africa, conquering countries which had been strongly Christian with such ease that people began to ask themselves whether God was on the side of these 'infidels'. It was very threatening to the Christian identity to see this younger, energetic religion that claimed to have superseded Christianity actually transforming the map and absorbing Christians into its empire. The *jihad* remained a bogey in the West for centuries. When, for example, Sultan Abd al-Rahman of al-Andalus made a raid into Southern France in 732, he was defeated by Charles Martel at the battle of Poitiers and this has been seen as a turning point of world history. Gibbon contemplated the consequences of an Arab victory with a shudder:

> the Rhine is not more impassable than the Nile or the Euphrates, and the Arabian fleet might have sailed without a naval combat into the mouth of the Thames. Perhaps the interpretation of the Koran would now be taught in the schools of Oxford, and her pulpits might demonstrate to a circumcised people the sanctity and truth of the revelation of Mahomet. From such calamities was Christendom delivered by the genius and fortune of one man.[66]

This is a distorted and exaggerated view. The Sultan was not continuing the *jihad* and had no intention of conquering Europe. He had been invited into Christendom by Eudo, Duke of Aquitaine, who wanted his help against Charles Martel. Muslim historians scarcely mention 'the battle of Poitiers' except in passing, where they refer to it as an unfortunate but unimportant little raid. They had no designs on Europe, which they saw as an undesirable place, with a dreadful climate and primitive, backward inhabitants who were on a level with the black barbarians of Africa. Indeed Muslims spoke of a statue in Narbonne which bore the inscription: 'Turn back, sons of Ishmael, this is as far as you go, and if you do not go back, you will smite each other until the day of Resurrection.'[67] Yet Gibbon's view of the battle of Poitiers is not unusual. Centuries after the theory was abandoned as a practical project by Muslims, it continued to be a buried phobia in Christendom and still affects our attitude to the Islamic world. There was a good deal of this kind of fear in the air during the OPEC oil crisis in 1973: the Arabs seemed to want to 'take over the world'.

Even before the *jihad* burned out, Muslims had learned to live alongside other religions within the House of Islam. When a country was conquered there was no pressure on the inhabitants to convert, any more than there had been when Mohammad conquered Mecca. Islam had always proclaimed the sanctity of the individual conscience and the Koran's teaching about the People of the Book gave the conquerors a rationale for their treatment of the Christians and Jews in their empire. Christians and Jews had to accept that Islam was the state religion and show their submission by paying a tax in return for military protection. Nor was there any persecution of Buddhists and Hindus, when the Muslims got to India. The *dhimmis* or protected minorities, as they were called, were not allowed to bear arms and there were humiliating regulations which required, for example, that they wear distinctive dress or bow to Muslims when they paid their tax. No church, synagogue or temple building should be higher than the mosque. But these regulations were not rigorously enforced and the *dhimmis* were allowed full religious freedom within the House of Islam. There was no tradition of persecution in the Islamic empire to match the persecution of the Jews in Christendom, for example. If there was an occasional persecution it was inspired by a Jewish or Christian uprising or it occurred when the House of Islam was invaded by Christians and Jews. Thus the position of the Christian *dhimmis* deteriorated during the Crusades and life for Jews only became intolerable in Islamic countries after the creation of the State of Israel.[68]

Many of the *dhimmis*, however, chose to convert to Islam of their own volition. In Northern Africa or Syria, where Christianity had been established for a long time, most of the inhabitants ultimately became Muslims. The religion was attractive because of its simplicity and its dynamism. Further, as Muslims conquered countries like Persia, Egypt or parts of Northern Africa they came into contact with an ancient learning and culture that they were eager to make their own. The first Muslims to emerge from Arabia had been unsophisticated, simple people, but very quickly the Islamic empire developed its own distinctive civilisation. The new converts to Islam were eager to 'Islamise' their own traditions and in this way Muslims were able to absorb classical and ancient learning that had been lost to Western Christendom during the barbarian invasions of the fifth and sixth centuries. This was an extremely attractive new culture and many of the newly conquered peoples wanted to identify more strongly with it and become Muslims themselves. For a brief period in about 700 the Caliphs actually had to forbid conversion by law; because the new converts no longer had to pay the poll tax, the economy was in jeopardy.

Despite its warlike theology, therefore, Islam was in effect a tolerant religion and its polity provided for peaceful coexistence. The Muslim policy of peaceful coexistence was dictated not only by tolerant idealism, but also by practical and political common sense. The Middle East had always been a place where there had been many different religions. When the Byzantines or the Zoroastrians of Persia had tried to impose a religious conformity on their conquered people and had persecuted religious minorities the results had been politically disastrous. When they first conquered a country the Muslims were always a tiny minority and it would have been rash and unintelligent to antagonise their new subjects by attempting to force conversion upon them. The religious liberty enjoyed by the *dhimmis* made them willing and even content to accept Islamic hegemony.[65]

One of the first countries to fall to Islam in 637 was Palestine, which had been part of the Christian Byzantine empire. The Caliph Omar entered Jerusalem mounted on a white camel, escorted by the magistrate of the city, the Greek Patriarch Sophronius. The Caliph asked to be taken immediately to the Temple Mount and there he knelt in prayer on the spot where his friend Mohammad had made his Night Journey. The Patriarch watched in horror: this, he thought, must be the Abomination of Desolation that the Prophet Daniel had foretold would enter the Temple; this must be Antichrist who would herald the Last Days. Next Omar asked to see the Christian shrines and, while he was in the Church of the Holy Sepulchre, the time for Muslim prayer came round. Courteously the Patriarch invited him to pray where he was, but Omar as courteously refused. If he knelt to pray in the church, he explained, the Muslims would want to commemorate the event by erecting a mosque there, and that would mean that they would have to demolish the Holy Sepulchre.[69] Instead Omar went to pray at a little distance from the church, and, sure enough, directly opposite the Holy Sepulchre there is still a small mosque dedicated to the Caliph Omar. The other great mosque of Omar was erected on the Temple Mount to mark the Muslim conquest, together with the mosque al-Aqsa which commemorates Mohammad's

Night Journey. For years, the Christians had used the site of the ruined Jewish Temple as the city rubbish dump. The Caliph helped his Muslims to clear the garbage with his own hands and there Muslims raised their two shrines to establish Islam in the third most holy city in the Islamic world. The Dome of the Rock and al-Aqsa will be important in our story and are a perfect expression of the position that Islam adopted towards the older religions. On the one hand they are a symbol of a dominant, victorious Islam rising out of the ruins of a superseded faith; on the other, they show a need to root the identity of this new religion deeply in the ancient Jewish religion.

It should be clear, therefore, that the holy-war pattern that developed in all three religions does not reveal an atavistic blood-lust nor does it reveal an inherent intolerance. Holy war was a response to trauma. The Hebrews experienced the trauma of slavery in Egypt and the Muslims the culture shock of a changing Hejaz. Both undertook migrations that were a journey towards a new self. They wanted to achieve a liberated, dignified and independent new identity. But there were other people in the way of this goal and inevitably these people became the enemies of the newly emerging identity. The Hebrews were threatened by the Canaanites, who lived in the land that they believed had been promised by their God to them. They were also deeply threatened by the superior culture and attractive religion of these pagan peoples and felt that their new Jewish identity was in jeopardy. Later Jews would feel threatened by the *am ha-aretz* or by the Romans and this led them to fight desperate holy wars against these essential enemies. The violence and rejection were seen to be holy because they were inseparable from the Jewish identity that they had been commanded by God to establish. Other Jews, however, gained a new confidence in the diaspora and felt secure enough not to need to root their identity physically in the Holy Land. They were able to adopt more open and tolerant relations with the *goyim* because of this confidence and found that this was enriching. The Muslims achieved this confidence far more quickly than the Hebrews because of their early success, which was in itself perhaps due to wiser management. The Muslims could afford to be more tolerant of the people they conquered and this enabled them to build a rich, new and distinctively Islamic culture and achieve a stronger Muslim identity that did not need to rely wholly on force. Confidence and a sense of security, therefore, led to toleration and peaceful coexistence. When the Jewish or Muslim identity has been gravely threatened, as it has in our own day, Jews and Muslims are very likely to turn to the archetypal holy war in their search for a solution.

There were no 'holy wars' in Christianity, however, until Pope Urban summoned the First Crusade, and even then it was another two or three years before the Crusaders really conformed to the archetype of the classic holy war. In the eleventh century, Western Christians were beginning to recover from the trauma of the Dark Ages and were trying to create a new Western identity which would enable them to shake off their sense of inferiority towards their more powerful and cultured neighbours. They were trying to achieve a new self and were beginning to feel a new confidence. The Crusades were an essential part of this process and perfectly expressed the new Western spirit. So deeply had Christianity been affected by the Jewish traditions she had inherited that these Gentile Europeans found themselves automatically moving towards the classic solution.

· CHAPTER TWO ·

Before the Crusade

The West Seeks a New Christian Soul

In CE 850 a monk called Perfectus went shopping for his monastery in the *souk* of Cordova. Here he was accosted by a group of Muslims who tauntingly asked his opinion of Mohammad and Jesus. It was a capital offence in the Muslim empire either to apostasise from Islam or to insult the religion or its Prophet, and at first Perfectus responded to the goading of the Arabs with commendable prudence and restraint. He could not answer any of their questions about Mohammad, he replied, but would be quite happy to talk to them about Jesus. The Arabs continued to press him and Perfectus suddenly snapped, breaking into a vitriolic attack on the Prophet. An angry group of Muslims gathered and swept the monk off to the Qadi. Perfectus was at first extremely frightened and tried to deny the whole incident, but the Qadi did not pass the death sentence because he realised that the Christian had been unfairly provoked. He put him in prison, but once he was in gaol Perfectus cracked again and began to attack Islam so scurrilously that eventually the Qadi was forced to sentence him to death. Perfectus was publicly executed during the celebrations of the end of Ramadan. That day a pleasure-boat capsized and its Muslim passengers were drowned. The Christians of the city at once declared that God had avenged the death of Perfectus. They salvaged his body, dismembered it and began to distribute relics of their 'martyr'. From this incident a new cult of voluntary martyrdom was born, which perfectly expressed the old paradigm of an early Christian holy war.

Perfectus had not actually sought his death; he seemed unable to control a suicidal tendency to modulate from restraint to vitriol. In his story we sense that relations between Muslims and Christians in Cordova were tense. The Arabs who taunt the monk and the furious crowds that gather 'like angry bees'[1] suggest a buried worry as well as an intolerance of a Christian who stepped out of line. Perfectus was equally strained, and found it quite impossible to keep back an excessive hatred of Islam. Yet this was not the whole story. The Qadi acted with charity and moderation. So did most Christians in the city, who were called 'Mozarabs' or 'Arabizers'; they seemed quite happy to live in the tolerant state of al-Andalus and were eager to imbibe Arab culture. They spoke Arabic, read Arab philosophy and literature, knew Arab legends and Arab songs. There was even some intermarriage between Muslims and Christians and some Christian children were given Arab names by their parents.[2] Yet there was a fringe group among the Christians which could not tolerate this fraternising. They not only loathed the Muslims; they also hated the Mozarabs. They were convinced that Christians and Muslims could not share a city and should not live peaceably side by side. Many of them had recently made an exodus from the city into the country surrounding

32

Cordova and there founded monasteries of zealots who were fanatical haters of Islam. As usual this exodus was a prelude to a holy war. These fanatical Christians were not only opposed to religious toleration of Islam. They also rejected the secular culture and were desperately seeking a Christian, Spanish identity that felt threatened by their Arab masters.

The real founder of this new cult was one Ishaq or Isaac, who seems to have been brought up to integrate with the Muslim establishment. He had been given a name that was acceptable to either a Christian or a Muslim and held an excellent post in the civil service. Suddenly he threw it all up, left the world of Islam and joined one of the new radical monasteries outside the city. There, however, hearing about the fate of Perfectus he felt that this monastic retreat was not enough. He came back into the city and presented himself before the Qadi, told him that he wanted to convert to Islam and asked if he would kindly expound the faith. When the Qadi was halfway through his explanation Ishaq cried suddenly, 'You have lied,'[3] burst into an hysterical attack on Islam and invited the Qadi to become a Christian. He was evidently in such a state of crazed euphoria that the Qadi imagined that he must be drunk and slapped him in the face. He was reluctant to sentence him to death, however, because he felt that the monk was not responsible for his actions, but the Amir insisted on the death penalty and had Ishaq's body cremated to foil the relic hunters. He realised how dangerous a martyr cult would be but he was too late, for this suicidal fanaticism spread quickly. Soon after Ishaq's death, the abbot of his monastery and six of the monks came into the city, publicly attacked Islam and forced the reluctant authorities to put them to death. During the summer of 851 about fifty martyrs died in the same way. The Mozarab Christians were most alarmed and the Bishop of Cordova condemned the martyrs, but they found apologists in a priest called Eulogio and a layman called Alvaro. They insisted that the martyrs were taking the only honourable and virtuous course and that the Mozarabs were themselves 'persecutors' for tolerating Islam.[4] Jesus had told Christians that they must confess his name before the tribunals of unbelievers, and it seemed quite fitting to Eulogio and Alvaro that this confession should take the form of scurrilous, inaccurate abuse of Islam and Mohammad. The martyrs, they said, were 'soldiers of Christ' who were fighting for his honour and the honour of the faith. They were 'gallant men and warriors' who were fighting a 'spiritual battle' when they attacked the Muslims and died at their hands.[5] This was a holy war.

The Cordovans had, therefore, spontaneously revived the old cult of voluntary martyrdom practised by the Roman martyrs hundreds of years earlier. It seems that such suicidal violence is the only way a minority group can fight a holy war against a threatening majority. We shall see this aggressive martyrdom again in the story of the Crusades and we have seen it in the holy wars of our own day. It is not clear that the martyrs believed that they were fighting in a cosmic battle to hasten the Second Coming of Christ like the Roman martyrs, although there may have been apocalyptic enthusiasm in the radical new monasteries. They produced the beautiful and strangely illustrated manuscripts of the *Commentary on the Apocalypse* by Beatus of Liebana that were later brought into Christian Spain by these monks and copied obsessively in Europe. But the martyrdom of the Cordovans was obviously deeply aggressive, and not only because they achieved their martyrdom by an enraged verbal attack: to force the Muslims to put them to death against their will was a profound moral assault, a violence that was difficult to combat because it was turned in upon itself and seemed to put the Muslims in the wrong.

The martyrs came from all classes of society. There were men and women, monks, priests and laymen, simple poor people and sophisticated scholars. Eulogio and Alvaro have preserved some of their anti-Islamic speeches and these show that they had an entirely false idea of the Muslim faith. Islam was accused of being a Christian heresy and a failed form of Christianity; Mohammad was presented as a depraved lecher who encouraged the Muslims to fornicate and practise various forms of unnatural sexuality; Islam was held to be an essentially violent religion, which forced conversion at sword-point and persecuted the Christian *dhimmis*; Islam was also described as a self-indulgent, easy religion that had none of the holy austerity of Christianity.[6] The fascinating thing about this Christian fantasy was that it appeared again in Europe virtually unchanged during the Crusades 300 years later. The twelfth-century scholars who attacked Islam had never read Eulogio and they had had no tradition of hating Muslims. Indeed until the twelfth century Christians in the rest of Western Europe seemed quite uninterested in Muslims or Arabs and they had very vague ideas of what the religion was about. But later when they wanted to justify the Crusades and explain Islam, scholars quite spontaneously produced the same fiction as the ninth-century Cordovans. The strange fantasy of 'Islam' created by medieval Christians obviously tells us more about the insecurities and neuroses of the European Christians than it does about the Prophet and his religion.

One of the things the Cordovans were doing in their violent polemic was creating an enemy at a time when some of them were seeking a new identity. The martyrs seemed very anxious not to be swamped culturally by the Arabs, and their hatred of the Mozarabs was as much provoked by Mozarab enjoyment of Islamic culture as by disapproval of their religious toleration. The way they turned instinctively back to the practices of the Roman martyrs shows that in their eyes 'Islam' was as threatening as the persecuting Roman empire had been to third-century Christians; it also shows a nostalgia for all things Roman, paradoxical as this may seem at first. Eulogio constantly presents the conflict as though it were happening in classical Rome. He calls the Sultan a consul, speaks of his accession as 'the day that he was adorned with the fasces', refers to al-Andalus as *respublica* and describes some Arab officials 'speaking to the lictors'.[7] He also seems to have tried to start a classical revival in Cordova to counteract the Arabisation of Spain. He made a visit to Pamplona in the Christian north and brought back to Cordova volumes of works by the Latin Fathers of the Church and Latin authors like Vergil and Juvenal. He obviously wanted to build a new Western, European identity for the Christian *dhimmis* in Muslim Spain. Some of the martyrs may have had a special reason to feel confused and insecure, as they came from mixed families. One of these was a young woman called Flora, whom Eulogio particularly admired.[8] She had a Muslim father and a Christian mother, had been brought up as a Muslim but had been instructed secretly by her Christian mother. When she left home to join a Christian community she clearly wanted to assert her Christian identity unambiguously, but this made her an apostate, which was a capital offence. It could well be that Perfectus may have come from a similar mixed background, and that it was probably the strain that this involved that caused him to veer so irrationally from restraint to hysterical abuse. Many of the other martyrs who seemed to have had Arab names could well have been in the same position. Other martyrs, like Ishaq, who had been brought up to assimilate with Islam, felt compromised by being identified with the Arabs, and Ishaq's exodus to the monastery was probably a quest for a distinct Christian identity.[9] Like other holy wars, this strange episode in Cordova also sprang from an inner crisis. To create an enemy whom you can hate unreservedly as the expression of all that you are *not* was clearly an important part of the martyrs' new self-definition, and must account for the fantastic portrait of Islam in their polemic.

The martyr movement did not last for very long in Cordova. In 859 Eulogio himself was martyred, even though he did not present himself for martyrdom voluntarily. Indeed, while he and Alvaro were very good at urging other people to seek martyrdom, it is noticeable that they were reluctant to do so themselves. But Eulogio was caught harbouring a young woman apostate and instructing her in the faith. The Muslim judges urged him to make a token conversion to Islam in order to save his life and not give in to this 'deplorable and fatal self-destruction' like the other 'fools and idiots'.[10] They promised that they would not pursue him afterwards if he continued to be a practising Christian, but Eulogio steadfastly urged the Qadi to sharpen his sword. The martyr movement died with its leader, but the rejection of Islam and the desire for a separate identity remained. In the early tenth century the monks of the radical monasteries made an even more dramatic exodus and migrated to the Christian kingdom of Leon. The King gave them land on the borders so that they could strengthen Christian presence in the no-man's land between Christian and Muslim territory. Their exodus had put the monks into the front line of the coming Christian holy war of the Reconquest of Muslim Spain.[11]

In Europe at this time there was a similar desire to establish a specifically Western identity, which created a different enemy: the Greek Christians of Byzantium. The barbarian invasions of the fifth and sixth centuries had left Western Europe in a vulnerable and weakened condition. The culture of the empire was lost, together with most of the wisdom of the ancient world. People could not even farm the land adequately and Europe became a primitive backwater where people gazed at the crumbling ruins of the Roman period as belonging to a bygone race of giants, whose achievements now seemed incredible. When the barbarians had invaded Europe it seemed at first as though Christianity itself would perish, because the various tribes were either pagans or else had been converted to heretical forms of Christianity. The faith survived in the fortresses of the monasteries, where the monks managed to conserve the writings of the Fathers of the Church and a few classical texts, but otherwise Christianity seemed to have been defeated by 'the world'. Yet Christianity not only managed to survive and re-establish itself more powerfully than before, but was the means whereby Western Europe rose again to a new power. The popes sent missionaries out to the barbarian kingdoms and sought to instruct them in the mysteries of Roman Christianity and they achieved some notable success. They managed to convert the Anglo-Saxons in Britain and the Franks in the old province of Gaul. But these new Christians tended to remain very ignorant of Christianity, with its complex doctrines and definitions, and their faith was often a confused jumble of pagan and Christian ideas. They were for the most part illiterate and uneducated people and it was clear that there was much to be done before Europe fully recovered from the loss of the Roman empire.

But Europe had a powerful Christian neighbour. When the Roman empire had been destroyed in the West, the Eastern part of the Roman empire, with its capital at Constantinople, had remained intact and was now known to the Europeans as Byzantium and to the Muslims as *Rum* (Rome). The Emperor of Constantinople, head of Church and state, was the descendant of the ancient Roman emperors. He still ruled a powerful empire and fought a shrewdly skilful diplomatic and military campaign to keep Islam at bay. As the only emperor left, he was now the ruler of Italy, which the barbarians had not yet wholly penetrated, and Byzantium had its administrative centre at Ravenna. The Greek empire of Byzantium, therefore, had enjoyed unbroken continuity and was the only place in the world where the old Roman Christianity had survived intact. The great Churches of Jerusalem, Antioch, Alexandria and Rome had either been swallowed up by Islam or gravely weakened by the invaders. Constantinople had not always been a great Church.

Originally it had been Constantine's imperial city and only a secular capital, but now it seemed the last powerful bastion of the faith and the guardian of theological purity against the twofold threat of Islam and the ignorant Western barbarians. The Patriarch of Constantinople acknowledged the spiritual primacy of the Pope, but the Emperor's court was felt to mirror the imperium of heaven, and the Byzantines liked to depict Christ as Pantocrater, the cosmic Emperor of the Universe.[12] This triumphant image of Christ reflected the confidence and serenity of the Greek Church. In the traumatised West the human image of the suffering Jesus would become more popular. But in Byzantium, the icons and mosaics of Christ and the saints also reveal the contemplative wisdom of the Eastern Church, which never became as belligerent as the Latin Church in the West.

One might perhaps see the Byzantine and the Western Churches as reflecting, respectively, the values of the ancient Greece and Rome. Even before Rome fell in the sixth century, the Latin version of Christianity tended to be more literal-minded and aggressive than the sophisticated Greek Church of the East. Its followers were more like the martial Romans, who had been practical men rather than intellectuals and had been conquered culturally by the Greek Hellenic tradition, which they could not match. Both Greek and Latin Churches had their eccentrics and fanatics, like any institution, but Greek or oriental Christians tended towards a more subtle interpretation of the scriptures than the Latins like St Augustine who took every story as factually true. Yet there was no doctrinal quarrel between Eastern and Western Christianity; the difference was psychological rather than intellectual. But after the destruction of the Western Empire, even though it was natural for the unscathed Eastern Church to feel responsible for the vulnerable Latins, the Western Church was still anxious to preserve its own Western, Latin identity and did not want to be swamped by the Greeks. Although nearly all the popes at this time were either Greeks or oriental Christians who were refugees from Islam, the Roman Christians were on their guard against the Latin tradition being lost. When Theodore, a Greek Christian from Tarsus in Cilicia, was appointed Archbishop of Canterbury in the new British Church in 668, a bishop from North Africa, who had been trained in the Latin rite, went with him to make sure that he did not introduce Greek customs into England.[13] Despite the powerful position of Byzantium and the precarious state of Western Christianity, the West was clearly anxious not to become a mere outpost of the Greek Church.

Interestingly the new barbarian converts to Christianity among the Anglo-Saxons and the Franks were particularly strong champions of the Latin rite. They resented the way the Greeks obviously looked down upon them and they hated the fact that Rome, the only glory left in Europe, should be dominated by the Eastern Church, that more Greek than Latin was spoken there and that the Pope, the successor of St Peter, was a Greek. They wanted the Pope to be a Westerner of the Latin rite and longed to rid Europe of the haughty Greeks. When St Wilfred, a leading English Christian, visited Rome in 704 to appeal to the Pope against the Archbishop of Canterbury, he was most distressed, after he had finished his speech in Latin, when the Greek Pope spoke to his advisers in a foreign tongue and when the court patronisingly 'smiled and said things that we did not understand'.[14] The Western converts did not want to create a separate Church; they simply wanted to be treated with dignity and respect and for the West to live according to the old Western traditions. The popes at this time were finding that the emperors of Byzantium were tending to limit papal claims. Slowly they began to realise that they had ardent champions in the newly converted barbarians, if they were ready to defy Greek control. When in 729 the Emperor actually dared to send Pope Gregory II a mandate restricting the placing of images of the saints in his churches, the Pope was furious and saw where his real supporters were: 'The whole West has its eyes on us, unworthy though we are. It relies on us and on St Peter, the Prince of the Apostles, whose image you wished to destroy, but whom all the kingdoms of the West honour as if he were God himself on earth.' He declared that there would be further missionary efforts in 'the most distant parts of the West'[15] and vowed that he would go himself to baptise these barbarian converts whose devotion to the papacy was such that they wished to be baptised by the Pope alone. Pope Gregory II did not in fact make this journey, but twenty-three years later a pope did cross the Alps and visited the barbarian Christians for the first time.

By the middle of the eighth century, the political situation in Italy had deteriorated. The Lombards had become established in northern Italy and weakened Byzantine power there, and this made the Pope himself more vulnerable and in need of a new secular protector, because even though the Emperor of Byzantium was still officially the temporal ruler of Rome he could no longer rely on his help. In 752 a Western Pope was elected who took the name of Stephen II and it was Stephen who made the momentous journey over the Alps in 753 to seek an alliance with Pepin, the new King of the Franks and the son of Charles Martel. In the Abbey of St Denis near Paris, Stephen crowned Pepin and gave papal legitimacy to the new Carolingian dynasty. Then he and Pepin made a treaty whereby the political power of Italy was divided between the Pope and the King of France. Pepin had effectively stepped into the shoes of the Emperor of Byzantium and this extremely important move on the part of the Western Pope was a direct affront to the Emperor of Byzantium and to the Greek Church. From this point the popes would be Westerners, and the papacy would become a Western institution which the Greek Church found increasingly difficult to accept. Stephen's action was of course highly treasonable and illegal, but he was transforming the papacy and declaring, for the first time, that the Pope was the ruler of Christian Europe not the Emperor. Pepin was not yet an emperor himself, only the Pope's client, but it must be significant that when he had greeted Stephen in Paris he had used the old ceremonial with which the Roman emperors had greeted popes in the past. The West was clearly getting ready to declare its political and cultural independence of Byzantium and even though there was still no thought of a schism between the two Churches it was inevitable that relations between them became very strained from this point. Naturally the Byzantines saw Stephen as a traitor and Pepin as a usurper and found it insulting that this illiterate barbarian should presume to take the place of the learned Emperor of Byzantium. But the new Christians in the West were well pleased with this symbol of their liberation from the proud and patronising Greeks. Pepin showed that he wanted to build Europe as a strongly united power once more and he dramatically extended his Frankish territories in a series of brutal wars, which forced more of the pagan peoples of Europe into Christendom at sword-point. As Europe began to revive and attempted a new period of power, she was asserting herself consciously against Byzantium, so that the first enemies of the new Europe were not the Muslims but the Greeks.

When Pepin's great son Charlemagne succeeded him in 771 he was the ruler of what is now France, Flanders and a large part of Western Germany. Charlemagne continued this Frankish expansion of Christendom into Eastern Germany and Eastern Europe, forcing the Saxons and Slavs into the faith at sword-point. He also tried to build the West culturally, initiating a renaissance of learning in his palace school, though he was never able to master the art of reading himself. He was a great builder and in his capital at Aachen he built the great Cathedral of St Mary which was modelled on the Byzantine imperial basilica at Ravenna. He was therefore setting himself up as the Western counterpart to the Greek Emperor. But he also inspired another comparison. In Aachen his throne was built according to the measurements of Solomon's throne in Jerusalem and his biographers constantly compared him to the kings and heroes of Israel: he fought as bravely as Joshua; he was a lawgiver like Moses; he was as dignified and saintly as King David and as great a builder as King Solomon.[16] In this new burst of confidence, the Franks were beginning to see themselves as a new chosen people and revealed the aggressive ambition of these new Western nations. Charlemagne's court was cosmopolitan and his biographers liked to present all the nations coming to pay tribute to Charlemagne at Aachen, the new Jerusalem. In particular they relished the embassy of Harun al-Rashid, the Caliph of Baghdad. These 'Persians', as they are vaguely called, are shown as awed by Charlemagne and are treated very sympathetically: the Sultan was said to have made Charlemagne the guardian of the Holy Sepulchre in Jerusalem.[17] But the Byzantine envoys get a very different treatment: they are shown as crafty but stupid, and certainly no match for the Franks. The extravagant chronicler known as Notger the Stammerer, who was writing in 885, is quite vitriolic in his tales of the Greeks at Charlemagne's court and shows them to be crushed and overwhelmed by the majesty of the Western King.[18]

The Franks saw Charlemagne as the great hope of the world, but the popes and Byzantines had a more realistic view of him. The Pope certainly did not intend to make him an emperor, equal to the learned Emperor of Byzantium, and in 787 a revealing incident shows how Charlemagne and the Franks still deeply resented this slighting comparison. The Second Council of Nicaea had met that year, attended by the papal legates and Eastern patriarchs. Although it was an ecumenical council, the Western bishops were not invited, because they were not theologically equipped to take part in the debates. Charlemagne was insulted and denounced the Council and the Greek Church as a 'filthy pond of hell' from which sprang 'streams of boastfulness and vainglory'. When he received a translation of the Council's decrees, he condemned them as 'errors', in 'the hope that the spineless enemy from the East may be repelled in the West'.[19] This behaviour was as unacceptable to the Pope as to the Greeks. It was absurd that an illiterate layman like Charlemagne should presume to lay down the law on abstruse doctrinal issues. But Charlemagne had wanted to make it clear that the Western Church was determined to be treated with dignity and respect. His action was also a veiled warning to the Pope. He should realise how much he depended on the Carolingians and he should not be so obviously in collusion with the Greek 'enemy'. It was not long before a pope discovered how much he needed Charlemagne.

In 800 a group of Roman citizens rebelled against Pope Leo III on the grounds that he had committed a crime. They threatened to cut out his tongue and gouge out his eyes to make him incapable of continuing in office. In the event, they bungled the gouging operation and only managed to damage one eye. As soon as he heard of the insurrection, Charlemagne marched on Rome with a huge army, crushed the rebellion and rounded up the rebels. In gratitude Leo crowned him Holy Roman Emperor of the West on Christmas Day. It was a deliberate affront to Byzantium, as Charlemagne was well aware. Einhard, his biographer, noted that the Byzantines regarded Charlemagne as a usurper and a threat, 'for he might well have been planning to take their own imperial power from them'.[20] They would continue to regard the Franks with deep suspicion, he wrote, and quoted a Greek proverb: 'If a Frank is your friend, then he is clearly not your neighbour.'[21] It seemed preposterous to the Greeks that this ignorant yokel should array himself in imperial regalia and consider himself their equal. It was also painful that a descendant of those barbarians who had destroyed the empire in the West was now sitting on the imperial throne. But to many of the people of Europe it seemed as though the West was now ready to take its destiny into its own hands and assert its independence of the haughty Greeks. It seemed that the days of Western humiliation were numbered.

None of these hopes was fulfilled. Charlemagne's empire and his achievements disintegrated after his death and during the ninth and tenth centuries Europe experienced the trauma of new invasions which halted her progress. The Vikings invaded from the north, the Magyars from the east and Muslim pirates raided in Italy and the south of France. But despite this distress, Europe never forgot Charlemagne; people looked back to him nostalgically as a symbol of Western dignity and independence. During the tenth century the Franks lost the leadership of Europe to the Germans, whom Charlemagne had conquered, and in 962 Otto I became the Holy Roman Emperor and initiated an exciting new renaissance of art and letters in his German empire. Yet again this was fiercely resented by the Byzantines, and there was a new hostility and contempt for the Western upstarts. The sensitivity on both sides is clear in the account Bishop Liudprand of Cremona wrote of his embassy to Byzantium on Otto's behalf six years after the imperial coronation. Liudprand had hitherto been a champion of Byzantium. He spoke fluent Greek and when he had made a previous embassy to Constantinople in 649 he had been at pains to explain Byzantine practice to Western people. But now that he went as Otto's envoy he got very different treatment and his account simmers with bitterness, anger and resentment. The climax came as he was leaving the country, when a customs official confiscated the purple silk that he was hoping to take home with him because, the official explained, the Emperor of Constantinople had decreed that the imperial purple could be worn only by the Byzantines 'who surpass other nations in wealth and wisdom'. It was a great insult to Otto, the Emperor of the West, and Liudprand wrote furiously to him of his new hatred of the Byzantines:

So you see, they judge all Italians, Saxons, Franks, Bavarians, Swabians – in fact all other nations – unworthy to go about clothed in this way. Is it not indecent and insulting that these soft, effeminate, long-sleeved, bejewelled and begowned liars, eunuchs and idlers should go about in purple, while our heroes, strong men trained to war, full of faith and charity, servants of God, filled with all the virtues, may not! If this is not an insult, what is?[22]

The Byzantines were seen as the antithesis of the Western identity. There was a new polarisation at a time when the West was making a new attempt to revive the old glories of the Roman empire, and as Europe defined herself anew the Greeks became everything that the Westerners were not. This stereotype of 'the Greeks' persisted throughout the Middle Ages. Their elegance and refinement (which the Westerners in fact deeply envied and knew was quite beyond them) have been distorted into an image of weak effeminacy. This scurrilous portrait, as fictional as the ninth-century Cordovan portrait of 'the Muslim', was a crooked mirror-image of Western deep-rooted feelings of inferiority and a projection of Western envy. The Westerners for their part were already cultivating an image of tough aggression and presenting it as virtue. They were opposing their brute brawn to the Byzantines' brains. It was still not a case of a religious split between the two Churches and both Greeks and Europeans would have found the very idea of a divided Christianity a shocking state of affairs, but there was an ever increasing tension between the two. From this point, as Europe really did begin to recover from the Dark Ages, this tension increased.

At about the same time as Otto was reviving the Holy Roman Empire in the West, the Church began an even more effective effort to reform the spirit of Europe. This reform started in the late tenth century in the Benedictine monastery of Cluny in Burgundy and in its many daughter houses. The Cluniac monks wanted to Christianise the people of Europe and educate them in the ways of true

Christianity. There was always a difference between what the Cluniacs intended and what the laity understood, but the reform was very successful. Many of the most powerful and successful popes of the eleventh century were Cluniacs and this helped to spread the ideals of the reform and made it official Church policy. Slowly Europeans became Christians in spirit as well as in name, but Christian in the spirit of Cluny. Pope Urban II was himself a Cluniac and his Crusade can be seen as one of the most dramatic results of the reform movement.

One of the most dramatic ways in which they gave Europe a new Christian identity was their ambitious building project, whose achievements have been compared to the building of the Romans.[23] This is very impressive when we remember how poor Europe was at this time. Hundreds of churches were built throughout Christendom, even in quite small villages or settlements. These impressive stone buildings in the Roman style towered over the humble shacks of the people and could be seen for miles around, giving a unified appearance to Europe that suggested a unified Christian spirit, and, perhaps, a revived Rome. Inside these churches the people heard Mass and were instructed in the faith. They learned important lessons in the Romanesque sculptures that depicted demons struggling with the soldiers of God. Life seemed to consist of an endless battle with the forces of evil and this reflected the spirit of the Benedictine monasteries, which had always seen themselves as fortresses, waging a holy war against the demons as the knights had fought against the Magyars, Muslims and Vikings who had invaded Europe. There was no thought of offering Christians reassuring or peaceful images, for life was still far too violent and dangerous in Europe and the churches were literally fortresses for the common people in time of war. During the eleventh century the invasions had ceased but there was a bitter and violent internecine feudal warfare. The knights were no longer the defenders of Christendom but, in the absence of an external foe, had turned against one another. During a battle, when the poor were caught between the armies of warring knights, they could barricade themselves into the church and find safety there. The Church was telling them very graphically that not only was she fighting a spiritual war on their behalf, but she was also protecting them far more effectively than the knights, who had no concern for their welfare. The common people should look to the Church for help and guidance, not to the barons and their soldiers.

Yet though this building project was undoubtedly very important, the people still had a great deal to learn about the basic facts of the Christian life and the Cluniacs sought to provide a more spiritual guidance and succour to the people than the purely physical sanctuary of the new churches. They believed, of course, that they were the only people in Europe who were living according to the spirit of the gospels and so naturally when they tried to Christianise the people of Europe they tried to teach them to live like monks. At first sight it seems that the Cluniacs in Europe were living very differently from the way Jesus and his disciples had lived in the land of Israel but the Cluniacs could argue their case effectively. Jesus had, for example, lived a celibate life and monks also lived lives of chastity. Part of the Cluniac reform was directed to enforcing celibacy on the secular clergy, who at this time were free to marry if they chose. The clergy put up a good deal of resistance, and it was not until 1215 that the Church was able to make celibacy obligatory for her priests. Again, Jesus had lived a poor life and the first Christians in Jerusalem had lived in community holding all things in common, so poverty was considered an essential monastic virtue. It is true that the Cluniac monks lived more comfortably than most poor people at this time and that the Cluniac monasteries were rich and powerful establishments, far removed from that early community in Jerusalem. But at least the Benedictines possessed no personal property and they lived communal lives, where the monks shared everything equally. A Benedictine monk also took a vow of stability, which meant that he promised to stay in one monastery for the whole of his life. Stability was an important value in the insecure world of the Middle Ages, where the primitive conditions made the whole of life seem fleeting and transient. In a world where agriculture was inadequate, people frequently died of starvation or malnutrition; beauty and health disintegrated very quickly; friends continually died and the community was very vulnerable to natural disasters like famines or floods. Life therefore seemed full of arbitrary change and disaster, which was seen not merely as the punishment for sin, but also as the experience of sin itself, in rather the same way as exile was seen by the Jews. By contrast, the monks in their walled fortresses which enshrined the gospel values permanently[24] seemed already to enjoy something of the safety and stability of heaven. Ideally people believed that everybody should be monks, but this was impossible. The Cluniacs therefore encouraged lay men and women to live like monks as far as they could.

How could this be done? One way was an attempt to regularise the sex lives of Western Christians. Tenth-century penitentials, guides for the priests about how to judge sins in confession, seemed to try to make married people as chaste as monks. Intercourse was forbidden during Lent and Advent, during menstruation, pregnancy and breastfeeding, on Ember Days, on Holy Days, on Mondays, Wednesdays, Fridays and Sundays.[25] We have no idea whether the laity put these formidable requirements into practice and it seems likely that this attempt to make Europe chaste was resisted by the lay people as steadily as it was resisted by the clergy. A far more popular way of forming the monastic character was the penitential pilgrimage, which became an extremely important part of the Christian life in Europe during the eleventh century.

Christians had always made pilgrimages to their holy places, but in the ideology of the pilgrimage promoted by Cluny it was the journey not the arrival that counted. This holy journey would be a journey to a new Christian self, because while he or she was travelling to the shrine, the pilgrim would be living according to the ideals and practices of the monks. The journey to the shrine was therefore a kind of novitiate, that formed and shaped the pilgrim and taught him what being a Christian really meant, according to the ideals of Cluny. At first sight, it might seem that nothing could be more different from life in a monastery. Instead of living a life of holy stability, the pilgrim was travelling from one place to another, exposed to the flux of the sinful world, so for the layman the religious life was essentially mobile. But in other respects the pilgrimage did mirror monastic ideals very accurately. Benedictine monasticism depended upon a conversion of life, whereby the monk turned his back on the sinful world and returned to God. Even when a monk was given to the monastery as a young child, he was expected to make that interior decision. Christ had said that nobody could be his disciple unless he was prepared to give up his family and friends and follow him to the ends of the earth, and to fulfil that command the monk made the exodus into the monastery. Similarly, the pilgrim literally turned his back on his old life for a time, leaving family, friends and everything with which he was familiar. In fact during the eleventh century, spiritual writers frequently compared the pilgrim's decision to migrate to a new life to Abraham's migration from Ur to the Promised Land or to the Exodus of the Israelites from Egypt.[26] At the outset of his journey, a pilgrim made a vow to pray at the holy place and he donned special clothes at the altar, just as the monk did at the outset of his religious life when he made profession of vows. Like the monk, the pilgrim joined a community dedicated to monastic ideals, for during the eleventh century the pilgrimage became a communual devotion. During the pilgrimage a pilgrim was expected to lead a celibate life, like the monk. Because the journey was often a harsh one, the austerities imposed the practice of monastic asceticism on the pilgrims. If the pilgrim was a rich man, he laid aside the comforts that cushioned him from the sufferings of cold, fatigue and weariness that beset the poor. If he was a poor man, the pilgrim discovered that his poverty was not a shameful state, but could have a spiritual value. During the pilgrimage rich and poor lived side by side in a community that, ideally, broke down the distinctions between them. Most importantly for our purposes, during the pilgrimage a pilgrim was forbidden to bear arms or to fight, just as the monk was. This holy journey became immensely popular during the eleventh century and it does seem to have changed the mentality of many European laymen. At the time of the First Crusade, many of the knights and poor people who answered the call to arms were imbued with these monastic ideals and lived fairly devout lives, whereas a hundred years earlier such ideals would have been entirely foreign to them.

But if the Cluniacs were more interested in the journey, for most of the laymen who took part in the pilgrimages it was the arrival that counted. The shrine or the holy place had been very important in the old Latin Christianity of late Antiquity. During the fourth century, when Christianity had become the state religion, new churches and basilicas had been built to house the bodies of the martyrs. Christians had come from far and wide to pray at their tombs, because they believed that physical closeness to these friends of God brought them nearer to heaven itself. They believed that the bodies of the martyrs were still imbued with a holiness that was felt to manifest itself physically. When the stories of their martyrdom were read aloud at the tomb, a sweet smell seemed to fill the basilica and the sick and crippled people who had gathered there cried aloud in ecstasy as they felt the power of the saints enter their bodies so strongly that their ailments were healed.[27] This fourth-century devotion to the holy place continued after the barbarian invasions in the new Christian kingdoms and naturally blended with the common pagan belief that certain places were instinct with godhead. Most laymen in Europe felt that 'holiness' was not a spiritual or moral state so much as a power that manifested itself physically like a holy radioactivity.[28] When the pilgrim finally entered the shrine at the end of his journey and prayed before relics of saints or at their tombs, he was exposing himself to a power that could kill a wicked man or heal a sick person. Relics were the most important element in the religious experience of Europe during the early Middle Ages. The establishment and the educated Cluniacs found this devotion highly dubious because it reduced religion to pagan magic but they could do nothing to change it. In the frightening world of the eleventh century, the relics gave to laypeople some of the stability and security that the monks enjoyed. Because the relic was linked to a man or woman who was now in heaven, it was a tangible bond with the next world. When, therefore, pilgrims prayed at the tomb of St Peter in Rome they felt an enormous safety in being so close to the man who opened the gates of heaven. People believed that the divine power was channelled to men through relics and so they were carried into battle, to help the army, and were used to bind oaths and treaties with the permanence of heaven.[29] The cult of the pilgrimage during the eleventh century necessarily also cultivated this devotion to the holy place, even though this had not been the original intention of the Cluniac reformers.

It follows that holiness was very local. A saint was only effective in the region where he had lived and died or in the place where he was buried. This is why people often stole the bodies of saints from a city; they wanted to appropriate this power for themselves. But the local character of holiness was problematic for Europeans because all the holiest shrines were obviously in the East, where Jesus had lived and died. This was why legends developed which maintained that after his death many of Jesus' friends had come to Europe and were buried there. St Peter was firmly believed to have come to Rome, even though there is not a shred of evidence for this. Similarly Mary Magdalene was said to have settled in the south of France and Joseph of Arimathea was believed to have brought the faith to England and to have been buried at Glastonbury.[30] Above all St James, who was called the brother of the Lord, was believed to have come to Spain and to be buried at Compostela. There was an ancient legend that said that James was Jesus' twin brother, so clearly having his body was the next best thing to having the body of Jesus himself. Compostela became the most holy place in Europe and during the eleventh century pilgrims travelled there in thousands to fill themselves with the holiness of St James.[31] Along the main pilgrim routes the Cluniacs built churches which housed other relics where the pilgrims could pray during their long journey to Spain, which was the end of the known world.

But obviously there could be no more holy place than Jerusalem where Jesus had died and risen again to save the world, and during the eleventh century there was a new passionate enthusiasm for Jerusalem and the Holy Land, which was seen by the laypeople as the holiest relic of all because of its physical link with the Son of God. The very soil of the land was believed to be pregnant with divine power, because Jesus had walked on it during his life. The Holy Sepulchre Church, which was believed to house the site of Golgotha and which contained the tomb of Christ, was filled with the immense holiness of the events that had redeemed mankind.[32] More pilgrims than ever made the arduous and dangerous journey through Muslim territory to the Holy Land. In Europe more Christians than ever before made donations to the Holy Sepulchre Church and dedicated the churches they built to the Holy Sepulchre. One of the earliest of these churches was at Loches in the Loire valley. It was built by Count Fulk of Anjou, who had made the pilgrimage to Jerusalem in 1009. When he had knelt to kiss the tomb of Christ he was said to have miraculously bitten off a chunk of stone. He had thus captured some of the holiness of Jerusalem for Europe, which he enshrined in his new church of the Holy Sepulchre back home. This legend tells us two things. First, a desperation had entered the European devotion to the Holy Sepulchre. More and more Western people felt acutely deprived of the holiness of the East.[33] The story is an excellent example of the literal-mindedness of Western Christianity and its obsession with the holiness of the physical relics of Jesus and the saints. This frantic and irrational love of the Holy Land was quite alien to the piety of the Byzantines, who found it typical of the primitive religion of the Western Christians. Second, Fulk's descendants would become very important Crusaders and in the twelfth century another Fulk of Anjou became King of Jerusalem. A passionate devotion to Jerusalem was one of the results of the Cluniac cult of the pilgrimage and was central to crusading. Though Urban II would have dismissed Count Fulk's passion for Jerusalem as superstitious and excessive, he did call the Crusade a pilgrimage and Crusaders would always call themselves pilgrims. In fact the word 'Crusade' did not become common until very late in the crusading movement.

But the pilgrimage was not the only element in crusading nor was it the only way the Church managed to transform the Western soul during the eleventh century. Before any real progress could be made in Europe it was essential that the internecine feudal warfare that was tearing society apart come to an end. The two centuries of invasion had militarised Europe and the knightly aristocracy had become extremely important as a defensive force. They had formed their identity on violence and warfare, which they saw as a glorious activity. But after the invasions ceased and there were no more legitimate external enemies, the system of defence that had evolved collapsed and turned in upon itself. Knights and barons started to fight each other. The country was devastated and property and crops vandalised. To counteract this the Church initiated a peace movement which was called the Peace of God. This began in the south of France at the end of the tenth century. Crowds of priests, knights and poor people gathered in huge 'Councils' and proclaimed a peace which they called the Truce of God. During this Truce all fighting was forbidden for a definite period and a group of knights volunteered to police this Truce and fight any of the knights and barons who broke it. All swore to keep the Truce in the presence of the relics, and the emotion at these gatherings was intense. They were similar to modern revivalist meetings and the people would cry 'Peace! Peace!' as they begged God to send them peace in their time. Slowly the movement spread and began to form public opinion. War and violence were depicted as unChristian and the common people felt that their hatred of the violent knights was justified. The knights themselves were taught that to fight other Christians was deeply sinful. During the Truce a knight adopted monastic practices, just as he might do if he went on a pilgrimage. He did not bear arms and did not fight, like a monk. To some degree he also lived a life of holy poverty during the Truce. The poor could not carry arms to defend themselves because they simply could not afford the very expensive equipment that made the knights a formidable fighting force. This made them frighteningly vulnerable and, by sharing this vulnerability for a time, the knights became poor men, as it were, and shared some of their problems.[34]

In the year 1033 there was a widespread famine, and an apocalyptic terror spread throughout Europe. As the Burgundian annalist Raoul Glaber wrote: 'Men believed that the orderly procession of the seasons and the laws of nature, which until then had ruled the world, had relapsed into eternal chaos; and they feared that mankind might end.'[35] They believed that God was about to destroy the world because of their sins, just as he had destroyed the world by flood in the time of Noah. The apocalyptic fear may have been enhanced by the fact that people believed that it was exactly a thousand years since the Crucifixion of Christ. To stave off this catastrophe the layfolk and the clergy marched in huge penitential processions, begging God for forgiveness, and this new terror entered the Peace of God, which suddenly spread that year all over France. At the Peace Councils, there was a new desperation. When they cried 'Peace! Peace!' people were no longer simply asking for an end of war. They were asking God to send a new and better world, free from plague, famine and flood. Glaber tells us that the peace movement now raised enormous hopes, which the Cluniacs and the establishment Church had not intended. The people now felt that they could change history and exercise some control over their own destiny. It was a pathetic glimmering of the concept of self-determination and, when the peace movement seemed to have failed them, Glaber says that thousands of people took a different and desperate course. First the peasants, then the more established classes of society and finally the rich nobles began to march in vast companies to Jerusalem in a mass pilgrimage: 'An innumerable multitude began to stream towards the Saviour's Tomb in Jerusalem,' says Glaber and was convinced that this meant a new apocalypse.[36] 'This vast crowd of people in the Holy City, of which no other century had seen the like, presaged nothing else than the coming of the miserable Antichrist, which must indicate the coming end of the world.' These pilgrims seemed to have believed that if they congregated in Jerusalem in large enough numbers, Antichrist would have to come and fight them and the battle with Antichrist would bring about the Last Days and the Final Redemption.[37] God would send down a New Jerusalem, which meant a new and better world. The pilgrims, therefore, were trying to force God to save them by acting themselves, and this will prove to be a crucial element in the holy war.

As in any time of stress, there was a great deal of apocalyptic fervour during the eleventh century. In about the year 1000 an old myth revived that would prove to be very important during the Crusades. The old Sibylline prophets of the late Roman period had said that before the end of the world, an Emperor from the West would be crowned in Jerusalem and would fight Antichrist there,[38] and people began to look around for an emperor who would fulfil this mission. There was a new feeling of purposefulness. Instead of waiting to be wiped out by another famine or pestilence, people were beginning to feel that they should try to save themselves by fulfilling these ancient prophecies. It was an initiative for self-determination. Thirty years after the great pilgrimage to Jerusalem in 1033, there was another massive exodus from Europe, when 7000 pilgrims left Europe for the Holy Land, probably with the same apocalyptic desire to force Antichrist to declare himself. When Pope Urban made his famous crusading speech in 1095 it was almost thirty years later and time for another such pilgrimage. When people heard that the Pope had urged the knights of Europe to march to liberate Jerusalem, many of them were probably inspired to join the Crusade in order to save the world and bring down the New Jerusalem. Urban himself, of course, would have had no truck with this kind of thinking, but he was unable to control the movement he started, for Jerusalem had been acquiring such rich and complex associations during the eleventh century.

But after the terrors of the first half of the century, the quality of life in Europe began to improve dramatically. There was an agricultural revolution and people felt that they had greater control over their circumstances. There was a new confidence in the air, which towards the end of the century began to express itself aggressively. Instead of cowering passively in land that they could not cultivate properly, Europe started to expand. The Normans had long challenged Roman and Byzantine power in the south of Italy and in 1061 Count Roger invaded the Muslim stronghold of Sicily and eventually conquered it for Christendom in 1091. In 1066 William of Normandy invaded the Anglo-Saxon kingdom of Britain and in 1085 Spanish Christians, with the help of Frankish knights, managed to conquer Toledo from the Muslims and pushed back the borders of al-Andalus. Although she was against war officially the Church was still anxious to harness this useful aggression and make it Christian. For many years monks had been encouraged to build monasteries in the no-man's land on the borders of Christendom and to push against the darkness of paganism and Islam that lurked outside the realm of Christ. Now that the knights were beginning to conquer the Muslims and push forward the frontiers of Christendom even more dramatically, the popes were anxious to keep control of the newly confident laymen.

Yet this involved an obvious inconsistency. Christianity had always been against violence and in the Peace of God the Cluniac reformers had been encouraging the people to see war as unChristian and to hate the knights. How could the Church now bless these new wars of aggression, as in fact she did? But for many years the popes had been preaching a double message. Some of the reformers had wisely felt that to antagonise the knights was foolish. In the Peace of God, knights had policed the Truce by means of violence, which in the interests of peace the Church had been prepared to sanction. In France and Italy other Cluniac reformers began to try to reform the institution of knighthood itself. Instead of harrying the poor and helpless, they taught that the Christian knight should come to the defence of the poor and needy and fulfil a Christian vocation. Other churchmen went further. They encouraged the knights in their diocese to form a militia to defend the local Church and the Christian populace in time of war. One of these bishops was the Bishop of Toul, who became Pope Leo IX in 1049. Two months after his consecration he formed a Roman militia to fight the Normans who were threatening to invade his lands and in 1053 he actually led his troops into battle himself.[39] Some of his contemporaries felt that this was too extreme, but the popes

continued to encourage these ecclesiastical companies. Twenty years later the Cluniac Pope Gregory VII invited the laymen of the whole of Europe to form a militia which he called the Knights of St Peter, bound to the Pope as its head and dedicated to the defence of the Church. In 1071 and 1074, in response to Turkish victories against Byzantium, Gregory called upon the Knights of St Peter to march to the East and liberate the Greeks from the infidels. Anybody who died on this expedition would gain an 'eternal reward', so that this would be a meritorious war, not sinful violence. Once the knights had conquered the Turks in Asia Minor they would march on to Palestine and liberate Jerusalem. Gregory promised to lead the militia himself.[40] There was very little difference between Gregory's proposals and Urban's Crusade, but during the 1070s nothing came of Gregory's project. Very few knights actually joined the Knights of St Peter and so there were no Crusades to the East. But when Urban made his appeal to the knights of Europe twenty years later, many of the Cluniac ideas had taken effect in a new way as well as other enthusiasms linked with the pilgrimage to Jerusalem.

The Church was, therefore, preaching a very confused message, and many of the knights were perplexed about their careers. Warfare was their life but they also wanted a Christian vocation. Tancred, one of the leaders of the First Crusade, was particularly worried, as his biographer Ralph of Caen recorded:

> Frequently he burned with anxiety because the warfare he engaged in as a knight seemed to be contrary to the Lord's commands. The Lord, in fact, ordered him to offer the cheek that had been struck together with his other cheek to the striker; but secular knighthood did not spare the blood of relatives. The Lord urged him to give his tunic and his cloak as well to the man who would take them away; the needs of war impelled him to take from a man already despoiled of both whatever remained to him. And so, if ever that wise man could give himself up to repose, these contradictions deprived him of courage.[41]

Tancred was obviously not convinced about the Cluniac vision of a reformed Christian knighthood, for he did not see it as the answer to the basic dilemma of Christian warfare. Other knights found their own solutions to the problem in their search for a new identity. Towards the end of the eleventh century, the Franks in particular were seeking a new identity and a new Christian vocation. They wanted to regain the leadership of Europe and build themselves anew, and as was natural they looked back to their past. But unlike the Anglo-Saxons or the Germans, who recalled their heroic pagan past in songs and poems, the Franks looked back no further than Charlemagne. In this respect, they had absorbed the message of Cluny: they wanted to be a Christian people, but they were also a warlike and violent people and they needed an aggressive religion.[42] In their search for a solution, they rewrote the history of Charlemagne, that great Christian warrior, to make him relevant to the very different world of the eleventh century. In an age which was passionately attached to Jerusalem, it was important that the founder of the Frankish dynasty should himself have a physical bond with the Holy City, so a new story developed that Charlemagne had made a pilgrimage to Jerusalem in the eighth century. Then Frankish poets and minstrels started to compose the *chansons de geste*, the songs of deeds, to celebrate the holy wars of Charlemagne, and again they made an important innovation. Charlemagne had considered his wars against the Saxons to be holy wars, because they had brought the Germans into the Church. But although he had fought in Spain, these were certainly not holy wars. He had merely gone to help one Muslim leader against another. Yet in the *chansons de geste* Charlemagne's Spanish wars became holy wars, because they provided the Franks with an enemy that could be attacked with impunity.

The creation of an enemy is very important as a foil to a developing new identity. The Muslims or Saracens provided a perfect 'enemy', even though it is quite clear that at this point the Franks had nothing personally against the Muslims and knew nothing at all about the religion of Islam. First, they knew that the Saracens of Spain were not Christians. This meant that they must be 'pagans' and the *chansons* ludicrously present the Muslims worshipping idols of Mohammad and Apollo. In the Bible, the crime of idolatry had justified Joshua's very savage holy wars and the poets of the *chansons* imagine Charlemagne and his Franks slaughtering Muslims with a real Israelite zeal. Fighting pagans was seen as a Christian duty, therefore: 'Never to paynims may I show love or peace,' Charlemagne says at the end of *The Song of Roland*.[43] But these 'paynims' are not the inhuman monsters imagined by the martyrs of Cordova. The second thing that the Franks needed from their enemy was that he should be a brilliant soldier. The Muslims were known for their military prowess, for their vast empire and advanced civilisation. To conquer the Muslims would greatly enhance the reputation of the Franks. Thus in the *chansons* the Muslims are often sympathetically imagined. They are brave soldiers, 'worthy and renowned'. Their only fault is that they are not Christians: 'Were he but Christian, right knightly he'd appear!'[44]

In the character of Roland we see the developing ideal of the new Frank. At the end of Charlemagne's campaign in Spain in 778, the Franks had been crossing the Pyrenees on their homeward march and the rearguard had been separated from the main army. It was ambushed and massacred at Roncesvalles by an army of Basques. Among the slain was Roland, Duke of the Marches and Brittany and the hero of the famous *Song of Roland*. In the poem, his history has been completely transformed, for the people who attack him are Muslims not Basques. In Roland we see the kind of Christian the Franks wanted to become. He has extraordinary physical courage and massive strength, is very aggressive but not particularly intelligent. The Franks did not want to be wise or intellectual Christians; they saw themselves as men of action above all. In the poem, the rearguard could have been saved if Roland had blown his horn to summon Charlemagne and the main army, but Roland steadfastly refuses to do so. His friend Oliver begs him to blow the horn, and, as they watch their men being slaughtered, Oliver bitterly tells Roland that this carnage is all his fault. He is undeniably right and Roland's refusal to call for help is

in fact a suicidal stupidity and irresponsibility. But the poet is on Roland's side: 'Roland is fierce and Oliver is wise,'[45] he says and makes it clear that Oliver's common sense is not quite the thing. Roland's most valued possession is his sword Durendal, and when he dies he bids farewell to Durendal before he commends his soul to God. He describes the relics on the hilt, which have made it a weapon of supernatural power: holiness has been put to the service of war.[46] With Durendal Roland had killed hundreds of Muslims, and the poet dwells on this slaughter in delighted but gruesome detail. Yet by means of this violence Roland had hacked his way into heaven, and during the Middle Ages he was venerated as a saint and martyr. At a time when the Byzantines still refused communion to a soldier during a campaign because of the blood he had been forced to shed in battle, Western Christians had taken the old cult of aggressive, suicidal martyrdom to its logical conclusion.

Urban II would have had no use for this Frankish ideal, but he did address his appeal particularly to the Franks. In the accounts of his speech, which were all written down some years after the First Crusade, Urban is made to call the Franks 'a race chosen and beloved of God', who should look back to Charlemagne for inspiration.[47] Certainly the Franks responded to his summons with intense enthusiasm and saw it as the answer to their problems: this would be the way they would become a great Christian people. Although crusading was always an international project, it was seen as a particularly Frankish exercise and the Muslim historians simply called the Crusaders 'the Franj'. But though Urban was ready to use this Frankish enthusiasm, his own idea of the Crusade was very different from theirs. It was a purely Cluniac vision and can be summarised in one word: 'liberation'. This notion of freedom had been a hallmark of the Cluniac reform, but it was a very specialised kind of freedom.[48] Cluny wanted to 'liberate' European institutions from the control of secular lords and place them under the direct control of the Church. Thus the monasteries were to be exempt from secular control and the popes also sought to 'liberate' the secular clergy from the control of the secular rulers. In Cluniac terms, 'liberation' meant freedom under the popes. It was synonymous, therefore, with the expansion of the power of the Church, and when he spoke about a war of liberation Urban meant the territorial expansion of Christendom. He had certainly referred to the Norman conquest of Sicily as a war of 'liberation' which had 'spread greatly the Church of God into Muslim territories'.[49] Similarly when the Spanish and Frankish knights began their war of Reconquest in Spain, he saw it as a similar war of 'liberation': 'the Church has been enlarged, the domination of the Muslims has been reduced.' After the conquest of Toledo, as part of the war effort, he encouraged the Christians in a new project of building and settlement in the old Roman city of Tarragona in no-man's land. This would become a liberated 'land of St Peter', he said, 'a wall and an ante-mural of Christianity against the Muslims'.[50] In 1098 he suggested that anybody who wanted to make a penitential pilgrimage should commute this into a period of working in Tarragona or should contribute financially to the building programme. Such Christians would then gain the same indulgence as they would have received had they gone on pilgrimage to Jerusalem.[51] Already Urban had been willing to link the pilgrimage to Jerusalem with a holy war of liberation.

But at the same time as Urban was encouraging the liberation of the extreme West, a new opportunity offered itself to liberate the East. Early in 1095 he had attended the Council of Piacenza and had received a deputation from the Emperor Alexius I of Byzantium. Twenty years earlier the Seljuk Turks, a barbarian people who had recently converted to Islam, had poured into Asia Minor, which was part of the Byzantine empire, and had seized a great deal of Christian territory. Since that time the power of the Turks had waned and their empire had been torn apart by internal quarrelling and dissension among the emirs and princes. Alexius had been making good progress in both war and a clever diplomacy, which played one Muslim leader off against another. A few vigorous campaigns might finish the Turks completely, but he simply did not have enough soldiers and he appealed to the Pope for help. Clearly it was a project after Urban's liberating heart. It would certainly expand the power of the Western Church dramatically, even though Alexius insisted that all lands conquered by Western soldiers should be returned to him. There had been a serious and official breach in the relations between the Eastern and Western Churches ever since a dispute about the nature of papal power in 1054, and Urban saw this request for military aid as a chance to extend the power of the papal Church more firmly in Byzantium, which had for so long had insufficient respect for the rising Western Church. It should also make for better relations between Rome and Constantinople. He agreed that he would encourage the knights of Europe to take an army of soldiers to the East, and when in November 1095 he spoke at the Council of Clermont, a council of the Peace of God movement, he summoned the First Crusade.

We have no contemporary account of Urban's speech, but it seemed that he began by calling for the Truce of God. Then he called upon the knights of Europe to stop fighting one another and to band together against the Turks in a twofold war of liberation. First they should liberate the Christians of Asia Minor from the Turks; then they should march on to Jerusalem to liberate the Holy Land. There would be the Peace of God in the West and the War of God against Islam in the East – a perfect solution to the problems of Europe! Urban seems to have called this expedition a pilgrimage, not simply because of the destination of Jerusalem, but because a large collective pilgrimage was the only model adequate for the massive offensive he had envisaged. The small feudal armies of Europe travelling only short distances could not compare with an army of thousands of Christian soldiers travelling 3000 miles to the Holy Land. Certainly Urban saw it as a Cluniac pilgrimage, where the soldiers would live like monks. He used the words of Jesus which had hitherto summoned monks into the cloister: 'Everyone who has left houses, brothers, sisters, father, mother or land for the sake of my name will be repaid a hundred times over' (Matthew 19:29).[52] He also seems to have reminded them that Christ had urged the Christians to be ready to die for his sake, as a Crusader would have to do. The Crusade would therefore demand a conversion of life and would be a dramatic journey to a new self. But hitherto the pilgrim had always been forbidden to bear arms during his pilgrimage. By giving these 'pilgrims' to Jerusalem a sword Urban had made violence central to the religious experience of the Christian layman and Western Christianity had acquired an aggression that it never entirely lost.

As soon as Urban had finished speaking, there was an explosion of enthusiasm and the crowd shouted with one voice *'Deus hoc vult!'* (God wills this!).[53] Yet this apparent unanimity was deceptive because the people seem to have had very confused and different views of the Crusades. Not all the laymen would have understood Urban's sophisticated Cluniac view of the Crusade. Some of the Franks would see it in the light of the *chansons de geste*, others would see it as an apocalyptic pilgrimage for a better world. Others certainly brought secular feudal ideas to the Crusade and saw themselves as fighting for the land of Christ their Lord just as they were bound to fight for the rights of their lord in Europe. Others would see it as a duty to fight for their fellow Christians who had been conquered by the Turks, just as knights were bound to come to the aid of their kinsfolk in a vendetta. One of the very early medieval historians of the Crusades makes a priest ask his listeners during a crusading sermon: 'If an outsider were to strike any of your kin down would you not avenge your blood relative? How much more ought you to avenge your God, your father, your brother, whom you see reproached, banished from his estates, crucified; whom you hear calling for aid.'[54] All these other lay ideas were very far from Pope Urban's vision of the Crusade, but the idea of a war for the Holy Land had unlocked a powerful complex of passions which he would not be able to control once the laymen responded to his call. This would lead the Crusaders to actions that horrified the Pope.

He had advised the knights to wait until after the harvests of 1096 so that the armies were properly provisioned, but thousands of Crusaders were too impatient. Popular preachers spread the news of the Crusade, bringing non-Cluniac and popular motivation to the fore and thousands of lay men and women volunteered to join their armies. The most famous of these preachers was the extremely charismatic Peter the Hermit, who inspired respect from people of all classes of society. 'Whatever he did or said it seemed like something half divine,' wrote the sophisticated monk–historian Guibert of Nogent, who knew him personally.[55] Peter wandered through France, attracting followers from all classes of society. Wherever he preached, his listeners were spellbound and reduced to tears, even when he reached Germany where nobody could understand a word he said. In Germany, two priests, Folkmar and Gottschalk, also stirred up some enthusiasm and in Germany too Count Emich of Leiningen, a robber-baron with a reputation for cruelty, proclaimed that he was the Last Emperor of apocalyptic myth, and began to gather an army, which joined up with other crusading armies from England and Flanders.

In March Peter the Hermit led eastward a band of about 10,000 nobles, knights and footsoldiers, which was accompanied by a large crowd of pilgrims. At the same time Walter Sansavoir of Poissy, a French nobleman, led an army of about the same size consisting entirely of footsoldiers. Shortly afterwards Emich set out with his huge army of 20,000 men, and two other armies led by Folkmar and Gottschalk started their journey through Eastern Europe towards Constantinople. Pope Urban was still preaching the Cross in France, while these armies began their journey, and five more armies were making their preparations at home, but it seems likely that these first Crusaders considered themselves an advance guard of the whole Crusade, not separate from their fellow Crusaders who would leave Europe in the autumn. Walter Sansavoir's beautifully disciplined troops marched straight through Eastern Europe and arrived in Constantinople in late July. The other Crusaders were not so fortunate. Because they were not adequately provisioned, these vast bands depended on local gifts of food. If this was not available, they had to resort to plunder and raiding. The people of the countries through which they were marching could scarcely provide enough food for their own population, let alone feed these thousands of soldiers and pilgrims. Fighting inevitably broke out and at the end of June Folkmar's army was destroyed at Nitra in Hungary by the angry Hungarians and very shortly afterwards Gottschalk's army was forced to surrender to the Hungarians at Pannonhalma. The Hungarians were so incensed by the Crusaders that they would not even allow Emich's army to enter their country. Emich's Crusaders tried to force their way in and they besieged the city of Weisenberg for six weeks. But they could make no headway and were at last forced to disband and return home in ignominy. Peter the Hermit's army was more successful, but suffered greatly during the journey. At Nish, in Byzantium, fighting had broken out in the markets where the Crusaders were trying to buy food and the army was badly mauled, but the survivors managed to reach Constantinople at the beginning of August. The Emperor Alexius, who had asked Urban for a conventional army, gazed at these huge masses of Crusaders and pilgrims with horror and swiftly conveyed them out over the Bosphorus and into Asia Minor. There, however, there was more looting because of famine and because discipline broke down in this alien country. Later in August nearly all Peter's and Walter's troops and pilgrims were massacred by the Turks.

The chroniclers did not approve of these first Crusaders and either omitted all mention of them in their account of the First Crusade or dismissed them as a mob of fanatics and peasants. It is very important for a holy war to be successful and the disastrous failure of these first Crusades called the whole movement into question. If a crusading army was the Will of God, how could it fail? This terrible defeat at the hands of the Eastern Europeans and the infidels in Turkey was not the prestigious victory that the West was looking for. The Crusaders were disowned and a popular legend of a 'Peasants' Crusade' grew up, quite at variance with the facts,[56] that these Crusaders were all fanatical peasants, and that while the barons and knights made their sensible preparations for the official Crusade, crowds of peasants simply wandered off to the East in a haphazard fashion, crazed by wild dreams of apocalypse and the New Jerusalem. Yet to dismiss these Crusaders simply because they failed is not entirely just. Providing food for the armies would be a major and frequently insoluble problem in the story of the Crusades. As many people would die of malnutrition during the journey as died in battle. The Crusaders who followed in the autumn benefited by their example and were careful to stop any plundering and raiding which would provoke the inhabitants of Eastern Europe. Later Crusaders would forget this lesson and meet with the same tragic fate as befell the first Crusaders in Turkey. In one sense the arrival of Walter and Peter was a great achievement. It was the first united and co-operative act of the new Europe and, for that time, a feat of organisation and dedication. It showed that the West was now ready to organise itself and act as a united whole to change history.

In another sense, however, the *legend* of the 'Peasants' Crusade' has an important message. Peter's army included some very important lords indeed and yet it was prepared to accept an impoverished hermit as its leader. We do not know much about Gottschalk and Folkmar, but they were not likely to have been rich, and Walter Sansavoir's name clearly indicates his impecunious material status. Crusading was from the start seen as a poor man's movement. Peter the Hermit survived the tragedy in Turkey, joined the First Crusade at Constantinople and became a very important leader of that campaign with a special responsibility for the poor. During the First Crusade the poor would be very important and would be able to influence policy dramatically – I will explain this more fully in Chapter 4. Crusading gave to the poor of Europe their first means of self-expression and their first practical power. It had sprung from monasticism, the pilgrimage and the Peace of God, which had all asserted the value of holy poverty. Even though Urban certainly had no thoughts of including the poor in his Crusade, he had spoken from within the framework of Cluniac movements which did include and foster the poor, so it was natural and inevitable that the poor would respond. In the popular mind, the Crusade would be the invention of Peter the Hermit, not Pope Urban.[57]

Yet if Peter stamped crusading with a positive image of the poor man he also bequeathed a far more deadly habit to the movement which became an incurable disease in Europe. The only thing we know for certain about the content of Peter's preaching is that it was strongly anti-semitic and inspired a series of pogroms in France. The Westerners, who were marching to the East to find their soul, had also found a new enemy. We have no eyewitness account of these first persecutions in Lorraine, but the French communities wrote letters to the German Jews in their communities in the cities along the Rhine. When they received these letters, warning them of an impending persecution, the German Jews simply did not believe them:

> When the letters reached the saints, the men of renown, the pillars of the universe in Mainz, they wrote to the land of France saying: 'All the

communities have decreed a fastday. We have done our duty. May the Omnipresent One save us and you from all the trouble and affliction. We are greatly concerned about your well-being. As for ourselves, there is no great cause for fear. We have not heard a word about such matters, nor has it been hinted that our lives are threatened by the sword.'[58]

Until Peter preached the Crusade there had been no systematic anti-semitism in Europe. The Jews had lived in separate communities, as was their custom in the diaspora, and lived at peace with their Christian neighbours.[59] In Germany the Jews felt so much at home that when they founded their cemetery in Worms, the bodies did not face Jerusalem in the usual Jewish way. They had developed a rich and unique Jewish tradition in Germany, and were already called 'Ashkenazi' (a corruption of 'Allemagne'). They themselves referred to German Jewry as SHUM after the three major Rhine cities where they lived in community: Speyer, Worms and Mainz. They simply could not believe that their Christian neighbours would persecute them.

Peter decided to spare them. In return for large donations of money and provisions he agreed to speak kindly of Israel while he was in Germany.[60] The Crusader who persecuted the German Jews was Emich. He believed that he was the Last Emperor and that his victory in Jerusalem would bring about the Last Days.[61] St Paul had said that before the Second Coming of Christ all the Jews would be converted,[62] so Emich proceeded to make sure that they were. In May and June 1096 on his way to Eastern Europe, he systematically attacked all the Jewish communities in Speyer, Worms, Mainz, Regensberg, Cologne, Trier and Metz. The Jews were given a choice: baptism or death. A few Jews allowed themselves to be baptised and their lives were spared, but most chose death. Fathers killed their wives and children rather than allow them to accept the religion of these murderous Christians. In each community, the Crusaders burned the synagogues and desecrated the scrolls of the Torah. Having purged Europe of the Jews who refused to be converted, Emich marched eastwards to save the world and to inaugurate the apocalyptic period of the Last Days. Some of the knights in his army, however, persecuted the Jews for other reasons. It seemed absurd to tramp thousands of miles in order to fight Muslims, about whom they knew next to nothing except that they owned the Holy City of Jerusalem, when the people who had (they thought) actually killed Jesus remained unscathed at home. They said to each other:

> Look now, we are going to seek out our profanity and to take vengeance on the Ishmaelites for our Messiah, when here are the Jews who murdered and crucified him. Let us first avenge ourselves on them and exterminate them from among the nations so that the name of Israel will be no longer remembered or let them adopt our faith.[63]

They had turned Urban's Cluniac Crusade into a vendetta and introduced a terrible element into crusading which would have grave repercussions. Every time a Crusade was preached there was an outbreak of popular anti-semitism. It was crusading which made anti-semitism an incurable habit in Europe that would survive long after the period of the Crusades, as I shall show in Chapter 12. The Jews of SHUM could have saved themselves by being baptised, but later secular anti-semites like Hitler took this Christian anti-semitism one step further and sought to exterminate all the Jews, whatever their religious beliefs. Crusading was thus originally responsible for the most shameful events of European history.

It must be said, however, that the official Church was at *this* time horrified by the pogroms. Urban had certainly not intended this persecution and many of the bishops in Germany tried to protect the Jews from the mob of Crusaders and gave them sanctuary in their cathedrals and palaces. The historian Jonathan Riley-Smith has suggested that the reason why these earlier Crusaders were disowned by the Church and why churchmen propagated the myth of the 'Peasants' Crusade' was shame and embarrassment about the persecution of the Jews. The official Christian position on the Jews was that they were an undoubtedly wicked people, who had lost their vocation of being the chosen people because they were God-slayers. They should be shunned by Christians and must accept an inferior position in Christendom; they were condemned to servitude eternally, *but* their lives were to be spared. This was the view of the Cluniac popes of the eleventh century, and in the thirteenth century this teaching would be enshrined in the *Summa Theologica* of St Thomas Aquinas, who dominated Catholic thought until relatively recently. As for Emich's idea of forcing the Jews to convert at sword-point, this was roundly condemned and the bishops taught the people that the Jews who had submitted to save their lives were not bound by their baptismal promises. These were not valid conversions.[64] It was not until the sixteenth century that the popes supported violent pogroms in Europe. But official disapproval was useless. Because of the usual gap between what the Cluniac reformers had intended and what the people had understood prevailed in the crusading movement, popular enthusiasms and beliefs invaded the monastic vision of the Crusade. The apocalyptic ambitions of Emich and the view of the Crusade as a holy blood-feud led to a persecution of the so-called enemies of Christ, and the Church was powerless to stop it.

It should be clear that there is a causal link between crusading and the modern conflict. The Crusades were originally responsible for embedding anti-semitism firmly in the Western identity. The first thing the Crusaders did on their journey to a new self was to slaughter Jews. Without European anti-semitism it is most unlikely that there would have been a modern State of Israel, which has been the cause of such suffering and dissension in the Middle East. Further, although the Crusaders were very vague indeed about the Muslims at this point, at the end of their journey to the Holy Land in 1099 they would slaughter 40,000 Muslim men, women and children and discover a new enemy of God, who threatened the Western identity simply because they stood in the way of the Christian possession of Jerusalem. The First Crusade was arguably the first co-operative act of Europe as she crawled out of the obscurity of the Dark Ages and entered international history once more and this act of self-assertion resulted in a shameful slaughter of Jews and Muslims. The Arabs and non-Arab Muslim people of the Middle East now see the Crusades as the start of a long history of Western aggression in the Middle East. It will be one of the arguments of this book that it is not enough to condemn the behaviour of either the Israelis or the Arabs in today's conflict but that the West must bear a good deal of responsibility for what has happened.

As yet the very confused expeditions had not achieved a clear ideology. There was a mixture of popular, monastic and secular motivation. It is true that by initiating the idea of a military pilgrimage, Urban had made a holy journey a prelude to a holy war according to the old paradigm that had first appeared when the Israelites had made their Exodus from Egypt and begun their long and fateful journey to the same Holy Land. But it would take three terrible years and the experience of the First Crusade to imbue the Crusaders with the true spirit of Joshua. The Crusade would not become a true holy war until 1099. I will now, therefore, leave the story of the First Crusaders, who left Europe in the autumn of 1096, until the second part of this book, which discusses the holy wars of the Crusades and the new holy wars today. I now want to look at the origins of the present conflict, which began as a deliberately secular struggle. On both sides there was a search for a new identity that was sometimes a deliberate rejection of religion, but which would ultimately give way to the old habit of the holy war.

CHAPTER THREE

The Present Conflict

Jews and Arabs
Seek a New Secular Identity

THE JEWS

On 14 May 1948 in the Tel Aviv Museum, David Ben Gurion held the ceremony of the proclamation of the State of Israel. It was the end of a long struggle by dedicated Jews to give their people a new home and a new identity. Instead of being despised aliens in the diaspora, threatened with persecution and extermination, they wanted the Jews to be proud and strong. They would shake off the weakness of their exile and create a new type of society in the land of their fathers which would be an example to the rest of the world. The new Jewish state had the backing of the United Nations, and within the next few days its right to exist was acknowledged formally by the United States and the Soviet Union. The surrounding Arab states, however, refused to grant a similar recognition. They argued that for over a thousand years Arabs had lived in Palestine and that the great powers had no right to give their land away to another people, to assuage their guilt about anti-semitism and to plant a Western-backed state in the Middle East. They vowed to annihilate the new state and on 15 May, when the British Mandate expired, five Arab armies invaded Israel.[1] It looked as though the little David would be devoured by the Arab Goliath, but the Israeli army was stronger and more efficient and was able to push back the invaders. During the hostilities and the 'cleaning up' afterwards some 750,000 Palestinians had left their homeland and have never been allowed to return.[2] The Wandering Jew had been replaced by the Wandering Palestinian and the salvation of the state had, in the time-honoured fashion of the holy war, led to the destruction of another people. The Jews who had been persecuted for nearly a thousand years in the Christian West had now made new enemies in the East and Arabs and Jews have been engaged in a deadly conflict ever since.

But this had not been the original intention of the first Zionists, who had begun to work for the return of the Jews to Israel in the late nineteenth century. The first Zionist settlers had no particular hatred of Arabs when they left their homes in the diaspora to settle in the land of their fathers. In this they were rather similar to the first Crusaders, who had been more preoccupied with their Western visions and problems than with hatred of the Muslims when they set off for the same land to make it their own. The first wave of Jewish settlers arrived in Palestine in 1882, the year after Tsar Alexander III had inspired a new bout of pogroms. Russia and Eastern Europe had had a long tradition of Christian anti-semitism, but these new pogroms were especially severe; they seemed to subside only to break out again in April 1903 when a brutal pogrom at Kishinev in Bessarabia shocked the world.[3] Despite the anti-semitic habit, Jews had still expected that eventually in the enlightened twentieth century it would die away, even in Russia, but the Kishinev pogrom showed that these hopes were futile. What was worse, there was a fresh outbreak of anti-semitism in Western Europe where the Jews had long been emancipated. In countries like France and Germany the Jews had thought that their problems were over and many sought to assimilate with Gentile society. If they felt a lingering anti-semitism in their Gentile neighbours, they looked forward hopefully to the new century when misguided Christian habits would be superseded by rational secularism or by a saner approach to religion. But these hopes were rudely shattered. In France, the first European country to emancipate the Jews after the Revolution of 1789, there was an hysterical outbreak of anti-semitism when the Jewish officer Alfred Dreyfus was (wrongly) convicted of treason in 1895. That same year the anti-semitic Karl Lueger was elected Mayor of Vienna. The reasons for this renewed persecution of the Jews in Europe will be discussed in Chapter 12. Now it is sufficient to say that since the Crusades Christians had made an enemy of 'the Jew', just as they had made enemies of 'the Muslim' and 'the Greek' in the early Middle Ages, producing a series of mythical stereotypes of the Jews which were shadow-selves of Europeans, reflecting their own fears and desires in a distorted mirror-image. The habit was too deeply entrenched to die away completely, even when Christianity seemed to be losing its sway in Europe. The European anti-semitism of the late nineteenth century was a secular version of the old Christian hatred of Jews. Instead of hounding the Jews to death for their alien religion, the Jews were now persecuted because they were of an alien race.

One of these anti-semitic myths should be briefly discussed here because it had an important effect on Zionism. The late nineteenth century was a period of intense nationalism, and Zionism could be described as Jewish nationalism. As the new nation states were created in Europe, people sought to create a new national identity for themselves and in so doing they made 'the Jew' the enemy of this national character. People who were fired with patriotism now blamed the Jews for having no country of their own. In Germany, for example, there was a new cult of the *Volk*[4] (the people) which linked the soul of the Germans to their land. This soul, people believed, was formed by the German landscape and this meant that the German spirit was alien to the city and to 'civilisation' (the culture of the city). This led Germans to see the Jews as the essential enemy of the German soul: they had no landscape of their own and so their souls could not develop naturally and this made them deformed human beings. Further, because Jews lived and worked in the cities, they were seen as the epitome of 'civilisation'. The new *völkische* craze created a youth movement, which roamed the countryside soaking up the German soul there. Naturally Jews were not allowed to join these, even if they regarded themselves as more German than Jewish. It also took over student society and students turned the Jews out of their clubs and refused to fight a duel with a Jew because he had no honour to lose. It appeared in many important novels, essays, scientific theories and philosophical works of the time. In this nationalistic climate it was natural for Jews to seek a national solution for themselves and many of the early Jewish settlers believed that only by re-establishing a physical contact with the land of their fathers could Jews discover their true selves.

But Zionism appeared first not in Western Europe but in Russia and here many of the Jews sought quite different solutions. Many of them turned to religion to give them strength to bear the pogroms. Others tried to flee. Thousands poured into Western Europe and inadvertently they increased the anti-semitism there. These refugees from Russia and Eastern Europe were different from the European Jews. Their strange clothes and manners and their apparently archaic beliefs reinforced the conviction that the Jews were essentially 'other' and horribly different from any other people in the world. Sadly the refugees found that they had not escaped anti-semitism and many of them and their children would perish in the Nazi Holocaust. Other Jews fled to the United States, where some of them were very successful but they would be very much aware of anti-semitism and even today, when American Jewry is very strong indeed, Jews there do not rule out the possibility of persecution. Other Russian Jews decided that more radical answers were needed and those who had received a secular education joined the revolutionaries who were conspiring to overthrow the tsarist regime, which had brought such suffering to their people. Some of these Jewish revolutionaries like Leon Trotsky and Rosa Luxemburg dissociated themselves from their people, following the example of Karl Marx himself, who wrote two frankly anti-semitic essays.[5] Trotsky and Luxemburg and their like believed that anti-semitism was simply the result of a corrupt economic system that would disappear like a bad dream after the revolution.

But some of the Jewish revolutionaries were unable to accept this. They suspected that their fellow Gentile revolutionaries were actually anti-semites and feared that Jews would fare as badly under the communists as they had under the tsars. In the event, they have been proved right. These secular Jews sought an entirely new solution in Zionism and began to believe that Jews would find no rest until they had a land of their own. In 1882, the year after the first pogroms, Leon Pinsker wrote *Autoemancipation*, which quickly made a great impact on young secular Jews. Pinsker insisted that the Jews had to acquire a country of their own, if they were ever to be dignified and free. Before the pogroms, Pinsker had been an assimilationist, but after them he was convinced that assimilation was impossible. A Jew would always be 'the Other' for the Gentiles: 'for the living, the Jew is a dead man; for the natives, an alien and a vagrant; for property holders, a beggar; for the poor, an exploiter and a millionaire; for the patriot, a man without a country.'[6] It was a firmly established Gentile tradition to make Jews the epitome of all that Gentiles were *not* and this meant that Jews could not live in countries ruled by the *goyim*. They had to take their destiny into their own hands and establish themselves in a country of their own, where they were not vulnerable to the passing anti-semitic whims of their fellow countrymen.[7]

It seemed a compelling solution and Pinsker strongly influenced a new Jewish organisation formed in Kharkov in 1882 which called itself the Lovers of Zion. Pinsker had had no decided views about where this Jewish state should be but eventually the Lovers of Zion convinced him that it must be in Eretz Yisrael, the Land of Israel.[8] Although they had usually had a secular education and were not religious people, the members of the Lovers of Zion had grown up in the *shtetls*, the all-Jewish towns and villages. As children they had sat in the synagogue and listened to the psalms and prayers which centred round the ancient land of their fathers. Maurice Samuel, who is an authority on the *shtetl*, has clearly shown the importance of Eretz Yisrael there:

> Half of the time the *Shtetl* just wasn't there: it was in the Holy Land, and it was in the remote past or the remote future, in the company of the Patriarchs and Prophets or of the Messiah. Its festivals were geared to the Palestinian climate and calendar; it celebrated regularly the harvests its forefathers had gathered in a hundred generations ago; it prayed for the Soreh and Malkosh, the subtropical [early and late] rains, indifferent to the needs of its neighbors, whose prayers had a practical, local schedule in view.[9]

In a time of crisis it is natural for people to look back to their roots. We have seen that this is what the Hebrews had done when they made the Exodus to the Promised Land and what the Muslims had done in seventh-century Arabia, and the

Lovers of Zion naturally thought of Eretz Yisrael when they wanted to make a new start. Because the Gentile world seemed committed to rejecting them, it was important that the Jews rose up to save themselves. As an early statement of the movement put it:

> Everywhere we are rejected, we are pushed out from everywhere. We are considered aliens. Is all hope really lost? Oh no! Judea [*sic*] shall rise again. Let our own lives be an example to our people. Let us forsake our lives in foreign lands and stand on firm ground in the land of our fathers.[10]

But many of the Lovers of Zion were not content with theory. About 6000 of them actually packed their bags, left their homes and families and settled in pioneering communities in Palestine. It was an extraordinary move and it was the Zionists' practical faith and courage in pursuing a very quixotic plan which made the State of Israel an established fact and surely one of the most startling achievements of the twentieth century. These first Zionist settlers showed others what to do and they would be known as the First Aliyah (the first Immigration). But besides the Lovers of Zion other Zionist groups began to form spontaneously. These were a disconnected network, often ignorant of each other's existence, but all shared the desire to return 'home', to escape from the terrifying conditions of the diaspora and save their people.[11]

But the man who gave coherence to Zionism and made it a factor on the international scene was not a Russian. Theodor Herzl was a sophisticated and charismatic Viennese Jew, who at the time of the Dreyfus affair was an established playwright and a correspondent in Paris for an Austrian newspaper. As a pressman he was present at Dreyfus' court-martial and left the École Militaire as the crowds were beginning to scream 'Death to the Jews!'[12] Herzl had been a firm believer in assimilation, but the shock of this new wave of anti-semitism converted him to Zionism. The intensity of this new hatred of the Jews convinced him that there would shortly be an even more terrible anti-semitic catastrophe and so he decided that the Jews must find a place of refuge where they could be safe. In 1896 less than six months after the Dreyfus trial, he published *Der Judenstaat (The Jewish State)*, in which he argued, like Pinsker, that the Jews needed a home of their own. He was not himself convinced that this had to be Palestine, however. Herzl had had an entirely secular upbringing: as Menachem Ussiskin, the Russian Zionist writer, said on meeting him, he knew nothing at all about Jews.[13] The Holy Land simply did not have the same instinctive pull for him as it had for Russian Zionists, who had been brought up in the intensely Jewish atmosphere of the *shtetl*.

For the next eight years Herzl literally worked himself to death in order to put Zionism – and the Jewish state – on the map. He began to meet the great statesmen of the world to interest them in the idea of a Jewish homeland, and was prepared to consider a homeland in Africa or the Sinai peninsula as well as in Palestine. His priority was to find a place – any place – where the Jews could shelter from the approaching apocalypse. He was prepared to find allies everywhere. He even talked to the dreaded Russian anti-semite V. K. Plehve, the Tsar's Minister of the Interior, who was masterminding the pogroms. After all, a Jewish state was in the interests of the anti-semites because it would get rid of the Jews. He talked to the Sultan of the Ottoman empire about the possibility of Palestine, to the Kaiser of Germany, to Joseph Chamberlain, the British Colonial Secretary, and to Arthur, Lord Balfour, the Prime Minister. Herzl was committed to the imperialist ideal and saw the future Jewish state as a colony of one of the great powers, 'an outpost of civilisation as opposed to barbarism', as he had written in *The Jewish State*.[14] He saw himself as the Jewish Cecil Rhodes, as bringing progress and Western civilisation to the primitive world. The interest he aroused in Chamberlain, who was deeply committed to the colonial ideal and saw great possibilities in the idea of a dedicated group of Jewish colonists who would serve the British empire, made Herzl certain that Britain would help him. Britain was, he said, 'the Archimedean point where the lever can be applied'; 'From this place the Zionist movement will take a higher and higher flight. . . . England the great, England the free, England with her eyes fixed on the seven seas will understand us.'[15] Events would prove that this instinct was a sound one. Without Herzl's political activities, it is most unlikely that there would have been a State of Israel. At a time when the great powers were carving up the world between them, the support of one of them was vital.

But just as crucial as Herzl's international work was his work within Zionism. In 1897 he gave the scattered Zionist groups a platform when he convened the First Zionist Congress in 1897. After the congress, which was held in Basle, he wrote in his diary: 'At Basle I founded the Jewish State. . . . Perhaps in five years but certainly in fifty, everyone will know it.'[16] When David Ben Gurion proclaimed the State of Israel in Tel Aviv fifty years and nine months later, a portrait of Herzl hung on the wall behind him. At the Congress Herzl's own charisma aroused deep feelings. Mordechai Ben Ami, the delegate from Odessa, described the emotion felt by the Congress when Herzl climbed on to the platform:

> Many eyes filled with tears. . . . Herzl mounted the rostrum calmly. . . . Not the Herzl I knew, the one I had seen only the previous evening. Before us was the splendid figure of a son of kings with a deep and concentrated gaze, handsome and sad at one and the same time. It was not the elegant Herzl of Vienna, but a man of the House of David, risen all of a sudden from his grave in all his legendary glory. . . . It seemed as if the dream cherished by our people for two thousand years had come true at last, and Messiah, the son of David, was standing before us.[17]

This description is significant. The delegates at Basle had no time for religion. They felt that Judaism had encouraged the Jews to sit back passively and wait for the Messiah, accepting and thereby encouraging their intolerable situation in the diaspora. Yet at almost every turn these secular Jews expressed themselves in religious terms. From its earliest moments, Zionism wore the mantle of religious Judaism, even though it was defiantly secular. For the Zionists from the *shtetls* the Jewish identity was inextricably bound up with the Bible and the Torah. In fact, this tendency expresses one of the Zionist dilemmas which, as we shall see in Chapter 7, has become agonising for many Israelis: how is it possible to be a secular Jew? The Zionists wanted to create a new kind of Jew, who would shake off the weakness of the diaspora, but it was essential that there should be a real continuity between the old Jew and the new. The new Judaism had to be rooted in the passions that had moved Jews for thousands of years or it would be unJewish, superficial and artificial. It would have no roots and would wither away. But these roots and ancient passions were essentially religious. Ben Ami was not wrong to see Herzl as a Messiah: he was a *Zionist* Messiah, because he dramatically expressed the basic Zionist belief in self-determination. Instead of abdicating their responsibility as human beings and leaving everything to God, the new Jews must take full responsibility for their fate and initiate their own secular salvation. But, as we shall so frequently see during the history of the holy war, religion is a powerful force that has laws of its own. Seculars who turn, however symbolically, to religion often find it difficult to control and keep within bounds.

The following year at the Zionist Conference, this symbolic and psychological Zionist link with their religious past led to a fateful decision. Herzl triumphantly announced that there was a real chance that they would be allowed to build a

Jewish state in Uganda. He was bewildered by his colleagues' absolute refusal to consider the idea. The Russian delegates actually walked out. Like the Lovers of Zion, they could see no alternative to Eretz Yisrael. They could not articulate their objections logically, because it was not a matter of logic but of such strong emotion and conviction that the necessity for Jews to return to the land of their fathers had the authority of a self-evident fact.[18] Their Jewish identity was inseparable from the Land of Israel and this made them inaccessible to reason and practical arguments. This inarticulate passion for the Holy Land will be another recurring factor in our story. Herzl was forced to accept that Palestine was the only place for a Jewish state if he wished to retain the leadership. He stood before the delegates, raised his right hand and quoted the words of the psalmist-exile in Babylon: 'Jerusalem! if I forget you, may my right hand wither!'[19] From that moment Zionism ceased to be a purely defensive movement concerned solely with finding a safe place for the Jews. It became committed to the return to Eretz Yisrael.

There were some Zionists who distrusted Herzl. People like Ussiskin were afraid that his activities might stir up more anti-semitism. If the Christians of Russia saw Jews colonising *their* Holy Land, who knew what terrible persecution might break out?[20] Zionists of this way of thinking saw the establishment of the Jewish homeland as taking place over a long period of time. Herzl was by temperament unsuited to such an undramatic solution, but he was also convinced that the situation of the Jews was far too dangerous to allow such gradualism because there simply was not enough time.[21] Future events would prove that his fears had been fully justified and after he died in 1904, worn out by his labours at the age of forty-four, the Zionist movement preserved his sense of urgency. But, more significantly, his overtures to Britain bore fruit. The Russian Zionist Chaim Weizmann continued Herzl's political activities[22] and cultivated the friendship of Arthur Balfour, who, for complicated reasons which I shall discuss more fully in Chapter 12, was very sympathetic to the idea of a Jewish Palestine. In 1917 the time seemed ripe for a firm declaration of British support for Zionism. Balfour hoped to enlist international Jewish support for Britain in her war with Germany; Britain was also looking covetously at the declining Ottoman empire and hoped to found more colonies in the Middle East after the Great War. These and other reasons convinced many of Balfour's colleagues and on 2 November the important statement that would be known as the Balfour Declaration was issued from the Foreign Office:

> His Majesty's Government views with favour the establishment in Palestine of a national home for the Jewish people, and will use their best endeavours to facilitate the achievement of this object, it being clearly understood that nothing shall be done which may prejudice the civil and religious rights of existing non-Jewish communities in Palestine, or the rights and political status enjoyed by Jews in any other country.[23]

Weizmann was disappointed.[24] The Declaration was deliberately vague about the nature of this 'national home': was it to be a political state, a colony or some sort of Jewish reservation? Further, it spoke only of a homeland 'in' Palestine, which could mean only a small part of the country, and there was that worrying phrase about the native inhabitants of the country, called euphemistically 'non-Jewish communities', as though to disguise the fact that Palestine was inhabited by a large Arab majority.[25] But despite Weizmann's disappointment, the Balfour Declaration was crucial to the establishment of the Jewish state. In 1920, after the demise of the Ottoman empire, Britain and France did indeed establish colonies, which they ingenuously called mandates or protectorates, in the Middle East. Britain took Palestine and the Mandate there was pledged to implement the Balfour Declaration.

Without this early British support the Zionist enterprise would probably not have been successful.

During the early years of the twentieth century, however, another radical development entered Zionism, which would also prove to have been vital. A young Jewish intellectual from Poltava in the south-west of Russia produced a tract called *The National Question and the Class Struggle*. Ber Borochov, who had been expelled from the revolutionary Social Democratic Party for Zionist deviationism, fused Marxism with Zionism and produced a socialist solution to the Jewish problem, translated into the language of *Das Kapital*. Because they had no land of their own, the Jews were inevitably pushed out of the 'primary' economic fields like agriculture into 'secondary' fields like commerce and light industry. This meant that they were essentially unproductive and that they were unable to take part in the class struggle. It was their poor economic status that caused the anti-semitism and the pogroms. It was no use emigrating to non-Jewish countries like America, because there would be the same problems there. The Jews needed a land of their own in an 'empty' or undeveloped country like Palestine, which was underpopulated – or so Borochov believed.[26] This socialist Zionism at once attracted many of the revolutionary young Jews who suspected their colleagues in the party of anti-semitism. Like the Lovers of Zion before them, these socialist Zionists were not content with theory and in 1902 the second wave of immigration began, which would later be known as the Second Aliyah. From all over Russia and the Ukraine, Zionists packed a bag and made the exodus to Palestine. Nobody organised this. It was not unlike the legend of the so-called 'Peasants' Crusade'. While cautious and responsible Zionists like Ussiskin stayed at home and while political Zionists like Weizmann worked to set up a Jewish state officially, other Zionists just got up and left. They provided a form of pioneering that was effective and unique and made a Jewish presence in Palestine an established fact. The socialists of the Second Aliyah believed that they were returning to their 'collective roots' in an independent homeland. In Palestine, the Jewish people would be redeemed from the weak position inherent in the diaspora and be given at last a new, strong identity. They would create an entirely new kind of socialist society, which would be an example to the rest of the world.

In 1904 the young David Ben Gurion arrived in Palestine. The year before he had written: 'We take with us young and healthy arms, the love of work, an eagerness for free and natural lives in the land of our forefathers, and a willingness toward frugality.'[27] In Palestine the Jews would create 'a model society, based on social, economic and political equality'. Zionism, he would write later, was not just a flight from anti-semitism but a positive attempt to create a new world and a new solution for the Jewish people. It was:

> a revolt against a tradition of many centuries, helplessly longing for redemption. We substitute a will for self-realization, an attempt at reconstruction and creativity in the soil of the homeland. We call for a self-sufficient people, master of its own fate. Instead of a corrupt existence of middlemen, hung up in midair, we call for an independent existence as working people, at home on the soil and in the creative economy.[28]

It was a secular version of the tendency that we have seen, in all three religions of historical monotheism, in the history of the holy war. The trauma of the diaspora had impelled the socialist Zionists of the Second Aliyah to act in order to change their destiny and change the world, and this activity took the form of a migration. It was revolutionary, in that it was a bid for independence and, like the first Muslims and some of the First Crusaders, a bid for a better world. Instead of seeing a messianic redemption and a heavenly apocalypse, Ben Gurion and his Zionists

firmly believed that the final socialist redemption was surely at hand.[29] The
perfect society that they intended to create in Eretz Yisrael would be a model for
the revolutionary struggle of other peoples.

The revolutionary socialism of the Second Aliyah had made Zionism, like
crusading, a poor man's movement. During the First Aliyah, the pioneers had used
cheap Arab labour and had been helped financially by Baron Edmond de
Rothschild, which were obviously methods that would be repugnant to Ben Gurion
and his like. But even the Lovers of Zion had warned settlers against building
Jewish Palestine on the 'rotten basis' of the old world order and one of their early
charters prophesied the *kibbutz*, which would be the important creation of the
Second Aliyah. There would be 'one fortune for the entire society. No man has
private property. Also his things, his clothes and whatever he may bring with him
or receive from his home belong to the entire society.'[30] When the Zionists of the
Second and Third Aliyah (1919–23) set up their *kibbutzim* they were picking up an
old trend in the Judaeo-Christian tradition and creating secular monasteries. In
these 'monasteries' a voluntary 'poverty' was cultivated.[31] The settlers wore the
clothes of Russian peasants or their old Russian student uniform until they were
quite literally rags. Food was kept deliberately simple and frugal and there were no
luxuries like alcohol or cigarettes. In this socialist Eretz Yisrael the Zionists firmly
believed that there would be no elite and, at least in the *kibbutzim*, no private
property.

The socialist Zionists also fell easily and spontaneously into a quasi-religious
mode of expression. Thus when Yitzhak Ben Zvi, who became the second
President of the State of Israel, describes his decision to make the *aliyah* in 1905,
he describes it as a sudden 'vision', a moment of self-discovery and conversion of
life. He had been speaking at a Jewish revolutionary rally when suddenly 'there
appeared in my mind's eye the living image of Jerusalem, the holy city with its
ruins, desolate of its sons'.

> At that moment I asked myself: *whom am I addressing?* Will my listeners here
> at Poltava understand me, will they believe? Are we, the Jews, *real partners*
> in this revolution and in this victory? Will this revolution, which promises
> salvation to the Russians, bring salvation for us Jews too? Why am I here and not
> there? Why are we all here and not there? As these questions arose in my mind I
> could no longer free myself from them; and as I finished my speech I no longer
> thought of this demonstration and of the victory of the Russian Revolution but
> of *our Jerusalem.* That very hour I reached the absolute decision that my place is
> in the Land of Israel, and that I must go there, dedicate my life to its upbuilding,
> and as soon as possible.[32]

Because the Zionists revived the sacred tongue of Hebrew for daily use, they often
used Hebrew religious terms to describe their ideals. *Aliyah*, for example, did not
originally mean 'immigration', it also meant 'ascent', the word traditionally used
for the pilgrimage to Jerusalem. The Zionists also called the immigrants *olim* or
'pilgrims' just as they do today. When the *olim* arrived at the port of Jaffa they
frequently knelt down to kiss the soil of Eretz Yisrael just as pilgrims did.
Frequently the *olim* spoke of their *aliyah* as a 'rebirth', just as a religious person
will often say that he has been 'born again' since his conversion. Often they
changed their names after making *aliyah*, a common religious habit after
conversion or vocation. Thus David Grien became David Ben Gurion (son of lions).
Frequently these new Hebrew names reflect the sense of strength and mastery that
the Zionists intended for the new Jews. Thus we have *Tamir* (towering), *Oz*
(strength) and *Lahat* (blaze). Some people named themselves after a part of Eretz
Yisrael in order to tie themselves more firmly to the land. Thus we have Sharon,

Golan, Karmi (Carmel) and Galil (Galilee). The name the settlers gave to their pioneering movement was *chalutzism* and in Hebrew *chalutz* had strong religious connotations of salvation, liberation and rescue.[33]

But this borrowing of religious terminology received no support from the Jews who remained loyal to orthodox religious Judaism. Nearly all the Orthodox rabbis in the diaspora condemned the movement, seeing it as a denial of religion and an impious aping of messianic redemption. They had learned over the centuries to believe that the Jews should stay in the diaspora until the Messiah led them back home and established a religious state in Eretz Yisrael. To establish a secular state there seemed blasphemous. Some rabbis even refused to make a pilgrimage to Jerusalem lest they condoned the Zionists. Thus Zadok of Lublin (1823–1900) wrote:

> I fear lest my departure and ascent [*aliyah*] to Jerusalem might seem like a gesture of approval of Zionist activity. I hope unto the Lord, my soul hopes for his word, that the Day of the Redemption will come. I wait and remain watchful for the feet of his anointed. Yet though three hundred scourges of iron afflict me, I will not move from my place.[34]

In Eretz Yisrael itself communities of religious Jews, who lived a devout life according to the Torah, were horrified by the *chalutzim* (the pioneers), and claimed that when Herzl had entered the Holy Land 'evil entered with him'. For their part, the Zionists turned away from their Orthodox brethren in disgust. These religious people, clinging to the Wailing Wall in their archaic clothes and long beards, seemed to symbolise everything that was wrong with the Jews. They wanted to liberate their people from anachronistic religious traditions that shackled them to attitudes of hopeless dependence and they created a new 'secular religion' of their own–a religion of Labour. It was by working productively on their own land that the Jews would redeem themselves from the corruptions of the old world. It was significant that the Hebrew word they used for labour (*avodah*) also meant religious ritual. As earlier Zionists had only been able to consider Eretz Yisrael as a homeland and had instinctively described Herzl in messianic terms, so now the new Labour Zionists replaced religious Judaism with a cult of work in Eretz Yisrael, but expressed themselves in traditional Jewish terms. Thus in about 1927 the young *chalutz* Avraham Shlonsky, who worked as a road builder, wrote this poem:

> Dress me, my own right mother, in a magnificent cloak of many colours
> And at the hour of morning service carry me to work.
> Light wraps my head like a prayer shawl.
> The houses stand upright like frontlets.
> And the roads, paved by labouring hands, run down like the straps of *tefillin*.
> Thus shall the fine city offer her morning prayer to her creator;
> And among the creators, your son Avraham, paving poet in Israel.[35]

The redeemed Jew of *chalutzism* does not need God; he is the creator.

In embracing the new religion of labour, the Russian settler A. B. Gordon slipped naturally into the terms and modes of thought of the old religion he had cast aside. He had once been an Orthodox Jew and a Kaballist, who had been greatly influenced by the nature mysticism of Tolstoy. He saw the Jews' reunion with their land in mystical terms. The Land of Israel was, in his view, superior to all others and had a spiritual power that was accessible only to the Jews and which formed the Jewish soul. In describing this power, Gordon used traditional phrases from the Kaballah:

The soul of the Jew is the offspring of the natural environment of the land of Israel. *Clarity*, the depth of an infinitely clear sky, a clear perspective, *mists of purity*. Even the divine unknown seems to disappear in this clarity, slipping from *limited, manifest light* into *infinite, hidden light*. The peoples of this world understand neither this clear perspective nor this luminous unknown in the Jewish soul.[36]

Gordon had experienced the diaspora as a trauma and his *aliyah* seemed like a moment of redemption, a liberation from the fallen state of alienation and a reunion with his deeper self. Yet at first Palestine did not seem like home to him and he found himself longing for the northern landscape of Russia, which was his *real* fatherland. What saved him was work (*avodah*), which connected him physically with Eretz Yisrael and made him conscious of a spiritual contact with it. This rebirth of his true self resulted in a liberation of universal love:

To the extent that my hands grew accustomed to labour, that my eyes and ears learned to see and hear and my heart to understand what is in it, my soul too learned to skip upon the hills, to rise, to soar – to spread out the expanses it had not known, to embrace all the land round about, the world and all that is in it, and to see itself embraced in the army of the whole universe.[37]

But in fact this religion of universal love did not embrace the whole world. It was essentially exclusive because the Land of Israel, in Gordon's vision, was only available to the Jews. The *goyim*, the Gentiles, could have no share in it. Gordon's exalted vision of the Holy Land made him unable to accept the people he found living there.

And it seems to you that the people who live here do not understand the natural phenomenon of the land of Israel, so remote and so different from it are they! This natural world, astonishingly magnificent, filled with grandeur – and its inhabitant, a kind of filthy, degraded creature, whose life is contemptible. This absence of culture, this spiritual desolation all bear witness to the fact that the local populace has not raised itself to the spiritual level of the land of Israel.[38]

As the settlers began to shape their new identity, they created an enemy. This was not a total fantasy, of course. The Palestinians really *were* the enemies of the Zionists, because they were extremely attached to their own country and naturally did not want to hand it over to the Jews. Yet Gordon's picture of the Palestinian is an exaggerated distortion that reflects an inner anxiety.

The very first settlers had been so intent on their own Jewish redemption that at first it seems that they really did not 'see' the Palestinians. It does not seem to have occurred to them that the 'people of the land' would be a problem. They saw Palestine as an 'empty' country. It is a habit of the colonial mind to regard any potential colony as empty, and the Zionists fell naturally into that way of thinking. In fact they had a slogan: 'A land for a people, for a people without a land'.[39] The discovery of the Palestinians was a shock, and most Zionists either ignored the Arabs or repressed the thought of them, hoping no doubt that they would go away. As early as 1891, however, the Zionist writer Ahad Ha'am realised that this myopia was dangerous. He warned the settlers not to underestimate the Palestinians, for if once the Arab thought he had been wronged or robbed 'the rage will stay alive in his heart.' Events have proved that he was right. Ahad Ha'am was disturbed at the way the settlers behaved towards the Arabs. They either hated them or behaved towards them in a hostile manner. Many Jews, he said, 'behave towards the Arabs with cruelty, infringe upon their boundaries, hit them shamefully without reason and even brag about it' or else they tended to ignore them altogether. Neither aggression nor repression is a balanced response and Ahad Ha'am suggested that the settlers 'were angry towards those who reminded them that there is still another people in the land of Israel that has been living there and does not intend at all to leave'.[40]

Throughout the history of the holy war people who stand in the way of the divine plan have been cruelly eliminated. The Zionists were not religious men at this point, but they would react to the Palestinians in a way that was quite inconsistent with their lofty idealism. Neither Joshua nor the Crusaders thought that the People of the Land deserved the human rights that God had commanded them to extend to other people. There is a story of one of the most eminent of the settlers of the First Aliyah which seems to give us some insight into why people behave like this. Eliezer Ben Yehuda could be described as a fanatical Zionist. A brilliant philologist, he was almost solely responsible for the creation of modern Hebrew. When his mother came to visit him in Palestine, he refused to speak to her because she did not know Hebrew and he believed that a Jew must speak only his own language in his own land.[41] Yet as early as 1882, when his ship had approached Jaffa, he had had grave doubts about whether the Land of Israel really was his country. He found himself watching the Arab passengers on board and suddenly he realised that they were far more at home in the East and in the Promised Land than he was. Whatever he might be in Zionist theory, he was in fact a foreigner there without political or national right and the country belonged to the Arabs. He could not bring himself to distort his view of them and make them a vile people unworthy of the land, as A. B. Gordon would do. The Arabs were, he wrote, 'tall, strong young fellows, dressed in the style of the country, but in expensive, elegant attire, and they were all merry and joyful, jesting and riotous.' Without warning 'an oppressive feeling of dread, as though I were confronting a fortified rampart, suddenly filled my soul.'[42] It made his return to the Land of Israel meaningless:

> Yes! this was the coast of the land of our fathers! And the feeling of dread grew yet stronger within me. Nothing else did I feel, no other thought was in my mind! I am afraid! After about a quarter of an hour my feet were standing upon the holy ground, the land of our fathers – yet in my heart was no feeling of joy, and in my head, no thought, no idea whatsoever! My mind seemed to have emptied itself or turned to ice; it would not budge. Only one thing filled my heart – that same feeling of dread. I neither rent my garments, nor fell upon my face, nor embraced the stones, nor kissed the ground. I just stood there in astonishment. Dread![43]

Ben Yehuda experienced the Arabs as a trauma, which he could not articulate but which clearly threatened him at a very deep level indeed. They threatened his very Zionist identity and integrity. They were not merely in the way of the Jewish state; they were in the way of his new self and were an implacable obstacle – a 'fortified rampart' – to all that he held to be most 'sacred'. Eventually he found that he could not swallow his doubts so he left Eretz Yisrael and became a Territorialist, believing that the Jews should seek a country in a land other than Palestine. Few people in our story had the moral toughness of Ben Yehuda and perhaps we should remember him, standing aghast as he gazed at the young attractive Arabs, when we read of the atrocities of the holy wars. This sickening, inarticulate dread will easily trigger an extreme reaction.

Most Zionists continued to believe for a very long time, despite the facts that were staring them in the face, that they would be able to build the Jewish homeland without violence. They believed that the final Marxist redemption was at hand and this made all Arab resistance to their plans seem either futile or else merely symptomatic of a pre-revolutionary consciousness that would wither away in the new socialist era. These idealistic Jews had no intention, at first, of fighting the Arabs; they honestly did not believe that it would be necessary. Some of them even persuaded themselves that they would be able to help the Arabs in a peaceful revolution. Shutting away the frightening reality of the Palestinians, they claimed that they would conquer the land by building it once more. In 1909 they began to build the city of Tel Aviv on the sand dunes opposite the Arab port of Jaffa, as their forefather Ezechiel had foretold. They believed that the renewed land would cause a dynamic spiritual and moral renewal of the Jewish people. One of their pioneering slogans went: 'We came to build the land and be rebuilt by it.'[44]

Yet things did not turn out as they expected. The exodus to Eretz Yisrael from the diaspora was intended to be a secular light unto the *goyim* as the world would be shown the first perfect society. Yet by the mid-1930s most of the idealists of the Second Aliyah, who were now the leaders of the community, had come to share the opinion of Yahweh when he gave instructions to Moses about the *goyim* of his day: 'they must not live in your country.' The peaceful building programme had been a prelude to a destructive war and to the exile of the Palestinian people from their homeland. Gradually Tel Aviv had grown until it had come to loom aggressively over Arab Jaffa, and *before* the Arab armies invaded in 1948 Jewish troops drove the Arabs from their city and looted it. After the war was over, the Arab villages that the Palestinian refugees had left behind were systematically destroyed, rather as Joshua had destroyed the cities of the Canaanites, making them a ruin for ever more. As Professor Israel Shahak has remarked sadly, some 400 of these villages were 'destroyed *completely* with their houses, garden-walls, and even cemeteries and tomb-stones, so that literally a stone does not remain standing and visitors are passing and being told that "it was all desert"'.[45] The new state would now be built not only in the land of the fathers, but on the ruins of the Palestinians' homes. We have to examine carefully how this new aggression came into Zionism.

For the Zionists who were engaged in 'rebuilding' the land, Labour Zionism was inspiring and exhilarating. Many of them were on a 'trip', a spiritual journey that was not a journey to God but the creation of a new self. In A. B. Gordon we can see the mystical dimensions of Zionism and we see it also in the *kibbutz* at Bittania in the Galilee where after their work in the fields the members would sit up all night and take part in highly emotional group-encounter sessions.[46] People would often fall into ecstasy or see visions of a transformed world. Even apparently sober Zionists like Ben Gurion were engaged in a visionary quest for a higher mode of being. He wrote rhapsodically to his wife of the 'vistas of a New World' that Zionism would bring about, 'a world of gladness and light, shining in the glow of an eternally young ideal of supreme happiness and glorious existence'.[47] This vision was mystical not in a theistic or religious sense, but in the sense that it was a process of self-realisation that sometimes takes a specifically 'religious' form.

When a person is engaged with his psyche at a deep level, he must accept the whole system. Otherwise it will not work. To outsiders the practices and forms of belief sometimes seem bizarre, but the 'believer' can envisage no other view of the world. We can see this clearly in the new 'religion' or 'enlightenment' of psychoanalysis, which was being created during this period by the great Jew Sigmund Freud in the diaspora. Psychoanalysis has parallels with Zionism in that both are disciplined processes of building a new self by delving deeply into the past, not just in a rational and cerebral way but by exploring the subconscious. It is very noticeable that when a person is engaged in intensive psychoanalysis, especially in the very early stages, he is often unable to see the 'outside world' at all. An innocent remark during a perfectly neutral social occasion can occasion a huge psychic explosion and an embarrassing drama because the analysand has not yet learned to dissociate himself from the process. An analysand will often refuse to accept any other view of the world but the analytical one, and finds it impossible to see the point of view of outsiders who only look at Freudianism objectively. This could well account for the blindness of the early Zionist settlers to the Palestinian position and their unshakeable belief in the rightness of their cause. Zionism was a quixotic movement; however practical and rational it appeared, it was highly emotional and psychological. In the West many people supported it, not just for rational and political reasons but for reasons that were similarly irrational and bound up with the Western identity. These will be the subject of Chapter 12.

A detached observer, however, particularly an outsider who is likely to be damaged by the movement, can see that Labour Zionism had two grave flaws. First was the conviction that Eretz Yisrael belonged to the Jews more than to the Palestinians. We have seen that to Zionists this conviction was deeply rooted and absolute. It is a conviction, however, that might have been understandable in the time of Joshua or the Crusaders but in the international world of the twentieth century one would have thought that it was nonsense and even dangerous. To maintain that you have a right to a land because your ancestors lived there 2000 years ago could set up a dangerous precedent. Celts in Ireland or Wales, for example, where there are strong nationalist movements, could demand to 'return' to parts of Kent and Sussex on the grounds that their ancestors had once lived there and that the current Anglo-Saxon–Norman inhabitants should leave. The Arabs could demand the return of al-Andalus in Spain. An outsider like the Palestinian would naturally find the Jewish claim to Palestine not only bizarre but mischievous and dangerous.

The second flaw in Labour Zionism was the ideal of the 'Conquest of Labour'. Even mystical Zionists like A. B. Gordon were aware that historically the Jews' claim to Palestine was weak. They would re-establish their ownership to the land by working on the soil. That was an additional reason why there must be no Arab labour in the *kibbutzim*. Yet this theory ignored the obvious fact that all around the *kibbutzim* the Palestinian Arabs, who formed a huge majority, were daily establishing *their* claim to the land by working on it and had been doing so for generations. To counter this threat the Labourites evolved myths about the Palestinians which further distorted the image of their enemy. They claimed, first, that the Palestinians had neglected their land and let it become a desert, which, in Zionist theory, would mean that they had forfeited their right to it. Yet this ignored the fact that, as even Israeli writers like Amos Elon point out, during the second half of the nineteenth century there had been considerable agricultural and economic development and improvement in Palestine. Another myth of Labourites was that the Palestinians had no attachment to their land and did not exist as a people. As Ahad Ha'am pointed out as late as 1920: 'Since the beginning of the Palestinian colonization we have always considered the Arab people as non-existent.'[48] These myths were not deliberate and malicious distortions, but an unconscious attempt of Labourites to justify their deepest instincts that the land belonged to them. Yet by 1920 the anti-Jewish riots in Palestine made it clear not only that the Palestinian people *did* exist but also that the Zionists would need more than myths and theories of a Conquest of Labour. Some Jews formed the Haganah, an underground corps which protected the settlements. Others favoured a more radical solution.

In 1923 Vladimir Jabotinski founded the Union of Zionist Revisionists and it was he who was responsible for militarising Zionism. 'We ought not to be deterred by this Latin word "militarism",' he argued; it was 'the natural defence of a people that had no homeland and faced extinction'.[49] Jabotinski had no time for Labour Zionism. He was an admirer of Herzl and shared his aristocratic vision of the new Jew. Revisionist youth joined his organisation *Betar*, striving for *hadar* or 'chivalry'. Jabotinski did not want the Zionists to be peaceful peasants farming the land but proud aristocratic Crusaders, exhibiting an unflappable confidence, dignity, a sense of honour and *noblesse oblige*.[50] When the *Betarim* arrived in Eretz Yisrael they did not work the land; instead they did two years' military service. Not content with seeking a socialist utopia in the Jewish homeland, Jabotinski sought a nation state on both sides of the Jordan. He was strongly affected by the racist nationalism of the day and his opponents in the Zionist movement frequently pointed out the likeness of his Revisionism to Nazi fascism.[51] Jabotinski wanted a state for the Jews so that they could preserve their racial purity and hence their unique creativity and integrity.

Because Eretz Yisrael would become a state, Jabotinski argued that the state needed an army. It was no use hoping that the Palestinians would acquiesce in the Zionist plans. 'They are not a rabble but a nation, perhaps somewhat tattered but still living. A living people makes such enormous concessions only when there is no hope.'[52] Herzl had also foreseen the Palestinian problem in Eretz Yisrael: 'We shall have to spirit the penniless population across the border by procuring employment for it in the transit countries, while denying it any employment in our own country,' he wrote in his diary, adding, 'Both the process of expropriation and the removal of the poor must be carried out discreetly and circumspectly.'[53] Jabotinski did not agree with this secretive spiriting away of the Palestinians, but he did agree with Herzl that Zionism was a colonial movement. No colony had ever managed to impose itself against natives without force, so Jews must now build 'an iron wall of Jewish bayonets' instead of settlements 'which the native population cannot break through'.[54] That, he insisted, was the only possible Zionist policy towards the Arabs. People like Ben Gurion had to give up their romantic dreams of Labour and face the fact that there was:

> an iron law of every colonising movement, a law which knows of no exceptions, a law which existed in all times and under all circumstances. If you wish to colonise a land in which people were already living you must provide a garrison on your behalf. Or else – or else, give up your colonisation, for without an armed force which will render physically impossible any attempts to destroy or prevent this colonisation, colonisation is impossible, not 'difficult', not 'dangerous' but IMPOSSIBLE. . . . Zionism is a colonising adventure and it therefore stands or falls by the question of armed force. It is important to build, it is important to speak Hebrew, but, unfortunately, it is even more important to be able to shoot – or else I am through with playing at colonisation. (1927)[55]

The Revisionists very quickly became important in Zionism both among the settlers in Eretz Yisrael and among the Zionists in the diaspora. After the shadow-boxing of the Labourites it seemed clear in the extreme. Jabotinski was adamant that a Jewish state must have a Jewish majority. Ideally there should be no *goyim* in it at all. How else should the state retain its racial integrity? Volunteers flocked into *Betar* and Jabotinski defiantly trained them on the Mount of Olives, right under the noses of the British. Zionism was acquiring the militant image that it would never lose. There was always a good deal of tension between the Labourites and the Revisionists, and Jabotinski would feel himself to be an outcast. He died in the diaspora in 1941 but even before his death Labour leaders in Palestine were coming round to accept some of his ideas. The Haganah acquired a new fighting edge and after his death Jabotinski's disciples would be largely instrumental in establishing the State of Israel. Jabotinski had always said that Judaea had fallen in blood and fire and in blood and fire it would rise again. His disciples made his prophecy come true and without this element in the 1948 war it is unlikely that there would have been a Jewish state.

The Zionists had to contend with two enemies in Eretz Yisrael. Besides the Palestinians they found that they had to confront the British, who had established their Mandate in the country in 1920. The Mandate was committed to implementing the Balfour Declaration and this should have been positive for the Jews, but the Declaration had also insisted that the rights of the Arab majority must not be endangered by the proposed Jewish 'homeland' in Palestine. This meant that the British in Palestine had an impossible task because the demands of the two peoples were irreconcilable. Today Israelis often accuse the British of favouring the Arabs and the Arabs insist that the British favoured the Jews. It seems that at different times the British showed contempt for both, but by the time the Second World War broke out in 1939 the Jewish community (the *Yishuv*) were in serious conflict with the British. The terrible news from Germany had changed the priorities of the settlers, increasingly preoccupied not with revolutionary socialism but with rescuing Jews from the Nazis. Yet still the British insisted on limiting immigration in Palestine so as not to endanger the rights of the Arabs by boosting the Jewish minority. The British continued this policy after the war, which resulted in ugly and tragic scenes; in July 1947, for example, the steamer *Exodus*, which carried 4500 survivors of the Holocaust, was forcibly turned back by the British when it reached Haifa and had to return to Germany. Naturally there was a new desperation in the *Yishuv* which increasingly expressed itself in violence against the Mandate.

Ben Gurion became aware of Arab nationalism in Eretz Yisrael in 1915, and from that moment it was no longer so easy for the Zionists to ignore or repress the Palestinian problem. It raised too many moral issues: could the Zionists conscientiously oppose another oppressed people who had similar aspirations to their own? 'It came down upon me like a blow,' Ben Gurion recalled years later. 'I said to myself "So there *is* an Arab national movement *here*" (and not just in Lebanon and Syria). It hit me like a bomb. I was completely confounded.'[56] Like Ben Yehuda before him, he felt the integrity of Zionism was threatened. Yet if the Zionist leader had kept his eyes open, Palestinian nationalism need not have come as such a bolt from the blue. One of the characteristics that impressed non-Zionist observers most forcibly about the Palestinian Arabs was their devotion to their land. They were forming a national identity, but twenty years too late. All around them they could see the British and the French giving independence to their Arab brothers in the new nation states of Egypt, Syria, Jordan, Lebanon and Iraq. The Palestinians were the only Arabs who were not being granted independence. They knew too that although it had been customary for the great powers to take control of a lesser people's land and control their destiny, these colonial attitudes were no longer considered so universally acceptable. Why were they alone being penalised in this way? It was also true that the Jewish settlers made their lives impossible. Not only were they frequently insulted by these foreigners, they were sometimes deprived of a livelihood. The settlers would buy land from one of the big feudal Arab overlords for their *kibbutzim* and would then turn the Arab tenants off the smallholdings that their families had often farmed for centuries. Because the *kibbutzim* were ideologically opposed to employing Arab labour, they were now both landless and unemployed. It was hardly surprising that the frustrations of the Palestinians exploded frequently into violence and bloodshed and, in 1936, into a rebellion against the British, who seemed to want to give their land away to the Jews.

The Palestinians suffered then and they continue to suffer in the propaganda war because beside the Zionists they seem ineffective and negative. Where the Israelis were building the land and making the desert bloom, creating a new tough image for their people, the Palestinians seemed perpetually to be saying 'no' to all this wonderful progress. They did not understand the nature of Zionism nor did they realise until too late that this farming was a Conquest, albeit a peaceful one, and that settlers like Gordon were claiming their title to Palestine by tilling the soil. Their attitude seemed mean and griping. Yet their position was extremely difficult. Their nationalism was twenty years behind Zionism, and the Jews therefore had a head start that proved crucial. It is not fair to accuse the Palestinians of being slow-witted here, as Israelis tend to do. Zionism was an extraordinary and idiosyncratic movement and peculiarly Western. It was not like a normal invasion or colonisation. Without a good, sound knowledge of Jewish history, Marxism, early nationalism and populism it would have been impossible for the average Palestinian to understand what these *kibbutzim* meant. By the time the Palestinians understood, Zionism was indeed well on the way to becoming an established fact, as the Second Aliyah had intended.

It was also true that while Zionism was very positive indeed for the Jews, it was *de facto* negative for the Palestinians. They were outside the great scheme and from the beginning of the Second Aliyah Zionism had adopted a menacing position towards the Arab inhabitants of Palestine, for all that it was such a peaceful movement. The *kibbutzim* were usually built in places that directly challenged an Arab village or group of villages, which is why they were so effective as military bases in 1948. A. B. Gordon's settlement at Degania, for example, was a challenge and a provocation to the Arab village of Umm Juni. Tel Aviv was a deliberate challenge to Arab Jaffa. The building of the land had in it an inherent aggression, even before the building project had become an overt act of war. Something of the spirit of this aggressive building manifested itself in the early 1960s in the new State of Israel. The city of Nazareth is the only major Arab city left in Israel and since 1948 the population had risen there from 8000 to 45,000. It was hopelessly overcrowded, but the government of Israel has done very little to build houses for the Israeli Arabs or to help the municipality. Nazareth was quickly becoming very run down. In 1960 the government forcibly appropriated Arab land in the hills surrounding the city as part of their 'Judaisation of the Galilee' programme. There they built 'Upper Nazareth' or 'Jewish Nazareth'. As the Israeli writer Yoseph Elgazi wrote in 1975, if the visitor goes to Jewish Nazareth:

> he will see over there the new buildings, the wide streets, the public lights, the steps, the many-storied [sic] buildings, the industrial and artisan enterprises, and he will be able to perceive the contrast: development up there and lack of care down there; constant development up there and no construction whatever down there. Since 1966 the [Israeli] Ministry of Housing has not built a single unit of habitation in old Nazareth.[57]

The exclusion and the menace that was once implicit in the *kibbutzim* was later present in the creation of Jewish Nazareth. It reinforces the positive image of the Jewish state against the negative stereotype of its enemy, the Palestinian, whom Israelis had been seeing as dirty, primitive and unworthy of the Zionist effort ever since A. B. Gordon had been lovingly cultivating the land.

Constantly the Arabs fought the Zionists for their country throughout the twenty-eight years of the British Mandate. Sometimes they made bad mistakes which would finally weaken them in 1948. They never succeeded in uniting themselves against the Zionists and they foolishly dissipated their strength by fighting the British. Their most damaging 'mistake' was, however, foisted upon them by the British. Sir Herbert Samuel, the British Governor, decided that the Palestinians needed a leader, so he invented the title Grand Mufti of Jerusalem, and the young Hajj Amin al-Husseini was one of the contenders for the post in 1921. He was in his mid-twenties and quite unqualified for the position. He was moreover a fanatical enemy of both the British and the Jews. The electoral college was moderate and sensible and, when the votes came in, Haji Amin was at the bottom of the list. To Sir Herbert's delight, Sheikh Hisam ad-Din, a moderate and learned man, was elected. The Hajj's family was not satisfied, however, and, a powerful family in Palestine, it stirred up a vicious campaign in Jerusalem. During the disturbances one E. T. Richmond, adviser to the Commissioner for Muslim Affairs and a rabid anti-Zionist, somehow persuaded Sir Herbert to make Sheikh Hisam stand down and put the Hajj in his place. That Sir Herbert agreed to this was tragic and from that moment it meant that there was no hope of a moderate, sensible or even a representative Palestinian leadership. The kind of man the Hajj was can be shown by the fact that he sought an ally in Adolf Hitler and thus linked the Palestinian cause with the fascist regime.[58]

In 1936 the British set up the Peel Commission to try and find a solution to the conflict between Arabs and Jews – its solution has in recent years come up for discussion again. It proposed two independent states. The Jews would have a small state in the fertile Galilee which they had already developed. The Palestinians would take the rest of the country. Hajj Amin, of course, would not hear of such a proposal and neither would Jabotinski and his Revisionists. However, the Labourites, who were still in the majority in the *Yishuv*, were willing to consider it. The rise of the Nazis in Germany had altered their priorities and they were now ready to abandon their old socialist ideals to the extent of creating a 'state'. In their discussions they showed that they had come around to yet another of Jabotinski's ideas: this state must have a Jewish majority. The *Yishuv* had grown, but the Arabs were still an overwhelming majority in Palestine. 'There is no hope that this new Jewish state will survive, to say nothing of develop, if the Arabs are as numerous as they are today,'[59] said the veteran Menachem Ussiskin, who thirty years earlier had been afraid that the *aliyah* would provoke the *goyim*. The liberal Labourite and propagandist Berl Katzenelson was more tolerant. 'I am willing to give the Arabs equal rights,' he said, 'if I know that only a small minority stays in the land.' He proposed a plan for the new state that included the provision to eliminate Palestinians from the state. 'Development means evictions,'[60] Joseph Weitz, the director of the Jewish National Fund, made the point of the Labourites clear. They wanted to rescue Jews from the anti-semites in Germany and were hoping that ultimately millions of Jews would make the *aliyah*. Where were they to go if the land was full of Arabs, and how were they to be settled if the Arabs owned most of the land? The deportation of the Palestinians from a Jewish state 'does not serve only one aim – to diminish the Arab population', Weitz wrote in a report. 'It also serves a second purpose by no means less important, which is to evacuate land now cultivated by Arabs and thus release it for Jewish settlement.'[61]

Herzl had airily imagined such a transfer of the natives of Palestine over thirty years ago, when most of the idealistic Zionists would have condemned the idea out of hand. Now they had stopped having visions of dream-worlds and had to face the cold light of this new anti-semitic dawn. It led to a new hardening. Even moderates like Weizmann and Ben Gurion were clear now that the new Jewish state meant the eviction of the Palestinians. Weizmann dreamed of buying a lot of land over the border in the Arab world and pushing the Palestinians into it, thereby presumably displacing more Arabs who would be forced to make way for the Palestinians.[62] He wanted Britain and America to put pressure on the Palestinians to go quietly. Ben Gurion also wanted the British to force the Palestinians out, but if necessary, he wrote in his diary, 'we must be prepared ourselves to carry it out.'[63] Jewish self-liberation was now determining the fate of others.

In 1936 the Peel Commission undertook to enforce the transfer of 250,000 Palestinians from the area of the proposed Jewish state. There were some voices in

Britain that opposed this transfer as immoral because there was no land for these deportees in the far less fertile proposed Palestinian state. The Palestinians, headed by the Haji, rejected the proposal out of hand and the Palestinians have been blamed for their negative attitude towards partition. Yet perhaps they were not negative so much as prescient. The *Yishuv* accepted partition. They were still staunch secularists and were prepared to accept land that had no great biblical connotations, just as long as the Palestinians were deported. The Zionist leaders had no intention, however, of remaining within the modest confines of their tiny state. When Weizmann was asked about the skimpy borders of the proposed state he replied cryptically, 'The Kingdom of David was smaller, under Solomon it became an empire. Who knows. *C'est le premier pas qui compte.*'[64] Ben Gurion was blunter. He told a Zionist meeting: 'I favour partition of the country because when we become a strong power after the establishment of the state, we will abolish partition and spread throughout Palestine.' The following year he wrote to his son:

> We shall organise a sophisticated defence force – an elite army. I have no doubt that our army will be one of the best in the world. And then I am sure that we shall not be prevented from settling in all the other parts of the country, whether through mutual understanding with our Arab neighbours or by other means.[65]

An unexpurgated text of this letter, only recently made available, adds: 'We will expel the Arabs and take their places.'[66] Labour Zionism had 'militarised' itself as Jabotinski had begged it to. In view of this it would have been suicidal for the Palestinians to agree to partition.

In fact, by refusing partition they appeared to have got what they wanted. In May 1939 the British abandoned the idea and produced a White Paper which envisaged Palestine as an independent Arab state. From now on the Jews would have to fight the British if they wanted their own state, even though in September of that year Britain declared war against the greatest enemy of the Jews. 'We shall fight the war as though there were no White Paper,' Ben Gurion promised, 'and the White Paper as though there were no war.'[67] In the last years that led up to the creation of the state the militant image of Zionism was coming more and more to the surface. It had consciously entered a new phase. The old revolutionary utopian messianism had been replaced by the apocalyptic messianism with its dreams of violent salvation. The peaceful *aliyah* was to become a war of annihilation.

A new type of Zionist appeared in Eretz Yisrael in the early 1940s. Menachem Begin, who became Prime Minister in 1977, had experienced the new anti-semitism in Poland and the Soviet Union. His whole family was murdered together with the entire Jewish community of his home town, Brest-Litovsk – some 30,000 souls. Begin was one of the few people to survive an interrogation by Stalin's NKVD unbroken; he survived a slave-camp in the Arctic circle, was released and walked to Eretz Yisrael through Central Asia. He was a tough, desperate man, committed to revenge. He was also religious. In 1943 Begin, a passionate admirer of Jabotinski, took command of the Irgun, the Revisionists' military army, and two months later started terrorist activities against the British administration. Begin repudiated the label 'terrorist' but, even though he condemned 'murder', he blew up CID offices, tax centres and the Immigration building, planted bombs and led raids in which Britons and civilian Arabs were killed.[68] Another terrorist organisation was Lehi, led by Avraham Stern. He was killed in 1942 but his colleagues carried on the organisation, led by Yitzhak Shamir, who became the Prime Minister of Israel in 1986. Begin regarded the Stern Gang as crude and stupid and would have nothing to do with such Lehi operations as the killing of six British paratroopers in their beds in 1946. However, the two groups were flung together following the assassination in 1944 by the Stern Gang of Lord Moyne, the British Minister for Middle East affairs.[69] Ben Gurion and the Haganah were appalled and started a campaign against both groups, capturing members and handing them over to the British. During this period underground, the Irgun and Lehi became closer and Begin became more desperate than ever, forming an organisation that would be ultimately proof against any attack or campaign.

At first, therefore, the *Yishuv* establishment disowned terror, but when the British raided the Jewish Agency on 29 June 1946, arresting 2718 Jews, the Haganah agreed to join forces with Begin. On 22 July that year the two groups blew up a wing of the King David Hotel, which housed the British administration. Ninety-one people were killed.[70] In the face of this new Zionism, the British decided to hand the problem of Palestine over to the United Nations. The Mandate remained, however, fearful that if it left Palestine to its own devices the Arabs would move in and exterminate the *Yishuv*. But Begin finally got rid of the Mandate. When three members of the Irgun were hanged by the British for terrorist activities in 1947, Begin hanged and mined the bodies of two British sergeants a few hours later. In Britain there were anti-Jewish riots in four major cities and in Derby a synagogue was burned down. The British decided to get out of Palestine as soon as possible.[71]

Without this terrorist activity it is not likely that there would have been a Jewish state in 1948. Britain was still restricting immigration with fanatical tenacity, even in the face of a thrice-repeated demand from the United States that survivors of the Holocaust be admitted. But terrorism was not only successful against the British. It was powerfully effective against the Palestinians. In April 1948 the Irgun and the Stern Gang attacked the Arab village of Deir Yassin outside Jerusalem in reprisal for raids against Jewish settlements. The attackers were supposed to warn the villagers with a loudspeaker so that the women, children and old people could be evacuated, but the loudspeaker van got stuck in a ditch and had to be abandoned. The Arabs put up strong resistance and the Irgun had to ask the Haganah for help. A squadron of commandos was dispatched and the village subdued. When the Haganah went home, Irgun and Lehi avenged their comrades who had fallen in the battle and began to loot and massacre for most of the following day. Two hundred and fifty men, women, children and old people were massacred and their bodies horribly mutilated.[72] The nightmare scenes were described by Meir Pa'il of the Haganah, who had gone along 'to get some estimate of these irregulars' combat capacities'. He came out with stories of obscene atrocity in 1972.[73] Begin sent out his congratulations 'on this splendid act of conquest. . . . As at Deir Yassin, so everywhere, we will attack and smite the enemy. God, God, thou hast chosen us for conquest.'[74] The spirit of Joshua had entered Zionism. On 25 April 1948 Irgun attacked Arab Jaffa. Again the Arabs fought bravely at first but had nothing with which to counter the Irgun's mortars and, with the memory of Deir Yassin fresh in everybody's mind, nearly all the 70,000 inhabitants of Jaffa abandoned their city and fled. There followed scenes of looting, destruction and pillaging.[75]

During the 1948 war many of the Palestinians followed the example of the people of Jaffa and left the country, fearing the cruelty of the Irgun. The Israelis have always maintained that they asked the Arab people to stay and that the Palestinians foolishly listened to the orders of the Arab leaders in the surrounding states who purportedly told them to escape from the Jewish state; nobody has ever been able to produce evidence of any such broadcasts from the Arab countries. Labour leaders had been maintaining for years that the Arabs would have to be forced out of Israel. The new post-Holocaust Zionism was desperate and determined to save the Jewish people from the dangers of the diaspora. They had to make way for the millions of Jews who would now return to the land of their fathers to live there in freedom and safety. Nobody had helped the Jews in Germany and nobody would help them in Palestine. The Zionists would have to 'do it themselves'. Their stories about the Palestinians' cowardly, stupid flight in 1948 is in line with their other myths about the enemy. They show that the Palestinians were not attached to their country and gave it up at the first show of force. Until recently the British, American and Israeli archives for this period were closed, and reports of UN observers in Palestine were little known. Lately, however, there have been studies of the 1948 Palestinian exodus, using archives as well as other sources, like the eyewitness accounts of Jewish veterans, only recently permitted to publish their memoirs, and the memories of Palestinian refugees themselves. These suggest the alternative view.[76] They suggest that many Palestinians fled because of the stories of Irgun cruelty; that Israeli soldiers terrorised many Arab villages, rounding up hostages in villages like Safsaf and Sa'sa and shooting them; that some Arabs were driven from their homes by brute force and then forbidden to return to the villages, which were either manned by Israeli soldiers or mined, and that many Palestinians were so attached to their land that they stayed on as refugees in their own country in great danger, until they were finally rounded up and sent over the border.[77] However one chooses to interpret the events of 1948, the creation of the State of Israel caused extreme and continuous suffering to the Palestinian people, which shows no sign of abating.

Once the State of Israel had been established in 1948, therefore, the Jews had achieved a new identity. The Zionists had proved that Jews were not timid weaklings, religious anachronisms and homeless aliens. The Israeli Jews were tough pioneers, brave soldiers and creative farmers. The State of Israel had brought Jews firmly back into the family of the nations and instead of being seen by anti-semites as relics of the ancient world, Jews were now vanguards of progress in the Middle East. In this respect Zionism had done great things for the Jewish people. The State of Israel must be one of the most extraordinary achievements of the twentieth century, a monument to dedication and resolution. The Zionists had turned an abstruse theory into an established fact and thus changed the world, and the State of Israel would be important for the identity of Jews in the diaspora as well as for Israelis. But some Jews were uneasy about the Jewish state and the Zionist enterprise. Albert Einstein, who took his Jewish identity very seriously, had written in 1938:

> I would much rather see reasonable agreement with the Arabs on the basis of living together in peace than the creation of a Jewish state.... my awareness of the essential nature of Judaism resists the idea of a Jewish state with borders, an army and a measure of temporal power, no matter how modest. I am afraid of the inner damage Judaism will suffer – especially from the development of a narrow nationalism within our own ranks.[78]

However positive Israel's new image, it was ambiguous. Behind the successful, victorious Israeli, lurked the suffering Palestinian who would become his shadow-self, repeating the Jewish experience of exile and persecution so exactly that it sometimes seems a cruel parody. This certainly troubled many Sabras, the native-born Israelis.

The Sabras were the first fruits of Zionism. It was hoped that because they had been born in the homeland, they would be more at home there than their parents, who had often found their 'return' traumatic and the homeland alien. Because they had been convinced that a physical and spiritual contact with one's homeland was vital for the new Jewish identity, the founding fathers decided that their children were to be formed and nurtured by the land of Israel itself. Their souls were to be shaped by it, just as the souls of their fathers had been liberated from the trauma of the diaspora by lovingly cultivating its soil. The creed of the importance of the land for the new generation of Sabras was memorably expressed by the Zionist poet Saul Tchernichovsky:

> Man is nothing but the soil of a small country,
> nothing but the shape of his native landscape,
> nothing but what his ears recorded
> when they were new and really heard,
> what his eyes saw, before they had their fill of seeing –
> everything a wondering child comes across
> on the dew-softened paths,
> stumbling over every lump of earth, every old stone,
> while in a hidden place in his soul, unknown to him,
> there's an altar set up
> from which the smoke of his sacrifice rises each day
> to the kingdom of the sky, to the stars. [c.1920][79]

The settlers decided that the land itself would educate the Sabras. Eretz Yisrael was to be the pivot upon which all educational activity turned and the child's senses, emotions and intellect were to be stimulated and shaped by his native landscape. The homeland would become an essential part of his integrity and identity. The young Sabras toured the country as much as possible, as they still do today, studying its geography and its flora and fauna. These field trips gave Sabras a formative and creative contact with the land. The children made excursions to important historical sites like Masada, where the Jewish resistance fighters had committed suicide rather than submit to the Romans in CE 73. A field trip or a trip to a place like Masada was – and still is – a kind of secular pilgrimage. The Israeli scholar Eliezer Schweid has written of these excursions:

> Anyone sensitive to the ambience of these trips can see that they are not merely another form of entertainment. There is something ceremonial, serious and elevated about the way the participants go about their preparations and about the trip itself, a kind of psychological attitude and devotion that give it an almost ritual character. In other words, the field trip is an act of symbolic significance; by means of it one accomplishes a higher purpose. It is the culmination of a process, the fulfilment of a hope. It embodies something of the whole meaning of life.[80]

This secular pilgrimage was imbued with a great deal of the spirituality that we have seen in early Zionism: it was a journey to the roots of the Jewish people and a way of taking possession of the homeland. Each new generation would establish the Land of Israel in its mind and heart in this way at a very deep level. The pilgrimages, excursions or hikes were complementary to the peaceful Conquest of Labour; this becomes clear when it is recalled that an annual march of citizens to Jerusalem has taken the place of a military parade on independence day.

Another way in which the Sabras established a deep and lasting contact with their land was by their passion for archaeology, which is probably unique to Israel. This passion has been given the Hebrew name *bulmus*, an old Talmudic term which denotes a ravenous hunger or mania.[81] Unpaid voluntary work on archaeological sites like Masada is one of the two main social services for which Israelis volunteer in great numbers. The other, significantly, is for dangerous duty in crack army units and for service in exposed border settlements.[82] It is not difficult to understand why this should be so. Freud himself compared archaeology to the process of psychoanalysis: in both pursuits people dig for hidden but important roots in the past and gain a new insight and new lease of life in the process.[83] Zionism itself had initiated just such a rebirth by means of a creative encounter with the past and it is clear that many Israelis find reassurance in discovering in the soil of Eretz Yisrael evidence that their forefathers really *were* there. Yigael Yadin, the great Israeli archaeologist, who is also a former general and chief of staff, has explained that this journey to the past has a quasi-religious element, and has claimed that it inspires the young Sabra to fight for his country: 'Through archaeology they discovered their "religious values". In archaeology they find their religion. They learn that their forefathers were in this country 3000 years ago. This is a value. By this they fight and by this they live.'[84] That this type of contact with the land can inspire a Sabra with a militant patriotism is clear when we remember that one of the most successful of the Israeli amateur archaeologists was Moshe Dayan, the hero of the Six Day War. In Dayan we have an example of an Israeli who had no doubts about Israel's right to Palestine. But other Sabras, who have received the same Zionist education, have always been more doubtful.

One of these was the novelist S. Yizah, whose great novel *Days of Ziklag* is set during the 1948 war. Yizah is clearly attached to the country, for the book is full of beautiful descriptions of the landscape, but the heroes of the novel have agonising doubts about their right to the land. They complain that Zionist rhetoric is like a millstone around their necks and that the sacred word 'homeland' is demanding, ambiguous and insufficient for the sacrifices they are expected to make.[85] In the *Tale of Khirbat Khisa*, which was written just after the 1948 war, a soldier describes the cold-blooded expulsion of the Arab villagers from their home and their inhuman dispatch to the 'other side'. It is a horrible revelation to the young hero of the consequences of Zionism. In words that recall the 'dread' of Ben Yehuda, he says: 'I felt within me a stupefying collapse.' When he contemplates the Arab village being absorbed into an exemplary Jewish settlement, he can find nothing positive about this 'rebuilding' of the land:

> We'll open a co-op grocery, a school, perhaps a synagogue. There'll be political parties. They'll discuss lots of things. The fields will be plowed and sown and reaped, and great feats will be accomplished. Bravo Hebrew *Khisa*! Who'll remember that there was once a *Khirbat Khisa* which we drove out and inherited. *We came, shot, burned blew up, repelled, pushed and exiled. What the hell are we doing here!*[86]

The last exclamation is also an agonised question, with layers of ambiguity.

The younger generation of writers also expresses this sense of 'stupefying collapse' at the same time as they remain committed to the State of Israel. The heroes of A. B. Yehoshua's novels and stories are similarly obsessed by the Arab past that lies beneath the rebuilt land and show constant doubts about the rights and wrongs of Zionism. In Yehoshua's first novel *Facing the Forests* (1963) the hero, who is writing a thesis on the Crusades, takes a job as a caretaker of a newly planted forest – one of the show-pieces of the Zionist enterprise. He finds himself increasingly haunted by the Arab village that the forest had obliterated and finally he helps one of the former villagers to burn the forest down in an orgiastic ecstasy of liberation. Yehoshua's heroes and heroines often feel a nagging guilt and constant worry and are frustrated in their attempts to make amends. When Yehoshua digs below the surface of the Jewish state, he does not find reassurance in its origins, as Yadin and Dayan both did. He sees the ruined Arab villages and finds that the roots of Zionism are tangled with destruction and pain. The only way out of this impasse is another tragic destruction – that of the Zionist achievement.

Amos Oz, probably Israel's finest writer, is a dedicated *Kibbutznik* who left home to join Kibbutz Hulda when he was only fifteen. He is committed to Zionism and very concerned that the Jewish state express the whole humanist Jewish tradition, not just a fundamentalist reduction of it. In his novels and stories we also see a love of the landscape and yet the Land of Israel is often sinister and threatening. There is a constant sense of dread, of siege and of frontiers. There is barbed wire; infiltrators raid on both sides of the border; jackals howl in the hills outside the *kibbutz* and enemy arc lights search the horizons. *My Michael*, Oz's most famous novel, was published in 1968 and at once it became a cult book in Israel. The picture is bleak. To Hannah, the heroine, Jerusalem is not a holy place but dangerous and threatening. Indeed, she cannot feel safe or at home anywhere in the country although she longs to identify with the Zionist hope. When she visits her mother for a Passover party in a *kibbutz* in the Galilee, she feels at first a wonderful sense of escape and freedom. The novel is set before the 1967 war and a trip north means that Hannah is in true Israeli territory and far away from the Arabs who hold the Old City of Jerusalem. The bus speeds through the rebuilt land; the passengers eat Jaffa oranges and admire the landscape, with Zionist reverence; Hannah's husband and son talk about the War of Independence and the government irrigation works; Hannah smiles prettily and affirms her faith in 'all the great works of irrigation'.[87] At the *kibbutz* she whirls round in the *hora* in a classic evening of Israeli togetherness. For a moment she feels at home and at one with her environment: 'I revelled. I was swept away. I belonged.'[88]

> But towards dawn I went out and stood all alone on the balcony of Emanuel's small house. I saw coils of barbed wire. I saw dark bushes. The sky lightened. I was facing north. I could make out the silhouettes of a mountainous landscape: the Lebanese border. Tired lights shone yellow in the ancient stone-built villages. Unapproachable valleys. Distant snow-capped peaks. Lonely buildings on the hill tops, monasteries or forts. A boulder-strewn expanse scarred with deep wadis. A chill breeze blew. I shivered. I longed to leave. What a powerful yearning.[89]

The Zionist yearning for the return has become a yearning to leave. Eretz Yisrael has become a prison instead of a land of liberation. The Israeli is caught there almost against her will; there is nowhere for her to go.

Throughout the book Hannah has fantasies of the Arab twins Halil and Aziz, who were her playmates when she was a child, but who have become terrorists in her dreams, training to destroy the State of Israel. They are at home in the country in a way that Zionist Hannah will never be and their terrorist activities are seen as an act of love and union that is far deeper than the hectic and conscious togetherness of the *kibbutz*. A bombing is an affirmation of their love for one another and love for their country, with which they are at one:

> Four lithe arms reach out. Matching as in a dance. As in love. As if all four spring from a single body. Cable. Timing-device. Fuse. Detonator. Igniter. Bodies surge down the hill and away, softly padding. And on the slope beneath the skyline a stealthy run, a longing caress. The undergrowth flattens and straightens as they pass. Like a light skiff edging through still, calm waters.[90]

Hannah knows very well that the twins are the creation of her fantasy: 'I sent them. To me towards dawn they will return. Come battered and warm. Exuding a smell of sweat and foam.'[91] The Israeli has created the Palestinian terrorist and is locked in erotic desire for her own destruction.

Hard-liners condemn the work of Oz and Yehoshua and the many others like them as defeatist and as evidence of the spiritual bankruptcy of the State of Israel which has lost the tough fervour of the pioneering days. Yet it seems that these writers are trying to prepare their fellow countrymen to make peace with the Arabs and to recognise the wrongs that Zionism has committed. They are acting as the conscience of the Israeli people. In the Hitlerian world, the founding fathers had not felt able to afford this luxury and many Sabras follow them in a refusal to consider the Arabs' point of view. Such Israelis usually speak about the Arabs with a regrettable and often offensive racialism. The 'Arab' has become the essential enemy of the Jewish people, just as the 'Jew' had been the enemy of European anti-semites. He represents everything that the Israelis feel they are not. The 'Arab' is dirty and primitive where the Israelis are modern and progressive; 'he' is fatalistic and irrational, where the Israelis are positive and rational; 'he' is a terrorist, where the Israelis are peace-lovers; 'he' is an essential child and a case of arrested development, where the Israelis are mature human beings. Such a creature cannot be taken seriously and 'his' point of view is therefore worthless. In the creation of a new identity, we have seen that a people often need a foil against which to measure themselves and this has been conveniently supplied by the 'Arab'. It is a sad fact of human nature that human beings tend to despise the unfortunate and the unlucky, especially those they may have wronged. This certainly affected the European's view of the 'Jew' and now it helps to shape the Israelis' view of the 'Arab'.

In such a neurotic climate a peaceful settlement seems a distant chimera, and yet there continue to be Israelis who try to return to the high moral ideals of early Zionism and point out that they are not compatible with the unfortunate *status quo*. Former hawks have dropped their old aggression and become peace-makers. One of these converted doves is the writer and politician Uri Avnery, who began his Zionist life as a Revisionist and a member of the terrorist Lehi group of Avraham Stern. Now he is the founder of a peace party and an outspoken critic of anti-Arab policies; he has helped to organise dangerous, secret and controversial meetings between Israelis and PLO officials in order to create a climate where *détente* is possible.[92] Another convert to peace is Professor Y. Harkabi, the former hawkish head of the Israeli Secret Intelligence, who now sees no hope for the Jewish state unless Israelis make important concessions to the Arab states and to the Palestinians.[93] It is important to remember that secular Zionism was originally a deeply moral movement and that its imperatives can impel people to change their mind and to make peace. The committed idealism of the *kibbutznik* can force a Zionist like Amos Oz to lay bare the essential ambiguity of the Jewish state and can make hawks like Avnery and Harkabi change their minds. As long as this secular Zionism prevailed there was always some hope, however remote, for a peaceful settlement.

But increasingly it seems that these secular ideals are giving way to religious extremism that absolutely rules out the idea of peace with the *goyim*. Menachem Begin was a religious man and he had brought the spirit of Joshua into secular Zionism. For many years after the creation of the State of Israel he was cast out into the wilderness and his political party Herut firmly pushed to the margins. Terrorism may have continued to be of use to the Zionists as they tried to establish their new state securely and there were other very dubious incidents committed by Israelis during the 1950s and early 1960s. But in the main, the higher, more humanitarian ideals of the Labour Party prevailed and before the 1967 war there was a spirit of *détente* in the country. After the Six Day War there was a religious revival in Israel and within Judaism and in 1977 Menachem Begin became Prime Minister only to discover that there were new religious Zionists who found his hawk-like policies shamefully and even sinfully weak. Constantly during its history, secular Zionism had adopted a religious posture and it has now given birth to an ardent religious Zionism that has created a climate in which a peaceful settlement is becoming an impossibility. The dangerous Zionist holy war will be discussed in a later chapter.

THE ARABS

On 26 July 1956 President Gemal Abdul Nasser was due to address the nation and Egyptians turned on their radios with excited anticipation, certain that something dramatic was about to happen. During the two years that he had been in power, Nasser had openly defied the imperialist West. He had denounced the Baghdad Pact of 1955, when Britain and America had made anti-Soviet alliances with Turkey, Iraq and Iran, as a thin device whereby the West sought to control the East. Nasser had retaliated by concluding a large arms deal with the Soviet Union to equip him in his struggle against Israel, who had launched a major raid against Egyptians in Gaza earlier that year. The following year, the United States curtly cancelled promised aid for the building of the Aswan Dam, and now Egyptians waited for their President to respond. They were not disappointed. Switching from classical Arabic into the fiery Egyptian dialect, Nasser laughed at the West and declared Egyptian independence. He announced that he was going to nationalise the Suez Canal; was it not 'our Canal', he asked, paid for at the cost of 120,000 Egyptian lives? Egypt did not need Western aid with such a major source of revenue. He would pay the shareholders full compensation, so that the transaction would be entirely legal, and the Egyptian Canal would pay for the Aswan Dam. Nasser could scarcely have made a more significant point; even his more cautious opponents in the Arab world were enthralled.[94] The Suez Canal was a classic symbol of Western exploitation of the people of the Middle East. It had been built by Europeans during the 1860s at quite a low cost but only 7 per cent of the shares were owned by the Egyptians, who scarcely benefited from this asset. By nationalising the Canal, Nasser was clearly telling the Egyptian people that they were now going to take control of their own fate and their own country. Britain and France were aghast, and the British Prime Minister Anthony Eden was reduced to incoherent, helpless rage.[95] Not only had this dynamic young President challenged the entrenched British belief that the Egyptians were a stupid race, incapable of self-rule. He had actually dared to deny that the Arab world was merely a subordinate part of the Western system and must, by the very nature of things, serve Western interests. Eden vowed to destroy Nasser and looked around for allies.

Suez, of course, was Nasser's great triumph. Later that year Britain, France and Israel formed a secret pact to effect a joint, concerted attack on Egypt. On 29 October, according to plan, Israel attacked Egyptian territory in Sinai. On the following day the United States' resolution in the Security Council calling for Israeli withdrawal was vetoed by Britain and France, who then attacked the Canal Zone on 5 November, ostensibly to separate the combatants. But this initiative collapsed completely under pressure from both America and the Soviet Union. Israel, therefore, was left isolated and was threatened by both superpowers. In March she was forced to withdraw from Sinai, having learned how perilous her situation was in the Middle East without the support of at least one friendly superpower. The whole shameful business was a diplomatic victory for Nasser: Britain, France and Israel had been humiliated, the Canal now belonged to Egypt.

The Suez victory has to be seen against a long, painful history of colonisation. For over a hundred years, Britain and France had been establishing colonies in the Middle East. This had begun in 1830 when the French had taken Algiers, and nine years later the British colonised Aden. As the Ottoman empire declined, this colonial expansion continued inexorably: Tunisia was occupied in 1881, Egypt in 1882, the Sudan in 1889 and Libya and Morocco in 1912. In 1915 during the First World War, the British responded to the Arab revolt against the Turks by promising the Arabs independence after the war, but the following year the notorious Sykes–Picot agreement divided the Middle Eastern lands of the Ottoman empire between Britain and France. Britain followed this with the Balfour Declaration in 1917, and in 1920 Britain and France marched into the Middle East and set up their mandates and protectorates. The Arabs often call 1920 the *am al-Nakba*, the Year of the Disaster. It was a lucid demonstration of their impotence before this Western colonising giant of insatiable appetite. There seemed to be no way to shake off this colonial domination, for although independence was formally guaranteed, in practice it was continually limited by various alliances and treaties that brought the area firmly under Western control. It seemed impossible for the Arab people to take their destiny into their own hands. The colonialists adopted modernising and Westernising policies that divorced the people from their cultural roots and introduced an alien and disturbing way of life. Furthermore, the occupying powers usually showed deep contempt for the 'natives', saw them as an inferior breed and seemed to assume that the Middle East and its inhabitants existed simply for the convenience of the West. This also applied to the non-Arab countries. In Iran the British had put Reza Shah Pahlavi on to the throne and were using the oil to fuel the British Navy. The Iranian people derived no more benefit from their oil than the Egyptians had from the Suez Canal.

The establishment of the State of Israel was the ultimate humiliation. Yet again the great powers had simply decided the fate of the Arab people over their heads. The abject failure of the Arab armies was a public demonstration of their powerlessness and was disastrous for the Arabs' self-respect. Finally, when 750,000 Palestinian Arabs were forced to leave their homes and poured into the surrounding countries, the rest of the world seemed absolutely indifferent. It appeared to be quite acceptable for thousands of Arabs to be crammed into hastily constructed refugee camps with no immediate prospect of returning to their homeland, while Israel systematically destroyed all trace of their former habitation. The Arabs felt singled out; it was as though they had been earmarked for special suffering, for in those sensitive years following the revelation of the Nazi obscenity, no other people could have been treated like that. The loss of Palestine, therefore, was not just a territorial matter. It assumed the same significance in the Arab world as the Holocaust assumed for the Jewish people. It symbolised the hatred and contempt of the rest of the world and the use of the Arabs as a scapegoat for Western guilt and neurosis. The Palestinian tragedy is likewise called *al-Nakba*, and is deeply linked to the colonial disaster of 1920. It was also called *al-Karitha*, a word which denotes terrible group catastrophe of near cosmic dimensions and just as the Holocaust became the subject of learned debate in the Jewish world, so too did the Palestinian catastrophe.[96] In 1948 Constantine Zurayk published his classic work *Maana al-Nakba* (Lesson of the Disaster) which began a tradition which has become known as the *Ilm al-Karitha* (the Science of the Catastrophe). In this tradition the Jewish state is seen as a crime against nature, as a 'cancerous growth' in the Middle East and an alien intrusion of unspeakable evil. Arabs regarded the Israeli Jews in the same way as Europeans had regarded Muslims and Jews for nearly a thousand years.

A significant part of the *Ilm al-Karitha* was a new Arab interest in the Crusades. Hitherto the Muslim world had not been very interested in the phenomenon of the Crusades, but now Arab historians argued that the Crusaders had been the first Western imperialists and the Jews were seen as new Crusaders and as the tools of Western imperialism. During the Crusades, the West had attacked the Arabs in Europe and in the Middle East, had driven them from their homeland in Palestine and Spain, had desecrated their holy places, massacred Arabs and seen them as inhuman vermin, who did not merit ordinary human rights. Cruel crusading exploitation was all that the Arabs could expect from the Western world. In addition to the crimes against the Palestinians, the Israelis were seen as the

The Present Conflict

79

representatives of the imperial West and surrounded with a nimbus of evil that belonged by rights to the colonial, crusading West.[97] An anti-semitism that was entirely new invaded the Middle East. Hitherto Jews may have been rather despised by the Arabs as an apparently powerless minority group, but there had been nothing like the phenomenon of Western anti-semitism. Now Arabs started to look back on those passages in the Koran which were composed while Mohammad was having to fight the Jews in Medina and ignored all the passages where the Koran speaks respectfully of the Jews as the People of the Book. The Jews were now seen as the essential enemies of the Muslims, who had fought against Islam from the first.[98] It was a view which ignored the fact that every single prophet venerated by Muslims had been Jewish, with the exception of Mohammad himself. But this was deemed insufficient and shortly the Arabs turned to the hated West for the one product of which she was most rightly ashamed. Fantasies of Western anti-semitism became current in the Middle East for the first time, and anti-semetic propaganda like the infamous *Protocols of the Elders of Zion*,[99] which was now taboo in the West, gained a new lease of life in the East. It is one of the great tragic ironies of the Middle East conflict that, by supporting the State of Israel, the West planted anti-semitism in the East. Once again the Jews were living surrounded by the old traditions of hatred, and the State of Israel, which was to have been a refuge, became one of the most dangerous places in the world for Jews. This new anti-semitism further demonised the Arabs, for when the Israelis heard a leader like Nasser talking like Hitler, he too became surrounded by a nimbus of absolute evil, which was in fact a Western not an Eastern evil.

Against this background of hopeless defeat and humiliation, the victory of Suez was intoxicating. Nasser seemed to have discovered a way to defeat the colonial powers and the dreaded State of Israel, and throughout the Arab world Nasserite ideologies were developed that were strongly anti-semitic and anti-Western. Egypt, which had hitherto been concerned mainly with Egyptian nationalism, now became the leader of the 'Arab nation'. It had not been easy to formulate an ideology that was acceptable and emotive enough to mobilise the Arab world against the West. Arabs were used to the religious polity of Islam, where politics was inseparable from religion, and found the Western, secular idealisms alien and difficult to assimilate. The first 'nationalist' leader, Jamal ad-Din al-Afghani (d.1897), had proposed a pan-Islamic solution to the problem of colonial occupation. He had wanted to use religion to cause a mass uprising and his ideas were still very popular during the twentieth century. But later movements for independence opted for the Western ideal of a secular nation state, which was alien to people brought up in the tradition of a united Islam. In 1908 the Young Turks had successfully staged a revolution in the Ottoman empire and immediately afterwards the Young Arabs held their first meeting in Paris. Arab nationalism had reached Palestine by 1915, when Ben Gurion first became aware of it. This secular nationalism reminded the people that they had been Arabs before they had been Muslims and urged all the people of the Arab world to unite together to form a solidly united front against the West. Arab nationalism was extremely strong in Syria, and during the 1940s became associated with a vision of a great Arab renaissance (*ba'ath*). Nasser's Suez triumph encouraged the Syrian Ba'athists in February 1958 to invite Nasser to form an immediate and comprehensive union between Syria and Egypt, which should be known as the United Arab Republic. In July of the same year, a revolution in Iraq toppled the strongest and most effective Western bastion in the Arab world. It looked as though the Arabs were indeed rising powerfully against their enemies and that Israel was being surrounded by strongly united and hostile forces.

Nasser had his own formula for Arab nationalism, based on the unique strategic position of Egypt. He saw Egypt as the centre of three circles of power: the Arab circle, the African circle and the Islamic circle. The first two circles of power are self-explanatory, given Egypt's position between Africa and the Arab countries. The third needs some explanation. Nasser's ideology was secular and in 1954, following an attempt on his life, he suppressed the extremist Muslim Brotherhood. He had no wish for an Islamic republic. But Nasser was a sincerely practising Muslim and was convinced that Islam was crucial to the Arab identity. He felt strongly that Arabs had to create their own distinctively Arab revolutionary ideology and should not borrow alien, foreign ideologies like communism or Western socialism. There was no need to turn to the communist East or the imperialist West, for in Islam the Arabs had their own distinctively revolutionary creed.[100] The idea came to him in 1953 during a visit to Saudi Arabia and centred on the pilgrimage. As he stood in front of the Ka'aba, reflecting on the vastness of the Islamic world, he became convinced that the pilgrimage must be politicised and should become 'a great political power':

> The press of the world should resort to and follow its news, not as a series of rituals and traditions which are done to amuse or entertain readers, but as a regular political congress wherein the leaders of Muslim states, their public men, their pioneers in every field of knowledge, their writers, their leading industrialists, merchants and youth draw up in this universal Islamic parliament the main lines of policy for their countries and their co-operation together until they meet again.[101]

To this end, with the approval of the Saudis, Nasser established the Islamic Congress, with Anwar Sadat as the first chairman. It was a bold and potentially powerful vision, but the Congress died as Nasser adopted a more revolutionary stance, which the more traditionalist and cautious Muslim leaders were not prepared to follow. This only made it all the more necessary for Nasser to emphasise the revolutionary aspect of Islam. Mohammad had been essentially a revolutionary, and in Nasser's Egypt Islam was presented as a religion which was implacably opposed to despotism and dedicated to the creation of a just and equal society.[102]

In the late 1950s, therefore, Nasser looked all set to form a powerful confederation of united revolutionary Arab states, but in fact the achievement of such a federation was too difficult at this particularly turbulent stage of Middle Eastern development. The Iraqis felt that having made their own revolution, they had no need of Nasser; and the Syrians, feeling oppressed by Egypt, seceded from the United Arab Republic in September 1961. By the middle of the 1960s, therefore, Nasser was isolated from the rest of the Arab world, though he was still unquestionably a world figure. The traditional and conservative states like Saudi Arabia felt threatened by his plans to modernise the Arab world, and Iraq and Syria, themselves in a state of turmoil, were against him. In 1966 the militant left wing of the Ba'ath Party effected a successful coup in Syria under Hafez al-Assad and Syria became a client state of the Soviet Union. During that year Syria backed guerrilla activity in Israel and taunted Nasser with cowardice. Jordan, Saudi Arabia and Iraq joined in and to retain the leadership of the Arab world as well as to retain credibility in Egypt Nasser was under great pressure to make at least a gesture of defiance against Israel. He had been anxious to avoid this, being quite aware of Egypt's military inferiority. But eventually the gesture of defiance that he was expected to make led to the Six Day War of 1967 and another crushing Arab defeat.

The Six Day War was the obverse of Suez. This time it was the Arabs who were humiliated by Israel. This time Israel was not deserted by the great powers, but had made sure of the support of Britain and the United States before launching the attack. This time Israel did not withdraw from the territory she had won but occupied the Sinai peninsula, the West Bank of the Jordan and the Golan Heights. The Arabs were powerless once more. In the years since Suez, the United States and Israel had formed a special relationship, in which Israel was not so much a client state as the representative of American influence in the Middle East and would ultimately come to dictate American policy there. Backed by this superpower, Israel was invulnerable to Arab attack, and the United States guaranteed to make her stronger in military terms than all the Arab states put together. If the influence of Britain and France had waned in the Middle East, their place had been taken by the United States, and the Arab world seemed further from independence than ever. Besides Israel, America had a client state in Iran and the Iranians had also felt their impotence before the American Goliath. When Mohammad Mossadeq had attempted to nationalise Iranian oil and had over-thrown the Pahlavi dynasty in 1953, Shah Mohammad Reza had swiftly been replaced by a CIA-organised coup. Mossadeq, a hero of independence, died in prison and Nasser, the one-time hero of the Arab world, was disgraced and discredited by the defeat of the Six Day War, even though the people of Egypt continued to love their charismatic leader. If the people of the Middle East wanted to assert their independence they would have to find a stronger weapon than secular nationalism would prove to be. Some of them would later discover that religion was precisely the weapon they needed and would revive the *jihad*. But in 1967 the Arabs found a new secular hero in Yasir Arafat, the leader of the newly organised Palestine Liberation Organisation, and it is important to give some account of this new form of secular revolution in the Arab world, which sought a solution for the peculiarly appalling difficulties of the Palestinian Arabs.

Naturally the Palestinians had suffered more than any other Arabs from the 1948 catastrophe. Crammed into their refugee camps, homeless and dependent the Palestinians suffered the trauma and vulnerability of exile. 'In twelve hours,' one of the refugees recalled, 'we had been changed from dignity to humiliation.'[103] The Arab leaders felt great sympathy for the refugees, but from the start they were also wary. Such an invasion of strangers was an embarrassment. Some Palestinians were able to support themselves and gain lucrative employment in Europe or the Gulf states, but many of the now destitute peasants and farmers were unable to be absorbed by states who had enough problems with their own poor. The refugees were also a painful reminder of the Arabs' humiliation and impotence before the combined strength of Israel and the great powers. Arab leaders like Nasser might make stirring speeches about throwing the Jews into the sea, but the crowded refugee camps were an eloquent witness of his real powerlessness. At a time when the Arabs were trying to restore to their people some dignity and self-respect, these thousands of pitiable refugees showed clearly the Arabs' real poverty and degradation.

The establishment of the State of Israel had inflicted upon the Palestinians the trauma and real dangers of exile. As the Jews had been shamed and humiliated in their diaspora, so were the Palestinians in theirs. The Jews had been scorned for being weak and homeless, and the Palestinians were similarly scorned by their new Arab neighbours. At a time of fierce nation-building, the Palestinians were derided for having sold their land to the Jews. The Palestinians had always been a proud people, but now found that they had a new, shameful identity. One refugee recalled their meagre food rations as a symbol of this new humiliation:

> I thought of our rations, this small quantity of flour we needed so as not to die of hunger. *This* was the Palestinian, a refugee, a person without respect, whom others summoned by gesture instead of by name, whom others portrayed as cowardly, though the opposite was the truth.[104]

Fawaz Turki, a refugee from Haifa, also had a bitter memory concerning the food ration that was such an obvious statement of dependency and of the loss of self-determination. He remembered joining a crowd in Beirut to watch a street entertainer with his performing monkey. The monkey was told to '"show us how a Palestinian picks up his food rations". I was a rough boy of fourteen, hardened to street life, but I could not suppress an outburst of tears.' It was especially hard to accept the constant accusation of cowardice. The local people would jeer at the refugees and depict them as people who had first 'sold their land' and then 'fled'. They would shout after them in the street 'Where are your tails?',[105] which is apparently a joke about cowardice (turning tail). Twenty years of this treatment had made the Palestinian people ripe for revolution – a revolution that would take the form of a rebellion against their fellow Arabs as well as against the State of Israel.

'I was a Palestinian,' Fawaz Turki wrote, 'and that meant I was an outsider, an alien, a refugee and a burden.'[106] As the Jew had become the Other in Europe, the Palestinian became a disturbing alien in the Arab world. This was the case even with Palestinians who were able to leave the camps and get very good jobs in the developing Gulf states, where they quickly became an elite. When he toured the Gulf states during the early 1970s, Jonathan Raban found himself immediately thinking of European anti-semitism when he heard people speaking of the Palestinians as a 'clever' people who were 'artistically talented' and 'very good at business'.

> They were not compliments; they were the seeds of a resentment which any European must spot with alarmed recognition. The most shameful thing in his own recent past started with words like that. If and when the Middle East goes through the same kind of economic crises which Europe suffered first in the 1870s and then in the 1920s and '30s, will the Palestinians escape the paranoid tide of loathing which engulfed the Jews?[107]

The situation is actually very different in the Middle East because of course modern anti-semitism did not actually 'start with' those kind of words but with the fantasies of Christians that had developed an image of the Jew as monstrously Other for nearly a thousand years. The Other in the Middle East today is not really the Palestinian but the State of Israel. Nevertheless Raban's comment is interesting because it reveals a view of the Palestinian as an alien who cannot easily be absorbed anywhere else in the world, now that he has lost his own country. He cannot easily acquire citizenship in some of the Gulf States, for example, because citizenship in some of these small, oil-rich states means that he would be eligible for very large grants of money, which, it would be argued, a Palestinian might use to support a Palestinian revolutionary movement like the PLO. The Wandering Palestinian has different problems from the Wandering Jew because the twentieth century makes bureaucratic difficulties for people who are stateless and finds it difficult to absorb a people associated with revolutionary activity. At a conference in America where Israeli and Palestinian intellectuals discussed possible peace and reconciliation, a man rose from the audience to pose a question:

> 'I am a Palestinian, a peasant. Look at my hands. I was kicked out in 1948 and went to Lebanon. Then I was driven out and went to Africa. Then to Europe. Then to here. Today (he pulls out an envelope) I received a paper telling me to leave this country. Would one of you scholars tell me please: Where am I supposed to go now?' Nobody had anything to tell him.[108]

The Palestinian's predicament is intolerable. He is either a refugee in a camp, derided and shamed by the local population of his host country, a deeply resented outsider in other countries of the Arab world or a homeless nomad wandering the world, desperate to find somewhere to settle. Because many of his people have tried to ameliorate the situation by a revolution, other difficulties have been created in the countries where he lives as an alien. It is Catch 22. The answer is clearly that the Palestinians need a country of their own, for reasons that are slightly different from, though just as pressing as, the problems that impelled Jews to find a land of their own. The revolution that would ameliorate the Palestinian's position in the diaspora would also be a nationalist movement and it is natural that, like Zionism, this national movement should take the form of a return home.

Although the Israelis have always maintained that the Palestinians had no feeling for their country, this was not the case. The love that they had always had for *Falastinuna* (Our Palestine) was naturally intensified by its loss. In the camps refugees from the same village naturally grouped themselves together in such a way as to recreate the lost village in Palestine as perfectly as possible. They would sit recalling life in their lost country with such vividness that even those refugees who had left Palestine as tiny children or who had been born in exile were familiar with every detail of village life before the disaster.[109] This was not just a nostalgic self-indulgence. 'In Palestine we were in paradise,'[110] one refugee woman declared. It certainly seems true that Palestinian society was a very happy one, but the woman's comment goes deeper than that. As they remembered Palestine they were creating a tradition and a folk history to counteract the lies and accusations that they heard in the outside world. The sense of exile was becoming a state of soul, just as it had in the Jewish experience. A young schoolgirl in the Lebanon remembered watching the Palestinians talking about their home:

> The conversation changed to the past, and how they used to live. And when they spoke, they wept, because of the attachment to their country. Whoever sits with them can understand more about Palestine than from going to meetings, because they lived the life. . . . But what affected me most was their weeping, because their land was so dear to them.[111]

They spoke about returning to the land, but this was a deliberately mythical return. They spoke of returning to a Palestine that was exactly the same as it had been before 1948,[112] yet they knew perfectly well that the country was daily being transformed into the modern Jewish state and that the villages they remembered had been destroyed completely and were now a part of the Jewish settlements. This denial of the reality of Israel was as psychologically necessary for them as the denial of the reality of the Palestinians had been for the first Zionist settlers. When they spoke about returning to their lost village they were really speaking about returning to a healthier way of life when they had been proud, free and their own people.

But it was not only the simple peasants in the camp who kept the memory of their homeland alive. The lost land has been a constant theme of Palestinian poetry since 1948. Even those who have a comfortable and prosperous life in the Palestinian diaspora see their life in exile as an unnatural state and yearn after their land not for material or political reasons but with a strong spiritual aspiration. Thus Jabra Ibrahim Jabra, who was born in Bethlehem in 1919 and settled in Iraq after 1948, is regarded as a leading poet, novelist and critic in the Arab world and has lived a materially pleasant life, but he sees his existence outside Palestine as a desert. Thus in the poem 'Deserts of Exile' (1953) he complains to his homeland about the misery of the Palestinians who are forced to wander from one place to another:

> O land of ours . . .
> remember us now, wandering
> among the thorns of the deserts,
> wandering in rocky mountains,
> remember us now,
> in tumultuous cities across the deserts
> and oceans.
> Remember us with our eyes full of a dust
> that never clears in our ceaseless wanderings.[113]

Tawfiq Sayigh, who has taught at prestigious universities in England and the United States, was only sixteen in 1948 but a longing for Palestine is one of the major themes in his poetry:

> My feet are torn,
> and homelessness has worn me out.
> Park seats have left their marks
> on my ribs.
> Policemen followed me
> with their suspicious looks.
> I dragged myself from place to place,
> destitute except for
> day-long memories of a home
> that yesterday, only yesterday,
> was mine,
> and except for evening dreams
> of my dwelling there again.[114]

The Palestinians have discovered that physical exile is also a spiritual displacement. It is not true that they would gladly settle in other countries were it not for the dishonest schemes of their leaders, as their enemies maintain. Deprived of their rightful place in the world, they are aliens and outsiders. Even those born in exile inherit this unnatural condition. Thus the poet Radi Sadduq, who was born in 1938, says that the new generation of Palestinians are as deprived and wounded as their parents. Addressing his new-born daughter Rula, he says:

> My little baby! you are a whole world here,
> but with no colour, downtrodden and vagrant.
> O Rula! Stranger you are,
> and the daughter of a stranger who
> is humiliated and a fugitive. (1963)[115]

Not all Palestinians were forced into exile, however. Today Palestinians make up 17 per cent of the population of Israel, where they live as second-class citizens. Where the poets in exile hear their land calling them to return, the Israeli Arab poets see it constantly but see it as possessed by somebody else. The well-known poet Mahmoud Darwish (born in 1942) addresses his country as his lover or as an obsession that he cannot shake off:

> You are my grief and joy,
> my wound and my rainbow,
> my prison and freedom.
> You are my myth
> and the clay from which I was created.
> You are mine with all your wounds,
> each wound a garden. . . .

You are my sun at its setting,
and my lightened night.
You are the death of me and the kiss of life.

When he compares the Zionists' love of their 'homeland' he sees it as artificial compared with the Palestinians' attachment to their country. The Zionists, he argues, saw Eretz Yisrael as a solution to their predicament in Europe or as an intellectual idea, but:

We excavated this home neither in mythical dreams nor in the illustrated page of an old book, nor did we create it in the way companies and institutions are established. It is our father and mother. We did not, either, buy it through an agency or shop, and we have been under no pressure to love it. We identify ourselves as its pulse and the marrow of its bones. It is therefore ours and we belong to it.

In a poem written during the late 1960s, Darwish gives perhaps the most telling insight into the Palestinian loss of identity after the disaster. It is a short poem called 'Identity Card', which is addressed to an imaginary Israeli official. Darwish speaks for all Palestinians, who by this time had politically been reduced to a name on an identity card, which hid a much more complex human reality. An Israeli Arab's identity card is marked with the letter 'B', a significant indication of his inferior status. The whole poem is governed by the imperative *'Sajil!'*, 'Record!', as the Palestinian demands that the Israeli takes note that the impoverished language on the card cannot express the full reality of the Palestinian condition:

Record!
I am an Arab
And my Identity Card
is number fifty thousand
I have eight children
and the ninth
    is coming in midsummer
Does this anger you? ...

Record!
I am an Arab
without a name – without title
patient in a country
with people enraged.

This last is an important point. Where the best Israeli writers are longing for a peaceful solution, Palestinian poets call their people to war. Their situation does not admit that they accept it without protest. Complaints and yearning for the homeland are not enough. Darwish's poem concludes:

Record!
I am an Arab.
You stole my forefathers' groves
and the land I used to till,
I and all my children;
and you left us nothing but these rocks
for us and all my grandchildren.
Yet, will your government take them too,
as is being said?
Then write down ... at the top of page one:

I neither hate others
Nor do I steal their property,
but if I become hungry
the flesh of my usurper shall I eat.
So beware . . . beware of my hunger
and of my anger.[116]

The younger generation was impatient with the passivity of their parents who had loved their land but not been able to defend it adequately. In the camps, the young became impatient with all the talk about Palestine and wanted action. These younger people started to form nationalistic groups. Many of them started to make raids into occupied Palestine and attack the Jewish settlements. They felt a desperate need to act and were increasingly aware that they would have to save themselves. The last thing that the Arab states wanted was a strong Palestinian nationalism in the camps. The raids of these *fedayeen* meant brutal reprisal raids by Israelis, who attacked and killed Lebanese, Jordanian or Syrian people as well as Palestinians. They were forcing the reluctant Arab states into precisely the kind of confrontation with Israel that their leaders were anxious to avoid at all costs. Consequently Arab officials began to come down hard on Palestinian nationalism in the camps. With the exception of Syria, the host countries started to police the camps, ruthlessly repressing any incipient nationalist fervour. Palestinians were told not to worry about liberating their own land but to 'leave it to the Arab armies'.[117] Repressing this nationalism meant new stern measures which were a further affront to the identity of the Palestinian and which demonstrated that he had lost the essential human privilege of determining his own political destiny. A refugee who attended a camp school in the Lebanon remembered how armed Lebanese patrols would surround the camps on days commemorating national Palestinian events:

> On those days they would make the school children walk in single file three or four metres apart, and we were forbidden to talk together. When we reached our street each one of us had to go straight to his home and stay there. We weren't allowed to listen to the Voice of the Arabs from Cairo or Damascus. Soldiers filled the camp all the time and used to listen at the windows to hear which station we were listening to. People used to put blankets over their windows to stop the sound going out.[118]

It was obviously only going to be a matter of time before the Palestinian people would throw off their humiliation and organise their revolution.

At the Arab summit at Cairo in 1964, the Arab leaders tried to appease the Palestinians by forming the Palestine Liberation Organisation, to muzzle Palestinian nationalism and keep control of the movement. They elected a chairman, Ahmed Shukairy, who would almost certainly prove ineffective and inefficient. It has been said that Shukairy's unsuitability for the post was the very reason that Nasser chose him. For Palestinians who were seeking to determine their own destinies this PLO was useless, and revolutionaries continued to join the older movements that had sprung up in exile.

Yasir Arafat is a shrewd man, with a strong practical intelligence that has enabled him to survive twenty years of the dangerous politics of the Middle East. He founded an organisation called Fatah, which was the name that Mohammad had given to the conquest of Mecca and which had since been used to describe the Islamisation of a land or a city. Arafat chose this name because he wanted to reassure the traditional states like Saudi Arabia that the movement would stick to good Muslim principles and not flirt with Marxist ideology as some of the other,

87

more extreme, Palestinian groups were doing. Arafat, however, had no intention of forming a religious movement. It was an avowedly secular nationalist movement which had one aim only: to liberate the homeland, by means of an uncompromising activism. Arafat and the members of Fatah were inspired by the liberation of Algeria from a colonial and occupying power by just such committed guerrilla activity. His revolutionaries were to wage war against the racist, fascist State of Israel, the tool of Western imperialism.

When the Jewish Irgun created their flag and emblem, it was the map of Palestine with a gun superimposed upon it. After 1948 this map had changed: whole Arab villages had been wiped out and new Jewish towns rapidly appeared. Nevertheless when Arafat created the emblem and flag of Fatah he chose the same pre-1948 map of Palestine and superimposed two guns upon it. This apparent coincidence reveals a strong similarity between two movements seemingly implacably opposed to one another. Neither a Zionist nor a member of Fatah would be able to see this resemblance and, indeed, would find the very notion of such a resemblance intolerable because the integrity of his movement depends upon the wholesale rejection of the other. Yet an outsider cannot fail to be struck by the similarity when he examines both movements objectively. It is not simply that both identify themselves with the same land. Both take as the basic point of departure the need for a persecuted people to take its fate into its own hands. Arafat would not wait for the Arab armies to liberate his country and save his people any more than a Zionist like Ben Gurion would wait for the Messiah to do the same job. Arafat resembled a Zionist like Ussiskin more than he resembled a more impatient Zionist like Ben Gurion. He foresaw a long patient struggle. The liberation of his people would be twofold: first his guerrilla troops would take military action against Israel in order to weaken her formidable war machine. Here he saw relentless skirmishing with Israeli troops on the borders as far more effective than the raids the more hot-headed *fedayeen* made on civilian settlements: such raids had no effect on the army and served only to unite the Israeli people round its leaders. Second, Fatah would seek to build the character of the Palestinian people anew by means of education and political programmes. The Palestinians should liberate their camps from the control of the host countries so that they could organise their own lives and become fully responsible human beings.[119]

A Zionist would scornfully point out that whereas Fatah and – later – the PLO were essentially violent, destructive movements, Labour Zionism at least had been originally a positive movement which sought to rebuild the souls of the Jewish people by reuniting them with the land. However, it seems that Arafat saw no alternative to violence and force any more than the Labour Zionists themselves did after the 1930s. The Palestinians could not conscientiously go out into the wilderness and rebuild their nation in an 'empty' country. This is what their enemies the Zionists had done and the Palestinians had been the victims of this peaceful, positive fallacy. Such a movement would offend the integrity of Fatah which was opposed to all such colonial movements. Arafat would argue that for the Palestinians to submit tamely and passively to their intolerable situation was shameful and an evasion of a basic human responsibility. When the European colonists had settled in the 'empty' lands of Australia and America, there had been no public opinion which had forbidden the dispossession and virtual annihilation of the Aborigines and the American Indians. Now the United Nations had declared that every people had an inalienable right to national existence and self-determination. It would be morally wrong for the Palestinians to sink into a subhuman state of passivity and dependence, and there was no realistic alternative to the use of force, as the Zionists themselves had discovered.

There were many other Palestinian groups apart from Fatah which sprang up spontaneously and quite independently of one another, rather as the first Zionist groups had sprung up in Russia. Two of these should be singled out for special discussion because they would be very important later. Like the Labour Zionists, these two groups sought a Marxist solution to the problem of the Palestinians. They believed that Arafat's simple nationalism was inadequate, ignoring problems in the Arab world that desperately needed a solution. The Palestinian disaster was not the fault of the Jews alone. It was also due to deep flaws in the structure of Arab society. George Habache, who founded the Popular Front for the Liberation of Palestine, argued that the liberation of Palestine had to be part of a revolution throughout the Arab world and that the PFLP had to fight the Arab regimes as well as Israel. Nayef Hawatmeh broke away from the PFLP to found a still more extreme and ambitious group. The Popular Democratic Front for the Liberation of Palestine saw the Palestinian struggle as part of the worldwide revolution against capitalism and imperialism. The Jews were not just lackeys of imperialism, they were themselves the victims of bad social structures. This was precisely the conclusion that Zionists like Ben Gurion and Ber Borochov had reached fifty years earlier. The revolution of the PDFLP was the first Arab organisation to recognise the State of Israel, albeit the recognition was a negative one. These two groups obviously found it difficult to get any support at all in the Arab world. The only state that would support them was Syria, whose fiercely anti-imperialist socialism closely resembled their own. Syria encouraged the *fedayeen* to make raids on Israel from Syrian territory, even though this meant that she was herself subject to Israeli reprisal raids. Syria maintained that this was the only possible position for an Arab regime and chided the more moderate states for their hypocrisy. In 1967 although Nasser was initially reluctant, Syria put so much pressure on Egypt that these countries were forced into the war that they had been seeking to avoid, in order to retain their leadership.

The Six Day War was an even greater humiliation for the Arabs than their defeat in 1948, and after the Israeli army's victory there was a new desperation in the Arab world. Israel had not only driven back their armies in a mere six days. She had also occupied strategic land belonging to Syria on the Golan Heights, from Jordan (who had also joined Syria's offensive) she had seized the West Bank and from Egypt she had taken the Gaza Strip and much of the Sinai peninsula. Despite clear instructions from the United Nations in Resolution 242[120] that these lands should be returned to the Arabs, Israel showed absolutely no sign of retreating and set up a military occupation in these large areas. This confirmed the Arabs in their view of Israel as an expansive and aggressive colonial power who seemed to be able to defy the rules that the rest of the world was supposed to obey. Yet again the world did nothing. Yet again there was a new exodus of Palestinian refugees: 400,000 Palestinians left the West Bank and settled in camps in Jordan; some had fled their homes in the 1948 disaster. Not surprisingly there was a new determination in the Palestinian revolutionary groups. The Arab leaders had demonstrated beyond a doubt that it was quite useless for the Palestinians to wait for the Arab armies to liberate their homeland. They would have to act for themselves. When Ahmed Shukairy was forced to resign from the leadership of the PLO in December 1967, completely discredited by his association with the Arab states, the Palestinian groups took control of the movement themselves. From henceforth the PLO would be an association of different groups with avowedly different ideologies. Yet though this meant that the movement was weakened by its diversity, it would have one great strength that would make it essential to the Palestinian people after their long humiliation. It was now their own movement. At last they had their own, autonomous leadership and had taken the first step in their process of emancipation from the Arab world.

In August the following year, the Arab world found a new hero. A squadron of special Israeli troops crossed the River Jordan and entered Arab territory in order to make a reprisal raid against the *fedayeen* in Jordan. There, however, they were opposed by a united group of Fatah men and Jordanians, who managed to resist the invaders for twelve hours and force them to return. They also destroyed some Israeli vehicles and aircraft. The Arabs were led by Yasir Arafat. It is very easy to understand how this partial victory was an event of extraordinary importance to the Arab world and to the Palestinians, even though Israelis do not rank the battle of Karameh (as the encounter became known) as a particularly important incident. For the Palestinians the battle of Karameh was as crucial and formative as the battle of Badr had been to Mohammad and the first Muslims in 624. Because of it, the prospect of return, which had hitherto been only a myth, acquired a new reality. Yet it was also crucial in developing the ideology of the new PLO. It is worth pondering on the comparison with Badr. After the battle of Badr, the prospect of the return to Mecca became a reality; after Badr Islam adopted the *jihad,* convinced by their success that God had been on the Muslim's side. Yet when Mohammad conquered Mecca he did so by means of a peaceful pilgrimage and no blood was spilt. In 1968 the PLO issued its charter which committed all its members to a war with Israel that would not cease until the whole of Palestine had been liberated. Yet the battle of Karameh led the PLO to abandon the old Arab solution to the Middle East problem. There was no talk in the PLO charter of throwing the Jews into the sea. The battle had ended not with a bloodthirsty dogmatism, but with a question. Dr Issam Satawi explained the experience like this:

> Until Karameh we were living a dream, the dream of 'return': return to the old Palestine, to our houses, our fields, and so on. We looked to the Palestine of the past. Karameh gave back the dimensions of hope to the Palestinian people; after Karameh, victory once again became possible for the Palestinians and then we (I am speaking from a collective point of view, of group psychology) saw the Israelis for the first time. And we asked ourselves, what are we going to do with them?[121]

In the PLO charter the Palestinians explained what they would do with the Israelis when they had liberated their homeland. They would be allowed to remain in the new secular democratic state of Palestine. Just as the Palestinians could not conscientiously colonise a so-called 'empty' land as the Zionists had done, they could not conscientiously drive out the Jews from their projected state. Instead, the new PLO under the leadership of the hero of Karameh would return to the old Muslim solution of peaceful coexistence. In January 1969 a Fatah leader put the position of the PLO very clearly in a statement to the *Tribune Socialiste*:

> There is a large Jewish population in Palestine and it has grown considerably in the last twenty years. We recognise that it has the right to live there and that it is part of the Palestinian people. We reject the formula that the Jews must be driven into the sea. If we are fighting a Jewish state of a racial kind, which had driven the Arabs out of their lands, it is not so as to replace it with an Arab state which would in turn drive out the Jews. What we want to create in the historical borders of Palestine is a multi-racial democratic state . . . a state without any hegemony in which everyone, Jew, Christian or Muslim, will enjoy full civic rights.[122]

This secular vision made a very important distinction that was also a positive innovation in the science of the disaster. The PLO was careful to distinguish in its charter and in its public statements between Zionism and Judaism.[123] The Palestinians said Zionism was racist, so they could not be racists themselves. 'We are not the enemies of Judaism as a religion nor are we the enemies of the Jewish race,' Arafat explained. 'Our battle is with the colonialist, imperialist, Zionist entity which has occupied our homeland.'[124] The PLO, therefore, was careful to abandon the anti-semitism that was so obviously damaging to the Arab cause. At the same time as the PLO charter declared war on Israel, therefore, it also took a small step towards peace and dropped the Arab propaganda of extermination which naturally filled every Jewish heart with horror and made the prospect of peace with the Arabs seem absurd.

There was, however, a flaw in the PLO charter. It argued that Judaism was a religion, a matter of private conviction, not a nationality: 'Jews do not constitute a single nation with an identity of its own; they are citizens of the states to which they belong.'[125] Fifty years ago that had been true but it had not been true for the last twenty years. The State of Israel *had* created a nation with a Jewish identity of its own, and the PLO charter, while careful to avoid other distortions of their enemy, denied that it existed. The following year, in 1969, Golda Meir returned the compliment in her famous but ill-judged statement which proved to be a tempting of fate: 'The Palestinians do not exist.'[126]

The Israelis soon discovered that the Palestinian people did indeed exist and had emerged as the new leaders of the Arabs in the conflict with the Jewish state. Fatah drew the Israeli army into a dragging war of attrition by skirmishing on the Sinai borders, with the result that the Israeli casualties in this new war soon exceeded their casualties in the Six Day War. They also found that they had a PLO new neighbour. With Syria's approval, Arafat moved his headquarters from Damascus to Amman, with King Husain's acquiescence. At that particular moment King Husain needed to dissociate himself from the disaster of 1967 and he actually called himself a *feda'i*. Yet the establishment of a semi-autonomous Palestinian entity in his own Bedouin kingdom was a threat to his personal sovereignty that he could not afford to sustain. Support for the PLO in Jordan depended upon Arafat's being able to mobilise support for the PLO among the Palestinian inhabitants of the Israeli-occupied West Bank, which had formerly been under Jordan's sovereignty since 1948. Arafat toured the West Bank on his motorcycle after the Six Day War trying to drum up support but he failed. As yet the Palestinians there were unpoliticised. This failure meant the end of Arafat's friendly alliance with Jordan. Husain simply could not encourage the Palestinian threat to his autonomy and even though he was ideologically committed to the PLO and to a policy that was rabidly anti-Israel, he could not conscientiously allow his own people to suffer from the brutal Israeli raids that would certainly ensue if the PLO carried out its activities from his kingdom. Accordingly he finally expelled the PLO from Jordan in what has become known as Black September 1970.[127] The incident revealed an inescapable difficulty in the Palestinian revolution. They were not conducting a liberation movement *in situ*. By the very nature of their new 1948 identity, the Palestinians had no territory and had to conduct their activities against another state in alien territory and they would inevitably subject their fellow Arabs in the host countries to the cruel reprisals of the State of Israel.

In September 1970, therefore, the PLO had to find a new home. Wherever it went it would be unwelcome, and this sharply demonstrated the essential problem of the Palestinian people: they had no home. The next home in which they tried to establish themselves was Lebanon, which had always tried to dissociate itself from the PLO because it feared reprisal raids from Israel.

However, these activities did not satisfy the extremists in the movement, who were impatient with Arafat's gradualism. They wanted more spectacular results. Members of the PFLP and the PDFLP were discontented with the nationalistic character of the PLO achievements and launched a campaign of international

terror. Just as extremist Zionists had turned to terrorism, so too did the extremist members of the PLO. Like the Zionist terrorists, they had an uneasy and ambiguous relationship with their centrists, Fatah and Arafat. At times, after a particularly repulsive act of terrorism, Arafat would dissociate himself from the extremists and denounce their terrorism as evil and inhuman, just as Ben Gurion disowned the Irgun and the Lehi. At other times, however, he had to co-operate with them, just as Ben Gurion and the Haganah had co-operated in the blowing up of the King David Hotel.[128]

Inevitably this terrorism gravely discredited the Palestinian cause. People were outraged at the spectacle of innocent people being murdered. There were obscene actions like that of the so-called Black September group during the Olympic Games of 1972 when eleven Israeli athletes were murdered. It seemed particularly disgusting because the Games represented the peace and harmony of nations which the terrorists had deliberately violated. The treatment of the elderly tourists on the *Achille Lauro* cruise ship in autumn 1986, who were terrorised and even murdered by four young Palestinians, was another obscenity. The terrorists seemed to have abandoned all the humanistic ideals that had originally inspired the PLO charter. Naturally sympathy for Israel increased and people began to forget the old terrorism of the Irgun, even though the Israeli commandos and members of the secret service often imitated the methods of the Palestinians when they made their reprisals. On 8 July 1972, for example, a car-bomb in Beirut killed Ghassan Kanafami, an important member of the PFLP, together with his young niece. Yet despite the dubious and lawless nature of this Israeli revenge, Israelis were now seen as the enemies of terrorism and the Palestinian became the terorist *par excellence*.

The terrorism also damaged the Palestinian civilians. When the *fedayeen* killed Israeli civilians in their raids or when terrorists killed Israeli citizens abroad, Israel's revenge took the form of massive air raids which killed large numbers of the civilian population of the camps, including women and children. It also endangered the rest of the Arab population and added a new reason for them to hate the Palestinian refugees. This has resulted in catastrophes like the massacre of Palestinian civilians by the Christian Phalange in the Lebanese camps of Sabra and Chatilla in September 1982. During the early months of 1987 the Shiite Amal troops in the Lebanon tried to get rid of the *fedayeen* by besieging the camps and refusing to let food in to the predominantly civilian refugees inside, who began to starve to death. Amal militiamen would sometimes shoot a woman through the head if she tried to escape from the camp to get food for her children. Despite the suffering, most of the Palestinians will not abandon the PLO. In fact it encourages more young men and women to become *fedayeen*. During some particularly brutal Israeli raids in April and May 1987 when the civilian casualties were unusually high, observers noted that all the young men in that part of Lebanon were members of the PLO.

The suffering of the Palestinians in incidents like these has, in a vicious circle, led to a new sympathy for their cause, at least in parts of Europe. Just as Israel benefited in 1946 and 1948 from the terrorism of the Irgun, so the early terrorist actions of the PLO were not entirely damaging to the Palestinian cause. They did at least mean that outside the Middle East people had to recognise that the Palestinian people existed.

The new Palestinian identity therefore was deeply ambiguous, just as the new Israeli image was ambiguous. Yet despite this association with ruthless cruelty, most Palestinians have found it impossible to dissociate themselves from the PLO, just as most Jews, perhaps, cannot entirely dissociate themselves from Zionism. It is too deeply bound up with the Palestinian struggle to survive and maintain an identity. Rosemary Sayigh has shown how for the camp Palestinian the PLO has become a symbol of the people and its destiny. The word *thawra* or revolution 'is used as a symbol of the life and destiny of the Palestinian people, reaching back into the past to cast new light on uprisings in Palestine, and pointing out a path into the future. Its reasons go far beyond the situation of the moment to a core of permanent identification.'[129] Without the PLO where is this 'revolution'? How can the Palestinian hope for a better world? 'The revolution gave me the answer to who I am,' one young boy said after the camps had been liberated in the Lebanon in 1969.[130] Another said, 'With the revolution we broke our handcuffs. Before I was living in a refugee camp, now I feel that it is a training camp.'[131] Even Palestinians who have become very successful in exile have found the revolution helpful in maintaining a positive Palestinian identity. As the Palestinian scholar Edward W. Said has explained:

> What all Palestinians refer to today as the Palestinian Revolution is not the negative distinction of being unlike others, but a positive feeling of the whole Palestinian experience as a disaster to be remedied, of Palestinian identity as something understandable not only in terms of what we lost, but as something we were forging – a liberation from nonentity, oppression, and exile.[132]

Though it is a flawed movement the PLO is an outward sign of this near-sacramental grace.

After the 1973 October war when the Arab armies were much more successful than they had been in 1967 there was a major change in PLO policy that was another step forward towards reconciliation. The inhabitants of the Occupied Territories of Gaza and the West Bank had been exerting pressure on the leadership. They had by now endured six years of Israeli occupation which had deprived them of certain basic rights, so that they could, for example, be arrested without warrant and were refused permission to form political parties. They were anxious not to be handed back to Jordan or Egypt in the event of the Israelis deciding to return the territories; twenty years of Jordanian rule had been quite enough. This certainly helped to create an important change of heart in Fatah. At the Palestine National Council of 1974, the same year that the PLO had been recognised by the Arab and Islamic summits as the sole legitimate representative of the Palestinian people, the PLO abandoned the old principle of all or nothing. Hitherto the charter had demanded the liberation of the whole of Palestine. Now they were ready to accept a homeland in part of Palestine, and plans were made to establish a 'mini-state' in the Occupied Territories.[133] This was an important concession: it was a tacit recognition of the State of Israel and expressed a willingness to live at peace beside the Zionist state. The second important decision of the conference was that plans were made for a meeting with the United Nations in Geneva. On 13 November 1974, Yasir Arafat addressed the General Assembly carrying an olive branch in one hand and a gun in the other. His speech was moderate and referred to the old vision of a secular democratic state in the whole of Palestine as a 'dream' that was simply a vision and inspiration for the future. He hoped that the United Nations would recognise the wrongs done to his people. At the end of the speech, however, he made a desperate plea:

> I appeal to you to enable our people to establish national independent sovereignty over its own land.
> Today I have come bearing an olive branch and a freedom-fighter's gun. Do not let the olive branch fall from my hand. I repeat: do not let the olive branch fall from my hand.[134]

After the speech Arafat received a standing ovation, with two notable exceptions: the representative of Israel was not present and the representative of the United States remained seated. On 22 November the General Assembly proclaimed the 'inàlienable rights of the Palestinian people in Palestine including (a) the right to self-determination without external interference, and (b) the right to national independence and sovereignty' (Resolution 3236).[135] In January 1976 the PLO was actually invited to take part as a full member in a meeting of the Security Council to discuss the question of Palestine. At the meeting the PLO expressed its demand for a Palestinian state alongside the State of Israel, but the document put forward at that meeting came up against the veto of the United States, who would not admit the Palestinians' right to establish an independent state.[136] But still Arafat seemed to have taken an important step forward in bringing his people into the family of nations.

Yet in the event nothing practical was achieved. Despite their recognition of the PLO, the Arab states have given no effective support and, in the Lebanon for example, there has been massacre and expulsion of Palestinians and members of the PLO. Israel and the United States have remained implacably opposed to the idea of a Palestinian state and in 1986 Israel made it a criminal offence for any Israeli citizen to meet with PLO officials to discuss the possibility of peace and compromise.[137] If many outsiders were impressed by Arafat at the United Nations, they were probably repelled by a new wave of PLO terrorism after 1974. The more extreme members of the organisation, headed by the PFLP and the PDFLP, felt that Arafat's approach was a betrayal of the revolution and were opposed to the idea of the mini-state on ideological grounds: how could Palestinians conscientiously ask to 'return' to territory that they had never lived in?[138] Most of the refugees had not come from the West Bank or Gaza but from other parts of Palestine which were now part of the Jewish state. For a time it seemed as though the PLO would split, but in May 1987 the Palestinians' isolation brought these rejectionist groups back under Arafat's leadership.

But this does not mean moderation. The Palestinians have suffered too long to give up their cause, and in December 1987 there was an uprising in the Occupied Territories that showed quite a new determination. On their television sets people throughout the world watched in a confusion of horror and admiration as young Palestinians stood up to the heavily armed Israeli soldiers with only rocks for weapons and Israelis gunned them down brutally. In December alone twenty-eight Palestinians were killed and more than 900 were arrested, but still the fighting continued and Palestinian spokesmen declared that this was only a dress-rehearsal for what was to come. For twenty years the Palestinians had endured the illegal and ruthlessly cruel Israeli occupation. The uprising began when a lorry driven by religious Jews who have illegally settled in Gaza drove into a truck of Palestinian workers, killing four of them. Rightly or wrongly, this was believed to be deliberate: rumours spread throughout Gaza that the driver of the lorry was the brother of a Jewish settler who had been stabbed to death in the centre of Gaza the day before and the demonstrations began. At first the West Bank Palestinians remained quiet, but one unit of the Israeli border patrols there decided to teach them a lesson. For three days these Israeli soldiers broke into homes at night, conducting searches at all hours, kicking down the doors, breaking furniture and beating people quite indiscriminately. When finally the soldiers harassed the worshippers who were returning from the mosque after the Friday prayers, the Palestinians decided that they had had enough and they began to throw stones. In return the soldiers opened fire on the unarmed crowd, killing an eleven-year-old child, a seventeen-year-old girl and a fifty-seven-year-old woman.[139] It is now clear that Israel is no longer the pathetic David facing the anti-semitic Arab Goliath.

The Jewish state is now Goliath. The high ideals that had inspired the Zionists have been lost. People in the Western world have grown accustomed to supporting the State of Israel, largely perhaps out of guilt for the atrocities of the Nazi Holocaust, but it must be clear that this kind of behaviour cannot be allowed to continue.

On both sides of the conflict, the new wave of implacable violence has been inspired and supported by religion. Where the secular leaders have shown themselves ready for compromise, religion sees any such tendency as deeply sinful. Hitherto Islamic groups in the Occupied Territories had been absolutely opposed to the PLO for religious reasons. Nationalism like that of Arafat and his organisation was anathema to a strict Muslim who believed that Islamic lands must be united under one leader, not divided up into a series of nation states. There should be only one Islamic state, which reflects the unity of the One God. The extreme Muslim Brotherhood and the various Islamic *jihad* groups were strongly opposed to Arafat's secular ideology, but the December uprising showed that religious and secular Palestinians were fighting side by side and for the first time all the Arabs in the Territories were firmly united. A leaflet by Islamic Jihad used Marxist language when it called upon 'the workers of Palestine to unite', and a famous slogan showed the new unity between the PLO and the *jihad* groups: 'He who throws a stone goes to heaven.'[140] The religious groups have come around to the idea of fighting with their secular brothers in order to liberate the Muslim people from tyranny, as Mohammad had fought the oppressive Qureish in Mecca, who had persecuted the first Muslims far less severely than the Israelis had persecuted the Palestinians. As for the seculars, they had gained a new respect for the religious groups in October 1987, when seven members of Islamic Jihad had been killed in two shoot-outs with the Israelis. Three of these religious Palestinians had escaped from an Israeli prison and the fact that they had bravely chosen to stay in the country and continue the struggle against the State of Israel won the Islamic groups a great deal of new support. In Iran in 1979 a similar alliance of religious and secular groups had managed to overthrow the powerful regime of Shah Mohammad Reza Pahlavi, which had strong American backing. It is an alliance which has greatly disturbed even the hawks in Israel, with good reason.

The conflict in the Middle East, which began as a secular movement, had often expressed itself in religious terms. Now religion seems to have become a central force in the conflict and this does not bode well for peace. It is now important to try to understand what this escalation of religious violence might mean for the Middle East and here the story of the Crusades and the Muslim retaliation they inspired can give us some valuable lessons, not because history repeats itself but because the Jews and Muslims who are fighting one another today have many of the same preoccupations and passions as the soldiers of God who fought for their religion when the Crusaders marched to Jerusalem to liberate the tomb of Christ.

PART TWO

Holy War

CHAPTER FOUR

1096–1146

The Crusade Becomes a Holy War and Inspires a New Jihad

In September 1096 Count Bohemund of Taranto saw an army of Norman Crusaders marching to the port of Brindisi to sail for the East and he was instantly inspired to join them. Although he was no longer a young man he was extremely handsome and master of the grand, flamboyant gesture that so frequently appears in the history of crusading. Immediately after taking the Cross in the Cathedral of Amalfi he strode down the great steps, tearing his scarlet cloak into ribbons, which he thrust to left and right into the eager hands of the captains of his army, so that they could make Crusader crosses for themselves. 'Are we not Franks?' he cried. 'Did not our ancestors come here from Francia and liberate this land with arms? What a disgrace! Will our blood relatives and brothers go to martyrdom and indeed to paradise without us?'[1] A few weeks later, Bohemund and his nephew Tancred set sail for Constantinople with a well-equipped and efficient army. Bohemund had pressing, worldly reasons for becoming a Crusader. His father Robert Guiscard had hoped to leave him a kingdom in the East, but his invasion of Byzantium had failed, so Bohemund had only a very small fief in the Duchy of Apulia. The Crusade was an obvious way for Bohemund to acquire an Eastern kingdom and it would be easy to dismiss Bohemund's typical Frankish piety as hypocrisy, which covered naked territorial ambition with the religious cant of the day. But this would be too modern a view, for in the Middle Ages people were less self-conscious about motivation than we are. For Bohemund, as for most of the First Crusaders, secular and religious motives existed quite easily side by side, and indeed the First Crusade was able to succeed only because of this fusion of strong piety and practical good sense.

Bohemund's claim to be a Frank is important, because he was really a Norman, a descendant of the Vikings who had terrorised Europe and then subsequently settled there, adopted a Frankish identity and converted to Christianity. They had their own duchy and had spearheaded the new expansion of Christendom of recent years. The Normans had made a conscious decision to ally themselves with the Europeans and in recent years Europe had acquired an exciting and dynamic self-confidence. This was largely the creation of the Church and Bohemund therefore would not have seen Christianity as a purely spiritual religion and a private affair, as we do today. He would have seen it as an ideology that led to progress and development, in rather the same way as revolutionaries embraced Marxism in Russia at the time of the 1917 Revolution. Bohemund seems also to have been conscious that the Norman 'Franks' were in the vanguard of the new expansion of Europe, because conquest and exploration were in their Norse blood, and it was easy for him to embrace this new Christian aggression because it

coincided so perfectly with his own needs and desires. He would become one of the most able leaders of the Crusade and was a shrewdly practical soldier, but he could quite simply tell his men that 'This is not a carnal war but a spiritual one.'[2] Bohemund's view of the holy war was not the Cluniac vision of Pope Urban but looked to *The Song of Roland*. In the Crusades the Franks would find a perfect way to unite their love of God with the love of war, and thousands of them would fight their way to paradise and to martyrdom. Certainly Tancred saw crusading as the answer to his long perplexity. His biographer wrote that as soon as he heard about the Crusade all his energies were released and doubts resolved in what amounted to a religious conversion of life: 'at last as if previously asleep, his vigour was aroused, his powers grew, his eyes opened, his courage was born.'[3] Everything suddenly came together for him in such a way that he literally had a new vision of life.

But Tancred had a practical problem. Crusading was a very expensive enterprise; a knight had to equip himself with horses, servants, armour and weapons for a very long campaign and Tancred could not afford it. His richer uncle Bohemund equipped him and helped him out financially and this would be an important feature of the First Crusade. Rich Crusaders felt it their duty to help poorer knights and everybody felt it a duty to give alms to the poor pilgrims. In this way the Crusade did express the Cluniac vision of the pilgrimage where rich and poor lived in community together and where the reformed Christian knights cared for the poor and the weak. The Cluniac ideal of holy poverty was very important to many of the Crusaders and showed how effectively Cluny had penetrated the conscious-ness of the West. Most Crusaders had to sell or mortgage property and land in order to be able to afford to go on the Crusade.[4] In Urban's terms they had been prepared to sell all they had in order to follow Christ. Godfrey of Bouillon, whose army was the first to leave Europe in August 1096, had sold his estates of Rosay and Stenay on the Meuse. He would become the first ruler of Christian Jerusalem and was felt to epitomise the ideals of the First Crusade. He had been born heir to the Duchy of Lorraine and was a descendant of Charlemagne, something that he and his fellow Crusaders took very seriously. He embodied the ideals of the *chanson de geste* in being a man of enormous physical strength and indifferent intelligence: the Emperor Henry IV had confiscated the Duchy of Lorraine from his family but had made Godfrey its administrator, a job that he so mismanaged that Henry was about to dismiss him. Like Bohemund, Godfrey had practical reasons for going on the Crusade, as there was no future for him in the West. But he was also a man of strong piety and in particular he lived a very frugal, simple life, showing that he had absorbed the value that Cluny set on holy poverty. In Godfrey too, the hero of the Crusade, we see a mixture of motive and ideology.

His brother Baldwin was a very different sort of man and was frankly secular in outlook. He had been destined for the Church and so had inherited none of the family estates, but he had proved to be quite unsuited for the life of a churchman and returned to the lay state. There was, therefore, no future for him in Europe and he took his wife and children with him to the East, clearly never intending to return. He was a great contrast to his brother in both manner and appearance and they were a dramatic and striking pair. Where Godfrey was tall, blond and of an equable, easy temperament, Baldwin was also tall but dark and autocratic in manner. He had none of Godfrey's austerity and enjoyed luxurious living. He was also by far the more intelligent of the two. His education in the cathedral school at Rheims had given him a taste for culture that was unusual in a layman at this time and during the Crusade he proved that he was a very able and shrewd soldier and politician. He was largely responsible for making the Christian Kingdom of Jerusalem an established state in the Middle East. For all its piety the Crusade would need and value secular pragmatists like Baldwin.

Shortly after Bohemund took the Cross in September 1096 another group of Normans led an army to the East and here again we see a mixture of motives and ideals. Robert of Normandy, the eldest son of William the Conqueror, was a very pious man and was genuinely moved by Urban's summons. He was a Crusader who certainly gave up everything to follow Christ on the Crusade. His father favoured his younger brother William Rufus and the two were constantly at war, and yet Robert was prepared to pledge his duchy to William in order to raise the necessary money to equip his army. It was because of the Crusade that he lost the throne of England and also his life and liberty. William seized the throne when his father died while Robert was still in the East, and when Robert got back he was thrown into prison, where he died, probably murdered, many years later. His brother-in-law, Stephen of Blois, on the other hand, had absolutely no desire to go crusading, and eventually deserted the army. In his family, however, his wife Adela made the decisions and she forced him to go. When he returned in disgrace, she made him take a second expedition to the East in 1100 which was massacred in Asia Minor and the reluctant Stephen died with his men. The third Norman of this group was Robert of Flanders, a good Cluniac. His father had made the pilgrimage to Jerusalem in 1086 and had then stayed on in the East until 1093, helping the Emperor Alexius to fight the Turks in Asia Minor and Anatolia. His son wanted to carry on the family tradition.

Raymund of St Gilles was also a Cluniac. He had been one of Gregory VII's Knights of St Peter and had fought the Muslims in Spain. It seems that Urban may have discussed his plans with Raymund before Clermont, because after the speech Raymund was the first noble to offer himself for the expedition. He was simply inspired by religious motives: he had no problems at home but was prepared to give up his rich and comfortable life for ever. At the time of the Crusade he was sixty years old and he vowed that he would spend his remaining years in the East. Yet Cluny would not have approved of all Raymund's piety. During the Crusade he showed that he was very credulous about relics and his army was accompanied by a large crowd of poor pilgrims who certainly affected his policies in ways that the Papal Legate, who travelled with Raymund, did not approve. Adhémar, Bishop of Le Puy, was committed to Cluniac ideals and was a man of wisdom and moderation. While he lived he was a valuable influence for good sense and made sure that the army observed the ideals of the Cluniac reform.

The leaders of the Crusade, therefore, were men with very mixed motives and ideals. Apart from the deserter Stephen of Blois and Hugh of Vermandois, second son of the King of France who got separated from the main army, they all fought bravely to the end under extremely frightening conditions. Even when the enterprise seemed hopeless, they persevered and finally managed to achieve an astonishing success. They were all dedicated men. Yet at this stage the Crusaders were not fighting a holy war in the classical sense and they were not yet imbued with the spirit of Joshua. They all had hopes of the Crusade and were making a journey to a new destiny, but they had very mixed ideas about what that destiny would be. They had Cluniac, Frankish, worldly ideals and ambitions and in some cases a strong personal piety. During the Crusade their practicality and their piety operated together very easily and they seemed sincerely to have believed that working for their own worldly success was quite in accordance with the will of God. The Crusaders were enthusiastic, but they had not yet created a clear crusading ideology that all the soldiers in the army could share. The common soldiers had very different hopes and ideals. Some saw the Crusade as a religious vendetta, others had apocalyptic hopes for a new world and some would have been attracted by the lure of the Holy City of Jerusalem. Many may have believed that

they would improve their lot and become rich and famous or they might simply have wanted an adventure, as well as having a strong piety. But all these mixed motives were transformed by the experience of the Crusade itself. Crusading turned out to be quite different from what anybody had expected and the terror and wonder of the campaign gave birth to an ideal of a distinctively Christian version of the holy war.

The First Crusaders had learned from the tragic fate of the five armies that had marched East in the spring. Some of the armies avoided the dangerous journey by land and went by sea. Godfrey and Baldwin, however, deliberately went by land, following the road that they believed that Charlemagne had taken when he had made his (legendary) pilgrimage to the Holy Land. They were consciously following the footsteps of their great ancestor as they sought a new solution, rooting their new selves firmly in the past.[5] But they did not abandon the practical realities of life in a filial dream. The armies that chose the land route had taken care to provision themselves adequately and the leaders were very strict indeed about forbidding looting and pillaging. They thus avoided arousing the hostility of the inhabitants and managed to arrive in Constantinople unscathed and in good order. Here the great armies camped around the city, ready to fulfil the first part of their mandate, which was to help the Emperor Alexius to recover the territories he had lost to the Turks in Asia Minor and Anatolia.

In Constantinople the Crusaders entered a different world and they gazed in astonishment at its palaces, churches and gardens, for there was as yet nothing as sophisticated and advanced in Europe. The city also housed the greatest collection of relics in the world and the Crusaders must have felt surrounded on all sides by the power and holiness of God. But they must also have felt jealous and resentful of the Greeks, who did not seem worthy of this spiritual treasure. The warlike Franks simply could not understand a people who thought war was unChristian and preferred to make treaties with the Muslims and seek a diplomatic solution rather than shed unnecessary blood. Nor could they respect Alexius, Emperor of Byzantium, who had let himself be trounced by the Turks. They lacked the political dimension to understand the skilful way in which the Byzantines had held Islam at bay for centuries, and could only see their policy as cowardly and dishonourable. For their part the Greeks were horrified by the Franks and their talk of the holiness of war. They found the massive crusading armies encamped in the suburbs threatening and could only see these Western Christians as ignorant barbarians. Alexius certainly did not trust the Crusaders and was worried that if they did succeed in reconquering any of his former territories from the Turks they would refuse to return it to him and keep it for themselves. He had heard that in Europe people bound themselves to one another by taking a feudal oath and he therefore suggested that while they were in the East the Crusaders should make such an oath to him and accept him as their overlord. But this sensible solution seemed shocking to the Crusaders. They saw it not only as a betrayal of their own overlords in Europe, but as against the whole Frankish spirit. Their glorious ancestor Charlemagne had bequeathed to them an aversion to the Greek Emperor and their Frankish identity had therefore been founded on a defiance of the Eastern empire. Alexius found that he had struck against something that was very deeply buried in many of the Crusaders and which exercised the power of an absolute veto. Godfrey, the heir of Charlemagne, felt so strongly about it that he attacked the suburbs of the city on Good Friday. This naturally seemed a blasphemy to the Byzantines, and Anna Comnena, Alexius' daughter, was even more horrified to see a priest, who handled the Eucharist daily, wielding a sword and shedding blood.[6] There could scarcely be a clearer example of the essential difference between the Greek Church and the Western Christian spirit. While the official Western Church would have disapproved of violence on a holy day, Godfrey would have seen nothing wrong with it. His piety was strongly coloured by the spirit of *The Song of Roland* and he would, therefore, have seen fighting for the honour of his people to be quite compatible with religion. This is also a very telling instance of the way that different levels of religion could exist in a Western Christian, who had not yet fully absorbed all the Cluniac ideals, though he certainly exemplified some of them. Godfrey understood the Cluniac teaching about holy poverty, but, as we have seen, the Church had given the knights a confused message about the Christian use of violence. Godfrey, a simple-minded man, preferred the clarity of *The Song of Roland.*

Eventually their common sense and the hard facts of the situation led the Franks to concede Alexius' demands. Leaders like Bohemund, who had fought in the East before, knew that unless they had the co-operation of the Greeks they would be unlikely to succeed in this war in unfamiliar terrain. The Greeks had promised to provision the armies as long as they were within reach of Byzantium and to come to their aid in a crisis. Eventually the Crusaders took the oath, but in the event showed little scruple about breaking it at the earliest opportunity. Urban had partly summoned the Crusade to heal the growing rift between the Eastern and Western Churches but in fact the Crusades would destroy any hope of a reunion. The Europeans had long hated the Greeks from afar, but when the Crusaders were actually confronted with the splendours of Constantinople and the elegance of its advanced culture, they felt inferior and this made them defensive and belligerent. During the ceremony of the oath-taking one of the knights sat on Alexius' throne and refused to vacate it when the Emperor entered, until Baldwin sharply rebuked him. Alexius then engaged the knight in courteous, if condescending, conversation and let him brag about his prowess in single combat. The Emperor then calmly advised him not to attempt any of those tactics when fighting the Turks, as he would find himself severely worsted.[7] The Franks constantly revealed themselves to the Byzantines as ignorant and uncouth poor relations, who fiercely resented their dependence upon Alexius and resented even more his mastery of a situation that left them floundering.

Once they had taken the oath, the armies were shipped across the Bosphorus and, 'at the gates of the land of the Turks',[8] the Crusaders all received the sacrament. At every important stage of their campaign and at each moment of crisis, the army turned to public prayer. These soldiers ranked liturgy on the same level as war councils and listened to sermons as carefully as they listened to military instructions. The Crusaders were soldiers who understood enough about the importance of nutrition to give their horses double rations before a battle, but would themselves fast for three days before an important offensive, even when they were already weakened by starvation.[9] At times of stress, Adhémar would urge them to give alms to the poor, even when most of the soldiers were themselves suffering gravely from want.[10] The prayer, processions, preaching, fasting and almsgiving gave this Crusade a distinctly monastic character; the armies seemed to their contemporaries to be vast military monasteries on the move[11] and gave the campaign the devotion of the pilgrimage that had given birth to it. It made this war different from all their other feudal wars.

In May 1097 the Crusaders and the Byzantines besieged the Seljuk capital at Nicaea. Alexius was probably aware that the Sultan Kilij Arslan I was far away at his eastern border and that this was an opportune moment for an attack. Kilij Arslan had heard about the Crusaders but had not taken them very seriously. It had been his troops which had massacred the armies of Peter the Hermit and Walter Sansavoir the previous year and he judged that this next Western assault would be just as easy to deal with. By the time he realised his mistake it was too late. He rushed back to defend his capital, Nicaea, which was manned only by a small garrison, and was soundly defeated by the Christians. He could do no more and sent word to his soldiers telling them to surrender as soon as their situation became intolerable. Eventually the Muslim garrison did surrender but they very wisely surrendered directly to Alexius, knowing that he would offer them acceptable terms. In the agreement, he promised that the city should not be looted. The leaders of the Crusade probably agreed with him that looting would be wasteful and dangerous to the Greek Christians of Nicaea, but their soldiers were furious and their resentment of Alexius grew. They watched incredulously as the Turkish nobles in the garrison were escorted to Constantinople with honour and heard in horror that they had been housed in one of the imperial palaces while awaiting ransom. But this was nothing to their fury when they heard that they had been forbidden to plunder the city. Their desire to loot did not spring entirely from greed. The army was already beginning to feel the pinch of want and some of the poor pilgrims had actually starved to death during the siege. Looting and pillaging would be the only way that the Crusaders would be able to sustain themselves once they were in Muslim territory. Even though Alexius tried to compensate them with very generous gifts of money – more gold than they had ever seen and ample to provision themselves – they still murmured angrily about his 'treachery', feeling deprived of an enjoyable raid and manipulated by an effete foreign power.

Nevertheless morale was high. The Crusaders had liberated a Christian city that had had a distinguished history; they had defeated the infidel in their first encounter and had redeemed the disgrace of the Crusaders' defeat the previous year. Their Crusade certainly seemed to be a viable enterprise. They were now ready for the next stage of the campaign, and at the end of June they set off on their long journey south through Asia Minor towards Palestine. Their objective was to liberate the pilgrim route to the Holy Land across Asia Minor, which had been infested with the Turks since the Seljuk victories in 1071, and to liberate former Byzantine territory around Antioch and in Armenia, and they had sworn to return these lands to Byzantium. It was important that there should be a strong Christian presence there and in northern Syria to support the Latin state that they intended to set up in Palestine. From this point they were on their own. The Emperor could not provision them so far from his capital, though he did send guides and advisers with them. The Crusaders were therefore entirely alone, surrounded by the hostile world of Islam, enclosed, as Professor Riley-Smith has said in a memorable phrase, 'in an alien, suffering world of their own'.[12]

The suffering and terror began on 1 July, days after they had left Nicaea. To ease the problem of supplies and provisions, the leaders had decided to march in two companies, and the vanguard set off one day ahead of the others, led by Bohemund, Stephen of Blois and Robert of Flanders, with Bohemund's army of Italian Normans and the armies from the north of France. The second army of southern French and the Lorrainers was led by Raymond of St Gilles. When the vanguard reached the plain outside Dorylaeum it pitched camp and thus fell into the ambush prepared by the Sultan, who had been lying in wait for them. At daybreak the Turks rushed out of hiding and fell upon the camp; at once Bohemund got the Christians organised. The poor and the non-combatants were put in the middle of the camp and the women were given the job of carrying water to the front line. Runners were dispatched to tell the rearguard to hurry to the rescue and Bohemund sternly commanded his troops to remain on the defensive and not to attack the Turks. Yet the horde of Turks seemed invincible and Fulcher of Chartres describes the paralysis of despair which fell on the Christians who sat in the centre of the camp expecting massacre. 'We were all indeed huddled together like sheep in a fold, trembling and frightened, surrounded on all sides by enemies,' he recalled. 'By now we had no hope of surviving.'[13] Instantly and as one, they turned to prayer. They decided that God had abandoned them because of their sins and, in the middle of a battle, there was a spontaneous liturgy of penance that could only have happened during a Crusade:

> We then confessed that we were defendants at the bar of justice and sinners, and we humbly begged mercy from God. The Bishop of Le Puy our patron and four other bishops were there, and a great many priests also, vested in white. They humbly besought God that he would destroy the power of our enemy and shed upon us the gift of his mercy. Weeping they sang and singing they wept. Then many people fearing that death was nigh ran to the priests and confessed their sins.[14]

Suddenly, when all seemed lost, the rearguard arrived. Kilij Arslan had believed that he had managed to trap the whole crusading army and the arrival of a huge army of fresh Christians completely caught him off guard. The Turks fled, hotly pursued by the Crusaders, who razed their camp to the ground. The Sultan had felt able to survive the loss of his capital at Nicaea, for his real capital was his tent, and the destruction of the camp was a far greater blow. He would not feel able to attack the Crusaders again and the hitherto unbeatable Turks had to recognise that they had a powerful new enemy.

The peril of the Christians had been so extreme that their sudden deliverance seemed 'a great miracle', as Fulcher put it: the Turks were put to flight because 'our comrades reinforced us *and* as divine grace was miraculously present'.[15] The sentence perfectly sums up the piety of these first Crusaders, who prayed as though everything depended upon God but fought as though they depended on themselves alone. The shock of Dorylaeum transformed their view of their mission. In Raymund's army, which had been with the rearguard and not present during the attack, an extraordinary rumour circulated. As the chaplain and chronicler Raymund of Aguiles recorded, the Crusaders had been protected by heavenly beings: 'Two knights clad in shining armour and of wonderful appearance advanced before our army and so threatened the enemy that they granted them no chance to fight in any way. Indeed when the Turks wanted to strike them with their lances they appeared invulnerable to them.'[16] As they continued their journey, the Crusaders excitedly asked each other who these warriors could have been, and finally decided that, as they were so far from their own patron saints, God had sent the local soldier–saints George and Demetrius to help them in their hour of need. From this point other pilgrims and soldiers began to have dreams and visions of these saints; they would also see St Andrew, the patron of the Greek Church, and the Eastern St Mercury. No Westerner had had a great devotion to these Eastern saints before, but now that they were in their territory and needed their protection they decided that God had sent them new patrons and protectors. St George would become the patron saint of the whole Crusade and a very popular saint in the West.[17]

The Crusaders desperately needed this reassurance: it was a way of acclimatising themselves to the frightening world in which they found themselves. The countryside was alien and filled them with terror: when they reached the Anti-Taurus range of mountains between Göksun and Marash, for example, the precipice they had to surmount filled them with utter despair. As the knights watched the horses and pack animals hurtling over the edge, wrote the author of the *Gesta Francorum* ('The Deeds of the Franks', an eyewitness account): 'they stood about in a great state of gloom, wringing their hands because they were so frightened and miserable, not knowing what to do with themselves.'[18] The Crusade became a chronicle of terror and suffering. The Turks destroyed the countryside so that the Crusaders could not find food, and men and animals began to die like flies. The poor pilgrims suffered particularly heavy casualties, as always, and depended totally on the alms of knights and soldiers who were themselves dramatically impoverished. As the horses died, more and more knights were reduced to the ranks because without a horse they could not perform their military function; others resorted to riding oxen, goats and sheep and to using dogs as pack animals.[19] They were experiencing a deprivation that went far beyond the secure holy poverty of the monk or the pilgrim back home and were moving into a terrifying new world where the bonds of society seemed to be breaking down. To comfort themselves they instinctively turned to religion and created the myth of the angelic warriors who were fighting on their side. The journey to Palestine had always been holy because it had been a pilgrimage to Jerusalem, but as they progressed the Crusaders felt themselves to be holy in their own right. They had a strong sense that God was, quite literally, marching with them: 'As we advanced we had the most generous and merciful and most victorious hand of the Almighty Father with us,'[20] wrote Raymund of Aguiles. He was leading them and preserving them just as he had led the Israelites during their long journey to the Holy Land. At the time of Charlemagne, the Franks had begun to see themselves as God's new chosen people and now the salvation they had experienced at Dorylaeum led them gradually to see themselves as taking up the vocation which the Jews had lost. Slowly too the Crusaders were being drawn together to see themselves as one people as they struggled through the desolate countryside. As Fulcher of Chartres said: 'Though we were of different tongues we seemed, however, to be brothers in the love of God and to be nearly of one mind.'[21] The Crusaders were being taught by their suffering to see themselves as the united people of God and this holy pilgrimage was forming an entirely new identity. The Franks in particular had been in search of a new vocation and crusading had given it to them.

Yet though they were beginning to see themselves as the chosen people they had not yet developed a Joshuan hatred of their enemy. Their image of the Turks was virtually the same as the portrait of the Saracens in *The Song of Roland*, except that they seem to have realised that they were not idol-worshippers. The Norman author of the *Gesta Francorum* admired them and considered them to be excellent soldiers; their only failing was that they were not Christians. He also felt a strong sense of affinity with them, and indeed the Turks and the Normans were very much alike. Both were barbarian peoples who had very recently fought their way through to the centres of an ancient civilisation and converted to the dominant religion. As the Normans and the Franks were at this time seeking a new Christian identity, the Turks were trying to build a new Islamic identity for themselves and were challenging the Arab establishment, which looked down on them with a certain disdain. After the battle of Dorylaeum, the author of the *Gesta* wrote:

> What man, however experienced and learned, would dare to write of the skill and prowess and courage of the Turks, who thought that they would strike terror into the Franks as they had done into the Arabs and Saracens, Armenians, Syrians and Greeks, by the menace of their arrows? Yet, please God, their men will never be as good as ours. They have a saying that they are of common stock with the Franks and are naturally born to be knights. This is true and nobody can deny it, that if only they had stood firm in the faith of Christendom and been willing to accept One God in Three Persons . . . you could not find stronger or braver or more skilful soldiers; and yet by God's grace they were beaten by our men.[22]

The Norman author is making the Turks the foil of Frankish eminence and greatness, just as the author of *The Song of Roland* had tried to do with the Spanish

Muslims. The Norman author is still very vague about his enemy: he still calls them 'pagans' throughout his history, as do the other chroniclers. He appears to think, mistakenly, that the Turks had been Christians at one time. He seems to think that the Arabs and the Saracens are different from one another. Had he known more about Islam, he might have mentioned another affinity. When fighting a *jihad*, Muslims combined piety with practicality, in very much the same spirit as the First Crusaders, and have continued to do so in the holy wars of today.

In September 1097 the Crusade split into two again. Before they went to the Holy Land they had to liberate northern Syria from the Muslims and restore these lands which the Turks had conquered to Byzantium as they had sworn to Alexius. They also needed to establish a Christian bulwark in this area to protect the pilgrim routes and the Christian state they planned to establish in the Holy Land. The main army, led by Bohemund and Raymund, marched to Antioch and encamped aggressively outside this powerful and strategically important city. A splinter group, led by Baldwin and Tancred, headed east towards Cilicia. On 21 September they took the city of Tarsus, and Tancred went on to conquer Adana and Misis while Baldwin briefly rejoined the main army and then set out east on his own towards Edessa.

Baldwin was probably the most secular of all the leaders: he was determined to get a kingdom for himself in the East and had no guilt about his oath to Alexius. He was careful to present himself to the Armenian inhabitants as a Christian liberator and in this he was supremely successful. As he marched towards the city of Edessa the Armenian Christians rushed forward to greet him ecstatically. In the face of this sudden Christian enthusiasm the Muslim garrisons either fled or were brutally conquered and massacred by the Armenians and Franks together. On 20 February 1098 he arrived in Edessa and was welcomed most warmly by the Armenian King Toros. Toros was anxious to get rid of the Turks but had no desire to return to the Byzantine empire. The Greek Orthodox had always despised the Armenian Christians and thought that they were heretical. Sometimes they had actually tried to suppress the native faith and the Armenians deeply resented them. They had no dreams of independence (they had been part of empires for so long) and had long thought that a Latin Western hegemony would be preferable. Baldwin seemed an answer to Toros' prayer and he adopted the imposing Frank as his son in a strange ceremony: he passed a huge shirt over Baldwin's head and, within its folds, the two men rubbed chests. Baldwin was now co-regent and heir to the throne. Yet, under most suspicious circumstances,[23] Toros was murdered on 10 March and Baldwin became head of state. At once he set about endearing himself to the Armenians and conquered the Turkish garrison of Samosata. There was no thought of returning this new territory to the Emperor, of course, and Baldwin had at a stroke greatly increased the size of his principality. In Samosata he discovered many Armenian hostages whom he returned to their families, greatly enhancing his popularity. Baldwin had established the first Western colony in the Middle East in circumstances that were as manipulative and ambiguous as most later colonial adventures in the area.

In the meantime the rest of the Crusaders were in extreme distress at Antioch; their experience here would be crucial to the Crusaders' understanding of the special nature of their mission. Despite the dreadful march, the army arrived at Antioch at the end of October 1097 in reasonable shape. Here they were replenished by supplies brought them by the Genoese fleet and there was, initially, a fair amount of food in the region. The Crusaders knew that they should try to take the city because Antioch had been one of the most important Christian cities in the early centuries of Christianity; St Peter had been its first bishop and it was here that the disciples of Jesus had been called 'Christians'. But the ancient Christian Church of St Peter had now been converted into a mosque; it was obviously the Crusaders' duty to liberate such a holy city, which would have been a major cult centre in Europe. To take the city and the country surrounding it would also consolidate the gains that Baldwin would make in Edessa. Yet there were grave doubts among the leaders. With winter coming on, would the army realistically have the strength to besiege such a powerful and well-defended city? Some of the leaders thought that they should wait for help from the Byzantines and for reinforcements from France. Others, however, including Raymund of St Gilles, had been powerfully affected by the new view of the Crusade:

> We have come here by the inspiration of God; through his mercy we obtained Nicaea, a very strongly fortified city, and through the same clemency we have obtained victory and security from the Turks. . . . Thus we should commit our lot to Him. We ought not to fear Kings, or the chiefs of Kings, nor yet places or times, when God has snatched us from so many dangers.[24]

The first part of that speech could be seen as conventional rhetoric, but the final sentence shows a willingness to put the crusading army outside the limitations that affect ordinary mortals. If God was fighting for the Crusaders why should they worry about the perils of winter or the impregnable walls of Antioch?

The decision to besiege Antioch almost finished the Crusade. To keep such a vast army of 50,000 soldiers with its crowd of poor pilgrims in one place for months at a time inevitably meant that the food available in the region was quickly exhausted. The country was stripped bare and severe famine set in. The efficiency of the siege was impaired because men were sent out further and further afield on raiding and foraging expeditions, sometimes as far as fifty miles away. Knights and poor people all started to die of starvation in great numbers. By January 1098 the famine reached its peak:

> The starving people devoured the stalks of beans still growing in the fields, many kinds of herbs unseasoned with salt, and even thistles which because of the lack of firewood were not well cooked and therefore irritated the tongues of those eating them. They also ate horses, camels, dogs, and even rats. The poorer people ate even the hides of animals and the seeds of grain found in manure.[25]

In January Peter the Hermit himself deserted the army. He was caught, brought back and the affair was quickly hushed up. It seems that Peter lost no real prestige among the leaders because he would soon be seen heading important missions to the Turks and preaching major sermons. The Crusaders were far more tolerant of deserters than the people back home because they knew what they had been up against. That same month even Bohemund thought that he ought to go home. He could not bear to watch his men and horses dying all around him when he himself was too poor to alleviate their sufferings. It was not only the rank and file who were dying; the leaders themselves had become poor and many important knights had been reduced to the ranks. By June 1098 there were only about 200 horses left in the entire army. Men who were wealthy and powerful in Europe were now riding donkeys and mules. The Crusaders really were shut off from everything they had known before in a strange, self-enclosed world of suffering.

If doughty Crusaders like Bohemund and Peter the Hermit lost faith for a time, why did the majority of the Crusaders decide to continue squatting before Antioch, watching their companions dying like flies of hunger and disease? We get some insight into what was going on in the minds of the Crusaders from a letter written by the bishops in the army: 'How one against a thousand? Where we have a count, the enemy has forty kings; where we have a regiment the enemy has a legion; where we have a knight they have a duke; where we have a footsoldier they have a count; where we have a castle they have a kingdom.' The bishops naturally felt that they were a tiny Christian island surrounded by a mighty Muslim ocean. The Crusaders stayed because they were deeply convinced that God would ultimately rescue them. The bishops continued their letter: 'We do not trust in any multitude nor in power nor in any presumption, but in the shield of Christ and justice, under the protection of George and Theodore and Demetrius and St Blaise, soldiers of Christ truly accompanying us.'[26] This was not a pious figure of speech. It was 'truly' a fact. Crusaders at Dorylaeum had seen these celestial warriors fighting for them. They now felt surrounded by an unseen heavenly army. To desert would be stupid; the deserter would be deserting Christ and his special friends. When the Crusaders started to refer to themselves as the 'army of God' or 'soldiers of Christ'[27] they meant this literally, and this meant that desertion was the ultimate apostasy. The malnutrition disposed the Crusaders to hallucinate and not surprisingly they began to 'see' more of these celestial warriors of God watching over the army, or else they dreamed of receiving heavenly messages of comfort which assured the Crusaders that 'the Lord is with you.'[28] This was not a pious fancy nor was it rousing rhetoric: they believed it was the literal truth.

The author of the *Gesta Francorum* shows the Crusaders fighting very hard indeed and making sensible stratagems; at the same time he shows us how they used to make a conscious effort to work up in themselves a sense of God's protection. After a particularly strong attack of the Turks outside Antioch, we see the Crusaders in his army gathered round their leader Bohemund:

> Angry at the loss of our comrades, we called on the name of Christ and put our trust in the pilgrimage to the Holy Sepulchre and went all together to fight the Turks, whom we attacked with one heart and mind. God's enemies and ours were standing about, amazed and terrified, for they thought that they could defeat and kill us, as they had done with the followers of the Count and Bohemund, but Almighty God did not allow them to do so. The knights of the True God, armed at all points with the sign of the Cross, charged them fiercely and made a brave attack upon them, and they fled swiftly across the middle of the narrow bridge to their gate.[29]

Just as the first Christian community in Jerusalem lived together with 'one heart and mind' so now this new community of knights in the army of the True God were united in their faith and commitment to fight the Turks, who were not simply their enemies but God's too. The author of the *Gesta* was certain that the Crusaders who died in this battle were not just casualties but martyrs. 'On that day more than a thousand of our knights or footsoldiers suffered martyrdom,' he writes, 'and we believe that they went to Heaven and were clad in white robes and received the martyr's palm.'[30] The author is aware that he is making a controversial statement. The Franks celebrated 'martyrs' like Roland, but this new kind of aggressive martyr was by no means generally accepted by most Christians in the West. Yet when a Norman knight like Roger Barneville died fighting and killing the Turks in an independent attack, he was buried by Adhémar with great pomp and ceremony and was believed to be a martyr by his fellow Crusaders.[31]

There is perhaps no better way of entering the mind of the Crusaders than by looking at the dreams or visions that they produced. It was natural for them to see their dreams as sent by God and we can see how they were ransacking their subconscious to dredge up any shred of comfort that they could. Just as before a battle they would prepare themselves by deliberately making themselves conscious of the presence and protection of God, so too in their sleep or in their visions they were convincing themselves that they had to stay on and fight to the bitter end. This end might be bitter in purely human terms but in the next life the Crusader would be among the most privileged Christians of all. When a notable Crusader died he would often be 'seen' by the knights and poor soldiers in battle as well as when they were in repose.[32] These martyred Crusaders would urge them to go forward bravely and tell them that the whole of the heavenly court was on their side: naturally this made them fight with a total belief in the protection of Christ and the saints. One of the best known of these visions was seen by the very pious knight Anselm of Ribemont the day before his own death. In one version of the story he saw the young knight Enguerrand of St Pol, who had died two months earlier. Enguerrand was glowing with an extraordinary beauty and assured Anselm that 'of course those who end their lives in the service of Christ are not dead.'[33] He transported the knight to heaven where he showed him his house there, beautiful beyond description, and told Anselm that he himself would be installed in an even more beautiful mansion on the morrow. In another even more telling version of the story Anselm found himself standing on a pile of filth,[34] gazing up at a splendid palace where he could see his former companions, who were so gloriously transfigured that he could scarcely recognise them. One of them, probably Enguerrand, told him that these were the crusading martyrs and that he would join them the next day. This is a useful insight into the mind of a noble but deeply pious knight facing his own death. The image of Anselm straining heavenwards from the pile of dung on which he was standing is a perfect emblem of the mental attitude of so many of the Crusaders.

So how did these soldiers of God explain their terrible sufferings? They naturally turned to the Bible, especially the Old Testament. They knew that God's special friends did suffer. Not only had the Israelites themselves suffered from hunger and sickness in the desert but there was also the example of Job. These sufferings had been sent by God himself to chastise his people as a father might chastise his child. Many of the Crusaders saw the unprecedented suffering outside Antioch as another proof that they too were God's special friends, marked by a special destiny. Fulcher of Chartres explained it thus: 'It is my belief that, pre-elected by God long before and tested in such a great disaster, they were cleansed of their sins, just as gold is proved three times and is purged by fire seven times.'[35] Anselm of Ribemont himself had written before his death that 'God, who "punishes all the sons he loves", trained us in this way.'[36] And Raymund of St Gilles and Bishop Diambert of Pisa in a joint letter to Europe said that 'for nine months God held us back . . . and humbled us outside Antioch, until all our puffed-up pride had turned back to humility.' In this view the Crusaders had got above themselves. They had marched into the East full of Frankish pride and self-assertion. Their victory at Dorylaeum had given them a heady belief that they were a special people. They were not mistaken in this, as events would prove, but first they had to be brought into a more truly Christian frame of mind and God only allowed them to win the city 'when such was our degradation that scarcely 100 good horses could be found in the whole army'.[37] Raymund and Bishop Daimbert were well aware of the importance of holy poverty. Now that they had suffered absolute degradation, when they were without horses, without money and without the basic means of subsistence, they were stripped of human pride and therefore able to do great things for God.

In the minds of the poor there was a different interpretation of these months of 1097. In many ways the perseverance of the poor pilgrims was quite extraordinary. They suffered more than the knights; they died in greater numbers despite all the almsgiving, and when the army was attacked by the Turks they were in a far more vulnerable position than the knights because they had no defence. The poor had no exalted code of honour which would make desertion difficult. They were used to the art of survival in harsh conditions, and that had to mean compromise. Similarly, what made knights who had been impoverished by the Crusade and reduced to the ranks persevere to the very end? There were many such knights: their horses died, they had to sell their weapons and equipment to buy food and finally resort to begging for bread at the tables of their former colleagues. It would be easy to imagine a knight in this position being filled with a great bitterness against the whole project and its dreams of earthly and heavenly glory. He might well feel like throwing up all his chivalric ideals and making for home. Half the Crusaders were dead and many had understandably deserted, but an enormous number stayed (probably about 50,000).

It seems in fact that through this experience the poor actually gained a new self-confidence during this winter – a confidence that would make them assert themselves against the rich and the powerful and dream of a day when the first should be last and the last first, when the poor would inherit the earth and be honoured by the rich. As they watched the rich haughty aristocrats begging for bread, riding clumsy mules as though they were peasants and sharing their own hopeless lot they must have had a new view of the ruling class. Never again would they see them as distant giants who were rendered immune to such ills by the security of wealth and privilege. They began to see the Crusade as a first step in that revolution foretold by Mary in the gospels when she sings that God had reversed the old world order:

He has routed the proud of heart.
He has pulled down princes from their thrones and exalted the lowly.
The hungry he has filled with good things, the rich sent empty away.

(Luke 1:51–4)

The belief that they were the vanguard of this new world led the poor Crusaders to seek a new and more powerful identity for themselves. The Frankish aristocrats were not the only ones with such dreams and visions for outside Antioch there was the first sign of the poor rising to new power and effectiveness. The initial indication of this self-assertion was that the poor now began to organise themselves into independent bands for their own protection. There was later a rumour that at this point in the Crusade a group of poor orphans formed themselves into a regiment and fought alongside the knights. The most remarkable of these was the band called the Tafurs, which had been founded by a knight who had been reduced to the ranks but became known as King Tafur.[38] It became a terrorist wing of the army which raided the surrounding countryside for food with such extreme savagery that they terrified most of the Crusaders. The Tafurs gave the Crusaders a fearful reputation among the Muslims in the area and it was rumoured that they even ate the flesh of their Muslim victims. In the darkest days of the siege this might well have been true. But the Tafurs were not just a menace: Guibert of Nogent is clear that they did the most exhausting work,[39] were tireless in battle and fought with exceptional bravery and ferocity. Pope Urban had not intended to make the poor militant; indeed the Cluniac reform had stressed the image of the poor man as being without a sword. Yet during the famine outside Antioch the poor men learned to assert themselves violently in order to survive.

Gradually the poor came to see themselves as an elite. A popular epic composed just after the Crusade helps us to enter into the visions and dreams of the poor as they struggled to survive outside Antioch. The *Chanson d'Antioch* shows that far from seeking holy poverty, the poor were dreaming of a greater share of the goods of this world: they wanted to bring about a fairer distribution of wealth. In the poem the poor of Provence gallop back to the camp and flaunt their booty 'to show their companions how their poverty is at an end; others, dressed in two or three silken garments, praise God as the bestower of victory and gifts.'[40] God was fighting for the poor to increase their status, just as, to them, he was fighting with the Crusade as a whole to defeat the Muslims. King Tafur cries to his men: 'Where are the folk who want property? let them come with me! . . . With God's help I shall win enough to load many a mule.'[41] This was not just greed but part of a conviction that by means of the Crusade God was bringing about a new world where a greater justice would prevail.

In the *Chanson* the Tafurs saw themselves as the elite of the Crusaders. At the same time as they were seeking to overthrow the old order, they flaunted their poverty as a badge and as a mark of privilege. King Tafur, in this legendary version of his life, was a Norman knight who voluntarily gave up his wealth and descended to the ranks of the poor people to lead them to glory. Such 'voluntary' poor were seen as belonging to the inner circle of Tafurs, for there was plenty of encouragement in the gospels to make the poor believe that they, not the knights, were God's chosen people and that they would take Jerusalem as King Tafur says: 'The poorest shall take it: this is a sign to show clearly that the Lord God does not care for presumptuous and faithless men.'[42] In the poem the Tafurs force the knights and the richer Crusaders to respect them at last. When the Amir of Antioch complains to the Crusader leaders about the Tafurs' terrorist activities, the leaders admit: 'All of us together cannot tame King Tafur.'[43] When the barons prove that they are not true Crusaders and show a real reluctance to push on to Jerusalem at one point, it is King Tafur who shames them into accepting his leadership. 'We are behaving like false pilgrims. If it rested with me and with the poor alone, the pagans would find us the worst neighbours they ever had.'[44] It is King Tafur who crowns Godfrey of Bouillon as King of Jerusalem and Godfrey swears to hold it as a fief from God and King Tafur alone. When the other Crusaders slink off home, it is the poor people who stay on to defend the Holy Land. Fantastic as this sounds it did contain a seed of truth and the poor did rise to a new power in fact as well as in fiction.

The movement of the poor Crusaders was strengthened by the visions of Peter Bartholomew, a poor servant in the army of Raymund of St Gilles.[45] On 30 December 1097 there was an earthquake. Some of the Crusaders even persuaded themselves that this terrifying occurrence was a sign of God's protection; they looked into the sky at the 'earthquake lights' and saw a glowing Cross. Peter, however, had another vision. He was praying in pure terror and it seems that the trauma of the earthquake tipped him into an hallucinatory state. Events would show that he was constantly ill – at one point he was losing his eyesight, which could have been due to starvation, so he was therefore disposed to visionary experience. As the earth rocked beneath him, Peter strained desperately to find some sense of hope and safety. Suddenly he saw a wondrously beautiful young man, whom he later identified as Jesus himself but who never spoke. This was a common feature of Christ in the Crusaders' visions. It may indicate an

Christians very early found it impossible to see their enemies as ordinary human beings and transformed them into monsters of unnatural evil, against whom their lives were a constant battle. These enemies were not just Satan and his demons: they could also be contemporary political powers. In July CE 64 the Emperor Nero began to persecute the Christians because he blamed them for the fire of Rome, and the author of Revelation describes the Roman empire as a hideous beast, whose seven heads represent the seven hills of Rome. The Beast is Satan's deputy and has been given near absolute power on earth. He has driven the New Israel (represented by the winged woman) into the wilderness and fights a deadly battle against the followers of Christ.

Centuries after the Roman menace had subsided, Christians were still haunted by the dangerous Beast. This French illuminator has actually added to the horror by giving it an extra head! The knights who have to fight the Beast as he manifests himself in their time cannot prevail against the overwhelming threat by using conventional weapons and methods. More deadly resistance is needed.

Revelation also foretold the arrival of another monstrous Beast, who would crawl from the depths of the earth at the End of Time, enthrone himself in the Temple of Jerusalem and rule most of the known world. Eventually the Christians would defeat him in a mighty battle in Jerusalem and Christ would return in glory. This struck a deep chord in evolving Christianity. The enemy of God was an inhuman monster who must be guarded against and destroyed. The Beast in Revelation is a deceitful figure, seeking to destroy and dominate the Christian world. From the depths of the Christian mind, submerged insecurity erupted in a fantasy of impending evil and in Europe the myth of the Beast developed into a belief in a figure called Antichrist. Again, Antichrist could be an ordinary human figure or institution, and Christians anxiously awaited his coming.

This Spanish monk–artist was working at the time of the First Crusade in the monastery of Santo Domingo of Silos, one of the frontier monasteries in the no-man's land between Muslim and Christian Spain. His style is quite different from the painting of other European illuminators and had been brought into Christendom in the tenth century by radical monks who, believing that Islam was deeply threatening to the Christian identity, had emigrated from Muslim Spain and settled aggressively on the borders. When the monk drew this sleek, powerful and energetic Beast climbing up to the Temple *(above)*, one wonders whether he recalled that Islam was also enthroned in Jerusalem and ruled a major part of the known world.

The same monk depicted the terrible vengeance that God would inflict on the enemies of the Christians. As the Last Days approached he would dispatch four horsemen who would ride through the world slaughtering the wicked by the four means foretold by the Jewish Prophets: wild beasts, war, famine and plague. The threat of absolute evil leads to dreams of extermination, and Christians could imagine only the most devastating methods as effective. Here *(left)* the Four Horsemen brandish the weapons which God has placed in their hands to effect their terrible task. The Horseman of Famine, for example, holds aloft a pair of scales which shows how anxiously food will be weighed. Behind the Fourth Horseman, who will kill by plague, sits a creature who is a complete travesty of nature. This is Hell, whom God has commanded to follow his *chevalier* in order to swallow the thousands who will die. It is as though the artist senses that there is something monstrous in this inhuman Christian violence. When the Crusaders talked about these Horsemen they would have called them *chevaliers* or knights, and many may have thought that they themselves were carrying out this prophecy when they slaughtered Muslims and Jews.

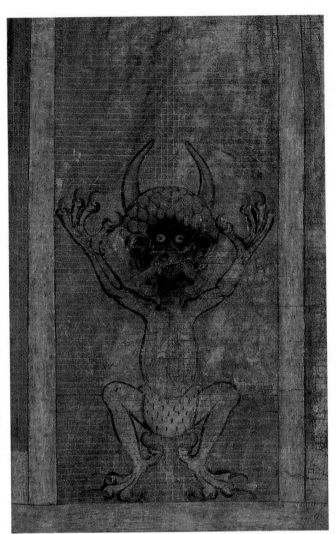

During the Crusades Christians identified Muslims as the monstrous enemies of God and saw their extermination as a divine duty. It became quite impossible to think of Muslims as normal human beings: they were regarded as travesties of good Christians and people of abominable evil (left).

According to the Prophecies, however, God was supposed to conquer the enemies of the Christians; instead Saladin managed to defeat the Christians and throw them out of Jerusalem. This must have been very disturbing: it threatened the integrity of Christianity itself, especially when Crusaders like Richard the Lionheart were unable to defeat Islam. After the failure of the crusading enterprise, this fourteenth-century illuminator cannot see Saladin rationally (below). The handsome, courtly Saladin has become a reptilian monster, sporting a black demon on his shield. But the artist makes Richard appear the stronger of the two, and it even looks as though he is about to unseat Saladin, whose horse cowers before the confident, thrusting steed of the Christian. This was wishful thinking at a time when Islam seemed to be going from strength to strength and had proved impregnable.

But gradually the balance of power changed. The West did eventually grow more powerful and confident and the Muslim world fell behind in the march of progress. Islam became less threatening and slowly the West seemed to forget all about it.

But in 1979 the Americans suddenly found themselves caught in the powerful fist of a revived Islam when their diplomats were taken hostage in their embassy in Tehran. Any Westerner who looks at this mural *(above)* naturally associates the American snake with the Devil, that monstrous projection of Christian fears. When we hear that Iranians call America 'the Great Satan' we assume that this is similar to the way in which the Crusaders had seen the Muslims – but now 'we' are the target.

It is certainly true that Iranians have turned their backs on the great powers and on Israel, the client of the West in the Middle East, because they have oppressed and exploited Muslims. These Iranians *(above)* have donned the white robes and red scarves of the martyr to show that they are prepared to die in a holy war of liberation because they believe it to be their Islamic duty to fight tyranny and persecution to the death. But they do not see their enemies as unmanageable foes: it seems that they believe that Islam can crush the great powers as easily as they have just walked over their flags. If Muslims all over the world join their struggle, Islam will be too powerful for its opponents to resist.

We must not interpret the images of the revolution as though the Iranians were Christians. In Shiite Islam Satan is a trivial creature, not a terrifying monster, President Reagan, represented here as the Great Satan *(left)*, is seen as a ridiculous figure who inspires derision, not dread. It will do Israel and Saudi Arabia (the two heads below) no good to be in the pocket of this outsize rabbit. We should note that the crowd is relaxed and laughing: they are not hysterical with manic, irrational rage. The Great Satan is the product of confidence, not of hag-ridden terror.

Westerners may think that this Iranian woman *(above)* looks weird and condemn her for perversely rejecting the freedom 'we' offered her. But *she* does not see the West as worthy of emulation. Here François Mitterrand is a one-eyed ape, Ronald Reagan a B-movie cowboy and Margaret Thatcher a pirate's moll. These allies of Israel have only puny little weapons: they cannot be taken seriously. It is difficult for us, with our inbuilt belief in the superiority of all things Western, to accept that Iranian Muslims think as contemptuously of the West as 'we' do of Islam.

Nor are the Iranians in the least intimidated by their powerful neighbours nearer home. The grinning Russian *(below)* is a buffoon who did not realise at that time that he was sitting on a time-bomb in Afghanistan, where the freedom-fighters had adopted the ideals and methods of the Islamic revolution. Similarly, the Israeli in the red beret of an elite commando unit *(below right)* fails to recognise the new Islamic danger to the Jewish State.

We must appreciate that these caricatures are not the visions of religious maniacs but that they express a view of the political world that challenges 'our' perspectives. The new power of both the Muslim and the Arab worlds has been very disturbing to 'us' in the West.

"I don't mind loading for the blighters to get a day's shooting—it's this 'Thine-guns-are-loaded-O-Great-One' that gets me."

This British caricature expresses the West's unease and is not nearly as confident as the Iranian murals. 'We' may think that we are making a tidy profit out of the wealthy but simple-minded Arabs (above), but actually it is the British who have to grovel before Arab wealth. Even the camel jeers at our outraged discomfiture that these 'blighters' are suddenly able to buy us up lock, stock and barrel, dragging us into a humiliating servitude because we need their oil. Arab oil wealth not only seems an affront to decent civilisation but also revives the old crusading fears that the 'Saracens' want to take over the world. This is pure racist stereotyping. Giles clearly differentiates the British from one another, but the Arabs are massive blobs, without necks, arms or legs. All is shrouded from view: even their faces are hidden by beards and dark glasses, and all we see is the sinister leer. The Arab gestures are menacing and inherently violent. Arabs then are not developed people like 'us' but are ranged above us in a threatening black wall. Nobody wants to look into their eyes or minds to find out what is really behind the stereotype.

Today in Israel Jews and Arabs are each part of the other's identity, and each needs the other to define themselves and their experience. When the Israeli boy looks at his reflection in the mirror (above) he sees 'the Arab' as a distorted image of himself – an image which monstrously semitic and violent. Buried worries about his own violent role in the Middle East can lead him to project that violence on to his enemy and then to dehumanise the Arab to justify his position. Jews in Israel and in the diaspora have all been traumatised by a thousand years of European anti-semitism, and the date (1979) of this American leaflet (left) shows that they are not wrong to fear a revival of anti-semitism in the West.

We have always preferred our fantasies of Arabs to the reality. J. S. Crompton's sentimental picture of desert life *(top left)* presents the Arabs as just like us and ignores their challenging differences in a way that is just as unrealistic as the Giles cartoon. The baby could be any British or American baby waving Daddy off to the office. But Western dreams of Arabia were not always so domestic. When most people in the West hear the word 'sheikh' they do not think of a Muslim leader but of the American-born Italian Rudolph Valentino *(above right)*, who acted out the ancient European myth of the over-sexed Saracen and made it acceptable by means of romance.

While we have always hated 'real Arabs', we want the Arabs we love to be Westerners. In England we had our very own Arab in T. E. Lawrence 'of' Arabia *(above left)*. Both Lawrence and Valentino became living legends, showing that they had touched a strong Western nerve. The Lawrence myth was boosted in the 1960s by David Lean's famous film, which became a popular classic and made Peter O'Toole our new 'British Arab'. The film remains popular even though we have since learned to hate the Arabs again, but this absurd still shows that a successful Western representation of the Arab will always be essentially stereotypical. Anthony Quinn's grotesque make-up makes him a farcically typical Arab with hooked nose and a brow furrowed from gazing into the sun as well as from scowling with rage. However, it is also true that Quinn could be Shylock in those productions of *The Merchant of Venice* which present Shakespeare's tragic Jew as fawning, venal, violent and morally repulsive. In some reach of the Western mind, Arabs and Jews are really all the same.

Hinter den
Feindmächten:
der Jude

The Crusaders not only left us with a hatred of Saracens. They also taught us to loathe and fear the Jews, a tradition which found its ultimate expression in Hitler's secular Crusade. This poster reveals the fear behind all Western fantasies of evil: 'Behind the power of the enemy lies the Jew'. The creation of monsters which inspire such dread that extermination is the only answer teaches us a frightening but salutary lesson: that those who dream these crusading dreams of hatred are themselves moral monsters who exceed their creations in unnatural evil.

unwillingness to give such a complete divine sanction to their insights and longings or may simply show that the saints were actually more vivid figures, at least to the lay Christians, than Christ himself. Alongside the beautiful young man a less intimidating old man appeared with sandy hair sprinkled with grey, who revealed that he was St Andrew. He told Peter Bartholomew that he had a message for the Count of St Gilles and for Bishop Adhémar. He strongly denounced Adhémar (most unfairly) for failing in his duty as a preacher and this showed that Peter did not share the general veneration of the Bishop. Count Raymund, on the other hand, was to be given a special task. In the ancient Cathedral of St Peter inside the city of Antioch, St Andrew explained, was the Holy Lance that had pierced Christ's side on Good Friday. When the city was taken, Raymund and Peter should take twelve Crusaders and dig for it. Then Peter was suddenly transported in spirit inside the besieged city and taken to the South Chapel of the Cathedral; at this point St Andrew disappeared into the ground and reappeared bearing the Lance aloft triumphantly. Peter was then returned to the camp outside the walls. This eccentric vision completely transformed the Crusade and that it should have done so shows how very much more powerful religion was than political ideas and motivation at this time. The Holy Lance, it must be remembered, would be a relic of such extraordinary power that it would in itself be an omnipotent weapon. Intimately bound up in the holy and powerful events which saved the world, its discovery would guarantee victory against the Turks.

But at first Peter was too frightened of the leaders to obey St Andrew and he did not deliver his message. St Andrew had to appear on no less than four further occasions, and he became more and more angry at Peter's delay. But Peter still hung back, because he was afraid that the barons would simply assume that he was trying to get extra food and would punish him for his blasphemy. Yet the persistence of St Andrew shows that however hard he tried to suppress this vision of hope, Peter was still clinging to it tenaciously. At this time he and his master were very busy trying to find provisions for the army; he was not simply sitting back passively and expecting deliverance to descend from heaven. Frequently St Andrew appeared when Peter was very actively engaged: on one occasion he saw St Andrew just as he was getting on board a ship that was to take him foraging in Cyprus. In the midst of these attempts to find a human, practical solution, Peter still turned to the vision of the Lance. St Andrew told him plainly that an army which carried the Lance into battle would never be defeated: Peter was struggling to convince himself that the Crusade could still be successful as a military and as a holy campaign, however hopeless it seemed at present. He even allowed himself to look forward past the disastrous period at Antioch to the day when the Crusaders would enter the Holy Land. St Andrew gave Peter a list of rather bizarre instructions for Raymund, when the army should reach the River Jordan in Palestine. Raymund was to cross the river on a raft, rebaptise himself and then preserve the underclothes he was wearing on that sacred occasion for ever and put them together with the Lance. Yet even though St Andrew was becoming more irate, Peter still could not bring himself to go to Raymund, but he probably talked to his less exalted companions and the story would have spread quickly. On one occasion, Peter's master claimed to have heard every word that St Andrew said to Peter, even though he did not see the celestial visitor. His master too was reaching and straining for a vision of hope. But Peter was not yet one of the self-confident poor, who were ready to challenge the rich. This early diffidence would change, but as yet Peter remained fearfully silent.

The Crusaders were making no headway against the city of Antioch, but they could not now abandon the siege and go on to the Holy Land, leaving this powerful enemy city undefeated in their rear. Finally in the summer of 1098 they heard some frightening news. Qawam ad-Daula Kerbuqa, the Turkish Emir of Mosul in Syria, had formed a mighty confederation of the princes in the area against the Franks. His large army had begun its march against the Christians and had made first for Baldwin's newly established Christian principality of Edessa. But by this time Baldwin was so firmly established and the Armenian Christians were still so delighted with their 'liberator' that Edessa seemed too powerful, and Kerbuqa felt that the half-starved army at Antioch would be an easier target to begin with. In fact, this confederation was not quite as threatening as it appeared. All the Muslim princes who had joined Kerbuqa were apprehensive about the power and prestige that he would gain if he managed to defeat the Franks. The dissension in Kerbuqa's army mirrored the dissension in the Suljuk empire at this date; it was this that made it difficult for the Turks to fight the Crusaders effectively. The Crusaders, however, knew nothing of this and when they heard of Kerbuqa's approach, some of them (including Stephen of Blois) despaired and deserted.

On 2 June, the night that Stephen left, the Christians made the crucial breakthrough. Bohemund had contacted a potential traitor inside the city through his Armenian spies. Captain Firouz was an Armenian Christian who had converted to Islam, but he was becoming dissatisfied with the regime and its religion and had made it clear that, for a price, he would betray the city. That night he sent word to Bohemund that he was ready to do the deed: the Crusaders should bring their ladders to the Tower of the Two Sisters and he would let them into the city. The Crusaders did indeed enter the city that night, crying aloud *'Deus hoc vult!'* They drove the Turks from the garrison and looted and pillaged the city. The starving Crusaders even ransacked the houses of the Armenian Christians as well as the Muslims, and the streets were filled with dead bodies. Against all the odds, the Crusaders had managed to liberate the venerable Christian city.

Their triumph was brief. On 4 June Kerbuqa's fresh and superbly equipped army arrived outside the walls and began to besiege Antioch. Unless the Byzantines came to relieve the Crusaders, as they had promised they would in a crisis, there seemed no hope that the exhausted Crusaders could survive in the spent city. But the Greeks never came: they had been misinformed and told that Kerbuqa had already conquered the Frankish army. The situation was desperate and on 10 June there was a night of panic. Crusaders began to desert the city and guards had to be posted at the gates to stop them leaving. Yet even in this darkest hour, some committed men stopped themselves giving way to fear. There was another outbreak of visions. In the very act of climbing the walls, Crusaders saw saints, angels or dead Crusaders who urged them to stay in the city and to trust in God: he had not forgotten his people and would deliver them from Kerbuqa.[46] During the past two years, the people had invested too much of themselves in crusading to abandon it, even in the face of such obvious danger. They could still summon up enough psychic energy to drive away their fear and reassert their conviction that God would intervene as he had intervened throughout their campaign. Though the Turks were at one point attacking the walls that night and seemed to be about to break into the city, Crusaders waited for deliverance.

During the panic and confusion a group of Christians went off to the Church of St Mary to pray for God's help. After what was probably an intense and exhaustingly emotional prayer session, most of the group fell into an exhausted sleep or trance. One priest stayed awake, or thought he did. Stephen of Valence suddenly saw a beautiful man standing before him.[47] Did Stephen recognise him? asked the man. Stephen noticed that behind the man's head was a cross and he asked if the man were Christ; the figure acknowledged that he was and asked Stephen a series of searching questions about the military organisation of the Crusade and reminded him of all the help that he had given to the Crusaders during their two-year struggle. But how had they repaid him? Christ asked sternly: with wantonness, fornication[48] and sinfulness. They had ceased to act like a Christian army and had profaned the holy pilgrimage with prostitutes. Why should Christ help them any longer? At this point Mary and St Peter both rushed to intercede for the Crusaders and Jesus relented. He told Stephen to go to the leaders and to get them to put the Crusade back on the path of righteousness by starting a campaign of liturgical prayer and a moral reform.

It is easy to understand this vision. In a state of heightened emotion where fear mingled with intense religious fervour, Stephen recalled the extraordinary events of the Crusade that he could only explain by divine intervention and then searched his soul for the reason for God's apparent abandonment. At the end of the vision, Stephen was consoled. Christ told him that within five days, provided that there was a moral reform, he would send help. While Bohemund was fighting back the Turkish army outside, inside the Church the priest sought a supernatural answer which he invested with a divine authority. Only thus could he reassure himself at this frightful moment and find the courage to approach and upbraid the leaders.

Meanwhile, outside, Peter Bartholomew was taking part in the fighting, even though he had just recovered from a serious illness. He was almost killed by being crushed between two horses, and at that moment of terror he had his fifth vision of the importunate St Andrew, who now spoke to Peter so peremptorily that the servant had to swallow his fears and seek an audience with Raymund and Adhémar. Though he seems not to have been totally illiterate, Peter was an uneducated man and would not have been able to come up with the more sophisticated solution of Stephen with its Cluniac concentration on reform and liturgical prayer. Peter sought the solution of the common people who saw relics as their major contact with the divine and felt that these relics partook of the security and permanence of heaven. In the chaos of Antioch during that night, neither Stephen's moral reform nor Peter's relic seem irrelevant to the appalling situation of the crusading army. How could either make Kerbuqa go away? Yet even though, in a twentieth-century view, these visionary solutions seem quite impractical, it is important to notice that there was nothing impractical about the visionaries themselves. Stephen not only contemplated the Crusaders' sinfulness, he also reviewed the history of the Crusade and made his Christ inquire about the military command. There was also a point to the moral reform. This was no time for the soldiers to seek a temporary oblivion in sex; they had to preserve their dangerously depleted energy for battle. Peter's visions had all taken place in a highly practical context. The last occurred in the heat of battle and in the very jaws of death itself. Both men had a very sound instinct. Military strategy was not enough at this point and the army had to raise its morale and find a new, shared vision. The other visions of the Crusaders that night which came as they were about to desert the city were important for the visionaries themselves because they made them return to the army, but a new group enthusiasm was desperately required. Searching their souls for reassurance and hope, Stephen and Peter actually saved the army.

The next day both visionaries went to the leaders. Peter met with scepticism, as he had feared. Raymund was deeply impressed, but Adhémar the Cluniac had no time for relics and was probably peeved about the aspersions cast by St Andrew on his preaching ability. Bohemund shared his doubts: why had St Andrew chosen a frequenter of taverns as his messenger?[49] He also suspected that Raymund, who also had his eye on Antioch, wanted to use this cock-and-bull story of a relic to get popular support. In this Bohemund was unjust. Raymund believed in Peter to the end of his life and when he got to the River Jordan he and his men faithfully carried out the absurd and meaningless rites that St Andrew had ordered. Other leaders beside Bohemund were sceptical and these included Tancred, Robert of Normandy and Robert of Flanders. But the common soldiers and the poor were ecstatic – literally. Nobody wanted to spoil the renewed surge of hope and confidence in the city caused solely by the promise of the Lance, not even Adhémar.

Adhémar was more disposed to look favourably on Stephen's vision. Stephen was a perfectly respectable priest and his vision was theologically sound. It called for a renewed commitment to the principles of the reform and for an ordered campaign of prayer to relieve pent-up terrors and anxieties.[50] Adhémar made Stephen swear on the gospels that his vision was genuine and then made the leaders swear that they would not desert the city. He decreed that the Crusaders daily sing the anthem *Congregati sunt* from the Divine Office and there would be a general moral rearmament. When the ordinary Crusaders heard about the vision and the oath they 'rejoiced beyond measure'.[51]

The following day Peter and twelve other Crusaders from Raymund's army started to dig for the Lance at the spot that St Andrew had pointed out. They dug all day and found nothing and Count Raymund went away dejected. Then suddenly, clad only in his shirt, Peter leaped into the pit and triumphantly produced a piece of iron that could conceivably once have been a lance. The joy and confidence that swept through the army was dramatic and extraordinary. The frightened rabble of only four nights ago had become an army of Christian soldiers who were ready to attack the enemy and were certain of victory. The discovery of the Lance was equivalent to the invention of a new deadly weapon to annihilate Kerbuqa. Now the ordinary soldiers and the poor were certain that they could not possibly lose, even though they were weak and exhausted.

Three days before the battle of Antioch, Adhémar ordered the usual fast and the near-starving men grimly abstained, at the same time as they gave their horses double rations.[52] There can be few examples of a battle fought and perhaps won by such determined mass will-power. On 28 June the Crusaders sallied out of the city accompanied by the Holy Lance itself and a crowd of white-vested priests who were praying aloud. They fell on the Muslims with supreme confidence. During the battle there was a mass hallucination of a whole army of celestial warriors led by St George, St Demetrius and St Mercury, who all lowered their standards to the Lance as it passed.[53] Crusaders claimed that anybody who was fighting in the vicinity of the relic was not injured. When the Crusaders actually saw the Muslim army scatter and flee before them, they were in such a state of exultation that they were not surprised. Kerbuqa and the Turks simply did not have a chance because God was fighting on the Crusader's side. 'Why did Kerbuqa flee, he who had such a large army so well provided with horses?' asked Fulcher of Chartres. 'Because he had dared to contend against God, the Lord perceiving Kerbuqa's pomp from afar utterly destroyed his power.'[54]

The Arab historians are quite clear that Kerbuqa made bad tactical mistakes during the battle and that one by one the other Muslim princes who were with him deserted and fled.[55] The frightening sight of these fanatical, desperate Crusaders must have been the final shock that split the alliance. Though the leaders might not have been ignorant of this, the ordinary soldiers and priests were far more likely to give absolute credence to the idea of the divine intervention. The trauma of Antioch confirmed the new vision of the Crusade that had been evolving ever since the battle of Dorylaeum. The Crusaders were filled with wonder and astonishment. They knew perfectly well that the odds had been stacked against them throughout the campaign. As Fulcher of Chartres said, 'Who could not marvel at the way we, a small people among such kingdoms of our enemies, were able not just to resist them but to survive?'[56] God may not have fed them with manna in the wilderness of Anatolia and Antioch but he had rescued them at Dorylaeum by a miracle: he had punished them for their sins, just as he had punished the Israelites when they disobeyed him during their Exodus from Egypt. Even though their plight in Antioch had looked as dire as the peril of the Israelites at the Red Sea, God had intervened and smashed the enemy just as he had destroyed the Egyptians. The Crusaders must be God's new chosen people; they had taken up the vocation that the Jews had lost. The Franks had indeed found their new Christian mission.

Yet after the success at Antioch the Crusade seemed grounded. At this point more than any other divided leadership crippled the Crusade as Raymund and Bohemund quarrelled. They were shattered by their experience and still physically weak. An epidemic of typhus broke out and on 1 August Adhémar died. His death was a grave loss and was a deep shock to the army. Many of the Crusaders had come to see him as their Moses leading them to the Promised Land and, of course, they recalled that Moses himself had died before the Israelites entered Canaan. He was buried with great sadness and pomp – ironically, given his scepticism, in the pit where the Holy Lance had been discovered. It was finally the poor who took the army in hand and told the leaders what to do.

Two days after the death of Adhémar Peter Bartholomew had another vision. He felt no sadness for he had never forgiven the Bishop for being so openly sceptical about the Holy Lance. In this new vision Adhémar appeared and told him that he had spent the last two days in hell because of his incredulity about the great relic, but the Lord had finally delivered him because he had once been kind to a poor man. Then Peter's old friend St Andrew arrived and gave Peter some advice for Raymund: if Bohemund was shown to be a sound Christian, and this was confirmed by one of the bishops, he should be allowed to take Antioch, and the rest of the crusading leaders and their men should march forthwith to Jerusalem and repent of their sins. If they did not depart immediately it would take them another ten years to reach Jerusalem. The message was clear. Peter was linking his visions with the view of the poor, who wanted their leader Raymund to lead them to Jerusalem. The poor had naturally seen the discovery of the Lance as particularly their own triumph, and Peter's new success and power transformed him from the servant who had been too timid to approach the leaders into a champion for the cause of the poor man who was ready to issue orders to the great and powerful. He had a vision of St Andrew and St Peter as paupers. St Andrew was 'dressed in an old shirt torn at the shoulders and in a cloak ripped at the opening of his left shoulder and he was vilely shod. Peter wore only a coarse and long shirt down to his ankles.' The saints explained that they had come in these odd clothes to show people how God should be worshipped. Then suddenly these poor men became glorified: 'nothing was brighter than they, nothing more beautiful.'[57] During the Crusade, the poor felt that their poverty had been transfigured.

As the legend of the Tafurs suggested, it was the new-found confidence that the poor had acquired at Antioch that eventually forced their leaders back on to the road to Jerusalem. In late November the Crusaders laid siege to Ma'arat in Syria and on 12 December the city fell. Yet still the leaders sat around quarrelling about who should lead the Crusade; the religious impetus seemed lost. But not for the poor, who on 5 January 1099 rebelled and began to tear down the walls of Ma'arat. They had not come to the East to conquer cities and forts, they cried. They had come as pilgrims to Jerusalem. The outcry was so great that on 13 January 1099 Raymund of St Gilles, barefoot and dressed like a poor man, led his army and a great crowd of pilgrim followers on the road to the south. He was followed the next day by Robert of Normandy and his army.

These two armies tried to take the city of Arqa but found they could make no headway, even when Godfrey of Bouillon and Robert of Flanders joined them. It was here that Peter Bartholomew finally went too far. In March he had a vision of

Christ (it closely resembled Stephen's, of which he had clearly been very jealous). Jesus gave to Peter a list of traitors to the cause and demanded their immediate execution; Peter was given the power to excommunicate the judges if he felt they did wrong. For some time the army had been getting very weary of Peter and his endless visions: for many the Holy Lance had done its work and the cause was now becoming discredited. There was a debate, and nothing so clearly captures the spirit of this Crusade than the spectacle of a Council of War passionately discussing the authenticity of a famous relic. To save his own honour Peter offered to undergo the ordeal by fire, the dramatic but standard practice of gauging God's will, and though he walked successfully over burning olive logs holding the Lance in his hand, he died twelve days later. He told Raymund of Aguiles that in the flames Christ had comforted him and told him that he would suffer because he had been so slow to obey St Andrew.[58] The death of Peter finished the Lance for most of the Crusaders, but a faithful remnant continued to cherish it. It continued to be led into battle and venerated until Raymund of St Gilles took it with him to Byzantium and it somehow disappeared. In Constantinople there was already a very well authenticated Lance, as Adhémar had pointed out from the first.

On 13 May the siege of Arqa was abandoned and the Crusaders began their march towards Jerusalem. Despite the setback in Arqa the Crusaders had won a formidable reputation for themselves. They were held to be unbeatable and wild stories circulated of their ferocity and apparently miraculous survival. These iron-clad giants from the West looked like monsters to the Turks and Arabs, who had heard stories of their cannibalism. The amirs and rulers of the cities granted them free passage and supplies, begging only that they might be spared. The Holy

Journey had ceased to be a nightmare and had become a triumphal procession. There were more visions: St George and other saints appeared to Crusaders with detailed instructions for finding their relics along the route. As their relic collection increased, the Crusaders felt a new power and mastery, and as they talked over their experience it seemed more and more incredible. Everything now seemed a miracle, even natural phenomena. The light wind that had sprung up when the Crusaders had entered Antioch and had muffled the noise they had been making was now seen to have been sent by God; when they had sallied forth to fight Kerbuqa it had been God who had sent the light rainstorm that had refreshed them. If a Muslim carrier-pigeon were intercepted it showed that even the birds of the air obeyed them.[59] They were now walking in a holy atmosphere where everything seemed divine.

This sense of the divine naturally increased when they arrived in Palestine and the Crusade took on even more the spirit of the pilgrimage. On 23 May they passed Tyre, a place that Jesus himself had visited. The Crusaders truly felt that they were standing on holy ground. The places became even more familiar as they passed through Galilee, Caesarea and what they took to be Emmaus. When they reached Ramleh, the administrative capital of Muslim Palestine, they had a breakthrough. The garrison and the townspeople fled in terror when they saw the fearful Christian army approaching and the Crusaders were able to occupy it without fighting. They had their first foothold in the Holy Land. At Ramleh they found the tomb of their new friend and patron St George; at once they created a bishopric of Ramleh in his honour and the shrine was solemnly venerated by the whole army.

Finally on 7 June 1099 the Crusaders arrived outside the walls of Jerusalem. Their first sight of the Holy City was marked by a new outburst of extraordinary fervour. After the agonies of the last three years, they had finally reached their goal, and in their highly-strung and exalted mood some may have felt that they were gazing at the Heavenly Jerusalem described in Revelation. The whole army wept and shouted aloud, gripped by a sudden mass hysteria.[60] But their cries were probably cries of pure rage. Then as now the imposing city in the hills with its powerful walls was dominated by the great mosques of al-Aqsa and the Mosque of Omar. The power and majesty of these buildings – so very much more imposing than almost anything in Western Christendom at this time – must have seemed an affront to God and to the true faith. It could also be that they felt something like the 'dread' that Eliezer Ben Yehuda would feel 800 years later when he saw that the Arabs were so much at home in the land of his fathers. The Crusaders had been told that Muslims occupied the Holy City, but now they could see it with their own eyes. They could hear the call to prayer echoing through the surrounding hills and valleys and it must have seemed a deliberate insult and deeply threatening to their whole enterprise on which they had staked their souls. These Muslims with their mysterious and false religion were polluting the Holy Ground. They were from Egypt and the Crusaders saw them very differently from the way they had seen the Turks in Asia Minor, not for any ethnic reason, but because in Jerusalem it was obvious that they were the enemies of God.

As usual the Crusaders adopted both a pious and a practical policy. They started to build two siege towers from which to attack the city walls and at the same time consulted a hermit about the best way to take the city. Following his instructions, the whole army processed seven times round the city walls, singing hymns and walking barefoot. They stopped at their holy places outside the city: there was Mount Zion where Jesus had eaten the Last Supper with his disciples, the Garden of Gethsemane where he had prayed in agony afterwards and the place on the Mount of Olives whence he had ascended into heaven. At these places, pregnant with divine power, they listened to sermons preached by Peter the Hermit and the other leading prelates. Finally the whole army flung itself on the city walls, convinced in their exaltation that they could conquer it by a miracle of prayer and fasting. The city remained proof against their prayers,[61] however, and as the Crusaders walked back to their camp, listening to the hoots and jeers of the Muslims, who had been watching all this incredulously from the city walls, these loud insults seemed directly aimed against Christ himself. They vowed vengeance.

On 15 July 1099 the Crusaders forced an entry to the city and conquered it. For two days they fell upon the Muslim and Jewish inhabitants of Jerusalem. 'They killed all the Saracens and the Turks they found,' says the author of the *Gesta*, 'they killed everyone whether male or female.'[62] The day after the massacre, Crusaders climbed to the roof of al-Aqsa and in cold blood they killed a group of Muslims to whom Tancred had granted sanctuary.[63] The Muslims were no longer respected enemies and a foil for Frankish honour. They had become the enemies of God and were thus doomed to ruthless extermination. They were polluting this Holy City and had to be eliminated like vermin, and from this point in the jargon of crusading the word given to Muslims is 'filth'. The famous eyewitness account of Raymund of Aguiles shows the Joshuan spirit in which this massacre was accomplished:

> Wonderful sights were to be seen. Some of our men (and this was more merciful) cut off the heads of their enemies; others shot them with arrows, so that they fell from the towers; others tortured them longer by casting them into the flames. Piles of heads, hands and feet were to be seen in the streets of the city. It was necessary to pick one's way over the bodies of men and horses. But these were small matters compared to what happened at the Temple of Solomon, a place where religious services are normally chanted. What happened there? If I tell the truth it will exceed your powers of belief. So let it suffice to say this much, at least, that in the Temple and porch of Solomon, men rode in blood up to their knees and bridle reins. Indeed it was a just and splendid judgement of God that this place should be filled with the blood of the unbelievers since it had suffered so long from their blasphemies.[64]

This killing was not just an ordinary battle of conquest; the Crusaders had fallen upon the Muslims of Jerusalem and slain them like the avenging angels of the Apocalypse. It was a judgement of God himself. It was a salvation like the salvation that God had effected at the Red Sea when he slaughtered the whole army of the Egyptians, a violent and ruthless separation of the just and the unjust. The Crusade had indeed become a holy war. The Holy Journey had ended in a righteous battle against evil in which the soldiers of Christ killed some 40,000 Muslims in two days.[65]

With tears of joy coursing down their cheeks the leaders of the Crusade processed into the Holy Sepulchre. It was a profound psychic encounter with the origin of their faith when they entered the holy atmosphere of the tomb from which Christ had risen from the dead. To celebrate the return of the faith to its most holy and powerful centre they sang the office of the Resurrection. Echoing the cadences of the Easter liturgy, which celebrates a new era that has broken upon the world, Raymund of Aguiles wrote:

> A new day, new joy, new and perpetual gladness, the consummation of our labour and devotion, drew forth from all new words and new songs. This day, I say, will be famous in all future ages, for it turned our labours and sorrows into joy and exultation; this day, I say, marks the justification of all Christianity, the humiliation of Paganism, the renewal of our faith.[66]

This glorious day happened also to be the feast of the Dispersal of the Apostles, who, according to an old tradition, had left Jerusalem to bring the gospel to the rest of the world. The Crusaders naturally saw this as far more than a coincidence. As Raymund explained: 'On this same day the children of the apostles regained the city and fatherland [*patria*] for God.'[67] The new chosen people were thus caught up in the drama of salvation history. The ancient home of the Jews had now become their own fatherland. They had conquered it by divine right in one of those dramatic events in which God had intervened in human history and used his holy people to save the world.

But the Crusaders knew that they had to establish themselves practically in the country and not get carried away by the thrill of victory. First, they needed a king for their Christian kingdom, and a week after the victory the electors, who were probably the higher clergy and some of the nobler knights, offered the crown to Godfrey of Bouillon. Although Godfrey was in some ways a weak and unintelligent man, he had the advantage of embodying the piety and values of most of the Crusaders. It was also moving for the Franks to see the descendant of Charlemagne sitting upon the throne of David and Solomon. But Godfrey refused the title of king: he would not wear a crown of gold, he said, in the place where his Saviour had worn a crown of thorns. He would be called the Defender of the Holy Sepulchre and was solemnly invested with this title in the ancient Church of the Nativity in Bethlehem, the birthplace of King David. Godfrey managed to establish the new Frankish state on a secure basis when he defeated an invading Egyptian army at the battle of Askelon on 12 August, while Tancred fought a masterly campaign to subdue the Galilee in the north. The great task had been achieved.

Pope Urban had died two weeks after the victory, but he would have been horrified by the massacre in Jerusalem. He had imagined an orderly war of liberation whereby the Western Church would have extended its frontiers and gained the prestige of conquering the Holy City. He would not have praised the fantasies of the Franks about being the chosen people nor would he have approved of the revival of Joshua's violence. It seems that many Christians were initially shocked by news of the massacre, which would never be forgotten by the Muslims of the Near East. When later, wiser Christian rulers tried to secure their kingdom by making overtures to the Muslims, the memory of the cruel bloodbath always stood in the way of true friendship. But in general the news of the conquest of Jerusalem was greeted ecstatically by the Christians of Europe. The new Pope, Paschal II, seems to have been caught up in the general euphoria, and wrote that the Crusaders had fulfilled the ancient biblical prophecies.[68] He spoke joyfully of the discovery of the Holy Lance and the relic of the True Cross, which the Crusaders had found in Jerusalem, and showed that he was well on the way to endorsing the popular piety of the Crusaders, who had begun to arrive home as conquering heroes.

After the state had been put on a secure military basis, most of the Crusaders returned home, as they had always intended, leaving only a few hundred knights behind. This alone shows that land-hunger was not a motive for the majority of the Crusaders. It is unlikely that any of them returned home rich men. Though much booty had been taken in Jerusalem and Askelon, large sums of money and treasure were given by the Crusaders to the churches in the Holy Land or were donated to the new Latin kingdom. In his exhaustive research on the matter, Professor Riley-Smith found only one Crusader who was reputed to have been made rich by the First Crusade. In fact, some of them were worse off.[69] Many of them returned home with damaged health after the traumas of the campaign. Some of them arrived home to face great difficulties that had developed while they were away. Flanders, for example, was in considerable disarray during Count Robert's absence in the East; other Crusaders found that people who had stayed at home had profited by their absence and seized their lands or titles. The most dramatic example of this was, of course, William Rufus' seizure of the throne of England while the rightful heir, Robert of Normandy, was on the Crusade. The chroniclers were not sympathetic to Robert's plight: they wrote that he had been offered the throne of Jerusalem but had refused it out of pusillanimity, and that was why he was punished when he returned home by life-imprisonment and by death.[70] Crusading offered spiritual rather than material riches and some of the Crusaders seemed to have come home with deep religious convictions: some actually became monks, others gave donations to churches or built churches at home to commemorate the victory and very many arrived home with relics, the true riches of crusading, which they donated to monasteries and priories, bringing some of the holiness of the East back to the West. Many of the Crusaders seem to have been venerated for the rest of their lives: Robert of Flanders was one of these. He was henceforward known as *Hierosolimitanus*, and other former Crusaders were given similar titles, which suggests that they received a prestige that was similar to that accorded in the Muslim world to those who have made the *hajj* or pilgrimage to Mecca and are called *hajji*.[71]

Indeed, instead of recoiling in horror from the massacre of Jerusalem, people in Europe were gripped by a new passion for crusading. The conquest of the Holy City stirred them as deeply as it had stirred the conquerors themselves, and Jerusalem and the Latin kingdom in the Holy Land became as important to the Christians of the West as the State of Israel is to many Jews in the diaspora today. The euphoria that gripped Europe after the victory of 1099 saw this as just the first in a series of new victories against Islam. As early as September 1099 Raymund of St Gilles and Bishop Daimbert of Pisa, in their joint letter describing the Crusade, wrote that 'the power of the Muslims and the devil has been broken and the kingdom of Christ and the Church now stretches all the way from sea to sea.'[72] There was talk of conquering Egypt, Asia, Africa and Ethiopia.[73] There seems also to have been an apocalyptic spirit abroad that saw the conquest of Jerusalem as a prelude to the Last Days.[74] It will be one of the themes of our story that a Holy Land or a Holy City can arouse deep passions and revive great hopes that are inarticulate but absolute and that any attempt to meddle with these feelings can be extremely dangerous for the other side.

For the next fifty years, crusading would be a central preoccupation and a popular pursuit in Europe. Long before there was any form of patriotism for the homeland or any sign of nationalism in the West, hundreds of thousands of people were ready to go to fight for their fatherland in the East. Indeed, immediately after the victory three large armies prepared to set out once more to reinforce the Crusader states and to help the few hundred knights there in their struggle to survive in the Muslim world. It was pointed out to Pope Paschal that many people who had taken the Cross in 1095 had not fulfilled their vows and had ignominiously stayed at home. The Pope at once said that any deserters, like Stephen of Blois and Hugh of Vermandois, as well as anybody who had avoided fulfilling his crusading vow must take the Cross forthwith. But besides these probably reluctant Crusaders, thousands of men and women, who had not thought of going crusading before, entered one of the three armies, inspired by the victory of 1099. This time the emphasis was naturally not on the liberation of the land, because that liberation had been achieved. On these Crusades of 1101 the aspect of the pilgrimage was stressed. It seems that the Crusades of 1101 numbered as many soldiers and pilgrims as the armies of the First Crusade. But this time the Turks of Asia Minor and Syria were ready for them; the shock of their defeat by the Franks at Antioch had pulled them together into a new unity. All three of the armies were massacred. But this did not deter future Crusaders from setting out for the East. Chroniclers put the blame for this disaster on the Crusaders, who, they said, had lacked the high seriousness of the veterans of the First Crusade, which became even more hallowed in consequence.[75] Smaller crusading expeditions were undertaken in Palestine and in Muslim Spain throughout the next twenty years of the new century, establishing crusading firmly in the European imagination.

One of the signs of the reverence with which people looked back to the extraordinary success of the First Crusade was that it inspired more literary effort than any other event at this time. In particular three learned monk–historians, who had not been on the Crusade, wrote accounts which adopted all the popular ideas of the Crusaders and showed that these had quickly been accepted by the establishment. Written within ten years of the conquest of Jerusalem, they show that the Christian Crusade had become a classic holy war. These historians – Guibert of Nogent, Robert the Monk and Baldrick of Bourgeuil – see the Crusade as a full-scale biblical war. For over a hundred years the monks of Europe had been trying to instruct and form the laity, but now the laymen of the Crusade had influenced the monks. In this canonisation of holy violence, there is no longer any vagueness about the Muslims. They are a 'vile' and 'abominable' race, 'absolutely alien to God' and meet only for 'extermination'.[76] After standing out so long against war and hatred, the official Church had accepted the violence of Joshua and canonised it. This 'holy journey of our men to Jerusalem' had been an event in salvation history, writes Robert the Monk, making the astonishing claim that there had been no more holy event since the creation of the world and the Crucifixion.[77] The journey to Jerusalem is described by these monks in terms of the Exodus of the Israelites from Egypt: just as the Crusaders had seen themselves as being led along the way step by step by God like the Israelites, so too did he lead and guide the Crusaders, wrote Guibert. The First Crusade, he says, was the greatest event of world history:

> If we consider the battles of the gentiles and think of great military enterprises in which kingdoms have been invaded, we will think of no army and absolutely no exploit comparable to ours. We have heard that God was glorified in the Jewish people, but we acknowledge that there is reliable proof that Jesus Christ lives and thrives today among our contemporaries just as he did yesterday among men of old.[78]

> We have said not once but many times, and it bears repetition, that such a deed has never been done in this world. If the children of Israel oppose this by referring to the miracles which the Lord performed for them in the past, I will furnish them with an opened Red Sea crowded with gentiles. To them I demonstrate, for the pillar, the cloud of divine fear by day, the light of divine hope by night. To the Crusaders Christ himself, the pillar of rectitude and strength, gave instances of inspiration; he strengthened them, without any earthly hope, only with the food of the word of God, as it were with heavenly manna.[79]

These three learned monk–historians show that the official Church was now ready and eager to revive the holy war of the Old Testament which the Jews themselves had abandoned centuries earlier.

The monks also saw the Crusade as a type of monasticism for the layman. Hitherto the only way to live the Christian life perfectly had been by entering a monastery or by going on a pilgrimage. Now by fighting and killing Muslims the Crusaders had discovered a 'new way of gaining salvation', Guibert explained.[80] The Crusaders themselves had come to see their pilgrimage in monastic terms, not simply because of the monastic practices that they had so scrupulously observed under Adhémar's leadership. It was natural. There had always been an inherent tendency to violence within monasticism, but the spiritual writers had stressed an interior quest that had nothing to do with fighting. A monk had been called a 'castellan of Christ' and monasticism had been seen as a knighthood of Christ in a holy war against the powers of darkness.[81] The way of the Cross had become a symbol of this monastic holy war and a symbol of the monk's vocation, just as it was for the Crusaders. In contemporary monastic writings, it is suggested that the monks are walking on a spiritual journey to a state which they call 'the heavenly

Jerusalem'. This union with God and subjection to his will was the goal of the Christian life, superior to the pilgrimage to the earthly Jerusalem. During the Crusade, however, the new 'knights of Christ' began to see their campaign in terms of this spiritual quest also. After the victory at Antioch they had written to the Pope begging him to come out to the East and join them in the last lap of their holy journey, and 'open for us the gates of both Jerusalems';[82] it seems that they believed that their holy pilgrimage was towards both the heavenly and the earthly Jerusalems and that it was not merely an exterior journey and war but also an interior conversion and a spiritual battle which brought them closer to heaven. The Crusade had canonised violence and made it a Christian vocation.

It was not long before the inevitable happened in the Crusader Kingdom of Jerusalem. The precarious states always suffered from a chronic shortage of manpower and desperately needed some committed professional soldiers, who would form a regular army quite independent of the usual feudal bonds. These regular soldiers would be the monks of the military orders. The Church finally gave monks a sword. This did not happen all at once. The Knights Hospitaller of St John had been founded before the First Crusade. Pious citizens in Amalfi had established a hostel in Jerusalem to care for the poor pilgrims, and a body of knights who bound themselves by monastic vows served the poor there and cared for the sick. This was fully in line with the spirit of Cluny, and now this charitable institution made the humbler acts of charity part of the aristocratic institution of knighthood. The Hospitallers in Jerusalem voluntarily became one with the poor, living lives of 'holy poverty' while at the same time remaining part of the noble order of chivalry. Their rule told them, for example, that they should always dress humbly 'for our lords the poor, whose servants we acknowledge ourselves to be, go naked and meanly dressed. And shameful it would be if the serf was proud and his lord humble.'[83] It is easy to see how, once the conquest of Jerusalem had made crusading a new quasi-monastic movement, this order of knights would be seen to express some of the loftiest ideals of the First Crusade. During the first half of the twelfth century, when Europe was ablaze with crusading enthusiasm, new recruits flocked into the order and so did donations of money. Soon the humble little community was very large and, ironically, very rich.

In 1108 a small group of knights who called themselves the Poor Fellow Soldiers of Jesus Christ presented themselves to the King of Jerusalem. They offered to act as a kind of police force in the Crusader states, protecting the pilgrims, who were unarmed, from marauding Muslims. Because they were given headquarters in the royal palace (the former mosque al-Aqsa which stood on the site of Solomon's Temple) they became known as the Knights of the Temple or the Templars. They too were clearly reformed knights of Cluny, dedicating their lives to protecting the poor and defenceless, but like the Hospitallers they were bound by monastic vows and a monastic rule. Like the Hospitallers again they lived lives of holy poverty, adopting a brutal, tough image and completely eschewing the fancy clothes and groomed appearance cultivated increasingly by the secular knights during the early twelfth century. They too became a very large and very rich order quickly, with houses in Europe as well as in the Holy Land. They owed allegiance to the Pope alone, so that they had liberated themselves from all secular control according to the principles of Cluny. The Templar dedicated his life to the defence of the holy Kingdom of Jerusalem.

Gradually these two orders took on more and more military duties, though the Hospitallers never abandoned their hostel work. The Templars soon acquired an invaluable knowledge of the topology of the Holy Land. They were also ruthless and efficient soldiers because they bound themselves to obey their superior (who was also their commanding officer). This meant that they were highly disciplined, something that we now see as basic to the military life, but this was not so in the Middle Ages when heroism like that depicted in *The Song of Roland* was the ideal. Knights would not obey their commander; they preferred individual acts of heroism and glory which could endanger the efficiency and even the survival of the army as a whole. Because of this military strength, the Templars were used more and more by the kings of Jerusalem in their wars against the surrounding Muslim states, until by degrees their old defensive policing duties were laid aside and they became the regular army of the Holy Land. This also happened with the Hospitallers, though their militarisation took longer and was even opposed by the popes until as late as the 1170s because it was felt their purpose was charitable work.

In order to establish themselves strongly against their Muslim neighbours, the Christians had to defend their borders in the Middle East. Therefore they either built their own castles or took over and adapted old Muslim castles that had been built at strategic points, and, increasingly, the kings of Jerusalem turned these castles over to the Templars and the Hospitallers because they alone had enough men and enough money to man them efficiently. The monastery had become a real fortress not just a symbolic one. Here these military monks were doing two things. First, they were rooting Christianity physically and powerfully in the Holy Land. In this respect they can be compared to the *kibbutzim*, for even though the Israeli conquest of the land was a peaceful one, we have seen that it had its aggressive aspects. The military orders' strict poverty was also in line with important ideals of the *kibbutz*. Second, by colonising the frontiers these new military monks were performing, and simply taking to its logical conclusion, a function that monks had been fulfilling in Europe for years. These monks were pushing aggressively against the frontiers of Islam and were in the front line of the holy war. One day the new chosen people would conquer Islam in Asia and Africa and these castles were originally seen as a springboard for future belligerent action. In the mean time the soldier–monks helped the secular knights who had settled in the Holy Land in their war of expansion during the first half of the twelfth century. They pushed forward the frontiers of the Crusader kingdom over the Jordan on the east bank southward into the Negev as far as Eilat and northward into Lebanon and Syria. It seemed as though nothing could stop the Franks from fulfilling their dream, and the military monks were an essential part of this success and were regarded as a crusading elite.

Few states in the history of the world could have had such an intense and idealistic religious foundation. Yet, in a great irony, the Crusader states rather quickly became more secular in spirit than any state in Europe at this time.[84] Pious, simple Godfrey of Bouillon died at the end of 1099 in an epidemic and he was succeeded by his brother Baldwin. Baldwin had spent the last two years in Edessa establishing a Western presence there. He and his knights ruled the city but used the Armenian people as high officials of the government and the civil service. Baldwin himself married an Armenian princess and adopted the lifestyle of an oriental ruler. It was a wise policy and helped the Armenians to adjust to this Latin rule. When Baldwin came to Jerusalem in 1100 he had no scruples about being crowned king. With his greater taste for luxury, he abandoned holy poverty and lived richly in a style that the Muslims could understand and appreciate. Egyptian delegates after the battle of Askelon had been astonished to find Godfrey sitting on the floor of his tent, bare-headed. Baldwin's autocratic manner, his strong rule and luxurious court was far more in the oriental mode than that of feudal Europe. Baldwin and his court began to adopt Middle Eastern dress, and slowly the Franks of Palestine learned how to adapt to life in the East, learned to take baths, to build in the Arab fashion and learned important lessons of Arab hygiene. These Western colonists were in the unusual position of having settled in a country that was far more culturally advanced than their own. The Crusaders, who had been trying to acquire a new Western identity, would in the East acquire an oriental one. 'Westerners,' Fulcher of Chartres wrote enthusiastically, 'we have become Orientals.'

> The Italian and the Frenchman of yesterday have been transplanted and become men of Galilee and Palestine. Men from Rheims or Chartres are transformed into Tyrians and citizens of Antioch. We have already forgotten the land of our birth; who now remembers it? Men no longer speak of it. Here a man now owns his house and servants with as much assurance as though it were by immemorial right of inheritance in the land. Another has taken to wife, not a countrywoman of his own, but a Syrian or an Armenian woman, sometimes even a baptised Saracen, and then lives with a whole new family. We use various languages of the country turn and turn about; the native as well as the colonist has become polyglot and trust brings the most widely separated races together.... The colonist has now become almost a native, and the immigrant is one with the inhabitants.[85]

This is a rather rosy view. The fierce cruel Crusader had not overnight become a tolerant coloniser. Indeed, when the oriental Christians had to take refuge in Crusader states because the invasion of the Franks had made their lives impossible in the Muslim cities, they were treated with great contempt and reduced to the level of second-class citizens. Curiously enough, something very similar happened in Israel. Jews had lived in the Arab countries for centuries. They spoke Arabic, dressed like Arabs and had adopted an Arabic lifestyle; they had known nothing like the persecution that the Jews had experienced in Europe. But after the 'disaster' of the creation of the Jewish state in 1948, there was a new anti-semitism and persecution and these oriental Jews had to take refuge in Israel. Here the Zionists from Europe despised them, seeing them as indistinguishable from the Arabs, and made them into inferior citizens. This treatment led to great bitterness, just as the oriental Christians in the Middle Ages came to hate the Franks and realise that they had been much better off under the Muslims.

The Crusaders' kingdom was, therefore, aggressive and belligerent. The Franks there fought a ceaseless war of expansion against the Muslims and despised the oriental and Byzantine Christians that they found living in their new territories. The state was dedicated to warfare. At a time when Europe was enjoying a period of great creativity and building a new culture, there was no similar cultural achievement in the Crusader states. There were some good historians and jurists, but nobody attained the standards of the scholars and artists back home. There was very little sculpture or architecture in the Holy Land, because the Franks' whole energy had to be concentrated on the war effort. The one great innovation that the Palestinian Franks did achieve was their castles, where they learned a great deal from the Arabs. Their building programme had to be part of their war effort, and the castles along the borders of their states made the crusading kingdoms into a fortress surrounded by hostile Muslims. It was a state of siege very similar to the situation of Israel today. How long would it be before these hostile Muslims started to fight back and attempt to recover their land from the Franks?

People in the Western world today who think of Islam as 'the religion of the sword' would probably expect the Muslims in the surrounding countries to have called a *jihad* instantly. This is not what happened. The idea of the holy war had become such a distant, stylised memory to the Muslims of the twelfth century that at first none of them seemed to see the Crusade itself as a Christian holy war. The twelfth-century Arab historian Izz ad-Din Ibn al-Athir saw the invasion of Syria in 1097 as part of a new phase of Western expansionism to which he attached no

particular religious significance. When he describes the sack of Jerusalem, Ibn al-Athir records the facts calmly. He explains that the population of the city was 'put to the sword', including a large number of Muslim scholars and ascetics 'who had left their homelands to live lives of pious seclusion in the Holy Place'.[86] There is no anguished rhetoric about the loss of the Holy Place, no vow to reclaim this Islamic land in the name of Allah, as the theology of *jihad* demanded. The Muslims of the Near East hated these Western invaders, naturally, but in the great heartlands of the Islamic empire there seemed a calm indifference about these distant incidents.

One ruler immediately proved an exception to this rule. After the sack of Jerusalem, those Muslims who managed to escape the slaughter began to flee from Palestine into the surrounding Arab countries. A few days after the tragedy of 15 July, refugees from Palestine began to pour into Damascus, carrying with them the Koran of Uthman, one of the oldest copies of the Holy Book. While some of them left out of sheer terror, others believed that exile was an Islamic duty in the event of occupation by non-believers. It was dishonourable for Muslims to listen to the insults heaped upon the Prophet by the Franks. As the first refugees stumbled into Damascus, they were greeted kindly by Qadi Abu Sa'ad al-Harawi. He told them that no Muslim should be ashamed to go into exile. The Prophet Mohammad, God's blessing be upon him, had been the first Muslim refugee when he had made the *hijra* from Mecca to Medina, and this migration had been the first step in the *jihad* he had undertaken to regain his homeland and free it from idolatry. Similarly, the Qadi explained, the refugees from Palestine must consider themselves *mujahideen*, soldiers in the holy war which they would fight to liberate their homeland and push the Franks into the sea.[87] At once al-Harawi led a crowd of Palestinian refugees to Baghdad, the capital of the Islamic empire, where they staged an angry demonstration. It was the month of Ramadan and al-Harawi and the Palestinians burst into the great mosque of the Caliph, the successor of Mohammad. Then al-Harawi began to eat ravenously and ostentatiously and was naturally surrounded by a furious crowd of worshippers, who were horrified to see him breaking the fast so blasphemously. Al-Harawi rose calmly to his feet and asked them why they were so upset about his breaking the fast when they seemed quite indifferent to the tragic loss of Jerusalem and the hideous plight of their Muslim brothers who had been forced into exile.[88] Weeping themselves, the refugees 'described the sufferings of the Muslims in that Holy City', wrote Ibn al-Athir, 'the men killed, the women and children taken prisoner, the homes pillaged'.[89] The Muslims of Baghdad wept bitterly in sympathy and the Caliph, who by this time had very little political power, set up a committee to look into the matter. As is the way of such committees, nothing came of it. Al-Harawi was disgusted and led the refugees through the streets shouting: 'I see the supporters of the faith are weak!'[90] His call to *jihad* met with complete apathy. Muslims were ready to weep for their brothers but were not prepared to take any practical steps to help them.

There are obvious similarities with the situation in the Arab world today, with one crucial difference. The Arabs and Muslims in the Middle Ages were in a much stronger position than their descendants today and had they united together they could certainly have crushed the isolated, poorly manned Crusader states. But they seemed chronically incapable of doing this. They were either frightened of alienating these monstrous Franks and attracting an offensive against their own city or they were busily engaged in fighting one another. As Ibn al-Athir admits: 'It was the discord between the Muslim princes that enabled the Franj to overrun the country.'[91] Furthermore, throughout the whole period of the Crusades the Arab and Turkish states of the Middle East seemed to find it impossible to found a secure polity. However strong a ruler was, his achievements were made null after his death because there was always quarrelling about the succession or infighting among the local emirs, and the new ruler would have to build up his sphere of influence from the beginning again. Furthermore, though it may seem surprising to those who see Islam as a warlike and violent religion, the Muslims do not seem to have been very good soldiers at this point and were not really serious in their campaigns. All this was naturally very much to the advantage of the Franks, in much the same way as the disunity of the Arab states today has been advantageous to Israel. This Muslim instability should have been checked because it simply meant more suffering and more refugees. In much the same way Arab apathy or downright hostility towards the Palestinians has played straight into Israel's hands.

The Franks, on the other hand, had no such disadvantage: they were still euphoric with victory and this made them formidable soldiers. Even the tragedy of the 1101 Crusades did not seem to have dimmed their confidence. There was a continuous flow of individual knights and barons from Europe, who brought small bands of knights to help the war effort, and for nearly fifty years the Franks seemed almost invincible. In 1104 they had taken Haifa, Jaffa and Acre, and more Palestinians were either massacred or driven from their homes to crowd into the neighbouring Muslim towns. At one point it seemed as though they might get to Baghdad itself, but in 1104 they were defeated at Harran, between what is now Syria and Iraq, but they took Tripoli in 1109 and Beirut and Sidon the following year. They now had a fourth state in the East, which became known as the County of Tripoli.

By 1111 the Muslims of the Near East saw no end to these Frankish victories. What was to stop them taking Tyre, Aleppo and Mosul? Another leader tried to raise a *jihad*. The Qadi of Aleppo, a city which felt particularly threatened and humiliated by the Franks, was Abdul Fadl Ibn al-Khashab. He was appalled by the passive and cowardly stand of the Amir of Aleppo, who tried to hold the Frankish scourge at bay by a policy of conciliation. On Friday 17 February Ibn al-Khashab decided to go to the heart of Islam as Ibn al-Harawi had done before him. Followed by a large crowd of Aleppans, including a number of Sufis and imams, he burst into the Sultan's mosque in Baghdad. The Arab historian of Damascus, Ibn al-Qalanisi, shows that this was a far more violent demonstration than the former one of 1099:

> They forced the preacher to descend from the pulpit, which they smashed. They then began to cry out, to bewail the evils that had befallen Islam because of the Franj, who were killing men and enslaving women and children. Since they were preventing the faithful from saying their prayers, the officials present made various promises, in the name of the sultan, in an effort to pacify them: armies would be sent to defend against the Franj and all the infidels.[92]

The response was still half-hearted, and Ibn al-Khashab and his supporters put no faith in this promise of a *jihad*. The following Friday they demonstrated in the mosque of the Caliph himself, smashing the *minbar* which was adorned with verses of the Koran and hurling insults at the Successor of Mohammad. In the streets the demonstrators shouted: 'The king of the Rum is a better Muslim than the prince of the faithful.'[93] The Aleppans were referring to the recent message from the Emperor Alexius, who had urged the Muslims to join him in a campaign to 'struggle against the Franks and expel them from our lands'.

Yet though religious leaders seemed apathetic towards the *jihad*, the Sultan of Baghdad himself was sympathetic to the plight of the demonstrators. He ordered Mawdud, the Amir of Mosul, to lead an army against the Franks and to strengthen Aleppo. Yet when this army arrived in Aleppo the Amir there closed the gates of the city against his 'liberators' and put Ibn al-Khashab and his supporters in prison. He frankly trusted Tancred more than Mawdud and in the event he was proved to be not entirely wrong. The army from Mosul promptly attacked the city and massacred many of their fellow Muslims. The following year Mawdud tried again: this time he decided to make Damascus the headquarters of his war against the Franks. His host, the Atabeg Tukhtigin of Damascus, pretended to be deeply honoured by the great role his city was to play in the *jihad*, but on the very eve of the expedition Mawdud was stabbed to death in the great mosque of Damascus and most people believed that this was the work of Tukhtigin himself. When the Sultan Mohammad, furious at this deliberate flouting of his authority, ordered all the princes of Syria to join him in the *jihad* against the Franks, he found that Tughitin of Damascus, feeling more intimidated by the Sultan than by the Franks, had actually made a treaty with King Baldwin of Jerusalem. The Sultan's great army thus opposed an army made up of Muslims and Franks: the troops of Damascus and Jerusalem were joined by the troops of Christian Antioch and Tripoli as well as by the troops of Muslim Aleppo. Unless this chronic disunity among the Muslims could be overcome, there was no hope that they would be able to dislodge the Christians from the Middle East.

It was not enough for dedicated *mujahideen* like Ibn al-Harawi and Ibn al-Khashab to try to revive the practice of the *jihad* in passionate demonstrations,

when plainly the Muslim leaders seemed to have lost all sense of a united house of Islam and were even ready to make common cause with the hated Franks. Some of them used warlike rhetoric against the Christian states and tried to appear thoroughly devoted to the cause of the *jihad* but they were not prepared to ally themselves with another Muslim prince because they were reluctant to enhance the power of another Muslim ruler. As a result of this the Franks were able to take control of the whole coastline of Palestine and the Lebanon in 1124.

The year 1128 proved a turning point. The Sultan of Rum in Asia Minor appointed the Turkish commander Imad ad-Din Zangi Atabeg of Mosul and Aleppo. Zangi was no paragon: he was often dead drunk and was as cruel and ruthless as most men of war at this time. Yet he brought very important new qualities to the area. First, he took his responsibilities very seriously and was no wild adventurer. When he arrived in Mosul he anchored himself in the city by marrying the daughter of the previous Atabeg and having his father's bones reburied in the city. He also got the Sultan to give him undisputed authority over Syria and northern Iraq and then had to make this potential empire an established fact by subduing the local opposition. Second, Zangi was able to impose a conformity and new unity on his army and on the territories he conquered. Discipline in his army was strict. Zangi made his men afraid of him and yet commanded their respect because he never asked anything of them that he was not prepared to do himself. Third, Zangi was the first serious ruler the area had had for years. Previous leaders had been preoccupied with looting and amassing riches; armies were demobilised after a year so that everybody could enjoy the fruits of the campaign and nothing permanent was ever achieved. Zangi never once dreamed of settling down in one of the palaces he conquered, but slept in his tent on a straw mat for eighteen years, a perpetual military nomad engaged in a ceaseless campaign to subdue the area to his rule. After a victory he would disdain to sleep in the newly conquered city but would camp with his men outside the walls. His army became an efficient and unstoppable machine in the area and slowly brought peace with its iron fist. Finally Zangi did not rely on force alone. He set up an impressive intelligence system and was thus aware of events in Baghdad, Damascus, Antioch and Jerusalem as well as within his own cities Aleppo and Mosul.

Ibn al-Athir's father was one of Zangi's closest friends and he and his historian son thought that Zangi was 'the gift of divine providence to the Muslims'. The country, ravaged by constant war (of Muslims against the Franks and of Muslims fighting other Muslims), had become a desert and the towns had become desolate. As Zangi steadily attacked his enemies for eighteen years, 'now this one, now that, making a conquest here, a treaty there',[94] he was bringing a new peace to the region, which could begin to build itself up again. Ibn al-Athir, drawing on the memories of his father, makes this clear:

> His subjects and his army went in awe of him; under his government the strong dared not harm the weak. Before he came to power the absence of strong rulers to impose justice, and the presence of the Franks close at hand, had made the country a wilderness, but he made it flower again. The population increased, and so did its prosperity. My father told me that he had seen Mosul in such a state of desolation that from the cymbal-makers' quarter one could see as far as the old Great Mosque, the *maidan* and the Sultan's palace, for not a building in between remained standing. It was not safe to go as far as the old Great Mosque without an escort, so far was it from human habitation, whereas now it is the centre of a mass of buildings, and every one of the areas mentioned just now is built up.[95]

There is a clear resemblance between the situation of the Near East in the early twelfth century and the situation of Europe during the eleventh century. The Turkish Seljuk barbarians had fought their way through to the centres of power and civilisation as the Germanic tribes had done in the fifth and sixth centuries and as the Normans had done in the ninth and tenth centuries. The Turks had settled and adopted the religion of the region, but their old warlike instincts militated against their building up a united, progressive society. Internecine war had prevailed and had devastated the country – although this Near Eastern 'Dark Age' had been of comparatively short duration. Now a strong ruler was beginning to impose a new order. The strong were no longer able to terrorise the weak and, in the aftermath of a series of bloody campaigns, Zangi was imposing a peace on the area which made progress possible. This expressed itself in a building campaign which would bring the Near East back into the civilised world. 'Mosul had been one of the most impoverished regions before Zangi's time,' Ibn al-Athir explained, 'but during and after his reign it blossomed with crops, sweet-smelling flowers and other plants as fruitfully as anywhere else in the world.'[96] By means of a warlike campaign, Zangi had made the desert bloom.

But one Arab leader stood firmly against Zangi. Muin ad-Din Unur, the Amir of Damascus, was determined that his great city should not fall prey to Zangi, and to preserve his independence he was prepared to renew the old alliance that Tughitin had once made with the Kingdom of Jerusalem. King Fulk of Jerusalem was equally worried about this new Muslim unity in the area and was quite ready to make a

treaty with Damascus to this effect, and the agreement was signed in 1140. The
Christians in the Crusader kingdoms were now ready to make an alliance with the
infidel in the interests of the security of the state, something that hardliners in the
West would never be able to understand. This treaty endured and would later have
fateful consequences, as we shall see in the next chapter.

Zangi, for his part, was equally determined to take Damascus, and in the course
of his relentless campaign he unwittingly changed the course of history. He
decided to make an attack on the Christian city of Edessa, not because he had any
religious hatred of the Franks but for strategic reasons. His intelligence system
informed him that in November 1144 Count Joscelin, the ruler of Edessa, had gone
on a pillaging raid along the banks of the Euphrates, one of those expeditions that
the poverty of the Crusader states made a constant necessity and which naturally
stirred up more Muslim hatred. Taking advantage of Joscelin's absence, Zangi
besieged the city on 30 November with an army that seemed to the civilians inside
Edessa to be 'as numerous as the stars in the skies'.[97] Joscelin dared not return to
confront it and Zangi urged the inhabitants to surrender. In the fifty years since
they had so enthusiastically greeted Baldwin as their liberator during the First
Crusade, the Armenian Christians there had come to dislike the Franks very much,
as did the other native Christians of the Near East. They decided that they would
be much better off under the Muslims and in any case there was no Frankish
commander there who was capable of fighting the Zangi's huge army. Still the
Franks of Edessa refused to surrender but their resistance was quickly crushed.
Zangi intervened to stop his troops massacring the inhabitants, made prisoners of
the Frankish civilians but executed the soldiers and released the Armenians. This
was a turning point. Zangi had achieved what no other Muslim leader had been
able to do. He had not only inflicted a severe defeat on the all-powerful Franks but
he had also destroyed the Christian principality of Edessa, which could not survive
the loss of its capital. His prestige in the Muslim world soared and the refugees
started to talk excitedly about the imminent liberation of their homeland. The
Muslims of the Near East saw themselves rising once more to a new powerful life.

Yet Zangi's victory also touched a deep nerve in the Islamic world. The Caliph,
doubtless relieved to be off the hook, heaped honorary titles upon him. Zangi
became 'the pillar of religion' and 'the cornerstone of Islam'.[98] It was assumed by
many people that he would now go on to liberate the city of Jerusalem, which the
Muslims called al-Quds, the Holy. But on 30 September 1146 he was assassinated
by one of his eunuchs, who was of Frankish origin. After his death it was clear that
he had become a Muslim legend that indicated the first signs of a popular revival of
the old *jihad*. Ibn al-Athir records two of the stories of the Zangi legend. One says
that on the day that Zangi conquered Edessa, the Christian King of Sicily had
successfully raided the Muslim city of Tripoli in North Africa. When he returned,
the King turned triumphantly to a Muslim sage in his court – a man for whom he
had a great respect – and asked him: 'What use is Mohammad now to his land and
his people?' 'He was not there [at Tripoli],' replied the old man, 'he was at Edessa,
which the Muslims have just taken.' The Christians all roared with laughter, but
the King reproved them: 'Do not laugh, for by God this man is incapable of
speaking anything but the truth.'[99] Zangi's secular war was beginning to be seen by
the people as a holy war: Mohammad was fighting with his people just as the saints
had fought alongside the Crusaders. The second story indicates that the *jihad* was
starting to be seen once more as a meritorious religious act. 'Certain honest and
goodly men have told me', Ibn al-Arabi wrote cautiously, 'that a holy man saw the
dead Zangi in a dream and asked him: "How has God treated you [in the after
life]?" and Zangi replied, "God has pardoned me, because I conquered Edessa."'[100]
Zangi himself had not been fighting a *jihad* but, as is so often the case in a holy

war, an unexpected victory or a sudden reversal of fortune can tip a secular war into a war of religion. It is also true that one holy war tends to inspire another in the other side and from this time the Middle East was caught up in an ever-escalating cycle of religious violence.

On the night that Zangi died, his second son Mahmoud entered the tent where his father's body lay, took the ring off the dead man's finger and placed it on his own.[101] He would continue his father's mission of uniting the Near East. But Mahmoud, who was usually known by his honorary title of Nur ad-Din, the Light of the Faith, was a profoundly religious man and his accession to power marks the beginning of a new chapter in the relations between the West and the Muslim world. After Zangi's death, the empire that he had so painstakingly built up looked as though it might disintegrate, as was always the way with Muslim empires. The unity that he had established had been based on fear rather than on a shared conviction, and Nur ad-Din would have to earn his own legitimacy and acquire the respect of his people. He chose to do so by presenting himself to them as a pious Muslim. He refused to live opulently, like many of the other amirs, but returned to the egalitarianism of Mohammad. His father Zangi had always practised a spartan frugality, but Nur ad-Din's asceticism was based upon Islamic principles. He would only levy taxes that were authorised by the Koran, and Ibn al-Athir, who remained devoted to the son of Zangi all his life, wrote in admiration of his simple lifestyle:

> His food and clothing and all his personal expenditure came out of income from properties bought with his legal share of booty and money allocated for communal Muslim interests. His wife complained to him of his austerity and so he allotted to her, from his private property, three shops in Hims that would bring her in about twenty dinar a year. When she objected that this was not much, he said: 'I have no more. Of all the wealth I have at my disposal, I am but the custodian for the Muslim community and I do not intend to deceive them over this or to cast myself into hell-fire for your sake.[102]

The ideal of holy poverty and community was central to Cluniac Christianity and to crusading and it is also certainly the hallmark of a Muslim ruler that he should create a just and equal society and does not live in luxury and splendour. This has been of crucial importance in the *jihad* of our own day. Nur ad-Din also presented himself to his people as a scholar, and in this he was quite different from the Christian ideal as expressed in *The Song of Roland*. In Christianity the word 'layman' was synonymous with 'uneducated, unlearned',[103] but in Islam the man of war was expected to be a scholar. Wherever he travelled the Sultan Nur ad-Din was accompanied by a crowd of learned imams and Sufis, whom he always treated with the deepest respect.[104] His court was known for its scholarship and after dinner Nur ad-Din used to enjoy a tough theological discussion with the most learned of the clergy. His scholars even accompanied him on a military campaign and would interpret its events and give him advice according to the principles of the Koran and the *Sharia*, Islamic law. By presenting himself as living scrupulously according to the principles of Islam, he gained the respect of his people, a respect that would prove far more durable than the terror that his father had inspired. In character, Nur ad-Din was quite unlike his father. He was a tall, dignified young man of twenty-nine when he came to power, and his expression was gentle and calm. Where his father had been somewhat raucous and effusive, Nur ad-Din's manner tended to be very formal and reserved.[105] But behind this quiet exterior, there was a stark tenacity of purpose.

In one respect, Nur ad-Din's image as a devout Muslim was an innovation. Although the Koran had denounced war, he would have been glad that a Muslim poet described him thus: 'He unites prowess in war with devotion to his Lord; what a splendid sight is the warrior at prayer in the Temple!'[106] Central to the Sultan's practice of religion was his devotion to the *jihad*. Nur ad-Din looked back beyond the early theology of the *jihad* that had been evolved in the first century of Islam but which had fallen into disuse to the Koran. Applying the principles of the Koran to the situation in the Near East, Nur ad-Din taught that it was the duty of every Muslim to devote his life to a *jihad* against the Franks. Although war should be avoided if at all possible, the Koran taught that it was sometimes necessary, because aggression usually needs to be repelled by force. The passages in the Koran which justify Mohammad's war with Mecca also applied with an uncanny accuracy to the present conflict against the Franks:

> Permission to fight is granted to those against whom war is made, because they have been wronged – Allah indeed has power to help them – to those who have been driven out of their homes unjustly only because they said 'Our Lord is Allah'.... If Allah did not repel aggression by means of those who fight against it, there would surely have been demolished cloisters and churches and synagogues and mosques, wherein the name of Allah is oft commemorated.
>
> (22:40–2)

The Muslims of Palestine had done nothing to harm the Franks before 1099, but still the Franj had travelled thousands of miles to attack them. They had not only driven Muslims from their homes and desecrated their holy places, but had massacred them; beside them, the ancient unbelievers of Mecca looked relatively beneficent! Lack of an effective Muslim resistance had enabled the Franks to go on committing one atrocity after another. The Koran emphatically decreed that 'persecution is worse than killing' and that Muslims must fight the persecutors 'until the persecution is no more' to secure the liberty and human dignity of the faithful (2:192). Obviously it was the duty of a sultan, the protector of the faith, to defend his people against these cruel and aggressive Christians. Hitherto Christians had been tolerated as the People of the Book but the Franks had forfeited this by their behaviour. It also seems that the Muslims thought that they were idolaters, not surprisingly when one recalls the Franks' devotion to statues and relics. The Muslim texts usually call them polytheists, people who worship more than one God, and this could also have been due to an understandable confusion about the doctrine of the Trinity, which states that there are three persons in God. Nur ad-Din taught that it was a disgrace to Islam to allow these 'unbelievers' to pollute lands that belonged to Muslims and fragment the unity of the Muslim empire by their alien state.

Muslims had declared war on the people of the West for the first time. Hitherto they had shown no interest in Europe and Western Christianity, but this marks the beginning of a long, sad history of hostility which still continues today. It is important to notice the difference between the *jihad* and the Crusade. The Crusade had partly resulted from the knights' desire to find a justification for their love of warfare and it had led to a canonisation of violence as a holy Christian vocation. There was a cult of violence for its own sake. But the Muslim *jihad* preached by Nur ad-Din and by Muslims today is essentially defensive rather than aggressive. The Koran is quite clear that self-defence is the only justification for war and that Muslims must not strike first (2:191), but St Augustine had ruled out the principle of legitimate self-defence and Christians had been obliged to find a more bizarre and unnatural rationale for a just war. The Muslim holy war is still essentially defensive in character and is either a retaliation or an attempt to prevent an injury or an assault. Jewish and Christian holy wars, however, both preach the holiness of an aggressive initiative. In later chapters we shall discuss these holy wars of today and see how some Muslims may be coming round to the Christian and the Jewish ideal.

The practice of the *jihad* was so moribund that if people were to fulfil their Muslim duty they had to be educated, and Nur ad-Din began a propaganda campaign as part of his war effort. He commissioned scholars to write books to develop the theology of the *jihad* and to spread the teaching to all the important imams in the cities, who would then transmit it to the other clergy. In their turn the clerics would transmit the doctrine to the people in the mosques and in the sermons that were preached each Friday. Nur ad-Din's methods are still used today by Muslims who want to summon a holy war, and in the course of this instruction and propaganda great stress is laid on the qualities of a true Muslim ruler. It is important to note that the emphasis is on reason and intellect rather than on the visionary fervour which finally dominated the First Crusade and which led the Crusaders to look forward to miracles. Muslims do not expect God to intervene and save them in miracles that suspend the course of nature. They believe that God will only help them when they have made every human effort to save themselves. 'Verily,' God says in the Koran, 'God will not change the state of a people unless they change the state of their own selves' (13:11). At first, the Crusaders had combined piety with practicality and fought as though everything depended upon themselves. The crusading theology that developed after the success of the First Crusade would lead other Crusaders to adopt less sensible policies.

The Crusaders had, therefore, inspired a revival of the *jihad* in the Middle East that was based on very different premises from their own holy war. When they had been struggling towards the Holy Land they had quite spontaneously turned back to the Old Testament and in seeing themselves as the new chosen people it was inevitable that the Crusade should share many of the preoccupations of the Jewish holy wars. One of the most important and crucial of these shared passions is the love of the same Holy Land. Indeed besides inspiring a new *jihad* it is also true that the Crusades helped to shape a medieval religious movement, which called upon the Jews to return to Zion and which rekindled their love of the Promised Land. In particular the writings of two Jews of Muslim Spain show that this religious 'Zionism' has many similarities with the Crusaders' devotion to the Holy Land.

Judah Halevi, the eminent poet and physician, had been a young man at the time of the First Crusade and had been personally affected by the new Christian enthusiasm for the holy war. The many increasingly religious campaigns in Spain during the early years of the twelfth century made life difficult for the Jews as well as for the Muslims, because the Jews tended to get caught as buffers between the two religions and it may well be that the anti-semitism inherent in crusading affected the attitudes of the Spanish Christians, who had hitherto had good relations with Jews. Halevi decided to emigrate to Cordova in Muslim Spain, where he felt he would be safer, but his emigration made him conscious of an essential homelessness. He began to argue that Jews could never feel at home in the diaspora; they could only be what God intended them to be in the Promised Land. In his great philosophical work *The Kuzari*, Halevi insisted that what distinguished the Jews from all other peoples was that they alone had the capacity to receive prophecy and vision from God, but that it was only in the Land of Israel that they could fulfil this prophetic destiny. Like the Crusaders, Halevi saw the Holy Land as pregnant with divine power. Only by being physically in contact with the land, by exposing themselves to this spiritual atmosphere, could Jews become prophets.

> The air of your land is the very life of the soul,
> the grains of your dust are flowing myrrh,

your rivers are honey from the comb.
It would delight my heart to walk naked and barefoot
among your desolate ruins where your shrines once stood.[107]

Halevi was profoundly affected by the new crusading pride in Christian Jerusalem and he told the Jews of Spain that this Christian initiative should make them feel ashamed.[108] The powerful, tangible holiness of God was accessible only to the Jews, and the Gentile inhabitants of the land could have no share in it. In his poem 'To the Rivals', Halevi scorned the Christians and Muslims who thought that *they* owned Eretz Yisrael: 'Why they are nothing but wild asses!'[109] he exclaimed; they would never find the prophecy nor would they encounter the Presence of God. Yet the Jews were doing nothing to recover their homeland. Even though Jews were in no position to organise a military expedition to liberate Israel, it must be a duty for Jews to make the *aliyah* to the holiness of God. In 1140, therefore, Halevi made his pilgrimage to the East and died there the following year. Only a few Jews followed his example, but Halevi's poems and writings were absorbed into the ritual and helped to nurture a sense of Eretz Yisrael as the Jews' real home. Halevi's conception of the Holy Land is not only very similar to the Crusaders' but it is also very close to that of a Zionist like A. B. Gordon.

When Judah Halevi made his *aliyah* to Eretz Yisrael, Maimonides was only about five years old. In 1148 he and his parents were forced to leave Cordova when the Almohads, a fanatical Muslim sect, invaded Spain and tried to get rid of the Jews. Maimonides ended up in Cairo, a scholar, physician and important man of affairs. In Egypt he encountered the holy wars between Muslims and Christians and for a time he was the physician to Saladin's son, when he became sultan. Maimonides' vision of the Holy Land is less poetical than Halevi's, but he certainly shares his sense of Eretz Yisrael as being crucial to the Jewish identity. The Temple Mount is the centre of the world, because it took the Jewish people back to their earliest origins, and to the origin of all mankind:

> Now there is a well-known tradition that the place where David and Solomon built the altar in the threshing floor of Arauneh was the same place where Abraham built the altar upon which he bound Isaac. This, too, was the place where Noah built an altar when he came out of the Ark. It was also the place of the altar upon which Cain and Abel offered sacrifices. There it was that Adam offered a sacrifice after he was created. Indeed, Adam was created from that very ground; as the sages have taught: Adam was created from the place where he made atonement.[110]

One day in the future, Maimonides foretold, the Jews would establish an independent state in Eretz Yisrael, governed by the Torah. Only when they ruled from the Temple Mount would a political order fully in tune with God's plan for the world come into being. Such a return of the Jews would thus be a light unto the Gentiles and the beginning of the redemption. Like the Crusaders, Maimonides saw occupation of the Holy Land as essential for the salvation of the world.

The Jewish and the Christian holy wars tended to follow a very similar pattern, and many of the religious Zionists, who see the present conflict as a holy war against Islam, think and behave today in ways that are remarkably similar to the Crusaders. If crusading contributed to the present conflict by producing anti-semitism in Europe, it also helped to form a religious Zionism that has surfaced again very powerfully and more aggressively today. One of the lessons of the First Crusade is that religion seems to be effective when all else fails. Without their religious faith, the Crusaders would certainly not have survived their traumatic journey nor would they have defeated the Turks. Although the Muslims were much slower to seek this solution, the *jihad* would ultimately prove to be far more effective in getting rid of the Franks than a purely secular war, and in the present conflict both Jews and Muslims have turned to the holy war because they see no other solution. In our own day religion has proved to be a very successful force. But religion also has its grave dangers and can result in failure as well as astounding success. The story of the Second Crusade gives us a clear indication of the different strengths and weaknesses of the Christian (and hence, later, of the Jewish) holy war and the new Muslim *jihad*.

CHAPTER FIVE

1146–1148

St Bernard and the Most Religious Crusade

The news of the fall of Edessa horrified the Christians of Western Europe and yet when Pope Eugenius and King Louis VII of France called a new Crusade the response was disappointing: people had heard too much about the horrors of the First Crusade fifty years earlier. But on 31 March 1146 Bernard, Abbot of Clairvaux, addressed a huge assembly of French barons at Vézelay and persuaded them that the fall of Edessa was not a disaster but part of God's plan. He had even 'allowed' or 'caused'[1] Zangi to conquer Edessa to give Christians a staggering opportunity. He would be with his people on their new Crusade, which was a revelation of divine love and one of the most significant events in salvation history.[2] Bernard was probably the most powerful man in Europe at that time. The King of France was in his thrall and the Pope a member of his religious order. He owed a good deal of his power to his charismatic eloquence. A contemporary wrote that his spiritual and emaciated appearance tended to 'persuade his audience before he had opened his mouth'.[3] When he had finished his speech in the presence of the King at Vézelay, there was as usual a holy pandemonium. The King knelt down and took the Cross and was followed by such a vast throng of people from all classes of society that the huge stock of ready-made crosses was exhausted and Bernard had to tear his garments to shreds and hand them to the clamorous crowds.

During the next few weeks Bernard toured France preaching the Crusade and at once barons, knights and poor pilgrims dropped everything and flocked into the King's crusading army. 'I opened my mouth; I spoke and at once the Crusaders have multiplied to infinity,' Bernard wrote complacently to the Pope. 'Villages and towns are deserted. Everywhere you see widows whose husbands are still alive.'[4] It seemed as though the whole of France was mobilising for the holy war in the same way as it had rushed to answer Urban's summons in 1095. Yet there was a great difference. Bernard's rhapsodic and mystical view of the Crusade was very different from Urban's sober Cluniac war of liberation. Bernard had been inspired by the new belief in the Christian holy war, which was now promoted by the establishment, and had taken it to its ultimate conclusion, and his mystical piety would make this the most religious of all the Crusades. To understand this Crusade we have first to understand Europe as she was in 1146, and why she had chosen Bernard as her spiritual and political leader.

We do not possess the text of Bernard's sermon at Vézelay but we do have some letters that he wrote to prospective Crusaders and so have some idea of what he probably said there. Bernard shared many of the same ideas as had inspired the First Crusaders. Like Urban he urged the knights to stop killing one another and engage in a holy war that would save their souls. Great sinners would also benefit from taking part in this campaign, he argued, because they would receive remission of all their sins. Bernard was deeply impressed by the holiness of the land where Christ had lived and died. It had been 'embellished by his miracles, consecrated with his blood and enriched by his burial'.[5] The fall of Edessa was a territorial disaster, and a cosmic disaster as well because now the holiness of this land was threatened by 'evil men'.[6] It 'really would be an inconsolable sorrow to all succeeding ages, because it would be a loss that could never be recovered'.[7] Bernard was convinced that its holiness was only accessible to God's chosen people, who were now the Christians. The Muslims, who might soon be 'feasting their eyes'[8] on the holy places, must be annihilated. Already 'the earth has been shaken and has trembled'[9] because of the victory of Zangi and if the Crusaders failed to rise to the urgent necessity of the hour it would be a 'boundless shame' and an 'eternal disgrace'.[10] Bernard's objection to Muslims was not based on any hatred of Islam as a religion, but rather on the fact that they were a threat to the Holy Land and therefore to the whole world.

This view of the Muslims and of the Holy Land is very similar to that of the Crusaders after the First Crusade and since 1100 had been fully endorsed by the Christian establishment. However, Europe was a very different place from the Europe of 1095; there was a greater stability, a new intellectual culture was emerging and, above all, the process of Christianisation begun by the reformers of Cluny had now taken effect. This meant that Europeans could now afford to think of themselves as individuals and this was reflected in the new Crusader piety. The first Crusades had been vast collective enterprises, but Bernard specifically preached the Second Crusade as a divine invitation of God to each individual Crusader. As he marched to the Holy Land he was answering a personal call and saving his own soul. God had made himself vulnerable by allowing the Muslim victory in order to make a Crusade necessary and this was a turning point in the history of the world. The new world-view of the Crusade makes the history of the world centre around the individual Christian soul. The Muslims are simply part of the divine plan, which cannot possibly fail. It takes the myopia of the holy war one stage further. Instead of seeing the Muslims as mere filth, they are now simply tools used and created by God to save his people's souls.

This new piety had sprung from Bernard's religious order – a new order of monks which had been formed by Cluny but which had rebelled against the Cluniac tradition and showed a development in the psychology of Europe. Instead of building up the piety of each monk, Cluny had been dedicated to building up a new Christian society. The great reformer Odilo, Abbot of Cluny, used to be fond of saying that if the Emperor Augustus had found Rome brick and left it marble, he had found Europe wood and left it marble.[11] The monk's life was busy and public and his spiritual life was largely communal and liturgical. There was not much time for personal, private meditation. Yet at the end of the eleventh century, when Cluny was most triumphant and when Europe seemed at last to be lifting its head after centuries of oblivion, individual monks within the Cluniac monasteries began to show a new restlessness; they wanted a new individual spirituality. This was rather similar to what had happened in Islam: the first Muslims had been primarily concerned to build a new Islamic society, and, when that had been established, the Sufis had built an Islamic mysticism of love.

In England at about the time of the Norman Conquest a monk of the monastery of Sherborne, who is usually known as Stephen Harding,[12] suddenly threw up the monastic life for reasons that are not clear and for years wandered restlessly throughout Europe in a private quest. Eventually he joined the new monastery at Molesmes in about 1091. Under its remarkable abbot Robert, Molesmes was engaged in a fierce internal debate. Most of the monks wanted to stick to the traditions of Cluny but, to their dismay, others wanted to cast aside the elaborate Cluniac order and return to the roots of the Benedictine tradition and to the roots of Christianity: they wanted to live a more simple life away from the massive structures and rich monasteries that Cluny had created. To the 'traditionalists' these new idealists seemed to threaten that stability which had been Cluny's greatest gift to Europe, to be flirting dangerously with the chaos from which Europe was just recovering. The rebels, who included Robert and Stephen, felt that the complicated rituals of Cluny were far from the spirit of St Benedict and of the primitive Church and that they wanted to make an exodus into the wilderness and build a new, perfect community. Accordingly in 1098, while the first Crusaders were struggling towards the Holy Land, Robert, Stephen and a few other monks left Molesmes and founded the monastery of Citeaux in Burgundy. It was a new reform movement.

In Citeaux the monks sought solitude and silence; they also wanted to live in a simple building and to return to the poverty of Christ and to a greater purity. In 1110 Stephen Harding became the Abbot of Citeaux and it was during his abbacy that an event occurred which made this obscure little colony the inspiration of Europe. In the year 1112 a troop of forty-eight young knights rode up to the door of the abbey and asked to become 'Cistercians'. These knights were led by the young Bernard and it was he who was responsible for making the Cistercian order the most powerful institution in twelfth-century Europe. His great piety and ability meant that he was elected abbot of a new daughter house of the order, at Clairvaux, in 1115, when he was only twenty-five years old. From that moment, joining the Cistercians became an irresistible trend in Europe. Bernard went round preaching the new Cistercian reform with his huge charisma; after just one sermon in a village, twenty or thirty young knights or wealthy noblemen would leave their families and follow Bernard and Christ (the two, of course, were identical!) into the Cistercian order. 'He is becoming the bane of wives and mothers,' a contemporary wrote of Bernard. 'Friends feared to see him approach their friends.'[13] Bernard had arrived at Citeaux leading forty-seven young companions; a few years later he had founded a new youth movement.

This huge influx naturally meant expansion, particularly since the rule stipulated that no monastery should contain more than twelve monks and an abbot. Besides being the size of the first Christian community of Jesus and his apostles, it was an attempt to build solitude into the very composition of the monastery. These monks wanted to make an exodus from the world and its entanglements and so naturally they went to the uncultivated outskirts of Christendom. On the extreme margins of Europe, therefore, new monasteries were frontier settlements like the *kibbutzim* in Israel later. Because these borderlands were a wilderness, the monasteries in effect became agricultural colonies.[14] To maintain their privacy and independence the monks had to tame the land and live off it, and because they could not do it all themselves and still have time for prayer they made an important innovation in the history of Western monasticism. With the monks lived a body of laymen who were called *conversi*.[15] The crusading armies had taken thousands of poor pilgrims with them in the quasi-monastic enterprise of the First Crusade, and now the Cistercians took them into their frontier monasteries. By offering the poor a stake in the monastic enterprise, they were offering them for the first time a cast-iron guarantee of salvation and a chance to live the religious life (the only Christian life) permanently. The Cistercians were thus continuing strongly within the Cluniac tradition at the same time as they were seeking to make an exodus from Cluny and go back to the roots of monasticism. Cluny had set out to 'liberate' the Church and the monasteries from secular control; the Cistercians in their fundamentalist monastic movement were making a more radical break with the world and were also continuing the association between monasticism and the poor that Cluny had initiated.

There was one respect in which Citeaux was very different from Cluny. In the older monasteries, most of the monks had been dedicated to the monastic life as young children and had grown up within the walls of these Christian fortresses. The monastic holy war waged against the devil and the powers of darkness was, therefore, manned largely by an army of conscripts. With our developed notions of freedom and the rights of the individual this seems an obnoxious idea, but in the less developed society of pre-modern Europe personal freedom was a luxury that people could not afford. This meant that most monks had never known the chivalric life. Yet when Bernard and his companions rode to the doors of Citeaux, they were young knights who had made an individual decision to embrace the perfect Christian life. This conversion of life was also made by the young men who followed St Bernard's call, most of whom would have once been knights.[16] As Cistercian monks they would never bear arms again, of course, but this new knightly influx gave the Cistercian order a certain chivalric and military image.[17] There was a military precision in its rule: where St Benedict had written only broad, general guidelines for his monks, the Cistercian rule legislated for every detail, even for the lifestyle of the monasteries' pigs.[18] There was a military edge to their piety and also to the new settlements they were making on the borders of Europe. These frontier colonies would need to be protected from the neighbouring pagans, and the *conversi*, who as laymen could bear arms, were easily mobilised into the monasteries' private armies. Along the outskirts of Christendom, therefore, the Cistercian monasteries were agricultural and military settlements taming the Godless wilderness and by degrees thus pushing forward the frontiers of Christendom. It is by this time easy to see why St Bernard, the moving spirit behind this new monastic reform, was able to preach the Crusade so effectively. He was already inspired by many of its ideals and practices.

Yet no fundamentalist movement entirely reproduces the original pattern to which it seeks to return; inevitably it makes innovations to meet the wants of the age. The Cistercians' simplicity was in spiritual terms a new departure. The Rule of St Benedict had been drawn up as Western Europe fell prey to barbarism, and its emphasis was on discipline, stability and defence. By stabilising his monks physically within the monastery and by subjecting the body and will through a communal discipline, Benedict sought to defend them against the chaos and evil of the rest of barbarian Europe. But by the end of the eleventh century, Europe was feeling confident enough to mobilise herself to attack and could abandon this old defensive posture. The First Crusade was the most dramatic of these aggressive projects but there was also a spiritual confidence. The old monasteries had been fortresses, warding off the forces of evil and conserving the old order. In the pioneering monasteries of the Cistercians, the monks were engaged in a spiritual struggle and quest. Resistance had given way to a mystical attack and a contemplative initiative, and the Cistercian was engaged on an inward journey or migration to God himself. In the early Benedictine and Cluniac monasteries, piety had been largely communal; now each monk in the Cistercian settlements was engaged in a personal quest. Hence too Bernard's emphasis on the individual call that God was offering to each Crusader.

But there was a basic ambiguity in Bernard's view of crusading, which sprang from his essentially elitist vision of the Christian life. He believed that ideally everybody should be a monk, because it was only monks who led a truly Christian life.[19] But clearly that was not possible, so God had entrusted the extraordinary privilege of a religious vocation only to the chosen few. Furthermore Bernard was convinced that no monks were closer to the Christian ideal than the Cistercians.

Fifty years earlier, Christians had been yearning towards the holiness of the East; in particular they had longed for the holiness of Jerusalem. Now Bernard taught that the Cistercian monasteries were holier than the Holy City itself. Once, an English pilgrim had made a vow to pray at the Holy Sepulchre Church in Jerusalem and on his way there he had decided that he would enter the monastery of Clairvaux instead and become a Cistercian. Bernard wrote that not only had this monk no need to fulfil his pilgrim's vow but that he had already fulfilled it, even though he had not got as far as Jerusalem:

> He has cast his anchor into the very port of salvation. His feet already tread the pavements of the Holy Jerusalem. This Jerusalem which is linked with the heavenly Jerusalem and which is entwined with her in all the deepest feelings of the human heart is Clairvaux.[20]

When Bernard spoke of the 'heavenly Jerusalem' he did not mean the city described in Revelation that would descend to earth at the end of time. He used the phrase as a symbol of that union with God that the Cistercian was striving to attain in prayer. It followed that this mystical state was far more 'holy' than any earthly city, no matter how deeply associated with Christ. For the Cistercian elite, holiness had become spiritual and removed from the physical world. Naturally a monk who was experiencing God himself in his cloister did not need the second-grade holiness of Jerusalem and the Holy Land. In fact, when Bernard was offered a piece of land near Jerusalem in order to found a monastery, he refused it.[21] His monks did not need a physical contact with the Holy City because they were already in possession of a far more significant holiness and a direct experience of God's love, which was inaccessible to the mere layman.

But for the rank and file the holiness of Jerusalem and Palestine was vital, because it was the closest that they would ever manage to get to God. It was, therefore, important for the layman to go on a pilgrimage there, not only because he would live according to monastic ideals during his pilgrimage, but because the land *was* undoubtedly holy due to its contact with the historical Christ. The layman could not achieve contact with God by means of contemplation, because this esoteric mysticism was only for the Cistercian elite, but he could take part in another secondary but very important Christian task in the Crusade. Crusading was central to Bernard's political vision of Christianity, which needed Christian soldiers. The Cistercians had laid aside their knightly duties for the more important Christian task of prayer; their monasteries were spiritual power-houses strengthening and sanctifying Europe, but those knights who had not been fortunate enough to be called to the cloister could fight for God in the world. That was *their* vocation. Europe was beginning to acquire a greater awareness of the power of her mighty neighbours, which seemed to threaten a Christendom that was still vulnerable for all its new confidence. Although neither the Byzantines nor the Muslims had any military designs on Europe, the massive power of these oriental empires made Europeans assume that they were just biding their time before they invaded and conquered their lands. Thus Guibert of Nogent could reproach the Archbishop of Mainz for the Germans' lack of participation in the First Crusade by saying that the Franks alone had defended Europe against the new barbarian invasions of the Turks, even though the Seljuks had neither the desire nor the ability to conquer Christendom.[22] The first Crusaders had had a very vague idea indeed of the Muslim world but now people were beginning to see poor little Christian Europe as an island of the true faith surrounded by hostile infidels. This view naturally affected the idea of crusading. Thus in about 1125 the English historian William of Malmesbury wrote a version of Pope Urban's speech at Clermont:

> The world is not evenly divided. Of its three parts, our enemies hold Asia as their hereditary home – a part of the world which our forefathers rightly considered equal to the other two put together. Yet here formerly our Faith put out its branches; here all the Apostles save two met their deaths. But now the Christians of those parts, if there are any left, squeeze a bare subsistence from the soil and pay tribute to their enemies, looking to us with silent longing for the liberty they have lost. Africa, too, the second part of the world, has been held by our enemies by force of arms for two hundred years and more, a danger to Christendom all the greater because it formerly sustained the brightest spirits – men whose works will keep the rust of age from Holy Writ as long as the Latin tongue survives. Thirdly, there is Europe, the remaining region of the world. Of this region we Christians inhabit only a part, for who will give the name of Christians to those barbarians who live in the remote islands and seek their living on the icy ocean as if they were whales? This little portion of the world which is ours is pressed upon by warlike Turks and Saracens: for three hundred years they have held Spain and the Balearic Islands, and they live in hope of devouring the rest.[23]

William's dates are wrong, but this remarkable version of Urban's speech shows a new twelfth-century view of the purpose of the First Crusade. Instead of being a war of liberation, it was a fight for survival. A new paranoia had crept into the Western world-view.

Christians had to fight back. Zangi's conquest of Edessa must in this view have looked like the first step towards an Islamic reconquest, just a preliminary to the invasion of Europe. In this natural but distorted view of Islam, the Crusader states were of enormous psychological importance to the people of Europe, who were just waking up from the nightmare of the Dark Ages. We have seen that when they had conquered Jerusalem, they had at first believed that they would one day settle the Muslim problem once and for all and would ultimately conquer the world, but they had also become more aware in recent years of the power of the Muslim giant. That was what had made Zangi's victory over the Frankish Christians at Edessa so threatening and why Bernard had described this as one of the turning points of history. Bernard, the former knight, was not just lost in mystical ecstasy in

Clairvaux. We have seen that, while the rest of his monks led secluded lives, he himself was heavily engaged in the political life of Christendom. He was fully aware of both the strategic and spiritual importance of the Holy Land and had long been convinced that, in order to fulfil its Christian mission in *this* world, Europe had to mobilise herself militarily to defend the faith. That was why he had always been such an enthusiastic supporter of the Templars. Although these soldier–monks were not as exalted as the Cistercians, they were engaged with them in a monastic partnership. In their monasteries in Europe the Cistercians stormed heaven and sought the heavenly Jerusalem in their lives of prayer and contemplation, while the Templars fought for the defence of the earthly Jerusalem. In their pioneering monasteries the Cistercians were pushing forward the frontiers of Europe, while the Templars in their fortresses in the East were pushing aggressively against the frontiers of Islam. Both sets of monks were occupied with the battle for truth, the difference being that the Cistercian elite fought on the spiritual plane and the Templars on the earthly plane. Each needed the other, as body and soul of the same entity. Now the Second Crusade gave the laymen a chance to join in this great monastic enterprise. Bernard had called it a revelation of God's love for the world and during the Crusade the laymen would experience this love for themselves, not by contemplating God like the Cistercians but by fighting for him like the Templars.

If the Cistercians were the elite of the monks, in Bernard's view, the Templars were the elite of the knights and of the active Christians, engaged on fighting God's battles for him in the world. He had given them his ardent support for twenty years. In 1126 King Baldwin of Jerusalem had sent two of the Templars to Bernard in Clairvaux and one was Bernard's uncle, André of Montand. The Order of the Temple needed to develop, and Baldwin wanted papal recognition for the Knights Templar, which Bernard made sure they got. Two years later, the Council of Troyes made the Templars an official religious order in the Church and approved their Rule, which was popularly believed to have been the creation of Bernard himself and was in fact very close to the Rule of the Cistercians. Fulk of Anjou and Henry of Champagne, two leading Templars, made a tour of Christendom to drum up support for the Templars and, at a time when crusading was vitally important to the people of Europe, the Templars immediately attracted a vast number of recruits. In 1129 Fulk and Henry returned to the Holy Land, taking with them, wrote a contemporary chronicler, 'so large a number of men as never had done since the days of Pope Urban'.[24] The order also gained a strong foothold in Europe and houses of Templars were established in France, Portugal, Scotland and England (the London Temple dates from this time). In their European houses the Templars looked after the interests of the Crusader states at home, and all over Europe these houses of soldier–monks appeared, dedicated to the defence of Jerusalem, uniting the two great Western passions of religion and warfare.

Bernard praised the Templars as ideal Christian soldiers. He saw the sophistication and refinement that was beginning to enter lay life in Europe and even into knighthood and chivalry, as effeminate and worldly – totally unfitting for a true Christian. In his treatise *In Praise of the New Chivalry* he admires the Templars for maintaining the rough values of his brutal view of Christianity:

> They come and go at a sign from their commander; they wear the clothes that he gives them, seeking neither other garments nor other food. They are wary of all excess in food or clothing, desiring only what is needful. They live all together, without women and children. No idlers or lookers-on are to be found in their company; when they are not on active service, which happens rarely, or eating their bread or giving thanks to heaven, they busy themselves with mending their clothes and their torn or tattered harness....

They crop their hair short because the Gospels tell them it is a shame for a man to tend his hair. They are never seen combed and rarely washed, their beards are matted, they reek of dust and bear the stains of heat and the harness.[25]

Europe was in a permanent state of war, in Bernard's view, and that meant that a serious Christian had no time for the softer pursuits or for the company of the vile sex of women. He had to be constantly ready for battle and his lifestyle should reflect this harsh and tough reality.

Bernard saw the violent enterprise of the Crusade as a revelation of the divine love and he also saw the Templars as fulfilling the ideals of Christian love, which was both tender and fierce:

These warriors are gentler than lambs and fiercer than lions, wedding the mildness of the monk with the valour of the knight so that it is difficult to know what to call them: men who adorn the Temple of Solomon with shields instead of crowns of gold, with saddles and bridles instead of candelabra . . . who in spite of being many live in one house, according to one rule, with one soul and one heart.[26]

They reproduced, therefore, the values of the first community of Christians who, the Acts of the Apostles said, lived in Jerusalem 'with one heart and one soul' (4:32), worshipping daily in the Temple, where the Templars had their head-quarters. They had replaced the old peaceful imagery of the Jewish–Christian tradition with shields and weapons, dedicating Christianity to truly martial values in the constant holy war for the true faith. Above all, having dedicated their lives to this war, they were daily and hourly prepared for martyrdom, the highest proof of love:

What in fact is there to fear for the man, whether he is living or dying, for whom to live is Christ and for whom it is a gain to die? He remains in this world faithfully and willingly for Christ; but his greater desire is to be dissolved and to be with Christ; this in fact is better. And so go forward in safety, knights, and with undaunted souls drive off the enemies of the cross of Christ, certain that neither death nor life can separate you from the love of God which is in Christ Jesus, repeating to yourselves in every peril, Whether we live or whether we die, we are the Lord's. How glorious are the victors who return from battle! how blessed are the martyrs who die in battle![27]

St Paul, whom Bernard quotes extensively here, would have been horrified by the Templars but Bernard was speaking at the end of a long tradition of aggressive martyrdom. In fact for Bernard the ideal Christian death was the death of one who died fighting and killing the enemies of God: 'Indeed whether a man dies in bed or in battle, no doubt the death of his saints will be precious in God's sight, but if in battle certainly his death will be that much more precious.'[28] The fact that these martyrs went to heaven slaughtering other people bothered Bernard not a whit. He never considered approaching the Muslims as a peaceful missionary and converting them by means of his famous eloquence. The only solution to the 'pagan' problem was the holy war. 'It would indeed be forbidden to kill pagans if one could oppose in any other way their violence and hatred and oppression of the faithful,' he explained to the Templars. 'But as it is it is better to massacre them so that their sword is no longer suspended over the heads of the just.'[29]

Urban had seen the Crusade as a political, military and territorial affair – a liberation of people and a liberation of a land. The First Crusaders had themselves often been inspired by secular motives as well as by religious ones and their campaign depended on piety and practical common sense. Bernard saw the Crusade as entirely the work of God. The Muslims were not real to him; he and his contemporaries misconceived their intentions as regards Europe and, more dangerously, assumed that they were already in the Christians' pocket because they were simply instruments that God was using for the glorification of the Christian West. If crusading was the revelation of that love of God which 'passeth all understanding', Bernard was manifesting a dangerous indifference towards the concrete political and military realities of the campaign he was dispatching to the East. He was teaching his protégés like King Louis to have the Cistercian attitude to life. It would, however, be perilous to bypass reason and practicality on the road to the earthly Jerusalem.

Shortly before the Crusade, Bernard had overthrown reason in the person of the great scholar and churchman Peter Abelard. Abelard was Bernard's rival for the leadership of the young men of Europe. He too had been destined for a military career and at about the same time as Bernard and his young knights had entered Citeaux, Abelard decided to give up military life and become a scholar. He quickly became a leading scholar and from all over Europe thousands of young men had left home and come to sit at his feet in Paris just as thousands of their contemporaries were entering the Cistercian monasteries. Abelard was a philosopher and a logician. He believed that religion should be an affair of the head as well as an affair of the heart. 'A religious man', he taught his young disciples, 'must always be able to give a reason concerning the faith that is in him.'[30] The young scholars who followed him had inquiring minds and wanted an intelligent quest instead of a scholarship that merely conserved ancient tradition. They supported their master with a passionate devotion. Abelard had become almost a mythical figure in France because of his famous and tragic love affair with Heloise and after that he had become one of the leading churchmen of his day. Bernard was determined to destroy him firstly because he was a rival and secondly because he challenged Bernard's mystical view of religion which saw the truth as an impenetrable mystery that had to be accepted by faith alone. Abelard, he said, referring to St Paul's famous hymn to charity, was lacking in Christian love: 'he sees nothing as an enigma, nothing as in a mirror, but looks on everything face to face.'[31]

Bernard wanted to condemn Abelard as a heretic, most unjustly since Abelard had no heretical views – indeed his religious ideas were conventional. Later the Church would come round to his scholastic methods, which were in part the methods of St Thomas Aquinas. Otto of Freising, a contemporary Cistercian abbot, accused his leader of unreasonable prejudice, suggesting that Bernard was improperly swayed by his hatred of scholars like Abelard and so lent too eager an ear to Abelard's enemies. Bernard summoned Abelard to the Council of Sens, which he packed with his own supporters; when the scholar arrived he found more of Bernard's supporters outside threatening him with violence. Abelard was simply not given a fair hearing and, when Bernard stood up and with his frighteningly persuasive eloquence condemned his teachings, he collapsed. He was by this time a sick man, probably suffering from Parkinson's disease, and he was prey to mental terrors brought on by the traumas of his life. He was condemned and his books destroyed so thoroughly that today we have only a few fragments of them. The Pope himself lit the massive pyre of Abelard's condemned manuscripts and Abelard never recovered from this. He died the following year at Cluny, where the kindly and scholarly abbot Peter the Venerable had taken him in. The event would have made a great impression on many of the Crusaders who marched out of Europe with a frightened and unnatural distrust of reason, which Bernard had dramatically taught them by destroying the great Abelard.

Bernard's preaching of a Crusade of love instantly gave rise to a new wave of anti-semitism. In Germany another Cistercian called Raoul started inciting Christians to attack the Jews and Bernard went into Germany to stop this persecution. Raoul, he said, had received no commission, human or divine, to preach in any way. 'A monk's vocation is not to preach but to weep,' Bernard thundered. He was 'inspired by the Devil, the father of lies'. 'Why turn your zeal and ferocity against the Jews?' he asked the Germans; 'they are the living images of the passion of the saviour.'[32] Yet the anti-semitic mechanism was already too strong. Bernard was not able to stamp out the pogroms and attacks on the Jewish communities continued; it seems that the people who stayed at home felt that harrying Jews was their contribution to the crusading effort.

While he was in Germany, Bernard achieved another of his objectives. The First Crusade had been seen as a Frankish project. Though Germany was by far the most powerful and unified state of Christendom, the Germans had been noticeably absent from the crusading effort of the official First Crusade, though they had sent three armies eastwards in the spring of 1096. In 1146 Conrad, the King of the Germans, had absolutely no desire whatever to go on a Crusade. He was, after all, an old man in uncertain health who was in no condition to survive the terrible journey to the Holy Land. He felt, with justice, that he was doing his part in the holy war by battling against the pagan Slavs and Wends of Eastern Europe. He was also helping Pope Eugenius fight his enemies in Italy and the Pope certainly did not want to lose him at this point. Both Pope and King, however, had reckoned without Bernard.

Bernard was determined that his Crusade should be international and that the whole of united Christendom should march against the Muslims to destroy Islam. In the autumn of 1146, after dealing with Raoul, Bernard preached the Crusade in Freiburg, Basle, Schaffhausen and Constance. There was the usual ecstatic response, even though few of the Germans could understand a word Bernard said. The holy pandemonium was such that people tried to tear Bernard's emaciated body to pieces in their rapture and at several points the frenzy was so extreme and violent that Bernard could not leave his house. There had been terrible famine the previous year and this may well have contributed to the outbreak of visionary fervour and 'miracles' of healing. People claimed to be cured of blindness as Bernard's shadow touched them or they threw away their crutches as they listened to his sermons.[33] They began to clamour for the New Jerusalem, in rather the same way as the half-starved Franks had done in the Peace of God councils during the famine of 1033. All this was most embarrassing for Conrad. On Christmas Day at Spier Bernard's crusading sermon failed to move him but two days later, when Bernard yet again addressed the court, the determined Cistercian turned his attention to Conrad and addressed him not as a king but as an individual. He imagined Christ speaking to Conrad on the Day of Judgement – a Conrad who had refused to go on the Second Crusade: 'O man,' Christ said, 'what have I not done for thee that I ought to have done?'[34] Like Abelard before him, Conrad collapsed, burst into tears and promised to take the Cross. Bernard's eloquent bullying had again achieved his objective.

The German triumph gave Bernard a new idea. In March 1147 he arrived in Frankfurt and dispatched a Crusade against the heathen Slavs and Wends. Shortly after this a humbler Crusade consisting of English, Flemish and Frisian Crusaders set out to join the main Crusade but they got waylaid in Spain where they stayed and helped the Christians there in their wars of Reconquest. They managed to conquer Lisbon and there was the habitual massacre of Muslims. St Bernard's loving Crusade had become a vast three-pronged assault on the Muslims in the East, the Muslims in Spain and the pagans of Eastern Europe. The first monks of

Citeaux had made their exodus into the wilderness and the new Cistercian houses had also migrated from the world. Now from the loving cloister of Clairvaux had issued a giant international attack on the non-Christian world by the newly mobilised Christendom.

At the end of May 1147 Conrad and his great army left Germany and began the journey through Eastern Europe towards Constantinople. Awed contemporaries spoke of a million men in his army and it seems that there may well have been 20,000 Crusaders. With Conrad went the two vassal kings of Bohemia and Poland and there was a contingent from Lorraine. The German nobles were led by the heir to the throne, Frederick of Swabia. It looked a formidable and impressive army and to an outsider it would have seemed an impressive image of a Christendom united solidly in an implacable hatred of the enemies of God. Yet the army was not so united: there was great trouble between the different ethnic groups and quarrels and rivalries between the German nobles. Conrad was not strong enough in temperament or in body to hold the army together and Frederick was still far too inexperienced to be an effective leader but nevertheless the army managed to journey without much incident through Eastern Europe, and on 20 July the Germans crossed into Byzantine territory, Conrad having first sworn an oath of non-injury to the Byzantine Emperor Manuel.

On 8 June the French army set out. Unlike Conrad, Louis had taken the Cross on his own initiative. He was a very devout young man of twenty-six and had been intended for the cloister until the death of his brother Philip had made him the heir to the throne. During a war with one of his vassals he had massacred all the inhabitants of Vitry in Champagne and had been plagued with guilt ever since. Bernard had advised him to make a penitential pilgrimage to Jerusalem, but when Louis heard about the fall of Edessa he resolved to lead a Crusade to Jerusalem instead: killing Muslims in the East would atone for his sin of killing Christians in France. Louis' beautiful young wife Eleanor of Aquitaine also took the Cross. She was one of the biggest landowners in Europe and had brought the whole of southern France more directly under the control of the King of the Franks when she had married Louis in 1137. The marriage was not a happy one. Eleanor had involved Louis in the war resulting in the Vitry massacre; she had managed to produce only one daughter – a source of great anxiety to the young couple and to Bernard, their guide. She found the gloomy court of Paris positively barbaric after the south and may have insisted on journeying east with the Crusade. Alternatively Louis may have insisted that she accompany him because he could not trust her at home: fidelity does not seem to have been her strong point and she was far too rich in land – and therefore too powerful – for anybody, even Bernard, to keep her in check.

As one may imagine, Bernard had absolutely no time for Eleanor. She had brought to Paris a refinement and sophistication that seemed to him a deep betrayal of true Christianity. The south had not taken to the Cluniac reform and had remained, though firmly Christian, more thoroughly secular in tone. The court of Poitiers, where Eleanor had grown up, was extremely sophisticated and Eleanor's grandfather, Count William the Troubadour, had filled it with the best poets and scholars of his day. Eleanor was far more intelligent than her husband, who had received only a narrow monastic education; she spoke several languages, wrote poetry and was patron to many courtly poets of the time who adored her and celebrated her in their poetry. When she arrived in Paris, she brought poets with her as well as a new fashion for southern clothes and refined southern manners. Eleanor began a little youth movement of her own in Paris; she taught the young people of the court that one did not have to behave like a boor or smell like a Templar to be a brave knight. Instead of despising or rejecting women, southern

courtly chivalry worshipped the lady, loving her from afar with no hope of physical possession. For her part the lady educated her knight, inspired him in his knightly duty to the noble ideals of chivalry and refined his manners. Bernard thought this courtly love was obscene and he was probably deeply worried that this woman was polluting the holy Crusade with her presence. She had brought to Paris a cool contempt for fanatical northern religion, and this attitude was beginning to be adopted by the young people. She taught her contemporaries in the court to play games like 'Confession', which involved the players in absurd and grotesque penances, and the 'Pilgrim Game', where one of the players was the saint in the shrine to whom the others prayed to try to make him laugh by obscene gestures or by tickling him. (The game was finally forbidden in 1240 by the Synod of Worcester.)[35] While most of the Crusaders had been properly schooled in true martial values by Bernard, Eleanor would bring quite a different perspective to the campaign and would throw light on some of its anomalies.

Eleanor used to say of Louis that she thought she had married a man but found she had married a monk instead.[36] In the measured eyewitness account of Louis' chaplain Odo of Deuil we can sense her exasperation with Louis' pious activities when he set out on the Second Crusade on 8 June. First he visited a leper colony to perform an act of charity and humility that filled Odo with admiration. Then he went to the monastery of St Denis where he prostrated himself like a novice before the altar and received the crusading banner from the Pope himself:

> Then when the banner had been taken from above the altar, after he had received the pilgrim's wallet a blessing from the pope, he withdrew from the crowd to the monk's dormitory. The crowds and king's mother and wife, who nearly perished because of their tears and the heat, could not endure the delay; but to wish to depict the grief and wailing which occurred then is as foolish as it is impossible. On that day the king and a few of his retinue dined in the refectory with the brothers, and, after receiving the kiss of peace from all, he departed, accompanied by the tears and prayers of all.[37]

There could not be a clearer image of the monastic origin of this Crusade. Louis certainly regarded himself as a pilgrim and as a kind of monk, living the religious life for the duration of the campaign, and this would have some important repercussions.

There had been some talk of King Roger of Sicily providing a fleet to take the Crusaders to the East, but neither the Pope nor Bernard trusted Roger, who later proved to have his eye on Byzantine territory. In any case, Louis and the French wanted to walk in the footsteps of Charlemagne and their ancestors the First Crusaders, so they took the land route. This was their first mistake. The Crusaders who had marched through Eastern Europe in the autumn of 1096 had been careful to prevent any pillaging. Conrad, however, showed no signs of learning this lesson. His army pillaged disgracefully once on Byzantine territory and on one occasion Frederick of Swabia killed all the Greek monks in a monastery near Adrianople to avenge the deaths of two of the Crusaders. When the Emperor Manuel, not unnaturally, remonstrated with him Conrad simply retorted that after the Crusade he would return and attack Byzantium itself. Once they had crossed the Bosphorus, the Crusaders continued their career of looting and vandalism and, having followed so closely in the dangerous footsteps of Peter the Hermit's Crusaders, most of the German army suffered their fate. On 25 October the Germans arrived at Dorylaeum. The knights dismounted to rest their exhausted horses and the infantry were weary and thirsty. While they were thus off-guard, the whole Seljuk army massacred nine-tenths of Conrad's army in revenge.

Louis' army kept better order and avoided pillaging, but their journey was difficult. The inhabitants had suffered enough from Crusaders. The food was finished, the local people hostile and the French began to mutter angrily against the Germans. Louis reached Constantinople safely, therefore, but he should have learned from the experience of the First Crusaders that to take the land route was a bad mistake. To wish to follow in the footsteps of Charlemagne and his ancestors was a pious wish but it was also dangerous and impractical. The journey across Asia Minor had almost finished the First Crusade and now it almost finished the Second.

The survivors of Conrad's army with their King joined the French and together the Crusaders began the dangerous journey. The First Crusaders suffered from the heat of summer; the Second Crusaders endured fierce winter storms, and at one point hundreds of German soldiers were swept away by a torrential flood. Otherwise, the Crusaders suffered the same horrors as their predecessors: the Turks had ravaged the countryside, so there was malnutrition and starvation; the poor pilgrims began to die in droves; the horses also died or else were killed for meat; knights were reduced to the ranks; the army was continually harassed by the Turks who inflicted heavy casualties. At one point at Kronos, the vanguard were almost wiped out because the leaders did not obey orders. The Second Crusaders were guilty of a culpable impracticality. They had wandered off in a pious dream, hopelessly unprepared. Bernard had failed to anchor his men in the practical realities of campaigning and the result was disorganised disaster, as at Kronos or Dorylaeum. The First Crusaders had managed their similar danger with instinctive practicality and military skill when their vanguard had been attacked by the Turks at Dorylaeum. Odo of Deuil was very well aware of the Crusaders' lack of preparation and throughout his account of the journey he gives practical tips to future Crusaders about what kind of carts to use, for example, or which towns were wealthy enough to provide good provisions: 'For never will there fail to be pilgrims to the Holy Sepulchre; and they will, I hope, be the more cautious because of our experiences.'[38] Their piety had precluded their common sense and the Second Crusaders would make still more dangerously pious mistakes.

Over a year later in February 1148 the exhausted army and pilgrims struggled into the Byzantine port at Attalia and camped outside the city. They had to make a decision: should they go the rest of the way by sea, continue with the land route or else divide forces, sending half by sea and half by land? They had realised that they could not go on land any longer and, without any justification, said that their difficulties had been much greater than those experienced by their predecessors. One of the difficulties they claimed was the 'treachery' of the Greeks.[39] Manuel, Emperor of Byzantium, like Alexius before him, had little reason to rejoice that a Crusade was coming to the East. The Germans had declared war on him and pillaged his territory and the French had proved difficult and truculent about taking the oath of loyalty. Having these huge Western armies to look after presented grave problems for Manuel – political, military and economic problems not easily solved. Manuel was fighting an endless war against the Turks, but when he had heard that the Crusaders were coming he made a treaty with Mas'ud, the Sultan of Rum. As usual, any treaty with the infidel shocked the Crusaders deeply, but Manuel knew from bitter experience that the presence of the Crusaders was bound to stir up fresh Turkish aggression in which he did not want to get embroiled. He was also being viciously attacked by the navies of King Roger of Sicily. He had, therefore, no reason to welcome the Crusaders or to feel positive about the West, and yet he was a decent man and tried to take care of them as best he could. The Crusaders complained bitterly that he did not feed them sufficiently,[40] yet no state at that time, even an efficient one like Byzantium, could adequately provision such a huge army during the winter. At Attalia, for example, winter stocks were very low and the Turks had ravaged the countryside. The Byzantine governor did what he could, on the instructions of Manuel, but there simply was not much food available. Instead of appreciating this fact, most of the Crusaders simply accused the Greeks of treachery. 'The Greeks betrayed us' is Odo's constant and bitter refrain.[41] But the Greek inhabitants of Attalia were also having to go without food, simply because of this Western army. Then, when the Crusaders were settled outside the walls of the city, the Turks swept down and started to attack the camp and the city. The Crusaders blamed the Greeks for not protecting them adequately, and it may well be that the people of Attalia made little effort to protect these belligerent and ungrateful Westerners whose presence meant that the Turks had come to attack their city.

Hostility to Byzantium was deeply imprinted on the Western identity but in the Second Crusade it reached new heights. The First Crusaders had constantly grumbled about Alexius and had treated him disgracefully, but the chroniclers criticise Alexius and his government rather than damn all Greeks *per se*. They were uncomfortably aware, for all their hostility, that Urban had called the Crusade to help their fellow Christians in the East and to heal the rift between East and West. The attitude of the Second Crusaders was far more bitter and distorted. Odo's measured and elegant pen drips venom every time he mentions the Greeks. He tells us that there were people in Louis' army who seriously thought it the duty of the Crusaders to attack Byzantium and to conquer Constantinople before they went on to the Holy Land. They tried hard to persuade Louis to take this course, but fortunately the King took the advice of the more humane bishops in the army and turned a deaf ear to the hawks. Odo also tells us that it was very difficult to prevent the soldiers from pillaging Byzantine territory because the Greeks 'were judged not to be Christians, and the Franks considered killing them a matter of no importance'.[42] In comparison with the Greeks the Turks seem neutral figures in Odo's account. His real enemies are the Greeks and he is convinced that the next duty of the West was to send another Crusade against Byzantium, to punish them for their treachery against the Crusaders. Diatribes like this are common:

> The Greeks degenerated entirely into women; putting aside all manly vigor, both of words and spirit, they lightly swore whatever they thought would please us, but they neither kept faith with us nor maintained respect for themselves. In general they really have the opinion that anything which is done for the holy empire cannot be considered perjury. Let no one think that I am taking vengeance on a race of men hateful to me, and that because of my hatred I am inventing a Greek whom I have not seen. Whoever has known the Greeks will, if asked, say that when they are afraid they become despicable in their excessive debasement and when they have the upper hand they are arrogant in their severe violence to those subjected to them.[43]

This prejudice and hatred shows that the siege mentality and paranoia of twelfth-century Europe was leading the West to a greater intolerance. No longer are Christians in Europe simply finding it difficult to live side by side with other religions, they are finding it more and more impossible to live alongside their fellow Christians in the East. Christian horizons in Europe were shrinking rapidly.

Eventually, after a good deal of agonised discussion, a terrible decision was made which was a crime against the whole Crusader ethos. It was finally decided that the army would proceed by sea from Attalia; ships were provided by the Greeks but there was not enough room for all the Crusaders. Only the knights, the aristocrats and some of the footsoldiers could sail. The rest of the infantry and the huge mass of French and German pilgrims were simply abandoned with their wives and children. Stranded outside Attalia, they disappeared from history, betrayed by their brothers. All were killed by the Turks or were taken into slavery or else starved to death. To abandon the poor may have been necessary for the survival of the Crusade but it gravely damaged its moral integrity. It would be a long time before crusading could attract the poor again and people looked back nostalgically to the vintage days of the First Crusade when a new, fairer world-order had seemed imminent. The decision at Attalia was bitter proof that the gap between rich and poor was greater than ever.

On 19 March 1148 King Louis and his army arrived at the port of Saint Symeon. Conrad had been taken ill the previous December and had had to return to Constantinople, where Manuel, with exceptional Christian forbearance, personally nursed the German King who had threatened to attack his empire, and early in March had him and his household taken to Palestine by a Byzantine fleet. In this saga of stupid, blind hatred, it is pleasant to record that Conrad and Manuel became the best of friends. So Louis was the only leader to land in the Christian Principality of Antioch, and as soon as Prince Raymund of Antioch heard of his arrival, he and all his household rode down to welcome him and escort him triumphantly up to the city. The next few days were spent in revelry and feasting and the Franks, stupidly, began to forget some of the perils they had endured and were lured back into an optimistic frame of mind.

After the dreadful journey, Eleanor was delighted with Antioch. She felt far more at home in the sophisticated and luxurious East than she did in Bernard's gloomy Paris, and at Antioch there was the additional delight of a reunion with Prince Raymund, who was her uncle and childhood companion, very close to her in age, and with whom she had years ago enjoyed a rather scandalous relationship before he had left to try his luck in the East. At once the two exiles from Poitiers began to spend a lot of time together and ugly rumours circulated. Louis became pathetically jealous. But Raymund expected far more than a chance for a flirtation from the Crusade. He was watching the steady rise of Nur ad-Din, whose city of Aleppo was only about fifty miles away and a serious threat to his Christian principality. Yet Nur ad-Din was still not invincible and a sudden surprise attack

by the mighty French and German Crusaders together with the Antiochene army would almost certainly finish him off once and for all. He suggested to Louis that they make such an attack.

To the utter astonishment of both Eleanor and Raymund, however, Louis flatly refused to do any such thing. He stoutly insisted that he was on a pilgrimage and could not undertake any major offensive until he had prayed at the Holy Sepulchre. This was the spirit of St Bernard as Louis had, with his limited intelligence, understood it and this type of impractical piety was peculiar to the St Bernard's most religious Crusade. None of the First Crusaders, even the most pious of them, would have committed this idiocy. Eleanor was furious with her husband. It was the last straw, she said. She had a much clearer grasp of the political reality than her monkish spouse and could not go along with this holy stupidity. If Louis wanted to set sail for the Holy Land, she told him, he would have to go by himself. She and her own personal troops from Aquitaine would stay in Antioch and would attack Nur ad-Din with Raymund. When she got back to Europe she would divorce her inadequate husband and take her great lands elsewhere. Driven out of his mind with jealousy, Louis forcibly abducted her at night, bundled her on board ship and set sail for Acre. Eleanor would remain by Louis' side for the rest of the Crusade but when she sailed away from Antioch she was, at last, pregnant.[44] There would be a silence about the paternity of this new daughter when she was finally born in Europe. By that time Raymund of Antioch had been killed while fighting Nur ad-Din. Eleanor would never forgive Louis.

At Acre, Louis and Conrad were reunited and were entertained with great pomp and circumstance by Queen Melisende and her son Baldwin III, who was only seventeen and reigned together with his mother. Acre had never seen such a splendid congregation of Western Christians and yet it would not have been an easy meeting. The Crusaders from Europe would have been shocked by their brothers who had grown up in Palestine and had adopted such a luxurious and oriental lifestyle. They seemed completely to have turned their back on the heroic, boorish Christianity of St Bernard. The final shock was that the Kingdom of Jerusalem was actually in alliance with one of the infidel: the treaty made years earlier by Unur of Damascus with the King of Jerusalem against Zangi still stood. Damascus had no wish to encourage Nur ad-Din's supremacy in the area and it had been mutually advantageous for Jerusalem and Damascus to oppose him with a united front. The Crusaders had bitterly condemned Manuel for his treachery in making a treaty with Sultan Ma'sud, but what were they to make of this Frankish abomination? When they looked around the Kingdom of Jerusalem they found that matters were even worse than they had realised. Some of the lower orders had married oriental women and had produced a race of half-castes, and others had Muslims as friends, would eat dinner with them, consult Arab doctors and speak with them in accursed Arabic. We learn about these Muslim–Christian friendships from Muslim sources,[45] not from the Palestinian Franks themselves in their accounts of their kingdom, and this could suggest that subliminally they felt guilty about hobnobbing with the infidel in the Holy Land. Their uneasiness and defensiveness would certainly have been aggravated by the unabashed horror of the Crusaders from home who would have seen them as polluting holy crusading ideals.

On 24 June 1148, after the Crusaders had prayed at the Holy Sepulchre, they met the Palestinian Franks in Acre for a huge council of war. It was here that the holy blindness of this religious Crusade of St Bernard's revealed itself with an astonishing clarity. Instead of going off to attack Nur ad-Din, their most dangerous and committed enemy in the Near East, the Christians decided to attack their one ally in the Muslim world: Unur of Damascus. Nobody has been able to explain this absurd and perilous decision which would ultimately prove fatal not only to this Crusade but to the future of Christian Jerusalem. The Christians had at their disposal the largest army that they had ever been able to deploy against the Muslims and together with the army of the Principality of Antioch they might well have been able to nip Nur ad-Din's holy war in the bud before it became rooted in the area as an established and valued method of dealing with the Franks. Instead, by attacking Damascus, they were strengthening the hand of Nur ad-Din, because faced with the treachery of his erstwhile ally, Unur would inevitably turn to Aleppo for help. The Franks' decision at Acre was an extraordinary stroke of luck for the Muslim leader and a tragedy for the Christians. It is easier to understand the reasoning of the Crusaders. They had throughout ignored the practical aspects of their campaign and had no understanding of the political situation in the area. They would scarcely have heard of Aleppo but Damascus was a city with hallowed biblical associations and was even believed to have been the site of the Garden of Eden. The fact that Unur was the ally of the Christians would seem shameful, not a reason against an attack. There were no 'good' Muslims – all were the enemies of God. But for the Palestinian Franks, who did understand the political situation, the decision to attack Damascus was one of utter folly. It may simply have been territorial greed that inspired them, or they may have been shamed into the decision by the Crusaders who had been so appalled to hear that they had a Muslim ally. It could even be that they were persuaded to make the attack precisely to purge themselves of this sinful alliance. Casting mere human prudence to the wind, they would have put themselves back on course in the holy war. A people led and guided by God himself does not need political prudence. It could, therefore, be the case that the decision was taken to make an act of faith, trusting to God and leaving mere human wisdom behind.

The siege of Damascus was a fiasco, lasting only a few days. At first the Crusaders made some progress and they conquered some of the orchards outside the city. Then the Palestinian Franks suggested that the Christians move their army under the walls, so that the Muslims from the city did not have cover of trees when they made an attack. The position chosen was so disastrous that the Crusaders accused their Palestinian brethren of being in the pay of Unur and indeed it may be that by this time the Franks of the Crusader kingdom had realised the lunacy of this campaign. When they saw Nur ad-Din's army arriving to come to the aid of Unur, they might have made a last-ditch attempt to remedy the situation and could even have accepted a bribe from their former ally. At all events, they finally persuaded the Crusaders that they should lift the siege and that the enterprise was hopeless. The army, which had suffered enormous casualties, limped ignominiously back to Jerusalem.

The story of the Second Crusade shows what Bernard's piety and distrust of reason could become in less gifted men: a belligerent irresponsibility. It also shows the danger of a holy-war mentality which believes that ordinary human intelligence and prudence should be cast aside on principle as an act of faith. Such policies are not only irrational, they are also suicidal. Thousands of Crusaders had lost their lives during this expedition and the huge enterprise of the Second Crusade had been entirely wasted. The Kingdom of Jerusalem was gravely endangered by this failure and Nur ad-Din must have felt that the Franks' absurd decision was an answer to his own prayers and a complete vindication of his own holy-war effort. Muslim morale in the area was henceforward much higher and Nur ad-Din would go from strength to strength, slowly building up an empire that would one day almost surround the Christian states.

The failure of his Crusade was a great blow to Bernard's prestige in Europe and people were right to blame him: by removing the Crusade from the realities of life and seeing it as solely the work of God he had encouraged a suicidal policy in the army. It was also a blow for crusading itself. How could a holy war fail if, as Bernard had promised, it was the work of God? Bernard himself was bewildered by the disaster and the only explanation he could find was that the Christians had been too sinful so that God had withdrawn his help. But the triumph of the 'pagans' over the true faith was for Bernard a cosmic disaster that was, literally, the end of the world. It seemed, he wrote to the Pope, 'to point an end almost to existence itself'.[46] The Crusaders themselves blamed the Greeks and that excuse was very acceptable to Bernard too, but other critics were more forthright. In Würzburg a monk who had talked to some of the survivors and had learned how the campaign had been mismanaged, concluded that the Crusade had not been inspired by God at all but by wicked and stupid men like Bernard and Pope Eugenius: 'Certain pseudo-prophets were in power,' he wrote, 'sons of Belial and Heads of Antichrist, who by their stupid words and empty preaching misled the Christians and induced all sorts of men to go against the Saracens for the freeing of Jerusalem.'[47] This angry monk was only one of the critics that began to express doubts about the Second Crusade at that time, but nobody yet condemned the concept of a holy war as such. They only criticised aspects of crusading or particular crusading episodes.

Nevertheless there were clear signs that people were seeking a less bloodthirsty religion and this is most obviously apparent in the cult of the Virgin Mary that Bernard himself was vigorously promoting. One of the most famous hymns to the Virgin was supposed to have been the work of two Crusaders: Adhémar of Le Puy and Bernard himself. It shows a bleak view of life as a vale of tears and a yearning for sweetness and consolation which is supplied not by Christ but by Mary.

> Salve Regina, Mater Misericordiae: Vita, dulcedo et spes nostra salve. Ad te clamamus, exsules filii Hevae; ad te suspiramus, gementes et flentes in hac lacrimarum valle. Eia ergo, advocata nostra, illos tuos misericordes occulos ad nos converte. Et Jesum, benedictum fructum ventris tui, nobis post hoc exsilium ostende. O clemens, O pia, O dulcis Virgo Maria.

> Hail Queen, Mother of mercy; hail our life, our sweetness and our hope. It is to you that we cry, exiled children of Eve; it is to you that we sigh, groaning and weeping in this vale of tears. Therefore do you, our advocate, turn your merciful eyes towards us and after our exile show us your son Jesus. O clement, O loving, O sweet Virgin Mary.

Even Christians dedicated to the holy war were seeking an alternative that was more loving than vengeful, and a mediator and advocate who would be more merciful and compassionate than Jesus, who made such terrible demands on his followers. Adhémar, who wrote most of this hymn, had experienced the terror involved in the service of the crusading Christ during the trauma of the First Crusade.

Other Christians, at the time of the Second Crusade, seemed to reject crusading altogether when they turned to the Virgin Mary. At Chartres, the lay people quite spontaneously created a counterpart and an alternative to the Crusade, when they decided to build a new church for Mary in their city at the same time as the Crusaders were leaving Europe. There had always been a shrine to the Virgin there, but this lay movement laid some of the first stones of the magnificent cathedral of Chartres which has made the city famous. A building association was formed that organised lay men and women, rich and poor, to quarry the stones themselves and convey them to the site. An awed monk wrote to a monastery in England of the extraordinary scenes he witnessed. Men and women yoked themselves to the huge wagons 'like beasts of burden'.[48] Nobody could join the building association unless he had reconciled himself with all his enemies, and even though a thousand or more lay people were working at a time together, there was absolute silence, save for the prayers of the priests who accompanied them, 'exhorting their hearts to peace'. The emphasis in this movement of the Virgin was on peace and reconciliation not on holy war. At the site of the church, the wagons were parked and the people formed 'a spiritual camp'. Relics were brought in and sick people who were carried into the camp in huge processions were healed. All night long there was singing of hymns and canticles. The similarity to the crusading armies is clear. It seems as though at a time when their fellows and neighbours were marching thousands of miles to the East, the people who elected to stay at home spontaneously set up a counter-Crusade dedicated to peace and to building up something beautiful at home. They were constructing a holy place in Europe instead of tramping to the Holy City of Jerusalem and were creating rather than destroying and killing. Chartres was not the only example of this constructive building. At the same time other building associations were formed, quite spontaneously and independently, in Normandy, Crusader heart-land.[49] All were centred on ancient shrines to the Virgin Mary. Whenever there was a new surge of crusading enthusiasm, there was another building campaign, but these building projects seem to be trying to separate themselves from the holy war and to be seeking a peaceful alternative, instead of being part of the war effort.

It is often true that the people who are not involved in a holy war tend to be more creative than their territorially minded brethren. We have seen that this is true in Judaism and in 1146 it was also true in Christianity. Indeed Bernard's crusading religion itself seems barren. Not only was his Crusade a disaster but he thwarted creativity at home. As a Cistercian he disapproved of beautiful architecture, and would have had no time for Chartres Cathedral; he destroyed Abelard's intellectual movement, and even his mysticism was elitist and exclusive and only for Cistercians. Francis of Assisi would later bring spirituality to the people and the friars would replace the Cistercians as the leaders of Europe in the thirteenth century.

In the second half of the century other people started to draw away from crusading and its values. Eleanor of Aquitaine, who had always opposed Bernard's holy war, spread the cult of courtly love throughout northern and southern France after she settled in her native Poitiers in 1170. Courtly love became extremely popular among the aristocracy, and it not only challenged the brutal values of crusading Christianity. It also exalted a love that had nothing to do with physical possession, but which idealised the lady who remained remote and distant from her knight. Crusading and courtly love had both been inspired by the love of distant objects: a distant lady and a distant land, but crusading had transformed this love into a lust for physical possession. Courtly love, on the other hand, had more in common with Bernard's view of the heavenly Jerusalem. Eleanor and her daughter Marie of Champagne became the patrons of many troubadour poets and one of their most important protégés was Chrétien of Troyes, who lived only thirty miles from Clairvaux. This proximity to the Cistercians was more than physical because Chrétien's stories show a marked closeness to the mystical ideals of Cîteaux. In his stories the journey has changed its character. Like the mystic, the knight is engaged on an individual quest that he undertakes alone, not in the massive Crusader armies. Journeying, seeking and suffering, the Knight roams all over the world but his journey has no end in this life. He is in search of love and it is far more important to suffer and even die for this love than to possess the beloved and reach an earthly fulfilment. He confidently expects a union of love that always remains in the future tense, a spiritual promise that inspires his quest for an ideal. Instead of being the prelude to a holy war, in the courtly myth, the journey has become a prelude to love. Instead of leading to an aggressive conquest of a physical land, the new journey of the courtly knight, like the journey of the mystic, has no physical end.

The last of Chrétien's romances was *The Story of the Grail*.[50] He never completed it, but later writers, including many Cistercians, became fascinated with the myth. The Grail sought by the knights was originally supposed to have been the cup used by Jesus at the Last Supper which contained his true blood (*sang réal*). There was an old legend that Joseph of Arimathea had brought the Grail with him when he came to England. In the new version, the Grail is no longer a relic but the mystical vision of God. The knights are seeking not the earthly city of Jerusalem but the heavenly city of Arras, which has no precise geographical location and is indeed out of this world. People were beginning to seek an ideology that was not obsessed with territorial possession or with a return to physical roots.[51] They sought to liberate the holy from the physical and to find an alternative to the suicidal violence of crusading religion.

At the beginning of his story *Cligés* Chrétien looks back to the past:

> From books that have been preserved we learn the deeds of men of old and of the times long since gone by. Our books have informed us that the pre-eminence in chivalry and learning once belonged to Greece. Then chivalry passed to Rome, together with that highest learning which has now come to France. God grant that it may be cherished here, and that it may be made so welcome here that the honour which has taken refuge with us may never depart from France: God had awarded it as another's share, but of the Greeks and Romans no more is heard, their fame is passed, and their glowing ash dead.[52]

This is a new source of Frankish pride. Seeing a new intellectual spirit in France Chrétien envisages a vocation of learning for his people. Instead of looking back only to Charlemagne, he is seeking to establish a connection with the Greeks and Romans, those heroes of the classical world who were not only great military powers but also beacons of learning. Chrétien is seeing the new Frankish revival as continuing this ancient tradition, and at this time scholars were indeed building a bridge back to the classical past that had been lost during the Dark Ages. As the Franks conquered land from the Byzantines or from the Muslims, Europeans were able to get in touch with men who spoke Greek and Arabic and who were familiar with the learning of the ancient world that the West had lost. Latin scholars hastened to places like Spain or Sicily, and between 1150 and 1187 scholars like Gerald of Cremona and his pupil Daniel Morely discovered a wealth of texts and a tradition of learning among the Arab scholars that they strove to make available to European students.[53] They began to translate texts from the Arabic and thus discovered the scientific works of Aristotle as well as the philosophical and scientific scholars of the Islamic world. Toledo was a particularly important translation centre; it contained Jewish and Arab scholars whom Daniel Morely found 'the wisest philosophers in the world'.[54] As we shall continue to see, when religion was not involved, Christians, Muslims and Jews could respect each other, because they shared a secular culture. The Arabs had absorbed the learning of the Hellenistic and ancient world and assimilated it in a form that was palatable and comprehensible to the other religions of Abraham. By translating these Arab texts Western scholars were returning Europe to her classical roots and discovering a rich and lost intellectual tradition. They also had much to learn from Arab philosophers and scholars like the philosopher and physician Abu Ali al-Husain ibn Abdalla ibn Sina (d.1037) and their great contemporary in Cordova Abu al-Walid Muhammad ibn Ahmed ibn Rushd (d.1198). These names were shortened to Avicenna and Averroes and the Muslim philosophers became new sages and guides to the struggling West, which built the new tradition of scholastic learning according to the methods of the Arabs, with an emphasis on grammar and logic.

During the period of the Crusades, therefore, some Christians were learning from Arabs and Jews instead of slaughtering them in the name of God and from this fruitful and positive co-operation a new intellectual life was born in Europe. The Arabs in particular were a light to the Christian West and yet this debt has rarely been fully acknowledged. As soon as the great translation work had been completed, scholars in Europe began to shrug off this complicating and schizophrenic relationship with Islam and became very vague indeed about who these Arabs really were. They were at a deep level unable to identify them with the Arabs and Muslims they were fighting in the Crusades and 'Arabs' tend to get lumped indiscriminately with other 'Gentiles' like the Greeks, Assyrians and the Chaldeans. It was rarely acknowledged that the Arabs were not 'Gentiles' or 'pagans' at all but believed in the God of Abraham. Ludicrous inconsistencies abounded: Thomas Aquinas would praise Avicenna and Averroes but simply dismissed their Islamic religion as pagan error. Others actually refuted 'Islam' by quoting Ibn Sina.[55] When Dante imagined the virtuous 'pagans' in Limbo in *The Divine Comedy* he duly includes Avicenna and Averroes but puts them right at the end of a long list of distinguished Greek or Latin scholars whom he prefers to celebrate as his intellectual ancestors.[56] During the Renaissance, this classical heritage was firmly established in the consciousness of Europe, and Arabic was dropped from the curriculum and denounced by the new Hellenes as a barbarous tongue. The relationship with Islam and the Arab world was far too complicated for people to cope with in a balanced way. Crusading had made a blind hatred of the Arabs an essential part of the Western identity. Scholars at the time similarly found themselves unable to realise fully that these Greeks that they were rediscovering so enthusiastically and claiming as their own were actually the ancestors of the hated Byzantines. These peaceful and creative movements at home on one level rejected crusading, at least implicitly, and built up new, exciting structures of thought and art at home. Yet even in the most positive of these attempts to approach the Greek and Arab world, there is an unhealthy repression and double-think about people who are at one and the same time guides, heroes and deadly enemies. This is very clear in the scholarship about Islam.

In 1141 Peter the Venerable of Cluny had made a tour of the Benedictine monasteries of Spain and there he met two other visiting monks: Robert of Ketton, an Englishman, and Herman of Dalmatia. Both men were seeking texts on mathematics and astronomy, but Peter persuaded them to co-operate with him on a project of translating major Muslim documents. Robert and Herman worked together with a Spanish Christian, Peter of Toledo, and a Muslim, Mohammad the Saracen, and together they produced a collection of documents that remained very important in the Western understanding of Islam until the sixteenth century. There was a translation of the Koran, a history of the world from a Muslim standpoint, an exposition of Mohammad's teaching, a collection of Muslim legends and an early work of polemic against Islam called *The Apology of al-Kindi*. Subsequently an annotator made some additions to these works, and these were taken by later students to be as authoritative as the texts themselves.[57] This seemed an enormously positive step forward and yet it would produce a tradition of polemic which, far from seeking an understanding of Islam, produced a distorted fantasy and helped to fuel the war effort. Peter the Venerable, a gentle and loving man, wrote a treatise which claims to reach out to the Muslims with love, but the title of his work shows the spirit in which it was conceived: *Summary of the whole heresy of the diabolical sect of the Saracens.*[58] It seemed impossible for Christians to see Islam as anything but a failed version of Christianity. The polemic against

the Muslims that developed in the Middle Ages and still continues to affect the way Westerners see Islam today perfectly reproduced the polemic of the martyrs of Cordova. The Muslim became the hated shadow-self of the Western Christian, hated therefore with an irrational and neurotic intensity.

The second half of the twelfth century was a time when people were beginning to draw back from crusading and to seek a more peaceful form of religion. Here and there isolated scholars in Europe were questioning the validity of the holy war. Thus the Anglo-Norman Crusader who took part in the Christian conquest of Lisbon in 1147, and who wrote an account of the campaign, reeled back in horror at the thought of further massacres of Muslims like the one he had witnessed. 'Stay now your hand, Lord,' he pleaded, 'it is enough.'[59] Isaac, the Abbot of Étoile, was extremely disturbed to hear about a new (unnamed) military order, which 'despoils licitly and murders religiously.' Isaac calls this order a *monstrum novum* (a modern abomination) and finds it impossible to square the cruelty of the order with 'Christ's clemency, patience, or manner of teaching'.[60] Walter Map (d.1209), Eleanor of Aquitaine's secretary, also found the military orders worrying. It was 'with the word of the Lord, not with the edge of the sword' that 'the Apostles conquered Damascus, Alexandria and a great part of the world'.[61] None of these writers condemned crusading entirely, but they do show that here and there people were beginning to see a deep contradiction between the Crusades and the teaching of Christ. Most people repressed this perception very thoroughly and Crusades continued to set out for the Holy Land, but it is significant that when the scholars of the period turn to the study of Islam they continue to see it as the religion of the sword, a view that is still accepted as a self-evident truth by large numbers of people in the Western world.

Islam, we have seen, is no more violent than either Judaism or Christianity and indeed set a pattern of peaceful coexistence and conquest early in its history. What the Western scholars of the twelfth century were doing was creating a fantasy that had very little to do with Islam, but which had a great deal to do with the problem of Christianity's violence. When Robert of Ketton translates the words of Sura 88 in the Koran, 'For thou art to be a teacher not a coercer', the Annotator leaps in with an astonishing attack on Mohammad:

> Why then dost thou teach that men are to be converted to thy religion by the sword? If thou art not a coercer but a teacher, why dost thou subject men by power, like animals and brute beasts, and not by reasoning like men? In fact, like the liar you are, you everywhere contradict yourself.[62]

The Annotator is commenting on words that state unequivocally that Islam is *not* a religion of the sword; he also had before him in the Koran Mohammad's positive teaching about the People of the Book and his admonitions to his followers to exercise restraint in their *jihad* against Mecca, which was to be a defensive and not an aggressive war. Yet although the Western scholar has evidence in front of him that contradicts his thesis, what he 'sees' is the violence of Islam. He cannot be convinced by the Koran: because Mohammad is a 'liar', you cannot trust a word he says and so the evidence of the Koran is worthless. Islam *has* to be a violent religion because Europe would have it so. Peter the Venerable, a kindly, tolerant man who accused St Bernard of a heartless intolerance when he took Abelard into Cluny after the Council of Sens, insists at the opening of his thesis that he wants to reach out toward the Muslims in love: 'I approach you, not as men often do, with arms,' he writes to the Muslim he imagines reading his book, 'but with words; not with force but with reason, not in hatred but in love. . . . I love you, loving you I write to you, writing to you I invite you to salvation.'[63] It is a positive approach, just as the translation work that he initiated in Spain was positive. Yet Peter will also ignore what is on the page in front of him and instead understand what he 'knows' at some deep but obscure level to be 'true' about Islam. Thus when he read Ketton's translation of the Koran, he had before him plenty of texts which show that Mohammad urged Muslims to speak courteously with the People of the Book and to stress their common ground: 'Our God and your God is one' (29:46). Yet Peter seems convinced that, alone of all religions in the world, the Koran refuses to discuss religion – unlike the Persians, the Greeks and the Romans who, in Peter's view, all sought the truth in peace. There was no substance in this belief. Muslims punished Christians who insulted Islam and the Prophet, but were perfectly ready to listen to a person of another religion expounding their religious views. Instead of reading the Koran as a whole, Peter will find an isolated verse in the Koran, take it quite out of context and then enlarge rhetorically on the meaning he extracts from this distorted text:

> For what is this? *If anyone wish to dispute with thee, say that thou hast turned thy face and the faces of thy followers to God.* O Mohammad . . . if you make no other reply, except about turning your face and the faces of your followers to God, shall I believe what you say to be true? Shall I believe you to be a true prophet of God? Shall I believe the religion which you delivered to your people to have been delivered to you by God? I shall indeed be more than a donkey if I agree; I shall be more than cattle if I consent.[64]

Words that refer to purely internal Muslim affairs have been taken as a general statement of exclusion of any other point of view. Instead, Peter claims, Islam imposes itself by the sword alone and with horrible violence. 'Words fail . . . at such bestial cruelty.'[65] Even a fair-minded man like Peter was impelled to lay aside reason and objectivity when he came to view Islam and still needed to see it as a violent and intolerant faith.

Neither the Annotator nor Peter the Venerable consider the Crusades. The Annotator does not recall Bernard's remark that the pagan problem can only be solved by the sword. Peter the Venerable could condemn the use of force and insist that he would approach Muslims only in a spirit of love, and yet when Louis VII left for the Crusade he wrote to him saying that he hoped he killed as many Muslims as Moses (*sic*) and Joshua killed Amorites and Canaanites. He wrote also to the Grand Master of the Temple, expressing his lifelong admiration of the order in its fight against the Saracens. It was a paradoxical and neurotic complex.

Just as it was impossible for Christians to see Islam as anything but a failed form of their own religion, so too it seemed impossible for them to see Islam as anything other than a violent religion, even though evidence to the contrary was staring them in the face. The Muslim had early established himself as the Christian enemy, and as such a part of the emerging identity of Western Christendom. He was, therefore, part of the Christian soul and was made to carry the burden of Western anxiety about Christian violence. Books and television programmes today that sport titles like *Sword of Islam* or *Militant Islam* are still reverting to that old stereotype, and the obstinacy with which people still cling to the idea of Islam as 'the religion of the sword' shows that at some level people *need* to believe it. Certainly in Israel today hawks like Raphael Eytan will justify taking a hard line with all Palestinians on the grounds that the religion of Islam teaches Muslims to believe that all men of all other faiths are their enemies and have to be destroyed with violence.[66] To make peace with them is, therefore, impossible and this means that Jewish violence is justified and necessary.

At the same time as some medievals in the West were worrying about Christian violence, many others were worrying about sex. Celibacy and chastity had been part of the Cluniac programme for the Christianisation of Europe. During the

St Bernard and the Most Religious Crusade

159

twelfth century the popes were still fighting a battle against married clergy and in 1215 would finally succeed in imposing celibacy. At the same time penitentials and pious sermons presented sex as an expression of Original Sin and as incompatible with holiness. Bernard himself illustrates the sexual neurosis of the period. He was a dedicated misogynist in a long tradition of Christian misogyny and was so unable to cope with his sexuality that, when his own sister came to visit him wearing a new dress, Bernard flew into a violent rage and called her a filthy whore and a clod of dung.[67] Even Abelard and Heloise, the two great lovers of the period, did not glory in their passion like Romeo and Juliet but were both convinced that their love was deeply sinful, that marriage was a dishonourable state and that they both richly deserved the tragedy they suffered.[68] Islam does not denigrate sexual pleasure, but considers it a great gift of God, and teaches that the married state is more natural and a higher state than celibacy. Indeed, the fleshly strain that we find in the poetry of some of the troubadours was probably influenced by Arab love poetry and Muslim mystical poetry,[69] which describe both the love of men and women and the love of God in frankly erotic terms. But the Christian scholars of the period could only condemn this appreciation of sexuality and therefore they attacked 'Islam' as a religion that had been deliberately set up to encourage promiscuity and lust. One biography of Mohammad by a Pisan author has Mohammad say to his followers: 'You have established me as king that I may furnish you with an easier religion, by which you may both serve God and freely enjoy the delights of the world.'[70] There is an ill-concealed envy in much of this. Biographies of Mohammad by Christians describe the Prophet's sex life in a manner that reveals far more about their own sexual problems than about the facts of the Prophet's life. The Koran was said, quite incorrectly, to condone homosexuality and to encourage unnatural forms of intercourse. One scholar claimed that the foulness of lust among Muslims was inexpressible; they were deep in this filth from the soles of the feet to the crown of the head.[71] Soon the Church would accuse any outgroup in Christendom of excessive and unnatural sexual practices and twelfth-century Christians stigmatised the 'heresy' of Islam by cursing what they considered its sexual laxity. Today we continue in this tradition: at a time when many people in the West are liberating themselves from the sexual repressions of their Christian past, Islam is constantly denigrated as a sexually repressive religion. We have completely reversed the old stereotype and not many people seem interested in the truth of the matter or wish to find out about Islam itself. They simply want to bolster their own needs against their long-established counter-image: 'Islam'. I will discuss this in Chapter 9.

By the time of Thomas Aquinas, therefore, Islam was considered a Christian heresy that encouraged sex and violence. The Muslim had acquired a new identity in the West that was entirely a Western creation and did not spring from any real contact with Muslims. In the Crusader states, writers did not produce these fantasies because they were surrounded by real Muslims who would have made such distortion impossible. At the same time as scholars in Europe were producing this image of Islam, the Devil was becoming a new force in the Christian imagination and gaining a power he never had in the Bible. He was becoming a monster of enormous power who was also a distorted human being. Often he had animal characteristics or monstrous genitals, aspects of humanity that the Church was teaching Christians to reject. One could say that one of the great problems of ethical monotheism as expressed by Christianity is that it encourages an unhealthy projection. Because it is axiomatic that there is no evil in God, this makes it difficult for Christians to accept what is either evil or what they are told is evil in themselves. They tend to reject this 'evil' and once they have rejected it, it becomes inhuman and monstrous with threatening power. The Devil is the greatest of these projections and is unique in its horror to Christianity. The monstrous Muslim is clearly a similar projection: Christians could not accept their holy violence or their repressed sexuality, so they projected all this on to the enemies they were fighting in the Holy Land, who were already seen as the inhuman enemies of God.

There were also new fantasies about the Jews, the other victims of the Crusaders. Although the official Church prohibited the persecution of Jews, churchmen had ambivalent attitudes which affected the people. Gregory VII pointed out that in their own Bible they had constantly sinned and God had to punish them. It also seemed inconceivable that the Jews who had witnessed Jesus' miracles and teaching could reject him, and this made people begin to see them as extraordinary beings – almost inhuman. This sense of the Jews' otherness was compounded by their use of foreign practices like circumcision, sabbath worship and special dietary laws which set them apart from their Christian neighbours in the diaspora. And, as with many such outgroups, myths and legends developed about the Jewish people: Jews were said to have secret tails, for example, or a peculiar smell. These fears and fantasies fuelled the wave of persecution that broke out each time a Crusade was preached.

In 1144, however, a new horror crept into the mythology about the people of Israel. Just before Easter and Passover a small boy called William disappeared from his home in Norwich, England, and his body was later found abandoned in the forest nearby, with many lacerations. His mother and a local priest accused the Jewish community of the murder and this was confirmed by some Christian servants who worked in a Jewish household. They claimed to have watched William's murder through a chink in the door and seen their Jewish masters crucify William and pierce his side. The local sheriff refused to believe these tales and hustled the Jews to safety in Norwich castle. Two years later, however, at the time of the Second Crusade a bishop was appointed to Norwich who approved of the cult of 'Saint' William, which had flourished because of the manner of his death. There was a new anti-semitic outbreak in the city and one Jew was killed. William's tomb now became an official cult centre with pilgrims and a profusion of miracles and this naturally led to a new hostility against his so-called murderers. At about this time another element crept into the myth. It was pointed out that the day the murder was discovered was 22 March, in that year the second day of Passover. It was well known that during this season Jews ate special unleavened bread and there was also a legend that from the moment that the Jews had sent Jesus to his death with the cry 'His blood be upon us and upon our children' they had been subject to a special curse. Jews had suffered from haemorrhoids and the only remedy that could save them was, their sages said, 'the blood of Christ'. The sages had meant that the Jews should be converted to Christianity but the Jews had misunderstood them, with their usual perversity, and decided that they had to murder a Christ substitute each year and mix his blood with their special Passover bread. In 1146 one Theodore of Cambridge, a convert from Judaism, came forward with a tale that linked William's death with this Jewish practice. Every year, he said, a Jewish council in Toledo appointed one of the Jewish communities in the diaspora to perform this murder and acquire the necessary blood and in 1144 the lot had fallen to Norwich.[72] Two anti-semitic legends thus became associated with William's shrine in Norwich: ritual murder and the Blood Libel. Stories like this circulated fast within England and Europe and every time a child disappeared in suspicious circumstances, the Jews would be blamed.

What was clearly happening was that, in a rather different way from the Muslims, the Jews were being made the alien and the enemy of Christians. New fantasies would be produced about both these crusading victims as the xenophobia of Europe increased and the Jews would suffer especially from the new craze for persecuting heretics in Europe, which will be discussed in Chapter 10. The Jews were becoming inhuman and monstrous beings and, like the Muslims, were acquiring a demonic identity. In pictures Antichrist was increasingly given Jewish features and even an intelligent man like Thomas Aquinas believed that Antichrist would be a Jew of the tribe of Dan.[73] The anti-semitic fantasies acquired a boost every time there was an outbreak of crusading enthusiasm, so that in the minds of the crusading generations the Jews and the Muslims were linked in a diabolical bond: both were monstrous enemies of Christ and of Christians and both were bound up with the Christian identity. Both were the creations of the unhealthy Christian subconscious, and the greed with which the mythology about Muslims and Jews was gobbled up shows that it was psychologically necessary to European Christians. That this should have been the case shows that, although Europe was making great strides in the direction of progress, the Western soul was unhealthily haunted by frightening fantasies that were neurotic projections of self. These fantasies would not die away as Europe became more confident. We shall see that they continued to grow as Europe developed and mirrored the process of change.

These fantasies, like the Second Crusade itself, reveal in the holy-war mentality a denial of human reason and a flight to forms of thought and to behaviour which, consciously or unconsciously, depart from normality. This seems to be a characteristic of both the Christian and the Jewish holy wars, which tend to develop along similar lines. This tendency has obvious perils. It precludes the possibility of peaceful coexistence with the monstrous enemies of God and means that the champions of the divine plan will feel justified in taking extreme and abnormal measures to see that it is enforced, even if this seems to court disaster. Normality and rationality are no longer appropriate when it is a matter of translating the supernatural values of God into human history: 'For my thoughts are not your thoughts, my ways not your ways – it is Yahweh who speaks. Yes, the heavens are as high above the earth as my ways are above your ways, my thoughts above your thoughts' (Isaiah, 55:8–9). To one who cannot share this perspective, the actions and policies of such a holy warrior seem not only fanatical but absolutely mad. Because they are by their very nature quite unpredictable, they can be extremely dangerous in a delicate political situation, like that which existed in the Near East during the Middle Ages, which is not at all unlike the situation today. In the anxious years that followed the Second Crusade, many of the Franks realised that if their kingdom was to survive they would have to exercise all their diplomacy and political astuteness. Others, however, felt that such rational pragmatism was unworthy and lacking in faith. The Holy Land must be defended in God's way, not according to the limited perspectives of prudence and reason.

The Muslim holy war continued to operate within a shrewdly political context. The year after the Crusaders' defeat at Damascus Muir ad-Din Unur died, and power passed to the nominal sovereign of the city, a young man of sixteen named 'Abaq, who was unable to establish an effective rule. Nur ad-Din marched to Damascus and camped outside the city, but his intention was not to conquer Damascus but to win it over peacefully, as Mohammad had conquered Mecca. He was more concerned to win the sympathy of the civilians, among whom he had become almost a cult figure because of his sober piety and spectacular military success: when rain fell after a long drought, shortly after Nur ad-Din had pitched camp outside the city, the people put it down to Nur ad-Din. The Sultan presented himself to the city as its protector against the Franks. In a letter to the leaders of Damascus, he insisted that this was not a siege, but that he had simply come because 'the complaints of the Muslims have induced me to act in this way, for the peasants have been despoiled of their goods and separated from their children by the Franj and they have no one to defend them.'[74] He could well understand, he

added shrewdly, why Muir ad-Din and his advisers had been forced to make a treaty with the Franks; they had not been in a military or political position to oppose them. But they had nevertheless 'criminally wronged' their 'poorest subjects' by this policy. The leaders still held out against Nur ad-Din, but the ordinary people, who had naturally been shocked and terrified by the Franks' treachery, took the point and from this time the Sultan's name was mentioned in the Friday sermons, right after the Caliph and 'Abaq.[75] Nur ad-Din continued this policy of discrediting 'Abaq, who had actually made a truce with the Franks against Nur ad-Din. In letter after letter he accused the young ruler of treachery and begged him to join his *jihad* against the Christians. Gradually 'Abaq became more and more isolated and public opinion in Damascus inclined strongly to Nur ad-Din, who seemed the truer Muslim. On 18 April 1154 Nur ad-Din and his army arrived outside Damascus again and, after a token assault, the city accepted Nur ad-Din as their sultan.[76] The following day he made a speech to the ulema, the qadis and the merchants, made some important tax cuts and brought along large supplies of food for the poor. For the first time in its history, the Kingdom of Jerusalem was opposed by both the great Syrian cities of Aleppo and Damascus, under a young and dynamic ruler who was dedicated to its destruction.

We shall see that this shrewd politicking in the name of God has continued to characterise the leaders of today's *jihad*, who like Nur ad-Din often present themselves as the friend of the poor, and discredit rulers by pointing out that they are colluding with the real enemies of the Muslim people. It is obviously quite a different approach from the irrational policies of the Crusaders. Yet at about this time another element of the *jihad* was establishing itself in Syria, whose methods have also been adopted by Muslims today in their holy war. These methods seem much more fanatical and closer to the Christian flight from normality. A sect of Muslim extremists from Iran who were known by their enemies as the Hashashin, because they allegedly used marijuana to achieve exotic mystical states, was beginning to occupy mountain fortresses in what is now Syria and the Lebanon Eventually they had what amounted to a mini-state in the mountainous region between the Muslim city of Hama and the Christian city of Latakia, on the coast. The Hashashin were Shiite Muslims; that is, they differed from the Sunni majority in refusing to accept the legitimacy of the Baghdad caliphate. They believed that the successor of Mohammad should be a descendant of Ali, the Prophet's nephew and son-in-law and it may be that they had come to Syria in order to be closer to Egypt, which at that time was ruled by a Shiite caliph. Although there were no real theological or religious differences between Shiites and Sunni Muslims, the Hashashin were implacably opposed to the Sunni rule and were working for the triumph of the Shia, which they believed would usher in a golden age. The sect had started during the tenth century, when the Seljuk Turks had begun to invade Iranian and Iraqi territory and imposed the Sunni tradition. The Hashashin made the *hijra* to inaccessible mountain fortresses, whence they prepared for a *jihad* according to the usual paradigm. In their formidable castles, they practised a form of gnostic mysticism, introducing the initiate to esoteric and secret knowledge which they claimed was the true Islam. But the Hashashin did not confine their activities to mystical prayer. They also fought a *jihad* of terrorism. Individual members undertook the murder of prominent members of the Sunni establishment in missions that were usually suicidal because of their extreme danger. Thus the Hashashin gave us our word 'assassin'.[77]

The Assassins became a deadly force to be reckoned with, because of an inherent weakness in the Islamic political system. When a leader died, there was usually a complete upheaval and the new ruler would not be able to establish his legitimacy automatically but would have to do so by means of his achievements. An empire like Nur ad-Din's would usually disintegrate after the death of its conqueror and this meant that assassination was very effective indeed in undermining the stability of the Sunni establishment. Though the Assassins may have looked like mindless fanatics, therefore, they were actually almost inhumanly rational and their suicide missions, like those of most of their counterparts today, were not conducted in blind, passionate fervour, but coldly and with full deliberation. Discipline was the keynote of their organisation together with an absolute loyalty and obedience to their sheikh. The arrival of the Assassins in Syria was actually very helpful to the Christians, because these terrorists concentrated on the Sunnis and were not very interested in killing Franks. Consequently in their struggle against the Crusaders, most of the Sunni leaders would henceforth be fighting with one very wary eye on the Assassins. In fact the first response of Westerners to Muslim terrorism was very reverential. Troubadours sang of their exemplary fidelity and loyalty and promised to serve their ladies as selflessly as the Assassins served their sheikh; they too would be ready to die in her service.[78] This Western admiration is not very surprising, because of the suicidal tendency in crusading. Further, the Assassins and the Templars had a good deal in common. Both vowed absolute military obedience to the leader, the Sheikh or the Grand Master, even if this were suicidal. The Templars' monasteries were also fortresses like the Assassins', and it has been suggested that the Templar practice of colonisation was influenced by the Assassin practice. Both used their fortresses not merely to establish borders, but to push their frontiers forward and to establish a new sphere of influence in enemy territory. In the sect of the Assassins, therefore, the Muslim *jihad* in some ways came quite close to the Christian Crusade.

In 1157 Nur ad-Din became seriously ill and did not recover his health for nearly two years. This gave him time to reflect on his future policy and he realised that he would now have to put his *jihad* into effect. His emirs urged him to start with an attack on nearby Antioch; Nur ad-Din refused, pointing out that Antioch had never belonged to the Muslims but had been a Byzantine city. He had no wish to antagonise the Emperor of Rum and indeed in 1159 Manuel had been able to reassert his suzerainty over the Frankish principality as well as over the Turkish states in Anatolia. This sudden resurgence in Byzantine military power held Nur ad-Din back from making a sweeping reconquest of the Kingdom of Jerusalem, for the Byzantines now threatened his borders to the north and Manuel would not allow Nur ad-Din to upset the balance of power in the Middle East any further. There seemed to be a stalemate, but suddenly the war between the Muslims and the Frankish Christians found a new theatre. King Amalric of Jerusalem woke to a sudden realisation of the strategic importance of Egypt and in 1162 he decided to invade the Shiite state. Nur ad-Din was obliged to send his general Shirkuh to Egypt to support its Shiite and suppress this new Christian offensive. From this point, Egypt would play a vital part in the story of the Crusades.

· CHAPTER SIX ·

1168–1192

A Religious Jihad *and a Secular Crusade*

In December 1168 Nur ad-Din got a desperate message from the ruler of Egypt, begging him to rescue his country from the Franks. In October King Amalric of Jerusalem had invaded Egypt, seized Bilbays and massacred all its inhabitants, Coptic Christians as well as Muslims. In terror, the citizens of Cairo had barricaded themselves into the new city and had burned down old Cairo to save it from the monstrous Christians: the fire raged for fifty-four days. This was simply the last act in a struggle for Egypt which had occupied Christians and Muslims for six years, and Nur ad-Din at once sought out his brilliant Kurdish lieutenant Shirkuh, who had fought an extraordinary series of campaigns in Egypt since 1163. A wild, obese, one-eyed, tough old warrior who was adored by his troops, Shirkuh jumped at the chance to finish the Egyptian problem once and for all. He turned to his nephew, who was standing beside him, and cried: 'Yusuf, pack your things, we're going!'[1] Yusuf could scarcely have been more different from his uncle. He was a slightly built young man of thirty-one, with handsome melancholy features that would suddenly break into a dazzling smile. He had delicate health and a sensitive temperament that moved him easily and frequently to tears. Yusuf had fought with Shirkuh in Egypt two years earlier and looked back at the campaign with horror, so when he heard his uncle's order, he recalled later, he was terrified: 'I felt as if my heart had been pierced by a dagger, and I answered, "In God's name, even if I were granted the entire kingdom of Egypt, I would not go."'[2] He pleaded the trauma of his last campaign in Alexandria and pointed out that he had financial problems. Yet Shirkuh insisted that his presence in Egypt was absolutely vital and Nur ad-Din peremptorily ordered the young man to go, giving him money to finance the campaign. Yusuf set off, 'like a man being led to his death'.[3] Yet this timid reluctant young Emir would become one of the most remarkable and dedicated heroes of the *jihad*. More usually known by his title Salah ad-Din (the righteousness of the faith), he was revered by both East and West and was the only Muslim hero to have been given a Western version of his name by his admirers in Europe. What happened to transform Saladin into a passionate soldier of Allah?

In the event there was no fighting in Egypt, for Amalric had been so appalled by the dedicated hatred of the Cairenes that he had withdrawn his troops, and Shirkuh was hailed by the Egyptians as a liberator. They were eager to accept him as their ruler for the affairs of Egypt were in chaos. The Egyptian caliphate had been very powerful and a great threat to the Crusaders when they first arrived in Palestine, but by the mid-twelfth century it was in decline. The Caliph possessed very little real power and Egypt was ruled by a vizier; none of the recent viziers had been able to establish a strong government. Ten days after he arrived in Egypt, with the full approval of the young Caliph, Shirkuh sent Saladin to assassinate the present Vizier and took the office himself. Shiite Egypt was now part of Nur ad-Din's Sunni empire, and this drastically altered the balance of power in the area. The Emperor Manuel and Amalric were appalled and decided to unite in a joint offensive against the formidable Shirkuh. God seemed on their side, for, just two months after he had become vizier, Shirkuh died of a massive bout of overeating. The Christians felt even more cheerful when the new Vizier had been appointed.

There were many doughty emirs in the army who would have done the job well and who had a strong claim to the honour because of their faithful service in the long Egyptian campaign. But the situation in Egypt was difficult. The Caliph's advisers obviously wanted an easily manipulated vizier who would not threaten the institution of the caliphate, and this solution also suited Nur ad-Din. The election of a strong Sunni leader at this moment could have been unnecessarily provocative, for some elements in the country were not entirely sure that they wanted to commit themselves to Nur ad-Din now that the Frankish threat had subsided. Nur ad-Din was also worried that a strong, ambitious vizier might threaten the unity of his empire. Egypt was a very long way from Aleppo and separated from it by the Frankish kingdom. If the new Vizier wanted to create a centre of personal power, he would not be easy to control. All in all it seemed wise to look around for a weak character who would do what he was told, and there was one obvious candidate. Ibn al-Athir writes: 'the advisers of the Caliph al-Adid suggested that he name Yusuf the new vizier, because he was the youngest, and seemingly the most inexperienced and weakest of the emirs in the army.'[4]

Yet this kind of reasoning is often dangerous. We have seen how a sudden unlooked-for reversal of fortune can make a whole people feel that it has a divine destiny and the same is undoubtedly true also of individuals. From being the most despised emir in the army, Saladin suddenly found himself with the title *al-malik al-nasir* (the victorious king). He was dressed in the white and gold turban of the Vizier and a scarlet-lined tunic; a jewel-encrusted sword was put into his hand, he was mounted on a splendid chestnut horse with a jewelled bridle and he found himself living in the Vizier's palatial residence. A sensitive man like Saladin found this astonishing and even shocking. He had not wanted to come to Egypt at all, yet now he was the Vizier. The only explanation he could find was that he had a special divine calling and from that moment Saladin became a deeply religious man. Despite all the splendid trappings of his new life, he started to live very frugally as befitted an Islamic ruler.[5] At the end of his life he left only forty-seven *drachmas*, even though he was the most powerful man in the Middle East. He gave away whole provinces to anybody who asked him and distributed everything he had to the poor. His long-suffering treasurers used to keep a reserve hidden from him to provide for emergencies. He also began a serious course of study with the leading *mujtahids* and got one of them to write a catechism of the Islamic faith for his own use, which he studied with passionate delight. His friend and biographer Baha ad-Din says that he was a confident theologian and always enjoyed a lively theological discussion.[6] But his faith was also distinguished by a strong personal feeling. Whenever he was free from affairs of state he used to love to read the *hadith* (the traditions about the life of Mohammad) and often he used to invite Baha ad-Din to read with him. The two men always made their morning prayers together and Baha ad-Din noticed how frequently Saladin would weep with emotion at prayer or when one of the *hadith* moved him. Tears would flow again when Saladin heard a particularly moving verse of the Koran recited, and he used to seek out the expert reciters of the holy book and sit eagerly at their feet.[7] From the moment he was elected vizier, therefore, he had a new identity: his whole life centred on the beliefs, the principles and the passions of Islam.

Yet Saladin did not simply feel called to return to religion and live as a good Muslim ruler; his vocation was far more specific. Years after he had been elected vizier he said: 'When God gave me the land of Egypt, I was sure that he meant Palestine for me too.'[8] He was convinced that Allah had called him to lead the *jihad* against the Franks. It is not surprising that when he turned to religion, he was inspired by the holy-war ideal. He had grown up in Nur ad-Din's court, and there the integrity of Islam was seen as inseparable from the *jihad* against the Christians. It was natural, therefore, that Saladin's new religious identity should measure itself against the enemy of Islam. What was astonishing was the passion with which he threw himself into the *jihad* and how deeply his religious conversion changed his personality. Baha ad-Din shows us that he became obsessed with the *jihad*:

> The Holy War and the suffering involved in it weighed heavily on his heart and his whole being in every limb; he spoke of nothing else, thought only about equipment for the fight, was interested only in those who had taken up arms, had little sympathy with anyone who spoke of anything else or encouraged any other activity. For the love of the Holy War and on God's path he left his family and his sons, his homeland, his house and all his estates, and chose out of all the world to live in the shade of his tent, where the winds blew on him from every side.[9]

What had happened to the timid Yusuf who had begged not to be forced to go to fight the Franks in Egypt? It seems that his old fears had left him completely. His whole life was now dedicated to warfare and, as Baha ad-Din records, he never left the front line even when he was ill – which happened frequently as his health was never robust. During the campaign he made it an inflexible rule that each day he would make one or two circuits of the enemy camp and 'in the thick of battle he would move through the ranks, accompanied only by a page with a war horse led on a bridle.'[10] This way he would traverse the whole army and create a sense of unity and common purpose. His religious conversion had obviously unlocked the complex of his former fears and touched reserves within him that nobody had imagined he possessed, least of all himself. He was quite clearly a new man, liberated from his old limitations and gripped by a compelling sense of destiny which made him suddenly powerful and formidable.

The new sense of confidence manifested itself very quickly. Within two months Saladin managed to secure his position in Egypt. He put down a revolt in the Egyptian army and smartly repelled the joint Christian attack of Amalric and Manuel, which fortunately for him had been very badly organised. He was clearly not the weak leader that his enemies had hoped. But soon he faced a new danger. Nur ad-Din, who had a hearty contempt for Shiite Muslims, demanded that Saladin abolish the Shiite caliphate and bring Egypt into Sunni Islam, which was obedient to the Caliph of Baghdad. Saladin had already got rid of the officials who seemed to be loyal Shiites and replaced them with Sunnis who were loyal to himself, but it seemed very risky to demote the Shiite Caliph, which might well antagonise the Egyptian people at this crucial time. He also suspected Nur ad-Din of being motivated more by politics than by religion. There is no religious or theological difference between Shiite and Sunni Islam: the difference is political and concerned with the Muslim leadership. There was no religious reason why Shiites and Sunnis could not live in peace together and engage in the same *jihad* against their common enemy, the Franks. Saladin had also become extremely fond of the young Caliph under whom he was serving, and he did not want to betray this friendship, especially as the Caliph was seriously ill at this time. But events were taken out of his hands. On Friday 10 September 1171 a Sunni visitor from Mosul (possibly planted by Nur ad-Din) climbed into the pulpit of a mosque in Cairo and said the prayer in the name of the Caliph of Baghdad, whom the Shiites considered a usurper. It was a direct challenge to the Egyptian caliphate and Saladin was forced to support it or become a traitor to the Sunna. The next Friday he gave orders that there was to be no further mention of the Shiite caliphs in the mosques of Egypt. By this time the Caliph was dying and Saladin forbade anyone to tell him. 'If he recovers,' he said, 'then there will be plenty of time for him to find out. If not, let him die untormented.'[11] Shortly afterwards the Caliph did die without learning that his dynasty had been abolished, and curiously enough there was no public outrage at this switch from Shiah to Sunni Islam. The caliphate – a political institution only – had been dead in fact if not in name for many years. Egyptians were enjoying the new security Saladin had brought to the country and were ready to accept the Sunni faith if this was part of the package. Nur ad-Din had hoped that abolishing the caliphate would bring Egypt more firmly under his rule but it actually gave Saladin himself much more power. Hitherto he had been not the official head of state but only the functioning head of state; now that the Caliph had gone there was only the Vizier.

A few months later Saladin began the *jihad* by leading a daring attack against the Frankish fortress of Shawbak on the east bank of the Jordan. The Franks were just about to surrender when Saladin heard that Nur ad-Din had arrived to join him in the holy war and at once he withdrew his troops and marched them back to Cairo. His official excuse was that he had wind of a sudden uprising in Egypt but his real reason was much more complicated. Saladin believed that *he* was the man called to liberate Palestine, but where did that leave Nur ad-Din, who had been calling for a *jihad* for over twenty years? At Shawbak, the Sultan would have tethered Saladin firmly to his own banner, yet that did not seem right to Saladin because he felt convinced that *he* should lead the *jihad*. Was Saladin just an ambitious young traitor, who was using religion as a cover for his own empire-building? His behaviour during these years is often dubious and Saladin himself was confused and worried about his position. One must not explain away his religious conversion wholly in this way, because his zeal lasted until he died in 1193, years after the threat from Nur ad-Din was over. His sudden departure from Shawbak also indicates a conflict in Saladin. He showed himself desperately anxious to avoid actually meeting his master, largely because he must have felt that his own conviction of righteousness would fade once he faced the saintly Nur ad-Din. By no stretch of the imagination could Nur ad-Din be reckoned one of the unworthy leaders whom it was an Islamic duty to reject. He was widely regarded as a Muslim saint: throughout Syria Muslims offered prayers in his name and saw him as the new saviour of Islam. He had created the form of Saladin's own new-found piety, with its emphasis on poverty and the *jihad*. There must have been a deep fear that, once he was face to face with this austere and formidable man, Saladin would become the frightened Yusuf once again and his new confidence and power would drain away.

As for Nur ad-Din himself, he was rightly suspicious and he threatened to come to Egypt in person to assert his authority. Nervously Saladin asked his advisers whether he should be ready to fight and, trembling with rage, his father Ayyub argued for loyalty to the great son of Zangi:

> I am your father, and if there is anyone here who loves you and wishes you well it is I. But know this: if Nur ad-Din came, nothing could ever prevent me from bowing before him and kissing the ground at his feet. If he ordered me to lop off your head with my sabre, I would do it. For this land is his. You shall write this to him: I have learned that you wanted to lead an expedition to Egypt, but there

is no need for you to do so. This country belongs to you, and you need only send me a charger or camel and I will come to you a humble and submissive man.[12]

Yet Ayyub was by no means as forthright and simple in private. In private he assured his son that 'if Nur ad-Din tried to take so much as an inch of your territory I would fight to the death against him. But why allow yourself to *appear* overly ambitious? Time is on your side. Let Providence act.'[13] He had a conflict too. On the one hand he was certain that Providence had marked his son for greatness but he was clearly aware that at the moment his position seemed dubious and 'appeared' ambitious. Saladin took his father's advice: he sent a submissive message to Nur ad-Din which seemed to satisfy the Sultan for the present. At the same time he sent his brother Shams ad-Daula to conquer the Yemen, which he did quite easily, to provide a place of refuge for the Ayyubid clan if things should get difficult for them in Egypt. He was clearly not as confident of victory as he sometimes appeared. In the event, however, the conflict with Nur ad-Din convinced him still more deeply of his divine election to the *jihad*.

In 1173 Saladin set out once again to attack the Franks east of the Jordan in a burst of confidence. Exactly the same thing happened as had happened two years earlier. Nur ad-Din set out to join him in the noble *jihad* and Saladin instantly turned back to Cairo. This time the excuse was that his father was dying, and in fact Ayyub had recently had an accident and was in a coma, but this did not satisfy Nur ad-Din. The Sultan decided that it was time to put this rebellious young Vizier firmly in his place and started to mobilise his troops for an expedition to Egypt. Saladin could only wait, certain now that he was finished. But then there was an act of divine salvation: in the midst of his preparations the Sultan Nur ad-Din died suddenly of a heart attack on 15 May 1174 at the age of sixty. To Saladin it seemed that God had spoken and confirmed him in his vocation. His astonishing luck could only be explained by divine providence.

He now began to assert his leadership against the supporters of Nur ad-Din's son al-Salih, who was only eleven years old. The death of his master seemed to have released a new level of aggression and confidence in Saladin: immediately he claimed the regency of al-Salih in a threatening and violent missive to the city of Damascus, where the young Sultan was in residence. The tone was so uncharacteristically fierce that it disconcerted al-Salih's supporters and they and the Sultan retreated to Aleppo when they heard that Saladin's army was marching to Damascus. When the Vizier of Egypt arrived, the city of Damascus opened its gates to him voluntarily and acknowledged him as the successor of Nur ad-Din. Saladin followed up this victory by conquering the cities of Homs and Hama, which put him in a powerful position in Syria. But Aleppo and Mosul still held out against him and rallied round al-Salih. They decided to call in the Assassins who were only too delighted to take on the man who had abolished the Shiite caliphate of Egypt. Early in 1175 three Assassins made an attempt on Saladin's life, but they were surprised by his guards and were all massacred. But on 22 May 1176 there was a much more successful attack. While Saladin was asleep in his tent, an Assassin rushed in and dealt him a dagger blow first on the head and then on the neck. Fortunately Saladin had taken to wearing protective mail underneath his clothes after the last attack and the blade did not penetrate. At that moment one of the emirs came on the scene and he killed the assailant, but another Assassin and then a third appeared and fell upon Saladin. They were massacred by the guards, who had been quickly alerted, and Saladin came reeling out of his tent unharmed. Naturally he saw his preservation as a divine act but he also decided to follow up this salvation by conventional practical methods.

In August 1176 his army marched into central Syria, Assassin-land, and besieged the great Assassin fortress of Masyaf. But then abruptly the siege was lifted under very mysterious circumstances and Saladin turned back without having struck a single blow. There are two explanations given. Ibn al-Athir says that Rashin ad-Din Sinan, the Sheikh of the Assassins, sent Saladin a note threatening to assassinate his whole family unless he abandoned the siege. It was a threat that nobody who knew anything about the Assassins would take lightly. The second story comes from the Assassins themselves: it says that one night Saladin woke up and saw a stranger leaving his tent, whom he was certain was Sinan himself. Beside his bed he found a poisoned cake and a note that read: 'You are in our power.'[14] Terrified out of his mind, Saladin ordered the retreat.

For another five years Saladin fought an endless war against Aleppo and Mosul, against the Franks and against other opponents in Iraq and Mesopotamia. It was an exhausting struggle, but it was clear that he was in the ascendancy despite his ignominious defeat by the Assassins. His power depended on a great deal more than force of arms. He was gradually being seen as the true successor of Nur ad-Din, even though he had fought the saintly son of Zangi during his lifetime. This was because he practised Nur ad-Din's virtues. He could be seen to be continuing his tradition and presenting himself to the Muslims of the Middle East as a more legitimate Islamic ruler than his opponents. He even surpassed Nur ad-Din in some respects. Like his former master he was zealous about living frugally and generously but Nur ad-Din had been a rather formal, distant man. Muslim tradition teaches that a ruler must not segregate himself from his people and Nur ad-Din had been genuinely loved by the people and devoted to their interests. But he had tended to withdraw into formality and inspired a certain awe. This disappeared in Saladin's much more informal court and Saladin frequently astonished his contemporaries by his friendly identification with the people. He always used to eat with his soldiers, and would retire from them only to pray. He demanded no special treatment and never behaved like an enraged *prima donna* or a divine despot as some oriental rulers did at this time.[15] His general affability and easiness constantly impressed Baha ad-Din, who was amazed when his mule kicked Saladin on the thigh and his master simply smiled. Another time his mule splashed the Sultan and ruined all his clothes but Saladin only smiled and did not make Baha ad-Din ride further back.[16] He tells us of a tedious servant who pestered Saladin to sign a petition, even when Saladin pleaded desperate weariness, and who actually ordered his Sultan to go into his tent to get an inkwell. Saladin calmly signed the petition and waved away Baha ad-Din's effusive praises.[17] He had probably learned a valuable lesson from his uncle Shirkuh, whose men had loved him because he had been their comrade and shared all their dirt, but his accessibility and friendly informality also had an Islamic importance, which was not lost on his followers, who saw him as a ruler in the tradition of the earliest and most authentic caliphs.

This informality was only one of the things that made Saladin deeply loved, and the love he inspired was a far more lethal weapon against the leadership of al-Salih than his military victories. Saladin was not just a sultan but a warm human being who was both vulnerable himself and quickly responsive to other people's suffering, and this naturally made him more popular than the distant Nur ad-Din. When his nephew Taqi ad-Din died, he summoned some of his sons and close friends to tell them the news and 'wept pitifully enough to move to tears even those who did not know the reason for his weeping'.[18] Eventually the whole group was sobbing bitterly, until Baha ad-Din reminded them that they were on a *jihad* and should pull themselves together. Saladin's famous tears flowed again when a Frankish woman came into his camp to plead for the return of her little girl who had disappeared during a recent raid. The woman had heard how kind the King of the Muslims was, and her trust and distress moved Saladin to weep and order the child to be found and returned immediately.[19]

As a general rule, however, Saladin was implacable in his determination to throw the Franks from Palestine, even though he could be very kind to individual Christians. Just as he had outdone Nur ad-Din in being an accessible ruler, close to his people, so too he outdid him in his zeal for the *jihad*. As soon as Nur ad-Din died he mounted a propaganda campaign, mobilising the people in a holy war as Nur ad-Din had done and as Muslim leaders have done in our own day. Books and treaties were composed on the duty of *jihad*; Sufis and imams preached the doctrine of the holy war in the mosques and during the Friday sermon and an education campaign was mounted in the army. For the first time in the history of Islam the *hadith* were read to the troops when they were drawn up for battle and the reading and discussion took place while the army was mounted in the saddle and advancing towards the enemy.[20] For nearly twenty-five years Nur ad-Din had been teaching the people of Syria that a true Muslim should be ready to fight the Franks. Saladin was able to build on this and was seen to exceed his master in zeal. It was this that was ultimately crucial in making people accept him as their true and worthy ruler, despite his rather shady past. His ultimate success was inevitable. In 1181 al-Salih died and in 1183 Saladin entered Aleppo as its conqueror. He was now master of the whole of Syria except for Mosul, and for the first time in its history the Crusader kingdom was surrounded by a tightly mobilised Muslim empire that denied its right to exist. Hitherto the Crusader kingdoms had been able to capitalise on the disunity in the surrounding Turkish and Arab world, in rather the same way as Israel has profited by Arab disunity. By 1183 the isolated Western state was facing a new Muslim giant. How would the Christians react?

The Crusader Kingdom of Jerusalem was as isolated in the Middle East as Israel is today, but it need not have been. Unlike the Israelis, the Christians had natural allies in the area in the Eastern Christians, but religious chauvinism had antagonised this potentially powerful support. The Crusades had gravely increased the tension that had long existed between the Western Church and the Greek Orthodox empire of Byzantium and this meant that the Crusaders could not always rely on the powerful Byzantine empire for support. The Kings of Jerusalem had often been aware of the need to enlist Byzantium as an ally, but the clergy loathed the Greek Orthodox and had turned the Greek clergy out of churches that had been in their possession for centuries, had stripped these ancient churches of their icons and replaced them with Western images and statues of Western saints. The Greeks soon realised that they had been much better off under Islam. The same applied to the oriental churches of native Eastern Christians. These Christians were the remnant of the powerful Eastern Christianity that had been destroyed by the mass trend of conversion to Islam after the Islamic conquest. They were Churches of great antiquity but they held beliefs that seemed heretical to their Western brethren. These heresies concerned the nature of Christ and were of an abstruse philosophical nature that few of the Crusaders, who were not the most intellectual men in the world, would have been capable of understanding. The Jacobites of Syria and the Copts of Egypt, for example, were monophysites. That is they believed that Christ only had one nature, the divine, whereas Greek Orthodox and Western Christians believed that he had two natures: human and divine. The Maronites of Lebanon believed that Jesus only had one will, whereas Westerners believed that he had two, a divine and a human will, on the same principle. These aggressive quarrels about doctrines that depend on human philosophical speculation rather than on divine revelation show the doctrinal neurosis of Christianity, which is deplored by both Muslims and Jews. It was certainly dangerous to the security of the Crusader Kingdom of Jerusalem. Again, the kings had realised the importance of this powerful oriental support, and had tried to encourage the Native Christians to settle in the Crusader states. But the religious chauvinism of the clergy and of the military orders hated to have 'heretics' in their country or their army.

Through a belligerent religious intolerance, therefore, the Franks in the Crusader kingdoms had effectively isolated themselves and had antagonised the Eastern Christians whose support could have been invaluable to them when they were facing Saladin's new *jihad*. They were totally dependent upon Western support in rather the same way as Israel is today and were desperate for a Crusade to come from Europe to fight this new Muslim threat. The Crusader states always had a chronic shortage of manpower; they could take on small armies of Muslims but Saladin was amassing a bigger army than they had ever had to fight before. The crusading army was manned by the old baronial families, by the military orders and by new immigrants from the West, but immigration had slowed down by the 1180s. Further, the disaster of the Second Crusade had given the West a distrust of large-scale crusading and when the desperate Palestinian Franks asked for Crusaders to come from Europe to help them to fight Saladin, nobody came.

At a time when their Muslim neighbours were uniting under a strong leader, the Christians in the Crusader Kingdom of Jerusalem were so bitterly divided by internal factions that in 1183 when Saladin became master of Aleppo there was grave danger of a civil war. Amalric had died in 1174 and had been succeeded by his son Baldwin IV, who was a leper. The Leper King was a young man of great courage and determination, but his illness meant that he was often too sick to rule effectively and had to give power to a regent. It also meant that he could not always control his barons effectively and these barons had divided themselves into two main camps, which could be described as the doves and the hawks. The doves were usually men who had been born and bred in the Middle East and whose attitudes were naturally more oriental than Western. They believed that they should make peace with Saladin in formal peace treaties. Because they had always lived surrounded by Muslims they did not regard them as inhuman monsters and felt that if the state were to survive the present crisis the Christians must try to keep the peace until a Crusade arrived from the West. The hawks were mostly new immigrants from the West, who were appalled by the oriental laxity they

discovered among their brethren in the Holy Land. They felt that any contact with Muslims or peace treaties with them were dishonourable, that the Lord would help the Christians and that they should not rely on human prudence alone. The hawks naturally attracted the religious extremists, while the doves took a more pragmatic and secular view of the conflict. Doves would feel it to be a matter of principle to keep to the terms of a peace treaty, but hawks would regard it a matter of honour to break peace treaties with the infidel even if that meant provoking a war that the Christians seemed most unlikely to win.

The hawks tended to cluster around the royal family. The royal family tried to woo these newly arrived dissidents to give them support against the barons, who wanted more power for themselves in rather the same way as barons were trying to control the kings in Europe at this time. Their leader was Reynauld of Chatillon, whose career in the Middle East had done a great deal to antagonise oriental Christians and Muslims against the Franks. He had arrived in the East after the fall of Edessa in 1147, full of the religious belligerence that would characterise the Second Crusaders and thirsty for gold, conquest and Muslim blood. After the death of Eleanor's uncle Raymund of Antioch in 1149 he managed to marry his widow and take on the leadership of the principality. His exactions soon made him deeply unpopular but he irrevocably damaged Western relations with the Eastern Christians in 1156. He claimed that the Emperor Manuel had not paid him money that was due to him and in revenge planned an attack on the Byzantine island of Cyprus. When the Greek Patriarch of Antioch refused to finance the expedition, Reynauld captured him, tortured him, coated his wounds with honey and exposed his body to the sun for a whole day so that he was ravaged by insects. Not surprisingly the Patriarch gave him the money he needed and Reynauld then devastated Cyprus so cruelly and thoroughly that the island has never recovered. Besides destroying buildings and crops, he massacred thousands of men, women and children and finally gathered the Greek monks together, cut off their noses and sent them to Constantinople. The act was not merely horribly cruel, it was also suicidal. Naturally Manuel had to respond, and when Reynauld saw the whole imperial army marching towards Antioch he realised that he had gravely endangered the security of his own principality. He asked pardon and Manuel accepted his act of penitence, but the local Greek Christians would never forget this outrage. The Christians were not the only people to suffer, however, for Reynauld made frequent raids of plunder and vandalism in Muslim territory and his greedy aggression must have helped Nur ad-Din's propaganda for the *jihad*. In 1157 he was captured by the Muslims while raiding the country north of Aleppo and he was not released until al-Salih let him go in 1175. His years in captivity had fuelled his hatred of Muslims and of Islam and he returned to the Crusader states full of increased aggression. Unable to recover the throne at Antioch, he married the heiress of Shawbak, Moab and Krak and installed himself east of the Jordan.

Another leading hawk was Gerard of Ridfort, who had arrived in the East in 1173. He had taken service under Count Raymund of Tripoli, the leader of the doves, and Raymund had promised him the hand of the next available heiress. But the following year, when a suitable heiress became available, Raymund broke his promise and gave the lady to a wealthy Pisan merchant, who ungallantly put her on a pair of scales and offered Raymund her weight in gold. (It appears that the lady weighed about ten stone.) Gerard was furious and never forgave Raymund. He left Tripoli in a huff and joined the Templars, rose quickly through the ranks and in 1179 became the Grand Master of the Temple and so very important in the kingdom. He was implacably opposed to Raymund and the doves and was full of the same belligerent chauvinism as Reynauld, as his subsequent behaviour showed.

In 1180 two new hawks became members of the royal circle. First was the newcomer Guy of Lusignan. King Baldwin's health was obviously cause for anxiety and to ensure the succession his sister Sibylla had been married to William Long-Sword of Montferrat in 1176. William had died of malaria later that year, but in 1177 Sibylla produced a son whom she named Baldwin, and who became heir to the throne. One heir was insufficient, so the barons looked around for a new husband for Sibylla, who was next betrothed to the important dove Baldwin of Ibelin. He was captured by the Muslims in 1179 but when he was ransomed and returned to Jerusalem, he found Sibylla had jilted him and was betrothed to the handsome young Guy of Lusignan. Naturally the barons were furious. It was a grave insult to the Ibelins, a venerable baronial family in Palestine, and Guy was obviously a weak fool. The possibility that he might one day be king was appalling. That same year there was another scandalous royal appointment. Agnes, the Queen Mother, secured the election of Heraclius Archbishop of Caesarea to the patriarchate of Jerusalem. His good looks seem to have been his only qualification for he was corrupt, a womaniser and venal. An arch-hawk, he had been elected illegally over the head of William of Tyre, a learned historian, a dove and a much worthier candidate. William would finish *Deeds Done Beyond the Sea*, his long history of the Crusader states, two years later, sickened by the state of the country and too disgusted to continue his work:

> Up to the present time, in the preceding books, we have described to the best of our ability the remarkable deeds of the brave men who for eighty years and more have held the ruling power in our part of the Orient, and particularly at Jerusalem. Now, in utter detestation of the present, amazed at the material which is presented before our eyes . . . we lack the courage to continue. In the acts of our princes there is nothing which seems to a wise man worthy of being committed to the treasure house of the memory, nothing which can contribute refreshment to the reader or confer honour upon the writer. Truly, we can lament with the prophet [Jeremiah] that there has perished from our midst 'law from the priest, counsel from the wise, and the word from the prophet.'[21]

Jeremiah had lamented the sins of the Israelites and had prophesied that the chosen people would lose their land. His prophecy had come true when the Jews had been deported to Babylon in 589 BCE. The Crusaders had seen themselves as God's new chosen people when they had conquered Jerusalem in 1099 and it seemed now that they might lose the Holy Land as the Jews had done before them, but entirely through their own fault.

The country simply could not afford this internal conflict, because they had already experienced the new determination of the Muslims under Saladin. In the first years of the Leper King's reign, Raymund of Tripoli, the leader of the doves, was the regent. Raymund looked more like an oriental than a Westerner, with his dark, tanned skin and his hooked nose. He spoke fluent Arabic, read Arabic and Islamic texts and was absolutely opposed to the belligerent chauvinism of hawks like Gerard of Ridfort and Reynauld of Chatillon. He wanted the country to survive and was not willing to sacrifice the national security by making the Kingdom of Jerusalem the aggressive vanguard of Western Christianity in its bid to conquer the world. While he was regent the country had been committed to a policy of appeasement and non-aggression and at this point Saladin was not strong enough to attack. In 1177, however, Baldwin took up his own kingship and Saladin invaded the country in an uncharacteristically rash and ill-advised campaign. He was soundly defeated and driven back by the Christian army. His prestige suffered greatly but still his empire continued to expand, united in its hostility to the Franj. Ardent Muslim converts to the *jihad* infiltrated the Christian states and harried the Franks by looting and pillaging, and to gain some relief King Baldwin asked for a truce. Saladin was glad to agree. The harvest had been bad and neither side could afford a full-scale war.

But Saladin would have been bound to make peace, even if it had not been convenient and here we see an essential difference between the extremists in a Christian Crusade and an Islamic *jihad*. The Koran says that war is an obnoxious and unnatural state. Provided that the conditions of peace are not harmful to Islam or to Muslims, if the enemy proposes a truce or asks for negotiations, the Muslims must co-operate, though in a *jihad* a truce against the 'unbelievers' must not exceed ten years (see 8:62–3). Saladin was anxious to expel the Franks from Palestine, but he could not present himself as a righteous Muslim ruler and refuse to sign an acceptable truce. He was always scrupulous about this and never broke a truce in his life. His Muslim integrity demanded it. But a Christian hawk like Reynauld of Chatillon felt that the truce was quite incompatible with his religious integrity. From his castle on the east bank of the Jordan, Reynauld could watch the rich Muslim caravans marching along the trade routes to the infidel city of Mecca and the sight was an intolerable temptation. In the summer of 1181 he attacked a large caravan of merchants, which was accompanied by pilgrims who were making the *hajj*. This was a flagrant breach of the truce and so released Saladin from his obligations. Even more shockingly, once he had secured his pile of booty, Reynauld and his men set off on the road to the holy city of Medina, intending to attack the infidels in their own homeland. Saladin quickly intercepted him, and his nephew Faruk-Shah drove Reynauld back home to Moab. But the whole incident had been a deliberate provocation to Muslim sensibilities. By violating the sanctity of the *hajj* and by threatening Medina, Reynauld had done far more than merely break the truce; he had made an unequivocal attack on the integrity of Islam. It would be a pattern that would be repeated on two more fateful occasions, and in the person of Reynauld we can see the danger of a radical minority like the Gush Emunim in Israel today. Reynauld had put the whole country at risk and declared war on his own initiative, just as some Gush fanatics threaten to do. At first Saladin simply asked for the booty back. Reynauld refused and the Leper King rather weakly let the matter drop, so Saladin made another move. A few months later a ship carrying 1500 Christian pilgrims to the Holy Land had been driven off course and forced to put in at an Egyptian port, not realising that the truce had been broken. Saladin threw the pilgrims into prison and then offered to release the hostages if the booty was returned. Still Reynauld refused and this gave Saladin every justification for renewing the *jihad*. He was still not strong enough to make a full-scale invasion but he could do a great deal of harm. No one knows what happened to the hostages: they probably became slaves. Villages and crops were devastated in the Galilee, the city of Beirut was besieged and the Muslims captured the Christian fortress of Habis Jaldack in the Transjordan. More importantly, Saladin's prestige increased in the Muslim world, while Reynauld had shown the Muslims that the Christians were indeed dangerous enemies to Muslims and to Islam.

As the Muslims grew more united, Christians were more divided. Feeling was now running so high between royalists and barons that there was almost civil war in 1182. Raymund of Tripolis had married the heiress of Tiberias in the Galilee and when he entered his new territory King Baldwin would not allow him to enter the kingdom. He had been persuaded by his hawkish advisers that this was a coup and that Raymund was plotting against the government. Only after furious protests by the barons would Baldwin consent to see Raymund, who managed to persuade him of his innocence. The incident showed how deeply the sick young King was being influenced by his hawkish advisers, who had also advised him to support Reynauld against Saladin in 1180. Later that year the King became desperately ill and though he did rise from his sickbed, it was clear that he was not capable of ruling any longer. Naturally the barons wanted Raymund to be regent, but this time the King appointed the weak and ignorant Guy of Lusignan, who had none of the decisiveness that usually characterised hawks and seemed to be without an independent thought in his head.

Later that year Reynauld made his most provocative assault on Islam. He planned an assault on Mecca itself, intending to raze the Ka'aba to the ground, drag the Prophet (whom he called the 'accursed camel-driver') from his grave and at the same time to raid and plunder. There was a flair and simplicity about the project that was remarkable. Reynauld built a fleet of collapsible ships, tested them on the Dead Sea, dismantled them, loaded them on to the backs of camels and conveyed them 130 miles over the desert to the port of Eilat on the Gulf of Aqaba. Eilat was in Muslim hands, but Reynauld managed to take the port quite easily and his navy of Christian pirates sailed down the Gulf of Aqaba into the Red Sea, looting and pillaging as they went. They attacked the port servicing Medina at Yanbuh, sank a pilgrim ship on the way to Jeddah and attacked the port of Rabiqh near Mecca. In the Holy City itself there was fear and terror. It was the first time for centuries that anyone had threatened to sully the holiness of Mecca, but fortunately Saladin's brother Saif ad-Din al-Adil rushed to the rescue from Egypt, defeated the Christian navy and carried the prisoners into Medina, lashed to the backs of camels. Reynauld had already returned to Moab, but his companions were all executed. When Saladin heard of this attack, he vowed that he would kill Reynauld with his own hands, and in the Muslim world Brins Arnat, as they called Reynauld, became identified with everything that was most threatening to the Muslim world. The *jihad* was seen to be essential. Saladin could count on the distant support of the Caliph of Baghdad and Muslims throughout the world. They might not be willing to fight themselves, but they could not ignore an attack on Mecca.

Reynauld's action was especially dangerous in view of the situation in Syria, for in 1183 Saladin had become the master of Aleppo and the most powerful Muslim leader in the Middle East. He could now turn his whole attention to the liberation of Palestine and the assault on Mecca would mean a full-scale attack. In September 1183 his army left Damascus, crossed the Jordan and camped by the fountain of Tubaniya, on the site of the ancient city of Jezreel. His soldiers began to raid the countryside and take over the little forts in the area. Instantly Guy mobilised the army of the whole kingdom, which marched from Sephoria to meet the Muslims, camped at the Pools of Goliath opposite Saladin, but then found themselves almost entirely surrounded by the Muslim army. Reynauld and the hawks urged Guy to make an immediate attack, and this view was naturally shared by the common soldiers. But Raymund and the Ibelin brothers Baldwin and Balian told Guy that it would be fatal to provoke a battle against an army that was numerically superior. If the Christian army sat tight, Saladin would be forced to retire. He could not hold his army together on hostile territory for long, especially as winter approached. They were proved right. Saladin kept trying to lure the Christians out, but Guy refused to engage with him. Eventually Saladin was forced to retire and on 6 October his army crossed the Jordan and returned to Damascus.

Yet this victory did Guy no good at all. Reynauld and the hawks sneered at him and the common soldiers saw him as a coward. Guy also quarrelled with the King, who dismissed him from the regency and reinstated Raymund of Tripoli. Baldwin was now determined that Guy should not rule the kingdom and to that end he had his little nephew Baldwin V crowned in readiness for his imminent death; he also made a will. When he died, Raymund was to remain regent, and if Baldwin V died before reaching the age of ten the successor to the throne of Jerusalem must be chosen by the Pope, the Holy Roman Emperor and the kings of France and England.

He also made a valiant attempt to unite the royal and baronial parties. In 1180 it had been agreed to marry the King's half-sister Isabella, who was also the stepdaughter of Balian of Ibelin, to the young Humphrey of Toron, the stepson of Reynauld of Chatillon. Isabella was now eleven years old and ready for the marriage. The wedding would be a powerful symbol of the unity of the doves and the hawks.

In fact the wedding of Humphrey and Isabella was devastated by the *jihad*. Reynauld had insisted that it should take place in his castle at Kerak in the Transjordan, which would one day be Humphrey's personal fief through his mother. During the celebrations, the wedding guests heard that Saladin was approaching with his army. Reynauld's castles were an obvious target for a raid, and Saladin set up eight catapults and began to bombard the walls with huge rocks. The story of the wedding of Kerak shows how very different things could have been between Christians and Muslims, for both sides responded to the situation with a courtly flair and imagination. Even though the rocks were making the mighty walls of the castle shudder, the celebrations gamely continued and the Franks courteously sent out some of the special wedding food for Saladin. They explained that a wedding was in progress, and Saladin gave orders to his men not to attack the wing of the castle where the young couple was spending the night. Eventually Saladin could make no headway against the powerfully fortified castle and had to retire. Baldwin IV, who had been too ill to attend the celebrations, had hurried to defend the castle with his troops and was carried into it on a litter in triumph.[22] The grand gesture of Kerak had come to have a different meaning from that which had been intended. It did not unite the wedding guests, who left the castle as bitterly divided as ever. The wedding had shown the vulnerability of the Christian state: now that the Muslims were determined to destroy the Kingdom of Jerusalem, the Franks would always have to be ready for battle. They could never relax completely in joyous celebrations, because the enemy was always at the gate. The incident also showed that Muslims and Christians actually shared many of the same courtly values and on this level could respond to one another very well. Sadly what drove them apart was their religion.

In March 1185 Baldwin IV finally died of his leprosy and his will came into effect. The little Baldwin V, who was only seven years old, succeeded to the throne and Raymund became the Regent. At a council of war he asked the barons what should be done. The country was in no state for war and the barons agreed that Raymund should ask Saladin for a truce. Saladin himself was glad of peace at this point; he was having some trouble with the city of Mosul and the *jihad* had reached an impasse. A truce was agreed for four years and the Crusader state tried to build up a new prosperity, encourage trade again and, above all, try to persuade the West to send a Crusade to help them. But the peace did not last long. In August 1186 Baldwin V died at Acre; Raymund was present at his death together with Joscelin the Seneschal and afterwards Joscelin advised Raymund to return to Tiberias and call an assembly of the barons to discuss the implementation of Baldwin IV's will, which had made provision for the succession. He himself would convey the little corpse to Jerusalem for burial.

Yet Joscelin proved to be privy to a palace plot and while Raymund was at Tiberias there was a coup. In the Holy Sepulchre, the Patriarch Heraclius with royal support crowned Guy of Lusignan and Sibylla King and Queen of Jerusalem. Gerard of Ridfort witnessed the ceremony. At first the barons tried to stage a counter-coup by presenting Humphrey of Toron and Isabella as claimants to the throne, but at the last moment Humphrey broke down and rushed to Guy to beg for forgiveness. The barons realised that all was lost and they all likewise submitted, except for Baldwin of Ibelin, who left the country in disgust, and

Raymund of Tripoli, who withdrew to his lands in the Galilee.

At this point, when the country was in no position to take on an external enemy, Reynauld of Chatillon broke the truce again. For the last few years he had been kept in check by Raymund but now that Guy was king his energies were unleashed again. Only a few weeks after the coup he attacked another caravan of merchants and pilgrims on their way to Mecca, massacred all the armed men and herded all the rest into captivity in his castle. One of the captives was Saladin's sister. When one of the prisoners actually dared to remind Reynauld of the truce, he scornfully replied: 'Let your Mohammad come and rescue you!'[23] The same pattern of events repeated itself. Saladin said that if Reynauld restored the booty and freed the prisoners, he would honour the truce. Naturally Reynauld refused and Saladin swore that he would slay him with his own hands.

Saladin now called a full *jihad* against the Franks, the enemy of Islam. Thousands of cavalry and infantry began to stream towards Damascus from all over his empire. Damascus was crammed with soldiers and waving banners, and surrounded by a mass of camel-skin tents which the soldiers used to shelter themselves from the sun. For the first time for centuries, Islam was now fully mobilised in an effective full-scale holy war. Yet still the Christians did not seem to appreciate their peril and continued to quarrel about their own concerns. Raymund saw the end of the kingdom approaching irrevocably, and to salvage something from the wreck he made a private treaty with Saladin, who in return promised not to attack Tripoli and the Galilee. This was treasonous and it gravely damaged the Christian resistance, because Guy was now deprived of all Raymund's troops. But as usual, the hawks acted with suicidal belligerence and set out with troops to attack Raymund at Tiberias. Balian of Ibelin, the brother of Baldwin (who had left the country) had to come forward and explain to Guy the obvious fact that if he attacked Raymund with his depleted troops, Saladin would attack them with his massive army because Raymund was his ally. The whole army would be destroyed. Guy tended to agree with the last person to speak to him strongly and he called off the attack.

Encouraged by this success, Balian decided to try to arrange a peace between Raymund and Guy, so that the Christians could meet Saladin with a fully united front. He went to Guy and explained to him how isolated he was. Antioch had made a truce with Saladin, to dissociate itself from the dangerous folly of the Kingdom of Jerusalem. Guy had lost his best knight in Baldwin of Ibelin. If he lost Raymund too, he was finished. Guy agreed to try to make peace and on 29 April 1187 a peace delegation, led by the Grand Masters of the Temple and the Hospital, set out for Tiberias, planning to meet Balian later in the Castle of La Feve in the Plain of Esdraelon in the Galilee.

On the 30 April Saladin's young son al-Afdal approached Raymund with a request: could the Muslims send a reconnaissance party through Galilee? Raymund could not refuse this embarrassing request from his new ally and gave permission for the Muslims to enter his territory, provided that they did no harm to any town or village and went back to their own territory before nightfall. Al-Afdal readily agreed and Raymund issued orders that all the people of Galilee should remain in their homes the next day. On 1 May he watched an army of 7000 Muslims ride past his castle in Tiberias into the Galilee. That evening he watched them ride back as agreed, leaving the country before nightfall. However, on the spear of each of the vanguard was the head of a Templar knight.

Raymund's orders had reached La Feve on the evening of 30 April and there was Guy's delegation, waiting for Balian of Ibelin who had not yet arrived. When Gerard of Ridfort heard that the traitor Raymund had ordered him to hide from the Muslims, it was more than his hawkish heart could stand. He sent out orders to all

the Templars in the area to join him at La Feve. James Mailly, the Marshal of the Temple, duly turned up with ninety knights, and the following morning forty secular knights joined them from Nazareth. The little band of Christians rode out to find the Muslims but, when they saw the large host watering their horses at the springs of Cresson near Nazareth, James Mailly and the Master of the Hospital quite sensibly wanted to turn back. Gerard was disgusted. He taunted the Master of the Hospital with cowardice and sneered at James: 'You love your blond head too much to want to lose it.'[24] Templars had vowed absolute obedience to their Master, and James replied: 'I shall die in battle like a brave man. It is you who will flee as a traitor.'[25] In the spirit of Roland at Roncesvalles, Gerard led the company in a suicidal charge against the Muslim army: it was a massacre. All but three of the Templars and knights were slain, and among the three survivors was Gerard of Ridfort.

The disaster of Cresson shook the whole kingdom. Inevitably there was an outcry against Raymund of Tripoli, who was accused of conversion to Islam. Raymund himself was shaken by the disaster so he agreed to break his treaty with Saladin and put his troops at the disposal of the King and the Franks began to mobilise their forces to meet the Muslim threat. The entire army of the Kingdom of Jerusalem gathered at Acre and then marched from Acre to Sephoria; but, says Ibn al-Athir, 'they were reluctant and demoralised.' The Muslims themselves were not entirely convinced that a pitched battle was a good idea. Some of the emirs advised Saladin to weaken the enemy by repeated skirmishes instead; others said that the Muslims were beginning to get impatient: when was this famous *jihad* going to be fought? Saladin himself concluded that the Muslims could not let this opportunity pass without 'striking a tremendous blow for the *jihad*'.[26] The battle must be fought before the autumn, which was the end of the fighting season, for the troops had to return home for the harvest. But would the Franks, who could be very cautious warriors, as he had discovered in 1183, be lured into battle?

He decided to lay a trap for them and prayed that the Franks would walk into it. On 1 July he took his army over the Jordan into Galilee, camped half of it near the lake and with the other half he attacked Tiberias, which fell to the Muslims after an hour of fighting. Raymund and his sons were at Sephoria with the army but the civilians of the city took refuge with the Countess in the garrison and she sent word to her husband to tell him what had happened.

Twenty miles away in Sephoria, the Franks engaged in a fierce argument about what should be done, and the doves and the hawks both tried to persuade Guy, who was dithering as usual, to follow their policies. Raymund was for staying put. He understood Saladin's plan and though Tiberias was his own city he was prepared to let it go for the time being. He knew that nothing dreadful would happen to his wife and the citizens of Tiberias. They would simply be taken to Damascus and could easily be ransomed later. If the Christians just stayed put, Saladin would have to go back home again, as he had in 1183, and then the Christians would easily reconquer Tiberias. At present it was better to lose one city than to risk the whole army and lose the whole Kingdom.[27] This was a disgusting policy to hawks like Reynauld of Chatillon. He accused Raymund of being a Muslim-lover, waved aside his arguments about the immense size of Saladin's army ('a large load of fuel will be good for the fires of hell!')[28] and urged the King to cast aside these timid, prudent policies and fling his army bravely against the enemy of God.

Guy himself was in a dilemma. He had suffered gravely when he had followed Raymund's advice in 1183 and he was bound, as a feudal monarch, to go to help his vassals in Tiberias. But after the shock of the Cresson massacre, he was less inclined to listen to Reynauld's suicidal belligerence and at the end of the council of war he decided to listen to Raymund. Unfortunately he listened to the last speaker to address him sternly, as was his wont. Late at night Gerard of Ridfort, the 'hero' of Cresson, went secretly to his tent and chided him severely for listening to the traitor Raymund.

> This is the first task which has fallen to you since you were crowned. And know well that rather than see that, the Templars would put on their white mantles and sell and pawn them lest the humiliation the Saracens have caused me and all of them together be not avenged. Go have it announced throughout the army that all should arm and every man go to his company and follow the standard of the Holy Cross.[29]

As usual Guy did what he was told; the army assembled itself and started to march towards Tiberias. Saladin could not believe his luck as he watched the Franks fall neatly into his trap. An extreme religious chauvinism that ignored normal reasoning and military and political good sense had pushed the whole Christian army into a battle that it was most unlikely to win. The fanaticism of a disaffected minority had prevailed over the more peaceful and sensibly secular policies of the barons, and the Kingdom of Jerusalem had been put at the mercy of an enemy that was determined to annihilate it.

The army trekked across the hills of Galilee in the blazing summer heat, burdened by its armour and equipment. A journey that should have taken only a few hours lasted all day. Saladin sent snipers to follow the rearguard and pick off any stragglers. He had cut off the normal water supplies and many wells and springs had been dried up, so the soldiers were half-crazed with thirst. Eventually they arrived at the Sea of Galilee in an exhausted state to discover that Saladin's camp had cut them off from the water. Some of the barons urged the king to fight their way through to the lake, but Guy was moved by the plight of his soldiers and the pleas of the Templars to pitch camp for the night. They camped on slopes near the hill called the Horns of Hattin, where Jesus was traditionally supposed to have preached his pacifist religion in the Sermon on the Mount. The barons thought that there was a well at the site of the camp, but on arrival they found that it was dry. Raymund of Tripoli cried aloud, 'Ah, Lord God, the war is over; we are dead men; the kingdom is finished.'[30]

The misery of the Christians, most of whom were becoming dangerously dehydrated, was increased by the Muslims who burned large fires which sent acrid smoke in their direction. Even worse were the sounds of jubilation from Saladin's camp. There the fresh, rested Muslims suddenly saw victory in their grasp in a reversal that they had not expected and, as one would expect, there was a new burst of religious fervour. The 3 July that year was the night of the 26/27 Ramadan, the holiest night of the Muslim year, for it was the night that Mohammad had received the first words of the Koran from God. As the Koran says this night of Qadr (destiny) is better 'than a thousand months':

> On that night the angels and the Spirit by their Lord's leave come down with his decrees.
> That night is peace, till break of dawn. (97:5)

As they waited for the dawn, the men of Saladin's army waited for a divine judgement. Saladin's secretary and chancellor Imad ad-Din al-Isfahani saw the night of Qadr that year as the separation of Good and Evil:

> Night separated the two sides and the cavalry barred both roads. Islam passed the night face to face with unbelief, monotheism at war with Trinitarianism, the way of righteousness looking down upon error, faith opposing polytheism. Meanwhile the several circles of Hell prepared themselves and the several ranks

of Heaven congratulated themselves. Malik [the Guardian of Hell] waited and Ridwan [the Guardian of Paradise] rejoiced.[31]

The approaching victory had increased the conviction of the righteousness of the *jihad*, as is always the case in a holy war. spontaneously the Muslims interpreted the coincidence of the date into a providential decree, just as the Christians had seen a divine significance in the date of their conquest of Jerusalem in 1099. This *jihad* was no ordinary war of conquest for Saladin's soldiers of Allah; it was a cosmic battle and an act of salvation history.

But Saladin continued to plan practically and carefully; he had no intention of abandoning wise policy for holy enthusiasm, and while his men were chanting hymns and praises, he deployed them round the Christian camp until it was completely encircled. As the chronicler says, not a cat could have slipped through the net. After the dawn had ended the peace of the Night of Qadr, the Muslim assault began. The Christian infantry could only think of water and they rushed down the hill towards the Sea of Galilee that was glinting invitingly. They were driven back up the hill and either slaughtered or taken prisoner; hundreds of men lay on the hillside wounded and with swollen, blackened mouths. The cavalry, however, fought bravely. Raymund of Tripoli led a charge that succeeded in breaking the Muslim line, but then the Muslims simply closed behind them and they could not rejoin their companions. Raymund escaped from the battle, but died of rage and grief soon afterwards. Balian of Ibelin also fought his way out and was one of the last Christians to escape. The cavalry continued to charge against the enemy and eventually Saladin and his son al-Afdal watched the royal tent overturned on the Horns of Hittin where the King had retreated. At that moment Saladin knew that his dream had become an established fact. 'My father dismounted and bowed to the ground,' al-Afdal recalls, 'giving thanks to God with tears of joy.'[32] The Christian army had been soundly defeated and the Kingdom of Jerusalem was lost.

After the battle, Saladin had two important prisoners of war brought to his tent: King Guy and Reynauld of Chatillon. Both men were half dead with exhaustion and made desperate with thirst. Saladin handed a goblet of water iced with the snows of Mount Hermon to Guy, who drank and passed the goblet to Reynauld. It is a custom in the Arab world that a host may not kill a man to whom he has given

food or drink and when Saladin saw Reynauld drinking he pointed out that he had not given *him* permission to drink. 'I am not therefore obliged to show him mercy,' he said, with a terrible smile.[33] He then took his sword and cut off Reynauld's head and dragged the corpse to the feet of the terrified Guy. Yet to Guy Saladin mildly remarked that one king did not kill another and he explained kindly that Reynauld had only been executed because of his great crimes and treachery. Guy was taken to Damascus for a time and then allowed to go free. This famous story perfectly illustrates Saladin's attitude, which is a new one in the holy war. He did not want to massacre all the Christians indiscriminately, on the Joshuan model. To individual Christians like Guy he could be kind, almost to a fault. To release the king of a people you have just conquered is not a very wise policy and Saladin would pay dearly for this kind of clemency. Reynauld, however, who had planned to attack Mecca, could expect no mercy. A few days later Saladin had all the prisoners of war who belonged to the military orders brought into his presence and massacred in cold blood. The Sufis in his army begged for the honour of killing one prisoner each and Saladin watched the executions smiling with joy. He rightly judged that of all the Christians in the Holy Land, they were the ones most dedicated to the war against Islam. Imad ad-Din, who was present at the massacre, wrote in his history of Saladin: 'On that day I saw how he killed unbelief to give life to Islam and destroyed polytheism to build monotheism.'[34] The massacre was a religious act of salvation.

Yet the Koran states clearly that prisoners-of-war must not be ill-treated in any way and that, once the fighting is over, prisoners should either be ransomed or released as a favour, as Saladin released Guy (47:5). Prisoners whose ransoms remained unpaid were to be distributed among those who had taken part in the fighting and were to be allowed to earn enough money to pay the ransom themselves; their captors were admonished to help them out of their own pockets (24:34), for the ransoming of captives was considered to be a highly commendable act (2:178). The *hadith* lay down even more stringent requirements. Mohammad directs Muslims to treat their prisoners as full members of their own family: 'You must feed them as you feed yourselves, and clothe them as you clothe yourselves, and if you should set them a hard task, you must help them in it yourselves.'[35] Ill-treatment became the prisoner's ransom and if a captive were cruelly treated he must be allowed to go free. In general the Muslims seem to have observed these practices and we have seen that others who, like Reynauld of Chatillon, were prisoners, were finally released and others, like Baldwin of Ibelin, were eventually ransomed. This was why Raymund of Tripoli was not worried about the fate of his wife and family when they were taken prisoner. But Saladin's massacre seems a flagrant breach of this humane code and marks a new level of intransigence in the *jihad*. The Koran does say that punishment can 'be proportionate to the wrong that has been done you' and it may be that the massacre was seen as a retaliation for all the savage massacres that the Christians had inflicted upon the Muslims, but the Koran immediately goes on to recommend forgiveness: 'It shall be best for you to endure your wrongs in patience' (16:127). However, the Koran is also very emphatic about the importance of steadfastness and determination in war. One way of limiting the horrors of war was to bring the fighting to a speedy conclusion and to that end Muslims must take firm measures to ensure that hostilities cease as soon as possible. To release or to allow to be ransomed people who had so recently shown themselves to be dedicated enemies of Islam, like Reynauld and the Templars, would mean that there would simply be more Christian atrocities and more fighting. Saladin seems to have been torn between his natural compassion and his determination to rid Palestine of the Christian menace and, as we shall see, this led him into trouble.

Because the whole Christian army had been destroyed at Hittin, there could be no major opposition to Saladin's occupation of the rest of the Kingdom of Jerusalem. Knights who escaped from the battle and civilians who fled from the occupying Muslim army began to congregate in Tyre, where they established themselves under the leadership of Conrad of Montferrat, the brother of Queen Sybilla's first husband. He had known nothing about the disaster of Hittin and had only been in the Holy Land by the merest chance. A resident of Constantinople, he had been involved in a murder there and hurriedly escaped as a 'pilgrim' to Jerusalem. As his ship approached Acre he noticed that the town seemed deserted and naturally he thought that this was odd. When he heard about the Christian defeat he immediately set off to Tyre to organise the Christian resistance there and it was due to his prompt action that the Franks managed to keep this last foothold in the Holy Land. Other committed knights did not merely seek a refuge in Tyre but went straight off to Jerusalem in order to try to save the Holy City from the infidel. Ibn al-Athir tells us that many survivors of Hittin concentrated there, together with the civilians in the area and the inhabitants of Ascalon. There was 'a great concourse of people there, each one of whom would choose death rather than see the Muslims in power in their city.'[36] Jerusalem was crucial to the Christian holy war and must be defended to the bitter end.

It had also become important to the Muslims and here again Saladin pushed the Muslim *jihad* into a new direction. In the Jewish and the Christian holy wars the idea of a holy land is crucial but this is not the case with the *jihad*. Indeed many Muslims right up to the present day would consider the veneration of a 'holy land' to be idolatry, because it is raising a mere physical reality to an unacceptably high status. Certainly Muslims regard Mecca as a holy city but their pilgrimage there is an affirmation of faith, not contact with a land which is intrinsically or physically holy. Mecca is sacred because of its associations with the roots of the religion and when the Caliph Omar conquered Jerusalem in 637 Jerusalem became the third most holy city in Islam and a place of pilgrimage for Muslims because it had associations with Mohammad and some of the earlier prophets. Yet Saladin and his *mujahideen* seem to have been inspired to fight the Franks because they were the enemies and oppressors of the Muslim people, rather than by a passionate devotion to Jerusalem like that which inspired the First Crusaders to undertake unbelievable dangers in order to liberate the Holy City. *Mujahideen* in our own day have preserved Saladin's priorities when they have fought a *jihad* against the current persecutors of Muslims.

But Jerusalem has important associations for Muslims and contact with this city of al-Quds (the Holy) was an imperative for the followers of Mohammad. When Saladin and his army arrived outside the city walls and camped on the Mount of Olives opposite the city, the Sultan at once asked to be taken to a spot where he could see the Dome of the Rock and al-Aqsa, the old Muslim shrines that dominate the city. He was aware that the conquest of *this* city was quite different from his conquest of the other cities of Palestine and he gave a rousing sermon to his army, reminding them of the importance of Jerusalem in the Islamic revelation. The very first Muslims had prayed facing Jerusalem, he told them; the Prophet Mohammad had made his Night Journey there in the years before the *hijra* to Medina: he had alighted on the ancient Rock and thence ascended to heaven and spoken with Moses and Jesus, linking Islam with the two older religions. Jerusalem was also associated with the ancient Jewish prophets of God's revelation, and with David, Solomon and Mariam, the mother of Jesus. At the end of his sermon, Imad ad-Din tells us, Saladin vowed to restore Jerusalem to Islam and 'took an oath not to depart until he had honoured his word and raised his standard on the highest point and had visited with his own feet the place where the Prophet had set foot.'[37] After

Saladin had finished speaking, his soldiers looked at the holy city of Jerusalem or al-Quds with new eyes and found a new motive for fighting the Franks, who had profaned the Dome of the Rock with a cross. When the Franks had conquered Jerusalem eighty years earlier, there had been no great outcry about its loss in the Islamic world and indeed most Muslims seemed to have been even more indifferent to its fate than they were about the massacres and the plight of the refugees. But, right up to the present day, actually confronting Jerusalem stirs up very deep feelings in people of all three religions. In the summer of 1187 Christians and Muslims prepared to do battle once more for the Holy City.

The Christians were desperately afraid and for good reason. However many thousands of people had congregated in Jerusalem, they could not oppose Saladin's powerful army effectively, because they had no knight there who was experienced enough to lead the battle and most of them were civilians. Would Saladin deal with them as they had dealt with the Muslims in 1099? Then, as if in answer to their prayers the distinguished baron Balian of Ibelin arrived. He had had no intention of taking part in the fight for Jerusalem. After Hittin he had had enough of war and, as a dove, he was not a fanatic about the Holy City. He had simply come back to collect his wife, who had been in Jerusalem at the time of the battle of Hittin, and to bring her back to Tyre. He explained this to Saladin and courteously asked Saladin's permission to enter the city; the Sultan granted his request on condition that he stayed there only one night.[38] Balian swore to observe this condition, and entered the city. Once inside, however, the people begged him to stay and lead them in their final desperate struggle. Balian felt deeply torn. He had a duty to protect his people and also a religious duty to defend Jerusalem, but he had given his word to Saladin that he would not stay in the city. To resolve his dilemma he took a course of action that gives us another clear example of the mutual respect and consideration that could have existed between the Muslims and the Christians, if only religious idealism had not come between them. He went to Saladin to explain his position and Saladin gave serious thought to the problem. Eventually he concluded that since Balian felt that he had a religious duty to stay, he would release him from his oath. Both men believed in the same code of honour; both respected the sanctity of an oath.[39] Balian did not think that religion absolved him from an oath with an infidel, as Reynauld had, and Saladin was able to enter sympathetically into Balian's position, even if this worked out to his disadvantage.

Saladin had made the Christians an offer. If they handed the city to him unconditionally, there would be no bloodshed. He was returning to the spirit of Mohammad when he had conquered Mecca. The Christians, predictably, refused this offer and the fighting began.[40] It was soon clear to them that they had absolutely no chance at all and would have to sue for peace, but now Saladin took a hard line. They had refused his offer of a peaceful solution so now, he swore, 'We shall deal with you, just as you dealt with the population when you took it ... with murder and enslavement and other such savageries.'[41] The whirligig of time had brought its revenge to the Christians and added a new twist of horror to the vicious cycle of the holy war. The Christians sat and waited for death, but then Balian came up with a solution. He went to Saladin again and made a desperate threat. There was a large number of people in the city, he said, but at the moment they were only fighting half-heartedly because they were still hoping that Saladin would spare them with his usual celebrated clemency. But if they saw that death was certain they would take truly desperate measures:

> If we see that death is inevitable, then, by God, we shall kill our children and our wives, burn our possessions, so as not to leave you with a *dinar* or a *drachma* or a single man or woman to enslave. When this is done, we shall pull down the

Sanctuary of the Rock and the Mosque of al-Aqsa and the other sacred places, slaughtering the Muslim prisoners we hold – 5,000 of them – and killing every horse and animal we possess. Then we shall come out to fight you like men fighting for their lives, when each man, before he falls dead, kills his equal.[42]

Saladin consulted with the imams and jurists in his army. Was it lawful for him to break the oath that he had sworn to take the city with bloodshed, if he could thereby spare the holy mosques? They decided that it was and Saladin prepared to occupy the city peacefully, but his financial advisers insisted that he take the Christians prisoner and demand adequate ransoms.[43]

On 2 October 1187 Saladin and his army entered Jerusalem as conquerors and for the next 800 years Jerusalem would remain a Muslim city. In the next chapter we shall see that its conquest by the Jewish state in 1967 initiated a fresh round of holy wars in the Middle East. By another holy coincidence that was fervently noted by the Arab chroniclers, Saladin's victory occurred that year on the day when Muslims commemorated Mohammad's Night Journey. Saladin kept his word, and conquered the city according to the highest Islamic ideals. He did not take revenge for the 1099 massacre, as the Koran advised (16:127), and now that hostilities had ceased he ended the killing (2:193, 194). Not a single Christian was killed and there was no plunder. The ransoms were deliberately very low, but still there were thousands of poor people who could not even afford them and who were therefore taken prisoner by the Muslims and disappeared for ever into the House of Islam. There were so many prisoners that it was said that a Frankish slave could be purchased for a sandal in Damascus. But large numbers escaped this fate because Saladin was moved to tears by the plight of families who were rent asunder and he released many of them freely, as the Koran urged, though to the despair of his long-suffering treasurers. His brother al-Adil was so distressed by the plight of the prisoners that he asked Saladin for a thousand of them for his own use and then released them on the spot.[44] All the Muslim leaders were scandalised to see the rich Christians escaping with their wealth, which could have been used to ransom *all* the prisoners. When Imad ad-Din saw the Patriarch Heraclius leaving the city with chariots crammed with treasure, he urged Saladin to confiscate it. But Saladin refused. The Koran said that oaths and treaties must be kept to the letter and it was essential that the Muslims should observe the legalities. 'Christians everywhere will remember the kindness we have done them,' he said.[45] Heraclius paid his ten-dinar ransom like everybody else and was even provided with a special escort to keep his treasure safe during the journey to Tyre. Saladin was right that the Christian world was impressed with his clemency. Even though it was Saladin who deprived Christianity of Jerusalem, he has been venerated in the West in a way that no other Muslim hero has been. Legends grew up that he had received Christian baptism and had been dubbed a Christian knight. People must have been subliminally aware that Saladin had behaved in a far more 'Christian' way than the Franks.

But his mercy earned him the disapproval of his own people. All the Christians that he released swelled the resistance at Tyre, and Saladin would find it impossible to dislodge them. Ibn al-Athir, whose loyalty to Nur ad-Din meant that he could never quite forgive Saladin for his behaviour to his master, is critical:

> Every time he seized a Frankish city or stronghold such as Acre, Ascalon, or Jerusalem, Salah ad-Din allowed the enemy soldiers and knights to seek refuge in Tyre, a city that had thus become impregnable. The Franks of the littoral sent messages to the others overseas [in Europe] and the latter promised to come to their rescue. Ought we not to say that in a sense it was Salah ad-Din himself who organised the defence of Tyre against his own army?[46]

In fact Saladin's clemency contravened the ruling of the Koran, because instead of ensuring that the conflict with the Christians was ended once and for all, he had unwittingly prolonged it. There would be more Crusades to the Holy Land for the recovery of Jerusalem, more bloodshed and massacre and it would be another hundred years before the Muslims finally evicted the Western Christians from the East. At the start of his career, Saladin had been a reluctant soldier and, despite the zeal for the *jihad* that he later developed, his emotional and sympathetic nature finally made it impossible for him to be a really efficient *mujahid* (soldier in the holy war). Yet in this long chronicle of bloodshed and horror, this failing must surely make Saladin one of the most attractive characters in the history of the holy war.

Once he was inside Jerusalem, Saladin set about purifying the holy places from their long pollution. Al-Aqsa had been the headquarters of the Templars, and they had built living quarters around and against the mosque and had taken up some of the sacred mosque itself with storerooms and latrines. On the Dome of the Rock there was a giant golden cross and as soon as the Muslims entered the city some of them had climbed up the cupola and taken it down – an event that caused an immense commotion. 'When they reached the top a great cry went up from the city and from outside the walls,' says Ibn al-Athir, 'the Muslims crying the *Allah akhbah* in their joy, the Franks groaning in consternation and grief. So loud and piercing was their cry that the earth shook.'[47] Inside the mosque, the great rock on which Abraham had bound Isaac and upon which Mohammad had alighted after his Night Journey had been hidden by the Franks with a marble covering and the mosque was full of statues and images, which the Muslims consider idolatrous. All these signs of Christian occupation had to be erased and the mosques returned to their former state. Workers purified the mosques, sprinkled them with rose water and on Friday 9 October the Muslims celebrated their Friday prayer in al-Aqsa so that 'Islam was restored there in full freshness and beauty.'[48]

But there was an intransigence in Saladin's *jihad* that was quite new in the Islamic tradition, so that it was an innovation as well as being a return to fundamental principles. Hitherto Christians had always been considered People of the Book. They had always been allowed to worship freely in Muslim countries. Now Western Christians were expelled from the Holy Land that Saladin had been able to conquer. The Greek and Eastern Christians, who had not fought a holy war against Islam, were permitted to remain in the Holy Sepulchre, but the other churches that the Western Christians had built were turned into mosques and madrassas. Notices were affixed above the doors stating that Saladin had conquered the building from the polytheists.[49] Western Christians were now seen as a pollution of the holiness of al-Quds and had to be purged. But this did not apply to the other People of the Book. While the Christians had reigned in Jerusalem, Jews had not been permitted to live in the Holy City, but now Saladin invited them back to live there side by side with the Muslims. Throughout the diaspora, Saladin was hailed as a new Cyrus and many Jews made the *aliyah* to the Holy Land, convinced that this new return was the first sign of the messianic redemption.[50] Jews like Judah Halevi had been making the *aliyah* from Europe for over forty years, but now that the ban on Jerusalem had been lifted the idea of a new return to the Promised Land took strong root and gave rise to a new burst of Jewish settlement in the country. In the light of recent events, it is surely ironic that this early religious Zionism should have been inspired and encouraged by an Islamic conquest of Jerusalem.

A holy war leads to a distorted view of the enemy, and just as the Christians had built up a distorted view of the Muslims, so now the Muslim *mujahideen* propagated a distorted view of the Frankish Christians. Imad ad-Din could understand their love of Jerusalem. He imagines them waiting for the arrival of Saladin's army and resolving to die for the Holy City: 'We love this place, we are bound to it, our honour lies in honouring it, its salvation is ours, its safety is ours, its survival is ours.' But he becomes deeply confused as he tries to explain this devotion of the 'polytheists', and sees it as an attachment to the statues or idolatrous effigies themselves as much as to the fact that Jerusalem was the site of the Crucifixion. In his account, the Franks say:

> Here are the effigies of the Madonna and the Lord, of the Temple and the Birthplace, of the Table and the fishes, and what is described and sculpted of the Disciples and the Master, of the cradle and the Infant speaking. Here are the effigies of the ox and the ass, of Paradise and Hell, the clappers and the divine laws. Here, they say, the Messiah was crucified, the sacrificial victim slain, divinity made incarnate, humanity deified.[51]

There is a muddled perception here of the place of images in the Christian life. There is a muddle also in the subject of some of these effigies. The simple and uneducated Christians who were living in the Hejaz in the seventh century believed in many apocryphal legends about Jesus and the Apostles and these influenced the picture of Christianity in the Koran. Thus the 'Table' that Imad ad-Din imagined the Christians venerating refers to a legend recorded in the Koran about Jesus, who asked Allah to send down a table filled with heavenly food to increase the faith of the people (clearly a distorted version of the institution of the Eucharist). The Koran also preserved a legend in which the infant Jesus spoke miraculously from his crib (19:31) and Imad ad-Din imagined Christians worshipping an effigy or idolatrous statue depicting this event, which does not appear in any of the gospels. From the start, therefore, Muslims had a muddled picture of Christianity, which had been given to them by primitive Christians who lived far away from the main centres of the Christian world. Imad ad-Din was reiterating and compounding this distortion, which had now been given a new intensity. Muslims and Christians could often understand each other very well indeed in secular ways, because they shared the same courtly values and at this time their societies were very similar in structure and preoccupation. Yet in religious ways they were receding from one another rapidly and aggressively and it seemed impossible for each to see the other clearly.

Saladin's *jihad* had begun as a defensive holy war twenty years ago: he was simply liberating a land that had been taken from the Muslims. Yet, like most holy warriors, after his victory his vision became more aggressive and expansionist. He now wanted to purge all the Franks from the face of the earth, not just the Franks of Palestine. Baha ad-Din related that one day he and the Sultan had been riding beside the coast of Palestine and were looking at the wild, wintry waves. The sea horrified Baha ad-Din, who had scarcely seen it before. He had just decided that anybody who went to sea voluntarily must be mad, when Saladin turned to him and said: 'I think that when God grants me victory over the rest of Palestine I shall divide my territories, make a will stating my wishes and then set sail on this sea for their far-off lands and pursue the Franks there, so as to free the earth of anyone who does not believe in God.'[52] Saladin could no longer believe that the Franks believed in the same God as he, any more than Westerners at this time could see Muslims as worshippers of the same God as themselves. Baha ad-Din was also convinced that the Franks all over the world were the enemies of Muslims and of God himself. He was deeply impressed by Saladin's project of attacking the West, not only because the Sultan was brave enough to face sailing on that 'terrible sea' but because he was 'not content with extirpating God's enemies from a certain part of the earth', but he also wished to 'purify the whole world'. The Muslims had never before considered invading Western Europe, but the Crusades had convinced them that Westerners were the essential enemies of the Muslim people of the East. The new hatred of the West introduced into the East by Saladin's *jihad* also inspires the *jihad* in the East today, when a new wave of Western aggression and exploitation has led the new *mujahideen* to see ejection of the West and enmity to the West as essential to the integrity of Islam and the Orient.

The *jihad* inevitably led, therefore, to a hardening and further polarisation of attitude even in a man as compassionate as Saladin. It led to the creation of new enemies, to further distortion of the enemy's image and a determination to purify the whole world of this enemy. The defensive *jihad* for a land had become a holy war against the Western Christian world. In a man who was less compassionate the holy war would lead to even greater cruelties and this we can see in the hatred and enmity on both sides of the conflict in the Middle East today. Just as the Ayatollah Khomeini has developed a new intransigence towards Muslims who do not share his beliefs, so Saladin also believed in exterminating heretics – a totally unIslamic idea. Baha ad-Din praised him for this zeal in persecuting dissident thinkers. After noting Saladin's orthodox belief in the truths of Islam, he said that he 'hated all philosophers, heretics, materialists and all the opponents of the Law'.[53] In 1191 Saladin ordered as-Suharwardi, the young philosopher and mystic of Aleppo, to be crucified for his heresy, a practice that was alien to the spirit of Islam. The first Muslims had been horrified by the cruelty with which Christians persecuted other Christians who did not share their beliefs, and the Koran condemns this intolerance. But the mechanism of the *jihad* had led Saladin (as it would later lead Khomeini) to look for enemies in the Muslim camp. The Crusade would also lead to a new zeal for persecuting heretics in the West.

It is not surprising that the Franks of East and West should have come into Saladin's mind when he looked at the Mediterranean, for very soon after his victory at Hittin new Crusaders began to sail to the defence of their brethren. King William of Sicily arrived very promptly and helped to consolidate Christian resistance at Tyre. He had died in 1189 but then there was a new threat. Guy of Lusignan had been set free that year, and when he arrived at Tyre there was a struggle for the leadership between him and Conrad of Montferrat. Guy strengthened his own position by a quite uncharacteristic display of daring and decisiveness. He sailed down the coast to Acre and managed to besiege the city, against all the odds. He was able to hold the siege only because a new wave of Crusaders from Denmark and Frisia arrived over the sea to Acre when they heard of this new Christian initiative. Preachers sailed from Palestine to Europe to recruit more help and Ibn al-Athir gives us an interesting insight into the new Christian propaganda, which produced distorting images of Muslims and of Islam to show that they were now the abominable enemy of Christ and the Christian people:

> To incite the people to vengeance, they carried with them a painting of the Messiah, peace be upon him, bloodied by an Arab who was striking him. They would say: 'Look, here is the Messiah and here is Mohammad, the Prophet of the Muslims, beating him to death!' The Franks were moved and gathered together, women included; those who could not come along would pay the expenses of those who went to fight in their place. One of the enemy prisoners told me that he was an only son and that his mother had sold her house to buy his equipment for him. The religious and psychological motivation of the Franks was so strong that they were prepared to surmount all difficulties to achieve their ends.[54]

These propaganda devices ring true. They are simply variants of those distortions used by most people who have wanted to recruit soldiers for a long and difficult war, and Islam was well established as the enemy of Western Europe and of Christ. Saladin was deeply impressed by these hordes of Crusaders who began to pour into the crusading armies to come and avenge the loss of Jerusalem. When he heard of these ardent Crusaders, he told his troops that they must match this Christian religious fervour: 'All they have done, and all their generosity, has been done purely out of zeal for him they worship,'[55] he said and pointed out that the Muslims were shamefully lacking in this zeal. Nobody in Baghdad or Persia had answered his appeal for help in the *jihad*.

Yet in fact these Crusaders who were beginning to answer Pope Gregory VIII's call for a Third Crusade were not as fervent as Saladin imagined. It is undoubtedly the case that the loss of Jerusalem was very shocking. It would be similar to the distress Jews in the diaspora would feel today if Israel lost the Holy City. The people of Europe cried out for their leaders to go to the East to recover the Kingdom of Jerusalem and to fight the enemies of God. The Muslim victory, as always, threatened the Western Christian identity at a very deep level. Why had God allowed the heinous Saracens to triumph? It is true that the poor people were not so eager to accompany the armies; after the Second Crusaders had abandoned the poor in Asia Minor and left them to be killed and enslaved by the Turks, there was not unnaturally a decline in crusading fervour among the poor. But they wanted their rulers to go and when they saw three huge armies finally leaving Europe, led by the most powerful monarchs in Christendom, chroniclers speak of a huge surge of hope. Surely this massive Christian assault could not fail to recover the Holy City and re-establish the Christian kingdom. The honour of Christ would be restored. Western Christians who decided to stay at home still kept their eyes on the East and waited breathlessly to hear news of a great Christian victory once the first armies arrived in Acre in the spring of 1191.

Yet that date in itself is significant. After William of Sicily's prompt expedition no major crusading army left Europe until 1189. The Christians were trying to maintain a toehold in the Holy Land at Tyre and Acre against very great odds. Their position was very precarious and the siege grim and desperate and yet, despite this new surge of crusading enthusiasm, no army came from the West to relieve the Franks in Palestine. When Bernard had preached the Second Crusade in 1146 it had been only a matter of months before Conrad and Louis VII took their armies to the East. But in 1187 the potential Crusaders were far too busy about their business at home in Europe to consider fulfilling the Crusader vows that public opinion forced upon them.

Three of these Crusaders were actually at war with one another. King Henry II of England and King Philip Augustus in France were engaged in a brutal war, and were ceaselessly invading each other's territories in France. Henry's son Richard (later called the Lionheart) began fighting with his father but later callously joined forces with Philip. The endless bloodshed horrified most of their subjects and the Pope and various churchmen tried unsuccessfully to make peace. In this climate there was no way that these three kings, who had dutifully taken the Cross, could think about going to the Holy Land. On 6 July 1189, however, King Henry died at Chinon, having agreed to sign a truce two days earlier because of his illness. It is doubtful that he ever intended to go to the East, but his son and heir was anxious to fulfil his vow. This was not out of religious zeal: Richard was an excellent soldier and the Eastern campaign was an exciting military challenge, which also appealed to his love of adventure. Philip Augustus was far less enthusiastic, but realised that it would be impolitic to delay any longer. He and Richard signed a treaty and agreed to leave for the East later that year. On 3 September 1189 Richard was crowned

King of England in Westminster. This meant little to him; he was always more of a Frenchman than an Englishman and, though he had inherited his father's shrewd ruthlessness, he was also very much the son of his mother Eleanor of Aquitaine, who had divorced Louis VII and married Henry II after her return from the Second Crusade. Richard had a secular, intelligent outlook, enjoyed life at Poitiers and was himself a courtly poet. He was never very interested in being a king of England and shortly after his coronation he left for Vézelay, where he had agreed to meet Philip.

But before he did so an old crusading pattern asserted itself. In the last chapter we mentioned the rise of anti-semitism in England and the hysterical myth of the blood libel. A deputation of wealthy Jews attended Richard's coronation and was attacked by the crowd. Crusading always brought the hatred of the Jews to boiling point. The loss of Jerusalem and the prospect of an English king for the first time leading an army to the Holy Land brought a new passion for the Crusade to England and inevitably the Jews suffered. As soon as they knew that yet again Christians were to fight Muslims in the East, they automatically began to attack the Jews at home. The mob then attacked the Jewish community in London. As one of the chroniclers puts it: 'Many of those who were hastening to go to Jerusalem determined first to rise against the Jews.' By now the Jews and the Muslims were fused together in the Western consciousness as the enemies of God. When you decided to attack one, it was now a reflex to attack the other.

Richard had no time for this anti-semitism. He took a purely secular view of the situation and we will see that he had no hatred of Muslims either: they were just military enemies like any other and he did not single them out in a special category like most Western Christians. Indeed, Richard had always favoured the Jews, probably because they helped to finance his expensive wars in return. He quelled the riots in London and permitted a Jew who had submitted to baptism to save his life to return to his faith and abjure his baptismal vows. Baldwin, Archbishop of Canterbury, remarked that if the Jew did not wish to be God's man he had better belong to the devil, which clearly expressed the attitude of the established Church, even though it still did not condone the pogroms. But the crusading habit of anti-semitism was too firmly established for Richard to control. As Easter and Passover approached the following year and as more Crusaders left their homes and went to join Richard's army, all the buried fear and hatred of the Jews exploded violently: they were the heinous people who had killed Christ on Good Friday and had cried: 'His blood be upon us and upon our children!' They murdered little children and baked their special Passover bread with their blood and to kill them was a holy duty for Christians at a time when their great King was setting off to kill the Muslims. Pogroms erupted all over the country. The most serious of these was at York, where the wealthy Jewish community was massacred, even though they had taken refuge in the castle. Norwich, which had an established anti-semitic tradition, also suffered. As the chronicler records, 'All the Jews who were found in their own houses in Norwich were slaughtered; some had taken refuge in the castle.'[56] Killing Jews was now an indelible Christian habit and the English massacres at the time of the Third Crusade were another milestone for European Jewry, and a presage of even more terrible things to come.

While Richard and Philip had been occupied with their own European concerns, a far more spectacular Crusade left Europe. On 27 March 1188 the Holy Roman Emperor Frederick Barbarossa took the Cross, but a whole year elapsed before he actually left. Dedicated as he was, he was still most concerned about his affairs at home. In early May 1189 he finally set out on the dangerous land route with the largest force ever to march to the East. Awed contemporaries estimate that there were 50,000 horsemen and 100,000 infantry. They were well disciplined and morale in the army was high. Frederick had revived very old Crusader hopes. He was the first emperor to go on a Crusade and inevitably, when they saw this vast army marching towards Eastern Europe, people remembered the old Crusader dreams of the Last Emperor, who would conquer the East and force the return of Christ and the Last Days upon the world. There was a sudden eruption of apocalyptic fervour, which certainly inspired many soldiers in Frederick's army. This was exactly what Frederick had intended. His ambition was to revive the old ideal of the Holy Roman Empire of Charlemagne and to rule Germany and Italy as the new leader of Western Europe. To this end, Charlemagne suddenly got a new German identity, as Frederick encouraged the people to think of him as their own ancestor. Frederick had got Charlemagne canonised in Germany, even though Charlemagne had fought the Saxons of Germany in his holy wars and dragged them into Christendom by force. Next Frederick commissioned a monk of Aachen to write a new version of *The Legends of Charlemagne*, which made much of Charlemagne's legendary pilgrimage to the Holy Land and his so-called holy wars in Spain. When Frederick assumed the imperial title of Charlemagne, he was naturally presenting himself to Europe as the new Charlemagne and when he went on a Crusade, walking in the footsteps of his predecessor, he was powerfully reinforcing that idea. He knew that an Emperor like Alexander the Great had become the ruler of the known world of his time by his conquests in the East. With his powerful army, there seemed no good reason why Frederick should not easily defeat Saladin, have himself crowned in Jerusalem and thus become the most powerful man in the world. Once again Westerners were pursuing a Western fulfilment at the expense of the East and certainly Saladin watched the approach of the Emperor with dread. It seemed that his new *jihad* would be crushed after all. He sent Baha ad-Din to Baghdad to try to make the Caliph call a *jihad* but there was no interest in the holy war in the Islamic empire, except in Egypt and Syria.

Then a totally unexpected event occurred, which seemed like a new salvation for the Muslims. The German army had made its way through Eastern Europe and then entered into a conflict with the Emperor Isaac Angelus of Byzantium, who was not as wise or patient as either Alexius or Manuel Comnenus had been. When Frederick sent his envoys to Isaac to arrange for his troops to cross the Bosphorus, Isaac threw them into prison, meaning to hold them as hostages for German good behaviour. Frederick, the new Western Emperor, could not possibly tolerate this from his rival and counterpart. At once he sent his son to take the town of Didymotichum in Thrace as a counter-hostage and wrote home to his son Henry to organise a Crusade against the Greeks and to collect a fleet to sail against Constantinople. Once again the crusade had begun with an act of war against Byzantium. Isaac hastily climbed down and apologised and Frederick accepted the apology. He was, however, reluctant to cross Anatolia in the winter and it was not until March 1190 that he set off south, using the road taken by Alexander the Great. The journey was as difficult as it had always been and many Crusaders died. On 10 June the army arrived at the river of Calycadnus in the plain of Seleucia. At that point, Barbarossa leaped fully clad in his armour into the raging river. He may have wanted to cool himself in the summer heat or it may have been a display of crusading bravado but the shock proved too great for his ageing body and he drowned instantly, dragged under by the swift current. It was the end of the Crusade. Without their Emperor, the German Crusade lost its special appeal and, leaderless, the German soldiers could not continue their campaign. Frederick of Swabia tried to carry the army forward, but he lacked the personality and the imperial cachet. There were so many deserters that only a tiny remnant of the vast horde that had left Germany limped into Antioch. Many stayed on there to enjoy the fleshpots and did not accompany the faithful few who struggled on to Acre, only to lose heart and sail straight home again. To Saladin, this event obviously

seemed arranged by Allah and his conviction of the righteousness of his *jihad* soared. The death of the Emperor was a great blow to the West. It had seemed certain that the massive German effort, backed up by the French and English Crusades, would easily drive back the Muslims and liberate Jerusalem.

Meanwhile, on 4 July 1190 Richard and Philip set out from Vézelay. It had been agreed that they would meet in Sicily and sail to Acre, avoiding the disastrous land route, but instead of proceeding straight to relieve the desperate army at Acre, the two monarchs spent the whole winter in Sicily engaged in their own private wars. Richard at one point captured the city of Messina and threatened to go on to capture the whole province because his sister Joanna, who had been the wife of King William, had been ill-treated by Tancred, the new King of Sicily. Once Philip had forced a peace upon Richard and Tancred, the two Crusaders then began to quarrel about their own private affairs, in particular about Philip's sister Alice whom Richard had refused to marry. By the time those differences had been sorted out it was mid-October and it seemed wiser to postpone the departure to Acre until after the winter. Richard settled down to enjoy the winter with his sister Joanna now released from her confinement by Tancred; he also received a visit from his mother Eleanor of Aquitaine.

Finally in the spring of 1191 the dilatory Crusaders set out for Acre. Philip arrived fairly promptly and he began to reorganise the siege and prepare new engines of war. It was decided to delay the assault upon the city until Richard arrived, but, intent upon his own personal adventures, Richard did not arrive until 6 June, having conquered Cyprus *en route* and having also captured a Muslim supply ship. It must have been very galling to Philip to see the extraordinary welcome he received. Richard's handsome appearance, personal glamour and ruthless cleverness made him a far more charismatic figure than the able and patient but coldly unattractive Philip. There were huge demonstrations of joy when he arrived with twenty-five ships bearing men, arms and equipment, and the Franks lit great fires among their tents to celebrate his arrival. Richard's reputation had spread among the Muslims. They had heard that he was a man of great courage and spirit, with many of the qualities they admired in a leader. 'He had fought great battles and showed a burning passion for war,' wrote Baha ad-Din. 'His kingdom and standing were inferior to those of the French King, but his wealth, reputation and valour were greater.'[57] His arrival and the noisy exaltation of the Franks caused a panic among the Muslims, which Saladin met firmly, urging his men to rededicate themselves to the *jihad* which had the support of God himself.[58]

The siege of Acre had been one of the most grim conflicts of the whole crusading movement. Inside the city the Muslim garrison and civilians had endured a siege of two years. Round the city walls were the Christians and behind them was Saladin's army, unable to reach the Muslims inside the city. The Christians had been able to make no headway; there was sickness in the camp, which was bitterly divided. The conflict between Guy of Lusignan and Conrad of Montferrat was still raging and the arrival of the Crusaders exacerbated this: Philip supported Conrad and Richard supported Guy. Philip and Richard themselves were very uneasy partners and as soon as Richard arrived he began to lure some of Philip's men into his own army with money-bribes. There had always been a good deal of contention during a Crusade, but the Third Crusade was remarkable in the proliferation of quarrelling and petty rivalries that had nothing whatever to do with the holy war. It was not only the leaders who had lost the religious spirit; the ordinary soldiers in the army were 'secular' crusaders, inspired by profane enthusiasms.

While Saladin urged his men to place their trust in God and Islam, to read the *hadith* in the ranks and to public prayer for divine help, Richard resorted to much more practical tactics. There were no rousing sermons and no fasts. Instead he offered gold pieces to any man in the army who could take a stone from the city walls, which the Crusaders were trying to pull down. This would have been unthinkable in any previous Crusade, but it was effective now and there was a new spirit and new energy in the army. But this energy was largely secular and materialistic. The holy war had changed sides: now it was the Muslims who were religious and the Christians who were the seculars, but their religious zeal could not help the Muslim garrison inside the city of Acre and on 7 July a swimmer brought Saladin a message: unless he could bring them immediate aid they would have to surrender. The Crusaders and Christians were making frequent attacks on the walls and though they had not yet managed to break into the city, the garrison simply could not hold out against these vast forces for long. Saladin's soldiers could not make the breakthrough and on 12 July the garrison surrendered; when Saladin saw the Christian banners being unfurled from the walls he cried like a child. His *jihad* was no longer invincible.

Negotiations began. This simple statement marks a turning point in crusading, for this secular Crusade was unique because of the Christians' readiness to resort to diplomacy with the infidel. This would have shocked many of their crusading predecessors, who had found the very idea of a treaty with the Muslims an abomination. But the disaster of Hittin had knocked some hard common sense into the Christians of Palestine, who had seen what damage the obduracy of Reynauld of Chatillon and Gerard of Ridfort had done. Richard and Philip, of course, were secular, pragmatic realists and found nothing amiss with diplomacy. Saladin was defeated and bound to accept terms, once the Christians had shown their readiness to talk. It was agreed that Acre be surrendered to the Christians with its contents and ships; 1500 Christian prisoners-of-war should be released by the Muslims; the Muslims were to make money payments and the True Cross, which had been captured at Hittin, was to be restored to the Christians. Then the Franks moved into Acre and began to sort out their internal affairs. It was agreed that Guy should remain king until his death and that afterwards the throne should pass to Conrad – plans which came to nothing as both Guy and Conrad died within two years and the crown passed to Richard's nephew, Henry of Champagne. Philip decided that he had done his duty and could go home. He had been continuously ill since he arrived. He promised Richard that he would not invade his French lands while

Richard was in the East and sailed for home. He left a large number of his men behind and the leadership of the Crusade passed to Richard, who now prepared to continue the campaign against the Muslims.

Though his men, thoroughly enjoying themselves in Acre, were not eager to begin a new campaign, Richard was anxious to continue the Crusade. The army was financially burdened by a large number of Muslim prisoners-of-war, and Richard showed how ruthless he could be. On 20 August, when there was some delay in the transfer of the money that the Muslims had agreed to pay, he had 2700 Muslims, including women and children, brought outside the city walls and killed in cold blood, in full view of Saladin's army. There have been several explanations of Richard's war crime. Chroniclers claimed that he had been trying to avenge the massacre of the Templars and Hospitallers after Hittin. Others said that he was trying to shock the Muslims into returning the True Cross, which they seemed to have lost, and still others suggested that Saladin was being dilatory about the money on purpose and that Richard wanted to teach him a lesson. The massacre seems, however, to have happened for pragmatic reasons. When Saladin had had too many prisoners he had released some of them, but this act of mercy had backfired and led to an effective Christian resistance. When Richard had too many prisoners at Acre, he simply killed them all and this also proved to have been a bad mistake. Instead of terrifying the Muslims, Richard had given them a new reason to fight the *jihad.* During the siege of Acre Muslim morale had become very low, but when the Muslims saw that the Christians were as ready as ever to persecute them gratuitously in horrifying massacres, they committed themselves to the holy war with a new grimness and determination which would make them fight Richard's Crusaders with fresh vigour.

So hostilities resumed. The Crusaders were not used to the heat and many men were lost through sunstroke: they fainted, fell from their horses and were killed where they lay. Nevertheless Richard managed to push forward to Caesarea but then he asked for a new round of talks, which Saladin was bound to permit, despite the new confidence of his troops. As Richard demanded nothing less than the return of the whole of the Holy Land including Jerusalem to the Christians, these were not terms that were acceptable to the Muslims of the Near East nor to Islam, so the peace talks broke up. On 7 September, Saladin attacked the Christians at Arsuf but was defeated by a narrow margin. Now Christian morale surged and the Muslims began to look askance at Saladin, who was no longer the conquering hero of Hittin and seemed to have lost his bearings. The Crusaders occupied Jaffa and again Richard opened negotiations and asked for a truce.

Both sides needed a rest from the fighting. Saladin needed to recover from his recent failures and had to fortify Jerusalem and the rest of the country. Richard, despite his success, was a realist: he knew perfectly well that the Christians were in no position to fight a full-scale campaign to liberate the rest of the country. The Franks of Palestine had been decimated and weakened at the battle of Hittin and would be in no position to keep the whole of the Holy Land once the Crusaders had gone home. Richard wanted to recoup some of the Christian losses by means of diplomacy, which would prevent further bloodshed. Al-Adil, however, was aware of the vulnerability of the Christian position and he advised Saladin not to come to terms too readily. During the negotiations, Richard talked to al-Adil. He was fascinated by Saladin and would have loved to have met him personally, but the Sultan declined, saying that it was not fitting for two kings to meet while they were still in a state of war. The negotiations were conducted in a very friendly spirit. Richard, the secular Crusader, certainly did not see the Muslims as monsters like the religious extremists and he soon became very fond of al-Adil, whom he called 'my brother and my friend'.[59]

But in spite of the cordiality and good will on both sides there was deadlock when they discussed the possession of Jerusalem. Richard insisted that the Holy City belonged to the Christians. 'Jerusalem is for us an object of worship that we could not give up,' he wrote to Saladin, 'even if there were only one of us left.' The same applied to the whole of the Holy Land: 'It *must* be consigned to us.'[60] Richard was honestly trying to be rational and practical and saw the situation realistically. But the 'holiness' of the country made it impossible for him to be rational, however hard he tried. He could not formulate a logical political argument, but spoke with the inarticulate urgency that we have seen Jews and Christians falling into when they speak about the possession of this land. Both have felt that their claims are self-evidently right, even though this claim cannot be backed logically. For all his secular attitudes, Richard was emotionally convinced that Christians 'must' possess the Holy Land, convinced at a very deep level, too deep for him to explain, because it was crucial to his whole Western identity. Saladin, however, had no difficulty about putting his case rationally in political as well as in religious terms:

> Jerusalem is ours as much as yours: indeed it is even more sacred to us than it is to you, for it is the place from which our Prophet accomplished his nocturnal journey and the place where our community will gather on the day of Judgement. Do not imagine that we can renounce it or vacillate on this point. The land was originally ours, whereas you have only just arrived and have taken it over because of the weakness of the Muslims living there at that time.[61]

It is another instance of the rationality of the *jihad*, when compared with the emotional nature of crusading.

Richard's next move was an extraordinary proposal that amazed both sides. He suggested that his sister Joanna should marry al-Adil and that they should rule in Jerusalem together as Muslim king and Christian queen.[62] Joanna would rule the coastal cities that the Christians had reconquered during this Third Crusade, and al-Adil would rule the rest of Palestine, which Saladin had won. Christians should have access to Jerusalem once more, so that they could pray at their holy places. The important point about this outrageous but inspired suggestion was that Richard would have suggested this solution in Europe. He did not put 'Muslims' in a human category of their own; he saw them as normal people and he dealt with them just as he would have dealt with Frenchmen and Englishmen. As one might expect, nothing came of this suggestion. Saladin simply assumed that Richard was making a good joke. A serious man himself, he found Richard's exuberance lacking in the gravity that befitted a knight, though he had come to respect him as a soldier. But the Christians were horrified and Joanna herself refused point-blank to marry an infidel. The churchmen supported her by saying that such a marriage would in any case be invalid. But, nothing daunted, Richard asked al-Adil if he would be willing to get round this by becoming a Christian, and al-Adil, who was by no means as religious as his brother, declined very politely but invited Richard to dinner at Lydda on 8 November.[63] The banquet was a great success and Christians and Muslims exchanged gifts and parted with warm demonstrations of affection and avowals of eternal friendship. Richard's solution of sharing the Holy Land was too controversial for anybody to accept and indeed in this matter we have not advanced beyond the medieval Crusaders and *mujahideen*. Most Jews and Arabs would find such a solution impossible today. Yet the fact that Richard was able to suggest it shows that he was different from previous Crusaders because he was ready to compromise with the infidel. He could see the futility of this religious warfare and realised that events were getting out of control. He had written to the Sultan: 'the Muslims and the Franks are bleeding to death, the country is utterly ruined and goods and lives have been sacrificed on both sides. The time has come

to stop this.'[64] When Christians and Muslims could get on together as well as he and al-Adil, this endless killing was ridiculous. But in a religious conflict, people are not ready to accept policies that recommend compromise and living together.

At the end of the year the talks had reached deadlock again, so the fighting resumed, but still both sides were in constant touch and ready to talk. Richard managed to conquer more towns along the coast as far as Askelon, but Saladin was always able to take back one city, whenever Richard had won another. It was a military stalemate. Twice the Crusaders advanced as far inland as Beit Nuba, which is only twelve miles from Jerusalem, and on both occasions the common soldiers became inspired for the first time by the old crusading passions. The mere proximity of the Holy City had, as usual, touched some vital nerve and they longed to go forward and conquer the city. Inside Jerusalem, the Muslims were certain that the Christians would advance and knew that in that case they would be in for a hard siege and perhaps even a defeat. They also knew that the Crusaders would not behave like Saladin and that there would be another massacre, perhaps even more violent than the massacre of 1099, as the Christians avenged Hittin. Although the emirs blustered and protested their loyalty, there was panic in the city and the leaders feared a massive desertion.

Saladin's reaction to this crisis gives us a telling view of the essentially practical nature of the Islamic *jihad*. He was deeply depressed by the events of the Third Crusade, for which he had to blame himself in large measure, and the first time Richard's troops reached Beit Nuba it seemed to him that all was lost. The enthusiasm for *jihad* was still very new in the Muslim world and had not taken deep root; he was very much afraid that his emirs would desert and all night long he and Baha ad-Din sat up, turning over all the possible courses of action and discussing first this solution and then that. They felt increasingly desolate: 'It was winter,' wrote Baha ad-Din, 'and we were alone but for God.'[65] Yet they could find no solution to their frightening predicament and Saladin seemed overwhelmed with despair. Eventually they went to bed, but scarcely had their heads touched the pillow when the muezzin called the faithful to the dawn prayer. Baha ad-Din went back to the Sultan's room to make his prayers with him as usual and found Saladin washing himself. Both men looked at each other blearily and admitted that they had not slept a wink. But that morning Baha ad-Din had an idea – an idea that would have occurred to a Crusader long ago. Why did they not pray about this? he asked. They had done everything they possibly could, exhausted all their human resources and there was nothing more they could do. Surely they should put the matter in God's hands. Ninety years earlier, when the First Crusaders had found themselves facing almost certain disaster in Antioch, they had turned instinctively to prayer and had saved themselves by finding a visionary solution. But Baha ad-Din clearly felt that prayer for divine aid was a rather controversial idea, for he seemed to need to argue it out:

> on this subject there is an authentic *hadith* of the Prophet, saying: 'My God, all my earthly power to bring victory to your Faith has come to nothing: my only resource is to turn to You and to rely on Your help and trust in Your goodness. You are my sufficiency, You are the best preserver!' God is too generous to let your prayers go to waste.[66]

It seemed a novel suggestion to Saladin too: 'How shall we do it?' he asked, a question that would have seemed patently unnecessary to a Crusader. Baha ad-Din did not suggest an outpouring of personal prayer or a mystical flight but a very formal and official petition. He advised Saladin to give alms privately and perform two *raka'at* (ritual prostrations) at the Friday prayers that afternoon at al-Aqsa. Saladin followed his secretary's advice. He performed two *raka'at* on the very spot whence the Prophet ascended to heaven during the Night Journey. 'I saw him prostrate,' Baha ad-Din recorded, 'with tears running down his white beard and on to his prayer-mat, but I could not hear what he said.'[67] The story shows us that, unlike the Jews and Christians in their holy war, Muslims do not expect God to intervene to save them. Theirs is a more self-reliant faith and they feel that God expects them to fight as though everything depended upon them. God will not help them unless they have made every effort to save themselves first.

On the very same day the captain of the advance guard brought Saladin some marvellous news. The Franks had left Beit Nuba and were marching back to the coast. The danger was over. But where a Christian would have seen that as entirely due to God and an answer to prayer, Baha ad-Din gives a very accurate account of Richard's own very practical reasons for withdrawing and not attacking the city. The Templars and Hospitallers had persuaded him that conquering the Holy City would be useless and ultimately even dangerous for the Christians who lived in Palestine. After the Crusaders had gone home, Saladin would certainly reconquer al-Quds and might follow that by a new offensive against the Franks in their coastal cities. Further, the winter rains were very heavy and the hills around Jerusalem almost impassable. Previous Crusaders would have scorned such prudence and caution and Richard's men, inspired for the first time by religious zeal, clamoured for him to go forward. Richard, the secular pragmatist, would not dream of leaving it all in God's hands and went back to Jaffa, persuaded by these eminently sensible suggestions. His secular crusading was in fact very close in spirit to Saladin's Islamic *jihad*, which turned to God only as a last resort. On the second occasion that Richard's army reached Beit Nuba, he managed to capture a large Muslim convoy carrying food and equipment to Jerusalem, taking rich booty and thousands of horses and camels. Yet still Richard would not capitalise on his victory for the same pragmatic reasons. One day, while he was riding in the hills that surround Jerusalem, he suddenly came within sight of the Holy City. Instantly he covered his face with his shield and turned away: he would not look at the city, he cried, that God had not allowed him to conquer.[68] This was a knightly gesture, but in reality Richard had no intention of jeopardising the security of the Christians in Palestine by pressing on to Jerusalem.

By August he was desperate for a settlement. There was absolute military deadlock between the two sides; his troops, having been twice balked of the chance of conquering Jerusalem, were furious and almost mutinous; he had bad news from home, where Philip Augustus – his former fellow Crusader – had invaded his lands in France, despite his promise. Finally Richard himself became ill. Saladin graciously sent him his own doctor and sent gifts of fruit and snow to make cooling drinks, but he remained adamant and would make no further concessions. Eventually on 2 September, Richard capitulated and a treaty was signed for five years, which showed that both sides had had to compromise from their original absolutism. Saladin had to accept that he was not going to be able to throw all the Franks into the sea and then pursue them into Europe. Instead, there would be a thin coastal kingdom stretching from Jaffa to Beirut which would have its capital at Acre, though its king would still wistfully call himself King of Jerusalem. Richard had to accept that he was not going to reconquer the Holy City but he had won the right for Christian pilgrims to pray there. Muslims and Christians had to recognise each other's existence in Palestine and in the Holy City.

The story of the fall of Jerusalem and the Third Crusade seems to suggest that where practical realism prevailed there was a possibility of peaceful coexistence and mutual respect. It was their religions that drove the Christians and Muslims apart. Otherwise they shared the same courtly values. Saladin and Richard both respected each other as knights. At one moment during a battle at Jaffa, when the

Crusaders' cavalry seemed exhausted, Richard himself led the spearmen in a charge against the Muslims, and Saladin was almost beside himself with furious admiration. When he saw Richard's horse fall under him, the Sultan at once sent his groom into the fray with two fresh horses for the brave King of England.[69] It is another example of the secular grace with which Muslim and Christian could respond to one another in gestures that both perfectly understood. In Europe there were many similar legends about the two great knights Richard and Saladin. In one of these, Richard entered Jerusalem *incognito* and dined with Saladin: they had a very amicable meal and in the course of conversation Richard asked the Sultan what he thought of the King of England. Saladin replied that Richard excelled in the chivalric virtue of bravery, but that he was sometimes inclined to spoil this by being too rash in battle. For his part, he, Saladin, preferred to cultivate the chivalric virtues of moderation, even in battle.[70] The story shows that in Europe Richard and Saladin were both seen as exemplars of the chivalric ideal. It is a criticism of Richard and a praise of the Sultan who conquered Jerusalem, but who was still seen as a true knight with qualities that Richard lacked. Instead of seeing the Muslim and the Christian as polar opposites, the legend shows them as two halves of the ideal knight.

The legend of Richard in Europe is revealing in another way. He must surely be one of the most famous of the English kings and yet after his coronation he spent only a few months in the country, which he bled dry to pay for his campaigns in France and in the Holy Land. Yet during his absence on the Crusade he became known as the Lionheart and is reputed to have been a great king of England simply because he led an army to the Holy Land. It shows that crusading was deeply important as a value in Europe, for all that it seemed to be becoming a rather secular pursuit. Perhaps one of the most famous legends about Richard concerns his favourite troubadour Blondel of Nesle. On his way home from Palestine, Richard was taken prisoner in Austria and Blondel wandered throughout Europe, searching for him. One day he sat beneath the walls of the castle where Richard was a prisoner and sang a song that he and the King had composed together. Halfway through he paused, and Richard, who had been listening in his cell, took the song up and Blondel could go to England and tell the people where Richard was. The story shows a yearning devotion to the Crusader King, who seems bathed in a highly idealised and romantic light, even though he was really a ruthless and even cruel pragmatist. For those who stayed at home, crusading was becoming a distant and glamorous affair, very different from the bloody reality. Yet there was another legend too that shows a buried worry about this new kind of Crusader who sailed home without bothering to go and pray at the Holy Sepulchre: he is reputed to have eaten Muslim flesh with relish – he had been sick unto death at the siege of Acre and developed a craving for pork. Because there was none available in this Muslim country, the desperate cook served up Saracen flesh instead and Richard not only found it quite delicious but was instantly cured. He rose from his bed immediately and went out to massacre a few thousand Muslims. When he found out what he had eaten, he simply roared with laughter. During the First Crusade, the Tafurs had been said to eat Muslim flesh, but they had not enjoyed it like Richard, who seems to break this taboo quite easily and feel no disgust. This story was very popular in France during the reign of Richard's enemy Philip Augustus, but it may reflect a repressed view of crusading as a monstrous activity, especially when one bears in mind the sympathetic legends that were developing about Saladin.[71]

The story of Richard's Crusade shows a certain cooling of the religious atmosphere among the Crusaders; similarly, after the death of Saladin in 1193, Muslims quickly lost their enthusiasm for the *jihad*, once the Christian menace had been reduced and cut down to size. Al-Adil eventually succeeded his brother

and showed that he was far more secular in spirit and was perfectly prepared to live side by side with the Franks in Palestine and Egypt. After 1193 Christians and Muslims found that coexistence could even be mutually enriching in purely secular ways. Both derived great benefit from trade and commerce with each other and were reluctant to jeopardise this by futile holy wars. Once there had been a religious *détente*, they might have gone on living side by side in peace, but the Crusaders from Europe made this impossible. Today, however, the people of the Middle East have turned once again to religion and we are now in a position to understand why this should have happened and what the consequences of this new cycle of religious warfare are likely to be.

CHAPTER SEVEN

1967

Zionism Becomes a Holy War

The terrifying weeks before the Six Day War in 1967 have become known as the *Hamtana*, the waiting period, in Israel. The Israelis were waiting to be exterminated. As they listened to Nasser vowing to annihilate the Jewish state and to their Prime Minister, Levi Eshkol, mumbling confusedly in his speech to the nation, it seemed that the perils of the diaspora in Europe had followed the Jewish people to the Middle East. Yet again they were surrounded by enemies who wanted to wipe their memory from the earth and the Jews seemed weak, passive and fatally ineffective. The Zionist enterprise had failed.[1] But when the Israeli army reversed the situation in the spectacular victory of the June war, it must have seemed like a salvation in the old sense, like the salvation at the Red Sea when God had saved his people from certain death and destroyed their enemies. We have seen that an unexpected victory or a dramatic reversal of fortune has often made people feel that they have a special divine destiny and the Six Day War marked a new stage in Zionism and brought a strong religious element into the old secular movement. There was another reason for this, besides the success of Israel, which had conquered a great deal of Arab territory: the Sinai peninsula and the Gaza Strip had been taken from Egypt, the Golan Heights from Syria and the area known as the West Bank from Jordan. The Holy City of Jerusalem had also been 'liberated' from the Arabs. Since 1948 Jews had not been able to enter the old city or pray at the Wailing Wall, and this reunion with Jerusalem stirred up those powerful emotions that we have witnessed before in our story. The tough young commandos who had fought their way through to the last remaining wall of the Temple laid their heads against its ancient stones and wept, even those who were not, at that time, at all religious.[2]

The Zionists had always turned instinctively to the religious values and customs of Judaism when they wanted to develop their movement, and they naturally did so once again. The philosopher Martin Buber compared the victory to the salvation of the Israelites at the Red Sea.[3] Yitzhak Rabin, who had liberated the Old City of Jerusalem, described the reunion with the Wailing Wall as a moment of religious illumination: it 'revealed as though by a flash of lightning truths that were deeply hidden'.[4] 'It was a truly religious movement,' the Israeli scholar Harold Fisch has written, 'the experience of a miracle. It had a special metaphysical character.'[5] The victory also had a profound effect upon the Jews of the diaspora, just as the Crusaders' conquest of Jerusalem had strongly stirred the Christians of Europe. 'God has had a dream,' wrote the American Zionist scholar Abraham Heschel, 'and the task of Israel is to interpret that dream.' He saw the victory as yet another example of God's continuous love affair with his people, of which the creation of

Israel was just the latest example: 'In the upbuilding of the land we are aware of responding to the Biblical Covenant, to an imperative that kept on speaking to us throughout the ages, and which never became obsolete or stale.'[6] Just as the Crusaders had seen their victory as an act of salvation history that had vital consequences for the whole world, Zionists began to feel that they had a religious mission and were acting out the divine plan. In this exalted mood, there was no question in the minds of many Israelis that they had a right to keep the territories they had conquered from the Arabs, even though the United Nations ordered them to evacuate them. Why should they obey the *goyim* when God clearly had other intentions for the Holy Land?

But not everybody shared this mood of triumph and national pride. Shortly after the Six Day War, some leftist intellectuals and writers interviewed the soldiers of the *kibbutzim* who had fought in the war and found a mood of disillusion and dismay. They recorded their findings in a book called *The Seventh Day*.[7] When they were asked why the Jews had more of a right to the Land of Israel than the Palestinians and the Arab states the soldiers had no answer and shook their heads blankly. Some of the younger soldiers who had been born after the creation of the State of Israel were shocked to discover that the Palestinians in the camps of the newly occupied territories were still yearning to return to the land that they regarded as their own. They found it baffling to hear these refugees talking about their homes in cities like Beersheba or Haifa, which were now completely Jewish. 'It made my blood boil,' one of them said, 'I remember I couldn't grasp it. After all nineteen years had passed. . . . How dare you say that you are from Beersheba . . . that you are from Rehevoth.'[8] We have seen that Sabras like S. Yizah and Amos Oz had questioned the Jews' 'right' to their land from the earliest days of the state. Despite their Zionist upbringing, these young people from the *kibbutzim*, which fulfilled the ideals of Labour Zionism in their purest form, had not been convinced that the land was theirs and were unable to make any coherent response to the Arab point of view.

Some of the soldiers interviewed in *The Seventh Day* had found themselves actually identifying with the Palestinians. The Nazi Holocaust had been crucial in forming the Israeli identity and has continued to be so. During the war some of the soldiers asked themselves whether the Jews were not persecuting the Palestinians. One soldier recalled 'a terrible feeling'[9] when he met the Palestinians in the Occupied Territories as a conqueror:

Kids, three or four years old, already knew how to raise their arms, to walk about town with raised arms. For me this was awful. Kids the age of my son walk with their arms above their heads. I remember that old men and women came to implore. It was an awful feeling, awful. It's a horrible feeling to have to explain to these women that nobody intends to kill their husbands. Horrible, and I can't free myself from it.[10]

Amos Elon points out that the soldier was probably subconsciously recalling the famous photograph of the terrified Jewish child holding his hands above his head in Nazi-occupied Poland, a photograph with which every Israeli is familiar. Other soldiers made the same connection. As one of them said:

'If I had a clear association with the . . . holocaust, it was in a certain moment, when I was going up the Jericho–Jerusalem road and the refugees were streaming down. . . . I felt directly identified with them. When I saw those children carried in their parents' arms, I almost saw myself carried by my father . . . my identification was precisely with the other side, with our enemies.' Still another soldier bitterly admitted that when he entered an Arab refugee camp in order to put down a disorder, he felt 'like a Gestapo man... I thought of home, I thought my parents were being led away.'[11]

The mood of these soldiers reflected the obscure distress and buried guilt felt by many Israelis after the Six Day War. If these Israelis turned to religion to express their feelings, they did so in a quite different spirit from their fellow countrymen, who saw the victory as yet another triumph for the chosen people. The poet Yehuda Amichai had fled Nazi Germany with his parents in 1936 when he was twelve years old and had come to Israel as a refugee. After the Six Day War he wrote the short poem 'On the Day of Atonement':

> On the Day of Atonement in 1967
> I put on my dark holiday suit, and went to the Old City in Jerusalem.
> I stood for some time,
> before the alcove of an Arab's shop,
> not far from the Damascus Gate,
> a shop of buttons and zippers and spools of thread in all colours,
> and snaps and buckles.
> A glorious light and a great many colours
> like a Holy Ark with its doors ajar.
> I told him in my heart that my father, too,
> had such a shop of threads and buttons.
> I explained to him in my heart all about the tens of years
> and the reasons and the circumstances
> because of which I am now here
> and my father's shop is in ashes there,
> and he is buried here.
>
> By the time I had finished,
> it was the hour of 'the Locking of the Gates'.
> He too pulled down the shutter and locked the gate,
> and I went home with all the worshippers.[12]

The prophets and sages of Judaism had taught Jews to examine their actions and exercise imaginative compassion for others. But some Israelis were returning to the spirit of Joshua and David, feeling that the land was theirs by divine decree and that the *goyim* had no right there at all. They spoke of the Six Day War as redeeming the land and liberating it for the Jewish people. From this time there would be a deep split between these hawks and the doves, who insist on a purely secular perspective. After the 1967 victory Amos Oz published an article in the newspaper *Davar* putting the secular point of view strongly:

> For a month, for a year, or for a whole generation we will have to sit as occupiers in places that touch our hearts with their history. And we must remember: as occupiers, because there is no alternative. And as a pressure tactic to hasten peace. Not as saviours or liberators. Only in the twilight of myths can one speak of the liberation of a land struggling under a foreign yoke. Land is not enslaved and there is no such thing as a liberation of lands. There are enslaved people, and the word 'liberation' applies only to human beings. We have not liberated Hebron and Ramallah and El Arish, nor have we redeemed their inhabitants. We have conquered them and we are going to rule over them only until our peace is secured.[13]

Religion does not have to be a dangerous element in politics. It can encourage morality and decency in public relations and foster a concern for others. A Judaism that returns to the tenet of Rabbi Hillel: 'Do not do unto others as you would not have done unto you'[14] will be concerned with the plight of other human beings. It forces people to make a connection which is the basis of a certain kind of morality and beneficence, however painful this connection might be. But to return to what Oz calls 'the twilight of myths' can lead to a complete distortion of realities. When people feel that they have a special destiny, everything that concerns them seems larger than life.

In the socialist periodical *Progressive Israel* the Israeli commentator Levi Morav explained this dangerous tendency, which he calls 'catastrophic', that entered Zionism after the Six Day War: 'Its starting point is that nothing is simply just what it is – everything is gigantic, tremendous, colossal, one-of-a-kind, exceptional.'[15] Thus he points out that the building of a bridge over a creek of muddy water in the Occupied Territories now tends to be described as 'proving the eternity of the Jewish people', the final answer to the schemes of the anti-semites. A new road cutting across a densely populated Arab area in the territories proves 'the eternity of the people of Israel's return to its historic and undivided homeland and a challenge to the genocidal schemes of Arafat and Company'.[16] The cornerstone of a new industrial plant is an historic stone, a return after 2000 years of exile:

> The danger to any people's spirit and soul lies first of all in the corruption of its language. A bridge over a stream has to ease traffic, a broad new road must cut the time needed to travel from one place to another, a new plant has to provide employment. Important and necessary plants have nothing to do with the eternity of Israel. Not every new drainage ditch is a singular historic event.[17]

Early Zionism, like early crusading, had been an intensely practical movement. But this tendency to consider one's every movement to be larger than life or even part of the divine plan has introduced an unreality that could be seriously damaging. The Crusaders who were inspired by St Bernard to see their Second Crusade as part of the divine plan found to their cost that a failure to see things as they are can be very dangerous, even fatal. There had always been an essential myopia in Zionism. At the same time as the settlers were labouring to make a Jewish presence in Palestine an established fact, they had at first been blind to the reality of the Palestinian people and had never taken their claims seriously enough. But some of their Sabra children had seen what they had done to the Palestinian people and they were trying to make their people aware of this. Amichai and Oz were still trying after the Six Day War. But the new sense of the 'holiness' of Zionism that entered Israel has meant that Israelis on the right, whether they are secular or religious, have such an inflated view of themselves and their state that the claims of the Arabs are seen as either ludicrously insignificant or else perverse and blasphemous, because they are standing in the way of the divine plan.

After the 1967 victory, some secular Zionists therefore remained unimpressed with the new hawks. In particular Ben Gurion did not see Jerusalem as a holy city and its recovery as a metaphysical event. He referred to the Israeli conquest there as the acquisition of so much real estate. He also felt that the Territories should be given back, because the Israelis had plenty of land for their needs. If anybody wanted new lands to conquer they should come and join him in the Negev (he was living on the Negev *kibbutz* Sde Boker) and reclaim the desert.[18] But in 1967 people in Israel were sick of Ben Gurion and were finding him bombastic and tedious.[19] Nobody was likely to take much notice of the former Prime Minister's condemnation of the new Israeli chauvinism.

We have seen that the Zionists had often used religious words to explain their movement, and after the 1967 victory the word 'holy' came into Zionism for the first time. When Prime Minister Levi Eshkol first entered the Old City, he said: 'I see myself as a representative of an entire nation, and of many past generations whose souls yearn for Jerusalem and its holiness.'[20] The secular Jewish state was becoming a holy land and while one might consider making concessions about ordinary territory, there is no question of returning 'holy' land, because that would be a betrayal of the highest and most sacred values of all. We have seen this in the conflict between Muslims and Christians during the Crusades. Moshe Dayan, the hero of the Six Day War, also demonstrated this new intransigent respect for the holiness of the new capital of Israel, when it was his turn to enter Jerusalem for the first time. 'We have returned to all that is holy in our land,' he said. 'We have returned to it never to be parted from it again.'[21]

Dayan continued this theme a few months later on 3 August when he presided over a ceremony on the Mount of Olives, which had always been a favourite spot for Jews to be buried because the Messiah was to appear there and the Jews buried on the Mount would be the first to greet him when they rose from the dead. Now that the Israelis had conquered the Mount of Olives, they had decided to reinter there the bodies of the soldiers who had died in the 1948 war. They had fought for the Jewish homeland and been a secular Messiah for the Jewish people, and Dayan spoke of the sacred dreams of the Zionists and of the return of the Jewish people to the West Bank, which had such hallowed associations:

> Our brothers, who fought in the war of Independence: we have not abandoned your dream, nor forgotten the lesson you taught us. . . . We have returned to the Mount, to the cradle of the nation's history, to the land of our forefathers, to the land of the Judges, and to the fortress of David's dynasty. We have returned to Hebron, Shechem, Bethlehem and Anatoth, to Jericho and the ford over the Jordan. Our brothers, we bear your lessons with us. . . . we know that to give life to Jerusalem we must station the soldiers and armour of the Israeli Defence Forces on the Shechem mountains and on the bridges over the Jordan.[22]

The West Bank was 'holy' in a way that the old State of Israel in the Galilee and on the coastal plain was not. It was biblical country, the country of Abraham, Joshua and King David. At Hebron was the great tomb of the patriarchs Abraham, Isaac and Jacob, venerated by Muslims and Christians as well as by the Jews. At Shechem (the Arab town of Nablus) Joshua had made a covenant between the tribes of Israel and God, after he had conquered the country and slaughtered the Amelecites. Bethlehem had been the birthplace of King David, who like Joshua had massacred thousands of *goyim* in his holy wars against the Philistines. At Bethlehem too was the tomb of Rachel, the wife of Jacob, who was said to have risen and wept as she watched the children of Israel passing her tomb on their way into exile in Babylon in 589 BCE. On the holy West Bank, the Israelis encountered a Judaism that saw the integrity of the people of Israel and their religion as essentially tied to the physical possession of the Land of Israel and to a violent rejection of the Gentiles. Just a few months after his acquisition of this Holy Land, Dayan saw Jerusalem as so quintessentially Jewish that the city would perish if the Israelis withdrew their forces from the 'Shechem mountains' and the Jordan bridges.

Yet for the Gentiles, who could not share this Jewish view of the Holy Land, the Israeli presence in the Occupied Territories was illegal, because it contravened the international law that stated that territory occupied during a war must be given back once the hostilities had ceased. When the Israelis showed that they had absolutely no intention of withdrawing from the Territories they had conquered, the Security Council of the United Nations issued Resolution 242 on 22 November 1967. This called for:

(i) Withdrawal of Israeli armed forces from territories of recent conflict;

(ii) Termination of all claims or states of belligerency and respect for and acknowledgement of the sovereignty, territorial integrity and political independence of every state in the area and their right to live in peace within secure and recognized boundaries free from acts and threats of force.[23]

But Dayan had made it abundantly clear that Israel had no intention of obeying this purely human law nor was he going to respect the rights of the Palestinian people in the Territories. He was not a religious man, but the 'holiness' of the Jewish past meant that the people of Israel operated on quite another plane from other people. Many Israelis absolutely endorsed this policy, as they do today. Immediately after the victory, the Israelis started to 'occupy' the Territories in the time-honoured fashion of the secular pilgrimage. Hitherto their trips in the Land of Israel had usually not been to religious sites, but now when they started to tour the West Bank they found themselves stirred by this return to their physical and religious roots as a people, when they visited the Tomb of the Patriarchs or the Wailing Wall. They felt as convinced that this land was 'theirs' as Richard the Lionheart, when he had inarticulately but passionately argued to Saladin that the same holy land 'must' be returned to the Christians.

But other steps had been taken to ensure that the Territories remained in Jewish hands beside the posting of the IDF along the new borders of Israel. The Labour government at once established twenty settlements along the valley of the River Jordan to ensure the 'security' of the State of Israel. These were new *kibbutzim* and were at one and the same time agricultural and military settlements. In the Sinai, General Chaim Bar Lev established a system of military defence against Egypt, which he believed to be impregnable. The old Zionist habit of making a Jewish presence an established fact by practical and aggressive measures came automatically into action. The army also had to tour the inhabited areas, putting down the unrest which naturally broke out, as the people of the Territories began to realise that the Israelis were there to stay. A draconian occupation was established, which brutally deprived the Palestinians there of basic human rights.

Yet besides these official, government steps to occupy the Territories, individual Israelis started to take a pioneering initiative themselves, just as the early settlers of the First, Second and Third Aliyah had done at the beginning of Zionist history. They would not wait until the Territories became Jewish officially but would do it themselves. Zionism had planted strong hungers and needs in the Sabras and pioneering was obviously deeply embedded in the Israeli identity, but many young Israelis felt that the *kibbutz* movement was not the same as it had been in the good old days of vintage Zionism. The early *kibbutzim* had been aggressive and had a military dimension that the new ones lacked since the state had been established officially. Indeed the *kibbutzim* had produced those disillusioned and worried soldiers whose revelations in *The Seventh Day* were scorned by the belligerent Zionists of the new right in Israel and were seen as a sign of the spiritual bankruptcy of the old Labour Zionism. As soon as there was a possibility of a more daring type of pioneering many young Israelis instantly responded to what they perceived to be a challenge to the proud Jewish self, showing how frustrated they had felt with the previous *status quo*. Immediately after the war, a group of writers, academics and politicians formed the Movement for the Land of Israel, which provided financial and moral support to any *kibbutzniks* who wanted to colonise the Territories. On 15 June 1967, days after the ceasefire, Kibbutz Merom Hagolam, the first of the Movement settlements, was established on the Golan Heights near Quneitra, very close to the new border and only fifty kilometres from Damascus.[24] These new settlers saw themselves as taking up the pioneering challenge that the old *kibbutzim* of the left had abandoned. They would lovingly cultivate the so-called Land of Israel and press aggressively against the frontiers of the Arab world as the early settlers had done sixty years earlier. Like the soldier–monks in the orders of the Temple and the Hospital in the Middle Ages, they had put themselves on the front line and were dreaming of future conquests in the Arab world. There was much talk of a 'Greater Land' of Israel and this new secular movement showed that Zionism was moving more explicitly towards a belligerent religiosity. [25]

The early settlers had wanted to build a Jewish homeland in the land of their fathers and they had achieved their aim in 1948 when the modern State of Israel was established. But this 'Greater Land' of Israel had no political or geographical reality in the modern world; it was a purely biblical concept. God had promised a land to Abraham that had extensive frontiers:

> That very day, the Lord made a covenant with Abram and he said: 'To your descendants I give this land from the River of Egypt to the great River: the River Euphrates, the territory of the Kenites, Kenizites, Kadmonites, Hittites, Perizzites, Raphaim, Amorites, Canaanites, Girgashites, Hivites and Jebusites.
> (Genesis 15:18–21)

Biblical scholars have described these frontiers as including parts of what are now Sinai, Lebanon, Syria, Iraq and Jordan. These frontiers had never been achieved and always remained a promise for the future. When biblical Israel achieved its greatest expansion under King Solomon nothing like these boundaries had been established, but the chosen people had only managed a kingdom that extended a little way from the coast into what is now Syria and Jordan. But the victory of 1967 had taken a dramatic step towards the realisation of that biblical promise. Israel was not yet at the Euphrates, but she was very nearly at the Nile. These new secular *kibbutzniks* were dreaming of future conquests that would realise this ancient, legendary promise and enable the people of Israel to fulfil their whole potential in a way that they had never managed before. Many started to plan a state on both sides of the Jordan. They somehow saw that land as 'belonging' to them, even though their fathers had never lived there, except as aliens and exiles. From the moment that the Second Congress of Basle had committed the first Zionists to a state in the ancient homeland they had introduced religion into their secular movement. How could you be a *secular* Zionist and still maintain that you had a right to settle in Palestine or on the West Bank, unless in some sense you endorsed the promise to Abraham? When Joshua had marched into the land and conquered it he had done so because God had commanded him and he had put the Amelecites to the sword because this was part of the divine plan. Because it was the will of God, Joshua had had no choice. Occupying the Promised Land had always been a divine commandment for Jews and never a natural right.

The new Greater Land Israelis of the right also adopted a view of Zionism which turned the movement on its head. The seculars had always maintained that the Jews had a choice: they could either wait in the diaspora to be persecuted or they could take their destiny into their own hands and save themselves. Now the aggressive right maintained that they had no choice and made the phrase *en brerah* (no alternative) a rallying cry.[26] Zionism, they insisted, was a purely reactionary movement and the Jews had been throughout coerced by their enemies so that they had had no choice but to act in the way they did. Hitler, the British and finally Nasser had attacked the Zionists and forced them to adopt one policy after another. Thus the veteran *kibbutznik* Yitzhak Tabenkin completely rewrote Zionist history after 1967:

We were coerced by history, left with no option. From scattered colonies to National Home; from National Home to a State in part of the Land and from that to the liberation of the Land of Israel as a whole. A process we did not initiate. At each stage we had no option (*en brerah*) but to respond to a demand made on us. We are manifestly coerced by the logic of tragedy and redemption.[27]

In this view, the Zionists were caught up in a providential plan. Tabenkin uses words like 'redemption' and 'liberation' to explain Israel's new lust for territorial expansion. Land that was not part of the State of Israel was to be 'liberated', even though it was inhabited by other people, who would therefore suffer. Because the Israelis were 'coerced' by the 'logic' of 'tragedy' they were in the grip of fate and need take no responsibility for their action. They certainly need not obey the United Nations and international law. 'There is no alternative of [*sic*] going back to the old boundaries,' said a Greater Land spokesman after the war; 'we are condemned to be strong.'[28] Like the Crusaders, after their conquest of Jerusalem in 1099, the Zionists of the right had fantasies of further massive expansion. 'Strength' no longer meant inner strength or liberation from the weakness inherent in the diaspora. It meant territorial integrity and expansion. In developing the amoral and quasi-religious theory of *en brerah* they had also turned their back on Jewish tradition of personal accountability and moral responsibility and had reverted to a more primitive view, which saw man as a helpless being who is quite unable to control his own life.

From 1967 to 1973 this belligerent chauvinism of the right prevailed and the voices of moderation were drowned. This newly intransigent Israel had no time for peace and pushed towards another war. On 4 February 1971, for example, President Anwar al-Sadat, Nasser's successor, made a startling peace offer. If Israel withdrew her forces in the Sinai to the passes, he would open the Suez Canal to Israel, withdraw Egyptian troops from the east bank of the Canal and enter into negotiations with a view to signing a peace treaty. For over twenty years, the Israelis had complained that the Arabs refused to make peace with them but now that the largest Arab state had actually offered to recognise the Jewish state, the offer was scornfully ignored.[29] Six months later Moshe Dayan, at that time Defence Minister, seemed to have 'forgotten' about it. He announced that he was 'forced' to establish a settlement at Yamit, in the Gaza Strip, to be manned by the members of Herut, the party of Menachem Begin. 'If the Arabs refuse to make peace, we cannot stand still,' he said, invoking the spirit of *en brerah*; 'If we are denied their co-operation, let us act on our own.'[30] Two years later in April 1973 at a ceremony on Masada, Dayan made a deliberately provocative speech which called for a Greater Israel: 'with broad frontiers, strong and solid, with the authority of the Israeli government extending from the Jordan to the Suez Canal.'[31] Only a few months later on 6 October 1973, Sadat's forces made their astonishingly successful invasion of the peninsula on the feast of Yom Kippur (the Day of Atonement). The Egyptians smashed through the apparently impregnable Bar Lev line while Syrian troops invaded the Golan Heights, taking Israel entirely by surprise. Although the IDF managed to push back the Arabs, they had a frightening demonstration of their isolation in the Middle East and they could no longer jeer at the Arabs' military inferiority. The old complacency was exploded and the trauma lent a new urgency to the Greater Land Zionists, who now felt that they had *en brerah* even more strongly. But the Yom Kippur War had a different meaning for the explicitly religious settlers, who believed that by colonising the holy land of the West Bank they were fulfilling a divine commandment. We must now see where these religious Zionists had come from.

In 1949 Rabbi Ignaz Maybaum wrote in his book *The Jewish Mission*:

Zion is the mountain of the Lord with the house of prayer for all the nations of the world (Isaiah 56:7). Zion is not yet. We must still pray for it to be established. The world is not yet redeemed. We must still wait, hope and pray. We are still in the *galut* (exile); the citizens of the State of Israel as well. The Kingdom of God has still to come....

There is no short cut to Zion whether the Jew is a citizen in the diaspora or whether he is a citizen of the Jewish State. Zion is not yet. The Mountain of the Lord is not yet established. We must still pray: 'Next year in Jerusalem.'

May the citizens of the State of Israel learn from history and understand that Jerusalem is situated where what is beyond history enters history.[32]

Rabbi Maybaum was a member of Reform Judaism, which had developed in Europe during the nineteenth century as an attempt to create a more liberal Judaism than the old Orthodox Judaism that had developed in the diaspora. But we have seen that the Orthodox rabbis would have agreed with the Reform that there was no spiritual significance in the Jewish state; indeed they had found it a blasphemous aping of the redemption. But from the very early days of Labour Zionism, there had been a few Orthodox rabbis who had quite a different view and they created a movement in 1903 which they called Mizrachi (spiritual centre) and which saw the Jewish settlement in Palestine as the first signs of the approaching redemption, in which Jerusalem would be the centre of a new world. They were not unlike those Crusaders who had seen a Christian presence in Jerusalem as the first stage in bringing about the Last Days. While the socialist Zionists of the Second and Third Aliyah settled in Israel, Mizrachi Zionists also made religious settlements. They were in a minority and were rather arrogantly ignored by the seculars, who saw them as an anachronism that would wither away in the course of time. But though many of them resented this attitude of their fellow Jews, the religious Zionists believed that dwelling in the land of Israel would bring the secular Jews back to religion. Living in Zion would touch some depths in the Jewish souls of the settlers and would force them back to the Torah. They have not proved entirely wrong for it was these Mizrachi settlers who finally produced the religious settlers who began to colonise the Holy Land of the West Bank after the Six Day War, together with the Greater Land Zionists.

A crucial figure in this religious Zionism was Rabbi Abraham Yitzhak Kook, the leader of the Mizrachi settlers. He did not feel at all antagonistic towards the secular settlers, and was not perturbed by their wish for a purely secular state which was not ruled according to the principles of the Torah. On the contrary, Kook's providential view of history saw the settlers as fulfilling God's plan without their realising it. He was always quick to praise the achievements of the early *kibbutzim* and their pioneering effort, seeing it as complementary to his religious plans for the Judaising of Palestine. 'We lay *tfillin*,' he was fond of saying, 'and the pioneers lay bricks.'[33] The religious settlers fulfilled the Torah and renewed the Jewish spirit, and the settlers, who were working on the sacred soil, were fulfilling a priestly task whether they realised it or not.[34] All Jewish activity in Palestine at this time, the early twentieth century, should be seen as 'the birthpangs of the Messiah'. They were bringing about the final redemption and were 'the light of the Messiah'.[35] In the view of the religious Zionists, Jews should not sit back passively to await the Messiah, but should force him to come by settling in Eretz Yisrael and this initiative would save the whole world: 'All civilizations will be revived by the renaissance of our spirit,' Kook wrote. 'All quarrels will be resolved and our revival will cause all life to be luminous with the joy of fresh birth.'[36] Kook's view of Eretz Yisrael was very close to that of Judah Halevi, the twelfth-century religious Zionist. By immersing themselves in 'the land's towering holiness' the Jews would

Religion not only transforms our view of history; it also gives us a new geography. In this map Jerusalem is placed at the centre of the world, and in the Holy Sepulchre Church the actual central point, the *Omphalos*, is clearly marked. There was a strong tradition that this was also the site both of the Garden of Eden and of Golgotha, where Jesus was crucified: man was created and fell, and was later redeemed and created anew in the same place. It was logical that this central event of history should have happened at the physical centre of the world. In this view not only did Christ rule the world, but Jerusalem was obviously a Christian city. Christians in Europe *knew* how far they were from Jerusalem; thousands of Crusaders had died on the long journey there. During the thirteenth century Crusades were fought in Egypt and people *knew* how close Egypt was to the Holy Land. But they *felt* so closely connected to Jerusalem that here Rome, France (*Galia*) and England (*Anglia*) are much nearer to Jerusalem than Egypt is. People prefer a mythical to a scientifically accurate map because religious geography speaks to fundamental emotions.

Jerusalem is also holy to Jews and Muslims, who believe that this rock *(above)* is the place where Abraham bound his son Isaac to sacrifice him to God. Solomon had built his Temple on this holy spot, which became the centre of the Jewish world. No Gentile was allowed here because that would have polluted its holiness. A Jewish tradition claimed that *this* was the pivot of the whole world and the site of Eden. The Jews lost their Temple when the Romans destroyed it in CE 70, but when the Caliph Omar conquered Jerusalem for Islam he built this mosque of the Dome of the Rock to sanctify the place anew and to manifest the Muslims' connection with their father Abraham. It is the third most holy place in the Muslim world, after Mecca and Medina.

A medieval Christian pilgrim sometimes compared his journey to Jerusalem with Abraham's migration to the Promised Land. This eleventh-century pilgrim *(left)* carries staff, wallet and palm, which had been blessed when he set off to show that he was a consecrated man and that his journey was holy. Jesus had walked beside his disciples on the road to Emmaus after the Resurrection, as shown in this stained-glass window at Chartres *(right)*, and pilgrims to Jerusalem believed that Christ was with them during their journey. Because Jesus had walked there, the Holy Land was imbued with spiritual power and by following in his footsteps they made a physical contact with the Son of God.

Today pilgrims still feel they are walking in Christ's footsteps when they walk up the Via Dolorosa towards the Holy Sepulchre Church. They identify with him as strongly as they can by carrying a cross as a symbol of their willingness to obey his command: 'No one can be my disciple, unless he takes up his cross and comes after me.' These sophisticated pilgrims *(above)* still see Jerusalem as the centre of the world in a very real emotional sense. Their behaviour may look eccentric to an outsider, like the Palestinian on the left, but they have their own vision of what they are doing, which makes it deeply significant, though not explicable in rational terms.

As this pilgrim *(below left)* gets closer to the tomb of Christ she becomes rapt in a spiritual journey that transcends ordinary time and space. On this Easter Sunday she feels that time has been annihilated and that she is with Christ on the first Easter morning when he rose from the dead in this very place. She is approaching the spot which is the centre of her faith and spiritual identity.

When pilgrims actually enter the tomb *(left)* and touch the spot where they believe that the body of Jesus lay for three days after his Crucifixion and then burst the bonds of death and redeemed the world, their rational, egotistical selves fade and they feel themselves at the heart of an entirely different world, central to their Christian experience. They have carried their crosses to Calvary and now they identify with the Risen Christ. As St Paul put it: 'I have been crucified with Christ, and I live now not with my own life but with the life of Christ who lives in me' (Galatians 2:19).

Non-Muslims are forbidden to enter Mecca, the heart of the Muslim world and during the *hajj* each year pilgrims from all over the world travel to the Ka'aba, which they believe was built by Abraham and Ishmael. At the centre of the emotional crowd, the pilgrim kisses the meteorite known as the Black Stone *(inset)*, set in the wall of the Ka'aba: at this moment he feels united with Mohammad, who kissed the Stone when he conquered Mecca.

The Wailing Wall *(right)* is the last relic of the Jewish
Temple, the destruction of which is a bitter symbol of
Jewish suffering. The Gentiles have sought to destroy
Judaism and to exterminate the chosen people. There is
a Kabbalistic tradition that the *Shekinah*, the Presence
of God which dwelt in the Temple, went into exile
with the Jews when they lost Jerusalem. This suggests
a metaphysical homelessness which has produced an
essential imbalance in the world because it affects the
very ground of reality. Only when the Jews are returned
to their land will the whole world regain its
equilibrium. Today, after their suffering in the
diaspora, Jews try to get as close as they can to the
Wall. Again, this looks strange to outsiders but
physical proximity to these stones represents a healing.
It is a return not only to the site of the Temple but to
the way things ought to be.

Peace and reconciliation are important pilgrimage
themes, but the picture below shows that this holy
place has created a problem which affects the political
conflict in Israel between the Jews and the Arabs. They
are finding it more and more difficult to share this area.
The exclusive nature of holiness means that the

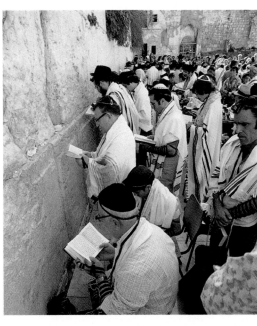

presence of unbelievers is a pollution, and Jewish terrorists have plotted to blow up the Muslim shrine
of the Dome of the Rock *(below)* so that they can rebuild the Temple. Religious emotion can lead to loss
of all rational restraint and, indeed, the conflict for the Holy Land today stirs feelings that are deeply
buried in the Jewish and Arab identities.

The struggle for
the Holy Land has
been desperate
ever since Moses led
the Israelites out of
slavery in Egypt
towards freedom in the
land that God had
promised to Abraham.
The salvation of the
Jews meant the destruction
of any other people who
stood in their way *(left)*:
Pharaoh and his army were
drowned in the Red Sea and
the Canaanites were
exterminated by the army of
the Israelites.

There was a new Exodus to
the Promised Land in our own century
when Jews fleeing anti-semitic persecution in the Soviet
Union and Nazi Germany set off for the land of their fathers *(below)*.

They struggled on foot through alien and desolate countryside, laden with tragic memories of cruelty and oppression *(above left)*. All were ready to risk everything and stagger to the end of their endurance. After the Second World War other refugees were ready to face the perils of a voyage on illegal immigrant ships, dodging the British, who were determined to restrict Jewish immigration to Palestine. These refugees could probably all have sought a refuge that would have required less suffering but they were not simply fleeing oppression. They called themselves *olim*, which is Hebrew for 'pilgrims'. A reunion with the land that was central to their Jewish identity would put their shattered world to rights and heal them by linking them with their past so that they could build a new life and a new self. The Belgian Jews on board the illegal immigrant ship *Auerbach (above right)* look happy and full of hope, even though they have suffered so much from the Germans. Their determination to settle in Palestine was not destroyed by the opposition of the British, who intercepted their ship off Tel Aviv and forced these *olim* into internment camps in Cyprus. In the face of this universal opposition, the Zionists resolved to take possession of Palestine whatever the cost to themselves or to others.

Once again, the salvation of the Jews meant the destruction of their enemies. The Palestinians' Exodus from their homeland meant endless exile and a cosmic homelessness, which seems writ large in the heavens:

Oh our village! I swear by your soil
we have not tasted sleep,
wakeful through remembering you,
tearful because of our separation from you.
And all the time we gaze at the sky
observing your sad face.
Oh, how sad your face has become.

(From Yusuf al-Khatib's 'The Lake of Olive Trees' (1957) in Khalid A. Sulaiman, *Palestine and Modern Arab Poetry* (London, 1984), pp. 123–4.)

But the Palestinian case *must* be considered. This family fled from Jordan in Black September 1970, having already had to flee at least once before. Where are they supposed to go now? Nobody wants them, for they are unwelcome and even persecuted as aliens in both the Arab world and in the West. The Wandering Jew, incurably homeless, has been replaced by the Wandering Palestinian. As the Palestinian poet Mahmoud Darwish asks: 'Where should we go after the last frontiers? Where should the birds fly after the last sky?' ('The Earth Is Closing on Us', trans. Abdullah al-Udhari, *Victims of a Map, A Bilingual Anthology of Arabic Poetry* (London, 1984), p. 13.)

When the Israeli army 'liberated' the Wailing Wall during the June war in 1967, the tough young paratroopers became pilgrims, clinging to its stones and weeping. It seemed as though a wound in the very nature of things had been healed when the Jewish people were reunited once more with their spiritual and emotional centre. Many Israelis feel such a powerful but inarticulate attachment to Jerusalem that they cannot consider the Palestinians' case rationally. Similarly, many people in the West find this restoration of the Holy Land to the Jews profoundly 'right'.

This is the city that has inspired such extraordinary fervour in Jews, Christians and Muslims that they have all been prepared to massacre thousands of people to preserve their holy places intact. Jerusalem is an apocalyptic city: the hill in the background is the Mount of Olives (now in the West Bank), which plays a major role in the mythology of the Last Days in all three religions. Apocalypse naturally introduces a note of extremity that tips easily into violence.

In this religious tradition holy places have to be built. They are not usually left as 'holy' springs or rocks, where the deity can be felt in nature. In Jerusalem it is noticeable how often people have established a holy shrine in order to lay claim to the city against its previous owners. King Solomon built the first Jewish Temple in Jerusalem in about CE 950, fifty years after David had won it from the Jebusites. The Wailing Wall is not part of Solomon's Temple, but the last relic of a temple built by King Herod shortly before the birth of Christ. The Wailing Wall was not really a wall but a dyke, and the Temple proper was the upper area now filled by the mosques of the Dome of the Rock *(to the left, with the gold dome)* and al-Aqsa *(to the right, with the silver dome).* These were built by the Caliph Omar after his conquest of Jerusalem in 637 and clearly reflect the Muslim position. Their roots are in the ancient faith of Judaism, but Islam is the ultimate revelation of God and therefore it is superior to the older religions of the Book.

To build such shrines in a holy city to which others feel they have a claim can be seen as an aggressive and provocative act. Certainly the First Crusaders found it very threatening, and when they conquered Jerusalem in 1099 they massacred men, women and children so savagely in this temple area that the blood came up to the horses' knees. They then celebrated their conquest of the city by building a new Church of the Holy Sepulchre to house the tomb of Christ, to liberate which they had slaughtered so many. (We cannot see the church in this photograph because it is some way behind us.) The Crusaders had no intention of allowing the Muslim mosques to remain in the hands of Islam. They were as exclusive about their Holy City as the Jews and Muslims had been about Jerusalem and Mecca: there was to be no Muslim or Jewish worship in it. They converted the mosques to Christian use, which was an assault upon Islam and also, in a different way, against Judaism. They thought that these Muslim shrines were *Jewish* sites and therefore as the new chosen people, they took them over for their own use. They believed that the Dome of the Rock was the old Jewish Temple, where Jesus had taught and prayed to his Father, so they made it into a church which they called the Temple of the Lord. When Muslims saw the cross on the cupola they quite correctly construed it as an act of war against Islam. The Crusaders turned al-Aqsa into the royal palace and the headquarters of the Templars, because they thought it was the old palace of King Solomon. They even put latrines into this beautiful mosque built to celebrate the Prophet's Night Journey, which had been a vision of the connection between Judaism, Christianity and Islam.

Some of the Crusaders' other building projects were more obviously aggressive. This is just one of the many powerful castles that created and maintained the frontiers of the Crusader states. Yet the fortresses were not just defensive: by subduing the surrounding countryside the knights were inching their way further into the House of Islam. In the last days of the kingdom of Jerusalem this castle at Shawbak, in what is now Jordan, was owned by the notorious Reynauld of Chatillon, and here and in his nearby castle of Krak he planned his raid on Mecca. His actions proved suicidal for the Crusader kingdom, but he was inspired by a passionate belief that the land belonged to the Christians and that compromise with the enemy was a religious betrayal.

When the Templars built the Church of Vera Cruz in Segovia (left) they modelled it on the Holy Sepulchre Church in Jerusalem. These round Templar churches, found all over Europe, show the centrifugal pull exerted by Jerusalem. But during the thirteenth century, when this one was built, Christians in Europe had to accept the bitter truth that the belligerent chauvinism of knights like Reynauld had lost them Jerusalem for ever. They found comfort in the shape of this church, which suggested that Europe could have holy places too. The relic of the True Cross, to which the church was dedicated, made it the shrine of some of the holiness of Jerusalem; similarly, the new thirteenth-century devotion to the Real Presence of Christ in the Eucharist meant that every church in Europe was a temple housing the Presence of God. But there was still an aggressive element: this Templar church was built in the wake of the Christian advance into Spain during the Wars of Reconquest; it proudly faces the great Muslim castle just opposite, which had been defeated by Christianity.

Building and settlement had long been part of the Christianisation of Europe. Monks such as the Cistercians had settled on the borders and in the no-man's land between Christendom and Islamic or pagan land. Settlement and colonisation had steadily pushed forward the frontiers of Europe and had planted a Christian presence in alien territory. In the pagan wilderness, monks worked the land and lived what they believed was the most perfect form of the Christian life. Thus they were conquering the land for the Church.

This religious Jew *(below)* would probably have no idea that he had anything in common with medieval monks; indeed he might be appalled by the idea. But in fact there is a similarity that goes far deeper than the primitive axe the Jewish worker is wielding, which is very like the one drawn by the Cistercian artist. Like the monks, this religious settler is working on alien land and conquering it for the true faith. This is the West Bank. In the background is an Arab village. The devout Jew is establishing Jewish presence in land that belongs to the Arabs in order to extend the borders of Eretz Yisrael.

This religious Jew has not gone into the desert to pray like a hermit: his prayer is an act of war and a bid for the conquest of territory. He was one of the settlers who illegally colonised Sinai while it was occupied by Israel. By living a Jewish life and studying the Torah in Arab territory, they wanted to Judaise it and make it impossible for Israel to give the land back to Egypt. They wanted to bind Israel to the land as firmly as they bind *tfillin* to their arms and foreheads when they pray *(right)*. Because God had promised Sinai to the Jews, they believed that settling there was a divine commandment, like the wearing of the fringed shawl for prayer. They would be the vanguard of Israel, making God's will an established fact by building settlements in disputed territory, no matter how provocative such ostentatiously Jewish activity was to the Arabs.

The horrible architecture of this West Bank settlement *(right)* is more than a visual assault, because this Jewish Holy Land is not a desert. Palestinians have lived here for hundreds of years, and they find these Jewish colonies a threat. Like Crusader castles, they are strategically positioned to establish a strong Jewish presence and are seen as the front line in a holy war for future conquest: religious settlers want to fulfil God's promise of land on *both* sides of the Jordan. Like Reynauld they see the

Holy Land as a divine trust and would consider it a religious duty to break any treaty that Israel made with the Arabs. Religious activity on the West Bank enables Israel to step up military presence there. These Jewish pilgrims to some holy place *(below)* need to be guarded because their pilgrimage defiantly proclaims that the land is Jewish and is an attempt to take possession of the Promised Land.

But there has been another building project in the occupied territories. Camps like this one on the Gaza Strip had to be built for the Palestinian refugees who fled their homes in 1948: the Holy Land of the Jews must exclude Gentiles who stand in the way of the divine plan. Twenty years of Israeli occupation in Gaza made the Palestinians there so desperate that children were driven to attack the heavily armed Israeli soldiers with rocks. The Israelis, in their turn, were ready to open fire on them and kill them. So sacred is the Land of Israel to their Jewish identity that they were impelled to actions that lie outside ordinary morality.

save themselves. In exile, Judaism had become weak, because it had lost the Temple. Without Temple worship, the Torah could not be entirely fulfilled, and because the Torah reflected the conditions of life in Palestine not the very different physical conditions of the diaspora, it was only in Israel that a Jew could live a fully Jewish life. In the diaspora Jews were inevitably infected by the corrupt, secular values of the Gentiles:

> The air of the gentile lands holds the Jews back. The impure soil that is everywhere outside the land of Israel is thus suffused with the stench of idolatry and the Jews there are worshippers of idols in purity. The only way in which we may escape the disgrace of idolatry is for the Jewish people to gather in the land of Israel.[37]

A religious Zionist like Rabbi Kook had a very similar attitude to a secular Labour Zionist like A. B. Gordon. Neither had any time for the *goyim*. Both saw Eretz Yisrael as the only place where a Jew could be truly himself; both saw themselves as redeeming the land and redeeming the Jewish people by means of *avodah*. The difference was that for Gordon *avodah* meant labour or work, but for Kook *avodah* meant keeping the 613 commandments of the Torah and working to rebuild the Temple.[38]

For the first twenty years of the history of the State of Israel, the religious Zionists were content to keep a low profile and the seculars scarcely seemed aware of their existence. But by 1967 the religious were very worried indeed about the Jewish state and felt that it was time to take drastic action. Instead of inspiring the Jews to return to the Torah, the State of Israel was becoming more and more materialistic, more polluted with secular idolatry than some of the diaspora countries. This was an abomination, for it was polluting the sacred soil of Israel, and naturally when the Arabs seemed about to wipe out the Jewish state, the religious Zionists saw this as a divine punishment. Three weeks before the outbreak of war, Rabbi Kook's son, Rabbi Zvi Yehuda Kook, gave his annual address on the anniversary of the State of Israel at the important Merkaz Harav yeshiva in North Jerusalem. Usually the Rabbi praised the labours of the state but this year his message was very different. 'We have sinned!'[39] he cried, and his audience, who were expecting to be exterminated in the near future, began to weep. The nation had been guilty of a grave religious infidelity, according to Rabbi Kook. How could a Jewish state allow the Temple Mount to remain in the hands of the *goyim*? How could the chosen people settle in the Negev and the coastal plain, when the true Holy Land was in enemy territory? What kind of Jewish state allowed the holy cities of Hebron, Nablus and Jericho to remain unliberated? When a few weeks later the IDF actually *did* liberate these holy cities, Rabbi Kook was hailed by his followers as a Prophet of Israel. The extraordinary victory naturally seemed to them an act of God and was seen as the first sign of the coming redemption.[40] Yet the Labour government seemed unwilling to capitalise on this splendid opportunity, so the religious Zionists of Merkaz Harav decided to take the responsibility themselves.

Immediately after the victory of 1967 Rabbi Moshe Levinger, a graduate of Merkaz Harav and a disciple of Rabbi Kook, became a pioneer. He went straight to the Holy City of Hebron and squatted in the Park Hotel for six months. Then he transferred to a nearby military camp which he refused to leave until finally the embarrassed government gave him permission to build a settlement and sent soldiers to guard it.[41] Together with Rabbi Eliezer Waldman, another graduate of Merkaz Harav, he built the settlement of Kiryat Arba (the biblical name for Hebron). Not content with this achievement, Levinger went on to build one new colony after another on the West Bank and very swiftly the Jewish settlers had established the Etzion Bloc between Jerusalem and Hebron, making the Jewish presence so strong in the area that it was difficult to imagine how it could ever be given back to the Arabs. In the Etzion Bloc another graduate of Merkaz Harav, Rabbi Haim Drukman, founded the important Bar-Etzion yeshiva. The method adopted by these new religious pioneers was always the same: they settled illegally and then, by skilfully playing one political leader against another, forced the government to make their settlements official.[42] Naturally the rabbis attracted the attention and support of the pioneers of the Movement for the Land of Israel. They also attracted other young people, who may not have shared their religious beliefs but who did respect the rabbis' decision and felt that they alone in Israel had the courage of their convictions. Obviously the Labourites felt very ambivalent about these pioneering rabbis and their followers.[43] They could not share their religious vision and yet they touched something very deep in their Zionist identity. Labourites like Shimon Peres were very supportive to the religious settlers, seeing them as picking up the pioneering torch which seemed to have fallen from the hand of Labour. The rabbis loudly challenged the Labourites: *they* were the true successors of the founding fathers, they claimed. Secular Israelis had got soft; they were filled with the weak ideologies of the Gentiles and of the diaspora.[44] The secular *kibbutzim* had produced those blasphemous soldiers of *The Seventh Day*, who sympathised with the *goyim* and who seemed to have no sense at all of the commitment that all Jews must feel towards the Land of Israel.

But though many Israelis respected the rabbis, others were horrified by them and felt that they were unJewish and contradicted every one of the decent ideals of true Zionism. They were astounded by this shrill religious Zionism which seemed to have grown in their midst, as a religious parody of their own movement. Amos Oz has recorded the shock felt by the secular liberals when they encountered this religious Zionism for the first time. The editors of *The Seventh Day* had produced their book largely because they were so distressed by the belligerent chauvinism that had gripped so many of their fellow countrymen after the Six Day War; they wanted to point out that all this nationalistic rejoicing was out of place and that Israel must face up to the moral responsibilities of the victory, which meant further Arab suffering. They went to visit the Merkaz Harav yeshiva in order to seek the advice of the religious students, hoping to tap the richer and more compassionate element in the Jewish tradition and to hear the teachings of the prophets and sages. Instead they encountered the newly triumphant messianic Zionism and heard for the first time the then unfamiliar rhetoric of the Zionist 'holy' war. Amos Oz was not present at the meeting but he had read the minutes. Instead of a religion of the heart, he says, the seculars heard about the 'ecstasy over the Wailing Wall and Biblical sites in the West Bank, the talk of victory and miracles, Redemption and the Coming of the Messiah'.[45] The Christian Crusaders would have understood this very well, even though they would have been appalled by this Jewish version of their own movement, with its apocalyptic hopes, its veneration of the 'holy' places and of 'holy' war. From its earliest days, crusading had attracted and inspired Jews like Judah Halevi to produce a religious Zionism. But for Oz and the editors of *The Seventh Day* crusading meant persecution of Jews, and this heartless and irrational Zionism seemed to contradict essential Jewish values. As Oz recalled, the religious students seemed:

> crude, smug and arrogant, power-drunk, bursting with messianic rhetoric, ethnocentric, 'redemptionist,' apocalyptic – quite simply, inhuman. And un-Jewish. The Arab human beings under our dominion might never have been. It was not an affair of, as it were, human distress, but of signs and oracles, of tidings of 'the end of days' and of the beginning of Redemption.[46]

This was the beginning of a bitter and increasingly violent dispute in Israel between religious and secular Jews.

Yet perhaps Oz should not have been so astonished at the appearance of this religious version of his movement. From the very beginning Zionists had used religion when it suited them and what the story of the holy war tells us is that religion seems to have its own laws and its own dynamic. It should be handled with care. Nurturing religious symbols and values can give rise to the 'real thing' and a religious revival that becomes a Frankensteinian monster, that will devour its progenitor. It cannot always be controlled. The secular Israeli dove A. B. Yehoshua gives us some idea of how this could happen to an individual in his controversial novel *The Lover*. The lover of the title is a rootless disillusioned Israeli who has moved to the diaspora. He feels uncommitted either to the State of Israel or to anything or anybody else. He describes himself shamelessly and defiantly as a lover of other men's wives. He returns to Israel simply to collect a legacy from his dying grandmother; while he is waiting for her to die, the Yom Kippur war breaks out and the lover is forced to join his regiment. To his horror he finds himself posted to a very dangerous position in Sinai and is determined to escape. Eventually he disguises himself in the clothes of an ultra-Orthodox Jew and finds that the secular establishment simply ignore him and that escape is therefore very easy. Because he is a deserter, the lover has to hide out in the Old City with an Orthodox community, dressing like them, praying with them and observing the commandments. He comes to have a fascinated respect for them. He never experiences a full religious conversion and remains an atheist, but he has been radically changed by the experience. His secular friends notice that phrases like 'Praise the Lord!' or 'God willing!' fall naturally from his lips. On a fast day he finds that he is quite unable to eat his breakfast and when teased about this he can only shake his head in embarrassed confusion.[47] Donning the outward form of Judaism, stroking his long ear-locks and eating Kosher food, and swaying backwards and forwards in the rhythms of Jewish prayer have all touched some hitherto unreached part of his Jewish identity.

Zionism also adopted the outward form of Judaism in its language and above all in its claim to settle in Eretz Yisrael. Zionists had always been mutely but urgently aware of there being 'no alternative' to Eretz Yisrael as a place for the Jewish homeland. But this was a purely religious value. The Zionists wanted to create a new secular Judaism, but their inability to conceive of any other homeland but Palestine demands the answer to the question: what does it mean to be a 'secular Jew'? Judaism is a religion not a nationality or a race. Jews have segregated themselves from Gentiles for thousands of years and lived according to a different set of laws which are religiously inspired. The Jewish way of life is religious and anybody who wishes to share it can convert to Judaism, even if he was not born a Jew. If somebody who calls himself Jewish does not believe in God, does not live according to the Torah or keep a Jewish home, what form does his Judaism take? Is it a devotion to the past? That past is a religious past. A devotion to past Jewish suffering only is surely rather negative. It is true that anti-semites have forced Jews to be 'Jewish' because of their racist attitudes, and have made it impossible for a Jew to escape his Jewish identity. But again, to accept the anti-semites' definition of oneself is a very negative foundation for a new Jewish self. It is true that Judaism has developed many truly admirable traditions, but side by side with these humane and enlightened traditions there exist other less positive traditions, which a fully observant Jew must take very seriously.

A religious Zionist has a very clear answer to the question about the validity of the Jewish claim to Palestine. He will say simply that God wants the Jews to live in that country. Seculars, however, have much more difficulty in arguing their claim over and above the Arabs' claim to the land, unless they adopt the quasi-religious mythology of *en brerah*. The *kibbutznik* soldiers in *The Seventh Day* were genuinely perplexed and disturbed that Zionism, which they had been taught was a deeply moral movement based on the Jewish respect for the inalienable rights of others, was producing such suffering. Many of these disillusioned Israelis would leave the country; others have worked for the establishment of humane values in Israel; and others have turned to religion for the certainty and absolution they felt they needed.

The Zionist use of religion was often ambiguous and sometimes the Zionists did not fully understand the complexity of some of their symbols. Thus when the Dead Sea Scrolls of the Essenes were discovered at Qumran in 1947, they were seen almost as title deeds of the new state. The archaeological discovery had resurrected the Jewish past from the very soil of Eretz Yisrael and 'proved' that this was indeed the land of their fathers. The scrolls were accorded the reverence that medieval Christians used to give to saints and relics. They were displayed in the grounds of the Israel Museum in Jewish Jerusalem in an extraordinary building which is called the Shrine of the Book, as though the scrolls were themselves 'holy'. The boldly phallic imagery of the Shrine, the womblike central chamber and the narrow passage that leads to it is a powerful Zionist and archaeological metaphor: the visitor feels that he or she is burrowing into the depths to experience a new life. Yet the scrolls that one meets at the end of this journey into the past speak of violent apocalyptic battles. The Jewish Essenes were religious extremists who would have had no time for the 'secular' Jews who had built this Shrine in their honour. They would have had far more in common with the religious Zionists of Merkaz Harav and the West Bank settlers.

Ten years after the Six Day War the Labourites lost their hitherto undisputed leadership of the party and Menachem Begin was elected Prime Minister in 1977, with the support of the religious parties.[48] He went to the election promising to work for a Jewish state on *both* sides of the Jordan. The expansionist, Herut party, which had been a distrusted minority party for nearly thirty years, had become the leaders of the people of Israel and brought religion firmly to the forefront of the movement, for Begin is a committed religious Jew, who had already brought the

spirit of Joshua into Zionism before the creation of the state. But he would find that
the religious Zionists were far more extreme than he was. After the trauma of 1973
there had been a new surge of religious passion. The trauma of the Yom Kippur war
was seen as a punishment or as a catastrophe that would usher in the messianic
era. Many diaspora Jews as well as Israelis returned to the full observance of the
Torah and joined the West Bank settlers, to ward off further divine punishment.
Rabbi Waldman explained this religious view of the history of the previous six
years:

> In 1967 God gave us a unique opportunity. But the Israelis did not seize it. They
> did not colonize the newly-conquered land. They left all the options open. It's as
> if they had refused the offer of the Almighty while at the same time thanking
> him. Therefore God inflicted upon Israel the sufferings of the Yom Kippur war.[49]

Where the secular Zionists of the Second and Third Aliyah wanted to save the Jews
without God, the religious Zionists who are now in the vanguard of the movement
have made God a major actor in the history of the State of Israel. Events can no
longer be seen from more than one point of view. A loyal Jew cannot worry about
the Arabs or about the morality of the occupation if God has arranged matters. He
must simply work to further this divine initiative. This is what the radical rabbis
and their followers intended to achieve. After the 1973 war they made a new effort
and the result was the creation of a set of religiously dominated parties on the far
right, which regard the policies of Begin and his successor Yitzhak Shamir as a
cowardly betrayal of Judaism.

In February 1974 Rabbi Levinger founded the first of these organisations. The
Gush Emunim (the Bloc of the Faithful) is not a political party seeking seats in the
Knesset but a pressure group dedicated to making the nation understand what they
regard as a vital truth: the redemption of Israel (and hence the redemption of the
whole world) is dependent upon the liberation of the Holy Land. Amana, its
colonising branch, is dedicated to planning new settlements on the West Bank and
urging diaspora Jews to man them. Unlike the secular settlers in the Movement for
the Land of Israel, the Gush Emunim do not avoid populated areas but make for
places with a religious significance. Thus settlements have been established in
Tekoa, the home of the prophet Amos, at Shiloh, the site of an ancient Jewish
temple, and at Ofra, near Shechem. Naturally this has angered the Palestinian
inhabitants, so there has been fighting, and because the IDF have to come in to
guard the settlers this makes the Israeli presence in the territories more aggressive.
This does not bother the settlers, because there is no thought of making peace with
the Arabs or trying to see their point of view. A Gush settler will either ask
incredulously, 'Who cares about the Arabs?'[50] or else simply see the Arab problem
as a trial whereby God, blessed be he, is testing the faith of the chosen people.[51]
Attempts to understand the Arab viewpoint are regarded as perverse and unJewish.
As Yisrael Harel, a settler in Ofra and chairman of the Council of Jewish
Settlements, has put it, there must be a return to a sense of 'absolute truth', which
admits of no valid 'other sides'.[52] The Arabs are the enemies of God and must be
fought to the death. If anybody asks Rabbi Levinger whether he is worried that his
movement is killing any hope of peace with the Arabs, he replies:

> No. The advance of the Jewish people, the fulfilment of the Redemption, of the
> morale and integrity of the Jewish people and Eretz Yisrael – these are more
> important than any hypothetical peace. It is through all this that the world will
> have peace.[53]

He is convinced that his struggle is paving the way for the Messiah, and so pursues
his course oblivious to its political consequences.[54] That the Arabs are the enemies

of the chosen people means that they are the enemies of all mankind and that they are not entitled to the consideration and respect of other human beings. It is the attitude of Joshua and of ardent Crusaders and it deeply worries a secular Zionist like Amos Oz, who has recently warned Gush members that 'he who denies the identity of others is doomed to find himself ultimately not unlike those who deny his own identity.'[55] It is this that inspires the seculars to accuse the religious chauvinists of introducing Nazi ideology into Zionism.

Far from being concerned about blocking the peace process, Gush members are implacably opposed to any peace. They maintain that the conflict with the Arabs is a holy war and like Reynauld of Chatillon they consider peace treaties to be a deep betrayal. The struggle for the territories is a holy war and must be satisfied with nothing but the final destruction of the enemy. As Harriet, an American Jew who is a member of the Tekoa community, told Amos Oz:

'In the Six-Day War, and the Yom Kippur War, too, we should never have stopped. We should have gone on, brought them to total surrender! Smashed their capital cities! Who cares what the goyim were yelling?' After some thought, she adds, 'But that wouldn't have brought peace, either. Maybe it would have given us some quiet, but not peace. Because this is a religious war! A holy war! For them *and* for us! A war against all of Islam. And against all the goyim.'[56]

If the Israeli leaders are cowardly enough to make peace, Harriet added, then the Gush should start another war of their own.[57] It would not be impossible for them to do this. In 1984 members of the Jewish underground in Israel were discovered to be plotting to blow up the Dome of the Rock and al-Aqsa, and the Gush rabbis found this quite acceptable. How could the Messiah return if the Muslims were on the Temple Mount?[58] It is an action not at all dissimilar to Reynauld of Chatillon's attempted attack on Mecca and Medina and would have provoked a frightening reaction from the Arab world.

Like the most fervent of the medieval Crusaders, the Gush members have laid ordinary rationality and political common sense aside, and this makes them as much of a danger to the State of Israel as Reynauld of Chatillon was to the Kingdom of Jerusalem. They are convinced that their settlements are bringing about the coming of the Messiah and naturally this puts them into an apocalyptic frame of mind where more cautious policies are irrelevant. It seems incredible that educated people can hold these essentially crusading views, but Dr Amiel Unger, a lecturer in political science, has no doubts on the matter. He points to the prophecy of Amos:

'And I will bring again the captivity of my people of Israel, and they shall build the waste cities, and inhabit them; and they shall plant vineyards and drink the wine thereof . . . and I will plant them upon their land which I have given them.' That's what he said. Now if you'd look at our community, if you'd look, from a philosophical perspective, at all the settlements in the country, you'd see with your own eyes the fulfilment of the prophecy. Word for word. We've even planted vineyards here. You'd have to be completely blind, God forbid, not to see that this is the beginning of the final Redemption.[59]

Because they are convinced that they are carried in the arms of God, as the Crusaders were convinced, the Gush members believe that ordinary human prudence should be laid aside. This proved to be a fatal and suicidal policy in the Middle Ages, and were the Gush's recommendations to be carried out they would prove suicidal to the State of Israel. The fact that an operation like the blowing up of al-Aqsa could lose Israel much Western support could only be an advantage in the Gush perspective. They believe that Israel should not rely on Western aid from the *goyim*; casting off these unworthy props would be an act of faith that would speed up the coming of the redemption, because God would have to step in to save his chosen people.[60] Secular doves like Amos Oz see the Gush as a terrible danger. The dialogue that religious and secular Zionists must begin, however distasteful to each, is in his view a 'matter of life and death'. The Gush could make of Israel a new monster like Belfast or South Africa, he says, and 'they may drag both me and my children with them, to kill and die in a perpetual and unnecessary war.'[61] When Oz looks at the settlement in Ofra, he does not see the birthpangs of the Messiah. He sees an ugly collection of pre-fab villas which bear witness to the terrible talent that Jews have for self-destruction, for they could easily lead to the death of the State of Israel.[62]

Obviously the Gush bitterly condemned Begin when he signed a peace treaty with President Sadat in 1979 and disbanded the settlements in the Sinai. They were not alone. The 'betrayal' of Camp David led a group of extreme secular and religious Zionists to form Tehiya, or Renaissance, the largest party on the far right. Tehiya, like the Gush and the Morasha party (led by Rabbi Drukman), is committed to work for the Greater Land of Israel, to settlement in the territories and to an unremitting war against the Arabs.[63] The leaders of Tehiya have in the past had strong connections with Jewish terrorism. Raphael Eytan was the chief of staff of the IDF during the Lebanon war and was severely censured for his dubious role in the Sabra and Chatilla massacres. Geula Cohen was a former member of the Irgun and published an autobiography called *Woman of Violence, Memoirs of a Young Terrorist, 1943–1948*.[64] Rabbi Eliezer Waldman was arrested on suspicion of instigating an attack on the Arab mayors of Nablus and Ramalla on 2 June 1980, when one mayor lost a foot and the other both legs in car-bomb explosions. The Rabbi was released because there was insufficient evidence against him, but has since maintained that the kidnapping of three Israeli officers in Beirut was God's way of punishing the Israeli government for arresting Jews for anti-Arab terrorist attacks.[65] Obviously in order to exist all these parties are forced to condemn terrorism, but they encourage their members to resort to terrorism on an individual basis.[66] The mere presence of these settlers in the West Bank provokes violence and the response of the settlers themselves, secular and religious, is swift and deadly. In November 1987 a group of schoolgirls in Gaza threw stones at a car of Jewish settlers, who promptly opened fire. One seventeen-year-old girl was killed and several were gravely injured.[67] This is the spirit of Joshua and the spirit of Reynauld of Chatillon. The new religious Jewish right feels no compunction about such acts, which contradict the spirit of so much of the Judaic tradition. As a religious spokesman for the far right has said: 'The God of Israel is a God of revenge. If somebody hurts a Jewish man he is hurting God, because we are the Chosen People. It is a desecration of the name of God if you don't take revenge.'[68]

This last brings us to an important point, which must be discussed if we are to understand the last speaker fully. Yossi Dayan is a member of the most radical religious party of all, which has the uncompromising name Kach (Thus it is!). An Orthodox Jew does not regard the first five books of the Bible as a human creation. The works of the prophets and the sages are important and certainly inspired by God, but Orthodox Jews believe that the Pentateuch, which they also call the Torah because it contains the 613 commandments, was dictated by God to Moses in rather the same way as Muslims believe that God dictated the Koran to Mohammad. Moses even wrote down the account of his death at the end of Deuteronomy, before it actually happened. This has very important consequences. A fully observant Jew in the Orthodox (but not in the reform) tradition will not see the story of the Exodus as a myth and the expression also of a primitive tribal theology, which Israel later outgrew to develop more compassionate attitudes. These stories are the literal truth and the words of God. When therefore God repeatedly commands his chosen people to fight a brutal war of extermination against the people living in the Land of Canaan this means that such a war is a *mitzvah*, a commandment. It is not an optional duty but a religious imperative to exterminate the Gentile inhabitants, who oppose the people of Israel's claim to their Promised Land. It is a *mitzvah* to tear down their homes and wipe their memory from the earth, and the chosen people are told by God that this is a condition of their election:

> Devour then all these peoples whom Yahweh your God delivers over to you, show them no pity, do not serve their gods, for otherwise you would be ensnared.
>
> You may say in your heart 'These nations outnumber me; how shall I be able to dispossess them?' Do not be afraid of them: remember how Yahweh your God dealt with Pharaoh and all Egypt, the great ordeals your own eyes have seen, the signs and wonders, the mighty hand and outstretched arm with which Yahweh your God has brought you out. So will Yahweh your God deal with all the peoples whom you fear. Do not be afraid of them, for Yahweh your God is among you, a God who is great and terrible. Little by little Yahweh your God will destroy these nations before you. (Deuteronomy 7:17–22)

When a religious Jew of the far right looks at the Palestinians and the Arab nations, he is bound to see them in this context and to feel no compunction about seeking to drive them out of the land. Kach is dedicated to this end.

Thus while the prophets preached of the duty of kindness to the stranger and of compassion and mercy, the Torah also taught Jews that holy war was a divine commandment that must be taken literally. From the ninth to the end of the eighteenth century, and still in Orthodox Judaism, Jews all observed the Halakhah, the legal system of classical Judaism developed by the rabbis and enshrined in the Talmud. Some of these rabbinical laws are directly hostile to Gentiles.[69] Thus where the murder of a Jew is a capital offence, a Jew who indirectly causes the death of another Jew is only guilty of what the Talmud calls a sin against the 'laws of heaven', to be punished by God rather than man. A Jew who kills a Gentile is only guilty of a sin against the 'laws of heaven' and to kill a Gentile indirectly is no sin at all.[70] In the past, various rabbis taught that the direction that killing a Gentile was a sin only applies to 'Gentiles with whom we [the Jews] are not at war',[71] and some drew the logical conclusion that in wartime *all* Gentiles in the opposite camp may or even should be killed, including women and children. After 1973 a booklet was published by the Central Region Command of the Israeli army, whose area includes the West Bank. The Command's Chief Chaplain wrote:

> When our forces come across civilians during a war or in hot pursuit or in a raid, so long as there is no certainty that those civilians are incapable of harming our forces, then according to the Halakhah they may and even should be killed.... Under no circumstances should an Arab be trusted, even if he makes an impression of being civilised.... In war, when our forces storm the enemy, they are allowed and even enjoined by the Halakhah to kill even good civilians, that is, civilians who are ostensibly good.[72]

This booklet for the guidance of religious soldiers was withdrawn by the secular Command. Similarly influential rabbis, who have a large following among religious army officers, identify the Palestinians with the enemies of the ancient Israelites, so that God's command 'you shall not leave alive a single living thing' (Deuteronomy 20:16) acquires a sinister topical relevance. Educational trips in the

Gaza Strip are not uncommonly conducted by such rabbis, and soldiers are told that the Palestinians there are 'like the Amelecites'.[73] It is easy to understand how an observant Jew could feel that terrorism against the Palestinians is a *mitzvah*.[74]

It would therefore seem that there is a strain in Orthodox Judaism which makes it lethal when it is applied to politics, just as there was in Christianity at the time of the Crusades. This does not have to be the case, however. There are Orthodox Jews who, to their great credit, disown any such sanctification of hatred. Notable among these is the controversial Israeli dove Professor Yeshayahu Liebowitz, who is also an Orthodox Jew. He advocates a separation of religion and politics in Israel, condemns the current aggressive nationalism as idolatry, insists that Israel must hand back the Territories and accept the idea of an independent Palestinian state and denounces the present policy as Nazi fascism. He has also founded a movement whose members refuse to serve in the Occupied Territories when they are doing their reserve army duty each year, even though this refusal can mean imprisonment.[75] But Liebowitz is a maverick in Israeli society. Religion is more and more used there as an aggressive weapon that forbids any peace or compromise and none of the radical religious right go as far as Rabbi Meir Kahane, the founder of Kach.

When in 1984 Kahane secured a seat in the Knesset with 1.2 per cent of the vote, there was widespread concern and disgust in all sectors of Israel. President Chaim Herzog refused to receive him, the left called him a Jewish Hitler and Yitzhak Shamir called him 'negative, detrimental and dangerous'.[76] He was even denounced by the rest of the far right.[77] He had come to Israel after a long history of violent religious zeal. In America he had been an FBI agent and had penetrated a conservative and allegedly anti-semitic organisation. He then founded the Jewish Defence League in New York, which mounted a terrorist campaign against young blacks who attacked Jews in the streets and against the anti-semitic Soviet Union. Then he decided that he had a duty in Israel, made the *aliyah* in the early 1970s and founded Kach. He and his party were soon associated with terrorist attacks on Arabs. Kahane totally approves of terrorism against Arabs: 'I approve of anybody who commits...acts of violence. Really I don't think that we can sit back and watch Arabs throwing rocks at buses whenever they feel like it,'[78] though like the other far-right parties he will not allow Kach's existence to be threatened by linking it officially with terrorist acts. It is widely believed that the underground Jewish movement TNT (Terror against Terror) is the military army of Kach, though nobody has been able to prove it.[79] As long as Kahane remained an outsider his extreme views seemed eccentric but harmless. He insisted that the only solution to the problem was that every single Palestinian in the country should be deported. This is a dream of many Israelis, but most cannot bring themselves to condone it because it is a blatantly racist solution and Jews have suffered too much from such racism and fantasies of elimination to encourage it among themselves. The fact that Kahane was actually elected to the Knesset, however, and that support for him and his policies has steadily increased, threatens the moral and human integrity of Zionism and the Jewish state. During the Palestinian uprising in Gaza and the West Bank in December 1987, commentators estimated that Kahane would get 5 per cent of the vote if there were an election, and that a third of all Israelis would agree that Palestinians should be deported (or 'transferred' as they prefer euphemistically to phrase it) from the Occupied Territories.[80]

Kahane argues with a relentless logic that is difficult to counter, because it takes on the central flaw in the Zionist argument: what right do the Jews have to Palestine that is not religious? Kahane's basic premise is that religion is the only possible way of being Jewish. The only reason for being a Jew and for living in Israel is the Torah.[81] He quite correctly points out that Judaism is not a racial religion. Anybody who chooses to convert to Judaism and live by the Torah is welcome to do so. Jewry is not a race or a people but a religious group.[82] This is also the only justification for the Jews to live in Israel. The only reason for living in what he has described as a most uncomfortable and inconvenient country is that God wants the Jews to live there.[83] He has said so repeatedly in the Torah, the first five books of the Bible, and should be taken literally. Jews cannot claim that they have a right to Eretz Yisrael simply because their ancestors lived there in the distant past. 'Who the hell cares where we lived 2000 years ago?' he asks, with a certain reason.[84] The Labour Zionists had based their claim to the land on their loving cultivation of its soil in the Conquest of Labour, and many Israelis today will argue that because they made the desert bloom and the Palestinians had done nothing for the land which matches the Jewish achievement, the Jews 'deserve' it. Kahane has no time for this reasoning.

> When certain Jews say to the Arabs: 'Look what we've done for you, we found a desert here and we transformed it into a garden,' the Arab replies with good reason: 'This may be true, but it was my desert and now it has become your garden.' So I understand the Arabs completely. It's insane to believe that you can buy them, that because you send them to Hebrew University they are going to turn into 'good Arabs,' in the sense that the Israeli Left means.[85]

Kahane argues that Israelis have 'such a sense of guilt' that they resort to dishonest arguments and policies towards the Arabs and Palestinians that are actually contemptuous. Kahane insists that he understands and respects the Arabs' position: 'The Arabs do not want peace. They want a country. And Zionism is not here to bring peace. It is here to create a Jewish state, and peace, of course, if at all possible. My main objective is a Jewish State, with or without peace.'[86] Anyway, as Kahane says, 'war isn't so terrible.'[87] It is a divine commandment to establish a state in the whole of Eretz Yisrael, including the Territories, and if that means war then the Israelis must fight as Joshua did.

When people accuse Kahane of being a racist, he has a swift and deadly retort: he isn't a racist but respects the Arabs; the real racist is the secular Zionist of the left. If Jews do not accept that their religion is the only reason for being Jewish then there is no other reason but race. It is a matter of a certain genetic inheritance: 'it is the biggest fascism...to believe that one has a right to come back here solely because one lived here 2000 years ago.'[88] The pillar of Israel is the Law of Return which guarantees instant citizenship to Jews. Kahane says that this is a racial law, which excludes Arabs because they are not of the right race. The only reason for keeping the Arabs out is because God commanded that 'they must not live in your country.' 'God wants us to live in a country of our own, isolated, so that we live separately and have the least possible contact with what is foreign, and so that we create as far as possible a pure Jewish culture based on the Torah.'[89]

There is nothing new in Kahane's accusation: Arabs and other opponents of the State of Israel have said that it is a racist, fascist state for years. The worrying thing about Kahane's accusation is that this time it is a Jew, basing his argument on the Torah, who throws down this gauntlet. It is a shameful and frightening thing that in the Jewish state, of all places, a member of the Knesset can get up and propose racist laws that are virtually indistinguishable from the Nuremberg Laws. Kahane would take all the voting rights away from Arabs in Israel; he would deprive them of citizenship; forbid them to buy property; forbid intermarriage between Jews and non-Jews; forbid sexual intercourse between Jews and non-Jews (penalty: fifty years' imprisonment); and introduce an apartheid system, whereby Arabs and Jews would have segregated beaches, for example.[90] Kahane is determined to deport all the Arabs from the State of Israel and the Occupied Territories. The Jews should offer the Arabs financial inducements to leave, but if that fails Israel will have to use force. 'I am not about to ask them to leave,' he has said. 'I want to make them leave...I want to scare them.'[91] When he visits an Arab town like Umm el-Fahm in the Galilee, he will talk about it as a Jewish city which, for the time being, has Arab residents. He will visit such a town to invite the Arabs to go. When there were riots in Afula and the Jewish population turned on the Arab residents in what can only be described as pogroms, Kahane visited the town and praised the citizens: they were not rabble-rousers, he said, they were 'good, loyal Jews'.[92] The Arabs are cruel, inhuman terrorists, he claims, who must be forcibly ejected. They are 'breeding like rabbits'[93] and within twenty years they will have attained a majority in the Greater Land of Israel. They will then be able to destroy the Jewish state: first they will force the government to change the Law of Return so that Palestinians can return to their homeland, and then, when the Palestinians have come flocking back, they will be able to drive the Jews into the sea.

The demographic problem is an Israeli nightmare. It is this that has persuaded Professor Y. Harkabi, a former hawk and head of Israeli intelligence, that Israel must give the Territories back simply in order to prevent an Arab majority in the so-called Jewish state. Because Israelis continue to refuse to do this, Harkabi has said that they have 'exercised their democratic right to commit suicide'.[94] Yet though Kahane's demographic argument is a powerful one, this is not the real reason why he disturbs Israelis. We have seen that there was an element in Zionism that actually nurtured and trained certain belligerent religious attitudes, so that Kahane's violent, Joshuan religion had been inherent in the Zionist solution from the start, though the seculars had determinedly eschewed religion. Similarly Kahane's racialism was inherent in Zionism from the very beginning in excluding non-Jews from the great Zionist scheme. It is true that the first Zionists did not arrive in Palestine with developed racialist prejudice against Arabs, though these did develop later. They had come with positive ideals, to build a model society and rescue their people from extermination. But in creating a Jewish state, where the Israeli Arabs were second-class citizens, they introduced a racist element into the heart of the Zionist vision. Further, Kahane's solution of driving the Palestinian Arabs from the country is not a new solution. There were vast exoduses of Arabs in 1948 and 1967. This caused many Israelis a great deal of moral anguish. Yet it continues to be true that many Israelis nurture a dream, whether or not they admit it, of an Israel without any Arabs and some still cherish the dream of a Greater Israel without Arabs. These are racist and impossible dreams which must not be indulged, and many of the *kibbutzniks* and leftists oppose Kahane's rhetorical evocation of this forbidden dream. Whenever he turns up to speak, many of them will gather to fight his supporters to stop his appearance. When Kahane spoke at Afula, local *kibbutzniks* were present with whistles which they blew throughout the speech to try to drown the flood of racist eloquence. But there were hundreds of young people there who were passionate Kahane supporters. A poll taken by the Smith Institute and published by the newspaper *Davar* in October 1986 revealed that 38 per cent of Israelis agreed with Kahane's opinion that the Arabs should be forcibly deported.[95] Kahane is not wholly foreign to the spirit of Zionism and many Israelis, secular and religious, either accept his vision or recognise with distress the threat to Zionist and Jewish integrity that Kahane offers the State of Israel.

Of all the far-right groups, Kach is the most blatantly reductive and monistic. Instead of seeing Judaism as a rich and complex tradition, Kahane sees the whole integrity of Judaism as dependent upon the State of Israel.

> There are not several messages in Judaism. There is only one. And this message is to do what God wants. Sometimes God wants us to go to war, sometimes he wants us to live in peace. . . . But there is only one message: God wanted us to come to this country and to create a Jewish State.[96]

Secular Israel is not an adequate solution; Kahane wants a state governed by the laws in the Torah. He has no time for Western humanism or for Western ideals like democracy, which he sees as incompatible with the Torah.[97] But, like the Gush Emunim, Kahane believes that the Messiah will come and that this is the messianic era. If the Jews become religious again and return to live in Israel, then the Messiah will come. But Kahane fears that, if this does not happen, the Messiah will come all the same but not in glory.

> If we deserve him, he may come at this instant, in glory and majesty. And if we don't deserve him, he'll come all the same, but in the midst of terrible sufferings. This is why I am fighting today. I am fighting so that the Jews become good Jews, so that there is not a catastrophe at the coming of the Messiah.[98]

The catastrophe will be a new worldwide outbreak of anti-semitism, that will make Hitler's Holocaust seem trivial in comparison. Kahane is quite unconcerned that his words and actions might well be stirring up buried anti-semitism in the Middle East and in Western Europe. He would almost welcome it. He thinks that such anti-semitism will force the Jews to come back to Israel and will thus help to realise the divine plan.[99]

Secular Jews also endorse Kahane's ideas. In 1982 Amos Oz interviewed a notorious hawk who preferred to remain anonymous, so Oz calls him 'Z'. When the article was published in the newspaper *Davar*, people accused him of making it all up, because Z's views were so extreme, but Oz claimed that he received many letters from readers who entirely shared Z's ideas. Z's basic argument is that the Jews missed a great opportunity in the early days of Zionism. Instead of cultivating the land and making the desert bloom, they should simply have come out to Israel and massacred a million Arabs. Then there would have been no Hitler, no Holocaust and a massive Jewish state of twenty million Jews, because there would have been such outrage and anti-semitism that all the Jews would have had to make the *aliyah*.[100] He was delighted with Israeli's dubious role in the Sabra and Chatilla massacres of Palestinians in the Lebanon earlier that year because he hoped it would make the civilised world hate the Jews.

> So now maybe we've finished once and for all with that crap about the Jewish monopoly on morality, about the moral lesson of the Holocaust and the persecutions, about the Jews who were supposed to have emerged from the gas chambers pure and good. We're done with all that garbage. That little destruction job we did in Tyre and Sidon, the job in Ein Hilweh (too bad we didn't wipe out that maggot's nest for good) and the nice healthy bombing in Beirut, and that mini-massacre – all of a sudden five hundred Arabs becomes a massacre! – in those camps [Sabra and Chatilla] (too bad the Christian Phalangists did it, and not us, with our own delicate little hands!), all those blessings and good deeds have finished off that bullshit about a 'Chosen People' and a 'Light unto the Nations.' Yes, bullshit! We're finished with that: not chosen and no light, and thank the Lord we're done with it![101]

Early Zionism had sought precisely to be a light unto the Gentiles, but this new Zionism of people like Z and Kahane wants to increase anti-semitism to bring the Jews to Israel and plunge the Gentiles into a Hitlerian darkness.

Z claims that he personally is prepared to do the 'dirty work' himself: 'to kill as many Arabs as it takes, to deport, to expel, to burn, to see that they hate us'.[102] After all, this is what the rest of the powerful nations have done, he argues.[103] Who now remembers the fate of the Australian Aborigines or the American Indians? Once that violent phase is over, then it is the turn of people like Oz to launder the past and make Israel a truly moral country, that sincerely laments its criminal record:

> I'll make a working arrangement with you: I'll do everything I can to deport the Arabs really far away, I'll do all I can to provoke anti-Semitism, while you write odes about the wretched fate of the Arabs and hold the buckets to catch the Zhids that I've forced to take refuge here. And then you can teach these Zhids to be a light unto the Nations. I'll wipe out the Arab villages and you can hold protest demonstrations and write the epitaphs. You'll be the family's honour and I'll be the stain on the family's honour. Be my guest. Is it a deal?[104]

A desperation and an amorality has entered Zionism that fills many Israelis with despair. But extremists like Kahane and Z insist that they cannot allow themselves the luxury of guilt. From the very beginning Zionism committed a wrong against the Arabs and excluded them from their plans for the Jewish state. There was an inherent violence in Zionism from the start and Kahane and Z would maintain that they are simply stating explicitly what the moderates are afraid to admit.

Certainly Israel seems to be moving steadily towards the right and away from any peaceful solution. When Peace Now, the peace movement, staged a demonstration against Israel's role in the Sabra and Chatilla massacres, an Israeli extremist threw a hand-grenade and killed the young Israeli scholar Emil Grunzweig. This gave Israelis a salutary shock and Grunzweig has become a symbol of great peril. Zionists had wanted to create a homeland where the Jews could live safely, and if Jews had begun to kill each other because of their conflicting views about this state then the whole Zionist enterprise had failed. But though all Israelis of the right and left agreed that there must be no terrorism against other Jews, this has not stopped Israeli violence against Arabs in Israel. At the same time as Israel publicly and sanctimoniously condemns terrorism, violent acts against Palestinians are condoned. Where a Palestinian boy of fourteen can be imprisoned for throwing rocks, Jewish settlers who have shot schoolgirls are

Holy War

released on bail, cheered by their supporters when they leave prison and given light or suspended sentences. The Western world seems to condone this behaviour, probably out of a residual guilt about anti-semitism.

Increasingly violence against the Arabs takes a religious turn. Israelis have held provocative prayer meetings in the Temple area, which is sacred to Muslims, and tear-gas has been thrown into the al-Aqsa mosque while Muslims are at prayer there. But there has also been fighting – though as yet no killings – between secular and religious Jews in Israel. Secular Israelis of the left have attacked Kahane's supporters. The ultra-Orthodox have started to fight secular Jews. In the summer of 1986 they burned down bus-shelters carrying advertisements that featured girls in swimming costumes, insisting that this violated the Torah. At once the seculars retaliated and even burned down a synagogue. In the late summer of 1987 Mayor Teddy Kolleck of Jerusalem gave permission for the screening of films on Friday evenings. Once again the ultra-Orthodox went out on to the streets. Prayer meetings were held at the Wailing Wall which were really a call to arms. There was fighting and street violence that was severe enough for the police to use tear-gas and jets of waters to disperse the crowds. The seculars responded with similar antagonism. Hundreds stood provocatively in the queues for Friday movies. In the last week of August 1987 Nahum Hunun, an eleven-year-old ultra-Orthodox boy was grabbed by a stranger in the street, who cut off his earlocks. As his father remarked, this was the sort of action that one might expect in Hitler's Germany but not in the Jewish state.[105] Some Israelis have even predicted a civil war between secular and religious Jews in Israel.

The seculars are not fighting because they hate religion, but because they argue that there are many different ways of being Jewish and that Judaism is *not* simply a religious tradition but a whole civilisation. They reject the right of other Jews to tell them how to live. In their turn, the ultra-Orthodox and the religious right accuse the seculars of being Nazi fascists, who seek to destroy the Jewish religion as Hitler did. Many of the seculars fear that religion will not only forbid Israelis to go to the cinema on Fridays, but will be used to encourage cruel and repressive measures against the Arabs and will make peace an impossibility. In the Crusader Kingdom of Jerusalem it was the religious extremists like Reynauld of Chatillon who refused to make peace and so brought about the destruction of the state. Secular Israelis feel that even if the religious right do not destroy the state politically they may do so morally. In the Crusader kingdom the Christians were on the brink of civil war, and indeed the holy-war mentality tends to divide societies bitterly. A final similarity between the current state of affairs in the Middle East in the Crusader Kingdom with the situation today was that this internal division in the Kingdom of Jerusalem took place in the context of a new enthusiasm for the Islamic *jihad.*

CHAPTER EIGHT

1979

Iran and the New Jihad: Muslims Demand an Islamic Identity

Shah Mohammad Reza Pahlavi of Iran seemed to rule one of the most powerful and progressive states in the Middle East; backed first by Great Britain and then by the United States, the Pahlavi dynasty appeared to be leading Iran firmly into the twentieth century. In an area where many regimes were aggressively hostile to the West, Mohammad Reza had made Iran a client state of the United States in rather the same way as Israel. His large and efficient army was equipped by America and trained by Israel; his secret service SAVAK worked hand in glove with the CIA and the MOSSAD, the Israeli secret service, using the same methods.[1] It seemed inconceivable that a dynasty enjoying such powerful local and international support could fall, and to many Western people Iran seemed an island of stability in the Arab wilderness of the Middle East. Yet on 16 January the unthinkable happened: the Shah was forced to abdicate and leave the country in disgrace. He had been toppled by a mass uprising of the Iranian people led by fiercely militant Muslims. Two weeks later the Ayatollah Ruhollah Khomeini returned to Iran after an exile of sixteen years. He was greeted by millions of Iranians from the poorer classes, who lined the streets shouting and crying for joy. Poets hailed his return as the beginning of a golden age where, after centuries of oppression and corruption, justice and righteousness would reign again in Iran and would spread to the whole world.[2] This bearded mullah, clad in the traditional robes of a Muslim clergyman, had inspired the most important and successful revolution since the Chinese revolution of 1949 and after centuries of colonial humiliation Islam had won a major victory. It was no longer possible to see religion as an anachronism, for the Ayatollah Khomeini's Islamic revolution challenged both superpowers and encouraged a new wave of religious militancy throughout the Middle East. The Ayatollah had changed the world and after 1979 East and West had to understand and absorb the meaning of this new Islamic *jihad*.

In the West, most people had watched this revolution with incredulity and dismay. For a year before the return of Khomeini they had been witnessing extraordinary scenes on their television sets. Thousands of virtually unarmed Iranians had poured on to the streets challenging the Shah's soldiers to shoot them: hundreds of them had been killed. Massive crowds of workers and people from the professional and middle classes had defied the curfew and charged the SAVAK forces, fired by the Islamic war-cry *Allahu Akhbah!* (God is great!) which echoed from loudspeakers on the rooftops. Hundreds of Iranian civilians had donned the white robes of the martyr, ready to die and go to paradise in this new *jihad* for Islam. Iranian women threw aside their Western clothes and shrouded themselves in the all-concealing chadar as a revolutionary act; they too rushed on to the streets

with machine guns or crude weapons crying 'Allah! Koran! Khomeini!' Religious processions in honour of the Islamic martyr Husain paraded through the streets, but the participants clenched their raised fists and shouted 'Down with the Shah' in such vast numbers that the Iranian soldiers did not dare to shoot at them. After the revolution there were still more shocking sights. Thousands of young men joined Khomeini's special Martyr regiment and wore a scarlet bandanna to show their dedication to Islam; plugged into cassette machines that were playing Khomeini tapes, they worked themselves up into an exalted state so that they could face almost certain death in feats of suicidal bravery in the Gulf War. Even more terrifying were the thousands of young boys who joined the junior martyr corps and charged over the minefields to clear the way for the revolutionary troops, blasting themselves into heaven with the cry *Shaheed!* (Martyr!). To most Western people it seemed that Iran had been gripped by a mass religious insanity. There was general ignorance about the nature of Islam, which now seemed a primitive and destructive force hurling individuals towards suicide and a whole people to destruction. Against all reason the Iranians had rejected the gift of progress and secular development that the West had offered them and were returning Iran to the barbarous darkness of the seventh century.

But in fact there was nothing new about the Iranian revolution, which seemed so monstrously other to Westerners. It was a classic revival of the *jihad* which Nur ad-Din and Saladin had called against the Christian Crusaders from the West. There was in this *jihad* nearly all the themes that fuel a holy war in all three religious traditions: a strong desire for self-determination; an effort to overcome a trauma; a dedicated struggle to create a new identity; a return to fundamental principles and to the past, which is also a creative encounter leading to a new lease of life; a fierce commitment to social justice and the desire to create a more equal society. In these respects the Iranian revolution was not so very different from early Zionism, which the West had not stigmatised but found sympathetic and admirable. But one theme was missing from the Iranian *jihad* which made it very different from Jewish or Christian holy wars. There was no cult of a holy land or a holy city. It is true that from the beginning of his revolutionary career the Ayatollah Khomeini had denounced Israel and Zionism, but that was because he saw it as an alien state, which had persecuted Muslims. He was not moved by a veneration for Jerusalem, such as had inspired both the Crusaders and the Israelis, because he would have felt that such excessive veneration was idolatry, a worship of something other than Allah.[3] Indeed Khomeini had no particular love of his own country and there was certainly no nationalism or patriotism in his desire to liberate it from Shah Reza. This probably does make the Iranian revolution unique among revolutionary movements. When the Ayatollah was boarding his plane in Paris for his return journey to Iran in February 1979, an unsuspecting French journalist asked him how he felt about going home to Iran, after an exile of sixteen years. Khomeini answered in one word: '*Rien.*' Nothing.[4] He was inspired only by Islamic ideals.

Khomeini's revolution was not uncharacteristic of the Iranian people, but he can be seen as the result of a very long Iranian and Muslim tradition of revolution and criticism of the establishment. To understand this tradition two things are necessary: first we need to look at the origins of Shiite Islam and the notion of a legitimate Muslim ruler, and then we must look briefly at recent Iranian history to see why millions of Iranians became revolutionaries in 1978. The revolution was very disturbing to the other Muslim countries, particularly those which had Shiites in their own territories. Many Arab leaders wanted to dissociate themselves from this Persian movement and stressed that Shiite Islam was very different indeed from the Sunni Islam followed by the majority of Muslims. Western journalists picked this up and produced a rather distorted view of Shiism, dwelling, for example, on the Shiite 'yearning for martyrdom' as though it was an essentially hysterical and masochistic religion. But even though different emphases of doctrine naturally developed in both the Shiite and the Sunni traditions, there is no theological difference between the two. The revolution has inspired Sunni Muslims in the Middle East as well as Shiites. Sometimes the Shiite–Sunni conflict is compared to the Catholic–Protestant conflict in Christianity, but this analogy is misleading. It is true that the Shiites have complained that they are often discriminated against in countries where they are a minority, as the Catholics were in England until the late nineteenth century, for example. But in Christianity there has always been an aggressive insistence on theological orthodoxy, which does not exist in either Judaism or Islam. Like Judaism, Islam has a very simple creed and is a religion of practice rather than theology, but the complicated doctrines of Christianity can very easily be 'misinterpreted' and this leads to bitter doctrinal disputes. Islam, like Judaism, does not allow the notion of 'heresy' and sees a man's theological beliefs as a private matter, not a matter for the establishment to control. The Christian yearning for intellectual conformity seems idolatry to Muslims, because it raises man-made ideas and human systems to an unacceptably exalted level. This is an important point, and one to which we will return in the discussion of Khomeini's ideology.

The Sunni–Shiite conflict began as a purely political dispute. After the death of the Prophet Mohammad in 632, the people elected his friend Abu Bakr as his Successor (Caliph). But there was a group of Muslims who believed that Mohammad would have wanted his cousin and son-in-law Ali to be the leader (Imam) of the Islamic community, because he had been closer to the Prophet than anyone else. Ali accepted the caliphate of Abu Bakr on the important Islamic principle that it had the support of the majority of the people, but his followers (the *Shi-ah-i Ali*, Partisans of Ali) did not and they regarded the caliphs as unlawful rulers. To be a Muslim ruler seemed a dangerous and unenviable job, however. Few of them died in their beds.

In 656 Ali was finally elected Fourth Caliph by the Sunni and the Shiites called him the First Imam. Like those of his three predecessors, Ali's reign was marked by political dissension as the *umma* underwent the huge upheaval of transforming itself from a desert society in the Hejaz into a rapidly expanding empire. The fanatical Kharaji sect (who were the first group to make the *hijra* or migration from the main *umma* and wage a *jihad* against the Muslim majority, whom they felt were betraying Islam) had been supporters of Ali and had then withdrawn their support. One of their members murdered Ali in 661 and at this point one Muawiyah seized the caliphate and founded the Umayhyad dynasty, transferring the seat of the Caliphate from Medina to Damascus. It was the end of an era. Despite their troubles, the first four caliphs were henceforth regarded as righteous or rightly guided (*rashidun*) and the Umayhyads and their successors the Abbasid caliphs were regarded by the people as *munafiqeen* (hypocritical) rulers. The restless period of the four righteous caliphs, who had experienced the problems that inevitably accompany the creation of a new society, was regarded as the Muslim golden age. It is natural for later generations to idealise the founders of a movement, but there was also good reason for Muslims to see the *munafiqeen* as lacking in the devotion and piety of the rightly guided caliphs. They proved to be men who were far more interested in personal power and the creation of a dynasty than in religion, and they soon lost the support of the masses.[5] The Shiah naturally continued their opposition to the caliphate and after Ali's death, they regarded his son Hasan as the Second Imam. But even the Sunnis dissociated themselves from the *munafiqeen* and the caliphate gradually declined as a real political or religious power.[6] In times of trouble Sunnis looked elsewhere for their leaders and put their trust in men who measured up more fully to the Islamic ideal. We have seen how the Sunni Muslims of the Near East despaired of the caliphs during the time of the Crusades and gave their support to local leaders like Nur ad-Din.

Nur ad-Din gained a strong popular support because he presented himself as an authentic Muslim ruler, who was living according to the ideals of the righteous caliphs. Sunnis and Shiites might disagree about individuals but they were fully agreed about what kind of man a true Muslim ruler should be and about what kind of leadership he should establish.[7] He had to be quite clear that the only true leader of the Muslims was God himself, and should rule as God's trustee; he must live frugally and simply and be at pains to create a just and equal society. Above all, he must not be a despot like the Ummayad and Abbasid caliphs, but should be the servant of his people.

As soon as Abu Bakr became caliph, he had made this clear. He told the people that if they noticed any unIslamic traits in his rule they must correct him: the Caliph must be controlled by Islam and by the people. Ali was even more explicit. He taught that 'the common people of the *umma* are the pillars of the religion, the power of Muslims and the defence against enemies.'[8] The Muslim ruler must not keep himself secluded from the people nor could he be a dictator but should rule by consultation with the people themselves. He must not create an elitist society and he must take special responsibility for the poor and needy, ensuring that wealth was fairly distributed in the *umma*. The ruler, Ali taught, must be a merciful and compassionate leader, ruling a just society. This ideal of the legitimate Muslim ruler is still a crucial factor that no leader of a Muslim country can safely ignore.[9] Many devout Muslims in the Middle East today would see their present political leaders as *munafiqeen* who have either set up a secular state or who live in luxury while the vast majority of the people live in extreme poverty.

It was inevitable that there would be a clash between the Ummayad Caliphs and the descendants of Ali, who were an obvious threat to their dynasty. When Hasan died, his brother Husain, the grandson of the Prophet, refused to accept the Umayhyad caliphate and became the Third Imam. This refusal was an act of revolution. In 680 Caliph Yazid resolved to destroy the Shiite Imam, who fled to Mecca, seeking sanctuary in the Holy City where violence was strictly forbidden. Caliph Yazid showed his true colours when he sent an assassin into Mecca disguised as a pilgrim. Imam Husain survived the attempt on his life but this flagrant violation of the holiness of Mecca shocked the whole Muslim world. The citizens of the city of Kufa in modern Iraq invited Husain to take refuge with them and promised to support him against the tyrant, and the Third Imam set out on a dangerous journey to create a just and truly Islamic society in Kufa. With him travelled a small band of loyal followers who joined him in his refusal of this unIslamic tyranny, which was a mockery of everything that Mohammad had stood for. Eventually in the desert of Karbala, just seventy kilometres from Kufa, Husain and his men were surrounded by the Caliph's huge army. He told his followers to leave him, but they all absolutely refused to leave their Imam, even though they had no hope of surviving the battle because they were so vastly outnumbered. Yazid attacked the Shiite band and Husain and all his followers were killed. They had chosen to die fighting oppression and unIslamic tyranny, not because they were unbalanced people yearning for martyrdom but because they had a revolutionary duty as devout Muslims to fight against unIslamic cruelty.[10]

Karbala added a new element to the Muslim paradigm of the holy war, and Shiites and Sunnis all look back in horror at the immoral slaughter of the devout grandson of the Prophet. Throughout the Muslim world, Husain's heroic story is kept alive during the month of Muharram in passion plays and recitations that

impress on all Muslims the duty of resisting tyranny to the death, however hopeless the struggle might be. Naturally Karbala was especially important to the Shiah and Muharram became a climactic moment in the Shiite year. Husain's willingness to die for Islamic values sanctified the imamate and after his death nine more descendants of Ali succeeded him as the imams of the Shiah. Of these, seven were murdered by the Caliphs and it was clear that accepting the position of Imam did not mean a life of luxury and ease but was the grim undertaking of a dangerous revolutionary duty. The Imams bravely provided an Islamic alternative to the despotic and unIslamic dynasties of the caliphs and were ready for martyrdom as part of their witness to true Muslim ideals. In 874 the Twelfth Imam went into hiding and after his death in 917 there were no further descendants of Ali to take up the revolutionary vocation of the imamate. Shiites believed that there was no more legitimate temporal rule, but instead the Islamic leadership tended to pass to those members of the clergy who were most learned in Islamic law and who expressed true Muslim values in their lives and teaching.[11] The Sunnis had also sought out their own leaders, but these leaders could be laymen and warriors. In the Shiah the leadership tended to be confined to the clerics – a fact of some importance in the Iranian revolution. In the Shiah an apocalyptic belief developed in the Twelfth or Hidden Imam, who was expected to return to inaugurate a golden age of Islamic justice. As in Judaism and Christianity, revolutionary striving for a new world became closely associated with an apocalyptic, messianic belief in a final redemption. Some Shiites felt that political action was wrong and that Muslims should sit back and wait for the Hidden Imam, but others decided that they had to take responsibility for the people's fate.[12]

In Iran, where Shiism had been the official religion since the sixteenth century, there was a strong revolutionary tradition among the mullahs, the Muslim clergy. Certain Islamic jurists, the *mujtahids*, felt that it was their religious duty to guide the people and to oppose monarchs of the Safavid and Qajar dynasties, who were autocratic oppressors and ruled by dictat and not by consultation. They were obviously *munafiqeen* and were acting in defiance of basic Islamic principles. The Prophet Mohammad had risen against the oppressive ruling class of Mecca and now the mullahs felt it was their duty to do the same. They also objected to the habit of the Qajar shahs (kings) to court the imperial powers of Britain and Russia and allow them to have undue influence in the country. This was not due to any incipient national feeling, because the mullahs would have disapproved of nationalism on Islamic grounds: they would not have wished Iran to be a nation state separate from its Muslim neighbours, because they believed that Islam should be a single entity, reflecting the unity of the One God. The Prophet Mohammad had given to the first Muslims a proud, new identity of their own, which had enabled them to throw off the great powers of their own time, who had long exploited the Arab people of the peninsula. Similarly, the Muslim leaders wanted the people of Iran to be free of these alien powers, who were exploiting Iran for their own ends and were also importing foreign ideologies that were opposed to the essential values of Islam.[13]

In particular they objected to the Western doctrine of 'secularism', which insisted that religion was a purely private and spiritual affair and must be kept quite separate from politics. This belief had grown up in Europe during the eighteenth century, and people now tended to regard the separation of Church and state as essential to the integrity of each. It is a prejudice that we still have today and people are rather suspicious of a religion that gets involved in political affairs, which they then dismiss as 'worldly'. This prejudice has probably made it very difficult for people in the West to understand the Iranian revolution. It is certainly true that religion and politics can be a dangerous combination, as we have seen in the last chapter, and also that a religion can become corrupt if it sullies itself with politics and the struggle for power. But too great a separation from 'worldly' affairs can also threaten the integrity of religion. Christians who have piously said their prayers and given tacit support to oppressive governments or who have encouraged the poor to accept their lot and wait for a future reward are also denying basic Christian principles. In England today there are some Christians who say that the Church of England should disestablish itself and separate itself from the unChristian Thatcher government, which does not live up to the teachings of Jesus and St Paul about equality and compassion. This is the spirit in which we should understand the Muslim involvement in politics. From the days of the Prophet, religion and politics had been inseparable: Mohammad had been striving to create a better world and each generation of Muslims felt it their duty to continue this struggle for a just and equal society that reflected the will of God. In Iran the Shiite clergy felt it their duty to go back to the spirit of the Imams and create an alternative Islamic Iran, which challenged the unjust and oppressive policies of the *munafiqeen*.

By the end of the nineteenth century, therefore, there was a tradition in Iran whereby in each generation certain *mujtahids* came to be accepted by the mass of the people as their true leaders. The people found it more and more difficult to identify with the monarchs of the Qajar dynasty, who had been infected with so many foreign ideas, but they could relate to the values of the mullahs, which were the same as their own. Muslim Iran became a real alternative to the secular establishment; it was almost a country within a country. Alternative Islamic Iran had its own institutions, which came increasingly to oppose the secular institutions of the government. The mosque had always been the centre of Muslim life. It was quite different from a Christian church, which is reserved for prayer. Ever since Mohammad had built the first mosque in Medina, it had been the central meeting place for all the activities of the Muslim community – political, military and cultural – as well as for prayers and sermons, because *all* these activities were religious. In alternative Iran the mosque was the local centre where the people were educated and trained practically and intellectually in the values of Islam, which penetrated their daily lives at all levels. In a time of political crisis, the mosque would become a centre of political underground activity, linked to other mosques in a natural but effective network.

Besides the local centre of the mosque, there were the madrassas, the Islamic colleges, where the important *mujtahids* taught and trained the clergy. To train to be a mullah, you needed a particular type of mind and to be able to handle logical and verbal distinctions in a way that is alien to much modern Western education. From all over Iran, adolescent boys who had proved in their local Koranic schools that they had this talent would become *talabeh* or seekers. They left their homes and families, sometimes for ever, and often travelled hundreds of miles away to study at one of the famous madrassas under the teacher of their choice. The young Ruhollah Khomeini left his obscure home town Khomein, on the edge of the Iranian desert, in 1918 when he was only sixteen. He came from a family of mullahs, so it was a natural decision for him. He could have chosen any number of madrassas, as far away as Najaf, in Iraq, or even in India, but in the end Ruhollah decided to study under Ayatollah Arakti in Arak, which is about 200 miles from Tehran and not far from Khomein. This does not indicate any special affection for his home town, however. Shortly after he came to power a delegation from Khomein begged him to visit the city, and Khomeini refused their elaborate and effusive invitation curtly: 'There will be no visit.'[14] Attachment to home was in his view an unworthy sentimentality, but he apparently offended some members of the Khomeini delegation, for all their veneration of him. It is interesting that for

a time Khomeini considered going to Tehran to study under the Ayatollah Beheshti, one of the revolutionary *mujtahids*, and probably decided against it because the Ayatollah was 'too political'.[15] At this time Ruhollah does not seem to have been very interested in politics. He was a solitary, rather distant and unapproachable young man, who used to write poetry in his spare time under the pseudonym 'Hindi'. Some of these poems, which were published in Tehran in 1979, show the uncompromising, stern religious vision of the younger Hindi:

> I know not in which book I read
> The story of Tamerlane's exploits:
> He who put young and old to the sword,
> He who ignored the commands of the Lord.
> At night he was struck by insomnia
> Crying aloud and writhing with pain.
> Doctors who came to offer him a cure
> Saw the wound of a sword around his neck
> Strangling him. That's the revenge of God.
> So as the Tatar pierced the roof with his cries,
> The Angel of Revenge chuckled noiselessly.
> There is One who lays the mighty low.
> There is He who chops the guilty to pieces
> To him is devoted 'Hindi' and to no other one. (*c.*1940)[16]

In Arak as in all the Iranian madrassas Khomeini and his fellow *talabeh* studied according to an ancient educational tradition, with methods and logic that would seem very strange to a Westerner today. But at the time of the Crusades Westerners would have found these methods very familiar. The Iranian *talabehs* are the last people in the world to study according to the scholastic methods and disciplines that produced scholars like Abelard and Thomas Aquinas in Christendom and Averroes in Muslim Spain. Like the medieval students, the young Seekers begin with grammar, rhetoric and logic, which in medieval Europe were known collectively as the *trivium*, the first three of the seven liberal arts. The teaching was not carried out by means of lectures, but by a question-and-answer discussion, that is much the same as the method of 'disputation' practised in the universities that were springing up in Europe at the time of the Crusades. The students have a text in front of them and sit on the floor around their teacher, who sits on a short flight of steps. He expounds the text under discussion and the students question and challenge him, in ways that most of us in the West would find difficult to follow because they depend on a logical method that is technical and on hair-splitting definitions of terms. In the time of Abelard, the disputation was often very aggressive and rude, but this is not so in Iran. A student has to introduce his query in a courteous and standard phrase like 'With your permission, an important point', and in a discussion between equals the debate is punctuated with elaborate and formal praise: 'God bless your fine mullah's mind!' In the madrassas the egalitarian structure of the classes and the methods of study meant that every student could go at his own pace and attain his own standard, whether he was a brilliant academic or destined for a humble village pulpit. There was no external 'syllabus' that everyone had to follow and no public examinations. This meant that a student could internalise his religious studies at a very deep level, and indeed he would be steeped in them night and day. The *talabeh* would continue their discussions and studies together outside class. They slept in long dormitories and wore a distinctive uniform, which meant that the madrassa was a strong symbol of the alternative Iran which was maintaining its separate Islamic identity.[17]

Yet no society has ever succeeded in maintaining complete equality, however dedicated it is to the idea of justice. Many of the mullahs were in fact Sayyeds or gentlemen, the aristocrats of Iran who claimed, improbably, that they were descended from the Prophet Mohammad. They were allowed to wear a green or black turban, instead of the white turban of the other Muslims. Khomeini himself is a Sayyed. This meant that despite the egalitarian structure of the madrassa, the mullahs did in fact constitute an elite. So too did the system of teaching. The student may have been taught according to an ancient tradition, but this did not mean that his studies were backward-looking because most madrassas encouraged the use of what is called *ijtihad* or independent judgement. Not everybody could exercise this. Only very learned *mujtahids* were able to amass the immense amount of knowledge required to build upon older traditions and on the ideas of contemporary scholars and at the same time take the Islamic tradition forward by exercising their own judgement. The people and the less learned and skilled clerics had to follow their leaders in a process that they called *taqlid* or emulation.[18] This did not mean emulation in matters theological, which Islam does not require, but in matters of practice governed by Islamic law, which is studied in the madrassas. In Iran, the jurists very often used *ijtihad* to examine contemporary problems in the light of Islamic teaching and sometimes these problems would be political. Thus although Islam proclaimed the importance of equality, it did mean that in fact decisions were made by only a small group of clerics. When a mullah had reached a certain status he was by a general consensus called 'Ayatollah' or the symbol of Allah. This meant that he was now entitled to make Islamic decisions and to act as a model and guide for the behaviour and practice of others. We shall see that some of the lay revolutionaries of 1978 felt that this clerical authority was unIslamic and claimed that they too had the right to exercise *ijtihad*. But most of the people and the *bazaari*, the merchant class, were content with the system. By the end of the nineteenth century, the *mujtahids* and the local clergy had attained a formidable power and two incidents show the tradition in Iran which would lead the people to rise as one to the leadership of Khomeini.

The first of these incidents was the tobacco crisis of 1872 when the Qajar Shah sold the monopoly over the production, sale and export of tobacco to the British in return for money and shares that went into his own pocket. This naturally incensed the Iranian merchants and they went straight to the chief mullah in Tehran, Hajji Mirza Hasan Ashtiyani. In the Western world no businessman would think of going to consult a priest or his local bishop about an unpopular government policy that affected his business. Priest and laymen would both consider that concern for such worldly and commercial matters is not fitting for a man of God, who is supposed to be dedicated to more lofty spiritual concerns. But, as this incident shows, things are very different in Islam, where clergy and laymen believe that any concern of a member of the Muslim community is a matter of concern to the clergy, whether it is a matter of body or soul. Hajji Ashtiyani was not fully qualified to make an Islamic ruling on the tobacco crisis, so he asked the advice of the great *mujtahid* Hajji Mirza Mohammad Hasan Shirazi of Najaf, who issued a *fatwa* (ruling) that forbade all Iranians to smoke tobacco. The effect of the *fatwa* was electrifying. Smoking as we all know is an addictive habit and it would be difficult to imagine any ruler, secular or lay, who by a single pronouncement would be powerful enough to stop a whole country from lighting up. But in Iran in 1872 public opinion banned smoking absolutely. Nobody dared to sell tobacco on the streets, and even the police and the Shah's wives were afraid to smoke. It was not that people were cowed by the authority of the Hajji, but because they could see that this was a positive act and that the clerics seemed far more concerned about the welfare of the ordinary people than their Shah. Posters appeared threatening a *jihad* and at once the people started to prepare arms and provisions for a military campaign. The tobacco industry had been completely sabotaged, the British were afraid to go out on to the streets and cowered in their homes. Eventually the Shah had to ask Hajji Ashtiyani for talks. Ashtiyani agreed to call off the *jihad* – nobody was serious at *this* point about a full-scale revolution – but not the ban on smoking, and when the Shah therefore threatened to expel him from the country the crowds swarmed on to the streets in such threatening numbers, braving the guns of the palace guard as they would do a hundred years later, that the Shah had no choice but to rescind the tobacco concessions.[19] The tobacco crisis showed that it was the clergy and not the Shah who controlled the masses and were in touch with the people. Alternative Islamic Iran was a challenge that no monarch could safely ignore.

The clergy also intervened in the constitutional crisis of 1906 when some secular intellectuals initiated a movement for reform which would control the Qajar shahs and secure some political participation. The Qajars were deeply opposed to any such reform and the movement would have failed had not some of the constitutionalists thought of asking the clergy for help. The *mujtahids* produced a *fatwa* which demanded a reform to limit the Westernisation and secularisation of Iran and imposed a limit to the Qajars' oppression of the people. The people were mobilised in much the same way as the people of the Near East had been mobilised in the *jihad* against the Crusaders by Saladin. The Constitution was preached in the mosques at the Friday sermon and a *jihad* against the oppressive government was called. The result was that overnight the Shah found himself threatened with revolution. He had to concede the demands of the constitutionalists and in their turn the constitutionalists had to agree that no legislation would be passed that was repugnant to Islam. A committee of *mujtahids* had the power of veto over the legislation passed by the Iranian parliament. The Shah now found himself controlled by dedicated religious Muslims.[20] But at this date he also found himself confronted by a new religious centre of power in the city of Qum, which was about fifty miles from Tehran and was just beginning to acquire a wholly new importance. It had always been a holy city because the Sixth Imam was buried there and pilgrims used to pray at the shrine.[21] But in the first years of the twentieth century the madrassas in the city suddenly became more prestigious and the chief *mujtahids* began to congregate there. The result was that Qum was now an alternative religious capital that was constantly in opposition to the Shah's secular capital in Tehran. Qum was unique in the Muslim world and a symbol of the independence and power of alternative Iran.[22] In 1919, when Ayatollah Arakti left Arak and went to Qum, his young and brilliant student Ruhollah Khomeini followed him there. For the next fifty years Khomeini taught in the Muslim capital at the important Faiziyeh Madrassa and acquired a formidable reputation in Islamic jurisprudence; but he was not at the forefront of the opposition to the regime. In 1942 he published his *Kashf al-Asrar* (Key to the Secrets) and earned the title of ayatollah, but he lived a quiet, unpolitical life, studying, teaching and composing poetry.

The more vociferous *mujtahids* at Qum were condemning the new phenomenon which was known as *gharbzadgi* or West-toxication. Western modes of life were entering the Middle East as first Britain and then France began to establish their colonies, protectorates and mandates in 1920. Britain had sought to control the shahs of Iran who had co-operated with the colonisers, offering them the tobacco concession, for example, and so the shahs were firmly linked with the West in the minds of the ordinary people. But the Western invasion was more insidious than that. Western dress, education and technology also brought 'progress' into the area. Many of the wealthier young Iranians went abroad to study in Paris, London, Oxford or America. They brought 'modern' ideas back with them and Western

enthusiasms like secularism, nationalism, atheism and Western amusements and entertainments that were quite alien to the traditional Iranian way of life.[23] The shahs also wanted their country to progress into this modern or Western world and were happy to allow the British to form the Anglo-Persian Oil Company in 1909, which meant that the recently discovered oil was produced and marketed by the British in their modern refineries. The British paid the shahs well for this but the Iranian people did not benefit from this new source of wealth in any way.[24]

The *mujtahids* at Qum condemned this exploitation by the West and they were also worried by their fellow countrymen who had succumbed to Western values. This is difficult for us to understand, perhaps, but we must try to come to terms with it for it is crucial to an understanding of the revolution. The mullahs were not atavistically turning their backs on progress and modernisation. They felt that this adoption of an essentially alien lifestyle would produce a culture shock. They described the Westernised Iranians as particles of dust suspended in the air, in touch with neither heaven nor earth.[25] They also saw the new Western idols of communism or socialism as doomed to disappoint. Indeed some of the Iranians who had returned home to Iran felt rootless and lost; they felt that they belonged neither in the East nor in the West. In their poetry and writings the frequency of themes like loneliness, nothingness, walls, fatigue and darkness show this malaise.[26] They felt that they had lost their identity. Once they had lost their sense of the old traditions of Iran and once the excitement with the novel Western way of life had worn off, many younger Iranians felt caught between two worlds and in need of a clear identity. It is a common problem that has surfaced all over the Third World in countries which were former colonies of Western powers and have lost touch with their natural way of life and have not been able fully to absorb the Western values nor to make more than a superficial use of the Western institutions we have left behind us. The *mujtahids*, therefore, as the spiritual leaders of Iran, were concerned about the plight of the nation, which seemed to be running after false gods that would ultimately betray them.

This hostility to the Shah naturally increased when the shahs began to try to cut down the power of Iranian Islam and became even more firmly controlled by Great Britain. At first the Qajar shahs had been happy about the oil deal with Britain, but as time went by they wanted a larger slice of the cake and the British started to look around for a new ruler whom they could manipulate more easily. They discovered Colonel Reza Khan, the founder of the Pahlavi dynasty and the father of Shah Mohammad Reza. With the support of the British, he overthrew the Qajar dynasty in 1921 and sold the British more oil concessions.[27] Not only had Shah Reza put the regime in the thrall of Britain but he declared himself at the outset to be the enemy of Islam. He realised that if he wanted to survive he could not allow himself to be controlled by the mullahs as the Qajars had been. At his coronation he declared that he was taking Iran back to its Aryan roots in the days before it had been conquered by the Arab armies and had converted to Islam. Iran would have an Aryan identity not an Islamic one. He claimed that he was reviving the ancient Persian monarchy of King Cyrus, the King who had allowed the Jews of Babylon to go home to Jerusalem in 538 BCE.[28] As if this were not enough, Shah Reza made his dynasty an absolute dictatorship and abolished the new constitution. He called himself King of Kings in defiance of the principles of Islam, and the Iranians suffered the double humiliation of a repressive regime and still more exploitation by Great Britain, who fuelled her navy with Iranian oil without the people of Iran gaining a penny.[29]

This return to Aryan roots was clearly influenced by the nationalist movements in Europe, some of which were seeking to return the people to their pre-Christian past. Actually Shah Reza seemed more concerned to Westernise his country than to revivify its ancient Persian glories. His model of an ideal state was the new Turkey of Mustafa Kemal Ataturk, and he imitated many of Ataturk's measures in an attempt to modernise and de-Islamise Iran. The wearing of the veil was forbidden and mullahs were forced to shave and wear the kepi instead of the traditional turban. Naturally this was viewed by the *mujtahids* as an act of war. This tyrant was forbidding them their liberty and subordinating religion to his own secular visions. A new era of intensified West-toxication began as Reza Shah made educational and legal reforms to modernise Iran. Universities were established on the American model, which were advised by fifty-nine universities in the United States.[30] It was a new kind of invasion. First the Iranians had felt their land invaded by British oil prospectors and businessmen, who were simply milking Iran for their own ends. Now they were invaded by American academics who were forcing alien methods of education and courses of study that filled the heads of the people with foreign ideas. Discontent increased in the country; even those Iranians who were secularised and Westernised felt dissatisfied and powerless in this absolute monarchy which denied them any real political participation. Like the Muslims, these secular Iranians wanted to take their destiny into their own hands. Things did not improve when Britain and Russia both invaded Iran in 1941 and Shah Reza – who had been loud in his support of Hitler – ws forced to resign and go into exile. His son Mohammad Reza was sworn in and, though he lacked his father's imposing physical presence, he soon showed that he was firmly committed to continuing his father's despotic and elitist dictatorship.

From the beginning of the Pahlavi regime there had been opposition among the people. Secular revolutionary groups that were inspired by nationalist or communist ideologies were formed but these lacked the support of the mass of the people, who found their ideas alien and incomprehensible. More serious was the opposition of Ayatollah Hassan Mudarris, who was elected as a deputy to the Majiles, the Iranian parliament. His passionate and eloquent speeches denouncing imperialism, colonialism and dictatorship made him extremely popular among the masses and he became such a threat that Shah Reza exiled him for eight years and finally had him poisoned by his agents.[31] Naturally the Ayatollah was revered as a martyr by the people, who saw him continuing the tradition of Imam Husain and the other imams who had been murdered by the *munafiqeen*. He was continuing the Iranian tradition of revolutionary Islamic leadership and had proved that he was ready to lay down his life for his people and fight tyranny to the death.

As soon as Reza Khan had left the country in 1941, Islam had sprung back to life, showing that his attempts to secularise the nation had been entirely superficial and had not touched the mass of the people at all. Traditional dress reappeared and the public Husain celebrations, which had been forbidden by Reza Khan, were enthusiastically resumed. In 1948 the clergy issued a *fatwa* forbidding women to go to market without a veil and the new young Shah Mohammad Reza was unable to control this rampantly militant defiance of his secularising policies.[32] New Islamic groups were formed that showed the Iranian determination not to allow the shahs to threaten their religion: never again would Islam be forced into the humiliation to which Reza Khan had subjected the clergy and people. The new opponents of the Shah seized their revolutionary vocation with a new desperation and violence. In 1945 Mullah Harab Safari founded the Fedayeen-e-Islam, an underground terrorist organisation, and demanded an Islamic state and a *jihad* against the Shah and the West, who were the enemies of the faith.[33] He and his colleagues were caught and executed in 1955 but the *fedayeen* survived underground and joined the 1978 revolution. In the early 1950s the Ayatollah Abdulqasim Kashani founded the Mujahideen-e-Islam, another terrorist group, and Kashani used to boast that at any one moment he could produce a million martyrs who were ready to sacrifice their lives in the fight against the Shah's tyranny.[34]

Ayatollah Kashani worked with the secular nationalist Mohammad Mossadeq in his campaign against the Shah and against the oil concessions to the British. In 1951 the *mujahideen* committed a series of assassinations which culminated in the murder of the Shah's Prime Minister Haj-Ali Rasmara and forced the Shah to rescind the oil concessions. Mossadeq became Prime Minister, but he would not allow his Islamic colleagues a greater share of power in his strictly secular movement, and Kashani had to break with him. These terrorist groups showed that they were actually not an effective means of fighting the tyranny of the Shah. Not only were they morally dubious, but they also lacked the support of the masses. The terrorists were ready to give their lives like Husain, but a campaign of assassination was a very different matter from the brave stand at Karbala and the martyr ideal was acquiring the aggressive edge it had acquired centuries earlier in Christianity and in the Shiite sect of Assassins. The terrorists were able to achieve a short victory but nothing long-term, and this applied also to the secular opponents of the Shah. In 1953 Mossadeq staged a successful coup and the Shah had to go into exile. Almost immediately he was re-established on his throne with the help of the CIA. The Iranians had exchanged British control and exploitation for American dominance. Iran now became a client state of the United States like Israel, and America began to enjoy the same oil concessions as the British had formerly enjoyed. Oil went into the American-owned multinational oil companies and, though money went into the Shah's pocket, the country derived no benefit from this great wealth. The secular coup had achieved nothing, and the lesson that both secular and religious Iranians had learned in the 1950s was that without the mass support of the people no revolution would be strong enough to stand up to the great powers.[35]

His new powerful American support made Shah Mohammad Reza even more repugnant to most of his people than his father had been. He was certainly aware that Islam was a threat to his dynasty, but at the same time he seemed to go out of his way to defy the ideal of a legitimate Islamic ruler and to embrace all the crimes of the *munafiqeen*. Like his father, he proclaimed an absolute monarchy based on the ancient dynasty of Cyrus, an ideal that denied the basic Islamic principle that God alone was the ruler of Muslims. Like his father again, Mohammad Reza sought an Aryan not an Islamic identity for Iran and he promoted the secularisation of the country. Tehran became a Western-style capital filled with visiting American businessmen, academics and oil prospectors who flocked into the bars, casinos and night clubs that shocked the Islamic sensibilities of most of the people.[36] Where the Islamic ruler was expected to care for the poor and needy, to live simply and be careful not to separate himself from the masses, the Shah lived a life of opulence in sumptuous palaces with solid gold telephones. In the south of Tehran the poor lived in shocking conditions: whole families were crammed into small rooms six feet by eight feet, and squatters hollowed dwellings for themselves in the massive garbage dumps that disfigured the shanty towns around the capital. Neighbourhood associations or trade union participation that might have improved the lot of the poor were forbidden.[37] Although this was appalling, this discrepancy between the rich and the poor would not in itself have caused the Islamic revolution. These policies of the Shah offended essential Islamic and Iranian values. When they rose up in the name of Islam to fight this ruler they were demanding an Islamic identity: that is, a decent and dignified life for everybody instead of this unjust and vulgar materialism that benefited only a very few.

Where an Islamic ruler was supposed to be compassionate and merciful and to consult the people frequently, the Shah was a cruel dictator, who ruled by means of a tiny dynastic elite and a system of personal loyalty to the chief. In 1955 with

American help, he founded SAVAK, which terrorized the Iranian people. It was dedicated to the discovery and destruction of all who opposed the Shah, and it killed and tortured thousands of Iranians; thousands more were imprisoned or forced into exile. Iranians were assassinated at home and abroad by SAVAK agents, with the help and knowledge of the CIA and the MOSSAD. SAVAK was particularly suspicious of intellectuals and the *mujtahids*. The Shah wanted to control the mind and spirit of his people.[38] Mullahs were prepared to fight this tyrant who was persecuting Muslims. This had been an Islamic duty since the days of the Prophet Mohammad and had been the reason for the revival of the *jihad* against the Crusaders in the Middle Ages. Now the clergy would lead their people against this *munafiq* and in some circles of mullahs it became a matter of honour to have been arrested or put in prison at least once for writing an article denouncing the Shah, for example, or by preaching a sermon against the regime. For years the Iranians had naturally looked to the clergy for guidance and now they did so again, seeing the mullahs as the champions of decency and morality.

In the early 1960s Ayatollah Khomeini emerged as one of the most dedicated of these revolutionary mullahs who fought the Shah in the name of Islam, and he appeared before the people as their leader and guide in the spirit of Ayatollah Mudariss, whom he greatly admired. From Qum he repeatedly attacked the regime of the Shah, which had been established with the help of imperialist powers and of Israel. He attacked the Shah's land reforms, which had impoverished the Islamic institutions and had not been helpful to the peasants. He attacked the bill which gave diplomatic immunity to US military personnel in Iran and which had put the Iranian people effectively 'under American bondage'. On 22 March 1963, during the celebrations at Qum for the anniversary of the Sixth Imam, a riot was provoked by SAVAK agents, who started shouting anti-Khomeini slogans. The police and the military were called in to quell the fighting, fifteen students of the madrassa were killed and Khomeini was arrested. Instantly riots broke out in all the major Iranian cities. When he was released Khomeini issued a *fatwa* that made it unlawful to co-operate with the government, which was tantamount to calling a *jihad*. On 4 June 1963 he was arrested again. There was a fresh series of riots and 15,000 people were killed by the Shah's army.[39] Finally in the autumn of 1964 he was exiled and first went to Turkey, but the mass of the Iranian people still regarded him as their leader. A network of Islamic revolutionary cells was established in Iran, and the Ayatollah continued to denounce the government from exile. He was particularly virulent during the celebrations of the twenty-fifth centenary of the Persian monarchy, when the Shah asserted that the 'creative genius' of the Iranian people was 'indissolubly linked to the fundamental principles' of the Aryan civilisation. Khomeini stated that the celebrations were, on the contrary, 'A means of extortion and plunder for the agents of imperialism. . . . Anyone who organises or participates in these festivals is a traitor to Islam and the Iranian nation.'[40] From exile in the holy city of Najaf in Iraq and later in Paris Khomeini continued to provide an alternative Islamic viewpoint, in the tradition of Iranian Shiism.

In fact his exile helped him a good deal, because he could be far more outspoken than most of his colleagues within Iran, who were vulnerable to SAVAK. In exile too he developed an original Shiite ideology to inspire opposition to the Shah. During the 1960s his opposition to the regime had simply restated the old traditional protest against imperialism, colonialism, secularism and foreign exploitation, but now he deepened his ideology and concentrated on creating a comprehensive ideal and a new Islamic vision to inspire his revolutionaries. Basic to Khomeini's thought is a horror of West-toxication. He taught the Iranians that if they wished to find themselves again, they must seek an Islamic identity and shed those foreign ideals that were being thrust upon them. 'We have completely forgotten our own identity,' he argued, 'and have replaced it with a Western identity,'[41] Muslims had 'sold themselves and do not know themselves'. They had become enslaved to alien ideals and only if they returned to their true Islamic roots could they be truly healed. The Iranian people did not want an Aryan identity because it meant nothing to them, but if they discovered their Islamic identity, they would find a new source of life and energy.

But this return had to dig for the true principles of Islam, because many Muslims had misunderstood their religion and had been corrupted by Western secularism. There were even eminent ayatollahs in Iran who taught that religion was a spiritual affair and that Muslims should leave politics to the experts; in any case no temporal government was valid in the absence of the Hidden Imam. In Khomeini's view this was nonsense: 'Were religion and politics separate at the time of the Prophet (peace and blessing be upon him)? Did there exist, on one side, a group of clerics, and opposite it, a group of politicians and leaders?'[42] This kind of thinking had emasculated Islam and perverted the Islamic identity of many Muslims, and it was essential that the original spirit of the Prophet be rediscovered. Khomeini looked back to the three great Muslims, Mohammad, Imam Ali and Imam Husain.[43] None of them had confined themselves to study and prayer, but had committed themselves to a revolutionary struggle (*jihad*) against oppression and idolatry.[44] True Muslims must follow their example and continue the *jihad* against the tyranny of *munafiqeen* like the Shah and the oppression of imperialism. They should fight against the new idolatry of false gods like materialism, socialism or nationalism which promised salvation but could not provide it. They must return to an active religion that united prayer with struggle:

> Islam is the religion of militant individuals who are committed to truth and justice. It is the religion of those who desire freedom and independence. It is the school of those who struggle against imperialism. But the servants of imperialism have presented Islam in a totally different light . . . intended to deprive Islam of its vital revolutionary aspect. . . . This kind of evil propaganda has unfortunately had an effect. Quite apart from the masses, the educated class . . . have failed to understand Islam correctly and have erroneous notions. Just as people may, in general, be unacquainted with a stranger, so too they are unacquainted with Islam: Islam lives among the people as if it were a stranger. If somebody were to present Islam as it truly is, he would find it difficult to make people believe him.[45]

Instead of retiring to madrassas to study, Muslim leaders should take up their revolutionary duty to fight corruption and oppression 'and to destroy the symbol of treason and the unjust among the rulers of the people'. From the day he was born, every single Muslim, cleric or layman, had a duty to take part in a *jihad* 'to create a victorious and triumphant Islamic political revolution'.[46]

There were many leading clerics who taught the people that in the absence of the Hidden Imam there was no legitimate political authority and that the ulema should not therefore set themselves up in positions of permanent power, but should continue to act as a pressure group and provide an alternative leadership. Khomeini countered this by his new theory of the *Velyat e-Faqih* or the Jurist's Trusteeship. Provided that they were very clear that they were only acting as God's trustees, the *mujtahids* could govern the state together with the people. They could eject the superpowers, who had formed a conspiracy against the Muslim people, by opposing their authority with the authority of God: the Islamic revolution would not simply replace one regime with another, but would set up a new Islamic order. The Islamic state would submit to God through the guardianship of the *mujtahids* and the people acting together; by living according to the Koran and the *Sharia* a just and equal society would be built up that had no need of foreign institutions like democracy or socialism but could simply return to Islamic principles, which were also the principles of God himself.[47]

This meant action and struggle. It would be necessary to fight to the death as Husain had done because 'death is better than a life of humiliation,'[48] Khomeini taught. Muslims must stop fighting one another and unite against the oppressive superpowers; if they would only unite together they would 'become a great power' that would be 'invincible and none of the superpowers will have the power to aggress or attack them'.[49] They should demonstrate this solidarity during the *hajj* to Mecca, the ancient symbol of the unity of Islam. The practice of the *hajj* had been perverted from its original political function, Khomeini argued. It was treated as a purely spiritual gathering by Muslims who had lost sight of the political dimension of Islam. 'They do not make an Islamic use of this gathering,' Khomeini complained. 'They have changed this political centre to a centre which represents a complete turning away from all the problems of the Muslims.'[50] From exile, Khomeini had one of his speeches circulated among the pilgrims at Mecca in February 1971. It expressed concern that 'the poisonous culture of imperialism is penetrating to the depths of towns and villages throughout the Muslim world, displacing the culture of the Koran.'[51] He was turning naturally to the old archetype: the pilgrimage was becoming a prelude to the *jihad* in which all Muslims had a duty to engage.

Khomeini had a special message to the people. The ulema had a duty to inspire the masses, but the people should not wait to be led into battle. They should rise up to save themselves. The people had enormous power and if they united together and formed a solid revolutionary front, 'the powers, no matter how great they may be, can accomplish nothing.'[52] Islam had always championed the cause of the poor, and the ideal ruler had been bound to care for the needy and the oppressed (the *mostazafeen*). America had claimed that she was a friend to the poor people of the world but how had she treated the *mostazafeen* of Iran? 'Is our country poor? Our country has an ocean of oil. . . . Iran is a rich country. But those so-called friends of humanity have appointed their agents to rule this country in order to prevent the poor from benefiting from its riches.'[53] The poor had a duty to stand up against this kind of tyranny and 'seize their own rights'. Neither the United States nor the Soviet Union had been a real friend to the poor despite their confident ideologies, and the people of the world needed an alternative to the capitalism of the West and the communism of the East. The poor must take their destiny into their own hands and initiate change by declaring war against the *mostakberin* (the ruling classes). Muslims should lead the way and be a vanguard for all the poor people of the world who had been damaged by the imperialism of the superpowers. The Islamic revolutionary *jihad* would bring about a new world order.[54]

Khomeini's active Islam is clearly very similar to the holy-war ideologies that we have been considering in this book. By taking his people back to their Islamic roots he had engaged them in a struggle (*jihad*) to form a new, healthier identity, to fight oppression in a war of liberation, to take their destiny into their own hands and strive for a new world order. It was the active militant faith which had inspired the Crusaders and the Zionists. Khomeini's revolt against passivity and quietism sprang from his theory of a faith which was not an abstract belief in the teaching of the Koran but a dynamic principle that joins man's will to the divine. 'Faith consists of this form of belief that impels men to action,' he wrote. 'Once faith comes, *everything* follows.'[55] He meant this quite literally. The active faith which would impel the Muslim to the *jihad* would make God's will a reality on earth. By embracing his revolutionary duty, therefore, a Muslim was actualising God's plan for mankind. In this Khomeini was very close to holy-war enthusiasts like St

Bernard, who believed that the Crusader was carried along in his holy war by God himself, who was using him to implement his divine plan for the world. More ironically, Khomeini's views are very similar to the zealots of the Gush Emunim, who believe that their West Bank settlements are actually bringing about the redemption. Khomeini believed that the *Sharia* and the Koran were formative. If men were forced to live according to these divine laws, a New Man shaped according to God's blueprint would infallibly appear. That was why it was so important to set up an Islamic state, where the people would be conditioned and formed according to the divine plan:

> Islam provides laws and instructions for all these matters, aiming, as it does, to produce integrated and virtuous human beings who are walking embodiments of the law, or to put it differently, the law's voluntary and instinctive executors. It is obvious then how much care Islam devotes to government and the political and economic relations of society, with the goal of creating conditions conducive to the production of morally upright and virtuous human beings.[56]

The creation of the Islamic identity, therefore, was a necessary stage in implementing God's plan for the world. The return of the Muslim peoples to their true Islamic roots was not a sentimental or merely cultural matter but a struggle to realise the divine order on earth. The creation of the Islamic state would be the first stage in a redemptive process in which Muslims would discover their true identity and would find new life and integrity, because they had been re-formed by the divine ideal. Like so many holy warriors before him, Khomeini was fighting for a completely new world.

Certainly he had inspired many of the Iranian people with these hopes and it is this dimension to his teaching which prompted the millions of people who greeted Khomeini on his return to Iran on 1 February 1979 to weep with joy. They were expecting a new world, not just a new regime. Some of these hopes were expressed by the poet Taha Hejazi, who calls for Khomeini's return in terms of the return of the Hidden Imam:

> The day the Imam returns
> no one will tell lies any more
> no one will lock the door of his house;
> people will become brothers
> sharing the bread of their joys together
> in justice and sincerity.
> There will no longer be any queues:
> queues of bread and meat,
> queues of kerosene and petrol,
> queues of cinemas and buses,
> queues of tax-payments,
> queues of snake poison
> shall all disappear.
> And the dawn of awakening
> and the spring of freedom
> shall smile upon us.
>
> The Imam must return . . .
> so that Right can sit on its throne
> so that evil, treachery and hatred
> are eliminated from the face of time.
> When the Imam returns,
> Iran – this broken, wounded mother –

will for ever be liberated
from the shackles of tyranny and ignorance
and from the chains of plunder, torture and prison.[57]

This vision of the new world points to a vital difference between the *jihad* and the Jewish–Christian holy wars, which centre on the liberation of the Holy Land. The cult of a Holy Land would seem idolatrous to Khomeini, who condemned even ordinary nationalism as a false god. When the Iranian poet talks about the liberation of the land, he is really talking about the liberation of the Iranian people. There was to be no cult of the Great Iran in the revolution. The *jihad* was simply the first necessary step in a worldwide Muslim revolution. The ideal was not a new nation but a pan-Islamic state which would defy the great powers and destroy the unIslamic boundaries and divisions that the imperialists had imposed upon the Muslims.

Khomeini inspired mostly the masses and the clergy, but the revolution could not have succeeded without the support of the middle classes and they were inspired mostly by the young lay scholar Dr Ali Shariati. Thousands of young people from the intelligentsia flocked to his lectures in the new free Islamic university, the Husainiyeh Irshad. They found his symbolic approach to Islam far more exciting than the more juridical approach of the clergy and were fired by Shariati's vision of the vocation of the Muslim lay man and woman. Shariati wanted to liberate the leadership from the monopoly that the clergy had acquired during the long revolutionary struggle in Iran. Naturally many of the clerics attacked him for this, but Khomeini remained silent and gave him tacit support. Shariati insisted that this clerical monopoly was elitist and unIslamic. It was absurd that the Muslim should have to emulate an elite of *mujtahids*; it was even dangerous. A more truly Islamic view was that every Muslim must 'do his own analysis, commensurate with his mental capacity and intellectual reserves'.[58] The enlightened intellectual (the *raushenfekr*) had a duty to seize the initiative and change the world as a dedicated Muslim. Shariati's great emphasis on the role of the intellectual did not mean that he was an elitist: he saw the *raushenfekr* as an emanation and expression of the people themselves. Like Khomeini, Shariati insisted that true revolutionary Islam was the property of the people. Thus even the simplest layman had a sound understanding of the faith. 'In fact,' he wrote, 'sometimes the comprehension of the uneducated for genuine Islam surpasses that of the *faqih, alem* and prestigious theologians.'[59] Until the coming of the Hidden Imam, it was the people who were the guardians of Islam and who had to establish a true Islamic society. They must designate the best among them to lead the *umma* and the enlightened thinkers among them would smash the idols of ignorance, keep the people informed of all the problems of the rulers and put themselves at the service of the people to initiate change. It was when Islamic thought became separate from the people that it degenerated into the passive quietism that was evident in some of the ulema, who sat in their madrassas discussing abstruse legal matters while the people themselves suffered oppression and persecution.[60]

Shariati was also convinced that the Iranian people had lost their true nature and had to return to their Islamic roots to be healed. Although he had had a Western education himself and had been greatly influenced by some Western thinkers, he was still certain that the only way Third World people who had suffered from the trauma of colonialism and imperialism could recover their true selves was by returning to their cultural roots, and for the Iranian people that meant their Islamic roots, 'not a discovery of pre-Islamic Iran'.[61] But Muslims had to be very careful to be clear about the kind of Islam they should return to. Did they want the Islam of the establishment and the *munafiqeen* or the Islam of the people?

It is not enough to say that we must return to Islam. Such a statement has no meaning. We have to specify which Islam; that of Abu Zarr or that of Marwan the Ruler? Both are Islam, but there is a huge difference between the two. One is the Islam of the Caliphate, of the palace and of the rulers. The other is the Islam of the people, of the exploited and of the poor. Which Islam do you advocate? Moreover it is not enough to say that you advocate an Islam that is concerned with the poor. True Islam is more than concerned with the poor. It struggles for justice, equality and the elimination of poverty. . . . We want the Islam of the fighters, not that of spiritual leaders.[62]

Like Khomeini, Shariati had no time for these clerics who taught that Islam was simply a spiritual and moral affair and that people should sit back and wait for the Hidden Imam. All Muslims had a revolutionary duty and this activist and dynamic faith in an endless struggle for social justice was the essence of the whole religion.

When Shariati taught his followers to return to their Islamic roots he did not mean that they should initiate a slavish imitation of the first Muslims in the Hejaz nor did he recommend a literal return to the spirit of the seventh century. They should follow the example of the Prophet Mohammad himself when he made the *hajj* an Islamic institution in 632. He had kept the pre-Islamic, pagan forms and rituals but had given them an entirely new Islamic meaning. He did not cut the Arabian people off from their roots by destroying the *hajj* to Mecca, but had enriched and reinterpreted those ancient, beloved rites, and given his people a new Islamic identity that grew creatively from the past.[63] Like the Zionists, Shariati was helping his people to rediscover themselves in a creative encounter with the past and to commit themselves to change by looking afresh at themes, ideas and attitudes that were deeply embedded in the Islamic identity of the Iranian people.

Iranians did not need to turn to foreign ideologies like communism or nationalism to achieve this change and salvation, Shariati taught. In Islam they had the most dynamic ideology in the world and the whole faith was an incitement to progress and development. The very word *umma* came from the Arabic root meaning 'to go, to move', whereas words used by other peoples (community, nation, state, tribe) lacked this essential dynamism and commitment to change. There were three important principles of Islam that were particularly conducive to this dynamic interpretation.[64] Over the centuries the clerics had narrowed down their potential but now they must be re-examined and given a new meaning. The first principle was *ijtihad* (or independent judgement). This should not simply mean the legal *ijtihad* practised by the expert jurists alone. The notion of *ijtihad* should encourage every Muslim constantly to correct and rebuild his ideas and engage in an endless process of constructive criticism of both himself and the *umma*. Properly understood, *ijtihad* was a call for a perpetual revolution and a refusal to allow individual Muslims or their society to stagnate and get trapped in stale habits that led to decay and decline. The second dynamic principle was the Koranic duty of 'commanding good and forbidding evil' (9:112). This duty was not only the duty of the clerics but had rather to be 'the mission and objective duty of all individuals – among the masses, the wretched, the intellectuals, the bazaar merchants'. All should have a say in the governing of the people and all should be able to suggest reforms and improvements in the *umma*. Real Muslims could never be satisfied with any one stage of achievement, but should constantly be striving for new heights. Finally there was the *hijra* or migration. This could be a physical *hijra* like Mohammad's *hijra* to Medina or it could be an internal *hijra* that committed each Muslim to an endless 'choice, a struggle, a constant becoming. [Man] is committed to a migration within himself from clay to God; he is a migrant within his own soul,' a 'being in the process of becoming' who was committed to endless quest. In Shariati's thought the *hijra* was an essential part of the 'struggle' *(jihad)* that must activate every Muslim in a ceaseless effort to build a new world.[65] Central to the Muslim identity was the *hajj* and for Shariati this holy journey was central to the dynamism of Islam. Setting out on this physical journey was an image of what Christian writers had called a conversion of life and what Shariati called the endless *hijra* of every Muslim. But it was a purposeful wandering. '*Hajj* is the antithesis of aimlessness',[66] he said. The Muslim has a definite goal: Mecca, the heart of the Islamic identity where he would encounter his roots. When he arrived at the Ka'aba, the pilgrim had to circle round and round the shrine and this was in itself a re-enactment of the dynamism of his faith. The great crush of people forced on the pilgrim a new sense of his identity with the people and freed him from his old passive selfishness and solipsism:

> As you circumambulate and move closer to the Ka'aba, you feel like a small stream merging with the big river.... Carried by a wave, you lose touch with the ground. Suddenly you are floating, carried on by the flood. As you approach the centre, the pressure of the crowd squeezes you so hard that you are given new life. You are now a part of the people.[67]

The *hajj* was, therefore, crucial in actually forming the Muslim identity, and this new sense of the pilgrim's solidarity with his people must commit him at every stage of his pilgrimage to the *jihad*. Thus as he stood in the *Maqam e-Ibrahim* (the place of Abraham) he committed himself to building up the *umma* creatively and to fight for the health of the people:

> you promise God that you will fight to save the people from being burned by the fire of oppression, ignorance and reaction. During the battle for the people's liberation *(jihad)*, throw yourself into the fire to save the people. Live the way Abraham did and be the architect of the Ka'aba of faith in your times. Help people to step out of the swamps of stagnated and useless lives. Awaken them from their stupor so that they refuse to suffer oppression in the darkness of ignorance.[68]

As he throws pebbles at the pillars of Mina, the soldier in the 'army of Abraham has to shoot seventy bullets at the enemies of Mina', the false gods of capitalism, despotism and ignorance. The pilgrimage has become a holy war according to the old archetype: 'If you are not a soldier,' Shariati warns, 'nor is your *hajj* valid.'[69]

The supreme example of the Islamic soldier in Shariati's teaching was the Imam Husain. When he had been killed at Karbala he had not just been fighting to restore the leadership to the descendants of Mohammad. He had been struggling towards the city of Kufa to build a perfect order for his people, the prototype of all societies that struggled to liberate themselves from tyranny. Like Khomeini, Shariati also saw the Islamic revolution as a movement that should be a vanguard for all other oppressed people of the Third World and, like so many other advocates of the holy war, Shariati saw his *jihad* as the first step towards the final redemption. Once the Shiah had encouraged the other oppressed peoples to unite together against tyranny, this universal *jihad* under the leadership of Islam would force the Hidden Imam to return and inaugurate a new world.[70]

Shariati was himself prepared to follow the example of Husain to the bitter end. He was pursued by SAVAK and had to go underground in 1973 but when his aged father was arrested Shariati gave himself up. He was tortured by SAVAK so mercilessly that his health was permanently impaired before he was finally freed and sent into exile. In 1977 at the age of forty-four he was found dead in his flat just outside London. It was widely believed at the time that he had been murdered by SAVAK agents, though later commentators believe that he simply died from the injuries he had sustained in prison. In either case SAVAK killed him and this is ironic. Although Shariati was hailed by all the revolutionaries as a martyr and a hero, it is not at all clear that he would have approved of the Khomeini clerical regime, nor even that he would have survived under it, as we shall see later in this chapter.

Like the Zionists, the Iranian revolutionaries were eminently practical and it was this translation of idealism into an established reality that made the Iranian revolution and the establishment of an Islamic regime one of the most remarkable phenomena of the twentieth century, alongside the State of Israel. The Muslim clergy and the radical followers of Khomeini mobilised the people, instructing them politically and religiously in the Friday sermon and, using the mosque as a centre, training them in the art of street warfare. The people were made aware of the iniquities of the Shah and saw their religion, with its demand for equality, as a powerful ideology that could rid Iran of this tyrannical regime. The practical and realistic mobilisation of the people was as effective as the Islamic propaganda of Nur ad-Din and Saladin had been, using the same methods, at the time of the Crusades. But this would not have been enough to enable the common people to face the heavily armed SAVAK and the Iranian army unless the people themselves had found a way of bringing the esoteric ideology of the mullahs into their own lives as a powerful emotional reality that did not owe its effectiveness entirely to reason and common sense.

Here I want to make what may seem at first to be a digression, but which I believe to be crucial to a true understanding of the Iranian revolution. We have seen that the First Crusaders would not have survived had they depended upon the intellectually sophisticated ideology of Pope Urban, which was foreign and outside the emotional and intellectual scope of most of the common soldiers. When they faced what seemed to be certain death at Antioch, they had persuaded themselves by mystical experience not to desert: they had produced visions that enabled them to transcend their fears and the rationally hopeless view of the situation. These visions of the Crusaders had sometimes got out of control: one need only recall the tragic career of Peter Bartholomew. They were not organised in any way but were individual, spontaneous and often undisciplined. There was a similar 'mystical' element in the Iranian revolution, but this popular mysticism was more controlled, albeit not always by the establishment. Since the time of the Crusades, Western Christians have come to associate mysticism with a quietist frame of mind, but we have also seen that in Islam mysticism could be associated with the holy war. The Sufis, the mystics of Sunni Islam, were among Nur ad-Din's most ardent supporters and mysticism inspired the Shiite set popularly known as the Assassins with a suicidal courage in fighting the Sunni establishment, which they thought was oppressing the Shiite minority. There would be a similar aggressive mysticism in 1978, but this was more controlled than the popular, sometimes personally dangerous mysticism of the Crusaders, but just as effective.

In his beautiful and scholarly book *The Mantle of the Prophet*, the Harvard Professor Roy Mottahedeh has told the story of an Iranian mullah of the younger generation, to whom he gives the fictitious name of Ali to protect his privacy and desire for anonymity. Ali, who was born in 1943 and who at the time of the publication of Mottahedeh's book in 1985 had recently attained the status of an ayatollah, was a Sayyed native of Qum, who had begun his studies in the prestigious Faiziyeh Madrassa, entirely through his own choice, at the age of ten. He proved to be a brilliant student who studied under Khomeini at Qum and later at Najaf. At a certain point during his studies, Ali decided that he wanted to undergo a mystical discipline, as his father had done before him. This was a controversial decision. The Shiites of Iran had condemned the Sufis, because they felt that their Islamic mysticism was an unacceptable innovation into the more sober and practical religion of Mohammad. Many Sunni *mullahs* felt the same but in both traditions Muslims have felt a need for a mystical dimension to their faith and in Iran there was a network of mystical experts who guided an initiate on the path of *erfan*, mystical knowledge. Ruhollah Khomeini had also been a disciple of *erfan*.[71] Ali's father gave him the name of a spiritual adviser and for some months under his guidance Ali followed his teachings during his daily prayers and attained some remarkable experiences,[72] which were not due to hysteria or to a suggestive imagination. Ali, as a devout Muslim, would not have claimed that he was reaching an experience of the transcendent God. But it seems that certain physical and mental disciplines can lead people to experience an alternative state of consciousness. The purpose of *erfan* is to lead the initiate to a state of mind where the boundary between himself and external realities has been destroyed. The climax of Ali's mystical career occurred while he was sitting in his courtyard for the dawn prayer, performing the exercise set by his guide:

> something new appeared inside him as well. The humming inside him was nearly in tune with the humming of the world around him, and he knew that his slight separation from this world was the only barrier between himself and pure existence. Like Husain he was willing to die, but Ali did not want to wait ... he longed to throw himself in the glowing pool in the middle of the courtyard and to exist entirely as part of the He that was the existence of everything.[73]

At his next meeting with his guide he was told: 'We're stopping here. This has been enough for you.'[74] His guide explained that Ali was not psychologically capable of any further mystical experience; his natural mode of life was intellectual not mystical. He could repeat the exercises he had been through as often as he chose, but must not venture beyond that final experience. Yet the experience stayed with Ali. After that moment in the courtyard, he said that he was never again afraid of death. Even when he later spent some weeks in prison for publishing an article hostile to the Shah's regime, he did not fear death. He sometimes feared that he would lose his mind, but he was not afraid to die.[75]

This kind of mystical teaching, therefore, controls the initiate so that his experiences do not exceed what he can bear, but do enable him to transcend his normal fears and limitations. The ordinary, uneducated people, however, could not manage the sophisticated mental discipline of *erfan* but they did develop their own folk mysticism. During the eighteenth century in Iran the people began to perform passion plays during the month of Muharram, which tell the story of the death of Husain. Over the years they have acquired a shape and spirit that is unique. They are performed by professional troupes, who take the plays into the most remote villages, and in the cities groups of people form their own troupes and perform in various locations. The plays are highly stylised and unrepresentational. A glass of water represents the Euphrates and when the Angel Gabriel appears carrying an umbrella, this means that he has just arrived from heaven. The audience responds empathically to the action. When there is a banquet, biscuits and cakes are passed around. They smile and weep with the characters. Because the outcome of the cycle of plays is known well, there is no suspense. The climax of the cycle occurs not when Husain actually dies, but when he puts on the white shroud as a sign that he is ready to die as a martyr in the struggle against tyranny. At that point the audience weep and groan and seem to have broken through a barrier that is similar to the mystical experience described by Ali.[76] This Muslim experience is not dissimilar to the Stations of the Cross in medieval Europe, which the common people followed every Good Friday and which helped them to a deeper understanding and experience of the sufferings of Christ. Nor is it unlike the bands of flagellant penitents of the fourteenth century, who toured Europe in vast bands, whipping themselves into a state where the barrier between the individual and the group had broken down and he had passed through to a new state of consciousness. In Iran, the people also listened during Muharram to stylised recitations of the death of Husain and beat themselves with chains and tore their flesh to identify themselves with Husain's state of mind.[77] The cliché 'to be beside oneself' gives some idea of their experience. They have escaped from the limitations of their normal selves and have attained an alternative state of consciousness. It is not that they identify with Husain. That would be considered blasphemous. Instead they have tried to enter into the spirit of his experience in order to be good Muslims themselves. The passion plays and Muharram recitations have been crucial in making Islam a central fact of life for the ordinary people. They cannot enter the esoteric system of study in the madrassas but have found a way of creating an Islam that has profound meaning for them. Without the passion plays it is doubtful whether Shiism would have survived as a strong force in Iran.

As one might expect, the clergy had mixed reactions to this popular religion, just as they had mixed reactions to the *erfan*. But some realised the potential importance of this folk mysticism.[78] Over the years the people had primarily felt pity and sorrow for Husain and they beat themselves and rent their clothing as an expression of compassion. They had also come to regard him as a patron, rather as the Crusaders regarded their patron saints. Because he was close to God people believed that he could get favours for them, as a powerful patron did on earth. It was a dependent form of religion, encouraging a rather passive frame of mind. But as the radical clergy preached against the regime in the mosques and Friday sermons, they taught the people that it was the duty of every good Muslim to fight positively against tyranny, as the Prophet, Husain and all the imams had done. The plays and recitations began to acquire quite a different meaning. Husain became an example of the revolutionary struggle. When he put on his white shroud, and the audience responded by doing the same, they were now declaring themselves to be ready to die as martyrs in the fight against the Shah, just as he had died in his struggle against Yazid. The emotional character of the plays gave this decision a resounding depth, just as Ali's mystical experience had done. They were no longer afraid to die and many of them would do so.[79]

By the time of the feast of Ashura in 1978, which celebrates the death of Husain, the people were ready for the final battle. A few days before Ashura a woman explained this fundamental change in the religious attitude among the ordinary Muslims:

> This ashura there'll be mourning but with a big difference. There'll be mourning with victory. Now we are more aware of the teachings of Husain. Now everybody knows *why* Husain went to fight Yazid. Before they didn't know. Three nights ago I went to a *rauzeh* [recitation] and the *rauzekhan* [reciter] called Husain *rahbar-e enqelab* [leader of revolution] – and he wasn't an educated *rauzekhan*, just a simple one. He'd never called Husain that before. Before they pitied Husain rather than admiring his courage. Now people are more aware of the whole meaning of religion.[80]

The 'whole meaning' of Islam meant a struggle (*jihad*) against the tyrant. The people had to fight the Shah as though everything depended upon themselves. Unlike the Crusaders they did not expect God to alter the normal course of nature for them. They knew that there was a good chance that they might die. As the same woman pointed out, Husain's message was stark: 'His message is – death. If you can kill, kill. If you can't, die in the attempt. Either kill or get killed, but like Husain fight against repression and tyranny.'[81] The people had not whipped themselves up into a state of mindless frenzy, as Western observers were inclined to comment. There was rather a purposeful determination that used the controlled mysticism of the passion plays and recitations to help them to transcend their very natural fear. There was a new spirit of comradeship among the people and a new slogan: 'There were no bystanders at the murder of Husain.'[82] The *jihad* demanded total commitment. During the revolution the people had discovered, deep within themselves, a new initiative and determination, which they could get from Islam but not from a foreign ideology like socialism. As in the Crusades, the poor were driven by desperation and mysticism to new heights of courage, self-expression and self-determination.

This ideal had also fired the middle classes who had been inspired by the teaching of Shariati to seize a new lay initiative. Just before the revolution Muslim lay groups were formed which were vitally important in mobilising support and disseminating intelligence. Some of these groups like Amal or the Liberation Movement had direct backing from the clergy but were manned by laymen from the professional classes. Others, however, were formed entirely on the initiative of laymen. Lay organisations like Jonbesh or the Movement of Militant Muslims not only played a crucial role in the revolution, but were also vital in the organisation of the Islamic state after the return of Khomeini.[83] These lay people had also acquired a new initiative and responsibility; instead of simply following the *mujtahids* and emulating them by *taqlid*, they were insisting on their own right to self-expression. The revolution had given the layman a new vocation in Iranian Islam, just as crusading had given the layman a new vocation and status in Christendom. Instead of seeing the revolution in Iran simply as the expression of mass hysteria, it should be seen as the result of a new, militant spirit of independence and personal responsibility among the poor people and the middle classes of Iran.

Crusading had originally been a mixture of secular and religious motives in the leaders and among the people and common soldiers. It is also true that without the support of the secular groups of communists, leftists, nationalists and socialists the revolution would not have succeeded. These people were ready to fight alongside the religious masses in a concerted effort against the Shah because they knew very well that they themselves lacked this mass support and that Khomeini was, therefore, the best chance Iranians had to get rid of the Pahlavi regime. Alongside the secular guerrilla groups fought the students, whom Khomeini had always seen as important allies in the revolution. The seculars hoped to have a share in the new republic, but perhaps they should have been warned by Khomeini's speeches that he had no time for any of their secular ideologies and that the new regime was to be purely Islamic.

During the late 1960s and 1970s a steady front of dedicated opposition to the Shah was building up in Iran, but it was not simply rejectionist. Certainly people wanted to get rid of the Shah and his regime, but they also had positive aims. The vast majority of the revolutionaries were coming to the conclusion that they did not want this Westernised dictatorship and were demanding an Islamic destiny. To turn the clock back to the dynasty of Cyrus and Darius was unrealistic, because it wiped out 1300 years of more recent history that had formed and shaped the identity of the Iranian people. Most of the revolutionaries were demanding an Islamic identity and saw a return to Islam as their only way forward to a healthier, independent life that was truly their own and which had not been foisted upon them by an exploitative imperialist power. In the time-honoured way of the holy war, the people were defining themselves against their common enemy in their struggle to assert their own individuality and integrity. The enemy was the Shah and the West.

The revolution finally erupted early in 1978. The Shah was determined to undermine Khomeini's influence and had an article published in a leading newspaper that was to have been part of a vicious smear campaign. It accused Khomeini of monstrous crimes and perversities, including homosexuality and drug abuse.[84] It was a stupid move and showed how little the Shah understood his own people. The day after the article was published there was a demonstration in the religious capital of Qum, which quickly developed into a battle with the police, and many of the students of the madrassas were killed. The ulema issued a *fatwa* which declared the government to be unIslamic and this was the call for a *jihad*. The people of all classes began to mobilise themselves. On 13 February, forty days after the battle at Qum, processions of mourning for the 'martyrs' who had died in the *jihad* against tyranny were held in most major Islamic cities. These naturally led to new riots with the police. In the city of Tabriz the police retaliated by locking the mosque, and the people instantly poured on to the streets wrecking banks, stores and cinemas and attacking the police with their crude weapons. Many people were killed and the revolution had gained more martyrs.

Forty days later a new day of mourning was held for the martyrs of Tabriz. There were demonstrations and processions in all the major Iranian cities and this time hundreds of people were killed. Forty days later, during 8/9 May, there was inevitably another day of mourning and riots exploded throughout the cities of Iran, and the death-toll rose, especially in Qum and Tehran. In between these Islamic celebrations of the martyrs, the secular groups had become active, taking to the streets and provoking new battles with the police. These riots brought out the Islamic poor in huge numbers, and secular and religious Iranians fought tyranny side by side.[85]

Faced with this widespread revolution, SAVAK resorted to more brutal methods. On 19 August they burned down the Rex Cinema in Abedan, killing about 400 workers.[86] Once again the poor exploded on to the streets and there were three nights of violence. Abedan became a military garrison, and tanks, armoured cars and jeeps tried to terrorise the workers to go back to work. Eventually, they were forced back but they worked to a go-slow. There was no rigid structure or organisation with definite leaders. By this time the poor and the workers knew how to organise themselves. When they were asked at Abedan who gave them their instructions they replied: 'No one in particular. Everyone agrees. There is really no organisation. . . . But by firing on us, the army has forced us to organise ourselves and even to arm ourselves. We listen to Khomeini.' They had learned from their leader that if they wanted results they had to seize power and effect change for themselves.[87]

The violence inspired by the Abedan riots forced the Shah to form a new government under Sharif Emami. It promised freedom of speech and made some concessions to the mullahs like shutting down casinos and bars and changing the old Iranian calendar to the Islamic calendar. But this gesture had come too late. The riots continued and SAVAK took no notice of the government's appeasement policy. Late in August they attacked the crowd at the Jabal mosque in Tehran and followed this by further attacks on mosques during the Friday sermon in most Iranian cities. Tension and violence mounted. SAVAK officers raped young girls or stripped them to the waist during these attacks and provoked a new hardened resolve among the people, who went into battle with the cry *Allahu Akhbah!* (God is great!) blaring from loudspeakers on the rooftops.[88] On 8 September there was a fresh tragedy. The army shot into a peaceful demonstration, killing hundreds.[89] The Black Friday massacre, as it was called, inspired a new wave of pitched battles between the people and the military. None of the army's powerful tanks or guns deterred the masses, who poured out into the streets wearing the white robes of the

martyrs, determined to fight tyranny like Husain.[90] Crowds of people were killed. It was clear that the Shah's soft line had not worked and Emami was replaced by Reza Azhari, who resorted to tougher measures. But by now the revolution had found its own momentum and seemed unstoppable. What could be done against revolutionaries who had no fear of death and who offered themselves to the guns of the army and police? Increasingly desperate, the Shah appealed to America and Britain for help, but none was forthcoming.

During the month of Muharram the revolutionary fervour reached its climax and this proved to be the crucial turning point. Again without official organisation, millions of Iranians took part in the great processions mourning Husain but these processions were indeed different. Instead of beating themselves with chains, the people marched with raised fists crying 'Down with the Shah!' Their mystical fervour demanded a revolutionary stance instead of the old passive mourning processions. They poured into the streets in such numbers that the military seemed paralysed and overawed. Some of the soldiers had also been affected by Khomeini's pleas to Iranians not to kill their fellow Iranians. The army fell apart as soldiers began to shoot commanding officers who urged them to fire on the people. The monarchy collapsed; General Bakhtiar of the secular National Front Party formed a government and on 16 January 1979 the Shah had to flee the country. But this did not satisfy the revolutionaries and there were more strikes against the secular regime of General Bakhtiar; the army was now in disarray; generals were following the Shah into exile; SAVAK officers were also deserting; no help was forthcoming from the United States. Within a fortnight of the Shah's departure, Bakhtiar resigned and the Ayatollah Khomeini returned to Iran.[91]

The Iranians had demonstrated with passionate dedication that they wanted an Islamic identity, not a Western one. It was the most spectacular victory Islam had achieved for centuries and gave 'Islam' a new image in the West. During the colonial period a new element had entered the Western stereotyping of 'Islam'. The faith was seen as an anachronism that encouraged a mindless fatalism: it was 'Islam' which had held Orientals back from progress and which made them submit passively to colonial rule. There had been no trace of this in the medieval fantasies of 'Islam' because at that time Islam was far too energetic and dynamic. After the Iranian revolution, however, it was no longer possible for Westerners to remain under this illusion. The revolutionaries had shown that Islam could very easily adapt itself to meet modern situations and that it provided the people of the Middle East with an ideology that was far more satisfying to them and far more effective than the Western secular ideologies that had inspired the struggle against imperialism in other Muslim countries. This was naturally very disturbing and Westerners tended to fall back on the old violent image of 'Islam', failing to see that this new violence had been inspired in large measure by the behaviour of the West in Iran. In the Middle Ages it had been the Crusades which had inspired a *jihad* in the Near East when the practice of holy war had been quite dead for centuries. It was the crusading zeal of Western powers like Great Britain and the United States which had provoked this new resurgence of *jihad* in the twentieth century.

On 4 November 1979 some students took the American diplomatic staff prisoner in the American embassy and demanded that the former Shah, who had just been admitted to the United States to receive medical treatment, be extradited. The action showed very clearly the new intensity of hatred for the West in Iran and was also a deeply symbolic act because for years the Iranians had felt that America had kept them prisoner in their own country. It also raised a number of other important issues. When the International Court of Justice gave a ruling that the holding of the hostages was illegal, Ayatollah Khomeini was very clear about his reasons for refusing to accept it: 'What kind of law is this? It permits the US Government to exploit and colonize peoples all over the world for decades. But it does not allow the extradition of an individual who has staged great massacres. Can you call it law?'[92] It was an uncomfortable question. Why should the rules regarding diplomatic immunity be so much clearer than those protecting a weak country against intervention and exploitation? Further, why had international law not been applied to countries like Israel, when they illegally kidnapped Nazis from South America or sent hit squads to assassinate Palestinian leaders abroad? President Jimmy Carter found himself in a desperate situation, but he seems to have been unable to understand that America was not guiltless and had brought this enmity upon itself. He was very quick to refer to America's behaviour in Iran as 'ancient history'.[93] Christian Bourguet, a French lawyer with ties with the Iranians who acted as an intermediary between the United States and Iran, described his meeting with Carter in late March 1980:

> At a given moment [Carter] spoke of the hostages, saying, you understand that these are Americans. These are innocents. I said to him, yes, Mr President, I understand that you say they are innocent. But I believe you have to understand that for the Iranians they aren't innocent. Even if personally none of them has committed an act, they are not innocent because they are diplomats who represent a country that has done a number of things in Iran.
>
> You must understand that it is not against their person that the action is being taken. Of course, you can see that. They have not been harmed. They have not been hurt. No attempt has been made to kill them. You must understand that it is a symbol, that it is on the plane of symbols that we have to think about this matter.[94]

But few people in the West seemed able to understand this. In the media, attention was focused on the hostages instead of on the complicated struggle within Iran immediately after the revolution and in general little attempt was made to comprehend its ideology.

Instead of understanding the symbolism of the hostage crisis, the West focused instead on the Iranian image of America as the Great Satan. Not surprisingly they interpreted this according to the Christian figure of Satan, a person of monstrous evil and seeming near-omnipotence. But actually the image was a very careful and accurate expression of Iranian feeling about America. Islam is a more strict form of monotheism than Christianity and would therefore never allow the acquisition of such terrible power. In the Koran, Shaitan is not a terrifying monster, but a fallen angel, who refuses to bow down and worship Adam and who tempts Adam away from true submission to God. In rather the same way America had allowed the Shah to try and tempt the Iranians away from Islam. In popular Shiism, Shaitan is seen as a poor trivial creature, who asks for benefits that Allah gives to man and is easily fobbed off with frivolous, secular trumpery. It was a triviality that was very like the casinos, bars and boutiques of the Shah's Westernised Tehran.[95] Instead of attempting to penetrate this symbol, Western politicians encouraged people to view the revolution as merely the result of mass hysteria; instead of recognising that the revolutionaries were genuinely inspired by rational ideas, the media encouraged people to view the revolution as hopelessly eccentric, unbalanced and paranoid. The huge crowds screaming their hatred of the West shocked Westerners, who had not considered Muslims as having an identity and force of their own.

In fact the Iranians had more to occupy themselves with than simply indulging their hatred of the West. They had to create a new Islamic society. Mohammad and the first four righteous rulers of the *umma* had had a difficult struggle and after this time the Islamic empire had fallen into the hands of the *munafiqeen*. Iranians saw themselves as returning to the spirit of the golden age. Khomeini established himself as the *Velayat-e Faqih*. It was not right that a cleric should exercise temporal power during the absence of the Hidden Imam, so he would not accept the role of Prime Minister or President, which was to be entrusted to lay Muslims. Instead he was the jurist who would advise the government on the Islamic propriety of their actions in building the new revolutionary state. Then the Islamic Revolutionary Party was formed, consisting of clerics and lay people who were dedicated to establishing an Islamic regime. Yet the IRP and Khomeini were both convinced that this must not be imposed on the people without formal consultation, because according to Islamic law true power and authority were vested in the people and the rulers must constantly turn to them for advice and direction. But the people also had to be healed of centuries of unIslamic oppression and despotism. They had to shake off the fetters of colonialism, take their destiny into their own hands and control their lives according to the Koranic ideal. This would mean a *jihad* against poverty and illiteracy. Not only did Islam demand the fair distribution of wealth, but the people had to 'change the state of their own selves' if they were to redeem themselves (Koran 13:11).

The young people were clearly crucial in this formation of a new Islamic Iran with a proud identity of its own. Three new institutions were created to recruit and form the young people according to the spirit of the revolution. First of these was the Revolutionary Guards, and young men flocked to join this military corps which was to replace the former Shah's corrupt army. The Guards embody the spirit of the revolution in rather the same way as the military orders expressed the spirit of crusading and the Israeli army expresses the image of the new strong Jew. The RG were dedicated to the *jihad* and would fight both the internal and the external enemies of the revolution.[96] They also saw themselves as the vanguard for other revolutions of oppressed people against colonialism and imperialism, and quickly formed contacts with about thirty-five other groups throughout the Third World.[97] The second youth movement was more peaceful, and was also reminiscent of crusading and Zionist institutions. Zionism developed the Conquest of Labour and Iran produced Construction Jihad, which was dedicated to nation-building. Young people took part in the rebuilding of the primitive rural areas and war-torn districts: there were projects in agriculture, cattle-breeding and building, and in cultural activities and health and medical education to improve the quality of life. New houses, bridges, roads and walls were built and peasants who had lived in mud hovels under the former Shah now lived in brick houses of two or three rooms. The Gulf War hindered this economic and constructive *jihad* so not so much was achieved as had originally been hoped. Finally University Jihad set up councils to supervise education, rewrite textbooks and root out the corrupt old secularism of the former regime. The West had assumed that the revolution wanted to deny progress and throw Iran back into the seventh century, but the revolutionaries did not want to return to a slavish imitation of Mohammad and the first caliphs. They simply wanted to return to their spirit and to produce a perfect Islamic society in twentieth-century terms, and that meant building up as well as pulling down.[98]

There were, however, a minority of Iranians who did not want a wholly Islamic society. The secular groups who had joined the Islamists because they knew that they were the only people who could get rid of the Shah were now unwilling to live in a *Sharia* state; they wanted a Western-style constitution that did not make the Koran and the *Sharia* the law of the land. Mehdi Bazargan, the first Prime Minister, was dedicated to the secular ideal and Khomeini and his ayatollahs were quite happy to use him to demonstrate to the people what the seculars were up to. On 30 March a referendum voted mass support for an Islamic republic and Bazargan and the secularists realised that their position was desperately weak. Within a month the nationalists went on to the streets to fight the religious Iranians, staging riots and demonstrations for a secular regime. They were quickly joined by the socialists and communists and fought by the new Revolutionary Guards. There were heavy losses on both sides in this fresh struggle. On 8 June 1979 the new Islamic constitution was proclaimed and the Islamic reforms began. Bazargan found himself in an impossible position, unable to stem the Islamisation of Iran. On 11 June eleven of his ministers had resigned and many of them went into exile. Khomeini's Revolutionary Council began to appoint its own members as deputy ministers. Bazargan realised that he had become a mere figurehead and resigned on 5 November 1979. The Revolutionary Council took control of the country and on 15 November announced the new government. There was one more bid for secular power. In the presidential elections of February 1981 Abdol-Hassan Bani Sadr was elected by 75 per cent of the vote. He had been a member of the Revolutionary Council and had declared himself in favour of an Islamic republic but in fact he had more secular aims and tried to form a coalition of the secularists who were opposed to a wholly religious regime. Yet he too found himself in an impossible position, because in the general elections that were held in May 1980 the Islamists took a massive majority of the seats. Mobilised in the usual way by the ulema, the people had voted for an Islamic identity. Bani Sadr was unable to survive politically in this parliament;[99] he was impeached in June 1981 and finally forced into exile as an enemy of the people.

The seculars continued their war against the religious. Groups like the communist Mujahideen-e-Khalq and the nationalist parties supported seculars like Bani Sadr with riots and a campaign of terrorism, and naturally there was an intensification of the *jihad* against them. After the impeachment of Bani Sadr there was a new outbreak of bomb attacks and terrorism. One particularly vicious attack on 27 June 1981 was the planting of a sixty-six-pound bomb in the office of the Islamic Revolutionary Party which killed seventy-two leading members of the party including Ayatollah Beheshti, who had played a crucial role in the revolution.[100] This attack horrified Khomeini and as *Velayat-e Faqih* he gave orders for a more ruthless hunting out of dissidents and enemies of the revolution. In July and August Mohammad Ali Rejai was elected President and Hojjat ol-Islam Mohammad Jabad Bahonar became Prime Minister. Both were committed to the Islamic Republic, and both were killed in bomb attacks on 30 August 1981.[101] Taking on the leadership was proving to be as perilous in revolutionary Iran as it had been for the Twelve Imams. The CIA recruited exiled opponents of the regime and also established links with the communist party Mujahideen-e-Khalq. In April 1982 a coup was planned and backed by the CIA and the Saudis. It was led by Sadeq Gotbzadeh, Bani Sadr's former Foreign Minister, and included, as an essential part of its offensive, a plan to assassinate Khomeini. The coup was discovered and Gotbzadeh was put on trial. Khomeini offered to save his life if he repented, but Gotbzadeh refused this offer of clemency and preferred execution.[102] The struggle against the Islamic regime was deadly and desperate, but the seculars could not succeed because they did not have the support of the people. Some 15 million people had voted for the Islamic constitution as opposed to 700,000 against and the assassination of beloved leaders actually did the seculars a disservice by putting the people even more staunchly behind Khomeini. The link with the United States also discredited the seculars with the people, who were firmly committed to condemning the Great Satan. The secular opposition was melting like snow.

Executions like the execution of Gotbzadeh were, of course, common. Immediately after the revolution, the revolutionary courts sought out, tried and executed the friends of the former Shah and the enemies of the true faith and of the Iranian people. People who offended the ideals of the revolution like prostitutes, pimps and drug dealers were also rounded up and executed, and later the secular enemies of the state were hunted down. Ayatollah Sadeq Khalkhali, who was the jurist supervising the courts, became known as Judge Death because of his excessive zeal in sentencing the enemies of Islam to death and Khomeini had to step in to moderate his enthusiasm.[103] In this respect Iran was no different from other revolutions which completed their victory with bloody purges. France, Russia and China all completed their revolutions by executing the enemies of the people.

A holy war nearly always exterminates the enemies of God ruthlessly, and victory in a holy war usually means the end of clemency and mutual respect. The idea of peaceful coexistence with the enemy seems impossible. Yet this had not always been the case in Islam. Mohammad had not followed his peaceful conquest of Mecca with a blood-bath and in the Islamic empire there had always been some tolerance of those people who held different beliefs. Khomeini claimed to be taking Iranians back to the Islam of the Prophet, and yet his *jihad* seems to have been a disturbing innovation and to have indicated a new intolerance. This may well have been a heritage of the revolutionary ethic of the Shiah. Khomeini and Shariati had virtually made the *jihad* one of the pillars of Islam, even though formerly only the fanatical Kharaji sect had considered *jihad* to be essential to the integrity of Islam in this way. The Iranian ideologists had committed Muslims to the idea of an endless revolution which had been necessary when the revolutionaries were fighting a mighty establishment, but a very different matter once the revolution had itself become the establishment. In 1979 the Shiites who followed Husain had their first complete victory and had to make a difficult transition from a state of revolutionary struggle and constant failure to resounding success. As *jihad* was part of the revolutionaries' identity and integrity, it was by now a way of life and it was not easy to stop the endless struggle.

The new Muslim intolerance was spotlighted by Khomeini's treatment of clerics who disagreed with his ideas. There were clergy who had supported the revolution, but who were not convinced that the clergy should run the state. Some of these clerics and ayatollahs had Islamic qualifications that were as good as Khomeini's and sometimes their standing as *mujtahids* was even higher than his. The Grand Ayatollah Mohammad-Kazem Shariatmadari, for example, was the leading *mujtahid* at Qum at the time of the revolution but he was hounded and penalised by the new clerical regime because he did not share its ideas. This *jihad* for intellectual conformity within Islam was a very disturbing innovation and one which was more characteristic of the Christian tradition than Islam's. Shariatmadari was convinced that religion should be separate from politics and that the ulema should act only as consultants to the professional politicians; now that the Shah had been defeated, the clergy should go back to their seminaries and leave the running of the country to the seculars. He was also in favour of a Western-style constitution and did not think that Islam should be imposed by law. When there were clashes in Qum and Tabriz between the supporters of Khomeini and those of Shariatmadari, the dissidents were overpowered by the Revolutionary Guards and their leaders were tried and executed. Shariatmadari was kept under house arrest in Qum, from which he has not yet been freed.[104]

Another very popular and charismatic leader was Ayatollah Mahmud Taleqani, who saw the possibility of creating a bridge between the religious and the seculars. Before the revolution he had been active in the lay Freedom Movement and had worked with Mehdi Bazargan. Early in 1979 he criticised aspects of the Khomeini regime, in particular its treatment of the Kurds, whom it was driving from the country. Later that year, after his children had been abducted (apparently with official approval) he was silenced and made to retract his criticisms publicly. In September 1979 he died of a heart attack, perhaps induced by stress.[105] Tough handling by the Revolutionary Guards was said to have killed Hojjat ol-Islam Lahuti,[106] and the Ayatollah Taher al-Sobai Khaqani also suffered a heart attack when he had been roughly brought to Qum under armed guard, after criticising some of the policies of the new regime.[107] Eminent religious leaders who had the power of *ijtihad* were being persecuted for their beliefs in a way that was quite new in Islam. It was also significant that those men who suffered could all see some possibility of peaceful coexistence between East and West, seculars and religious, or Iranians and Kurds.

In Khomeini's new Islamic state there was to be an ideological conformity. Although Islam had upheld the principle of liberty of conscience since Mohammad had made the *hijra*, Khomeini believed that the success and integrity of the revolution depended upon what he called 'unity of expression'.[108]

> The scent and hue of faith and of Islam, which is the foundation of victory and strength, will be eradicated because of the quarrels and siding with carnal desires and ignoring the commandments of the exalted God, while unity in truth and the unity of expression and the expression of God's oneness, which is the fountainhead of the greatness of the Islamic community will guarantee victory.[109]

Khomeini's view of monotheism only allows one point of view and ideological uniformity is an image of the oneness of God. Khomeini saw faith as an actualisation of God's truth and in this view deviation in ideology meant deviation from God. There could only *be* one truth. Muslims who oppose the *Sharia* state get in the way of God's plan and must be misguided; this deviation can only be explained by Khomeini as due to foreign influence or even satanic intervention. Khomeini's *jihad* quickly became a *jihad* against other Muslims who did not accept his ideas, which he claims to be the same as God's.

Khomeini had always seen the *hajj* as crucial and in 1979 he reminded the Iranian pilgrims on the *hajj* of the necessity of 'unity of expression': 'You Muslims of the world and you followers of the school of monotheism, the secret of all the problems of the Muslim countries is the difference of expression and the lack of coordination. The secret of victory is unity of expression.'[110] The *hajj* had always been the highest symbol of Muslim unity: whatever his ethnic origin or whatever his personal theological beliefs all Muslims were brothers because Abraham was their father. Khomeini and Shariati had seen the perception of this solidarity of the *hajj* as a prelude to the holy war and in this spirit Khomeini repeatedly urged Iranians to make the *hajj* 'a vibrant *hajj*, a crushing *hajj*, a *hajj* that condemns the criminal Soviet Union and the criminal America'.[111] Yet soon the *hajj* was seen as part of a *jihad* against the Muslims of Saudi Arabia. In 1982 Ayatollah Husain-Ali Montazeri insisted that only 'true' Muslims should administer the shrines of Mecca and Medina. The Saudis were 'a bunch of pleasure-seekers and mercenaries', he said. 'How long must Satan rule in the house of God?'[112] The following year, when the Saudis sought to impose restrictions on the pilgrims from Iran, Mohammad Musavi-Khoeniha, who had been the students' mentor during the hostage crisis, continued this belligerent propaganda: 'If a bunch of Saudi rulers should be able to dictate policies for the *hajj*, then we must ask if the government of Saudi Arabia is qualified to administer the holy sanctuaries.'[113] The Saudis were not only *munafiqeen* like all the other Arab rulers, they had actually co-operated with the Great Satan in an attempt to assassinate Khomeini in 1982. In 1986 Iranian pilgrims were caught trying to smuggle suitcases of explosives into Saudi Arabia to be used during the *hajj*.[114] The peaceful pilgrimage had become a holy war.

During the *hajj* of 1987 pilgrims from Iran seemed to have abandoned Islamic values altogether. In a 'unity rally' calling for deliverance from the infidels

America and Israel, Khomeini called for 'two splendid demonstrations' at Medina and Mecca during the *hajj*. Pilgrims should 'not refrain from giving expression to their hatred of the enemies of God and man'.[115] From the very earliest days of Islam, the Prophet Mohammad had respected the sanctity of Mecca by forbidding and deliberately refraining from the use of violence in the Holy City. The pilgrimage had always been an expression of Muslim unity. The identical pilgrim uniform, the performance of the same ancient rites and the recollection of Ishmael, the father of all believing Muslims, had always emphasised that whatever their race or class all Muslims were one and that this unity reflected the unity of the One God. Even the smallest act of violence was forbidden not only against human beings but even against plants and animals.[116] But now Khomeini had urged his revolutionaries to shatter this ancient tradition as a demonstration of 'true' Muslim values. On 21 July, the Iranian pilgrims violated the Muslim prohibition of images during the *hajj*, by carrying pictures of Khomeini through Medina, burned effigies of Ronald Reagan and chanted anti-Israeli slogans. Ten days later in Mecca the Iranians burned more effigies of Reagan, set cars on fire and attacked other pilgrims and Meccan citizens. The Saudi police were forced to use tear gas and baton-charged the demonstrators; during the stampede through the narrow streets that followed, about 400 people were killed. Muslims had killed other Muslims during the holiest rite of Islam. The Iranians carried home the coffins of the Iranian 'martyrs' who had died in the stampede and held more angry demonstrations against the Saudis, whom they claimed had machine-gunned the pilgrims.[117] This is most unlikely to be true, as the Saudis have always been very scrupulous about avoiding all violence in Mecca. The *hajj* had become a *jihad* in a shocking distortion of the ancient Muslim paradigm, in order to realise Khomeini's essentially unIslamic 'unity of expression'. This catastrophe in Mecca must call the Islamic integrity of the Iranian revolution into question.

We have often seen that, once the initial victory has been achieved in a holy war, people begin to dream of expansion and even of world domination. One of the new creations of the Iranian revolution was the World Congress of Friday Prayer Leaders and at its first meeting in December 1982 President Ali Khamene'i called upon the other prayer leaders from forty countries to mobilise a world campaign. They should make their mosques into 'prayer, political, cultural and military bases' which would 'prepare the ground for the creation of Islamic governments in all countries'. The preamble of the Iranian constitution refers to the 'ideological mission' of the army and the Revolutionary Guards to 'extend the sovereignty of God's law throughout the world'.[118] When, shortly after the revolution, Iraq invaded Iran to settle a territorial dispute that had been raging between Saddam Husain's government and the Shah for some years, Khomeini was quick to turn this into a holy war. Victory for Iran would be a victory for Islam against Saddam's secular government. The Islamic republic would be enlarged. This was not a nationalistic sentiment. Khomeini was not calling for a larger Iran but rather for an expansion of the frontiers of 'true' Islam. In this holy war there can be no talk of peace or compromise, because, Khomeini says, the Islamic government does not allow 'peace . . . between a Muslim and an infidel',[119] even though we have seen that the Koran does in fact teach that Muslims must make peace if the unbelievers show signs of wanting it (8:62–3). In the same way, although he has received Yasir Arafat, Khomeini is not interested in supporting their nationalist movement and he would have had no time at all for their vision of a secular, democratic state in Palestine. He sees the conquest of Jerusalem as part of his *jihad* against the imperialists and their clients, the Zionists.[120]

Although there were ambiguities in Khomeini's view of Islam, the Iranian revolution has been important to Muslims throughout the Islamic world. Many

saw it as a sign of the resurrection of Islam, a victory after centuries of degradation and humiliation, a promise of future power and glory and a victory over the imperial powers that none of the other states in the area had been able to achieve. The appeal was felt not only by Shiites, but also by Sunnis. It gave new impetus to extreme Islamic groups in Egypt, as I shall show in the next chapter. On 20 November 1979 (the first day of the Muslim year) the dawn prayers in the Great Mosque at Mecca were interrupted by a group of Sunni Arab Muslims with guns who proclaimed one of their number as the Mahdi or Messiah. They barricaded themselves into the Mosque and defended themselves against the Saudi troops for five days, and in the cellars and retreats for a further ten days. By the time the rebels surrendered 127 people on the Saudi side had been killed and the Saudis' reputation as Guardians of the Mosque had been gravely damaged. The Islamic identity of this revolution was obviously marred by the fact that it had violated the sanctity of the Mosque as the Iranians would do eight years later. But there were many Arabs in Saudi Arabia who could see that the uprising did have Islamic authenticity but had been misdirected. In the toilets of Riyadh University a graffito appeared in the spring of 1981 that echoed the feeling of many people. Addressing the leader, it read: 'Juhaiman, our martyr, why didn't you storm the palaces? The struggle [*jihad*] is only beginning.'[121] Saudi Arabia might hitherto have considered itself as the bastion of Islamic orthodoxy, but after the Iranian revolution the huge inequality of wealth appeared a great blot on its Muslim integrity. The success in Iran had shown the Arab masses that it was not impossible to topple the mighty from their thrones and provided a paradigm of revolution that none of the leaders in the Arab and Muslim states, where wealth is often unfairly apportioned, can afford to ignore.

But the revolution was most successfully adapted to another Arab people during the Lebanon war among the Shiite population. As soon as the Israelis invaded the Lebanon in the summer of 1982, Iran sent a contingent of 400 Revolutionary Guards, who set up an office in Beirut and preached a return to Islam. The Shiites there were passionately opposed to the Israeli invasion, but their most spectacular victory was, like the Iranian victory, against the United States. The American peace-keeping force had promised that they would be a neutral element in the Lebanon, but during fighting between Shiites and the Christian Maronites, the Maronites panicked and appealed for help which the Americans foolishly gave, opening fire against the Shiite militia. Shortly afterwards in April 1983 a Shiite car-bomber blew up the American embassy in a suicidal raid. The Shiites clearly saw this as an act of self-defence, according to the principles of Islam. 'If Americans kill my people,' said Hussein Musawi, the leader of Islamic Amal, 'then my people must kill Americans.'[122] In October 1983 another Shiite suicide raid bombed the barracks of the American marines and other buildings housing French and Israeli personnel, killing nearly 300 people. Violence is justified by the Koran as long as it is used to bring hostilities to an end, and in this these suicide raids were successful. The new determination and display of pure enmity forced the United States to withdraw; Islam had achieved its second victory over the Great Satan. The next Shiite offensive was mounted in the south of Lebanon against that other hitherto unbeaten enemy, the State of Israel.

Unlike the Shiites in Beirut, the Shiites in the south had no real hatred of Israel. Since their area had become the base for PLO activity, they had come to hate the Palestinians almost as much as the Israelis. When Israel first invaded and managed to eject the PLO, the Shiites saw her as a liberator, until they discovered that the Israelis did not intend to leave. They had exchanged one invading enemy for another. Tension mounted in the south and erupted during the Ashura celebrations in October 1983. The Israeli soldiers stupidly drove their tanks through the praying crowds, who, in their state of heightened emotion, threw themselves violently upon the Israeli soldiers, who then fired upon them. Later that day in Beirut, the Higher Shiite Council issued a *fatwa* which made it a sacrilege to co-operate with the Israelis and the *jihad* began. Two and a half weeks later, on 4 November, a suicide car-bomber killed twenty-nine Israelis and thirty-two Palestinians and Lebanese prisoners in the headquarters of the IDF in the south. This led to other similar attacks. There was no rigid structure of organisation here, any more than there had been during the Iranian revolution. Yet again, the Shiite Muslims knew what they had to do. Mosques became centres of mobilisation, as usual; a cadre appeared very rapidly and suicide attacks against the Israelis became an irresistible and unstoppable wave of violence that has been estimated to have killed 900 people.[123]

The suicide bombers were not impelled by a 'yearning for martyrdom' but by grim determination, in much the same spirit as the Assassins. The Koran told them that, when they were attacked, Muslims must use every effective means at their disposal to fight the oppressors and not let up until hostilities ceased and a normal state of peace could ensue. The Shiites of south Lebanon had seen how extremely effective this tactic had been against the Americans, once the Americans laid aside their neutrality and joined the Christian Phalange in their fight against the Muslims of Beirut. Once the Israelis had attacked the Shiite Muslims in the south, the Shiites made use of their religion to help them to transcend their natural fear of death in order to expel these invaders. The defensive character of this *jihad* was expressed very clearly by Khalil Jaradi, who organised many of the operations and eventually became a martyr himself.

> We fight Israel not because our religion is Islam, but because they are occupying our country, the same as we fought the Phalange and we fought the PLO. Our religion gives us a good means and a strength to fight back at the Israelis when we are treated in an unjust way and feel we must do something.[124]

The people of Iran had managed to eject the former Shah's American-backed regime by drawing upon the folk mysticism of the passion plays and fighting the heavily armed soldiers with bare hands. In the Lebanon, the Shiites had found an even more effective weapon. They were not fighting Israel because she was a Jewish state but because she had become their deadly enemy. To defend themselves they found that Islam gave them 'a good means and a strength' to face certain death. Their extreme dedication finally made these religious *mujahideen* the first Arabs to inflict a defeat on Israel. In June and July 1985 Israel began to withdraw her troops from the Lebanon. Yitzhak Rabin, the Israeli Defence Minister, spoke of the 'tragedy' of the war that 'let the Shiites out of the bottle'. It had surprised everybody, Rabin said, and he had been unable to find any trace of it in intelligence reports beforehand. The Shiites had proved to be far more formidable enemies than the PLO: 'in twenty years of PLO terrorism, no one PLO terrorist ever made himself into a live bomb.'[125] The secular PLO had not had the weapon of mystic exaltation.

After their success, the Shiites became aggressive instead of just defensive; during the first days of Israel's withdrawal from Beirut, a new slogan appeared which summoned the soldiers of God 'On to Jerusalem'.[126] This was not to be a war for Palestinian or Arab independence, but a *jihad* like Saladin's for the liberation of the Holy City. They also called upon the Muslims in the Occupied Territories to join them in this holy war, and we have seen that by the autumn of 1987 the Muslims there had indeed formed *jihad* groups and were fighting the Israeli army, armed only with rocks and stones, alongside their secular brothers. In September, one group was arrested on suspicion of having planned suicide car-bomb attacks in a Jewish settlement in the West Bank and in Israeli Jerusalem.[127]

The new Islamic *jihad* has a frighteningly aggressive image but originally it began as a response to aggression, the aggression of the Shah, America and Israel. It is a war of defence, fuelled by desperation and mysticism. During the time of the Crusades, religion proved to be a very powerful weapon when there seemed to be no hope. Secular means of getting rid of the Shah had failed in Iran, just as secular opposition to Israel and the United States had been ineffective in the Lebanon. By turning deliberately to religion, Iranian and Lebanese Shiites found a new strength with which to fuel their struggle against their seemingly omnipotent enemies. The revolutionaries and the martyrs found that they were able to push themselves past normal barriers and beyond their natural instinct for self-preservation by a religion which helped them to transcend themselves. The terrifying violence that has ensued must be taken as a measure of the despair and desperation of the Muslim people in their unequal struggle.

And yet the violence does make one quail. In Iran the child-martyrs seem to have been wantonly sacrificed in a manner that is quite opposed to the spirit of the Koran, which specifically says: 'Do not destroy your children' (17:32), condemning the pre-Islamic habit of infanticide in the Arabian peninsula. The cruelty of the Revolutionary Guards towards their fellow Iranians has made them terrifying successors of SAVAK. But even more significantly, at the time of writing the Ayatollah Khomeini has given signs of replacing the Shah as the enemy of Islam. On 7 January 1988 he claimed that his version of the Islamic government overrides even the Koran. This could be an extremely important claim, for if he persists in this attitude and encourages the Shiites in Iran and in the Middle East generally to follow him, it will mean that they are no longer Muslims and that the Iranian revolution is no longer an Islamic revolution. The pronouncement should be quoted at length, because it could be one of the most momentous events in the entire history of Islam:

> I must reiterate that our government is a branch of Mohammad's absolute vice-gerency, and is one of the first precepts of Islam. It takes precedence over all religious practices such as prayer, fasting or the *hajj* pilgrimage.... I openly say that the government can stop any religious law if it feels that it is correct to do so.... The ruler can close or destroy the mosques whenever he sees fit.... The government can prohibit anything having to do with worship or otherwise if [these things] would be against the interests of the government. . . . The government can unilaterally abrogate its contracts with and obligations towards the public whenever such contracts are against the interests of the country and Islam. . . . The government can prevent its citizens from performing the *hajj* pilgrimage which is one of the divine duties. . . . Government is an institution ordained by the Almighty and founded with absolute power entrusted to the Prophet and as an entity it supplants secondary statutes of the canonical law of Islam.[128]

It would be difficult to imagine a more unIslamic statement. Most astonishing is the Ayatollah's claim to be allowed to stop the Muslim practices of prayer, fasting and the *hajj*, three of the five pillars of Islam and the most fundamental of the Koranic practices. To forbid these practices, to close down mosques and to impose an absolute authority separate from the people in Iran would be effectively to destroy Islam in the country. It is a complete reversal of all the revolution stood for.

Various political explanations have been given for this astounding statement.[129] It has been said, for example, that it is part of a continuing battle between the Ayatollah and President Khamene'i and a move in the succession struggle. It has also been said that Khomeini wants to boycott the *hajj* as a move against the Saudis, who were about to impose strict curbs on Iranian pilgrims to prevent another sacrilegious assault. But other commentators have insisted that this pronouncement must be taken very seriously; certainly the mullahs and students at Qum have been horrified and have staged urgent demonstrations against Khomeini. But some of his student supporters have shouted in the streets of Tehran: 'Khomeini's command is as good as that of the Prophet.'[130] Hitherto there has been no question of 'heresy' in Islam, as we have seen. But Khomeini's statement and the students' slogan is pure heresy against the cardinal religion of Islam, which sees the Prophet Mohammad and the Koran as God's ultimate revelation to the world.

Yet when we take a broader look at this statement of Khomeini's and see it in the context of the history of the holy war in all three religions, perhaps it is not so surprising. In the very first holy war of all, we have seen that Joshua disobeyed the basic commandment 'Thou shalt not kill', albeit in response to a new command of God. When the Crusaders first marched to Jerusalem the original idea was that they would learn to live the Christian life during their long journey and indeed after the Crusade the Crusaders were seen as the elite of the Christian laymen. Yet there was nothing Christian about the Crusaders' behaviour in Jerusalem, which not only disobeyed the commandment 'Thou shalt not kill' but also entirely contradicted the loving and pacifist teaching of Christ. During a holy war, people tend to disobey crucial tenets of their religion and create a new martial faith, in absolute defiance of essential principles. In the new religious Zionism of today, extreme members of Israel's far right have flown in the face of the old ideals of Labour Zionism and have also distorted the nature of their religious Judaism, reducing it all to a commandment to inhabit the Land of Israel and ignoring the centuries of Jewish humanism. When, therefore, Khomeini makes a pronouncement that defies all the sacred teachings of Islam and flouts essential principles of the Koran, he is doing what Jews and Christians have done for centuries. Khomeini is unique, because he actually spells it out.

Another typical and tragic feature of the holy war that is revealed in Khomeini's heretical pronouncement is that it will inevitably set Iranians against other Iranians, Shiites who accept Khomeini's new stand against Shiites who reject it, and Shiites against Sunnis. During the holy war, the hatred that is unleashed is not confined to the enemy. It also becomes directed against one's own people. This happened in Judaism and Christianity. We have seen that when the exiles returned from Babylon in 538 BCE they started to fight other Jews, and this division has continued ever since. It is particularly evident in the bitterly divided Israel of today. Similarly at the time of the Crusader kingdom, the Christians were in a state of incipient civil war when Saladin was about to invade their kingdom. In Chapter 10, we will see that the Crusade would lead Christians to hound one another to death in Europe. Until this point, there has been no doctrinal quarrel between Shiites and Sunnis, but if the rest of the Shiah accept Khomeini there will be an absolute rift. A society which is in some way dedicated to war and the destruction of enemies not only makes the prospect of peace with the enemy very remote, but it also leads to the creation of enemies within. We shall see this very clearly in the next chapter.

CHAPTER NINE

1981

The Death of President Anwar Sadat: Holy War and Peace

On 6 October 1981 President Anwar Sadat was officiating at the victory parade celebrating the October War against Israel in 1973. Suddenly one of the trucks in the parade pulled out of line just in front of the presidential stand and when Sadat saw First Lieutenant Khaled Islambouli jump out and run towards him, he assumed that the young man was going to salute him and stood up to receive the tribute. Then a second officer threw a hand-grenade and there was a burst of machine-gun fire as the four assassins mounted a formidably efficient attack. Khaled shot round after round into the body of Sadat, even after he had himself been wounded in the stomach, crying: 'Give me that dog, that infidel!' After fifty seconds the security officers managed to stop the attack, but not before seven other people had been killed besides Sadat and twenty-eight others wounded.[1] The assassination of Sadat shocked the world in much the same way as the assassinations of President Kennedy or Martin Luther King. Sadat was the first Muslim leader in the Western world since Saladin to gain the respect and admiration of the West, but where Saladin had been a hero of the holy war, Sadat was a hero of peace. His historic journey to Jerusalem in November 1977 had become a twentieth-century legend of peace in an increasingly violent world, but the young men who shot Sadat did not see him as a hero and neither did millions of his own people. The date of his death is significant: it was the anniversary of his October War that had given back to the Arabs the self-respect they had lost in 1967. In the Islamic calendar, Sadat died on the feast of the Eid el-Adha, which commemorates Abraham's sacrifice, and he had made his journey of peace in 1977 on the eve of the very same feast. His assassins shot Sadat because he was an infidel ruler, who had abandoned the sacred duty of the *jihad* and made a shameful peace with the enemies of God.

The comparison with Saladin is fruitful. Until the twentieth century Saladin had actually been more widely revered in the West than he was in the East, even though he had been the sworn enemy of Western Christendom. Sadat had been a friend to the West and had signed a treaty with the vanguard of the West in the Middle East, but when he died his own people did not mourn him. When Nasser had died in 1970 thousands of people had poured on to the streets of Cairo, weeping and tearing their garments for the Arab hero who had staunchly defied Israel and the West. On the night of Sadat's death, the streets of Cairo were eerily silent, even though he was already being mourned and eulogised on news programmes in Europe and America.[2] At his funeral on 10 October Western leaders flocked to pay tribute to a great man. At their head were three former Presidents of the United States, Secretary of State Alexander Haig and Defence Minister Caspar Weinberger.

Prime Minister Begin of Israel was there, with his Interior Minister Yosef Burg and his Defence Minister Ariel Sharon, the dedicated hawk and Arab-hater. There were Chancellors, Prime Ministers and Presidents from Europe, and Prince Charles represented Britain. But there were no dense crowds of Egyptian mourners and no other Arab leaders at the funeral: after Sadat had signed the Camp David Treaty, Egypt had been expelled from the Arab League. It seemed that his death could not simply be ascribed to a few unbalanced fanatics but that at some level it had been endorsed by the whole Arab world. Why was this man of peace so deeply hated by his own people? The story of Sadat shows that, despite Camp David, there was no real will to peace on either side of the conflict and it also shows how deeply religion has inflamed the originally secular conflict in the Middle East. When Saladin and Richard had signed their treaty in 1192, it marked the beginning of a *détente* in the holy war, but 800 years later new holy wars on both sides have made peace seem dangerous and impossible. Sadat's tragedy shows that a man who has presented himself as a religious president cannot safely become a president of peace.

When Sadat came to power in 1970, the Egyptians did not hate him but they did not really take him very seriously. He lacked Nasser's strength and stability, perhaps because of his traumatic childhood. His father had married a black woman and had five children by her, of whom Mohammad Anwar was the second. But later, when he moved his family from the village of Mit Abu el-Qom to a four-roomed flat in Cairo, he married a white Egyptian girl, and had fifteen children by her. Sadat's mother was reduced to the level of a slave, and moved into a room with her five dark-skinned children, who frequently saw her beaten and humiliated. Throughout his life, Sadat was obsessed by his dark skin and always had a desperate need to be liked and accepted.[3] In addition to these misfortunes, he seems to have failed to get into one of the better schools, as his elder brother Taalat had done, and so he clearly lacked Nasser's intelligence.[4] His basic insecurity made him enjoy belonging to a close group and this got him involved in some dubious and rather foolish cloak-and-dagger conspiracies before he joined Nasser's group of Free Officers, which successfully staged the revolution of 1952.[5] Some of the members of this group were opposed to Nasser's recruiting Sadat,[6] because they felt he was a lightweight, but Nasser seems to have been genuinely fond of him, though he was aware of his shortcomings. People do seem to have liked Sadat and his eagerness to please was one of his endearing characteristics. The Free Officers probably felt that their reservations about Sadat were justified, however, on the night of the coup in 1952. Sadat had been ordered to come to Cairo from Gaza, where he was stationed, and to await instructions, but instead he took his wife Jihan to the cinema and when he got back to their apartment he found a stiff note from Nasser to say that the coup had taken place and where was he?[7] During Nasser's rule, Sadat was the Speaker in the Egyptian parliament for ten years, largely because of his histrionic talents. He always had a love of the theatrical and one of his earliest ambitions had been to become an actor. Nasser gave him the job of Speaker because he said that Sadat had a good voice and could orate with as much rhetoric as the Syrians.[8] In 1969 Sadat became Vice-President because Nasser felt that it was his 'turn' – all his colleagues had had a chance at the post and everybody enjoyed seeing Sadat's obvious delight in the job.[9] Nobody thought to remove him from office, because the last year of Nasser's life was a very hectic and indeed tragic year in the Arab world. In any case Sadat was associated in people's minds with Nasser. In the last years of his life, when Nasser was constantly depressed by the catastrophe of the Six Day War and was in failing health, he liked to spend his evenings with Sadat, who was an old and undemanding friend. Sadat himself always seemed devoted to Nasser and used to call him *mu'allan* (teacher).[10] When Nasser died unexpectedly in 1970 Vice-President Sadat automatically took over until the election of a new President, and many people assumed that he was just a caretaker. In rather the same way, nobody had thought much of Saladin when he had become Vizier of Egypt.

But, like Saladin, Sadat managed to gain the political support of the Egyptian people and become a strong leader. He won the presidential election of October 1970 by presenting himself to the electorate as the successor of Nasser, as Saladin had presented himself as the successor of Nur ad-Din. Like Saladin, Sadat had to put down a revolution in the army after coming to power and was thus able to demonstrate that he truly was the master of Egypt.[11] Now he had to justify his power by means of his achievements. In Western democracies a leader derives his legitimacy from the institution itself and from the state, but in a Third World country a leader derives his legitimacy from what he manages to achieve. Once Sadat had secured himself in power, he had to produce achievements equal to Nasser's, but this was difficult. Nasser had been revered all over the Arab world and was almost a legend. What could Sadat do that would not seem an anti-climax?

Despite Sadat's apparent love of Nasser during his life, he seems to have harboured a deep resentment of his leader and after Nasser's death this surfaced quite violently. The successor of Nasser began to tell his people that Nasser had made terrible mistakes and that he, Sadat, was the saviour of Egypt. This was naturally very confusing to the people, who had been told that everything was wonderful during Nasser's rule.[12] Sadat began to reverse Nasser's policies. Nasser had sought to make the Arab people proud and independent and had rejected the Western imperialists as the Arabs' enemies. Now Sadat sought to make Egypt a client of America in rather the same way as Israel and Iran: soon he would call Mohammad Reza Pahlavi 'my friend the Shah'.[13] In 1972 he expelled the 1500 Russian advisers that Nasser had installed in the country, clearly hoping to endear himself to the United States, and at first this seemed to give the Egyptians a new power and independence. His high-handed treatment of the Soviets made them respect and fear Sadat: in 1973 they gave him far more arms than they had given Nasser in 1967. In the early years of Sadat's rule, he began to show the Egyptian people that he had a power and strength that they had not seen in him before.

Sadat knew that he must find a popular power-base to rival the popular support that his Nasserite or Marxist rivals enjoyed, and so he turned to religion. Saladin had taken an Islamic identity as soon as he had come to power, and Sadat also presented himself to his people as the Pious President. He liked to be photographed praying in the mosques, wearing traditional Muslim clothes with the ash-mark on his forehead, proving that he was a good Muslim who bowed to the ground in prayer five times a day. He gave Egypt a more obvious Islamic identity than Nasser had done.[14] New mosques were built and the rich were encouraged to take part in this holy building project by large tax cuts. Islamic laws were reintroduced. It became a capital offence to apostatise from Islam, for example, and there was talk of punishing thieves by chopping off their hands. The sale of all alcohol was prohibited in the streets and confined to bars and night-clubs. An Islamic radio station presented recitations of the Koran and Koranic sermons all day, and the muezzin would interrupt the secular radio and television channels five times a day. Sadat constantly referred to God in his speeches, which acquired a distinctly pious tone. All this was a reversal of Nasser's policies. Nasser had ruthlessly suppressed the Muslim fundamentalists of his own day and in 1954 the Muslim Brotherhood had made an attempt on his life. The Brothers had been put into prisons and concentration camps. But though extremists condemned Nasser as a *munafiq* the common people could see him as a legitimate Muslim leader because he did appear to be trying to grapple with Egypt's appalling economy and to create a more equal society, and he had shown himself to be ruthlessly opposed to the enemies of Islam. In 1971 Sadat began to release the Muslim Brothers and, though he would not let them exist as an official body, he did allow them to publish their own magazine *al-Da'wa* (The Call). It was a clear demonstration to the people that he was not a *munafiq* like Nasser but was the friend of Islam.

Islam had a very strong appeal because after the Six Day War there had been a religious revival in Egypt, rather as there had been in Israel. People tried to make sense of the Egyptian disaster by returning to their religion and there was a general feeling that the Jews had won because they had been more true to their religion than the Muslims. Many young Coptic Christians became monks and Muslims joined Sufi mystic orders. Between April and July 1968 thousands of Copts and Muslims claimed to have seen Mary, the mother of Jesus, at Zeitoum in northern Cairo. Mary, they believed, had come to comfort them for the loss of Jerusalem and people felt that the apparitions were a sign that God had relented towards Egypt and would lead them to victory.[15] The struggle with Israel was becoming a religious struggle at a deep popular level and the people spontaneously sought a visionary comfort in their distress, as the First Crusaders had done. When Sadat presented himself to his people as the Pious President and began to give Egypt a more Islamic identity he was responding to this religiosity and encouraging it. But religion can be a very dangerous weapon. It has mechanisms and passions of its own that are not always amenable to political control.

Naturally the new religiosity changed the spirit of Sadat's October War against Israel. The code name for the operation was Badr, after Mohammad's first victory against the Meccans, and the battle-cry was *Allahu Akhbah!*[16] The war against Israel had become a *jihad*, and the Egyptians would call it the Ramadan War in much the same way as the Israelis refer to it as the war of Yom Kippur. Because the operation was so much more successful and demonstrated to an astonished world how much the Arab armies had improved, Egyptians naturally saw this success as God's endorsement of their cause. They turned to religion even more fervently because it had been found to be such a powerful weapon.[17] Sadat could turn to his opponents and point out that, where Nasser had disgraced the Arabs by the humiliating failure of the Six Day War, he had redeemed Arab honour. Yet Sadat

wanted to go one stage further. He wanted to be able to say that where Nasser had lost the Sinai peninsula in 1967, he had recovered it for Egypt. Now that he had vindicated the honour of the Arab nation on the battlefield and proved that Egypt was a force to be reckoned with, he indicated to Kissinger during the negotiations after the war that he was seriously thinking of renewing the peace offer he had made in 1971, which Prime Minister Golda Meir and Defence Minister Moshe Dayan had so contemptuously rejected.[18]

In 1973 the Arabs seemed set for a new, victorious phase in their history and it really looked as though they might be about to recover from the centuries of colonial humiliation. They had distinguished themselves on the battlefield and discovered a new weapon in their oil, which many religious Arabs saw as Allah's gift to his chosen people. When OPEC announced their embargo to force the world to take the plight of the Palestinian Arabs seriously, the whole world suddenly seemed at their mercy: the superpowers were rendered helpless, if enraged, and Western Europe was distraught. Old buried hatred of the Arab world, which had been firmly embedded in the Western consciousness since the Crusades, surfaced again, and it looked as though the Arabs still wanted to take over the world. In fact, the Arabs were no more eager to do this in 1973 than they had ever been. They simply wanted to take their destiny into their own hands, right the wrongs that they felt had been done to their people and force the world to respect them again. None of these hopes materialised, however, and for this failure Sadat and his peace policy must bear a good deal of responsibility.

After the war, Sadat told his people that they were at the beginning of a new, exciting era and he initiated an economic policy that he promised would bring wealth and success to Egypt. But Sadat was no economist. As the Americans would discover later he had no interest in or understanding of the subject, so it was not really surprising that his new policy turned out to be a disaster. He called it *infitah* or Opening and it is one of the ironies of Sadat's tragedy that his plans for peace and reconstruction often fell into the pattern and idiom of the holy war, like an accidental but uncannily accurate parody. *Infitah* comes from the same Arabic root as *al-Fatah*, the name given to Mohammad's conquest of Mecca. *Al-Fatah* had been the long climax of Mohammad's struggle to achieve an independent and essentially Islamic identity, but *infitah* meant a new foreign invasion. *Infitah* opened Egypt up: foreign currency, foreign investment and foreign imports were encouraged and great tax benefits lured many Western investors. Unfortunately this also meant that Egyptian businesses and goods went to the wall, and Egypt seemed to be acquiring a new subservience to the West and a new Western appearance. It was here that Sadat's image as the Pious President began to tarnish: many Muslims started to see him as a *munafiq* who had sold the honour and independence of his people as no true Muslim should.

A Muslim ruler must create a just and equal society, but in Sadat's Egypt there was an unacceptable amount of corruption and a new gap between rich and poor.[19] The only people to benefit from *infitah* were the foreigners and the Egyption millionaires, not the smaller Egyptian businessmen. Only 4 per cent of the young Egyptians would find well-paid employment and a successful future in this new Egypt. The rest faced a harsh alternative. If they stayed in Egypt, they faced unemployment or miserably paid state employment and permanent homelessness, because even the smallest flat was extremely expensive. It became impossible for Egyptians to marry and start a family until they had acquired some capital, and people began to feel hopeless and despairing. The only way to improve their lot was emigration. In the developing and wealthy Gulf states, young Egyptian intellectuals and skilled labourers were able to earn a great deal of money and thousands of Egyptians left their country for long periods, sent money home from the Gulf and saved for their own future. In exile, they joined the Palestinian refugees who were also doing well in the Gulf, and with them formed a new elite in the Arab world that was often resented and feared. Thousands of peasants also left Egypt to work in other Arab countries, where they could find just enough money to build a house or buy a tractor when they returned home. Sadat was forcing many of his fellow countrymen to make a *hijra* from their homeland because he had made it impossible for them to live there.

Clearly a policy like *infitah* did not look well coming as it did from the Pious President. Sadat's own lifestyle also belied his claim, because he was living in grossly unIslamic splendour: he had 120 rest homes, many of which had been refurbished at a cost of millions of Egyptian pounds; he started to wear clothes of expensive Western designers; and he was increasingly seen hobnobbing with capitalists like David Rockefeller.[20] His wife Jihan dressed like a Western woman and adopted Western manners, which shocked many Egyptians. She went down very well indeed in the West and when state visitors arrived she would often kiss them on the cheek, which seemed frankly scandalous to the newly pious Egyptians. A true Muslim ruler should never become isolated from his people, but Sadat led a very secluded, luxurious life. He developed a strange restlessness, and was constantly on the move from one of his resthouses to another, travelling by helicopter and accompanied by only a few cronies and his family. If problems arose he would often take off alone to ponder in private, as though a solution would drop directly from heaven instead of arriving during a consultation with his colleagues.[21] Sadat's isolation was not only unIslamic but dangerous for any ruler. Mohammad Heikal points out that from a helicopter Egypt looks a particularly peaceful land, but Sadat did not have his feet sufficiently on the ground to see the real dangers he faced in his own country.[22]

In their distress many young Egyptians naturally turned to religion, and this continued the religious revival which had begun in 1967 and which might otherwise have died a natural death. They flocked into Islamic groups which the Pious President encouraged and protected. This was especially true in the universities, where the Islamic student associations (the *jama'at islamiyya*), began to control the campus after the October War and Sadat encouraged this because they were proving powerful opponents of the Nasserite and Marxist unions. In 1975 he issued new decrees which enabled them to take over the student unions completely and by 1976 they had become the leaders of the students.[23] The campus took on an Islamic appearance. Young men wore beards and wore the gallabiyah, and women shrouded themselves in the chador. They insisted on the segregation of the sexes, on separate classes and buses for men and women and began to hold huge prayer gatherings. All this seemed perverse to most people in the West. It looked as though these students, who were often among the most intelligent, were throwing off the freedoms and humanism of the enlightened West and turning back to an outdated, puritanical religion which subordinated women to men and condemned sex as impure, shrouding the bodies of these young men and women from view. Something similar has also happened among the religious Jews in Israel. In recent years there has been a far greater emphasis on the separation of Jewish men and women there. A few years ago practising Orthodox Jews of the religious parties would very often organise an outing which would include mixed bathing, but now this would be unthinkable. Similarly more women are keeping their heads covered with a scarf and refuse to wear short sleeves than was common among religious Jewish women not long ago.[24] We in the West tend to find this very disturbing, so it is important to see what it means, even though this will entail a digression from our story.

People who come from the Christian tradition assume that the segregation of the sexes and the assumption of concealing dress in both Judaism and Islam springs from a hatred of sex, because Christianity has been very negative about human sexuality throughout its history, as I have shown at length elsewhere.[25] Despite the official teaching that sex and marriage were part of God's plan, a neurotic hatred of sex grew up that was quite distinct from the doctrine and which meant that marriage was regarded as a distinctly inferior Christian vocation and that sex was a disgusting, unholy activity. The hatred of sex survived the Reformation and Luther brought it firmly into the Protestant tradition. This distrust and fear of sex is unique among the major religions of the world and there is nothing like it in either Judaism or Islam. Judaism has always stressed the holiness of married, family life, which is why it punishes adultery so severely. Perhaps the Jewish attitude to sexuality can be best understood by considering briefly the command-ments that forbid a man and wife to have intercourse while the woman is menstruating and for seven days afterwards, when she takes a ritual bath. This 'purification', as the Hebrew word is translated in English, suggests that the woman is dirty or 'unclean', but in fact this is not so. There is a strong rabbinical tradition that says that the period of abstinence is required in order that the couple will enjoy sex more afterwards and that the man does not take his wife for granted as a sex object: 'Because a man may become overly familiar with his wife, and thus repelled by her, the Torah said that she should be a *niddah* [sexually unavailable] for seven days [after menses] so that she will be as beloved to him [afterwards] as on the day of her marriage' (Niddah 3lb).[26] Before going to the synagogue on Yom Kippur or one of the major festivals, a man is told to take a ritual bath, *not* because he is unclean, but in order to be more holy for the holy time during the service. Similarly menstrual blood is not dirty or a defilement, but after a period of separation a woman 'purifies' herself to make herself more holy for what happens next: sexual relations with her husband. The idea that sex could be holy in this way is quite foreign to the Christian world-view.[27]

It is also true, as I have said earlier, that Islam has a very positive attitude to sexuality. The Prophet himself seems to have been a highly sexed and passionate man, who saw no value at all in celibacy, and is said to have decreed that there was to be no 'monkery' in Islam.[28] Yet in the West we tend today to think that Islam is a sexually repressive religion, because 'we' are trying to free ourselves from the repressions of Christianity. The barbaric practice by *some* Muslims of clitori-dectomy encourages this belief.[29] In the last century, this disfiguring operation was performed on English Christian girls, with the approval of society, but it was performed for quite different reasons.[30] A Muslim may insist that his daughter has the operation because he owns her, and is afraid that her normal sexual urge might lead her to wander off with other men before she is given to a husband. It comes from a primitive impulse that seems common in many societies. It made some of the Crusaders lock their wives into extremely painful and dangerous chastity belts while they were in the Holy Land. In Victorian London, however, the girl usually had the operation because she had been found masturbating and enjoying her sexuality, which would have horrified her parents because they were terrified of sex.[31] The practice has not been upheld by a majority of either Muslims or Christians and it must be condemned for whatever reason it is performed. But the difference is important. Clitoridectomy is certainly not laid down in the Koran, any more than it is in the gospels. On the contrary Mohammad is said to have told Muslim men that they have a positive duty to satisfy their wives sexually; some of the rabbis told the Jews the same.[32] This is quite contrary to the spirit of the Fathers of the Church, who told Christians that if a man enjoyed sleeping with his wife too much he was committing fornication.[33]

The second thing that distresses Western people is that, at a time when the progressive West was promoting the ideal of the equality of the sexes, some Jews and Muslims today seem to be retreating to the old inequalities. It must be said that no religion in the world as far as I know has in practice been very good news for the position of women. Religions have until recently been male affairs like most other institutions. But people from the Christian tradition rather enjoy saying that Judaism and Islam are particularly repressive of their women. Again, this needs qualification. Judaism is a religion that proclaims the holiness of things by separating them. The Torah separates sabbath from the rest of the week, milk from meat, and Jews from Gentiles. The 'holiness' of the Land of Israel should probably be considered in this context; it is partly for this reason that the *goyim* are forbidden in the Torah to live there. The Torah also separates men from women; in Orthodox synagogues men and women sit separately and men and women have different religious duties. As one would expect the women's duty centres on the home, and the husband's on prayer and study. The Bible and the Halakah teach that women are blessed by God, but each morning in the synagogue a Jew must thank God for not making him a Gentile, a slave or a woman.[34] Jewish feminists, who want to preserve the ancient traditions, will argue that the Torah is not wrong to encourage a separation of the roles of men and women because this way it preserves and celebrates the holiness or identity of the sexes as different and distinct. But they still argue that Halakah must be developed so that women are no longer forced to take an inferior position in the community.[35]

In the West people are particularly wedded to the idea that Muslims oppress their women by divine command. But in fact Mohammad's first converts were women, who found the religion liberating.[36] The Koran gives women divorce rights and inheritance rights, which are not the same as those of men, but which women in the enlightened West would not receive for over a thousand years.[37] In the early Muslim community, Mohammad's wives were very powerful people, and after his death were consulted about religious matters, particularly Aisha, his favourite wife. There is nothing about the veiling or separation of women in the Koran; this practice did not creep into Islam until the third or fourth generation after the Prophet and it has been suggested that it came from Christian Byzantium, which had always treated its women in this way.[38] Certainly a Muslim feels he 'owns' his wife, but many Western men would feel the same. The Koran and the hadith both tell men to love their wives tenderly and live with them happily (see for example, Koran 30:22).

The return to traditional values in Judaism and in Islam today in the Middle East has been due to different reasons. In Israel it has been inspired by the desire to establish a strictly religious identity and is just part of a general return to minute observance of the Torah. Religious women who now cover their heads will also forbid their children to watch television, because of the prohibition of images in Judaism. In Sadat's Egypt, however, the young people of the *jama'at islamiyya* who returned to Islamic dress and the segregation of the sexes had a rather different reason. The Muslim student unions were encouraging their members to improve their lot by their own practical efforts instead of waiting for the government to help them, as the Koran enjoined. Egyptian universities are not like their counterparts in Europe and America. They can be heartless, mechanical factories. In Arabic they are called 'Universities of large numbers' and there is indeed vast overcrowding.[39] Students attending the compulsory lectures would often have to sit two or three to a seat. Only a few lucky people in the front rows would be able to follow a demonstration on a blackboard and if the loudspeakers broke down hardly anybody could hear a word that was said. Because success in the examination meant regurgitating these lectures accurately, lecture manuals had to be bought at some cost, and learned by heart. There was little intellectual freedom. The students who achieved the best grades when they graduated from high school were automatically placed in one of the 'elite' subjects like engineering, medicine or pharmacology. If a bright student wanted to study literature or law, which were not elite subjects, he would have to accept the fact that he would be studying with inferior teachers or classmates and that his chance of success after university was even more remote than it was already. This was a relic of the Nasser period; it was modelled on the Soviet system and was designed to produce a nation of technicians not scholars. In addition to these other difficulties for the students, there was great overcrowding in the dormitories, which made studying impossible in the evenings, and the students would be transported from these inhumanely huge student blocks on hideously overcrowded buses.

The success of the *jama'at islamiyya* was that its members addressed these problems effectively and practically, as good Muslims should. They used to hold revision sessions in the mosques before examinations, where students could study in peace and quiet and they issued cheap versions of the lecture manuals. Above all they tackled a particularly distressing aspect of the overcrowding. Because young Egyptians could not afford to marry until very late and because the sexual revolution that happened in the West during the 1960s did not spread to Third World countries, one of the great problems of Sadat's Egypt was sexual frustration among the young. For young men and women to sit crammed together on the same seat during lectures or jammed together on buses was clearly intolerable for both. Women found themselves harassed by desperate young men, who found that they could not stand this tantalising promiscuity. In these extremely difficult circumstances, the message of the Islamic segregation of the sexes was music in the ears of many of these strained young people. Women would find themselves freed from unwelcome attentions in the chador and it seemed to make good sense for men and women to live and study apart.[40]

But, given that Islam values sex so highly, why did these young people not use contraception? Why did the women not go on the pill? Some certainly did, but the members of the *jama'at islamiyya* felt that this was an unacceptable solution. Contraception and the permissive society were Western products and therefore unacceptable for most of the young people, who, with good reason, felt that the West was not their friend. But it was not simply a negative rejection. These Egyptians wanted to keep to their *own* family and social traditions, which would be undermined by this Western way of life. Muslims in the Middle East were not as enamoured as Westerners were about this Western 'freedom'. The way sex was used to sell products and was trivialised and commercialised seemed to denigrate an important value. Iranians also had rejected the triviality of the Great Satan and had expressed their separation from it by reverting to their own traditional dress. In the case of women, Egyptians felt that Western clothes were not always liberating. They can reduce a woman's dignity by making her a mere sex object and it is undeniably true that while we are rightly proud of the freedom and respect that we have *begun* to give to women in Western countries, this liberation has not halted that Western habit of enslaving and exploiting women through a heartless advertisement and sex industry that pays very little attention to human dignity. Many Western feminists would agree with this.

Clothes are, of course, extremely important in expressing one's identity and it is interesting that in Israel, Egypt and Iran the assumption of a different costume has naturally symbolised the assertion of a new self. Similarly the relations between men and women could be said to express most clearly the values of a society, so that it is natural when one society feels threatened by another that one of the first signs of a desire to resist this foreign coercion should centre on issues of sexual morality and the position of women. Yet the extreme measures to which Muslim men and women have been willing to go to express their distance from the Western point of view is very disturbing to us. This entire rejection of our way of life seems unbalanced because our way of handling the relations between men and women is very crucial to *our* sense of self. No society has as yet found a really satisfactory solution to these problems. In Western countries we have tended to swing from a period of sexual freedom to an extreme sexual repression. This phenomenon, which is unique to Western society, shows that we tend to be particularly sensitive on this issue and to have ambiguous views. This may make us more stridently convinced that our current way is the 'only' way of managing these matters. We should not condemn Muslim people for choosing to go their own way, rather than to follow us in our confusion.

The Death of President Anwar Sadat

But the return to Islam did not end there. Resuming traditional dress touched a deep chord in the Islamic identity of these students. Sadat may have praised and encouraged these Muslim groups and thought that he was establishing a popular power-base for his regime, but he was actually creating a Frankensteinian monster that would devour him: Khaled Islambouli, his assassin, was a member of the *jama'at islamiyya* when he was at university. One began by opting not to sit next to a woman and found that one was beginning to make a radical break from the regime. During Islamic festivals, the *jama'at islamiyya* would hold 'camps', like the similar camps held by their rivals, the Nasserites and the Marxists.[41] Here they did not simply spend their time studying the Koran; there was also a great deal of sport and practice in self-defence. The camps were trying to recreate a perfect Muslim society lived according to the spirit and values of the *rashidun*, the righteous caliphs. It was a retreat from the unIslamic world of Sadat's Egypt, and an experiment in the Islamic utopia, the creation of a perfect alternative world. Naturally this involved discussion of the regime in Egypt, which seemed to have no concern whatever for the fate of these young people. There would be lectures criticising the regime and condemning it as *jahiliyya*, the term used to describe the barbarous pre-Islamic period in Arabia, before Mohammad gave the Arabs power and a new identity. Egyptians had been told for years that their identity was anti-Western and now the Pious President seemed to be inviting the West to invade the country and drive out the Egyptians themselves. By returning to their own Islamic, unWestern roots, the students were beginning to recover a sense of self-respect and a new source of personal power.

However radical the *jama'at islamiyya* was naturally and inevitably becoming, there were other young Muslims who sought an even more radical answer; a new Muslim underground was being formed, and it sought a more extreme solution than the Muslim Brotherhood, which now co-operated with the regime. Many Muslims had been profoundly influenced by the writings of Sayyid Qutb, a Muslim Brother who had in his turn been influenced by the Pakistani Brother Abu el A'ala Mawdudi, who was also being eagerly read by young radicals in Iran. Qutb had been imprisoned by Nasser in 1954 and had read Mawdudi's book *The Four Expressions* while in prison. It had a great effect on him. Mawdudi told Muslims that they must refuse to compromise with the corrupt regimes which oppressed Muslims throughout the Islamic world and which violated essential Koranic principles. Muslims must be ruled by God alone and must reject the idols of false ideology and values placed before them by the *munafiqeen*.[42] Sayyid Qutb himself wrote several books which developed Mawdudi's ideas. He returned to the old paradigm of the *hijra–jihad*. In *The Shadow of the Koran* and *Signposts on the Road* he taught that there were two necessary stages in the struggle for a truly Islamic society. First was the period of weakness (*istidhaf*) when devout Muslims were in no position to fight the regime effectively. Instead they should withdraw from the corrupt society as Mohammad had withdrawn from his period of weakness in Mecca and made the

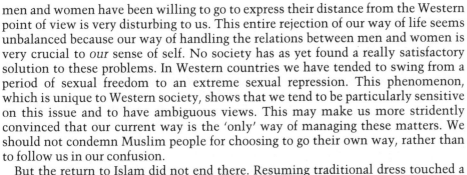

hijra to Medina where he gained a new power. Once Muslims were truly separate from the unIslamic world, they should build an alternative Islamic society where they would recover the strength necessary to end the period of *istidhaf* and wage a *jihad* against the infidels.[43]

The Egyptians who became disciples of Qutb were divided about how to interpret his teachings. Some formed the *jama'at al-uzla al-shu'uriayya* (Spiritual Detachment Group). They secretly pronounced a decree of excommunication (*takfir*) on the corrupt society, but because they were still in the period of weakness, they would conceal their views and pray before an imam whom they actually condemned as an infidel because he supported the government. Thus concealed and spiritually separated from society, they would wait for the period of power when they could fight a *jihad* against the infidels with a good chance of success.[44] Others felt that this was not a sufficiently radical solution and followed Sheikh Ali Abduh Ismail into the small Society of Muslims, but the group disintegrated in 1969 when Sheikh Ali defected and the sect was left with only one member.[45] Shukri Mustafa was a young, poorly educated Muslim from Middle Egypt, whose inhabitants are usually considered simple rustics by their fellow countrymen. He had been imprisoned by Nasser in 1965 but released in 1971 as part of Sadat's new approach to Islam. This did not endear the regime to Shukri, however, and he was soon preaching with such success in the hamlets and villages that by 1972 the police were already watching him carefully. They called the group the *takfir wal hijra* (excommunication and *hijra*) because Shukri declared that Sadat's regime was an infidel regime and he condemned any Muslim who supported it. He urged his followers to withdraw from Sadat's Egypt and openly form an alternative Islamic society. For a time the members of his group lived in the desert, but later most lived a communal life in flats in the poorest areas of the cities, which necessarily associated the Society of Muslims with the poor and outcast people of Egypt.[46]

Shukri preached a fundamental return to the Koran and denied that the later Islamic tradition had any value: imams who had written learnedly about the Koran had idolatrously elevated their purely human learning and made it an idol. Many imams had actually supported the infidel and hypocritical regimes of the *munafiqeen*. As examples he cited Sheikh Mahmud Shaltut of the al-Azhar Madrassa, who had in Nasser's time issued a *fatwa* which declared banking interest to be legal, even though many Muslims condemned it as usury, or Sheikh Su'ad Jala who had recently declared that Muslims were allowed to drink beer. Shukri taught that no Muslim who was serious about his religion could continue to live in this regime; the State of Egypt, he said, was as dangerous an enemy to the Muslim people as the State of Israel and none of his followers should contaminate themselves by joining the Egyptian army or taking any state employment. All contact with the state was strictly forbidden. Many young Egyptians who were confused by the *volte face* of Sadat's new Western Egypt and who found their lives miserable and hopeless took comfort from this absolute denial of the state and this return to old Islamic values. Shukri taught that the Muslims were too weak to stage a *jihad* against the regime and that when they were confronted with as powerful an enemy as the State of Egypt they should flee, as Mohammad had very wisely fled from Mecca when he had been persecuted there. In seclusion they would find new strength to fight the unbelievers.

The young people who followed Shukri and made the *hijra* into the communes were desperate with misery and in the new Islamic world that they tried to create they found their lives entirely changed. They had accommodation they could afford, they were able to marry young and the diplomas and certificates they had painfully acquired in the universities were condemned as worthless rubbish. There were many educated people in the movement, even though Shukri condemned education as worthless.[47] This was not a purely negative position but a confused comment on the economy. Most state employees with education earned far less than an unskilled worker and could only keep their families at subsistence rate; an illiterate country girl who became a lady's maid could earn more than an assistant professor. In these circumstances, Shukri argued, it was indeed pointless for Egyptians to learn to read. There was a similar clumsy extremism in his solution to the marriage problem, which shocked many of his opponents. Shukri reintroduced the old village habit of arranged early marriages. Members of his group were married very young and the match was arranged by Shukri himself. Several young couples shared a room in curtained-off cubicles. The group supported itself by manual labour and growing vegetables, but this was not enough, so Shukri sent his young men to the Gulf in turn in a new *hijra*. There they joined the thousands of their countrymen who had been forced to emigrate, and sent money home to the community. On their return they were entitled to a wife.[48] Shukri's policies seemed eccentric and bizarre but he was implicitly pointing to serious abuses in society. The movement was a passionate rebellion of the poor and oppressed, which presented an alternative Egypt on the margins of the great cities. Shukri's communities were actually creating a distorted mirror image of Sadat's Egypt, where people could marry young instead of suffering frustration, could reject the new secular values and materialism the regime was encouraging and return to Islam, and the men who made the *hijra* to the Gulf called attention to the fact that life was impossible for most people in Egypt.

The *hijra* of Shukri and his many disciples was itself an aggressive act because it was making a powerful statement about the miseries of many Egyptians who found their life intolerable. But the *hijra* ultimately led to a more direct *jihad*, even though Shukri insisted that his followers should flee from a confrontation with the enemies of Islam. The first indication of this new *jihad* against the state was an unsuccessful dress-rehearsal for Khaled Islambouli's operation in 1981 and it was carried out not by Shukri but by one of his rivals. In 1974 Saleh Sarrieh, a young PhD student who belonged to a group called the Islamic Liberation Party, led a band of followers to the Military Technical College, where they collected arms and volunteers. Then they marched on to the government headquarters. Their aim was to assassinate Sadat and to establish an Islamic state, but the movement was hopelessly small and was very easily crushed.[49] It demonstrated that Muslims were indeed too weak to undertake effective action against Sadat, and that Shukri and his followers had been quite correct when they confined themselves to the *hijra* and to creating an Islamic world of their own where the values of modern Egypt no longer applied. But Sarrieh's coup also proved fatal to Shukri. One of the members of his party who was imprisoned after the attempt decided to become a member of the Society of Muslims, but challenged Shukri's leadership. Another member who was released tried to lure some of Shukri's followers into a rival group of his own. There was a period of crisis in the community and Shukri decided to take action against the 'apostates', as he called them, by attacking their homes on 18 and 22 December 1976.[50] This was a fatal decision, because Shukri had now made himself vulnerable to the law by attempting to kill Egyptian citizens. The police stepped in and arrested fourteen of Shukri's followers and a warrant was issued for Shukri's arrest. Until this point the Society of Muslims had formulated no very clear tactics about how to deal with the state but now they saw their movement condemned on the front page of the official Cairo newspaper *al-Ahram* as 'a group of fanatical criminals'.[51]

During the first six months of 1977 Shukri tried to counter this attack peacefully and to give his group a more positive image. He tried, without success, to publish a book called *The Caliphate*, to issue communiqués which explained the true nature of his group, and to deliver statements on radio and television. None of these measures worked and Shukri felt his leadership in danger. In July members of the movement kidnapped Sheikh Mohammad el-Dhahabi, a former minister of the religious endowment, and published a list of demands: they wanted the lies that had been published against them retracted, they demanded that their fourteen 'martyrs' be released and that a 'committee of experts' be set up to examine major government institutions, something that was quite impossible in Sadat's Egypt. The Egyptian government refused to negotiate with these terrorists and when the Sheikh's body was discovered on 7 July there was a public outcry. This type of religious extremism was quite new to Egypt. What kind of Muslims would murder one of their co-religionists? Shukri and a large number of his disciples were arrested and Sadat convened a special military tribunal to try the case.[52]

At the same time as Sadat was releasing the Muslim Brothers imprisoned by Nasser, he found himself filling up the gaols with new Muslim prisoners who declared themselves hostile to the regime of the Pious President. It was a delicate and uncomfortable position and as the tribunal hearings proceeded he found that the establishment had declared war against Islam. Abdul Halim Mahmoud, the Sheikh of the al-Azhar mosque in Cairo, rejected Shukri's ideas, but explained that because Egypt had long been governed by people whose political philosophy was not rooted in the religious tradition of the country, many of the young people were muddled and disorientated. It was this that caused Shukri and his companions to see Sadat's Egypt as *jahiliyya*. The military prosecutor took quite a different line. On 11 October the military prosecutor explained the phenomenon as being due to the spiritual vacuum in the country. The ulema of Egypt had failed in their duty to instruct the youth in their religion and the root of the problem lay in al-Azhar's failings, not the government's. Naturally the ulema were furious and issued an angry reply; a new rift opened between the government and the religious establishment at a most important time.[53] Shukri was hanged with four other companions shortly after the conclusion of the trial in November 1977 and it is deeply significant that at that time the newspapers presented two main stories and pictures to their readers. One was of young, desperate bearded Muslim extremists who were being presented as the enemies of the state; the other was Sadat's historic journey to Jerusalem on 8 November 1977. The Pious President was about to become the President of Peace.

Early in 1977 there had been another eruption which showed alarmingly how desperate the Egyptian people were becoming and this was causally linked to Sadat's decision to go to Jerusalem on a mission of peace. Paul M. Dickie, the American Director of the International Monetary Fund in Egypt, had recently recommended drastic measures to rescue the economy, which included the devaluation of the Egyptian pound and a great reduction in the subsidies that the government paid every year on staple food and clothes.[54] Most of the impoverished Egyptians depended on these subsidies for their life and the members of parliament were horrified at the possible consequences of putting a fresh financial burden on the people. They also pointed out that there were wider political implications: if Egypt allowed her economic policy to be dictated by the United States she would inevitably isolate herself from the rest of the Arab world and lose the leadership which Nasser had established. Sadat, who remained frighteningly impervious to the plight of his own people, and who never fully appreciated Egypt's uniquely important strategic position in the Middle East and North Africa, turned a deaf ear to these protests. On 17 January the government announced that there would be a substantial rise in the price of twenty-five essential goods and on 18 January the people went on to the streets; the police could not control them and 160 people were killed. Sadat himself was in Aswan that day and astonishingly did not hear about the riots until 4 o'clock in the afternoon[55] (a telling indication of his isolation from the people) when the crowd charged against the rest-house in Aswan. Sadat had to escape by helicopter, and a plane stood by, ready to take the Sadats to Tehran. The next day, however, the army was brought in to quell the riots and Sadat restored the food subsidies. Clearly his credit was running low and he realised that he would have to regain the support of the people by doing something really dramatic, which would lead their minds to higher things. The answer was the peace process.

During President Jimmy Carter's first year of office, there was renewed effort in Washington to bring peace to the Middle East, but the Arabs were naturally suspicious of the interference of a great power friendly to Israel, and Israel had recently demonstrated that she was ready to make no concessions over the Territories. In 1977 Menachem Begin had been elected Prime Minister and had dedicated himself to the establishment of Greater Israel on both sides of the Jordan. The prognosis for peace was not good, but Carter manfully persevered and began a preliminary round of discussions with individual Arab and Israeli leaders. He favoured the 'comprehensivist' approach, which sought an overall agreement between Israel, the Palestinians and the Arab states, and did not want a series of separate peace treaties between individual states and Israel, which would almost certainly ignore the Palestinian problem.[56] Carter was distressed to find that Begin was most reluctant to take part in a conference that would put pressure on Israel to evacuate the Territories as an essential part of the peace process, and he found Sadat's eagerness for peace attractive and impressive. It was very worrying indeed to many Israelis when the US State Department issued a peremptory public statement, which showed none of the usual deference to the Israeli position:

> The status of the Palestinians must be settled in a comprehensive Arab–Israeli agreement. This issue cannot be ignored if the others are to be solved. Moreover, to be lasting, a peace agreement must be positively supported by all of the parties to the conflict, including the Palestinians. This means that the Palestinians must be involved in the peace-making process. Their representatives will have to be at Geneva for the Palestinian question to be solved.[57]

Israel's bogey of a Palestinian state seemed to be coming perilously near.

Sadat rescued Israel. He had his own misgivings about a Geneva conference, which would be far too helpful to his rival President Assad of Syria. First, it would naturally involve the participation of the Russians, his protectors, and Sadat had tried to limit the role of the Soviets in the Middle East. A renewed Russian influence in the area was not in the interests of the United States, and Israel was able to make great capital out of this in her opposition to Geneva. Secondly, since Assad had intervened in the civil war in the Lebanon and acquired power there, he had also made himself master of the PLO, who had their headquarters in Beirut and a power-base in the South. Assad had probably refused to allow Arafat to speak to the Americans during the preliminary talks. He was noisily loyal to the Palestinian cause and would make certain that before the conference access to the PLO would have to come through Assad himself, which would greatly enhance his prestige. It looked as though Assad would emerge as the Arab leader of the Conference and Sadat sought to pre-empt this.[58] He resolved his dilemma by reverting to the classic principle of a holy war: he would not wait for the Americans and Russians to bring peace to the Middle East but would do it himself. His peace policy would come to be called the Initiative, but this Initiative was supposed to be a prelude not to a holy war, as was the way of such initiatives, but to a full and lasting peace.

On 9 November 1977 Sadat addressed the members of the Egyptian parliament and promised them that he was ready to go 'to the ends of the earth for peace. Israel will be astonished to hear me say now, before you, that I am prepared to go to their own house, to the Knesset itself, to talk to them.'[59] The delegates and Arafat, who happened to be present, all assumed that this was Sadatian rhetoric and applauded loudly.[60] Others thought that, because Israel would certainly refuse, Sadat was unmasking 'the true face of Israel, who presents herself as a lover of peace',[61] as a broadcaster put it. It is true that at first Begin's response to the offer was grudging but on 15 November he seemed to grasp its historic importance and invited the President of Egypt to come to Jerusalem the following week. Sadat accepted, despite the bitter opposition to his plan among the Arab leaders. As Pious President, he might have claimed that he was bound by the Koran to respond to any overture for peace (Koran 8:62).

When Sadat had equated Israel with 'the ends of the earth' he had pointed to the immense psychological distance that had developed between Israel and the Arab states since 1948. Ezer Weizmann, the Israeli Defence Minister at the time, has written that in the twentieth century there have been two great journeys: the journey of the first men to the moon and President Sadat's journey to Jerusalem.[62] In emotional terms it was one of the longest and bravest journeys that have been described in this book, but this time it was seen as a prelude to peace not war. When Sadat landed at Ben Gurion airport, just after the end of the Jewish sabbath, he made an almost magical impression: tall, beautifully dressed and with a powerful presence, he seemed a dignified ambassador from a distant world, who was breaking down the wall of hostility and arriving as a vanguard of peace. Glued to their television sets, Israelis and Egyptians watched their leaders talk together with apparent cordiality. It seemed that an unimaginable event had come to pass: the monsters had become human beings, who could converse together and perhaps live together in peace.

The theme of the peaceful pilgrimage continued the following day. By one of the holy coincidences that recur in the story of holy war, it happened to be the Eid el-Adha (which commemorates Abraham's offering of Isaac) and Sadat went first to the Temple Mount, the site of Abraham's sacrifice, and prayed in al-Aqsa. Then he visited places sacred to Christians and Jews: the Holy Sepulchre and Yad Vashem, the Holocaust Memorial. He began his speech in the Knesset that afternoon with a reference to the importance of the Holy Land to all three religions: 'We all love this land, the land of God, we all, Muslims, Christians and Jews, all worship God.'[63] This set the deeply religious tone of his appeal for peace. Constantly Sadat called for religious coexistence: the presence of the Christian and Muslim shrines in Jerusalem showed that 'politically, spiritually and intellectually'[64] Christians and Muslims look to Jerusalem with reverence and see the 'city of peace' as centrally important. He insisted that it was time to abandon the intolerance of the Crusades, and to return to the spirit of Caliph Omar and Saladin,[65] who had encouraged peaceful coexistence in the Holy City.

The theme of coexistence was central to the speech and this meant that, as Sadat saw it, the Arabs were now prepared to live alongside the Jewish state. Many Knesset members wept when they heard Sadat's extraordinary words: 'You want to live with us, part of our world. In all sincerity I tell you we welcome you among us with full security and safety. This in itself is a tremendous turning point, one of the landmarks of a decisive historical change.'[66] Politically, his speech was pure comprehensivism. He insisted that he had not come to conclude a separate treaty between Egypt and Israel but to settle the problem of the Arabs and Jews. The Israelis must evacuate the Occupied Territories and there could be no peace without a just settlement for the Palestinians, who were the crux of this problem.[67] Even the United States, Israel's first ally, had decided to face up to the Palestinian question:

If you have found the moral and legal justification to set up a national home on a land that did not all belong to you, it is incumbent upon you to show understanding of the insistence of the people of Palestine for establishment once again of a state on their land. When some extremists ask the Palestinians to give up this sublime objective, this in fact means asking them to renounce their identity and every hope for the future.[68]

This would not be welcome to the ears of his Jewish listeners, and yet Sadat asked them to recall, on this feast of al-Adha, their common ancestor Abraham who was prepared for sacrifice, even the sacrifice of his own son. It was a characteristically religious appeal but, given the increasingly religious nature of the Arab–Israeli conflict, a powerful one. Abraham had given his descendants an example of the sacrifice that the Arabs were asking the Jews to make – a sacrifice of lands and ideals that were precious to them and central to their identity: 'Abraham went, with dedicated sentiments, not out of weakness but through a giant spiritual force and a free will to sacrifice his very own son, prompted by a firm and unshakeable belief in ideals that lend life a profound significance.'[69] Begin had no intention of making any such sacrifice, but in his reply to Sadat he was content himself to point to a connection between Arabs and Jews, which concentrated upon Sadat's journey:

> The flight time between Cairo and Jerusalem is short, but the distance between Cairo and Jerusalem was until last night almost endless. President Sadat crossed this distance courageously. We, the Jews, know how to appreciate such courage, and we know how to appreciate it in our guest, because it is with courage that we are here and this is how we continue to exist, and we shall continue to exist.[70]

There was a defiance in the last words that Sadat would probably have understood very well. Yet on 20 November 1977 Sadat was the star: by his dramatic journey he had attracted the attention and sympathy of the world away from Israel towards the Arabs.

Yet the Arabs were not appreciative of this and events would very shortly prove that they were right to distrust the Initiative. At first, however, their rejection was muted. When President Assad of Syria formed the Front of Steadfastness against Egypt, only three countries and the PLO responded. Yet none of the Arab leaders went to the conference Sadat summoned in Egypt on 14 December. Sadat really thought that his Initiative could achieve a comprehensive peace, but when the American and Israeli delegates met at the Mena House Hotel, the empty seats of the Arab delegates showed the world that only Egypt was interested in making peace with Israel. It soon became apparent that, though Sadat may have been the first to take the initiative, he would not be able to retain it. Flags of all the invited delegations were in position all round the conference table; Eliahu Ben-Elissar, the head of the Israeli delegation, insisted that the Palestinian flag be taken down, and Sadat was forced to obey. Despite his insistence in Jerusalem that the Palestinians were the crux of the matter, the Israelis were saying no to direct negotiations with the PLO and no to an independent Palestinian state. Ben-Elissar then insisted that the Palestinian flag be taken down *outside* the hotel and Sadat was forced to order that *all* the flags be lowered so that his ditching of the Palestinians should not be so dramatically apparent to the outside world.[71]

Sadat's next meeting with Prime Minister Begin on 25 December showed even more strikingly that the Israelis had managed to take control of the peace initiative. Begin began by taking documents from his briefcase that purported to prove that, when a country had been provoked to attack, it was lawful for the attacked country to keep territory gained during the war. Nasser had attacked

Israel and threatened to throw the Jews into the sea, and, Begin concluded: 'So, Mr President, you agree that this makes us legally justified in keeping the territory we conquered.'[72] He was prepared, however, to consider returning the Sinai, as long as the Israeli settlements remained, under armed guard. Sadat decided to bring this humiliating open session to a close, but it was now quite apparent that he had been manoeuvred into making a separate peace with Israel, and that nothing was to be done about the West Bank, or 'Judaea and Samaria' as Begin provocatively called them in the open session. Then came a press conference when Begin made Sadat read out the conclusions of the meeting. Never again would Israel and Egypt make war and as for the West Bank: 'The position of Egypt is that in the West Bank and Gaza a Palestinian state should be established. The position of Israel is that Palestinian Arabs in Judaea and Samaria (namely the West Bank of the Jordan) and the Gaza Strip should enjoy self-rule.'[73] Mohammad Heikal recalled the devastating effect that this had upon most Egyptians. To see their President, flanked by Begin and Dayan, talking about 'Judaea and Samaria' was profoundly disturbing and showed an Egyptian weakness and willingness to compromise on essential principles that was entirely new.[74]

What Begin meant by 'self-rule' for the Palestinians was shortly revealed in what became known as the Begin Plan. In Gaza and the West Bank, Arabs should be given 'autonomy'; this was not autonomy in the usual sense of the word, but a political dependence and subservience. Israel would keep sovereignty of the region and asked that 'for the sake of agreement and peace' the problem of these territories be shelved for the present. In the mean time, the Palestinians would be able freely to elect their own 'administrative council', but security and public order would stay in Israeli hands. In other words, the army and the police would remain in the West Bank. Next, the 'Palestinians' should choose either Israeli or Jordanian nationality.[75] What 'autonomy' meant in effect was that there would be no 'Palestinians' left on the West Bank or in the Gaza Strip. It also meant that to make good Israel's claim to these territories, more settlements would be established there. On the subject of Sinai, Begin remained suggestively silent.[76]

On 4 January Carter and Sadat had met at Aswan and jointly declared that there could be no peace in the region unless the Palestinians were given self-determination, and on 18 January Sadat withdrew his delegates from the peace talks. It seemed that on the subject of the Palestinians he was too far in spirit from the Begin Plan to continue negotiations. But in fact Sadat was moved to withdraw by quite a different problem. He had got wind of the secret Israeli decision to 'bolster' the Israeli presence in the Sinai by establishing six more settlements there. Sadat had already shown that he was prepared to lower the flags of Palestinian independence and go for a separate deal, but on the subject of the Sinai he remained immovable. He would let the West Bank go and leave the Palestinians out of the discussions, but if there was to be peace the Sinai had to be returned whole and entire to Egypt. As he said to Ezer Weizmann: 'I am ready to conclude a contractual peace treaty, with ambassadors, with freedom of navigation, everything. But you are getting out of Sinai! That includes all the settlements! They've got to go!'

At this point the peace process slumped. The Arabs were unanimously agreed that the Initiative simply meant another defeat at the hands of Israel, who had no intention of discussing the Palestinian problem seriously and no intention of returning any territory. Many Israelis simply did not want peace if that meant handing over any land. Seculars saw the territories as necessary to the security of the state, but most people felt with the religious right that the West Bank and Gaza 'belonged' to the Jews and were essential to the Jewish identity. Ezer Weizmann noticed in the eyes of many of his fellow countrymen 'a strange glint of satisfaction' that the peace process had failed.[77] But other Israelis were ashamed that their country was lagging behind on the road to peace and it was during this period that the Peace Now movement was founded.

Yet America was determined to push the peace process through somehow, although only one leader in the whole of the Middle East felt that peace was either possible or desirable. When Sadat made his visit to America in 1978 he got a hero's welcome, but Begin, who followed him, got a very chilly reception. Israel seemed grudging and ungenerous beside Sadat, and Carter found it hard that Begin, whom he respected as a religious and sincere man, should be so unwilling to make peace. A period of tension between Israel and the United States is always uncomfortable for both parties, and it was clear that a compromise must be found. Finally Moshe Dayan and Cyrus Vance discovered a way to break the deadlock. Instead of going all out for a comprehensive solution that seemed impossible to achieve at this point, there should be a separate peace treaty between Israel and Egypt which could be negotiated now, and later further negotiations would settle the problem of the West Bank and the question of the Palestinian inhabitants. In the mean time, the Begin Plan should be accepted as a *framework* of principles that would govern the interim, transitional period before the full peace was signed. Sadat was by this time ready for a separate peace and this was also less threatening to Israel, because it shelved the problem of the West Bank in a way favourable to the Jewish state.[78]

From 5 to 18 September 1978, Begin, Carter and Sadat and their officials conferred at Camp David in the Maryland hills and finally, after a great deal of tension, Begin and Sadat signed the Camp David Accords. These would be ratified by the full treaty the following year. They stated that there would now be peace between Israel and Egypt and that Egypt would take back the Sinai. Israel would withdraw her troops and evacuate the settlements in stages and would be allowed free passage through the Straits of Tiran and the Suez Canal. Besides the peace treaty between Israel and Egypt, there was a 'Framework for Peace', which looked forward to future hypothetical negotiations between Israel, Egypt, Jordan and the 'representatives of the Palestinian people', who were clearly not going to be members of the PLO. These discussions would decide the fate of Gaza and the West Bank and the fate of the 'inhabitants' of the country, who would in the mean time choose between Israeli or Jordanian citizenship. The Framework foresaw a transitional period of five years, when the Territories would be governed according to the principles of the Begin Plan, with the inhabitants of the land enjoying 'administrative autonomy'. The land itself would still belong to Israel.[79]

To Begin's credit he had always made his position perfectly clear. He had no intention of giving up the holy lands of the Jews, and when he announced on the day that the treaty was signed that the government was going to establish twenty new settlements on the West Bank, nobody could accuse him of being inconsistent.[80] He knew very well that none of the Arab states would accept the Framework for Peace, that there would be no future negotiations with Egypt, Jordan and Palestinians and that things would continue as they were for a long time to come. In the mean time, settlements would establish the fact of Israeli occupation and make it very difficult to return the Territories back to the Arabs at any future date. When all the other Arab states, including Jordan, joined Syria's Front of Steadfastness after the signing of the treaty, he must have been delighted. Yet we know that other Israelis saw this hard line as a betrayal of the Jewish people. After Camp David, the far-right Tehiya Party was founded and members of the Gush Emunim would never forgive Begin for forcibly evacuating the Jewish settlers in the Sinai. They had seen the settlements there as the front line of the chosen people in the holy war against Islam. The peace treaty with the *goyim* was a sinful treaty with the enemies of God.

Had Sadat simply gone for a separate peace treaty, he might have suffered less from his Arab brothers, who denounced the Framework for Peace as a betrayal of the Arab people. It had sold out the Palestinians, betrayed the PLO, which all the Arabs had decided were the only valid representatives of the Palestinian people, and had betrayed essential principles of Arab unity by colluding with the United States and Israel, the enemies of the Arab people. They pointed out that Israel was daily saying that the Jews would never withdraw from the West Bank and Gaza and that the Framework for Peace was, therefore, a farce. Camp David had given Israel the chance to build more settlements and continue the draconian occupation of the West Bank and Gaza. As President Assad said:

> To us, peace means that Arab flags should fly over the liberated territories. Under the Camp David accords, peace means that the Israeli flag should be hoisted in an official ceremony in Cairo, while Israel is still occupying Egyptian, Syrian and Palestinian territory and is still adamantly denying Palestinian rights. [81]

On 31 March 1979 the Arab summit issued a communiqué which threw Egypt out of the Arab League, severed all diplomatic relations between Egypt and the other Arab countries and transferred the headquarters of the League from Cairo to Tunis. Egypt was now quite isolated from the rest of the Arab world. Instead of being its leader, she had become a pariah. Arab unity had been gravely damaged and the position of the Arab people consequently weakened.[82]

The Egyptians themselves became increasingly unhappy about Camp David. Many people were as distressed as their Arab brethren about the implications of the Framework for Peace. When Sadat tried to encourage Egyptians to visit Israel as tourists to help the process of 'normalisation', the Egyptians voted with their feet and refused to visit a country which was mistreating their fellow Arabs. They were also distressed by their isolation from the rest of the Arab world.[83] Egypt was now forced away from her Arab identity and the isolation of the country meant that she was inevitably thrown under the shadow of the West. This was very disturbing to a people who had seen their Arab identity as essentially anti-Western and they resented the increased Westernisation of their country after Camp David. They were disturbed by the procession of Western superstars through Egypt. When Frank Sinatra gave a concert at the foot of the Pyramids, many felt that this cheapened Egypt, which seemed to be abandoning its ancient dignity and becoming the playground of the West.[84] When Elizabeth Taylor visited Cairo in 1979, people were disgusted that Sadat greeted her as the Queen of Egypt because she had once played Cleopatra, and the army officers who were guarding her hotel and escorting her round the country felt degraded. 'My God,' one of them said. 'What are we doing here, guarding an actress?'[85] Sadat himself seemed to have become a Western superstar, jetsetting with wealthy capitalists and playboys. The adulation he received in the West started to go to his head: he became over-concerned with his own personality cult, treated the nation to long, rambling talks about his life, spent as much time discussing the filming of his autobiography with a director as he spent on affairs of state and had himself constantly, obsessively photographed.[86] Opposition to Sadat and disillusion with Camp David grew in Egypt, but none of his opponents watched the Pious President of Peace more critically than the religious.

The Muslim Brotherhood had not opposed the regime, but had tried to enter the centres of power themselves and effect a reform from within. Thus their magazine *al-Dawa* had not criticised Sadat or his policies. But the Camp David Accords broke this tradition abruptly. On 20 September 1978 an article bitterly attacked the Framework for Peace for the same political reason as the other Arab leaders, but the prime cause of the Brothers' disapproval was that such a treaty was a violation of the *Sharia*. Israel was now part of the House of War and no regime that claimed to be Muslim could make such a peace. 'If the Muslims renounce the effort to recover any part of their alienated land when it is possible for them to do so, they are all in a state of sin,' the author declared absolutely. 'History will judge the present generation harshly, rulers and ruled alike, for having preferred material well-being to honour and religion.'[87] Camp David was incompatible with Islam and the *jihad* was essential to true Muslim integrity. *Al-Dawa*'s cover for May 1981 depicted the Dome of the Rock, chained with a padlock stamped with the Star of David. A hand clutching a hatchet was about to smash the lock.[88] The Egyptian state might have signed a peace treaty with the Jews, but for Muslims the old problem remained: the third most holy shrine in Islam was under the control of the enemies of God. Sadat could be a Pious President in 1973 when he was fighting a *jihad* against Israel, but not when he wanted to make peace. The Koran did *not* countenance a peace that harmed Islam and continued the oppression of the Muslims of Palestine.

In 1979–80 *al-Dawa* published a series of articles on the children's page entitled 'The Four Horsemen of the Apocalypse' which identified the four enemies of the Muslims and suggested, by implication, that the Muslim lands faced an apocalyptic situation and that the Last Judgement was approaching. This feeling is shared by most Muslim extremists and naturally this gives a new edge to the *jihad* effort today, as it has done throughout the history of the holy war. The first of these four horsemen was the Crusader (the Christian or the Western imperialist – the two, for obvious reasons, are one). Not all Christians are Crusaders, the author points out, but many of them invade the lands of Islam and poison the minds of Muslims with alien ideas. Some of them assume a pious disguise and come as missionaries, evangelists or ecumenists; the orientalists spread doubt and confusion and discredit the name of the Prophet and of Islam with lying tales; and above all the imperialists seek to subjugate and persecute the Muslim people.[89] The second horseman is the Jew and he is quite different from the Crusader because all Jews are essentially evil. The author asks his readers if they have ever wondered why God had cursed the Jews, when he had once preferred them to all other peoples. Quoting heavily from the Koran, the author answers his question:

> His preference was met with ingratitude and denial of divine power. *The Jews say: 'God's hand is chained.' May their own hands be chained! May they be cursed for what they say* (5:64). It may happen that a man lies or falls into error, but for a people to build their society on lies, that is the specialty of the children of Israel alone! *The Jews who listen to the lies of theirs and pay no heed to you* (5:41). *They listen to falsehoods and practise what is unlawful* (5:42). Such are the Jews, my brother, your enemies and the enemies of God.[90]

Instead of making peace with the Jews, Muslims should 'annihilate their existence'. In the new, religious Egypt, the Muslim fantasies about Jews that had surfaced in the very early days of the conflict were being revived. This Islamic anti-semitism was a distortion of Islam itself as much as it was a distorted picture of the Jewish people, and by quoting the Koran out of context, Mohammad's early vision of coexistence with the People of the Book had been lost. In this view, Muslim integrity depends on a pious extermination of the enemies of God just as it depends upon a fight for the holy city of al-Quds. This hatred of the Jews also surfaces in the portrait of the last two horsemen of the apocalypse: the Marxist and the Secularist. The author points out that Karl Marx was a Jew and that Marxism is therefore part of the Jewish conspiracy to take over the world. The first Secularist was Kemal Ataturk and the author argues that he was a secret Jew who overthrew the Ottoman sultans to punish them for not giving Palestine to the Zionists.[91] A president who had not only made peace with the diabolical Jews but who was also courting the Crusaders could not be a true Muslim. In the Crusader Kingdom during the 1180s religious extremists had found peace treaties with the enemies of God intolerable and had insisted on war, and in Sadat's Egypt as in Begin's Israel new religious extremists adamantly rejected the possibility of peaceful coexistence, which they saw as a fundamental threat to their religious integrity.

Sadat had preached peace in the Knesset by evoking the old Islamic ideal of coexistence but the Egyptian Muslims saw the President of Peace as the enemy of Islam and Sadat perversely went out of his way to reinforce this impression. The peace process was from start to finish accompanied by a new offensive against Egyptian Muslims. His journey to Jerusalem had coincided with the execution of Shukri and the attack on the ulema. When he got back from Camp David in 1978 he started to curtail the power of the *jama'at islamiyya*, denouncing its members and suppressing their achievements such as the cheap lecture manuals. The students simply hardened their opposition to the regime. In 1979 at the end of Ramadan they staged a formidable demonstration which showed the government that they were still very much alive and the neo-Muslim Brother Yusuf al-Quwardi made a passionate plea for an Islamic identity for Egypt:

> Egypt is Muslim, not pharaonic; it is the land of Amr Ibn al-As [the Arab commander who conquered Egypt in 640] and not of Ramses.... the youth of the *jama'at islamiyya* are the true representatives of Egypt and not the Avenue of the Pyramids, the theatre performances, and the films. . . . Egypt is not naked women, but veiled women who adhere to the prescriptions of divine law. . . . Egypt is young men who let their beards grow . . . it is the land of al-Azhar![92]

The students did not want the West and they made sure that it would not penetrate the campus, which from 1979 to 1981 became an Islamic oasis in the desert of Sadatian Egypt, as Shukri's communities had tried to be. Films, theatre and art of Western origin or which presented the Jews sympathetically were forbidden; couples who violated Islamic law were physically attacked. The *jama'at islamiyya* fought against the West defensively by withdrawing from the world in a *hijra* and fighting against the alien values that besieged them. In 1980 this *jihad* became a more direct offensive against Sadat.[93] On the feast of al-Fitah which ends Ramadan, the students held a huge prayer rally outside the President's house exhorting him to rule as a good Muslim. On the Eid al-Adha they were forbidden to hold a camp on the Cairo campus, so they left the university, marched over the Nile and occupied the Saladin mosque for twenty-four hours. In the mosque built by the truly devout Muslim hero of the holy war, they denounced Camp David and condemned Sadat as a Tartar, because like the Mongols who had converted to Islam in the thirteenth century he was a Muslim only in name.

The Islamic opposition was not confined to the students but was spreading to the common people.[94] As in Iran, the mosques played a crucial role and did what the newspapers had been able to do in times of greater freedom. Certain sheikhs like Sheikh Mahalawi, Sheikh Eid and Sheikh Kishk became noted, popular critics of the regime and in their Friday sermons they regularly preached to huge audiences on forbidden topics like the Shah, corruption, Camp David and the iniquities of the Jewish people. Cassettes of their sermons sold like hot cakes and were suddenly ubiquitous: they would blare from tape recorders all over Egypt, in the fruit-juice stores, in restaurants and in garages. Egyptians drank in these fiery denunciations of the regime as eagerly as the Iranians had imbibed the message of Ayatollah Khomeini. The cassette recorder had become a powerful weapon in the holy war. As they listened obsessively to these militant sheikhs, Egyptians were learning to see Sadat, the Jews and the Western Crusaders as essential enemies.

In his book *The Hidden Pillar*, which was privately circulated, Abed al-Salem Faraj takes this new belligerent Islam to its logical conclusion in a way that is quite new.[95] He argues that the *jihad* was one of the 'pillars' of Islam and was central to it. This was an extraordinary innovation that, in those days of heightened tension, many Egyptians were prepared to accept. A Muslim's first duty was the war against the Jews for the recovery of al-Quds, but first Muslims must fight a *jihad* against their Tartar rulers who were all 'apostates from Islam, nourished at the table of colonialism, be it Crusader, communist or Zionist'.[96] Once they had Islamised their countries, Muslims could fulfil their sacred duty of fighting a *jihad* against the rest of the world. Where the Islamic students' union and Shukri's followers had begun by tackling their own acute problems and had become enemies of the regime at a later, secondary stage, Faraj's starting point was not *hijra* but *jihad*. He thus limited Islam to one aggressive doctrine and excluded many other more complex traditions, in the same way as Crusaders and religious Zionists had produced caricatures of their religion. Faraj's militancy was closer to the post-revolutionary militancy of Khomeini in its focus on the *jihad*. Saladin certainly saw the *jihad* against the Franks as central to the Islamic identity but he was quite prepared eventually to sign a peace treaty with Richard. His *jihad* had been inspired by the aggression of the Franks, but Faraj's book was a reaction against the new peace. Before 1977 the 'Tartars' had at least been committed to the struggle against Zionism, he explained, but now that Sadat had betrayed Islam the people must take the initiative and make war themselves.

The members of the Jihad group to which Khaled Islambouli belonged had Faraj as their spiritual guide and dedicated themselves to the *jihad*. The organisation of the movement was both compact and loose. Members belonged to cells and each cell was called an *anqud*, a bunch of grapes.[97] If one *anqud* were plucked from the vine, the others could continue to thrive. Secrecy was now essential, for belonging to any controversial organisation was extremely perilous. Sadat had become obsessed with the need to uproot all the opposition that was building up against him in Egypt, and in 1978, during the peace process, he declared war against thousands of his own people by issuing what he called the Law of Shame. Any deviation in thought, word or deed from the establishment line was punished with loss of civil rights, withdrawal of passports and sequestration of property. Citizens were forbidden to criticise Islam, the state or its policies. (In Sadat's eyes 'Islam', of course, meant something very different from the way extremists saw religion.) Egyptians were also forbidden to join organisations, take part in broadcasts or issue publications that threatened 'national unity or social peace'. Private criticism of the regime was also forbidden and anybody who gave 'a bad example to the young' in word or deed was subject to the Law of Shame. This was naturally as repugnant to the Islamists as Camp David and increased the determination of men like Khaled Islambouli to rid Egypt of the tyrant.[98]

In the last months of his life, Sadat's iron-fist policy tightened its grip. On 5 September 1981 he arrested 1536 of his opponents: cabinet ministers, politicians, journalists, judges, intellectuals, sheikhs and members of Islamic groups were rounded up and thrown into prison without trial. Sadat seemed out of control. At a press conference he announced that his security forces were still rounding up the last of his enemies. When an American journalist asked him if he had cleared his action with President Reagan during his visit to the United States the week before, Sadat completely lost his temper: 'If this was not a free country,' he said, 'I would have you shot.'[99] Realising that he had made a dreadful impression, he tried again on 15 September in a televised fireside chat to the nation which lasted four and a half hours and which became an incoherent rant. During the last hour he attacked

his Islamic opponents in a way that gave grave offence. He sneered at the girls in their 'black tents' and the bearded young men;[100] he attacked Sheikh Mahalawi viciously and concluded: 'Now this lousy Sheikh finds himself thrown into a prison-cell, like a dog.'[101] One of the Islamists in prison was Mohammad Islambouli, the brother of Sadat's assassin.

On 23 September First Lieutenant Khaled Islambouli was told by his commanding officer that he had been chosen to take part in the victory parade commemorating the October War of 1973. At first he protested: it was the Eid al-Adha and he had been going to spend the day with his family. After some more argument, the officer repeated his order and Khaled said: 'Very well; I accept. Let God's will be done.'[102] He had taken up the duty of the *jihad*. First he went to consult Faraj, who issued a *fatwa* ordering the assassination. Next he consulted Colonel Zumr, the military head of his *anqud*, but the Colonel opposed the plan: killing the President was not enough. The *jihad* group was dedicated to overthrowing the whole regime and would be unable to do that before 1984 at the earliest. The *fatwa* took precedence over Zumr's judgement, however, and Khaled and Faraj went ahead with their plans. Faraj produced three companions for him and on the day of the parade Khaled managed to send the officers who were supposed to be in the procession with him on leave, replace them with his fellow conspirators, hide the grenades under the seat of the truck and carry the guns through the inspection points into the procession without removing the strikers. The four young men then rode forward to kill the President of Peace and achieve the crown of martyrdom.[103]

At his trial, Khaled gave three reasons for murdering Sadat. The first was the suffering of Muslims under Sadat's regime of oppression and tyranny; second was the Camp David agreement with Israel; third, the imprisonment of the Muslim clergy and faithful on 5 September. When he was asked if he had considered the effect his action would have on his parents, he replied, 'I thought only of God.'[104] Khaled, Faraj and the other three assassins were executed and eighteen other members of his *anqud* were sentenced to seventeen years' hard labour. The religious passion for the *jihad* is still not dead, however: during the summer of 1987 three leading members of the government were assassinated by members of *jihad* groups like Khaled's. There are frequent violent Islamic rallies where the demonstrators burn the Israeli flag and call for a resumption of the *jihad*.[105]

When Anwar Sadat signed the Camp David treaty he was signing his own death warrant. He must have been aware of the risk he was taking. On 20 July 1951 King Abdullah of Jordan was murdered on the steps of the al-Aqsa mosque in Jerusalem by Palestinian nationalists and supporters of Hajji Amin. The reason given was that dedicated to the *jihad*, and their members will permit no peace with the enemies of his grandfather die and has always shown a very healthy respect for the delicacies of the peace process between Israel and the Arab countries. But Sadat's death was different from King Abdullah's because it was inspired not solely by Arab nationalism but by religion, and the death of the Pious President has now set a precedent that no future Arab leader can ignore. In all Arab countries there are cells dedicated to the *jihad*, and their members will permit no peace with the enemies of God. Sadat's death shows how thoroughly the old secular struggle has become a religious conflict and it also shows that the holy-war mentality is stronger in the 1980s than it was in 1192, when Richard the Lionheart and Saladin could make peace with each other and still be honoured by their contemporaries.

In 1987 the prospect of further peace talks seems remote. On both sides of the conflict any peace move is opposed by the religious extremists and Israel is as reluctant to come to the conference table as she was ten years ago. Peace is becoming very dangerous for other people as well as presidents. PLO veteran Issam

Satawi, who had taken part in private discussions with Israelis, was murdered by more extreme Palestinians, who accused him of being an agent of Israel, the CIA and British intelligence.[106] In 1986 the Israeli government made it illegal for Israelis to take part in such peace initiatives and three Israelis who defied that law and met PLO officials in Romania were arrested on their return. As Uri Avnery, who masterminded these meetings, remarked sadly: 'Meeting for peace is now a crime. Meeting for war remains a virtue.'[107] Arabs and Jews both expressed a strong reluctance to make peace after Sadat had made his journey to Jerusalem in 1977, and this reluctance has given place to an absolute veto.

The new religious movements on both sides of the conflict are in many ways remarkably similar, though there are differences of emphasis between the Jewish and the Islamic movements. The faith of the Israeli right focuses largely on the ideal of the Holy Land which God promised to his chosen people, while the new Islamists tend to focus on the Islamic ideal of the just society, though they seem to be making towards Saladin's view of the Holy City. But both Jewish and Islamic enthusiasts insist upon replacing secular government with a religious government, both are convinced of an impending apocalypse, both are anxious to shake off Western patronage and to return to the rule of God and all are ready to take unreasonable risks or even to face death in the holy cause. Jews and Muslims both denounce each other as the enemies of God and see the annihilation and destruction of these enemies as a prime religious duty. It is a more extreme religious enthusiasm than that which inspired even the most fervent of the Crusaders, who shared some of these enthusiasms with their modern counterparts. Even the most zealous Crusaders were content to live under a secular form of government in the Holy Land. These religious groups may not prove as powerful as the Ayatollah Khomeini's Islamic revolution, but they apply formidable pressure that no Arab or Jewish government can ignore, and they also exacerbate the tension in the area, giving the struggle an absolute quality, which must affect their more secular countrymen.

It seems that holy war is now so deeply embedded in the area that a peace initiative is simply a prelude to a new holy war. Sadat's journey to Jerusalem led inexorably to the New Jihad Group and the holy-war initiative of Faraj and Khaled. In 1982 the Israelis launched Operation Peace for Galilee, that was described by Ariel Sharon as a defensive action to free Israelis near the northern borders from PLO terrorist attacks.[108] But this peaceful initiative was the prelude to a brutal and aggressive invasion of the Lebanon. It seems that Sadat's journey to Jerusalem was also a prelude to this offensive: it is likely that without the Camp David treaty Israel would not have been able to undertake such a massive invasion, because this would have left the Egyptian border undefended.[109] During the Lebanon war, the new Shiite *jihad* against the United States and the Israelis introduced a terrifying new religious element into the conflict. In the Middle Ages one holy war led to another, but today a peace initiative also seems to lead to a new holy war. In this increasingly religious climate, values become more and more absolute and bound up with ideals that are seen as sacred to national and religious integrity. Where seculars on both sides have shown that they can be willing to make peace, the religious absolutism on both sides is making peace impossible.

The story of Anwar Sadat, like the story of Mohammad Reza Pahlavi, indicates that many Muslims see the Western world as quite as dangerous as the State of Israel. But it is important to note that Islam is not a religion that puts the values of the 'East' against those of the West. Islam is a universal religion: it has European and West Indian members as well as Asians and African. Islam is not against the West *per se*, but during this century the West has been inimical to the Muslim world, by implanting the State of Israel and continuing to support it despite the suffering of the Palestinians, by a project of ruthless colonialism and then of blind exploitation of Muslim countries. It is no accident that Muslim fundamentalists call Western imperialism *al-Salibiyya*, the Crusade, for in the Crusades they suffered their first Western invasion.

Yet Carter would not have seen himself as an imperialist when he organised Camp David. He is a devout Christian baptist, firmly committed to the cause of peace. He would have thought that he was doing good and must be horrified to see how his efforts have backfired. He genuinely seems to have personally liked Sadat more than Begin, rather to the latter's chagrin. But in his public addresses Carter showed very clearly where his sympathies in the conflict really lay. In 1978, at the time of the Accords, he said: 'Israel is a return at last to the Bible land from which the Jews were driven so many hundred years ago, the establishment of the nation of Israel is the fulfilment of biblical prophecy and the very essence of fulfilment.'[110] They are words that could have been spoken by a member of Gush Emunim. Carter's Christian perspective and his biblical heritage made it impossible for him to see the land as anything but the Land of Israel. In this Carter seems the very obverse of a medieval Crusader, who persecuted the Jews. But Carter's words do show a blindness to the Palestinian claim, because he completely ignores the 1200 years of Arab Palestine. In this he was a true Crusader.

Even though he was harassed by the hostage crisis in Iran at the time of the Camp David treaty, Carter never stopped working for the peace between Israel and Egypt. Where the Crusader wanted to bring war to the region, Carter wanted to bring peace. His was the last American initiative for peace. His successor Ronald Reagan has shown himself to be far more blind to the Arab, Muslim world. His peace-keeping contributions were the brutal bombing of Libya in April 1986, as part of his Crusade against 'international terrorism', and the overtures to what he was pleased to call 'Iranian moderates' which led to the scandal of the Iranian arms deal and the deflection of the money to the Contra terrorists of Nicaragua. He has made it quite clear that he will not countenance an independent Palestinian state,[111] and during the worst days of the Palestinian uprising in Gaza in the winter of 1987/8, his administration made it clear that there was nothing Israel could do, however cruel, which could endanger her friendship with America. It seemed to American reporters, who had been horrified by the behaviour of the Israeli soldiers during the uprising, that Secretary of State George Shultz had no idea of what had been going on in the Occupied Territories during the past twenty years. He replied hotly to an incredulous journalist who asked if there were really no limit to the administration's support for Israel:

> Israel is a democratic country seeking stability and peace and the ability to pursue its destiny. And we support those objectives. And we work closely with Israel. Occasionally we disagree, but through all of that, this relationship, as I have said, is unshakeable – that's what that means.[112]

For Reagan, peace involves violence, cynical manipulation and full support for Israel, no matter how brutally she behaves. Reagan has also allied himself with fundamentalist 'born again' Christians. Carter was a genuinely decent man and would not have resorted to these tactics, but he shared Reagan's blindness to the Arab viewpoint and a total identification with Israel. In trying to force a peace and encouraging Sadat to isolate himself from the rest of the Arab world, he was actually handing him enough rope to kill himself. Carter may not have been as violent a Crusader as Reagan would be, but he still wanted to manipulate the Middle East to fit *his* vision of how the world should be, even though that meant ignoring the wishes of the vast majority of its inhabitants. In that he was a classic Crusader, and his peace initiative not that much different in intention from Reagan's.

What America has been doing, with tragic results, is to ignore the Arabs and identity with the Jews. She is not maintaining the 'triple vision' that is essential to a basic understanding of the Jewish, Christian, Arab problem. Carter and Reagan, representatives of 'Christianity', are not eccentric figures. They are the result of a long Western tradition of crusading. Over the years, this crusading changed somewhat, but the essential spirit remained. We have now looked at the holy wars between Jews and Muslims in the Middle East today, and have noted the weaknesses of both movements. But we must now look at our own contribution and assess the Western weakness. In order to do that I want, in the next two chapters, to return to the story of the Crusades. The Crusades of the early thirteenth century show that though crusading was changing, it was still deeply important to Western Christians. When the direction changed, it simply found new forms of expression and it would continue to do so after the Crusades stopped going to the Holy Land. These new Crusades also show us the beginning of the creation of a new Western identity, as well as teaching us some last, hard lessons about the holy war. We shall then, in the last chapter, watch the crusading spirit as it continued to thrive after the Crusades to the Holy Land ceased. After all this we will be in a better position to understand how Carter and Reagan both spring from a long line of Crusaders, as do all those in the West who support their policies in the Middle East. Indeed in the very next chapter we see the origins of this aggressive Western 'peace-keeping'.

PART THREE

Crusading and the Western Identity

CHAPTER TEN

1199–1221

Crusades Against Christians and a New Christian Peace

It is a long time since we left the story of the Crusades, so it is important to recall the relative positions of Christians, Muslims and Jews after the Third Crusade had ended in 1192. The situation was the reverse of that which pertains today. At that time it was the Muslims who were in the ascendant, and the Christians and the Jews who were in a weak position. Saladin had conquered Jerusalem from the Christians and almost succeeded in ejecting them all from Palestine. Even though he had made some serious military mistakes, he was deeply loved by his people and there were scenes of loud lamentation when he died the year after the Crusade in 1193. After his death there was the usual Muslim squabbling about the succession and the unity of his empire fragmented, but this did not affect Muslim supremacy in Palestine. Indeed after Saladin's death, the Muslims relaxed and the *jihad*, which was never as firmly established as the Crusade was in Christendom, died away and was replaced by a more secular toleration of the Franks. The Muslims were no longer threatened by the Christians in the Middle East, and they may well have thought that a *jihad* was no longer justifiable. The Koran was clear that a *jihad* must be defensive and a response to persecution and oppression. But the Christian Franks in their fragile little Kingdom of Acre, that stretched along the coast of Palestine, were no danger to the Muslim world and were clinging precariously to the very fringes of the House of Islam. Even though the Principality of Antioch had remained virtually unscathed, the power of the Christians was drastically reduced from the substantial Western bloc they had established a hundred years earlier at the time of the First Crusade. As for the Jews, they were severely persecuted in Christendom and their position would further deteriorate during the thirteenth century, but in the House of Islam their lot had improved: Saladin had invited them to come back and settle in their Holy City of Jerusalem and this had given a new impetus to many Jews to return to the land of their fathers. This medieval return to Zion, which would continue throughout the thirteenth century, was supported by Islam, but had been bitterly opposed by the Christians from the West – again, an ironic reversal of the situation today.

In Christendom itself, however, there was greater confidence, and Pope Innocent III was about to lead the Church to fresh worldly glory; under him the papacy reached the zenith of its power. There was more building, more culture and more wealth: the powerful maritime cities of Venice, Genoa and Pisa had opened out trade and they were beginning to strike out their own path. Their attitude was more and more secular and when they traded with Muslims they did not see them as the enemies of God but as partners and business acquaintances. This was another manifestation of the more secular spirit in Europe that had also appeared in the Third Crusade. In this era of prosperity and power one might have expected there to be a decline in enthusiasm for the holy war, as there was among the Muslims of Palestine. We have seen that the holy war usually begins as a reaction to trauma and can often die away when the threat disappears. But this did not happen in early-thirteenth-century Europe. It is true that it was much harder to get an expedition to the East together. The loss of Jerusalem had greatly diminished the appeal of the Crusade, but the old hatred and intransigence towards Muslims remained. More significantly, perhaps, was the emergence of new types of Crusade at this period. Crusading was a practice so firmly embedded in the Western Christian identity that it would never entirely die. It diverged from its original, classic form of pilgrimage to Europe at this time and discovered new forms – some of which entirely contradicted the spirit of the early Crusaders a hundred years before. But this abandonment and indeed reversal of old values and aims is something that we have also noticed in the holy wars that are being fought today.

Yet a desire to recover Jerusalem was still very strong in many Western Christians, who continued to go on conventional Crusades for another sixty years. People tried to work out what had gone wrong with crusading and why an enterprise that had been so spectacularly successful a hundred years before should have failed in modern times. God must be punishing later Crusaders and condemning the worldly and secular attitudes that had characterised the Third Crusade. In this spirit a group of French and Flemish barons started to plan a Fourth Crusade in 1199; they wanted to return to the ideals of the First Crusade, the only Crusade that had been entirely successful. They had been inspired to lead a Crusade to the East by a popular preacher called Fulk of Neuilly, and their leader, Tibald of Champagne, approached Pope Innocent III with the project. Innocent was delighted: the loss of Jerusalem had wounded the integrity of the Western Church which in all other respects was rising to a period of new power and glory. He liked the idea of a Crusade led by barons, who might be more amenable to Church control than emperors and kings, and he probably remembered that the First Crusade had been a baronial Crusade. It seemed a good omen and he dispatched Fulk of Neuilly and Abbot Martin of Pairis on preaching tours of France and Germany, so that they could draw the laity into Tibald's army. But times had changed since Peter the Hermit and Bernard of Clairvaux had set Europe on fire with zeal for Jerusalem. Fulk and Abbot Martin both preached very movingly and drew large audiences, but the numbers of laymen who took the Cross were very disappointing, reflecting the current malaise.

In 1201 Tibald of Champagne died and Boniface of Montferrat took over the leadership. Boniface came from good Crusader stock: his father had gone to settle in the Holy Land at the end of his life, his brother William had married Queen Sibylla and fathered Baldwin V, and his brother Conrad had led Christian resistance to Saladin at Tyre after the disaster of Hittin. In August Boniface held a conference with his colleagues at Soissons where they discussed strategy. Richard the Lionheart had believed that the next Crusade should attack Egypt and find a new power-base in the Middle East from which to attack Muslim Jerusalem,[1] and though many Crusaders were disappointed not to be sailing straight to the Holy Land it was eventually decided that Cairo would be the immediate target of the Fourth Crusade. This was a very ambitious project: to attack a foreign power miles from any friendly base had not been attempted since the First Crusade and it required a great deal of planning and money. A fleet would be necessary to convey the soldiers across the Mediterranean, and already Geoffrey of Villehardouin had been sent to open negotiations with Enrico Dandolo, the blind Doge of Venice. After the meeting at Soissons, Boniface went to Germany to stay with his old friend Philip of Swabia, who was the son of Frederick Barbarossa and the brother of the Emperor Henry VI.[2] Henry had died in 1197 but Philip shared many of his ambitions and now he made a suggestion to Boniface that would ultimately change the direction of the Crusade.

When Henry VI had conquered Sicily from the Norman dynasty in 1195, one of his prisoners of war had been Irene Angelina, the daughter of the Emperor of Byzantium who was also the widow of Roger, the dispossessed Crown Prince. Henry had married Irene to Philip and the arranged match developed into a love match, which naturally involved Philip in the affairs of the Emperor Isaac Angelus of Constantinople. The sons of Barbarossa were deeply hostile to the rival dynasty in the East, and Henry had long planned to lead a Crusade against Constantinople so that he could be the Emperor of the East and the West. In 1201 a new opportunity presented itself. A few months after the marriage of Philip and Irene, the inept Emperor Isaac had been unseated in a coup led by his brother, who became Emperor Alexius III. The ex-Emperor Isaac was blinded and he and his son, also called Alexius, were thrown into prison. In 1201, however, Prince Alexius managed to escape and he sought the protection of his brother-in-law in Germany. Philip introduced Alexius to Boniface at the end of the year and made a very interesting suggestion. He was anxious to help Alexius to recover the throne, because this would make the Eastern Emperor a client to his rival in the West. He pointed out that Byzantium could be a valuable detour on his way to Egypt. By unseating the Emperor Alexius III and installing the young Prince Alexius, he would have a grateful emperor obliged to support the crusading effort. Boniface did not immediately commit himself. There were too many other necessary plans to be made before the Crusade got off the ground.

In April 1202 the Crusaders made a treaty with the Venetians, who hoped to make a considerable profit out of the holy enterprise. Enrico Dandolo agreed that for the sum of 85,000 marks he would provide transport and food for 4500 knights, 9000 squires and 20,000 infantry. Innocent was not happy about this arrangement, which let the entirely secular and materialistic Venetians play such a key role in the Crusade, and he deeply distrusted Dandolo. He was quite right to do so: Dandolo had no intention of fighting any Muslims because this would ruin his profitable markets in the East. At the very time he was making his treaty with the Crusaders, his agents had been making another treaty with the Sultan al-Adil, who had not retained his brother's enthusiasm for the *jihad* and preferred a profitable peace with Christians. Dandolo promised the Sultan that he would not counte-nance any attack on Cairo: he hoped to use the Crusade for his own nefarious purposes. An opportunity soon presented itself. By June 1202 the Crusaders had assembled in Venice, but unfortunately only half the number they had expected had taken the Cross and only two-thirds of the money they owed Dandolo had been collected. When Dandolo found that they could not pay him in full, he took control. He crammed the Crusaders on to the tiny island of St Niccolo di Lido and threatened to cut off their food supplies unless they paid up or else helped him in a project of his own before they went to the East. Venice had recently been in conflict with Hungary for the control of the Dalmatian trade routes, and the Hungarians had just seized the key port of Zara in modern Yugoslavia. Dandolo wanted the Crusaders to capture Zara for him with their huge army. To their credit, some of the Crusaders were disgusted by the idea of attacking a perfectly innocent Christian city and they left the Crusade, but those who stayed on to co-operate with Dandolo were probably more confused than wicked. Like many modern Crusaders, they would have felt, when they turned their Crusade into a Crusade against Christians, that the end justified the means.

On 8 November 1202 the Crusade sailed out of Venice and arrived in front of Zara three days later. There was a battle and the city surrendered on 15 November

and was sacked by the Crusaders and Venetians. Innocent was very distressed and at first excommunicated the whole Crusade – an unprecedented disgrace – but then he relented, realising that the Crusaders had been exploited. Dandolo remained under the ban but was entirely unperturbed, especially as Philip of Swabia had approached the Crusaders again with a very interesting offer. If the Crusaders put Prince Alexius back on his father's throne, Alexius would pay the money to the Venetians, would send 10,000 imperial troops to Cairo with the Crusaders and supply them with food and money. Finally he promised to make the Greeks submit to the Pope and the Latin rite. This was a very attractive idea: to restore the Greeks to the true faith would justify an attack on Constantinople and would be a great victory for the Crusade, which was now definitely under a cloud. Dandolo was delighted with the scheme, not because he cared a jot about the heresy of the Greeks but because he saw a great opportunity for Venice. He hated Byzantium, which offered him very poor trading terms, and could never forget that it was during a brawl in Constantinople that he had lost his sight. The Crusaders approached Innocent with the idea and, though the Pope was very doubtful about any project managed by Dandolo and Philip of Swabia, he could not resist the idea of a newly united Christendom with himself at its helm. The First Crusade had partly been summoned to heal the rift with the Greek Orthodox and if Alexius did force them to submit to the papacy, the Crusade would at last have fulfilled this important objective.

After spending the winter in Zara, the Crusaders and Venetians sailed eastwards in April 1203, occupying some important ports on their way to Constantinople. They found the country largely undefended, for the position of the usurping Emperor was very weak indeed. The imperial army now consisted mainly of mercenaries, many of whom were Franks whose loyalty clearly could not be trusted in this instance. The Emperor was not a man to inspire great personal loyalty and, when he saw the crusading fleet sailing up the Bosphorus, he realised that all was over and fled from the city with his family. The young Prince Alexius had assured the Crusaders, most unrealistically, that the Byzantines would greet them as liberators, but the Byzantines had bad memories of Crusaders and were outraged by this new Western interference in their affairs. They firmly closed their gates to the Crusaders and brought the blind former Emperor Isaac out of prison and reinstalled him as emperor. Now that his father was back on the throne, they told Alexius, there need be no more trouble. Up to this point, Alexius had behaved as though his father did not exist, but he could not very well quarrel with this. But the Crusaders were not satisfied because they needed Alexius to be in a position of power to accomplish their grand design. They insisted that Alexius should be a co-emperor and on 1 August 1203 Alexius was solemnly enthroned in St Sophia as his father's colleague.

But once he was on the throne Alexius discovered that he could not keep the promises he had made to the Crusaders. Naturally the Greeks refused to submit to Rome and the Latin rite. Neither could Alexius pay the Venetians: his father had been a very extravagant ruler and the Empire was in financial straits. He also found that he needed the Crusaders to stay on in Constantinople simply to keep him on his throne, so the Crusade was grounded again. An intolerable situation developed in Constantinople that winter. The Greeks hated to see the Franks strolling arrogantly through their city as though they owned it; drunken Crusaders often pillaged the villages of the suburbs and there was a very dangerous fire in the city when the Crusaders piously set fire to a mosque which had been built for visiting Muslim traders. The new emperors proved to be quite inadequate and were hated because of their connection with the Franks. Finally in February 1204 there was a palace revolution: Alexius was strangled and Isaac died of grief a few days later, helped on, no doubt, by ill-treatment in prison. Alexius Musuphlus, the son-in-law of Alexius III, ascended the imperial throne as Alexius V.

The revolution was a direct challenge to the Crusaders. For some time Dandolo had been trying to persuade them that the only way out of the mess was a full-scale assault on the city and now they decided to follow this advice and put a Frankish emperor on the imperial throne. Any pretence that this Crusade was going to get back on course and fight Muslims in Egypt was abandoned, and the Fourth Crusade became a holy war against Greek Orthodox Christians, who had been the first official 'enemy' of the West, ever since the distant days of Charlemagne.

The Crusaders attacked the city on 6 April. At first the Greeks fought back energetically but they were demoralised by the years of internal revolution within their empire and the mercenaries became quickly exhausted and could fight no more. Within ten days the city had submitted to the Crusaders, who entered the city in triumph. Boniface and the Doge were installed in the imperial palace and gave their troops permission to loot and pillage Constantinople, which for centuries had filled the Christians of Europe with envy and a burning sense of inferiority. The sack of Constantinople was one of the great crimes of history. For three days the Venetians and Crusaders rushed through the streets, raping, killing and pillaging with a horrible eagerness. Women and children lay dying in the streets and nuns were raped in their convents. The Venetians knew the value of the treasures that they carefully purloined to adorn their own cities, churches and palaces, but the Crusaders from northern Europe simply went on the rampage. In the great basilica of St Sophia drunken soldiers tore down the great silk hangings and trampled the sacred books and icons underfoot, and a prostitute sat on the Patriarch's throne singing bawdy songs. Palaces and hovels alike were vandalised. The chronicler Geoffrey Villehardouin wrote that never since the creation of the world had so much booty been taken from a city: no one could possibly count the piles of gold, silver and jewels or the bales of precious materials.[3] Nothing could have better illustrated the deep hatred which had always filled Crusaders when they confronted the magnificent capital of the Eastern empire that belonged to the Greeks, whom they had so often accused of treachery, effeminacy and cowardice, but who had really made them feel their own weakness too acutely for comfort.

After the carnage, the Crusaders and Venetians appointed Count Baldwin IX of Flanders and Hainault (a compromise choice) to be the Latin Emperor of Byzantium and he was crowned with great pomp in the pillaged St Sophia. For fifty-seven miserable years there was a Western Emperor in Constantinople and a Western empire in the East which the Latins called Romania. It seemed to the exultant Crusaders that the whole of the East was about to submit to the Roman Church and that the power of Western Christendom had been dramatically enlarged. With such a magnificent new power-base in Byzantium, the reconquest of Jerusalem and the Holy Land would surely be only a matter of time. The Crusaders had always coveted the great relic collection in Constantinople and had considered the Greeks unworthy of this spiritual treasure, but now the Crusaders had captured this holy power for the West and many priceless relics were taken back to Europe. The Crusade seemed to have enriched Christendom spiritually and materially. Pope Innocent III, who had been horrified when he heard about the sack of Constantinople, still could not conceal his satisfaction when he contemplated this victory over the Eastern Church, which had for so long refused to submit to the ever more powerful Western Pope.[4] Now the Greeks had been brought to heel and their humiliation would surely hasten their conversion. For 150 years there had been tension and hostility between the Eastern and Western Churches, but now there would be a newly united Christendom.[5] But later, when he heard that his papal legate had absolved the Crusaders of their vow to journey to the Holy

Land, he began to have serious misgivings.[6] The Crusaders now wanted to divide their new territories up among themselves into fat fiefs, on the European model. They wanted to enjoy the spoils that they had stolen and bring the relics home to their grateful fellow Christians, who would be spiritually enriched by their powerful presence. The Crusade had shown itself to be an expedition whose only aim was to conquer Christian territory and would do nothing to win back Jerusalem.

As Innocent realised only too well subliminally, the Fourth Crusade was a travesty and a crime, which completely negated all the old idealism. Its leaders had wanted to return to the spirit of the First Crusade, but had in fact flouted some of the most essential aims of Pope Urban, when he had summoned that first expedition. Urban had told the Franks that it was criminal and shameful for Christians to fight other Christians. This had always been Christian teaching from the time of St Augustine. Urban had wanted the knights of Europe to stop fighting one another and expend their murderous energies on the Muslims. Further, the Crusade was to have been an act of love: the Crusaders were going to *help* the Greeks to recover their land from the infidel and to liberate these fellow Christians from the Muslim scourge. Now this Crusade had killed Christians, robbed them and destroyed the Greek empire. It was, therefore, a dramatic abandonment of the early crusading idealism, similar to the moral and religious reversals we have seen in the new holy wars today.

The Latin empire of Romania did not survive the century. In 1261 the Greeks managed to fight the Latins, drive them out and put a Greek emperor on the throne of Byzantium once more. But the ancient empire had been fatally wounded during this alien occupation. By parcelling up portions of the great united state into fiefs as they would have done in Europe, they undermined the strength of the country in such a way that it was very difficult for the Greeks to recover it later.[7] Further, during their occupation, the Europeans were just not sophisticated enough to understand the complex role that the Greeks had been playing for years in fending

off the Muslim advance. Crusaders had always been angered and scandalised by the
way the Byzantine emperors had played off one Muslim ruler against another and
had preferred to negotiate when war could be avoided. But in this way the
Byzantines had been able to conserve their internal strength instead of indulging in
bloody and wasteful wars, as well as weaken the strength of the various Muslim
empires. They had thus been a bulwark between Islam and Western Christendom.
But this subtlety was quite lost on the Latins and it may be that their conquest of
Constantinople gravely weakened the Greek empire and hastened her final defeat
by the Ottoman Turks in 1453. If this is so,[8] the Crusade would have actually
helped the cause of Islam and in this it certainly reflected the feelings of some past
Crusaders who had often hated 'the Greeks' more than the Muslims.

Byzantium can be seen as one of the greatest casualties of the Crusades.[9] The
Crusaders had helped to destroy a great and noble empire, which had remained far
more true to the spirit of the gospels than the Western Church. The Greeks had
never abandoned the ideals of pacifism, had never indulged a cult of war and,
though they had sometimes made serious mistakes, they had survived for
centuries living side by side with other great cultures in the East. Byzantium had
lived alongside the Zoroastrian pre-Islamic Sassanid empire of Persia, beside the
ancient non-Christian cultures of the Near East and had finally coexisted in
relative harmony beside Islam, as a respected and powerful neighbour. The Greeks
had been enriched by these contacts with other cultures and had developed a
tradition of learning, art, scholarship and love of the intellect that was peculiarly
their own. During the long and bloody history of the Crusades it is often refreshing
to read of the forbearance and good sense of the Greek emperors in not only putting
up with but actually trying to help the churlish Crusaders from Europe. Now the
Latins had deprived themselves of all this Greek wisdom. Instead of living side by
side with other cultures, the Crusaders had opted for a far narrower perspective and
demonstrated graphically that they not only wanted no contact or coexistence
with Islam; they did not even want to live side by side with their fellow Christians.
The sack of Constantinople, of course, put paid to any hopes of unity between the
Eastern and Western Churches, which both sides had confidently expected until
this date, whatever the tension. The Greeks could never forgive the Fourth
Crusade and the West had caused the scandal of a permanently divided
Christendom. The hatred of the Latins for the Greeks still survives in our use of
the adjective 'byzantine' to describe a frame of mind or type of behaviour that
prefers pointless and arcane subtlety for its own sake to plainer, more straight-
forward dealings. This is clearly a distortion that has come down to us from the
Crusaders themselves.

The next Crusade was an even more shocking flouting of the rule that Christians
should not kill other Christians. It is as though Christian aggression was
frustrated, now that the new Muslim power made crusading less desirable and so
needed new outlets, nearer to home. It was another example of the way that a
holy-war mentality tends to turn inwards upon itself and create either a civil war
or serious religious conflict and division. This new type of Crusade was instigated
by Pope Innocent III, and here we see a new type of Western leader, who turns a
blind eye to inconvenient realities and manipulates events to further his own
projects. Innocent uses language that is perhaps alien to us, who may not be so
familiar with Catholic or biblical imagery. But he is also a very familiar figure
indeed in his organisation of this infamous diversion of crusading from Jerusalem
to Europe. This Crusade was called to fight not the Muslims in the Near East but
Christians in the south of France. It has been suggested that Innocent continued to
feel very guilty about the sack of Constantinople and that this prompted him to
summon the new Crusade in 1209 against 'heretics',[10] who lived a devout

*Crusades
Against
Christians and
a New
Christian
Peace*

293

Christian life but who held different beliefs from the Catholics. However strongly Innocent felt about this heresy, two wrongs do not make a right. He could not absolve his own conscience for the crimes done to the Greeks by this new crusading initiative which slaughtered hundreds of other Christians and also led to a long and painful civil war in which many orthodox Catholics were killed.

From the middle of the twelfth century,[11] missionaries had travelled from Eastern Europe and had preached to Westerners a different form of Christianity which they claimed to be the true religion of Jesus. They found a particularly receptive audience in the region of Toulouse and Languedoc and there was soon a thriving rival Church down there, which continually attracted new converts. Languedoc had never been much affected by the Cluniac reform and the clergy there tended to be too complacent to encourage spiritual fervour in the laity.[12] The courtly culture of the south had developed independently of the Church and had made the region more secular in spirit, but the southerners were a deeply religious people and the new religion satisfied a strong spiritual hunger.

These new Christians called themselves the Cathari or the Pure Ones. None of their writings survived the Crusade, so our only source of knowledge about their faith is the polemic of their Catholic enemies, who may have distorted their teaching.[13] It seems that Catharism was another form of a dualistic religion that went back to the very first days of Christianity. It had inspired the Gnostic Christians of the second and third centuries and also the Manichees, who had come from Persia and converted many Christians during the fifth and sixth centuries. St Augustine had been a Manichee before his conversion and had fought the religion bitterly for the rest of his life. The Church has always tried to suppress this religion but has never succeeded in stamping it out entirely: there are still Manichees in parts of Eastern Europe today. Like the Gnostics and Manichees, the Catharists believed that God was engaged in a constant battle with an Evil Principle who was not divine himself, but who had created the world. The world was, therefore, essentially evil, but God had sent Jesus to save mankind from the world of evil matter. The Cathars did not believe that Jesus was God. He was an angelic figure who had not really taken a tainted human body, of course, but had only appeared to do so. Because he could not therefore suffer and die, he had only seemed to die on the Cross and had redeemed the world not by his Crucifixion but by being a spiritual teacher or missionary from above.

The Catharists spent their lives trying to purify themselves from the physical and seeking the spiritual world. They were not baptised because water was matter and evil, but they had a sacrament which they called the *consolamentum*, which severed a man or woman absolutely from the world.[14] Once you had received this sacrament you had to live a life of such exceptional purity that most Catharists received it only on their deathbeds. There were, therefore, two ranks in the Catharist Church. First there were the elite, who had received the sacrament and who were called the Perfect.[15] They lived lives of complete chastity, great austerity and strict evangelical poverty. Because food was evil, many of them were said to fast to death in a martyrdom called the *endura*.[16] The Perfect did not lock themselves away in rich monasteries, but toured the countryside in pairs, begging their bread, like the apostles. Even those southerners who were not converted by the Catharist missionaries were most impressed by their holy lives, which certainly put the orthodox Catholic clergymen to shame.[17] Less heroism was demanded of the Followers, who formed the second rank and the majority. They worshipped with the Perfect in a liturgy of repentance and lived according to the moral precepts of the Catharist Church, preparing for death and the final purification. They were not expected to be celibate, but marriage was forbidden as it was felt to give a hypocritical holy veneer to something inherently evil.[18]

Despite their obvious differences, the Catharist and the Catholic Churches were very much alike. The Catholics also believed in a struggle between God and a very powerful evil spirit, whom they called Satan or the devil. They renounced the world and the flesh, like the Catharists. The Church may have preached that marriage was a holy state but most Catholics *felt* that sex was evil, whatever the dogma. Heloise's letters to Abelard deplored their marriage as being worse than their previous fornication for reasons that were pure Catharism. In the Catholic Church ascetics were encouraged to fast themselves into a dangerous emaciation and some women saints actually ruined their heath and died due to this fasting. The orthodox also divided themselves into two ranks, with monks and nuns living the full Christian life and the laity living a diluted version.

Yet in very important ways Catharism opposed the whole ethos of crusading Christianity. Crusading was based on the cult of the Cross and the Holy Sepulchre, but the Catharists did not believe that Jesus had died on the Cross. Pilgrimage to the tombs of saints and veneration of relics had been crucial to Crusader piety, but a Catharist would not venerate either a tomb or a relic, because the dead body was a shameful husk, which the purified spirit had left behind. Because the world was evil, the idea of a Holy Land or a Holy City were contradictions in terms. But even more basically than this, Catharists were strictly pacifist and non-violent. They were also very tolerant people and seemed to have enjoyed disputing with the Catholics in open debate, and instead of spreading their religion by the sword they relied on peaceful missionary work.[19]

The Catharists were not the only heretics in Europe. In the north of France there was a similar return to basic Christian principles and a denial of the rich, powerful Church of Innocent III. The Waldenses and the Poor Men of Lyons also practised strict evangelical poverty and roamed the countryside preaching to the common people. The particular danger of Catharism was that unlike these northern 'heretics', Catharism was not a disorganised, popular movement, but had actually succeeded in creating an alternative Church in the south of France. Catharists had their own bishops and dioceses and their religion was not confined to poor people on the margins of society but had penetrated many of the great southern families and households and was accepted and even respected by the Catholic nobility.[20] This state of affairs could not be allowed to continue and at first Innocent tried to fight it by sending the Cistercians to preach against the heretics, but the Cistercians had changed since the vintage days of St Bernard; having abandoned their former austerity, they had become very rich and were now identified with the establishment. The southerners were simply not impressed, and thought that the Catharists were far more Christ-like. Then Innocent tried to provide a Catholic alternative to the Catharists. A young Spaniard called Dominic Guzman had recently founded an order to fight against heresy by peacefully preaching to the people, instructing them in the truths of the faith so that they would be proof against the blandishments of the heretics. Dominic and his followers lived lives of evangelical poverty as the Catharists did and his Dominicans toured the countryside as mendicants, barefoot and begging for bread. This was the new Christian ideal of the thirteenth century, which would replace the old Cistercian elite. The Dominican was a new kind of monk who called himself a friar, a brother. Instead of seeing himself as part of an elite that was separate from the people, he saw himself as one with them and his way of fulfilling the gospel precepts was quite different from the way that monks had traditionally followed. Instead of making an exodus into a monastery or into the wilderness to pray, the friar went out to the people. Instead of taking a vow of stability and living in one monastery all his life like the Cluniac or the Cistercian, the friar was constantly on the road, sharing the lot of the poor laymen. The Dominicans showed a new thirteenth-century desire to imitate the life of Christ more closely and literally than the Cluniacs had done, and it was this desire that was also attracting people to the Waldenses, the Poor Men of Lyons and the Catharists. Dominic seemed the perfect answer to the Catharists, but though his Order of Preachers was accepted in Languedoc more readily than the Cistercians had been, and though the Dominicans were able to put up a good fight against the heretics in public debate, they actually made little impression.[21] There were very few converts from Catharism to orthodoxy, and the heresy continued to spread.

Innocent now felt that there was no other solution to the problem but the sword, and on 17 November 1207 he wrote to King Philip Augustus urging him to take an army to fight the heretics in the region of Languedoc, offering him indulgences that were similar to those given to people who went on a Crusade to the Holy Land to fight the Muslims.[22] For the first time in Europe, a Pope was calling upon Christians to kill other Christians: Innocent was setting a precedent for a new kind of holy war that would become an incurable disease in Europe. It looked forward to the wars and persecutions waged by Catholics and Protestants against one another, to the wars of religion in the seventeenth century and to the bitter, endless struggle in Northern Ireland today. It is important to understand how Innocent tried to justify his Crusade against Christians.

The letter to Philip is not a calculated, rational response to a political threat, but Innocent had recourse to the same imagery that we have seen used by Arab writers to describe the State of Israel today: the Catharist Church in the region of Toulouse was an abomination of nature and a rampant cancer in the body of Christendom. The heresy of Catharism, he wrote, 'gives birth continually to a monstrous brood, by means of which its corruption is vigorously renewed, after that offspring has passed on to others the canker of its own madness and a detestable succession of criminals emerges'.[23] This hysterical description bore no relation at all to the devout Catharists, but Innocent seemed unable to be rational. He responded to them in language that others have used later to describe an alien presence in their own lands that is threatening and traumatic in a way that defies rational analysis. Innocent could not see that the heretics had a point of view of their own. Even the Catharists' virtuous lives and wise arguments were satanic traps to entice the hapless Christians into a pit of bottomless evil.[24] This alien growth, gnawing away at the body of Christendom, he explained, cannot be cured by means of a poultice but only by the knife, so Philip must arm himself strongly and 'eliminate such harmful filth'.[25] The great difference between the Arab polemic against Israel and Innocent's polemic against the Catharists is that Innocent is writing not about people who belong to a different race or religion, but against his own fellow Europeans who profess to be Christians. Hitherto in crusading jargon 'filth' had meant only Muslims: in 1207 other Christians had become 'filth' meet only for extermination. A new paranoia was surfacing in thirteenth-century Europe, which narrowed the circle of what was acceptable and which introduced a new level of intolerance against co-religionists which was unique to Christianity until it appeared recently in Khomeini's new Iran.

Philip Augustus was a hard-headed man who was not likely to be moved by such fantasies, but he was not averse to strengthening his hold over his vassals in Languedoc by a show of force. Many of his barons, however, were very responsive to this rhetoric and at a time when the enthusiasm for a Crusade against the Muslims in the Holy Land seemed on the wane, frustrated Crusaders were eager to exterminate the heretics of Languedoc. Chief among these was Earl Simon of Montfort, who had joined the Fourth Crusade but had left when Boniface had decided to attack Zara, disgusted by the prospect of Crusaders killing other Christians. Yet he had no doubt that the Christians of Languedoc were inhuman filth. Despite this eagerness, there was no holy war in 1207. Philip asked the Pope for guarantees that the Pope was in no position to give, so the campaign was deferred for the time being.

At the same time, the Pope also instructed Count Raymund VI of Toulouse and Count Raymund-Roger of Béziers and Carcassonne to root out the heretics in their lands, but to his horror both refused to do so. Neither of them was a Catharist himself, but they respected the devotion of their fellow countrymen and certainly they were not going to slaughter them to satisfy some whim of Pope Innocent. Southern integrity seemed at stake, and when the two superpowers of the papacy and the King of France seemed to unite against the Catharists of Languedoc, many Catholic southerners rallied behind their leaders. Feelings ran very high and the holy war was precipitated by an act of terrorism. On 13 January 1208 Count Raymund invited Peter of Castelnau, the papal legate, to Toulouse for discussions. At first he seemed to waver, but then adamantly refused to accede to Innocent's demands and he threatened Peter and his colleagues with death as long as they remained in his lands. The next day one of his supporters stabbed Peter in the back after Mass and the legate died of his wounds. It was a clear warning to the papacy, and naturally Innocent saw this as a sign of the growing cancer in the south.

It is at this point that Innocent reminds us forcibly of modern leaders and statesmen denouncing 'terrorists' as inhuman monsters who are a peril to humanity and must be annihilated, but completely ignoring the part that they or their clients have played in producing the situation that made some people desperate enough to resort to terrorism. On 28 March 1208 Innocent wrote to the faithful Catholics of the south, telling them the story of Peter's death and presenting him as a martyr.[26] Raymund, he said, had quite clearly colluded with this murder. He had not only threatened the legate publicly but had also received the murderer with great warmth. This was very flimsy and circumstantial evidence on which to build such a serious charge, which had fateful consequences.[27] Innocent blithely drew the conclusion that the Cathars were not simply a threat to truth, but were also a direct threat to the peace of the region. 'For if pestiferous men of this sort are trying not only to ravage our possessions but also to annihilate us ourselves,' he explained, 'they are not only sharpening their tongues to crush our souls but they are also in reality stretching out their hands to kill our bodies: the perverters of our souls have also become the destroyers of our flesh.'[28] Yet if anybody was perverting truth here it was not the Cathars but Innocent himself. The Cathars, we know, had no such murderous intentions but were strict pacifists. Yet this did not seem to matter to Innocent, which reveals another flaw in his position: either he did not think truth mattered 'in a good cause' and that the end justified the means if it stirred up hatred against the Cathars in the south, or he did not know much about the Cathar doctrines. If this latter was the case, then the only 'heresy' he could legitimately accuse them of was a failure to submit to Rome and not, strictly speaking, a matter of 'truth' at all. Either way, Innocent was cynically manipulating the realities of the situation to suit his own ends. Having 'proved' that the Cathars were a danger to the faithful, Innocent summoned his Crusade for Peace: clearly it was his duty to annihilate this enemy, because the Catholics were going about in terror of their lives. The Church would move in to defend the faithful and, as a first step, he would excommunicate Count Raymund and his supporters, which meant that the Catholics were now released from their feudal oaths to him. But if this mild sanction failed, Innocent warned, 'we will make it our business to take more serious action against him.'[29]

It is quite true that the assassination of Peter of Castelnau was an immoral and dangerously provocative act. But the Pope was patently ignoring the obvious fact

that he had *himself* threatened the peace of the region four months before, when he had written to Philip Augustus urging him to invade the south. The terrorist may have killed one man, but the Pope had earlier urged Raymund to kill hundreds of southerners. Again one cannot help comparing this myopia of Innocent's with the one-sided view of participants in today's holy wars. When Americans accuse Iranians of 'terrorism' in taking hostages but ignore the fact that they condoned and encouraged the terrorism of SAVAK, when Israelis denounce Palestinian 'terrorism' but forbear to mention the terrorism that the Israelis have committed from the 1940s to the present day, when the Arab leaders condemn the Israelis but persecute and manipulate the Palestinians themselves, they are all indulging in this convenient loss of memory. Further, in Innocent we see the new, coldly manipulative Crusader, who is the first great aggressive 'peace-maker' of the West. In his letter he mounts a ruthless, lying attack on the Cathars, who are about to 'annihilate' his powerful Catholic Church:

> Since the Church in that region sits in sadness and grief with no one to comfort her after the death of that just man and it is said that the faith has disappeared, that peace has perished, that the plague of heresy and the fury of the enemy have grown stronger and stronger and that, unless she is strongly supported against such a new attack, the ship of the Church will seem to have been wrecked in that place almost completely, we advise all of you most urgently, encourage you fervently and in so great a crisis of need enjoin you confidently in the strength of Christ, granting you remission of sins, not to delay in making haste to combat so many evils and to make it your business to bring peace to those people in the name of him who is *the God of peace and love*.[30]

The new paranoia in the West caused the most powerful institution in Europe to feel deeply threatened by a sect of men and women who refused to touch a sword. These people, Innocent declared, were now 'worse than the Muslims', and must be treated as ruthlessly.[31] Innocent prepared his violent reprisal.

In 1209 the Crusade was ready. Philip Augustus, who was having difficulties with the English at this point, was unable to lead the Crusade so Arnauld-Amalric, the Abbot of Citeaux, rode at the head of the large army of Crusaders. The south watched the advance with dread and Count Raymund tried to free himself from the catastrophe at the last minute by submitting to the Pope, but the Pope was unforgiving. 'Once he is isolated and dependent on his own forces alone,' he said to Arnauld-Amalric, 'we can deal with him last of all and strike him down without much difficulty.'[32] On 22 July the army surrounded the city of Béziers and demonstrated the deadly determination of these new Crusaders, who were prepared to wipe out this southern vermin as cruelly as they had exterminated the Muslims and the Jews. When the city surrendered and the Crusaders went to deal out the judgement of God, it is said that the soldiers asked the Abbot how they could distinguish the heretics from the Catholics and that Arnauld replied: 'Kill them all; God will know his own.'[33] Every single inhabitant of the city was massacred. The terror this inspired meant that the Crusade met with no further resistance until it reached Carcassonne in August. To save his people Count Raymund-Roger gave himself up to the Crusaders, was thrown into prison and his fief was given to Simon of Montfort. In November Raymund-Roger conveniently died in prison, and in a letter Innocent hinted that he had been murdered.[34] Simon, who was clearly anxious to establish himself as a legitimate ruler, exhibited the body to the people and had it buried with great ceremony. He then continued the Crusade, capturing one Catharist centre after another, burning the heretics, and replacing the local aristocracy with a northern nobility. The Crusade was becoming an efficient army of occupation and when in 1212 it began to attack the area north of Toulouse, the southerners appealed to Peter of Aragon to come to their aid, preferring his rule to the rule of these cruel, ruthless northerners.

Simon had become one of the richest and most powerful landowners in France during the Crusade. Every time he conquered a city, he automatically became its overlord and gave it as a fief to one of his dependants. Yet it would be a mistake to see him as a secular Crusader, who made use of the Crusade to further his own worldly ambitions. He was a Crusader of the old type who certainly considered this war against French Christians to be just as holy as a war against the Muslims. Before he fought and defeated Peter of Aragon at the battle of Muret, the chronicler Pierre des Vaux-de-Cernay described him praying with real crusading piety:

> Having prayed at length and with great devotion, he grasped the sword hanging by his side and laid it on the altar, saying 'O good Lord, O Gentle Jesus! You have chosen me to wage your wars in spite of my unworthiness. It is from your altar that I receive my arms today, so that in the moment of fighting your battles I may receive my weapons from you.'[35]

But however holy Simon's motivation, the southerners increasingly saw him as an invader who was taking their land away from them and threatening their own peculiarly southern identity. There had always been some tension between northern and southern France; southerners had always prized their own sophisticated courtly culture and tended to see the northerners as crude and uncivilised. After Simon's victory over Peter of Aragon at the battle of Muret the southerners began to fight back on their own behalf. To talk about nationalism is anachronistic, but there was certainly an element of a nationalistic war here.[36] It could be argued that the first spontaneous nationalistic movement in Europe arose in response to the new Crusade. For nearly twenty years southerners fought against the northern representatives of their King, even though their struggle was hopeless. It would be 1229 before a later Crusader brought 'peace' to France and took the Crusade against Christians into a frightening new phase.

Innocent's dealings with the Catharists had shown the hidden insecurity of the thirteenth-century Church, which was at the zenith of its power during his pontificate. This neurosis meant casualties and the Catharists had shown how dangerous pacifism and non-violence could be in a world dominated by the habit and paranoia of a holy war. But the Catharists were not the only poor people taking to the road during these years. At the beginning of the thirteenth century, Europe was undergoing economic and agrarian upheavals which were bringing her into a new period of prosperity and power, but this inevitably meant that some weaker people went to the wall. In some parts of northern France and Germany many poorer peasants could no longer make their farms sufficiently productive or else found that they lacked the capital to bring them up to the working standards of this newly efficient Europe. Many of these were forced to sell their farms to better-off peasants and found themselves homeless and reduced to beggary. During these years a new class appeared. Whole families of men, women and children were forced to live wandering, mendicant lives on the margins of society.[37] Often they would be drawn to the new heretical sects that stressed the value of holy poverty and which told these poor people that their suffering had a value: it was *they* who were truly imitating Christ, not the rich monks and clerics of Innocent's Church. From this point, sects like this mushroomed throughout Europe, often becoming increasingly belligerent towards the establishment which was indifferent to their plight.[38]

When they first took to the roads, these wandering bands of poor people were often called the *pueri* (the children) in rather the same spirit as black servants are often called 'boy' by white South Africans, and in the year 1212 the *pueri* formed a

*Crusades
Against
Christians and
a New
Christian
Peace*

religious protest movement of their own.[39] A young French *puer* called Stephen had a vision of Jesus, who appeared to him in the guise of a poor pilgrim begging for bread. He gave Stephen a letter for Philip Augustus, in which he pleaded the case of the poor. There was a sudden surge of hope and excitement: it seemed that Christ had not forgotten the poor after all. He had shown that he was a poor man too and identified with them; he was ready to plead their cause against the rich and the powerful. At about the same time a similar movement sprang up spontaneously in Germany, led by a *puer* called Nicholas. In each country about 30,000 *pueri* formed massive processions, carried large wooden crosses and tramped through the countryside and through the towns and villages. They transformed their enforced wandering into a holy journey, following the Cross of the poor and suffering Jesus. These processions were also a powerful demonstration of the plight of the *pueri* and a dramatic way of pointing to their identification with Christ, who had had nowhere to lay his head. The chroniclers of the time tell us that as they marched they sang: 'Lord God, raise up the Christian people and give us back the True Cross.'[40] But these holy journeys were not a prelude to a holy war. At the end of the summer the *pueri* disbanded peacefully and seemed to disappear from history. Many doubtless joined some of the new and more belligerent heretical sects like the Waldenses who also preached a return to apostolic poverty, and as a distinct class the *pueri* disappeared.[41]

Yet they rose to a posthumous new life thirty years later when they became Crusaders. When later chroniclers read about these strange processions, they naturally translated the word *pueri* as 'children', without understanding its special social significance, and the strange story of the Children's Crusade was born.[42] In these later versions of their story, Nicholas and Stephen were children whom Jesus had inspired to lead Crusades to the Holy Land: they would succeed where their elders had failed, because Christ preferred their weakness to the arrogant, worldly strength of the older Crusaders who seemed unable to recover the Holy Land. Nicholas promised that he would conquer Islam by a peaceful missionary campaign. The children should march through Europe, cross the Alps and continue until they reached the Mediterranean. Then the waters of the sea would open for them as they had opened for the Israelites, and they would cross the sea dry-shod, conquering the Holy Land miraculously by divine power alone. Of course it didn't work out like that. The children suffered tremendous hardship on the journey, the later chroniclers related. Many died and many dropped out. Only about a third of the children survived and when they rushed down to the Mediterranean, the sea did not open for them. The German children began their miserable journey back from Genoa but most died during their return home. Some of the French children stayed on in Marseilles, still desperate to get to the Holy Land. They were picked up by unscrupulous merchants who promised to transport them to Acre, but who actually sold them as slaves to the Muslims in North Africa and Egypt. Years later one of them returned home to tell their sad story.[43]

The tale of the Children's Crusade is probably one of the most fascinating and popular of all the crusading stories and this recent explanation does make very good sense. Perhaps the creation of the myth is as interesting as the story itself. It shows how deeply embedded crusading was in the consciousness of Europe. When the later chroniclers read about the great processions of *pueri* who carried crosses and prayed for the return of the True Cross which had been lost at the battle of Hittin, they automatically assumed that they must have been Crusaders who were marching to Jerusalem. In some respects, the chroniclers saw these 'children' as fundamentalist Crusaders who were returning crusading to the pious days of Peter the Hermit. Stephen and Nicholas both presented themselves as Prophets who had been divinely inspired, and Stephen actually had a letter from Christ as Peter was said to have had. Like Peter the Hermit's Crusaders, the 'children' had a tragic fate. But in other ways this myth showed a longing for a Crusade that depended upon God, as earlier Crusaders had done. There was also a new pacifism in this myth of the children: Nicholas wanted to convert the Muslims by preaching to them, which was quite a novel idea in 1212.[44] The miraculous journey to the Holy Land would be a prelude not to a holy war but to a peaceful preaching campaign. At a time when people were becoming more and more disillusioned with conventional crusading, they were still not prepared to abandon the holy war but were seeking an alternative Crusade, which would bring God back as the focus and which made peace instead of war. But the fate the chroniclers dreamed up for their child Crusaders in the 1250s showed that there was little thought then of any such alternative being really viable.

There had been a similar dissatisfaction and frustration with crusading in 1212 and people had tried to imagine a different kind of holy war. The Crusade against the Catharists had been one of these new alternatives, but other Christians were imagining peaceful Crusades instead of a Crusade for Peace. Peter of Blois, the secretary of Eleanor of Aquitaine, wrote of the great hope and enthusiasm he had felt when the Third Crusaders had left Europe. It seemed impossible that this mighty show of Christian force could fail to conquer Islam and regain the Holy Land. But when he heard of the disaster that had befallen Barbarossa's army and of the military stalemate that made it impossible for Richard to recover Jerusalem, he had been convinced that a new solution must be found: in the future it would be the poor people, not the rich and powerful kings and emperors, who would conquer Jerusalem. They would rely on the power of God instead of their own worldly power.[45] At this time also the preacher Alan of Lille argued that in future a Crusade would only succeed if it were inspired by poor people, who like Jesus had nowhere to lay their heads.[46] Alan and Peter both thought that the new Crusades would somehow take Jerusalem peacefully and not by the sword. There was a link between this kind of thinking and the peaceful demonstrations of the *pueri* who had instinctively turned to the imagery of the pilgrimage and the Crusade to express their plight. Originally crusading had been a poor man's movement and had given the poor their first real sense of power during the First Crusade. The *pueri* would not be the last poor people to seek to change their lot in the context of a Crusade. The transformation of the story of the *pueri* into the legend of the Children's Crusade shows that people were beginning to dream of a peaceful Crusade and to seek an alternative Christianity which was closer to the life Jesus had lived on earth than the powerful Church of Pope Innocent.

There may have been no child Crusaders in Germany in 1212, but in that year Europe did witness the almost miraculous journey of an eighteen-year-old boy who quickly became known as Puer Apuliae (the Boy of Apulia) or simply Puer Noster (Our Boy). Frederick Hohenstauffen, the only son of the Emperor Henry VI, had been born in the south of Italy to Queen Constance, the Norman heiress of Sicily, on 26 December 1194. From the very beginning this child had been a controversial figure. The poet Geoffrey of Viterbo prophesied that the boy was destined to be the Last Emperor, who would unite the East and the West and establish a lasting peace,[47] but the Cistercian prophet Abbot Joachim of Fiore foretold that Frederick would prove to be Antichrist, who would wage war upon the Christians and be the scourge of the world.[48] Yet for the first years of his life Frederick lived in danger and obscurity. His father died in 1197 and Philip of Swabia rode south to collect the little Emperor and bring him back to Germany, but there was a revolution in northern Italy against the hated German rule which made him turn back, and Frederick passed his childhood as the King of Sicily, protected by Pope Innocent III. In Germany Philip of Swabia fought with Otto the Welf for the throne of Germany and the Germans forgot about Frederick; though the Pope had promised to protect Sicily, he did not push his ward's imperial claims.

But in 1210 some Germans remembered Sicily to further their own ambitions and Kaiser Otto IV, who had managed to gain the ascendancy, set off to conquer the kingdom for the house of Welf. As he watched the imperial army march through northern Italy and approach his own domain in the south, Frederick was convinced that he was finished. He had neither the army nor the support necessary to sustain such an attack but suddenly, at the eleventh hour, he experienced a salvation. Pope Innocent, who had been watching Otto's progress with considerable anxiety, suddenly excommunicated the Kaiser who was attacking his ward and gave encouragement to the anti-Welf faction in Germany. In September 1211 the German nobles, egged on by Philip Augustus, deposed the excommunicated Emperor and elected Frederick in his stead. When Otto heard the news he panicked and instead of pressing ahead to destroy his rival, he turned back and rushed home to Germany to save his throne.[49]

Frederick was saved. Within a matter of days he had been rescued from certain destruction and elevated to the pinnacle of power. Not surprisingly he regarded this salvation as a miracle, which proved that he was the chosen one of God, and to the end of his life he remained convinced that he had a special divine destiny.[50] His advisers urged him to refuse the imperial title: he could realistically rely only on the papacy for support and most of the Germans still supported Otto. Naturally Frederick waved aside such human fears and in mid-March 1212 he set out on a journey to Aachen, accompanied by a small band of retainers and trusting only in the power of God.[51] Europe watched the progress of this sunburned and raggedly dressed youth with astonishment. In April he arrived in Rome, where Innocent solemnly blessed his young ward and then he set off for the dangerous imperial land in the north of Italy. At Pavia, the story goes, the Milanese tried to assassinate the young Emperor, but he simply jumped on to his horse and swam across the river. The people of Cremona saw his survival as miraculous and greeted him ecstatically as the Angel of the Lord.[52] From that moment his safety in Italy was assured but the real test lay in Germany. Otto had journeyed southward to meet his rival, and his servants, who had ridden ahead of him, were actually preparing a meal for him in Constance when suddenly Frederick appeared before them and demanded their support. His dramatic arrival seemed another miracle,[53] and when Otto arrived three hours later he found the city barred against him. By this time the people of southern and central Germany were ecstatic about this astonishing child, who seemed able to defeat the rich and powerful by trusting only in the Lord, and in December 1212 he was crowned King of the Germans in Mainz. Innocent himself called him a David, who had defeated the giant Otto the Welf, and the people of Germany were convinced of his divine election. 'The child has conquered the Welf with heavenly rather than with earthly might,'[54] one poet wrote, and another troubadour sang 'Behold the power of the child' in his rhymed chronicle:

> Now comes the Pulian Child along –
> The Kaiser's sword is twice as strong,
> Whom yet the Child did overthrow
> Without a single swordsman's blow:
> The people's love towards him did flow.[55]

It was certainly true that the people of Germany took the child to their hearts; he had an irresistible glamour and yet at the same time he seemed one of themselves.[56] His homely face and clothing offset his foreignness, which could have been a fatal disadvantage, and the people remembered that, despite his southern blood, he was the grandson of the great Frederick Barbarossa.

It was this connection that finally persuaded the people of the imperial city of Aachen to open their gates to Frederick in mid-July 1215 and the young Boy of Apulia was solemnly crowned in the cathedral and sat on the great throne of Charlemagne. He then amazed his people again: immediately after he had received the imperial diadem from the Archbishop, Emperor Frederick II suddenly and unexpectedly took the Cross.[57] The effect was magical. The child's miraculous rise to power, his apparent divine election and his relationship to Barbarossa, who had lost his life during a Crusade, raised everybody's hopes. Frederick was already a young David who had cast the mighty from their thrones: would he now become King David who conquered Jerusalem?[58]

Yet in fact it proved more difficult to draw a Fifth Crusade together than anybody had expected. After the great Lateran Council in 1215, Innocent had sent travelling preachers all over Europe to preach a Crusade and had been quite confident of a success. He had actually written to al-Adil to warn him of the wrath to come and to advise him to hand over Jerusalem peaceably.[59] But though the common people were eager to take the Cross, the nobles seemed even more reluctant to sail to the East than they had in 1202. It really did seem as though conventional crusading was a dying enthusiasm and an anachronism. When Innocent died in May 1216, his successor Pope Honorius III found it very difficult to organise a Crusade: only a few nobles set out that year with King Andrew of Hungary. Honorius was also disturbed by a report he had recently received from the Kingdom of Acre, which seemed very worrying.

The popular preacher James of Vitry had recently become Bishop of Acre and he was dismayed by what he found in the Holy Land. The Franks did not want a Crusade, he told the Pope. They were wary of endangering the security of their tiny state and were afraid that a holy war would destroy the excellent trading arrangements they were currently enjoying with the Muslims.[60] The Muslims were also enjoying the new trade with the West, and their passion for the *jihad* had died a natural death after Saladin's death in 1193. Al-Adil had no desire to call for a holy war, though he was taunted for this by a few of the officers in his army, and his son al-Malik al-Kamil, the viceroy of Egypt, fully shared his views: he had excellent relations with the 3000 Pisan, Venetian and Genoan merchants and traders who lived and worked in Cairo.[61] It seemed that this secular contact had made it possible for Christians and Muslims to live together in peace to their mutual advantage, but it seemed quite immoral to the newcomer, Bishop James of Vitry. He was also disturbed by the Franks' oriental lifestyle and seemed to equate the Franks' abandoning of a Western cultural identity with a denial of the Christian faith itself. The Franks had gone native, he wrote in disgust: they were fitter for the baths than for battle; they did not let their wives go to church more than once a year, but would send them to the baths three times a week; the knights had love affairs with Muslim women, wore soft, effeminate clothes and were completely given over to lust and idleness.[62] They were very worried that a provocative Crusade from the West would ruin all this.

At first there seemed little danger. In 1217 Duke Leopold of Austria brought an army to the East to join the Hungarians, but nothing was achieved beyond a few desultory raids in the Galilee. Most of the time the Crusaders wandered around collecting relics and early the following year the Hungarians went home. Muslims and Franks both relaxed. But in 1218 three fleets from Frisia, France and England arrived in Acre and decided to revive the old plan of capturing Egypt. In May they sailed for Damietta, taking the Muslims there quite by surprise, and in August they actually managed to capture the city. The shock of the loss of Damietta was too much for the ageing Sultan, who died a few hours afterwards of a heart attack. To try to prevent a quarrel about the succession, he had arranged for the Ayyubid empire of Saladin to be divided among his three older sons: al-Kamil was to take Egypt, al-Ashraf was to have Jizra and al-Mu'azam would take Damascus and Jerusalem. But there was still dissatisfaction, and while al-Kamil was away defending Egypt from the Franks, some Cairenes took advantage of his absence to put one of his younger brothers on the throne. Al-Kamil had to abandon the defence of the country and rush back to Cairo to put down the coup. The Crusaders had arrived in Egypt at an opportune moment and there was panic in the Muslim world. Sultan al-Mu'azam sent a message to Baghdad asking the Caliph for help and a vast army was promised, though it never arrived.

In September the Spaniard Cardinal Pelagius arrived in Damietta as the papal legate and he provided the leadership that the Crusade desperately needed. He found that morale was low despite their initial success: the Crusaders were dying of an epidemic that turned their skins black and which killed one-sixth of the soldiers. Pelagius insisted that action was the best remedy, and in February the Crusaders managed to occupy the city of al-Adilya. The Muslims were now becoming desperate. They had heard that the Emperor Frederick was on his way to the East, once he had settled his affairs in Germany. Al-Mu'azam began dismantling the walls of Jerusalem and other forts in Palestine in case he was forced to hand them over to the Christians, but in fact morale was still low in the Christian camp. After the battle of al-Adilya there was a military stalemate and the epidemic continued to rage in both armies.

When Pelagius had addressed the troops before the victory at al-Adilya he had made a suggestion that was quite new to crusading. Once they had conquered the Muslims, he said, it might be possible to convert the 'perfidious and worthless people' to the true faith.[63] Hitherto no Crusader had ever thought of trying to convert Muslims; they had previously thought that the only solution was massacre, as St Bernard of Clairvaux had written a hundred years earlier in his treatise on the Templars. But we have seen that in the thirteenth century there was quite a new enthusiasm for preaching in Europe. This was largely due to the heretics like the Cathars. The Cathars had travelled around preaching to the ordinary people, who were still so ignorant that they were very vulnerable to the heretics. They naturally saw these Cathar or Waldensian preachers, who preached a return to poverty, as much more concerned with them than the official Church, who had been content to leave them in ignorance, and it had been to counteract this that Pope Innocent had encouraged St Dominic to found his Order of Preachers, to instruct the poor laymen as the heretics were doing. But not all the preachers went to the poor. Some started preaching to the rich and to the middle classes and gained quite a following. One of the most popular of these charismatic preachers was James of Vitry, who had now come out to Acre, with the idea of preaching to the Muslims. It was an adventurous idea, but as we have seen already, James did not see this as a substitute for the Crusade, which he regarded as essential, as did Pelagius. Preaching could only be enforced by the sword. James had, however, managed to convert two Muslims and, though he had never been permitted to enter Muslim territory, he used to preach sometimes on the borders of the Christian kingdom, taking the word of God to the front line of the holy war. Occasionally he sent letters in Arabic over the border, to explain the Christian religion to Muslims and when children had been taken as hostages in the raids made by the Crusaders in Galilee in 1217, James had baptised them and sent them home over the border: by filling them with the life of Christ by means of the sacrament he had made them Christian infiltrators in enemy territory.[64]

Preaching and conversion was in the air, therefore, but suddenly a new arrival in Damietta took a much more radical approach. During the stalemate after the battle of al-Adilya one of the most famous popular preachers in Europe asked

This friendly picture shows what might have been. In Spain, where this chess manual was written, Christians enjoyed very fruitful contact with Muslims, and even at the worst moments of the Crusades Christians and Muslims showed that they shared the same courtly values and were able to respect and admire one another. The game of chess itself is worth considering. It has become so much a part of our tradition that we probably seldom consider that it is just one of many gifts that the West has taken from the Muslim world. The very fact that the game was able to be adapted to the Christian world and needed only minor alterations to suit European players shows that Christians and Muslims lived in very similar societies, ruled by kings, knights and religious leaders in castles, which were fortresses against the enemy. Chess is a stylised battle where the protagonists face an enemy exactly like themselves, not monstrous enemies of God. But Christians and Muslims had even more in common with the Jews than with each other. Both worshipped the Jewish God and venerated Jewish Prophets and heroes. All three religions could, therefore, have lived peacefully side by side to their mutual enrichment, but instead they were torn apart by holy wars.

This picture *(left)* expresses the energy of Islam, which insists that Muslims must take action and make an effort to change the world. Sometimes this could be achieved only by war and early Muslim jurists developed a theology of the *jihad* – a word which means 'struggle' but which came to refer to the holy war for Muslim world domination. But it would be wrong to see Islam as 'the religion of the sword'. After the beginning of the eighth century Muslims abandoned their dreams of world conquest and formed normal relations with their non-Muslim neighbours. Within the Islamic empire Jews and Christians enjoyed full religious liberty.

We have no pictures of Jewish medieval soldiers, because by this time Jews lived as small minorities and had had to abandon their early holy wars. Jews seemed peaceful people, who enjoyed quite good relations with their Gentile neighbours.

This peaceful co-existence ended for ever when Peter the Hermit preached the Crusade in 1095 *(below)*. Pointing towards Jerusalem he inveighed against the 'Saracens', who were polluting the holy places there, and against the Jews, who had crucified Christ. As a result of his preaching thousands of men and women set off to the east to fight the Muslims, and some attacked the Jewish communities at home in the first pogroms in Europe. After that date Western people saw Jews and Muslims as the enemies of God.

But how could Crusaders square this violence with the pacifism of Jesus and believe that butchering Muslims and Jews was 'holy'? This picture *(above left)* reminds us that besides being the loving Saviour of the Gospels, Jesus had a more frightening role. Here he is the Word of God, whose coming is foretold in Revelation. In his mouth he carries a sharp sword to kill the pagans and has opened the Book of Life, which decrees that his enemies will suffer in a burning pit for all eternity. He and his army wear white, the colour of victory, to show that resistance to divine wrath is useless (Revelation 19–20). That is why heaven blesses the Crusaders: they are uttering God's dread word to the pagans and effecting the Divine Judgement by punishing the wicked. But to concentrate on only one violent tradition and ignore all those scriptures which preach the paramount importance of love is to distort the religion entirely.

In Christianity, however, violence had come to stay and the knight *(above right)* is a familiar figure in Christian art. *(Below)* The Christian Crusades inspired a revival of the Muslim *jihad*, which in some respects reproduced the pattern of the Christian holy war. But enthusiasm for the *jihad* waned in the Middle East, after the crusading threat had abated, only to revive in our own day in response to a new Western offensive.

The Crusades gave birth to the Inquisition; indeed religious violence tends to turn in upon itself and sets people of the same faith implacably against one another. This nightmarish scene *(opposite)* is played against a black, lurid sky and suggests the massed powers of darkness that the Inquisitors fear will overcome the light of the faith. Yet such dread does not appear in the faces of the judges, who assume expressions of studied calm and serenity. One has even fallen asleep; only one has noticed that people are actually being burned alive and he shows merely a well-bred surprise. When people commit such atrocities in the name of religion they cannot afford to *see* what they are doing. Instead the Chief Inquisitor wears a halo: they see their violent cruelty as 'holy'. They have condemned five heretics to be burned at the stake. Two are already burning and the ambiguous representation of their extraordinary sexual organs show that the faithful see heretics as perversions of nature, with the monstrous qualities that people had once attributed only to non-Christians like the Muslims. This dehumanising fantasy was inspired by a deep dread and insecurity about the Christian faith. The heretics are dressed in a special uniform to mark their separation from the rest of humanity. One has repented and been taken in hand by orthodoxy; the others await death with the unnatural calm of their judges. One turns away from the crucifix and seems obdurate to the end; he is right to feel that this frightened religion has nothing to do with Jesus but is haunted by inner demons.

This ultra-orthodox Jew in Jerusalem *(left)* is probably a member of *Neturei Carta* (the Guardians of the City), which accuses Zionism of being a Jewish heresy: true Jews should wait for the Messiah before setting up a State in Eretz Yisrael. They await the imminent destruction of the State and have withdrawn from it completely in districts like this, which exactly reproduce the old European *shtetls.* They are tiny circles of orthodoxy in the darkness of the secular Jewish State, which they believe seeks to destroy Judaism. In the placards on the wall the ultra-orthodox denounce Zionist leaders as 'Hitler' and 'Nazis'. Haunted by fear of annihilation, they cannot *see* that these are monstrous things for one Jew to call another. But secular Zionists like Amos Oz are filled with their own irrational dread when they see these *shtetls*, because their Zionism was based on a rejection of the Judaism of the ghettos. Oz flees the district horrified by 'the incredible vitality of this Judaism, for as it grows and swells, it threatens your own spiritual existence and eats away the roots of your own world, prepared to inherit it all when you and your kind are gone.' This mutual dread has led to strife and bloodshed as religious and secular Jews clash and fight each other in the streets of Jerusalem.

Other religious Jews have Judaised the old secular Zionism. As they dance the *hora* these settlers *(right)* are not expecting a socialist utopia but messianic redemption. The new religion of Zionism centres on the gun: outside this little circle of godliness is the darkness of the Gentile world. Jews must not try to *see* the Arab point of view, because this is outside God's plan. Instead they must fight a holy war against them until the Messiah arrives; then the world will have peace, for the light will go forth from Zion to the black world of the *goyim.* Secular Israelis of the Left accuse this religious Zionism of narrowing Judaism to such a tiny compass that it is no longer recognisable and fear that it will drag Israel into an endless, suicidal series of holy wars.

This Iranian crowd *(top right)* is not relaxed and cheerful like others we have seen but full of dread and dismay as the people carry home the bodies of Iranian pilgrims killed in a riot in Mecca during the *hajj* of 1987. They cry for vengeance against Saudi Arabia and the United States, whom they claim were to blame for this terrible and blasphemous bloodshed in the Great Mosque where all violence is forbidden. But they do not seem to *see* that it was the Iranian pilgrims themselves who were responsible for the carnage – for it was the pilgrims who instigated the riot and began the fighting. Instead they regard Iran as a haven of true religion surrounded by powerful enemies who seek to destroy Islam and the revolution. What has happened to that early Iranian confidence, and why can this crowd not *see* how deeply unIslamic their behaviour at Mecca was?

Pictures like this shocked the West. These Revolutionary Guards *(right)*, wearing the red bandana of the martyr, have volunteered for specially dangerous missions in the Gulf War and will seal their readiness to face almost certain death with a ceremonial drink, which will bind them together in close communion. They are listening to cassettes of the Ayatollah Khomeini's sermons. It seemed to us that a whole generation of young men was being brainwashed; but they are not the first young idealists who have been ready to die for a revolutionary cause. Further, this is not a Nuremberg rally. Khomeini is not whipping up mob violence and crowd hysteria; each of the martyrs has his own cassette and makes an individual decision. Each listens to his leader with a different expression. *(Below)* Soldiers remember their sacrifice today at the Fountain of Martyrs.

The cult of martyrdom in Iran is not a morbid yearning for death; there is vigour and energy in it *(above)*. Without this spirit the revolution against the Shah's powerful army could not have succeeded. Thousands of men and women donned the white robes of the martyr and braved the soldiers' guns to bring about a brave new world. But in those days Khomeini had called upon Sunnis and Shiites to unite against the enemies of the Muslims. These martyrs, however, will die fighting the Muslims of Iraq, who have different religious and political ambitions from the Islamic Republic. The former ideal of Islamic unity has been lost and Khomeini is waging war against Sunni Islam. More and more Iranians are becoming sickened by the torrents of blood that have been shed uselessly over so many years in the Gulf War, which Iran seems incapable of winning but will not abandon. It is ruining the economy of the country and wasting thousands of lives in a suicidal belligerence which springs from a narrow, dogmatic interpretation of the faith.

One of the saddest aspects of this seemingly endless strife is that even thousands of children, like this little girl *(right)*, have volunteered to be martyrs and have died on the battlefields. Surely the Prophet Mohammad, a deeply compassionate man, would have been horrified to see children being exploited and killed in a war against other Muslims. Khomeini's regime offends basic principles of religion and morality, and such a state can result in a sickening loss of integrity and an irrational feeling of dread.

When he prays at the holiest place in the Jewish world, this soldier finds it quite natural to carry a gun at the same time as wearing his prayer shawl and *tfillin*. Prayer is one of the commandments of the Torah; he may believe that defending Eretz Yisrael is a commandment of equal importance. Although we usually think that religion and violence are entirely incompatible, Judaism, Christianity and Islam have all, at different times and in different ways, seen warfare as a holy duty. Today in the Middle East the conflict is becoming more and more religious and this makes the possibility of a peaceful solution increasingly remote, even though we usually think of religion as a force for harmony and reconciliation. Some forms of religion encourage people to gaze only at their own traditions and discount those of others. They also limit their own traditions to a belligerent orthodoxy which will admit of no compromise.

Pelagius for permission to cross the enemy lines and preach to the Sultan al-Kamil. Most people would probably consider Francis of Assisi, who made this startling suggestion, as one of the most perfect Christians who ever lived. The gentle saint who wandered around Italy wedded to absolute poverty and preaching to birds and trees seemed to have broken through the hatreds of institutional religion and made peace with the whole world. He would seem to be far in spirit from the violence of crusading and yet it was no accident that he happened to be present in Damietta in 1219. Francis was devoted to the Church, unlike most of the other European Christians who were returning to the practice of absolute poverty and an exact imitation of Christ. This had enabled Pope Innocent to make Francis' Friars Minor an official religious order, bringing the poverty movement within the established Church. Francis had made the 'heresy' legitimate and when the greatest Poor Man of Europe had joined the Crusade in Egypt, he had been a powerful reminder that crusading should really be a poor man's movement. Like King Tafur, Francis had voluntarily renounced his wealth and joined the ranks of the poor. Like the very first Hospitallers and Templars, Francis and his disciples devoted themselves to the service of the poor, while they practised a strict poverty themselves. Francis was simply the most recent expression of the reverence for holy poverty which had inspired the most fervent Crusades and there is no reason to suppose that Francis disapproved of the Crusades. Indeed there is a story that records his praise of the 'holy martyrs' Roland and Oliver, who had died in Charlemagne's wars against the Muslims.[65] Like any fervent Templar, Francis dreamed of conquering 'all peoples, races, tribes and tongues, all nations and men of all countries'.[66] He intended his friars to do this by preaching and missionary work and he had devoted a whole chapter of his rule to the mission to Islam, but he probably saw the Crusade as having a useful role to play in this offensive. The first major Christian missionary approach to the Muslims took place in the context of a Crusade, and Francis seems to have found this quite appropriate.

Once he had been given permission for his brave peace initiative, Francis went into the enemy territory quite unarmed, but 'strong in possession of the buckler of his faith', wrote James of Vitry.[67] The Muslims seized him on his way to the Sultan's tent and seem to have been rather impressed by this ragged and dirty fellow, who had come on this impossibly brave mission. Provided that Francis did not insult Mohammad or Islam, al-Kamil would have had no objection to listening to him expound the gospel message, and it seems that he listened to Francis for three days and offered him precious gifts at the end of his visit. Francis naturally refused, even when the Sultan urged him to give them to the Churches and the poor Christians, and told the Sultan that God would look after the needs of the poor. When Francis left, al-Kamil is reported to have said: 'Pray for me, that God may deign to show me the law and the faith that are most pleasing to him.' Then he sent Francis back to the Christian camp, 'with every mark of respect and in complete safety'.[68] Needless to say, the Sultan was not converted, but the story does make a peaceful oasis in the story of the holy war.

The Fifth Crusade dragged on and al-Kamil was ready to make peace. Egypt was threatened with famine that year and could not withstand a long campaign, and both al-Kamil and al-Mu'azzam were worried about the activities of their brother al-Ashraf in the far north. At the end of October the Sultan sent two Frankish prisoners of war to Pelagius with extraordinarily generous terms: if the Crusaders would leave Egypt, he would return Jerusalem, all central Palestine and the Galilee.[69] It is a sign of how very dead the lust for *jihad* was at this point. Al-Kamil saw Jerusalem purely in political terms, not as a Holy City. Naturally King John of Acre urged Pelagius to accept these terms, but just as naturally Pelagius refused. At a time when Christians in Europe had begun to hound other Christians to death, it was not likely that they would make peace with the infidel. The military orders agreed with Pelagius for strategic reasons: the forts in Jerusalem and Galilee had all been dismantled and it would be impossible for the Christians to maintain them once the Crusaders had gone. The holy war was resumed and Pelagius waited confidently for the arrival of the Emperor Frederick.

Yet the Emperor never arrived. He fully intended to leave for the East but was not prepared to leave Europe until his empire was absolutely secure. Pope Honorius, who had once been his tutor, began to wonder whether this former papal client was really going to be as amenable as Innocent had hoped. Meanwhile the Crusader army was grounded in Damietta, bored Crusaders began to return home and there were bitter disputes between Pelagius and King John about the management of the campaign. In February 1220 John and his army returned to Acre, and spent the rest of the year fending off Sultan al-Mu'azam, who had invaded the Christian kingdom: the new Crusade had put an end to the peaceful coexistence of Muslims and Christians in the Middle East. In Egypt, none of the troops would fight without John, because he was the only leader that all nationalities would obey. By July 1221 Pelagius could not wait any longer for Frederick and planned an attack on Cairo. King John arrived with troops from Acre, full of gloom but not wishing to be accused of cowardice. On 12 July, the Crusaders set out with 630 ships, 5000 knights, 4000 archers and 40,000 infantrymen.[70]

The Egyptian army had come to meet the Christians but when they saw the size of the army they hastily retreated and many of the citizens tried to escape from Cairo. But al-Kamil was now very confident. Both his brothers had sent armies to help him, and they blocked the Crusaders' line of retreat to Damietta. As he watched the Crusaders march ever nearer to Cairo, the Sultan smiled to himself, hardly able to believe his luck. The Westerners did not notice that the waters of the Nile were rising. By mid-August the ground was so soggy and slippery that the Crusaders had to halt their advance and finally make a retreat. As soon as the retreat began, the Muslim soldiers demolished the dykes, troops moved to cut off the exit routes and within a few hours the Christian army was ignominiously imprisoned on an island of mud.[71] Pelagius had to sue for peace to save his army from annihilation and naturally this time al-Kamil's terms were far less generous. The Crusaders must sign a truce for eight years and leave Egypt immediately; in return they could sail home unmolested.

The Fifth Crusade had been a humiliating failure and the prospect of the reconquest of Jerusalem seemed even more out of reach than it had thirty years earlier. In the same way the Crusade at home against the Catharists was proving ineffective: even though heretics were still burned in large numbers, the heresy continued to spread and seemed ineradicable. Indeed by making the heretics into martyrs for their cause (and in some sense for their country) the Crusaders were actually encouraging the heresy. Crusading did not seem to work any more but this did not mean that the idea could be abandoned, because the habit was now an indelible part of the Western identity. In fact the holy war had diversified and discovered new forms and outlets. In the Middle East today, the Jewish and Islamic holy wars began as offensives against the Godless enemy, but then diversified so that today Jews are fighting holy wars against other Jews as well as against Muslim Arabs, and Muslims are fighting other devout Muslims as well as Jews and *munafiqeen*. This is precisely what happened in the Middle Ages in Europe, where a new habit of internal holy war had been created which would prove to be incurable. Nor could people abandon the conventional Crusade: after the failure of the Fifth Crusade, people looked for a scapegoat and found one ready to hand in the Emperor Frederick, who would be pressured to lead a Sixth Crusade to the Holy Land eight years later.

At the time of the Fifth Crusade a new movement towards the Muslim world had begun that at first sounds very positive. Before Francis of Assisi left Europe for Egypt, he had sent a party of Friars Minor to preach to the Muslims in Spain and Africa. After the Fifth Crusade other Franciscans went to the Holy Land to preach to the Muslims there. More encounters like the meeting between Francis and al-Kamil would probably have been a very good idea and we are so accustomed to the notion of spreading the faith by means of missionary activity that it seems incredible that nobody thought of this before. A missionary campaign which seeks to explain and share the truth sounds the obverse of the military campaign that seeks to conquer and kill. Yet in fact this peaceful project proved to be a new type of Crusade. The Franciscans went into Islamic lands not to save the souls of the Muslims but to achieve martyrdom. As soon as the first group of friars arrived in Seville, they resorted to the tactics of the Martyrs of Cordova. They tried to break into a mosque during Friday prayers, and when they were driven away they stood outside the Amir's palace and shouted abuse against Mohammad and Islam. They were not reaching out to the Muslims in peace and love but mounting an aggressive assault. The Muslim authorities were forced to arrest them, even though they were reluctant to do so. To avoid publicity, they moved the friars round from one prison to another and eventually had them deported to Morocco. Here the Franciscans went straight into a new offensive, behaving in exactly the same way, and were deported from one area to another on two more occasions by the embarrassed authorities. On one occasion the local Christian community pressured the Muslims to get rid of the friars, because they did not want to be associated with these fanatics and naturally feared that this might cause trouble for them. Finally the authorities were forced to execute the Westerners who were so flagrantly breaking the law of the land. They tortured the friars, and offered them wealth and honour if they would repent of their behaviour and convert to Islam. Finally they were executed.[72] When Francis heard of their 'martyrdom' he is said to have cried: 'Praise be to Christ! I know now that I have five Friars Minor!'[73] It seems that even though his peaceful embassy to al-Kamil had not been aggressive, he did not disapprove of this other violent missionary offensive. This would prove to be the way the Franciscans would continue to preach to the Muslims. James of Vitry noticed these methods in the Holy Land:

> The Saracens listen willingly to the Friars Minor when they speak of the faith of Christ and the teaching of the Gospels. But when their words openly contradict Mohammad, who appears in their sermons as a perfidious liar, they strike them without respect, and if God did not protect them marvellously, would almost murder them and drive them from their cities.[74]

It was, therefore, wholly appropriate that the first mission to the Muslims occurred in the context of a Crusade, for missionary activity was a child of crusading and part of the war of the West against the East.

It seems that the aggression that inspired these missionaries was not always confined to a moral assault on the Muslims. Instead of seeking to save the souls of the Muslims they 'preached' to, the Franciscans actually sought to compound their damnation. In 1227 a group of seven Franciscans who had preached their way into prison in Ceuta, Morocco, wrote home to say that the main object of their mission had been 'the death and damnation of the infidels'.[75] Jesus had said that anyone who rejected the faith would be damned: 'He who believes and is baptised will be saved; he who does not believe will be condemned' (Mark 16:16). By ensuring that the Muslims were not only forced to reject the faith that was presented to them so insultingly but also to imprison, torture and kill Christ's ambassadors, the missionaries saw to it that they were damned indeed. None of the first missionaries seems to have been concerned with real conversion.

The Dominicans followed the Franciscans in preaching missions to Muslim countries, but they did not go there to seek voluntary martyrdom, did not insult Mohammad and confined themselves to preaching the word of God. Yet it seems that actually converting Muslims was not their first object. When Raymund of Peñafort, the great thirteenth-century Dominican missionary, was asked to justify his missionary initiative by churchmen in Europe, he gave five benefits that could accrue from his work. Missionaries, he said, can take care of the spiritual welfare of the knights engaged in a Crusade; they can preach to the oriental Christians; they can reform Christian apostates; they can prove to the Muslims that Christians do not worship idols and so improve their position in the Muslim world. Finally, very much at the bottom of the list and almost as an afterthought, Raymund suggests that his preaching might make a good impression on the Muslims there and there just might be one or two conversions.[76] In other words, his mission was not for the Muslims but for the Christians. It is interesting that Raymund should have been asked to 'justify' going into the House of Islam. Today most Christians would assume that this was a laudable enterprise but, as I shall show in the next chapter, during the late twelfth and throughout the thirteenth century Christians in Europe were being told to have no contact at all with either Jews or Muslims and this was being enshrined in rigid Church legislation. In this climate, Raymund's missionary initiative could only be viewed with suspicion because it brought him into dubious and perhaps unnecessary proximity with the infidel.

This very strange, aggressive and exclusive attitude was obviously born of the Crusades and it is therefore fitting that the most spectacular crusading venture – that of St Francis – should have happened in the context of a military campaign against Islam. It is surely one of the ways that crusading has survived right up to the present day. We have seen that radical Egyptian Muslims call Western imperialism *al-Salibiyya*, the Crusade. They also give this name to Christian missionary work. The connection is obvious. When Europeans began their colonising ventures during the eighteenth, nineteenth and early twentieth centuries, missionaries followed in their train and were encouraged by the colonialists, some of whom had no religious beliefs, as a valuable part of the Westernising process. I am not decrying the work of all these missionaries, of course. Many were brave and committed men and women, but it must be said that trying to impose Western Christianity and morality on people who had quite different religious and cultural traditions was impertinent in that it often showed very little respect for local traditions. The missionaries believed that they were bringing 'the truth' to these lost people; they saw *their* way as right and the religions and traditions of the people they were evangelising as wrong. This meant that they were 'saving' them. There is an arrogance in this assumption and even an aggression when one remembers the colonial context, with the Europeans' obvious contempt for 'the natives'. There is in this view much of the spirit of the first Franciscan and Dominican missionaries. European colonialists tended to force their cultural wares on the 'natives' whether they wanted them or not, rather like the Franciscans, and were as indifferent to their real needs as the Dominicans, seeking only to advance the cause of their own country and its traditions. The French call the secular version of this spreading of the good news of Western values *mission civilisatrice* and we have seen that in the Middle East today many people have been traumatised and put into cultural shock by this spreading of Western 'progress' among people who had venerable and distinguished civilisations of their own. The United States has taken on the 'mission' of spreading the gospel of Western culture today, and backs it up by bribes of 'aid' and 'arms', rather as the religious missionaries offered the benighted natives beads, medical aid and education. We have seen that America has been just as manipulative and exploitative as the old European colonialists. American activity in Iran has shown all the old missionary zeal to force the Western way of life on a people, whether they want it or not, for their own 'good', and at the same time showing a blind indifference to the people of Iran and a real lack of concern for their welfare.

The early years of the thirteenth century, therefore, reveal a new crusading impetus in Europe. At a time when the conventional Crusade to the holy land was unable to arouse the old enthusiasm, other forms like missionary activity were beginning to appear. At the same time these years show an increased narrowness in the Western outlook. Europe was determined to destroy not only Muslims, but also Eastern Christianity and even some forms of European Christianity. Western Christians were closing their doors to anything that challenged their insecure orthodoxies and frightened doctrines and were fighting these infidels and heretics with an aggressive righteousness, in the name of peace. This distrust of outside influence would surely contribute to the idea that the Western way of life was the only way, a crusading attitude that still exists today. Crusading would continue to be important to the identity of Western people and would continue to find new forms, right up to the present day. But in the thirteenth century people had not yet abandoned the old idea of a Crusade to the Holy Land. The miserable defeat of the Fifth Crusade made them very impatient for the Sixth, which would turn out quite differently from what anybody had expected.

CHAPTER ELEVEN

1220–1291

The End of the Crusades?

When the armies of the Sixth Crusade began to assemble in southern Italy in August 1227 there was a man in Europe who was a committed Christian but who also spoke fluent Arabic, corresponded with Muslim scholars and made it clear all his life that some of his best friends were Muslims. Through his Muslim friends abroad, he brought the first giraffe into Europe and sent the first polar bear into the Middle East. At a time when most people spoke at best only three languages, he spoke nine and wrote in seven. When to be a layman was, almost by definition, to be unlearned, this layman was a student of mathematics, jurisprudence, philosophy and natural history. When most Christians were encouraged to accept the 'Truth' blindly, he never stopped asking difficult and disturbing questions. Yet this man was not an obscure intellectual eccentric. He was Frederick II, the Boy of Apulia, who had become the Holy Roman Emperor of the West and ruler of Sicily and Germany. His contemporaries, who had been stunned by him as soon as he appeared on the international scene, called him Stupor Mundi, the Wonder of the World.[1] It was on Frederick that all the hopes of Europe were centred in 1227 when he finally fulfilled his crusading vow and set off to the East to win back Jerusalem from his friend, the Sultan al-Kamil.

Frederick was a man born out of his time and in the wrong place. In Europe people were quite unable to understand him, because they had no category in which to place him. He seemed prodigious to his contemporaries, even monstrous. Some people saw his exceptional linguistic talent as a mark of the inspiration of the Holy Spirit, who had descended upon the apostles in tongues of fire and enabled them to speak strange languages, but others saw this gift as a mark of Satan, who had inspired the confusion of languages at the Tower of Babel.[2] Terrible stories circulated about Frederick's behaviour which seemed scarcely human, let alone Christian. It was said that on one occasion when he was having an argument with a priest about the immortality of the soul, to prove his point he had nailed one of the priest's disciples into a barrel. When the unfortunate man died, Frederick pointed out that his spirit must have died with him, because it could not have escaped from the vat. One of the most distressing aspects of this story, for a medieval, would have been the fact that Frederick could question the idea of the immortality of the soul at all, which was believed implicitly as absolute truth by the vast majority of Europeans. Frederick's insatiable curiosity was thought to be very threatening. Another story said that Frederick had once wanted to prove whether Hebrew, Greek, Latin or Arabic had been the original tongue given by God to Adam and Eve in the Garden of Eden. This was a question that would have had grave theological implications if Arabic, the sacred tongue of Islam, should have proved to be the original tongue. He had a number of children brought up in absolute solitude by nurses who were forbidden to speak to them, because he was curious to see if and when the children did speak they would use the language of their parents or the original tongue. The experiment failed because all the children died; as the contemporary historian Adam of Salimbene said, they were starved of affection.[3]

These stories may or may not have been true, but they do tell us important things about Frederick. First, he was a man who inspired these kind of tales because he confounded basic assumptions and seemed a law unto himself. Second, although Frederick has often been hailed, quite rightly, as the first man of the Renaissance and although his learning was astounding by the usual standards in Europe at that time, in fact he was a crude, amateur scholar. Certainly the Muslim scholars he consulted considered him so, though they were impressed by his open, inquiring mind. Third, Frederick was ready to exploit anybody. It is important not to sentimentalise his friendship with Muslims: Frederick would exploit Muslims as he would exploit anybody else. The story of his 'experiment' with the children shows that his interest was entirely self-indulgent and often ruthless. But that he was able to see Muslims as normal and often admirable human beings was a great achievement, for he was living in a period of great intolerance.

For the past fifty years, European Christians had been commanded by the Church to have nothing whatever to do with Muslims or Jews, the two victims of the Crusades, and legislation was made which linked the two together explicitly as a common foe. In the next chapter I shall show how important this attitude would continue to be. The Lateran Councils of 1179 and 1216 issued directives which cut people off from Muslims and Jews and forbade normal contact or coexistence. Any Christian who took service in the house of a Muslim or a Jew was to be excommunicated, as was anybody who looked after their children; anybody who traded with Muslims, who took merchandise to Islamic countries and sailed in their 'piratical' ships was to be excommunicated and his property confiscated. Only missionaries, whose activities we have seen to be regarded suspiciously, were allowed to eat with Muslims and Jews. Pope Gregory IX, the cousin of Innocent III who succeeded to the papacy in 1227, issued decretals which added some new prohibitions and reissued the old Lateran decrees. Muslims and Jews living in Christian countries were to wear distinctive clothing to distinguish them clearly from the Christian population. It was a way of isolating and stigmatising the enemy and looked forward to the yellow star that Jews were forced to wear during the Nazi regime. On Christian holidays, Muslims and Jews were not to appear in the street lest they contaminate the holy day and offend the faithful; they must not hold public office in a Christian country and Muslims were not allowed to assail the ears of the faithful by the call of the muezzin.[4]

But not everybody had succumbed to this group view. By an accident of history, Frederick had been brought up in the Mediterranean world, where a very different attitude prevailed. The merchants of Venice, Genoa and Pisa, for example, had no intention of obeying the Lateran decrees; for a long time they had been trading with Muslims and making treaties and agreements with them. In cities like Cairo, Muslim and European merchants enjoyed excellent relations to their mutual profit. Frederick had been brought up in Sicily where Muslims, Greeks, Normans and Germans lived side by side in reasonable harmony. The Norman conquerors of Sicily had actually encouraged the Muslims and made great use of their superior intellectual talents. Many Muslims held important positions at court. The court Arabs were allowed to pray in the direction of Mecca at the proper times and keep the Ramadan fast, even though the Normans had destroyed the most important mosque in Palermo. The policy had been to make war against Islam but to live in peace with Muslims. Muslim presence naturally meant that many scholars had come to Sicily during the late twelfth century and a good deal of useful translation work had been done. Frederick had grown up in a cosmopolitan atmosphere, therefore, which made it impossible for him to believe in only one point of view. Most royal children in Europe had a strictly monastic education, but Frederick was left very much to his own devices. Wandering round Palermo as a child, he came into contact with Arab and Byzantine scholars, who opened his naturally inquiring mind to ideas and concepts that were quite alien to the narrow scholastic intellectual world of the rest of Europe. Frederick was always convinced that ultimately Christianity was the true religion, but that did not mean that he hated the Muslims or the Byzantines nor did he consider them infidels and heretics. When he had left Sicily in 1212 for Germany, he encountered an intolerance and ignorance there that was quite alien to him and which he would despise all his life. This would make him feel more at home in the Muslim East than in Christendom, because the Muslims valued learning and scientific inquiry as he did, and his difference from the vast majority of his fellow Christians in Europe would naturally increase his sense of being specially singled out by God.

But there were signs that paranoid intolerance was about to take hold of Sicily. Towards the end of the twelfth century, the great Arab traveller Ibn Jubayr had noticed that although Muslims were very successful in the court of Palermo, they seemed frightened and uneasy.[5] They had good reason. At the beginning of the thirteenth century the Sicilian population declared open war on the Muslims: they expelled them from the cities and settlements, and then drove them from the fertile plains into the mountains where they lived as virtual outlaws.[6] When Frederick returned to Sicily from Germany in 1221, he knew that he had to deal with these enemies of the state, who were now waging guerrilla warfare from their mountain strongholds, and his solution was brilliant but callous. Frederick wanted the Muslims out of Sicily but he also wanted to use them for his own purposes, so he would not wage a war of extermination against them, although in the end that was what his policy would ultimately mean for the Arabs of Sicily. He began to force them down from the mountains, and by 1223 he wrote that most of the Muslims of Sicily had been forced into internment camps on the plains,[7] though in fact the fighting continued until 1245. From the camps the Muslims were shipped across to the mainland and were interned in the old fortress city of Lucera in Apulia. Here they were allowed to build their own independent city state. They had their own amir, their own qadis, sheikhs and imams. They built mosques and the muezzin sounded loudly and freely. Within the city, Frederick built a scientific institute for the study of all branches of speculative science, and he made the Muslims of Lucera his favoured court officials. 'Most of his officials and courtiers were Muslims,' wrote the Arab historian Jamal ad-Din Ibn Wasil, 'and in his camp the call to prayer and even the canonic prayers themselves were openly heard.'[8] The Arabs themselves were fanatically loyal to Frederick and called him their sultan.

Lucera and Frederick's private Muslim army were a scandal in Europe; they seemed a blot of Godlessness on the face of Christendom. Yet although Frederick certainly enjoyed Lucera and his Arab friends there, this was a policy not of toleration but of exploitation. Lucera was certainly a city where Islam was tolerated and protected: Frederick would not allow papal missionaries there to harass the Muslims. But Lucera was also a refugee camp and a reservation. The Muslims *had* to live there and had no choice but to be loyal to Frederick because he was their only protector. Events proved that by concentrating his Muslims in one place, Frederick had taken the first step to their final extermination.[9] They were safe during his reign and during the reign of his son Manfred, but when his territories were taken over by the French King Charles of Anjou at the end of the century they did not survive. When Charles spoke of Lucera, he used the imagery that we have seen used in our own day to describe an intolerable alien presence: it was 'a nest of pestilence . . . lurid in pollution . . . the stubborn plague and filthy infection of Apulia'.[10] In 1301 the French attacked the city, massacred its Muslim inhabitants, turned the mosque into a church and renamed Lucera the City of St Mary.

Most people found Frederick's association with Muslims blasphemous and disturbing, but others found this breaking of a strong taboo fascinating and even liberating. Frederick inspired a great devotion all over Europe in people who felt that all was not well there. The establishment of Muslim Lucera and the blasphemous tales of his intellectual and scientific experiments made him a living legend and put him above ordinary mortals in the imagination of many people. But nothing excited such awe and fascination as the great processions of his imperial court that followed Frederick round Europe as he travelled from one of his castles to another. Nobody in Europe had ever seen anything like this unbelievably opulent and exotic spectacle. It was far more like the cortège of the oriental caliphs and sultans, who were denounced as *munafiqeen* by devout Muslims because of their unIslamic splendour. Poets and chroniclers in Europe wrote of these processions in a state of stupefaction, unable to believe their eyes. First there was Frederick's famous menagerie, a collection of strange and exotic beasts that always travelled with him. This was not just a publicity stunt: Frederick was passionately interested in natural history and indeed once wrote a book on the Arabic sport of falconry. Lynxes, leopards and lions were borne through the streets in gilded cages or were led by slaves on silken ropes. Then came the famous giraffe, which must have been a shocking sight to people who had never conceived of such a peculiar animal. Brunetto Latini, the Florentine politician and man of learning, wrote in astonishment of the huge elephant that he saw picking up an ass in its trunk and dashing it to pieces.[11] People stared in fascination at this monstrous beast, waiting for its bones to change to ivory before their very eyes.[12] This spectacular and, perhaps, frightening procession of animals naturally stirred the imagination of the awed crowds. Some people said that these were the strange beasts that were prophesied to accompany Antichrist, for many of his contemporaries thought that Frederick was a man of such evil that he must be Antichrist. It seemed the only explanation for this extraordinary man. But other people claimed that these beasts represented the first sign of the messianic era, foretold by the prophet Isaiah when all manner of strange animals would live together in peace, the wolf lying next to the kid.[13] In this view, Frederick was a Messiah figure and a saviour. He seemed lifted above the common human lot on to a plane between God and man. People also convinced themselves that he must be the Last Emperor, who would arrive at the End of Days and establish God's Kingdom on earth. When Frederick announced his intention of going to Jerusalem in 1227, it is easy to imagine the excitement that must have prevailed. His presence in Jerusalem, be he Messiah or Antichrist, would surely be an event of profound significance for the whole world.

There was a second aspect of these imperial processions that contributed to Frederick's myth. The elephant had come to Frederick as a gift from the Sultan al-Kamil and indeed the whole court had an oriental appearance. This brazen display of coexistence with the infidel was disturbing, but also obscurely thrilling to many people because it flirted with the forbidden. In particular the veiled Muslim girls aroused avid speculation. Did Frederick keep a harem?[14] The popes certainly believed that he did and so did many of his supporters. Frederick, on the other hand, always insisted that these girls were just kept in the court because they worked as domestic slaves; their skills in needlework or dancing and singing were useful and entertaining, in the same way as the rope-dancers, jugglers and snake-charmers that were also part of the court. The fact that nobody ever knew for certain whether this harem existed made the idea of it even more tantalising. Other members of the household were eunuchs and Arab male slaves, exquisitely and splendidly dressed, leading camels, laden with treasures and riches. This was an emperor that many Europeans could be proud of. At last they had a ruler who was the equal of the sophisticated Muslim rulers or of the Greek Byzantine emperors, who had scorned European Christians for so long. The procession was also a sign that Islam could be dealt with and controlled. These Muslims were Frederick's slaves and his Arab army was under his control. At a time when the Muslims seemed frighteningly powerful, Frederick's court seemed somehow reassuring to his supporters.

It was also true, as we have seen, that many people at this time were far from happy with Innocent III's powerful Church, and those who did not want to go so far as to join one of the heretical sects that were springing up at that time hailed Frederick with enthusiasm because he was offering an alternative. Innocent III had taught that the fullness of power (*plenitudo potestatis*) resided in the papacy and that kings and emperors received their power from God through the mediation of the Pope. That was the meaning of the symbolic imperial coronation, when the Pope or his delegate placed the crown on the head of the new Holy Roman Emperor. This meant that the Pope was the temporal and spiritual head of Christendom and could remove a ruler from power if that king or emperor behaved in a way that was displeasing or detrimental to the Church. Frederick would have none of this. We have seen that he believed that he had a special divine mission; that meant that he received his power straight from God and certainly did not need the mediation of the Church. He had made this clear at his coronation, even though he had been the ward of Innocent III. It will be remembered that he caused great excitement in 1215 when, after receiving the crown, he had unexpectedly taken the Cross and summoned a new Crusade. This was actually a direct challenge to Innocent, because hitherto the only people who could officially summon a Crusade were the popes, but Frederick had made his Crusade not only a lay enterprise but a lay initiative. Throughout his life he continued to challenge the Pope and many people all over Europe supported Frederick, however awesome and bewildering his behaviour. Pope Honorius had already found that he could not control the young Emperor and one of the most flagrant signs of Frederick's cool refusal to obey the Church was that the Pope could not force Frederick to fulfil his crusading vow and join the Fifth Crusade. When Honorius died in 1227 he was succeeded by Pope Gregory IX, who would issue the legislation ostracising Muslims and Jews. Clearly he would have found Frederick's consorting with Muslims frankly blasphemous. He was very much of the same mind as his cousin Innocent III, and was determined to quash Frederick's claim to be the temporal head of Christendom, leaving the Pope as ruler only in spiritual affairs.[15] He decided to use Frederick's unfulfilled

Crusader vow as a weapon and said that if the Emperor did not take an army to the Holy Land forthwith, he would be excommunicated and this meant that his subjects could withdraw their allegiance from him.

In fact Frederick was himself eager to go to the East, for his own reasons. He wanted to be the new Alexander the Great, who had made himself lord of the world by gaining an empire in the East and the West. It was for this that he had been called by God, he believed.[16] This motive marks Frederick out at once from previous Crusaders, because there was not a shred of the usual religious desire to liberate Jerusalem. Even as secular a Crusader as Richard the Lionheart had been convinced that Jerusalem belonged by right to the Christians, but Frederick did not see Muslim presence in the Holy City as contaminating. His desire to go to the East was simply part of his own, divinely inspired career. It must be remembered that if his contemporaries could only explain Frederick in terms that were larger than life, it was equally difficult for Frederick to explain to himself why he was so very different from anyone else in Europe: his isolation led him to see himself as God's chosen one.

Frederick had already been making preparations for his Crusade for some time. He had rewritten the constitutions of the Teutonic Knights, the German military order founded by Barbarossa.[17] Where other military orders were directly dependent upon the Pope, the Teutonic Knights were now dependent only upon the Emperor, as befitted Frederick's imperial theory. In 1226 he sent them into pagan Prussia to conquer it for Christendom and wrote a constitution that would put the country under the direct control of the knights and hence of the Emperor. This again was a direct challenge to the Pope, who was planning a papal state in Prussia and to this end had sent the Cistercians to make settlements there for some years.[18] Frederick's Crusade, manned by his Teutonic Knights, would be an Emperor's Crusade, not a papal Crusade.

The year before, Frederick had made another move that naturally thrilled crusading Europe and which gave him once again a legendary aura. He had married Princess Yolanda, the heiress to the throne of Acre and Jerusalem. The fate of this poor sixteen-year-old girl shows Frederick's cool, ruthless cruelty. Yolanda left Syria for the strange world of the West, weeping bitterly, and was married to her frightening husband at Brindisi on 9 November 1225. On the wedding night Frederick seduced Yolanda's cousin, and eventually sent the girl off to Palermo, where she lived pining for her home in the East until on 25 November 1228 (while Frederick was in the East) she gave birth to a son, Conrad, who became heir to the throne of Jerusalem and the light of his father's life. Having done her duty, Yolanda died six days after the birth. Most people in Europe, however, would have shed few tears for Yolanda, who, as a member of the despised caste of women, did not merit much attention. But the marriage itself greatly enhanced Frederick's status.[19] When he went to the East, he would go as the King of Jerusalem, so many people believed that this proved he was the long-awaited Last Emperor. But Frederick's conviction of his divine vocation did not blind him to practical reality: he knew that no Crusade had been successful since 1099 and that his chances of conquering Jerusalem militarily were slim. Then, however, shortly after his marriage to Yolanda it appeared that there was another way he could proceed.

During the Fifth Crusade, the Sultan al-Kamil had heard a lot of talk about the powerful Emperor from the West who was hourly expected to arrive in Egypt, and naturally he was anxious to know how serious a threat Frederick presented. The reports he was getting back from his informants in Sicily seemed astonishing: here was a Christian Emperor who allowed the muezzin to summon Muslims to prayer, whose most powerful officers and court officials were Muslims, and who spoke fluent Arabic. When he heard of Frederick's marriage to Yolanda, he felt that it was time to look into the matter more closely and he sent the learned emir Fakhr ad-Din al-Shaykh to Palermo. The Emir reported back in astonishment that all the rumours were true. Frederick spoke Arabic fluently, his courtiers and bodyguards were all Arabs, and the muezzin sounded freely in Palermo. The Emperor was full of contempt for the barbarous Europeans, especially for the Pope of Rome. This sounded very reassuring and al-Kamil began to correspond with Frederick. They discussed Aristotle, jurisprudence, the immortality of the soul and astronomy, and the Sultan sent animals as gifts for the menagerie. It transpired that neither Frederick nor the Sultan had any time for the useless and fanatical practice of the holy war and in 1227 the Sultan suggested that Frederick came out to the East. He had recently quarrelled with his brother al-Mu'azam, ruler of Damascus and Jerusalem, and told Frederick that he would be very happy to help him conquer Jerusalem from his brother. A friendly buffer-state between al-Kamil's Egypt and al-Mu'azam's Syria seemed highly desirable. Al-Kamil had no passionate feelings about the Holy City, unlike his uncle Saladin. Provided that it did not affect public opinion, al-Quds was only of military or political importance.[20] This was excellent news to Frederick, who had just been threatened by Gregory with excommunication for failing to fulfil his crusading vow. The conquest of Jerusalem would be a pure formality, he thought, but his coronation as King of Jerusalem would give him a prestige in the West that would greatly enhance his position against the Pope.

These arrangements were kept a closely guarded secret, of course, and when the crusading army gathered together in August it was assumed that this was a perfectly conventional Crusade. Of course when people saw that Frederick was taking some of his Muslim soldiers from Lucera to fight alongside his Teutonic Knights many people – clerics and laymen – were scandalised and it increased their fear that Frederick must be Antichrist: there were ancient prophecies which said that the Muslims would be the attendants of Antichrist, when he enthroned himself in Jerusalem. It also seemed to make a mockery out of the whole idea of a Crusade and was yet another example of Frederick's prodigious behaviour that trod mercilessly on people's most cherished beliefs and prejudices.

The Crusade set sail with 3000 knights and 10,000 pilgrims but the heat and the press of crowds led to an outbreak of malaria. Frederick himself became ill and was forced to disembark at Otranto, while the rest of the Crusade sailed on to Acre without him. Pope Gregory was furious when he heard that Frederick had left the Crusade and was convinced that this illness was simply a ruse and another delaying tactic. He promptly excommunicated Frederick and prepared to invade his lands in the south of Italy in a 'Crusade' – a disgraceful debasement of the ideal and one which put the people of southern Italy firmly behind Frederick. Frederick, however, remained untroubled. He assumed that the excommunication was just a routine matter and apologised humbly, offering to do penance. But Gregory was determined to press his advantage. He would lift the ban of excommunication only if Frederick accepted him as overlord of Sicily and southern Italy. This Frederick naturally refused to consider, but he was in a difficult dilemma. As an excommunicate, he was technically forbidden to go on a Crusade, but if he delayed any longer he would look absurd and lose face. He decided to put Gregory very subtly in the wrong and wrote a calm and dignified circular letter to the rulers of Christendom, apologising for the delay and hinting – with the greatest possible respect – that Gregory was holding up the crusade by refusing to lift the ban of excommunication simply to further his own territorial ambitions. It was imperative, he concluded, that he join his army in Acre and did not hold up the work of God, so he would set sail immediately, trusting confidently that the Pope would lift the ban. Early in 1228 he set sail from Brindisi, putting Gregory in a very embarrassing position. 'We have just left Brindisi for Syria,' he wrote piously to the

kings of Europe, 'and are speeding along before a favourable wind with Christ for
our leader.'[21] Gregory reacted furiously by excommunicating the Emperor again – a
pointless act, because it was like sentencing a man to death twice. He also actually
invaded his Italian lands, a move which aroused a great deal of support for
Frederick all over Europe, even though he was in the unique and grotesque position
of leading a Crusade as an excommunicate.

When he arrived in Acre, Frederick expected the recovery of Jerusalem to be a
mere formality, but the situation had changed since he had made his arrangement
with Sultan al-Kamil, who was now very embarrassed by Frederick's arrival. While
Frederick had been ill, al-Mu'azam had died, leaving Damascus to his very young
and inexperienced son al-Nasir. It now looked as though al-Kamil would be able to
conquer the whole of Palestine and Syria without making an unpopular treaty that
would give al-Quds back to the Christians. But he was a man of honour and
continued to feel obliged to keep his word to Frederick if he possibly could.
Frederick, for his part, was desperate. His lands at home were in danger and he
badly needed the coup of recovering Jerusalem to give him popular support in his
struggle with the Pope. But he had arrived in Palestine with a modest army that
was quite insufficient to liberate Jerusalem by force of arms. 'I am your friend,' he
wrote to al-Kamil. 'It was you who urged me to make this trip. The Pope and all the
kings of the West now know of my mission. If I return empty-handed, I will lose
much prestige.'[22] It was a very frank expression of Frederick's uniquely selfish
reasons for wanting to conquer Jerusalem.

The Sultan, however, was touched by Frederick's letter and realised the justice of
Frederick's claim upon him. He sent Fakhr ad-Din to the Emperor with gifts and a
message: he too had to take account of public opinion, he explained. To give up
Jerusalem without a fight would be politically dangerous, because of the devotion
the Muslims felt for the Holy City.[23] But he did not want to fight a wasteful war
with his friend, which in terms of loss of life would be damaging to both of them
and would delay his own conquest of his nephew al-Nasir's territory. Like
Frederick, al-Kamil had his own selfish and entirely unreligious reasons for
wanting to make a settlement. Fakhr ad-Din hinted that if it could be made to
appear that a treaty concerning Jerusalem would stave off a bloody war between
Christians and Muslims, that might solve everybody's problems. Frederick smiled
and took the hint, thanking his friend for the good advice.[24] At the end of
November 1228 he and the Christian army of Acre marched down the coast
towards Jaffa. It was not a very threatening force and the army was ludicrously
vulnerable. Because Frederick had been excommunicated, the Templars of Acre
could not ride with him, so they took a parallel route: they were not really
following Frederick, they just happened to be riding in the same direction.
Al-Kamil, however, played his part with great conviction and warned the Muslims
to prepare for a long and terrible war with the Christians. When, therefore,
Frederick asked the Sultan for peace talks, al-Kamil was naturally bound by the
principles of the Koran to negotiate for peace, if that was possible. Negotiations
began in strict privacy, a privacy which was highly offensive to the Franks of Acre
because they felt that Frederick should consult them instead of autocratically
acting on his own initiative. Frederick and Fakhr ad-Din took no notice of this
Christian objection and worked out the terms of a treaty, which they signed on 29
February 1229.

The treaty must be one of the most extraordinary diplomatic achievements of all
time. Without fighting a single Muslim, Frederick had managed to win back
Jerusalem; by means of peaceful co-operation he had achieved what no other
Western Crusader had managed with mighty armies. There would be a truce
between Muslims and Christians for ten years and the Christians would take back

Jerusalem, Bethlehem and Nazareth, together with the western part of the Galilee that adjoined Acre. The Muslims would evacuate Jerusalem, but they would keep the Dome of the Rock and al-Aqsa and a small group of imams and ulema would remain there. Muslims would be able to pray at these shrines and visit the city as unarmed pilgrims.[25] Frederick and al-Kamil were offering the solution of peaceful coexistence. Instead of fighting a series of pointless, destructive wars, Christians and Muslims should share the Holy City. Yet the howl of protest on both sides showed that they had gone to the limits of what was possible, as we have found in our own day. The Franks of Acre had not wanted a holy war with the Muslims at the time of the Fifth Crusade and had learned to form normal relations with their Muslim neighbours in secular matters. But once they were within reach of the Holy City, old, intolerant mechanisms at once went to work. The idea of a Christian monarch on a Crusade making friends with Muslims – and indeed feeling more obviously at home with them than with his own co-religionists – and allowing the Muslim filth to pollute the Holy City with their presence seemed an obscenity. In vain did the master of the Teutonic Knights point out that the Muslims who remained behind were a few old men who were closely surrounded by the imperial guard. The Franks replied that it was abominable that a holy Christian shrine should be contaminated by a pagan presence. Nobody seemed to understand that the two mosques had never had any Christian significance. It was generally believed that the Dome of the Rock was the old Jewish Temple, where Jesus had been presented to God and blessed by Simeon and where he had taught every day during the last week of his life. When the Christians had owned Jerusalem, the mosque had been a church called the Temple of the Lord, and had been the seat of a Christian patriarch. Now it was the seat of Mohammad, and Christian ears would have to listen to the sound of the muezzin and to the chanting of Muslim prayers without being able to object.[26] Muslims and Christians might be able to live together anywhere else and make compromises about any other matter, but not about the Holy City.

Al-Kamil had an even more difficult time. As soon as the treaty was announced, says Ibn Wasil, 'the lands of Islam were swept by a veritable storm.'[27] The people poured on to the streets in Baghdad, Mosul and Aleppo and at meetings in the mosques denounced al-Kamil as a traitor to Islam. The Sultan explained to the people that this was only a temporary measure. All they had given to the Franks were 'some churches and some ruined houses' but the mosques remained in Muslim hands. Once he had sorted out the political situation in Palestine and Syria, he could easily 'purify Jerusalem of the Franks and chase them out'.[28] These rational justifications were of no avail and in Damascus al-Kamil's nephew and rival al-Nasir made political capital out of the general dismay and ordered Sheikh Sibt al-Jauzi to preach a sermon in the Great Mosque lamenting the loss of Jerusalem. The whole population of the city crammed into the mosque and the crowd wept and groaned aloud. 'On that day one saw nothing but weeping men and women,'[29] wrote Ibn Wasil. In his prolix history *Mir'at az Zaman* ('The Mirror of the Times'), Sheikh al-Jauzi wrote that his sermon dwelt on the grief and shame that al-Kamil had inflicted on the Muslim people: 'O shame upon the Muslim rulers!' he cried, as the sobbing in the mosque rose to a crescendo. 'At such an event tears fall, hearts break with sighs, grief rises on high!'[30] Some forty years earlier, Richard and al-Adil had been able to sit down together to negotiate and both had been honoured by their contemporaries. Saladin had not been castigated for signing a treaty with Richard because that treaty had not sullied the integrity of al-Quds. It seems that once the habit of the holy war has been established, it is impossible for either side to make any concession at all about a holy city or a holy land. That is a sobering thought for us today.

Undismayed by these lamentations, Frederick marched to Jerusalem for his coronation, accompanied by the Teutonic Knights and the largely Arab imperial guard. More absurdities ensued. The Bishop of Caesarea was horrified that Jerusalem should open its gates to an excommunicate emperor, so he rushed there in Frederick's wake and put the holiest city in the world under an interdict. Frederick marched straight to the Holy Sepulchre Church and, because no priest nor prelate would crown him, strode to the high altar, seized the crown and placed it on his own head.[31] It was a superb affirmation of his position: he received his power from God and did not need the mediation of the Church. But the coronation of a Western emperor in Jerusalem was an event that was surrounded with a nimbus of hopes, fears and yearnings. *Was* Frederick really the Last Emperor and had he succeeded in establishing the Kingdom of God, as he claimed when he cried 'Behold, now is the day of salvation!'[32] in his coronation speech? Or was Frederick Antichrist, who had allowed Islam, the abomination of desolation, to establish itself in the Temple and who had made a mockery of the Pope of Rome? Nobody could decide.

Muslims were just as puzzled by Frederick as Christians were and this again tells us something important about the holy-war mentality. Tolerance is not prized or appreciated, even if this means the enemy treating the true religion with respect. After the coronation, Frederick went to the Temple Mount to visit the Muslim shrines, an event that was as shocking to the sensibilities of *both* sides as if President Sadat had prayed at the Wailing Wall during his visit to Jerusalem, or if Prime Minister Begin had joined him in prayer at al-Aqsa. Frederick seemed to feel no tension at all, and assumed that these Muslims were as warmly disposed to him as his friends Fakhr ad-Din or the Luceran Muslims. He jested with them in Arabic and spent a long time admiring the mosques, being particularly delighted with the pulpit in the Dome of the Rock, which he climbed to the very top. When he came down, he affectionately took the hand of Shams al-Din, the Qadi of Nablus, who was acting as the official guide, and walked with him towards al-Aqsa. When he saw a priest entering the mosque with a New Testament, Frederick beat him up: 'By God, if one of you dares to step in here again without permission, I will pluck out his eyes!'[33] That night the Qadi had ordered the muezzin to be silent as a mark of respect for the Christian Emperor, and Frederick was bitterly disappointed. The only reason he had wanted to sleep in Jerusalem, he said sadly the next morning, was to hear the muezzin in the Holy City.[34] This was neither appreciated nor understood by the Muslims. In a society in the throes of a holy war, toleration is not respected. Sheikh Ibn al-Jauzi, who had preached the inflammatory sermon in Damascus and who deeply disapproved of the treaty, had a very low opinion of Frederick during this visit. He was red-faced and undistinguished to look at, he wrote disdainfully. 'Had he been a slave he would not have been worth 200 *dirham.*'[35] The only way that the Sheikh could explain his attitude was by deciding that he was a cynic: 'his Christianity was merely a game to him.'[36] A secularly minded political Muslim like al-Kamil could appreciate an exchange of views and could respect and like Frederick. But these Muslim clergymen on the Temple Mount, whose lives were dominated by religion in the Holy City liberated by Saladin, could find toleration only incompatible with true religion. The question of Jerusalem was such a sensitive religious issue that on both sides most Christians and Muslims believed that their religious integrity demanded an absolute rejection of the enemy, who became the 'other'.

Frederick and al-Kamil had offered the Franks in Palestine their last chance; but on neither side was there any real will to peace, once the identity of Jerusalem was in question, an issue made fraught by one hundred and forty years of holy war. Where secular interests could unite Muslims and Christians, religious obsessions convinced both sides that it was impossible for them to share a society. Like President Sadat in our own day, Frederick learned how dangerous it was to make peace with the enemy and to meddle with religious issues. While he was making a private visit to the Jordan valley, the Templars contacted al-Kamil, told him that the Emperor would be unguarded and suggested that he have him assassinated. Al-Kamil was absolutely disgusted and warned Frederick, who decided that he should go home as soon as possible. He returned to Acre and tried to leave the city early in the morning before anybody was about. But the butchers were already in the market cleaning the meat and they followed the Emperor down to the harbour, pelting him with entrails and excrement.[37] The peace treaty that he had made had revived the old religious chauvinism that had helped to destroy the Kingdom of Jerusalem in 1187. This would prove suicidal, and when Frederick sailed away from the Holy Land, rejected and covered in filth, the fall of the Kingdom of Acre was only a matter of time.

Yet Frederick was not rejected by everybody in Europe, even though he remained a deeply controversial figure until he died in 1250 at the age of fifty-seven. To his supporters, his coronation in Jerusalem naturally added to his glamour, even though Frederick never returned to the East, and when his son Conrad came of age he preferred to stay and rule under his father in Germany. Frederick managed to sort out his difficulties with Pope Gregory when he returned to Europe, and signed the treaty of San Germano with him in 1230. But he continued to provide an alternative to papal Europe and battled with the popes for the secular leadership. He was seen by discontented Christians who hated the popes as a liberator and their champion against Rome, which was unnaturally refusing to admit the supremacy of this new Caesar. His struggle with the popes assumed almost cosmic proportions, and he was hailed by prophetic poets as an apocalyptic figure:

> Fate is still as the night. There are portents and wars
> In the course of the stars, and the birds in their flight.
> I am Frederick, the Hammer, the Doom of the World.
> Rome, tottering long since, to confusion is hurled,
> Shall shiver to atoms and never again be Lord of the World.[38]

The passion that Frederick inspired meant that, even though he fulfilled none of these hopes, shortly after his death in 1250 a belief developed that he would return and save the world. He would be a Christian Messiah, who would fight in the name of the poor, cast the mighty from their thrones and overthrow the Pope and the rich clergy who were a scandal to Christendom, because they oppressed poor Christians. People in the Holy Roman Empire prayed to him after his death as though he were indeed an almost divine figure: 'Our forefathers looked no more eagerly for the coming of Christ than we do for thine,' wrote a governor whose troops were in danger. 'Come to free and to rejoice us. Show us thy countenance and we shall find salvation!'[39] Frederick had stirred the imagination of Europe so deeply that the belief in his Second Coming became very popular among the disenchanted people in Europe, who wanted a different kind of Christian identity. They made him the symbol of their own longings and, inevitably, produced a highly idealised portrait of this difficult and frequently cruel man.[40] Frederick had been as ready to exploit the poor as he was everybody else and would have put down any revolution in his own territory very brutally. But to his devotees he became the champion of the poor and in the next chapter I shall show that this belief in the Second Coming of Frederick was one of the ways that crusading was kept alive long after Crusades had stopped going to the Holy Land; it produced ideas of which Frederick would not have approved, but which had sinister repercussions in the twentieth century.

It is important not to idealise and sentimentalise Frederick, as his supporters did. But it is important, as we leave him, to notice that he offered an alternative that could have involved more than throwing off papal and Church supremacy in Europe. He showed that it was possible to respect and live with Muslims. Admittedly he was willing to exploit them when it suited him, but while Europe was grimly shunning all contact with Islam Frederick saw Muslims as ordinary human beings with whom he frequently felt more at home than with his narrow-minded, fanatical fellow Christians back home. This was not because he was a freethinker. Frederick was a convinced Christian, and when he heard of al-Kamil's death in 1238 he mourned that his friend had never been converted to the true faith. He scoffed at religious superstition, but as a despot he would not allow heresy in his empire and persecuted heretics fiercely for their heterodox beliefs.[41] He understood the relation between heresy and revolution very well. But he could see the nobility and beauty of Islam and had no time at all for the absurd fantasies of 'Mohammadanism' that were believed implicitly by his contemporaries. Neither was he an anti-semite. Frederick once wanted to carry out a survey to prove that the anti-semitic myths of cannibalism, the blood libel, ritual murder and the like were all false. He thought that Jews who had converted to Christianity should be questioned about these matters. They would have no reason to lie, because they had now abjured Judaism, and the myths would be scotched once and for all.[42] Frederick was as cruel as the popes and their crusading Church, but at least he was free of the terror that made Europeans conceive of Muslims and Jews as the enemies of God. Had this view prevailed in the West and the cold light of rationality been allowed to fall on the emotional mythologies surrounding Jews and Muslims, much tragedy might have been spared, not only in the Middle Ages but also today, as I want to argue in the following chapter.

But by this time most people were already staunchly committed to a deep loathing of both Jews and Muslims, and Frederick's extraordinary Crusade filled the popes and their supporters, who constituted the majority, with disgust. Frederick had been regarded as Antichrist for years, but his contact and treaty with Muslims gave a new force to this belief. He was now surrounded with much of the aura of horror that surrounded 'Mohammadans'. In 1239 Pope Gregory wrote to the Archbishop of Canterbury, quoting Revelation: 'A beast arose out of the sea, filled with the names of blasphemy . . . it opened its mouth to utter blasphemies against God.' This spectre of evil, lurking in the depths of the Christian subconscious which would emerge and destroy the world was now seen to be Frederick.[43] Matthew Paris, who had once been the English secretary of Eleanor of Aquitaine, wrote that Frederick felt closer to Islam than to Christianity. He wrote in horror of Lucera, of Frederick's 'harem' and in 1247 wrote that he had made a treaty with the Sultan, who was his close friend, 'to the confusion of all Christendom'.[44] This was not true of course but people were not ready for Frederick's vision of coexistence with Islam. They were already irrationally convinced that Islam was poised ready to wipe out Christian Europe.

In the years that followed his death, Frederick's supporters became heretics and rebels, but his enemies became the establishment and intolerance of Muslims became an indelible habit in Europe. More scholars wrote about Islam and the Prophet Mohammad during the thirteenth century, which drove this hatred home. They built on the work of the twelfth-century Cluniac authors and Peter the Venerable, to produce ideas that would be considered self-evident facts well into the nineteenth century and which many people in the West would not find strange today. They claimed to be accurate and authoritative experts on Islam. Thus the thirteenth-century Spanish scholar Mark of Toledo produced a translation of the Koran that was indeed a considerable improvement on the work of Robert of

Ketton. Other scholars, like Roderick of Toledo who wrote *Historia Arabum* and the *Cronica de Espagna*, and the Dominican Ramon Marti who wrote the *Fourfold Condemnation*, also claimed to be serious, objective works of scholarship. But the title of Ramon Marti's work shows their attitude: they were not writing to understand but to condemn.[45] They wanted to induce a certain emotional response in their readers and create a state of mind which would lead Christians to see Islam as an absolute evil and an unmanageable danger.

These new works on the religion that they insisted on calling 'Mohammadanism' repeated all the old myths and added some of their own. They often relied on Christian and Muslim legends which bathed the Prophet and his religion in a bizarre and disreputable light. The picture of Islam that they created bore no relation to the reality but was a purely Western fantasy, which had already acquired the status of absolute truth. Thus at the end of the century the Dominican scholar Ricoldo da Monte Croce travelled in Muslim countries and was impressed and edified by the devotion and sincerity with which Muslims prayed and conducted their lives. They put Christians to shame, he wrote. But when he came to write his *Disputatio contra Saracenos et Alchoranum*,[46] he simply repeated the old myths recounted by Ramon Marti years earlier. The Christian image of Islam had an authority that easily overcame any objective contact with real Muslims. Riccoldo's absurdly prejudiced and inaccurate account of Islam would be used and implicitly believed by Western scholars until the very end of the seventeenth century.

The Christian scholars were at a loss to understand how Mohammad had managed to inspire such a loyal following in the Arab world, and so they presented him as an impostor or a fraudulent magician, who concocted false 'miracles' that took in the simple-minded Arabs. Thus there was a story about the Koran miraculously appearing between the horns of an ox or a cow, straight from heaven. Again, Mohammad was said to have trained a dove to sit on his shoulder and pick peas from his ear. To his poor deluded countrymen, it looked as though the dove was whispering in his ear and they thought that the dove was the Holy Ghost. The scholars explained Mohammad's ecstasies during his revelations by claiming that he was an epileptic, which was at that time tantamount to saying that he was possessed by the devil. He was also presented as a sexually obsessed pervert who attracted his followers into a religious cult that pandered to man's basest instincts.[47] The Muslim practice of polygamy was held to be purely bestial and was said to have reduced all Muslims to the level of animals,[48] and the Koranic description of paradise as a place of sensual delights was claimed to prove definitively that the religion was a cult of licensed self-indulgence.[49] It was by now implicitly believed to be an absolute truth that Mohammad had set himself up as a prophet in order to conquer the world and that most of his closest friends and followers had known that he was an impostor, but had kept quiet about it because of their own base ambition.[50] This meant therefore that every Muslim was essentially a hypocritical, untrustworthy aggressor and sexual pervert, and somebody like Frederick who had serious and friendly dealings with them was tainted by the same evil and suspected of the ultimate betrayal.

These new critics of Islam simply could not break free from their Christian limitations and view the religion objectively. They could not see, for example, that it would be very easy for somebody who was anti-Christian to see Jesus as an impostor and to view his miracles as fakes. They could not see that to accuse 'Mohammadanism' of being essentially violent and aggressive laid *Christians* open to a charge of hypocrisy and bad faith during the period of the Crusades. The thirteenth-century scholars were quite unable to see Islam outside the Western Christian context. They were still convinced, for example, that Mohammad was a

Christian heretic, who had founded a new Christian sect. They recounted a legend of a heretic called Sergius, who had fled orthodox Rome in the early years of the seventh century and had taken refuge in the Arabian desert. There he had met Mohammad, instructed him in his faith and coached him to be a prophet.[51] In this view, pre-Islamic Arabia was not a place in the Middle East with its own problems and preoccupations. In this imaginary geography, the Arabian peninsula was seen as a region in the outskirts of the *Christian* world of Europe and the haunt of Christian schismatics and heretics who had to flee from the centre of Christendom. So immersed were these scholars in Christian history that they were compelled to see Mohammad as a part of this history. They knew about the great heresies that had flourished in the Eastern empire in places like Alexandria and Ephesus. They had met the descendants of some of these heretics in the Middle East. From the third to the fifth centuries the orthodox Church had been involved in a series of bitter political and theological disputes with the Arians, the Monophysites, the Monothelites and the Nestorians, and when scholars encountered Islam, whose teaching about Jesus, for example, was not dissimilar to that of a heretic like Arius, they assumed that it was the last of these heresies.[52] They called it after its founder, just as they had in the case of Arianism, and ignored the name that Mohammad and Muslims used. Indeed, even though Muslims find it offensive, it is still common for people in the Western world to call Islam 'Mohammadanism'.

At the same time there was a development in the European hatred of the Jews during the thirteenth century. In 1243 near Berlin, the Jews were for the first time accused of stealing the Eucharist from churches and tearing the wafer to shreds. At once this became another standard charge against the Jews, and came up with the same regularity as the charges of child murder and cannibalism. The Jews were accused of a dedicated and murderous desire to wound Christ anew. To have crucified him once in Jerusalem had not been enough for them; they had constantly to lacerate his body again in the Eucharist. Nobody was able to reflect rationally that, since the Jews certainly did not believe that Jesus was present in the Eucharist, they would have very little interest in breaking into churches and desecrating the Host.[53] The devotion to the Real Presence of Christ in the Eucharist was new, and so automatically did people consider the Jews to be the enemies of Christ and of religion that they spontaneously made them the enemies of this new devotion. The accusation also expressed the Christian conviction that the Jews really 'knew' perfectly well that Jesus was God and was present in the Eucharist, but that they maliciously and perversely refused to submit to the truth. This made them worthy of persecution, and pogroms sprang up all over Europe when Christians believed that the Jews had committed this new eucharistic crime. Pope Gregory did not approve of the pogroms but we have seen already that he had no love of the Jews and put them on a par with the Muslims. In 1240 he condemned the Talmud, a book as heinous to the Christians as the Koran. On the first Sunday of Lent he sent a letter to all the kings of Europe, telling them to seize the copies of the Talmud, which was now a forbidden book in Christendom, while the Jews were in the synagogue on the sabbath. The books should be put in the custody of 'our dear sons, the Dominican and Franciscan friars'. There was not much response to this appeal. The Emperor Frederick, as one might expect, completely ignored it. But the King of France sprang to the task zealously. He ordered a certain Nicholas Donin, who was a convert from Judaism and was now a fervent Franciscan, to interrogate Rabbi Jehiel, a learned rabbi who was to represent the Talmud and the Jews in a public 'debate', which was really a trial of Judaism. This was a horrible perversion of Frederick's plan to use the Jewish converts to Christianity in order to *help* the Jews. But Frederick had reckoned without the irrational nature of

Christianity, which could so powerfully affect the imagination as to convince even converted Jews of the evil of their former faith. Because Donin knew the Talmud well, he was able to take the Rabbi through all those passages which were insulting to Christians, even though he knew that they represented only a tiny portion of the whole and could not possibly be said to be representative of Talmudic Judaism. Thus he managed to produce a distorted picture of the Talmud, as a work that was wholly intent on a dedicated hatred of Jesus and his followers.[54] In 1242 the Talmud was condemned and the books were burned in the presence of the King. This action of the King of France was typical of the man who was to be the last great Crusader.

King Louis IX of France could not be a greater contrast to Frederick. He was considered by the vast majority of people in Europe to be a perfect type of Christian king and was an example of the ideal Christian of the thirteenth century. It is significant that while Frederick's supporters became heretics and outcasts after his death, Louis was regarded as a saint by popular acclaim and was canonised by the official established Church. Even though he often behaved in a cruel, simple-minded, petty way, he is still called 'St Louis' today. He has a feast day on 25 August each year when a special Mass is celebrated in his honour. The readings from Scripture that have been chosen for this Mass include a reading from the Book of Wisdom (10:10–14) in the Old Testament, which is usually read on the feast day of a martyr, and we shall see that Louis did indeed die a pointless death on an extremely ill-conceived Crusade. The gospel reading (Luke 19:12–26) is the long parable of the talents where Jesus explains how a Christian should use his gifts fruitfully in this life, and the final prayer after the communion still celebrates Louis as a Christian soldier: 'O God, You gave Your blessed confessor Louis renown on earth and glory in heaven; we pray You, appoint him a defender of Your Church.'[55] Other prayers during this Mass recall St Louis' utter dedication to the values of heaven, his holy contempt of this life and his love of Christ. My missal quotes with approval the praise of the seventeenth-century Catholic writer Jacques Bossuet: 'He was the holiest and most just king who ever wore the crown.'[56] Louis therefore is still venerated by millions of Catholics all over the world as an example to all kings and rulers, and also as a man who made the best possible use of his life and who died a holy death. Yet Louis was an anti-semite and a cruel persecutor of heretics, and he was so consumed with loathing of Muslims that he led not one Crusade but two. There could scarcely be a more telling example of the way crusading values are still upheld subliminally by the official Church.

Where Frederick had presented himself as a rich and exotic ruler, Louis had a much simpler style. He used to sit cross-legged under a tree in his court at Vincennes, with his advisers around him, and encourage the people to bring their problems and difficulties to him.[57] In fact, even though he hated Jews, he thought of himself as one of the old kings of Israel. He judged his people like Solomon, and like Solomon he was also a great builder. Churches and monasteries sprang up all over France built in the new Gothic style. The most spectacular of his building achievements was La Sainte Chapelle in the royal palace, which he began to build during the early 1240s when he was also organising his campaign against the Talmud. As in King Solomon's day, building went hand in hand with warfare. La Sainte Chapelle was very much like Solomon's Temple in that it was built to enshrine the holiness of God. Louis had bought the important relic of the Crown of Thorns from the Latin Emperor of Constantinople, along with a large piece of the True Cross, some fragments of the Holy Spear, the Robe worn by Christ, the Holy Sponge and the Holy Shroud. The Emperor of Constantinople could not manage the economy of the empire he had seized from the Greeks during the Fourth

Crusade and so had to sell these priceless relics which the West had long coveted. Louis was able to profit from the crime of the Fourth Crusade and build a new holy place in the West.[58] The Crusades had violently wrested the 'holiness' of the East and carried it in triumph to Europe making a new holy place there. When we look at the almost miraculous beauty of La Sainte Chapelle, which was actually built to look rather like a reliquary and a crown, we should remember that it is one result of the Crusades. Without the bloodshed, violence and destruction of a Crusade, the chapel would never have been built.

Here it is important to recall the importance of relics in the piety of Western laymen. They were a physical contact with heaven and a source of valuable power. Holiness was still locally conceived and bound up with the physical and tangible, rather than a spiritual and pious state of soul. A good Christian king was not expected to have Solomon's proverbial wisdom and religious insight, but he was expected to build beautiful churches to enshrine relics. When a Christian like Louis went to pray at La Sainte Chapelle, he was probably not engaging in contemplative, internal prayer of the sort we automatically associate with Christian devotion today. That type of interior devotion or mysticism would not become common among laymen until the fourteenth century, the age of Julian of Norwich, Richard Rolle of Hampole and Walter Hilton. Christians of the period of the Crusades went into churches to encounter the holy power of the relics and expose themselves to the presence of God that was concentrated in a special place. It is in this light that we should view the new devotion to the Eucharist. At a time when the Christian possession of Jerusalem was problematic, it was important to have holy places at home and the new celebration of the Real Presence made each church as holy as Solomon's Temple had been.

Louis' friend and biographer John of Joinville gives us some insight into what it meant to be a Christian in Louis' court. Since the Cluniac reform in the eleventh century, the religious experience of the layman had been shaped by performing certain external rites, like the pilgrimage or indeed the Crusade, which were supposed to form certain attitudes and values. By the middle of the thirteenth century we see in Joinville's account that these values had 'taken', especially the value of poverty. He records long debates in the court about the type of clothes a Christian should wear, the merit of washing the feet of the poor and the importance of almsgiving.[59] When Joinville describes Louis' daily Christian regime, he simply lists the number of monastic offices he attended throughout the day.[60] Laymen were still encouraged to live the monastic life as far as they could. But this piety remained an external matter. Joinville does not show the Christians of Louis' court as being at all concerned with spirituality or with an inner attitude. Religion was still a matter of performing certain external gestures and rites in honour of Christ.

During our story, we have seen that some religious orders had been making Christianity an inner mystical quest. The Cistercians had given the lead here in the early twelfth century and the Franciscans had also introduced a more affective, interior religious life, where the practice of holy poverty went hand in hand with an intensive prayer-life. This was also the case with some of the heretical sects that were springing up in Europe during the thirteenth century. But to read Joinville's biography of Louis makes one aware that this was still not the case with most laymen, and I think that this will give us some idea of the mentality of many of the Crusaders. When Joinville writes about Louis' 'charity' we see very clearly that he is not talking about a state of mind whereby Louis was filled with affective love towards his fellow man, nor was he engaged in a struggle to suppress 'uncharitable thoughts'. For Joinville and Louis 'charity' meant practical almsgiving and care for the poor. He always had 'six score poor persons fed in his house with bread and

wine and meat and fish',[61] wherever he travelled. Every day he had some 'old and decrepit men'[62] dine with him at his table, and he daily gave 'countless generous alms'[63] to poor religious, hospitals, fallen women and distressed gentlefolk. This is all very laudable, of course, but when Christians today talk of 'charity' they usually mean more than generosity to the poor; they mean a state of mind, which must be cultivated by constant interior attention. Louis and his court do not seem to have arrived at this degree of moral sophistication. Indeed the moral discussions in the court are at a very basic level: Louis will spend some time explaining to Joinville that Christians must learn to repent and set their lives in order, because otherwise they will not gain such a great reward in heaven.[64] Although monks and friars were clearly aware of the interior implications of Christianity, this was not yet the case for the layman. His religious emotions and 'mystical experiences' were very clearly tied to a visit to important places like La Sainte Chapelle or, pre-eminently, Jerusalem. They were not cultivated by a daily regimen of disciplined contemplation. Mystical vision was often experienced in emergencies, as we have seen. But a layman's daily Christian life was still largely a matter of exterior practice.

Indeed serious thought of an independent nature was actually discouraged. This was because one of the most severe battles a Christian had to fight was a war against Satan, who constantly tried to destroy his faith. Louis told his men that they must suppress any doubts they had very violently, because these came from the devil. One must cry: 'Be off! You shall not tempt me from my firm belief in all the articles of the faith, even though you were to have all my limbs cut off!'[65] Faith was often a fearful struggle in which a man sometimes had to do violence upon himself because he saw his own natural thoughts as satanic if they questioned articles of faith. In this battle for the faith, a Christian could come to distrust and fear his own mind. Judaism and Islam are also religions of practice but they have simple creeds and Muslims and Jews do not have to do themselves such violence to believe them. But Christians were asked to accept very irrational dogmas, as, for example, that Christ was truly, physically present in a piece of bread. Joinville tells us of a knight who went in despair to the Bishop of Paris, unable to control his tears because he was losing his faith. Try as he would, he said to the Bishop, 'I cannot force my heart to believe in the Sacrament of the altar as Holy Church teaches.'[66]

He knew this was a temptation from the devil and it made him absolutely miserable. It is not surprising that he found it difficult to believe that the body of Christ was truly present on the altar. Such a belief throws all rationality aside; it is contrary to the way we learn to understand the world and the laws of nature. It is noteworthy that the Bishop did not attempt to convince the knight intellectually. He simply told him that whereas he personally had no doubts at all on the matter (a fact which is a telling indication of the simplicity of the Bishop's own state of mind), the knight's struggle was more pleasing to God. Interestingly, he illustrated this by means of a military simile. It was as though, during a war, he, the Bishop, were defending a safe castle, while the knight was defending a castle on the front line that was continuously under assault. Holding on to the faith was, therefore, 'a woeful struggle'.[67] Christians who 'forced' their minds to submit to these irrational doctrines had to do so on very flimsy grounds. Joinville tells a story of Louis' somewhat simplistic advice:

> He asked me a question: 'What was my father's name?' I told him, 'Simon.' He then asked me how I knew. I answered that I thought I could be certain of it and believe it, since my mother had been my witness. 'Then,' he said, 'you should believe no less firmly in all the articles of the faith, of which the apostles are your witness, as you hear sung every Sunday in the Creed.'[68]

Louis also liked to tell the story of Simon of Montfort, the crusading hero who fought the Catharists. When he also encountered people of southern France who did not believe in the Eucharist, the Count replied that, because he believed implicitly, he would have a richer crown than the angels when he got to heaven, because they did not need to have faith; they saw everything for themselves.[69]

Joinville gives quite a lot of space to the problem of faith; he shows that it was a difficulty and that people were, not unnaturally, finding it a struggle. I think that this tells us two important things. First, Christians who forced their minds to accept, without question, basically irrational and incredible doctrines were doing their minds no good at all. A person who accepted without a qualm that the bread of the Eucharist was the body of Christ was denying the evidence of his senses and the ordinary laws of nature. He was putting his religion into quite a separate category and not only was he learning to repress doubt violently, he was also learning not to relate the natural with the supernatural nor to make potentially dangerous connections and comparisons. When, therefore, he heard in the gospel that Jesus told him to love his enemies, a Christian like Louis would not connect this with the Church's view that he should kill them. Such lack of connection was part of his Christian make-up. The second important lesson we learn about this view of faith was that it was a very fragile state of mind. We have seen that such insecurity very often leads into a holy war.

Louis himself gives us an insight into the way this insecurity led to an instinctive belligerence. He liked to tell a story about a debate that had been planned at Cluny between Jews and Christians. Staying in the monastery as a guest was a knight who had recently been wounded. He asked the Abbot if he might open the debate, and the Abbot agreed, with some misgivings. The knight then asked the chief Rabbi if he believed that the Virgin Mary was the Mother of God. Not surprisingly, the Rabbi replied that he did not. The knight then simply hit him on the head with his crutch and knocked him out. That was the end of the debate. In terror, the Jews picked up their unconscious leader and fled, much to the annoyance of the Abbot, who rebuked the knight, telling him that he had been extremely foolish. The knight replied that in his view the Abbot had been a much bigger fool for arranging the debate in the first place. Many good Christians might have been deceived by the Jews' lying arguments.[70] Louis entirely agreed: 'No one who is not a very learned clerk should argue with Jews,' he commented. 'A layman, as soon as he hears the Christian faith maligned should defend it by the sword, with a good thrust in the belly as far as the sword will go.'[71] The kind of faith that requires an unnatural suppression of normal reasoning processes is inherently fragile. If a Christian hears doubt cast on essential but unnatural doctrines like the Incarnation, he may well feel the 'dread' that we have seen in our story to arise from a deep threat to personal integrity and identity. We have seen in other circumstances that a person feeling this threat cannot understand the 'other' point of view. A Crusader like Louis, whom his mother had seen was brought up surrounded only by religious men,[72] would respond to Jews with violent aggression, as a reflex. It would also lead him to be prepared to fight the spectre of 'Mohammadanism'.

In 1244 Christendom heard the dreadful news that the Christians had lost the Kingdom of Jerusalem once again. The Khwarazmian Turkish dynasty had been dislodged from Central Asia by the Mongol hordes and ran amok, fleeing westward to get as far as possible from the terrifying Mongols, destroying cities in their panic. When they arrived in Syria, 10,000 of them attacked Damascus and then rushed on to Jerusalem, occupied the city and drove out the Franks, before sweeping on to Gaza where, together with an Egyptian army, they defeated the Christians of Palestine in a decisive battle. The loss of Jerusalem was the usual trauma and threat to the integrity of Christendom. That year Louis fell ill in Paris, and Joinville relates that he was so bad that one of his nurses thought that he had died and wanted to cover his face, but the other stopped her, certain that the King's soul had not yet left his body. At that moment, wrote Joinville, God intervened: 'Our Lord worked in him and soon sent him back his health. He had lost the power of speech, but as soon as he was again fit to speak he asked for the Cross to be given him, which was done.'[73] He had been reprieved from death in order to recover Jerusalem.

Hopes were high and Louis' three brothers and most of the nobles also took the Cross. With an accredited saint at the head of God's army, it was felt that the Seventh Crusade could not possibly fail. Louis wanted to take crusading right back to its fundamental principles. There would certainly be no fraternisation with the infidel and his army would be as pious as the First Crusaders. Frederick watched the organisation of this new crusading initiative with deep cynicism and wrote to Louis, warning him that the enterprise was hopeless, but of course Louis completely ignored this advice. Frederick then wrote to his friend, Sultan as-Salih Najm ad-Din Ayyub, who had succeeded al-Kamil as Sultan of Egypt, warning him to prepare for this Seventh Crusade.[74]

Yet although Louis was a fundamentalist Crusader, returning crusading to its roots, his would also be a modern Crusade making use of the latest technology. It would be another four years before the Crusade was ready to leave because of all the elaborate preparations. He began by building a great harbour in the previously uninhabited bay at Aigues Mortes, where he gathered an enormous fleet. In his army were skilled engineers and bridge-builders, who played a crucially important part in some of the battles, so that this Crusade has been called the Engineers' Crusade.[75] At Cyprus Louis began to collect huge supplies of wheat to ensure that the Crusade would be adequately provisioned, and Joinville described the towering wheat-mountain that had been grassed over on top.[76] In this sense too Louis was returning to the spirit of the First Crusaders, who had prayed as though everything depended upon God, but had fought and planned with every human skill they could muster. Eventually the preparations were complete and the fleet sailed for Egypt on 28 August 1248. Louis put in at Cyprus on 18 September and was advised by the barons of Acre to spend the winter there to avoid the storms and the treacherous winter conditions in Egypt. They also hoped to persuade Louis to take advantage of the quarrels among the Muslims to try to negotiate the return of Jerusalem. As one might expect, Louis would have nothing to do with any diplomatic initiative with the infidel, and urged the Templars, who had begun negotiations, to break them off immediately.

Yet Louis was quite prepared to consider another diplomatic initiative to the murderous Mongols, who were threatening the Muslims in the East. Already in 1245 Pope Innocent IV had sent two missions to the Khan trying to ward off the coming destruction by suggesting that they convert to Christianity. He had heard that some of them were Nestorian Christians. The first embassy had returned discouraged, and told the Pope that the Mongols were not interested in conversion but only in conquest. But the second returned with Nestorian envoys from the Mongol general Baichu, who was planning to attack Baghdad and was quite happy to encourage the Christian Crusade to distract the Muslims of Syria. But no permanent alliance seemed forthcoming and the two envoys were sent back to Baichu in November 1248. A month later another two Nestorians arrived in Cyprus, as envoys of another Mongol general, Aljighidai. They told Louis that the Mongols were deeply interested in Christianity, and Louis was delighted.[77] He sent two Dominicans on a mission to the Khan, bearing gifts. One of these presents was a little portable altar, with relics,[78] decorated with pictures that illustrated gospel scenes. Louis was bitterly disappointed three years later when the Dominicans returned with the sad news that the Mongols showed no signs of sympathy for Western Christianity, but that they were prepared to consider an alliance with the French King. Louis should send further gifts as tribute.[79]

At first this strange episode seems rather refreshing. At last crusading Europe was reaching out sympathetically towards another culture – a culture which was entirely alien to Christians because it did not derive from any of the three religions of Abraham. In fact the Dominican and Franciscan envoys were very interested and excited by what they saw of the Mongols and seemed able to describe these strange people quite objectively, without any of the solipsistic fantasies that distorted the Christian view of Judaism and Islam.[80] Yet this new quest for contact was really inspired by the desperate needs of the holy war against Islam. At the time of the Crusade the Mongols were drawing nearer and nearer to the Islamic empire. Muslims had seen and suffered from the panic of the Khwarazmian Turks, in their headlong flight from these terrifying foes, who massacred and devastated wherever they conquered. With the Mongols to the East and Louis' Crusaders to the West, the Muslims felt caught between Scylla and Charybdis, and Louis' missionary initiative was, as usual, part of a deadly war against Islam.

Louis and the Pope were both so cheered by the thought of a new way of getting rid of Islam that they could not see that the Mongols were far more of a threat to Christendom than the Muslims had ever been. So deeply ingrained was the Western paranoia that the revelation of a far more ferocious race of Orientals did nothing to modify Western fantasies about 'Mohammadanism', which people seemed to need as emotional ballast for their own view of themselves. In the eighteenth century we shall see that a similar revelation of a new Orient made absolutely no difference to the way people saw Islam. The old medieval prejudice flourished unchanged, while people enthusiastically and appreciatively studied an Orient that was far more challenging to the Christian world-view.

In May Louis' beautifully equipped, modern army sailed from Cyprus to Damietta in Egypt. As soon as the banner of St Denis had been carried ashore, Louis pushed past the papal legate, leaped into the water which came up to his armpits and waded to the beach, lance in hand. As soon as he saw a host of Saracens on the beach, Joinville recalled, 'he couched his lance under his arm and put his shield before him, and would have flung himself upon them had not his wiser companions held him back.'[81] Instinctively Louis presented himself in a posture of unthinking aggression towards Muslims, just as he had with Jews. It was exactly the same response. But this gesture was also a deliberate harking back to the days of vintage crusading in *The Song of Roland*, and there would be a good deal of this dangerous and irresponsible chivalry during this Crusade, which might work all right in an eleventh-century poem, but was impossible in the real world of the thirteenth century. Yet a Crusader like Louis, like many holy warriors today, could deliberately close his eyes to rationality and common sense in an absurd and dangerous gesture. In fact he had arrived in Egypt at a favourable moment. The Sultan was dying and his son and heir Turanshah was far away in the Jezireh. There was a very good chance, therefore, of a palace revolution and this could be very beneficial to the Crusaders. The Muslims were so lacking in confidence at this bad period that the citizens and the garrison simply fled Damietta and the Crusaders could occupy the city without a battle. The news of the loss of Damietta spread fear and consternation throughout the Muslim world; their position seemed hopeless. The dying Sultan made the same offer as his father al-Kamil had made thirty years earlier: he would give Jerusalem back to the Christians if Louis would evacuate Egypt. Naturally Louis refused to deal with the infidel and confidently waited for the Nile waters to subside before he continued his campaign. Yet this confidence would prove to be as ill founded in reality as the heroic gesture of flinging himself upon the Muslims single-handed.

Their new desperation gave the Muslims a grim determination, realism and political astuteness that would ultimately prove superior to the rather old-fashioned crusading heroics. This was a terrifying new world for the Muslims and they could no longer afford the chivalrous generosity of Saladin in their fight for survival. When a strong detachment of Crusaders marched on Mansurah on 20 November, the Muslims braced themselves for the coming struggle, and when the Sultan finally died three days later, the Sultana Shajar ad-Durr acted swiftly and efficiently and kept his death a secret. By the time the news leaked out Fakhr ad-Din was firmly in control of events and Turanshah was already on his way to Egypt. Louis still hoped that a government led by a woman and an old man would shortly collapse and began to plan an offensive. On the night of 8 February 1250 the Crusaders managed to ford the canal that separated them from the Egyptian camp, make a surprise attack and put the enemy to flight. They were now in a strong position to take the city but threw away their victory in one of those anachronistic acts of foolish chivalry. The attack had been made by a vanguard, led by Louis' brother Robert of Artois and a contingent of Templars, and the Grand Master of the Templars strongly advised Robert not to attack the city until Louis and the main army had managed to ford the canal. But Robert would not wait and charged once more through the fleeing Egyptians and into the city, followed reluctantly by the Templars. Fakhr ad-Din, who had been in his bath, had rushed out into the streets without his armour and was set upon by the Templars and killed. But the Turkish Mamluk troops led by the slave–officer Rukn ad-Din Baibars quickly organised themselves and caught the small crusading force in an ambush. Robert and the Templars were massacred: there were only five survivors.[82] Louis and the main army managed to hold back the Muslims and establish themselves in the former Egyptian camp, but were not strong enough to take the city, which was equipped with better war-engines than their own. The Crusaders sat for a further eight weeks outside Mansurah and the campaign seemed to be falling into the same pattern as the Fifth Crusade. On 11 February the Muslims attacked the camp and inflicted grave casualties; Turanshah arrived and there was no palace revolution; an Egyptian fleet cut off the food supplies and there was famine in the Crusader camp which was quickly followed by disease. The glamorous expedition had become a nightmare.[83]

Now that he had come face to face with reality, Louis offered to negotiate with Sultan Turanshah, but it was too late because the Egyptians knew very well how precarious his position really was. The situation was hopeless and at the beginning of April Louis and his officers decided to retreat. The sick were sent by ship up the Nile to Damietta and the army began to return along the road they had travelled so hopefully a few weeks earlier. But the Muslims followed the army, harassing them on all sides, and the Crusaders were too exhausted and ill even to resist them. When Louis himself succumbed to the sickness, his officers took the responsibility and surrendered to the Muslims. The whole army was taken into captivity.

It was a unique and difficult situation for both Muslims and Crusaders. The Egyptians were embarrassed by the vast numbers of prisoners, whom they could not afford to feed, and every day a hundred of the weaker soldiers were killed off. Yet, while both sides negotiated for the conditions of the ransom, they had a chance to look at one another at close quarters. To Joinville the Muslims seem to have become human beings. He recalled the kindness of an old Muslim soldier who used to carry one of the sick Crusaders to the latrines every day on his back;[84] he remembered the kindness of the Emir with whom he was billeted: Joinville had eaten meat on Friday by mistake and the Emir was at pains to reassure him that God would not punish him for this accident.[85] For their part the Muslims were impressed with the behaviour of many of their prisoners and especially by the bearing of Louis himself. They even suggested, no doubt in jest, that he should be their next sultan. Louis seemed to have taken this seriously and told Joinville that he would have accepted the position.[86] Joinville wrote that the emirs said:

> that the King was the most steadfast Christian you could find. They gave as an example of this that when he came out of his lodging he used to lie on the ground in the form of a cross and so made the sign of the Cross with his whole body. They said too that had Mahomet allowed such misfortunes to befall them they would never have kept their faith in him; and that if their people made him their Sultan, either they would have to become Christians or he would put them to death.[87]

If this really is accurate, it would seem that the emirs had summed up Louis's Christianity rather well – a religion of gesture and simple acts of devotion, which had very little to do with the love and pacifism of Christ. Louis most certainly would have forced any Saracen subjects to convert at sword-point.

Eventually terms were agreed: Louis' wife Queen Margaret (who had remained with the garrison at Damietta) and the Templars managed to raise a million besants for the release of the King and most of the prisoners. But on 2 May there was a setback, when the palace revolution that the Crusaders had longed for actually happened. The Turkish *mamluks* or former slaves, who had played such an important part in the defence of Mansurah, now demanded a greater say in the government, and when this was refused they assassinated Turanshah and took control. From this point the Mamluks would be the principal enemy of the Crusaders in the Holy Land. After the assassination, the emirs rushed to their Christian prisoners with the blood still on their hands and swords and threatened to put them to death.[88] In fact, however, the Mamluks had absolutely no intention of losing the enormous ransom and on 6 May Damietta was handed back to the Muslims and the sick and weary Crusaders sailed back to Acre. For two more years Louis and a number of the French barons remained in the Holy Land, building and repairing fortifications. The Crusade of the Engineers had ended as a building project; the complete fiasco of the Seventh Crusade made it clear to many people

that it was impossible to conquer Jerusalem from Islam and that crusading should be abandoned. Joinville was one of these: after 1250 crusading seemed to him a useless, self-indulgent exercise, actually damaging the Kingdom of France, which had been gravely weakened by the absence of the King and most of the knights. But one knight of Christ never gave up. After his return from the Holy Land in 1254 Louis led a devout life of penance, so that never again would he wear fine clothes and he was always very moderate at table. The failure of his Crusade, he was convinced, could only be explained by God's wishing to teach him humility,[89] a characteristically simple-minded explanation of a disastrous campaign which had cost thousands of Christian lives. He was determined to lead an army to the East again, even if he waited another twenty years. It was his duty to fight the Muslims, who were an absolute danger to the Christian people.

But in fact the Muslims of the Middle East were at that time in very great danger themselves. In 1257 the Mongol army led by Hulegu, the grandson of Genghis Khan, began to march towards Baghdad. Before this vast army Caliph al-Mustasi'un had no choice but to surrender on 10 February 1258, but the city was sacked and the population exterminated. It seemed as though Louis' hopes were to be realised and that the Mongols really would destroy Islam; there was great rejoicing in the Crusader states. In January 1260 Aleppo was destroyed, Damascus was taken and occupied and in March the Mongols swept into Palestine and took Nablus and Gaza. As the horrified Muslims watched the destruction of one city after another, they naturally associated these destroyers with the Christian menace, which had attacked them relentlessly for nearly 200 years. Hulegu himself had Nestorian Christian connections and Damascus was now ruled by three Christian Mongols. But the Christian rejoicings were entirely misplaced and were based on a quite fictitious view of the Mongols. The Mongolian conquests were always accompanied by total devastation and extermination, unless the cities surrendered immediately and unconditionally; Hulegu would have made short work of Acre and Antioch and might even have gone on to invade Europe. Instead of neurotically inventing fantasies of Muslim conspiracies to conquer Europe, the Europeans should have been worrying about a far more dangerous enemy.

After the Mongols had conquered Gaza, they naturally looked towards Egypt and an envoy was dispatched to the Mamluk Sultan to order his capitulation. After the envoy had finished speaking, the Sultan simply struck off his head.[90] There was now a new harshness in the Muslim spirit and throughout the devastated Islamic empire people began to look to the tough Mamluks as their only hope. Sultan Saif ad-Din Qutuz seized the first chance that offered. Hulegu had to return to Persia after the death of his brother Möngke, the Supreme Khan, in order to cope with the inevitable problems of the succession, leaving only a few thousand horsemen in the country under the command of his lieutenant Kitbuga. In July 1260 Qutuz invaded Palestine, realising that this was Islam's last chance. By this time some of the barons in Acre, though not in Antioch, were becoming thoroughly alarmed by the Mongols' ruthless brutality, and although they would not fight alongside a Muslim army they agreed not to attack the Mamluks from the rear. When a revolt broke out in Damascus at the end of August, Qutuz had time to deploy his troops very carefully at Ain Jalut in the Galilee, and on 3 September the two armies met. By a brilliant ambush tactic, the Mamluks defeated and massacred the whole Mongol army, and this battle, which truly changed history, marked the end of Mongol supremacy.[91] It was an ironic reversal of Louis' hopes. Instead of the Mongols saving Christianity from Islam, it was the Muslims who saved Christendom from the Mongols and instead of the Mongols converting to Christianity they would finally settle in Persia and Palestine and become Muslims.

Only two months after the great victory at Ain Jalut, Baibars, the hero of the

battle of Mansurah, assassinated Qutuz and became the Mamluk Sultan. It seems a
sad reflection on the Mamluks, but many of them had always considered Baibars to
be their natural leader. Baibars could not forgive the Franks at Antioch for
colluding with the Mongols and in 1265 when Hulegu died he took advantage of
Mongol quarrels to invade their territory in Palestine to establish a new base there.
In 1268 he conquered Beaufort Castle near Acre and on 1 May he rode on to
Tripolis. The ruler Count Bohemund, who was also Prince of Antioch, prepared for
a long siege. But instead Baibars travelled swiftly northward and on 14 May his
army surprised the city of Antioch, massacred the population and reduced the great
and ancient city to ruins. He then sent a letter to Bohemund, telling him what had
happened: 'Be glad that you have not seen your knights lying prostrate under the
hooves of horses, your palaces plundered, your ladies sold in the quarters of the
city, fetching a mere dinar apiece – a dinar taken, moreover, from your own
hoard!'[92] This was quite a new Islam. The trauma of recent years had produced a
new cool ruthlessness and desperate determination to survive. Now that he had
effectively destroyed Bohemund's power, Baibars was prepared to make a treaty
with him. But still the Franks did not seem fully to have understood the
precariousness of their position. Baibars had sent his chronicler Abd-al-Zahir to
Acre to draw up the treaty. During the negotiations, when the Mamluks were
proving to be quite inflexible, the King of Acre told Abd-al-Zahir to turn around.
When he did so, he saw the whole Frankish army drawn up in battle array.
Unperturbed, he said to the interpreter: 'Tell the king that there are fewer soldiers
in his army than there are Frankish captives in the prisons of Cairo.' The King
nearly choked and the terms of the treaty were quickly agreed.[93]

Yet Baibars was not simply a destroyer. The battle of Ain Jalut had made him
master of Damascus, Aleppo and Cairo, which meant that for the first time since
Saladin the Ayubid empire was united under a single ruler, and it represented a
rebirth and a new power after the Mongol trauma. Like Louis, Baibars was a great
builder, and there was a cultural renaissance under the Mamluks so that Egypt and
Syria became centres of art and learning once more.[94] But to preserve the security
of this revived Muslim empire required constant vigilance. Baibars knew that he
had nothing to fear from the Franks in Palestine any longer, but there was always
the possibility of a new Crusade from the West. Indeed shortly after the destruction
of Antioch he heard some terrible news. King Louis of France had set out for the
East at the head of a huge army. This time, to the Muslims' astonishment, he had
made for Tunisia, an entirely new location for Crusaders. The Sultan Abu
Abdullah Muhammad al-Mustansir bi-llah, ruler of Tunisia, prepared to meet this
Christian attack and offered 8000 dinar for peace: his whole country was at this
point weakened by plague and famine.[95] Baibars waited in Palestine with
trepidation. If Louis succeeded in establishing a base in Tunisia, he was certain
that he would then attack the Mamluks in the Near East, who were themselves
also weakened by their long struggle, caught in a frightening vice between the East
and West. Anxiously Baibars watched the progress of the Crusade from Palestine.
The Christians took the money the Sultan offered them, but did not make peace
and started their Crusade. They had, the Egyptian historian Taqi ad-Din al-Maqrizi
tells us, 6000 cavalry and 30,000 infantry. 'The Muslims kept up the fight until
mid-Muharram, the end of August, with violent battles in which many of both
sides died.'[96] The Muslims of Tunis were almost defeated, when God suddenly
seemed to step in and liberate them, and the Mamluks and the Tunisians could
breathe again. Louis' army succumbed to the plague that was rife in Tunisia and on
25 August 1270 King Louis himself died. The King of France, wrote Maqrizi, as an
epitaph, 'was an intelligent man, cunning and deceitful'.[97] That was one Muslim
view of the most Christian King.

We have noted that in fact intelligence was not Louis' strong point and nowhere do we see his simple-minded irresponsibility more clearly than in the story of this last Crusade. When he had set off from Paris, against the advice of many of his barons like Joinville who were furious about this last Crusade, he was a very sick man. He was indeed so ill that Joinville had to carry him on the first leg of his journey in his arms.[98] Joinville himself had refused to take the Cross this time because he knew that he, like the King, was badly needed in France.[99] Had Louis stayed at home he might have lived a few years to do much useful work, but with an obstinate, almost pathological refusal to face reality that we have so often seen during the Crusades, he set out to endure the rigours of a hard campaign in an unhealthy climate, where there was already a major pestilence. It must have been obvious, even to Louis, that he would not live long, but it seems that he wanted to fight the Muslims to his very last gasp. Nothing, I think, illustrates his fanatical hatred of the Muslims more clearly than this suicidal expedition. The fall of Antioch must have filled Louis with such sickening dread that he was ready to make himself in effect a voluntary martyr to ward off the horror of an encroaching Islam.

Certainly Western Christians at once acclaimed Louis as a martyr and he was deeply lamented and revered as a Crusader, even though both his Crusades had been such dreadful failures. It was impossible for the crusading army to survive in Tunisia, once it had been decimated by the plague, which appears to have been a chronic form of dysentery. Scarcely able to believe their luck the Muslims of Tunisia watched the Christians making their preparations to go home, and sent the good news to Baibars, who could also relax. Yet the local people were charitable enough to erect a small shrine in Louis' memory, for they could see that, even though he hated them to his last breath, he was a genuinely religious man. Louis would not have reciprocated this gesture. He was not of course buried in Muslim territory, and Louis, who had brought so many relics home from the East, now returned from the House of Islam as a relic himself. Because the Crusaders were afraid that the body would decompose, they boiled the flesh off the bones, which they enshrined in a casket which they buried as soon as they arrived in Christendom. By a strange irony, this meant that Louis was buried in the same Church of Monreale in Palermo as Frederick, his crusading predecessor.

That was the last Crusade. Small armies did cross the Mediterranean, as we shall see, to try to save the Kingdom of Acre, but as a mass movement the project was now dead and seen to be impractical. This Christian failure called into question the whole integrity of the faith and we can see some of this fear and dread in a poem written at about this time by a Templar in Acre:

> Rage and sorrow are seated in my heart, so firmly that I scarce dare stay alive. It seems that God wishes to support the Turks to our loss. ... Ah, Lord God! Alas the realm of the East has lost so much that it will never rise up again. ... Anyone who wishes to fight the Turks is mad, for Jesus Christ does not fight them any more. They have conquered, they will conquer. For every day they drive us down, knowing that God, who was awake, sleeps now, and Mohammad waxes powerful.[100]

Had God deserted his chosen people? The success of the early Crusaders had been a glorious affirmation of the faith, and it had led to Christians regarding Muslims as polluting filth, who could be exterminated like vermin. But what did their new success mean? Muslims began to pose a terrible unanswered question to Europeans and were surrounded with a new aura of dread.

Yet ultimately the Christians in the East proved to be their own worst enemies. In 1271 Baibars had conquered the great Krak des Chevaliers in Syria, which not even Saladin had been able to overcome. The little Christian Kingdom of Acre and County of Tripolis now consisted of only a few cities along the coast and their position was obviously precarious. But when Baibars died, Sultan Qalawun, his successor, seemed to go out of his way to befriend the Franks.[101] In 1183 he renewed the treaty that Baibars had made with the Franks, and Acre, Athlit and Sidon were at peace with their Muslim neighbours. But Tripolis stood aloof and still preferred to side with the Mongols, who were themselves trying to make a comeback during these years. Hulegu's grandson Il-Khan Arghun approached the Pope and the rulers of Europe in 1287 with a new offer of an alliance and proposed a joint offensive against the Mamluks in January 1191. When news of this reached Qalawun, he realised that the presence of the Franks was a permanent threat to Muslim security, but he still refused to break the truce. Instead he decided to make an example of Tripolis, which paraded its Mongol sympathies,[102] and which he besieged in March 1289; he took the city by storm on 27 April. The historian Abu l-Fida described the events tersely: the civilians fled to the harbour and a few managed to take refuge on a small island just off the coast, 'but most of the men were killed and the children taken captive.'[103] The city was looted and razed to the ground and the Muslim troops then swam out to the island on horseback to kill those who had taken refuge there. For months it was impossible to land there, because of the stench of putrefying corpses.[104] The whirligig of time had brought its revenge. Desperation had reproduced in the Muslim soldiers the ruthless spirit of the Crusaders who conquered Jerusalem in 1099.

Yet even though many of his officers urged Qalawun to attack Acre, the Sultan refused to dishonour the truce. He urged Muslims to make use of Acre as a trading port and the city had never been so busy and even prosperous. Everybody had been able to benefit by this secular co-operation, and many of the more realistic barons were delighted with this turn of events. Perhaps Acre would be able to survive after all. But there was an aggressive party of religious chauvinists in Acre in 1289 as there had been in the Kingdom of Jerusalem a hundred years earlier and they urged King Henry to ask the Pope for another Crusade. In the summer of 1290 a crusading fleet from Italy sailed into the port of Acre. The Crusaders were fêted in an extremely alcoholic banquet and then they rushed drunkenly through the streets of the city, attacking merchants from Damascus and any man who wore a beard, which meant that some Christians were killed.[105] Qalawun was appalled by this fresh assault, yet he was still unwilling to destroy the city and offered to make a new treaty. But Acre had been overtaken by a crusading madness and refused to make peace, so Qalawun, driven beyond further endurance, swore on the Koran that he would not lay down his arms until he had thrown the Franks into the sea.

As the Christians watched the huge army assembling in Cairo, they woke up to the reality of their position. But it was too late. The army left Cairo on 4 November 1290 but on the following day Qalawun, who was now an old man of seventy-seven, died and the army had to turn back and deal with the succession. Qalawun was succeeded by his son al-Ashraf Khalil, who continued his father's offensive. In March 1291 the army set out again and this time reached Acre, camping outside the city walls at the beginning of May. There was a siege of a few weeks but finally on 17 June the Muslims broke into the city and once again Christians experienced the Muslim intransigence that they seemed to have gone out of their way to create. There were terrible scenes in the city. Prisoners who had surrendered in good faith were mercilessly beheaded; the men were all killed and, in the light of the burning buildings, women could be seen running and weeping through the streets. The Muslim soldiers killed babies at their mothers' breasts and slaughtered pregnant women. During a truce, some Muslims rounded up a group of women and massacred them like vermin.[106]

The End of the Crusades?

335

The contemporary Muslim historians saw a vicious circle in these events, which they interpreted as a manifestation of the justice of God. Abu l-Mahasin ibn Taghribirdi points out that according to the Muslim calendar the Franks had conquered Acre from Saladin on Friday 17 Junada II at the third hour of the day in the Muslim year 587. After terms had been agreed, Richard the Lionheart had massacred the Muslim prisoners that he had undertaken to spare. By a strange coincidence the Muslims had conquered Acre from the Christians on 17 Junada II, and the Sultan al-Ashraf also massacred the prisoners he had undertaken to spare. 'Thus Almighty God was revenged on their descendants,'[107] he concludes. There was a coincidence too in the Christian calendar, for the Franks at Acre were defeated almost 100 years to the day since they had defeated Saladin at the Siege of Acre. We have noticed the uncanny coincidences about the dates of events during the story of the holy war. If this coincidence means anything it must surely throw up the frightening cycle of religious violence, which eventually in the Middle Ages came round full circle. The Franks had invaded Palestine in 1099 and there they had slaughtered thousands of Muslims who had done nothing to harm them, except that they were living in Jerusalem. So aggressive was the Frankish assault that eventually the *jihad* of Nur ad-Din and Saladin arose as a response to this Christian holy war. One holy war continuously led to another for a hundred years, until finally it looked as though the Christians had reproduced the murderous cruelty and hatred that they had felt for the Muslims in the hearts of the Muslims themselves. This was perhaps one of the most tragic consequences of the Crusades. The Crusaders' violence in 1099 had horrified the Muslim world in the Near East; now at Acre the Christians experienced the new Muslim violence that they had implanted in the area.

Yet another Muslim chronicler puts a slightly different emphasis on the events of 1291. Abu l-Fida writes:

> With these conquests the whole of Palestine was now in Muslim hands, a result that no one would have dared to hope for or to desire. Thus the whole of Syria and the coastal zones were purified of the Franks, who had once been on the point of conquering Egypt and subduing Damascus and other cities. Praise be to God![108]

In this view, the Muslim purging of Palestine was not a mechanical cycle, but a matter of cause and effect. The Koran, we have seen, teaches that a war of self-defence is a Muslim duty when faced with oppression and aggression. The Franks had wanted to throw the Muslims out of their cities and conquer their lands. Therefore the Muslims had had to fight them back until the peril was eliminated. In rather the same way Western aggression in our own day has also produced a fresh round of Muslim intransigence and some religious Muslims have used the most desperate means of ejecting the current Western invaders from their lands. This is not just because 'history repeats itself' in a deterministic cycle of fate. It is because there has been a similar Western aggression which has produced a similar effect in Muslims of the Middle East in our own times.

The Crusades also had an effect on the Jews, which is likewise very familiar to us today. They had made life intolerable for the Jews in Europe and we have seen that this led some Jews to dream of a return to Zion. Ever since Saladin had invited the Jews to come back to Jerusalem there had been large Jewish migrations there from Europe. These people did not just see themselves as refugees, but they regarded their return as a positive religious duty. Throughout the thirteenth century there had been mass migrations, from Normandy, England, Provence and Languedoc.[109] One group from Paris led by Rabbi Yehiel at the time of Louis' Crusade had intended to rebuild the Temple in Jerusalem.[110] In 1268 Rabbi Meir of Rothenburg

was moved by the dramatic failure of the Crusades to reclaim the land for the Jews and tried to lead a great exodus from Germany but he was captured and imprisoned by Rudolph of Habsburg: at this time the Germans were finding the Jews too useful to their economy to allow them to leave. Rabbi Meir died in prison in 1293, an early martyr for the return to Zion.[111] We get some idea of what these Jews were feeling and thinking in the writings of the great Rabbi Nachmanides, who made the *aliyah* in 1267, after he had been exiled from Spain. He wrote that settlement in Eretz Yisrael was an absolute religious duty 'incumbent upon *each* generation, binding upon *every* one of us, even in time of exile'.[112] The land, he wrote, was beautiful but was now a desert: the Christians and Muslims had devastated it in their brutal wars. Eretz Yisrael, therefore, would not accept any other people but her rightful owners, the Jews: 'For ever since we departed from it, it had not accepted a single nation. They all try to settle it but it is beyond their power.'[113] It might even be the case that to fight a holy war for this land would also become an absolute religious duty and the Gentiles would only be allowed to stay on in Eretz Yisrael on carefully defined terms.[114] One of Nachmanides' disciples saw the fall of Christian Acre as the birthpangs of the Messiah, but was convinced that the redemption could not occur while there were any *goyim* left in Eretz Yisrael: 'Let no man think that the King Messiah will appear in an impure land; and let him not be deluded either into imagining that he will appear in the Land of Israel among Gentiles.'[115] It is obvious that this religious Zionism is identical to the current extremist fervour for Eretz Yisrael today. In the next chapter I want to suggest that, like the medieval version, modern Zionism might also be a response to a crusading West.

The great crusading adventure was over. The dream took a long time to die and for another 200 years there would be crusading projects. The last Crusader was Pope Pius II in 1464.[116] But none of these projects came to anything and there would be no Western hegemony in Jerusalem until the establishment of the British Mandate in 1920. For almost 200 years, as the West found her soul, crusading had been a central passion. Millions of Jews, Christians and Muslims had died in these savage holy wars; it is probably impossible to estimate exact numbers. Crusaders had massacred and driven Jews and Muslims from their homes, had carved themselves an empire in the Islamic wilderness, but were eventually ejected through their own fanaticism. The Muslims now owned the whole of the Near East and a significant part of Anatolia had been conquered from the Christians of Antioch. In 1261 the Greeks had managed to oust the Latins from Byzantium and so Constantinople was now in Greek hands, but Byzantium had been severely wounded in the struggle with the West. In Europe there were still some Muslims left. In Spain the Christian wars of Reconquest had proved very successful during the thirteenth century: the Christians took Cordova in 1236 and Seville in 1248, but there was still a small Muslim kingdom in Granada. In 1301, as we have seen, Charles of Anjou would exterminate the Muslims of Lucera. Christendom was now striving to purge herself of Muslims as Muslims had striven to purge Syria and Palestine of Christians and was making life so unbearable for Jews that some of them were trying to leave Christendom too.

During the thirteenth century it seems that Europe made a decisive choice and the two last important Crusaders give us some idea of what that choice involved. There was the path offered by the Emperor Frederick that envisaged an acceptance of Jews and Muslims and the setting up of normal relations with them. Sometimes these relations might be exploitative or even antagonistic, but they were governed by the ordinary rules that shape human relations. There could also be a possibility of great friendship. The other way was the way epitomised by 'Saint' Louis: this saw Jews and Muslims in a manner that was quite different from the way Western Christians judged every other people (even one as savage as the Mongols) and put them in a separate category. Louis saw Jews and Muslims as the essential enemies of religion and civilisation and could only approach them in a spirit of absolute antagonism. Neither Frederick nor Louis was perfect and nor were their methods: both were cruel, ruthless men. But the story of the last three Crusades makes it clear that Europe had opted for Louis' way and violently rejected Frederick's. Even though Frederick had many supporters these people were more truly in sympathy with his struggle against the papacy than with his policies of coexistence, though some may have been stirred by them on the level of fantasy. But Europe had committed herself to Louis' way since the First Crusaders responded to the call of Pope Urban and 200 years of holy war had burned an absolute hatred of Jews and Muslims into the Western identity. In the last chapter I want to argue that this abnormal way of regarding Muslims and Jews is still a Western habit and is a legacy from the Crusades.

After the Crusades stopped going to the Holy Land, Europe still followed the path of 'Saint' Louis, even when Europeans became more sophisticated and more spiritually aware. A single example makes this clear. Most of us would agree that one of the most evil of all Christian institutions was the Inquisition, which was an instrument of terror in the Catholic Church until the end of the seventeenth century. Its methods were also used by Protestants to persecute and control the Catholics in their countries. These methods were that 'heretics' should be hunted out by a panel of inquisitors, who in the Catholic Church were usually Dominicans. This gave them a new nickname for they were called *Domini canes*, the hounds of the Lord. These bloodhounds of orthodoxy sniffed out the heretics in the community and people who held unacceptable views or were accused of 'unChristian' practices were arrested and flung into prison. There they would be tortured with unbelievable cruelty and made to 'confess' their crimes. Frequently they were also accused of far more than heterodox opinions: they were forced to confess that they worshipped the devil or took part in monstrous sexual orgies; once they had been tortured beyond endurance, they had no further strength to deny the charges. The inquisitors themselves were genuinely convinced that these abominable practices really were committed by 'heretics' and this shows that Europe was still haunted by the same inner demons as had inspired Christians to make the Muslims and Jews monsters of evil in the Middle Ages. Four hundred years after the Crusades, sophisticated Europeans felt a sickening dread when they contemplated a challenge to their faith and this led them into this violent persecution. Once the heretic had confessed his error he might be released, but that was not always the case. After confession, the heretics were handed over to the secular authorities and were then either hanged or burned at the stake. Sometimes they were so badly injured that they could not walk to the pyre and the executioners tried to hide their dreadful wounds from the spectators.[117]

This obscene institution was the creation of that most saintly Christian king, 'Saint' Louis. In 1229, when he was only fifteen, Louis organised the first Inquisition to eliminate the heresy of Catharism in the south of France. The military Crusade of Simon of Montfort had not proved as effective as had been hoped and the heresy continued to flourish, so Louis instructed the Dominicans, who had originally been created to preach peacefully to the heretics, to persecute them instead by inquisitorial methods.[118] The Inquisition continued to operate in the south until 1247 when Louis and his army massacred the last remaining Cathars in cold blood at Montségur. But once Catharism had been wiped out, there were many other heresies to extinguish and the Inquisition continued, as we have seen. It was not surprising that this noxious offspring of the Crusades was eventually used to persecute Muslims and Jews living in Christian territory, who had been forced to convert to Christianity. In the early part of the next chapter, we shall examine this next phase of crusading activity against Jews and Muslims in the Christian West.

CHAPTER TWELVE

1300 to the Present Day

New Crusaders in the West

The year 1492 has been called the beginning of the modern period, and, while this is obviously an oversimplification, it is certainly true that for our purposes three very important things happened that year in Spain, which had seemed free of the intolerant neurosis that plagued the rest of Europe. In January King Ferdinand and Queen Isabella finally defeated the Muslim Kingdom of Granada, the last stronghold of Islam in Europe. With deep emotion, crowds watched the Christian banner being ceremonially raised on the city walls and throughout Europe church-bells pealed joyfully to celebrate this purging of Muslim filth. Three months later the Jews of Spain were given a terrible choice: they either had to convert to Christianity or leave the country. Many were so attached to Spain that they chose baptism, but about 100,000 Spanish Jews began a new period of exile and homelessness and the Jews of Europe mourned the destruction of Spanish Jewry as the greatest disaster since the loss of Jerusalem in CE 70. But the year 1492 is most famous for another apparently different but in fact deeply connected reason. Present at the ceremony of liberation at Granada was a man whose name was Christopher Columbus and in August he sailed across the Atlantic hoping to arrive in India, but accidentally discovered the New World instead. In India Columbus had hoped to establish a new Christian base from which to attack the Muslims, and his diaries show that years later he was still preoccupied with the reconquest of Jerusalem.[1] As Europe sailed into the modern period that would in so many respects be an entirely new world, she was still obsessed with the old crusading hatreds and enthusiasms that would not die away. They would also cross the Atlantic and take firm root in America, and we must now examine the survival of crusading long after Crusades had stopped going to the Holy Land.

Intolerance of Jews and Muslims had been building up in Spain for some time. For 800 years, Jews, Christians and Muslims had, for the most part, been able to live in Christian as well as in Muslim Spain quite amicably side by side. Together they had been able to build a rich and dynamic culture. Spanish Jewry had enjoyed a glorious renaissance during the twelfth century and it was from Spain that the West recovered the cultural heritage she had lost during the Dark Ages. But the crusading virus was too strong to resist and Spain would become even more anxious to purge herself of alien elements than any other country, as if to atone for the long period of sinful coexistence. There had been outbreaks of anti-semitism in Christian Spain since the end of the fourteenth century and more and more Jews had been pressured to convert to Christianity.[2] The rabbis warned their people that they would find no rest among the Christians and they would prove to be right, for the converted Jews, who were called the *marranos*, inspired a new paranoia. Many

of the *marranos* became sincere Christians but it is quite possible that others
secretly remained true to their old faith and during the fifteenth century Christians
became obsessed with the fear of crypto-Jews, lurking unseen in the midst of
society, eating away from within. In 1483 Ferdinand and Isabella established the
Spanish National Inquisition to seek out these hidden enemies of God. The
Dominican and Franciscan inquisitors could not touch the Jews who had not been
baptised, but the *marranos* could be arrested, tortured, forced to confess their
deviance and to denounce other crypto-Jews. Within twelve years 13,000 people,
most of them Jews, had been killed by the Inquisition and, when the Jews were
finally told to go in 1492, this led to a fresh inquisitorial purge of the new
marranos.[3] In 1499 the Muslims were given exactly the same choice of baptism or
expulsion and many of them chose conversion. This made the converted Muslims,
the *moriscos*, subject to the Inquisition in exactly the same way. As they had
received no instruction in the Christian faith, many *moriscos* remained true to
Islam, and Christians became terrified of crypto-Muslims spreading their poison
unseen and unnoticed and contaminating Christendom by their very presence.[4]

It is important to notice that the hatred of both Jews and Muslims was connected
and followed the same pattern. This would continue to be the case right up to the
present day. It is also important to notice that this new intolerance in Spain was
taking new forms in the post-crusading era. It continued long after there was any
territorial dispute with Muslims and long after there was any religious reason for
persecution. Not even sincere conversion could save the *moriscos* and *marranos*,
who could, for example, find themselves denounced to the Inquisition for refusing
to eat pork – a habit that is very commonly retained after conversion or
assimilation. Converted Jews would be arrested for lighting a candle on the sabbath
eve and converted Muslims were burned to death because they had refused to drink
wine. So deep was this neurotic craving for conformity in Spain that practices
which were neutral in themselves became capital crimes because of their mere
connection with the Torah and the Koran. Sometimes the accusations had no
religious significance at all but were merely Moorish customs, like throwing cakes
and sweets at a wedding or using henna.[5] It seemed that Moors and Jews could not
be assimilated into Christian Spanish society and that coexistence was an
impossibility. The religious conflict was becoming a racial conflict in Europe
centuries before the racial explosion of anti-semitism in the late nineteenth
century. As early as 1449 the Strictures of the Purity of Blood had been
promulgated in Spain to define exactly who was a racially pure 'Old' Christian and
who was a tainted 'New' Christian of Moorish or Jewish extraction. New
Christians were suspect and vulnerable to the Inquisition until the seventeenth
century, long after they had had any real contact with either Judaism or Islam.[6] The
Spanish phobia could not be assuaged by forced assimilation of outsiders; even
after conversion Jews and Muslims were objects of an irrational dread.

It was no better in the other countries of Europe. In fact the end of the Crusades
marked a new paranoia. In 1348 the Black Death struck and decimated the
population and there was a new wave of pogroms. People instinctively turned
against the Jews when faced with this overwhelming threat. Jews were tortured
and made to confess that they had poisoned the wells and springs in order to wipe out
the population of Europe. The Pope and bishops tried to stop the pogroms, which
continued even though people could see that the Jews were suffering from the
plague just as badly as the Christians. The masses were quite beyond reason and
killing Jews seemed to be the only way they could deal with their fear and grief. By
the time the pogroms ceased at the end of 1349 there were hardly any Jews left in
Germany and the Low Countries, and their position there would always remain
precarious.[7] Throughout the fourteenth century, Jews were expelled from one city

after another and the Wandering Jew became even more 'other' and alien because it was so clear that he had no permanent home in Europe.[8]

There was also a new terror of Islam. The failure of the Crusades had made 'Mohammadanism' frightening in quite a new way, because the Muslim victory cast grave doubts on the integrity of Christianity. In 1453 Islam became even more of a threat to Europe, when the Ottoman Turks conquered the Christian empire of Byzantium and Europeans felt even more vulnerable before this Muslim giant. The Ottomans followed their conquest of Constantinople with further conquests in Syria, Egypt, Tunis and Algiers, and without the rampart of Byzantium Europeans felt newly naked before this huge Islamic empire at their gates. The Turk became a symbol of terrifying power. He was 'the terrible Turk' or 'the unspeakable Turk' who had revived the old medieval nightmare and who was now poised on the very threshold of Europe, waiting to swallow up poor little Christendom. For over a hundred years the frontiers of Europe moved alarmingly backward and forward, while the Europeans grappled with the Ottomans in a series of naval battles. The battle of Lepanto in 1571 finally prevented any further Turkish conquests in Europe, but it was another century at least before the Ottoman threat declined into the Eastern Question. During this time there could be no real understanding of Islam: 'Mohammadanism' was an unspoken threat, too terrible to be voiced aloud.[9]

In the period immediately succeeding the Crusades, therefore, 'the Jew' and 'the Muslim' had become surrounded with an aura of absolute dread. Both were seen as capable and desirous of destroying Christendom totally and the external threat was becoming interiorised and institutionalised. This intolerance could not be controlled by reason or common sense; it had become too deeply embedded in the Christian identity and was part of the way people in the West saw the world. During the crusading period, Western Europe had created a new self. This self had pulled Europeans out of the Dark Ages and would soon impel them to conquer the world. But it was not a very healthy self for it contained a massive repression and paradox. People had sincerely believed that the Crusades were an act of love. Right up to the end of the Middle Ages nobody had seriously questioned the morality of this cruel and aggressive Christianity and if people objected it was usually for more pragmatic reasons. Yet the whole notion of a Crusade was obviously opposed to the loving pacifism of Jesus, who had told Christians to love their enemies. To believe that a war of extermination was an act of love involved a huge suppression and it would seem that this led to the neurotic projection of Christian anxieties on to the Crusaders' victims. In the Christian imagination both 'the Jew' and 'the Muslim' were monstrously violent and bloodthirsty. Surely this must reflect a deep worry about Christian violence? As they groped for a new understanding of who they were and what they stood for, Christians in Europe got used to seeing Jews and Muslims as symbols of all they were *not*. The fantasies they created bore no relation to the objective reality but were unhealthy creations expressive of a flaw in Western integrity. At each stage of Europe's development, Europeans redefined the image of the Jew and the Muslim to make them both the complete opposite and a distorted mirror-image of the Western self. It is a habit they acquired from the Crusaders.

Crusading ideology would continue to have an effect in the popular imagination and traces of this appeared horribly in the twentieth century. For years German Catholics had expected Frederick II to return as the Last Emperor and during the fifteenth century the Church came to regard hopes for the Second Coming of Frederick as a dangerous heresy. In the early sixteenth century it appeared again, led by a man who was known as the Revolutionary of the Upper Rhine. He produced a book called *The Book of a Hundred Chapters*, and its importance does not lie in the influence it exerted, which was very small, but in the influences that its author absorbed, which would seem to have continued for another 400 years, long after the crusading motif had been lost and become a part of the German sense of self. The Revolutionary introduced a new note of racial chauvinism into the old Frederick fantasy. He rewrote history and claimed, like the Crusaders, that *his* people were the chosen people, not the Jews, but he went on to claim that the Jews had misled the world and robbed the Germans of the respect that was their due. In this reworked history, the Germans, he said, had long ago 'lived together like brothers on earth, holding all things in common'. They were the descendants of Noah's son Japhet, and had made their way to Europe after the flood and inspired an empire at Trier which had ruled the whole of Europe and initiated a golden age. This empire had been destroyed by the Roman empire, and the Latins (the Italians and the Franks) had continued to oppress the Germans to this day. Fortunately Frederick would soon return, subjugate the Latins and purge Europe of the wicked in huge crusading massacres. Then he would re-establish the German empire at Mainz, which would last for a thousand years and usher in the Last Days. Once he had conquered Europe, Frederick would go on to crush the Ottoman Turks and would then march on to the Holy Land, liberate Jerusalem and destroy 'the society of Mohammadans' in a new series of massacres. Then the Germans would rule the world once more, throw off the old humiliating past and re-establish the pure German culture, and the world would see that they really were the chosen race.[10] It must be stressed that the historical Frederick would have condemned this theory, but in the mind of the Revolutionary, Frederick, grandson of Barbarossa, had been mythologised. He was now an expression of the pure German spirit, which was struggling to realise its unique destiny. His myth still inspired Germans 400 years later: it is surely not an accident that the classic and certainly the most exuberantly enthusiastic biography of Frederick was written by Ernst Kantorowicz, a patriotic German scholar, who published his *Frederick the Second* in 1931.

Sixteenth-century Germany was the home of the Protestant Reformation and it is important to make clear from the outset that, though the Crusades to the Holy Land were a Catholic project, Protestantism had its own forms of crusading and these would be crucial in forming modern Western attitudes towards Jews, Muslims and the 'Holy Land'. The Reformation may have banned relics, devotion to saints, pilgrimages and the love of holy places, which had all been crucial in crusading religion, but it would continue the crusading tradition of seeing Muslims and Jews in an abnormal way and made its own distinctive and damaging contribution to this Western mythology. Protestantism was a very aggressive religion. Luther in particular was a passionate and vituperative man, who believed, for example, that all rebellious peasants should be massacred[11] and that the Pope was Antichrist.[12] Later Protestants would persecute Catholics and fight religious wars against them, while the Puritan tradition in Protestantism could be very cruel and repressive. If Luther and his colleagues made important reforms in Western Christianity, they did not make it a religion of peace.

Luther hated Muslims as vehemently as any Catholic Crusader. He was deeply disturbed by the Turks, but saw 'Mohammadanism' not merely as a political threat, but rather as an interior state of alienation and an image of absolute wickedness on a par with the Catholic Church.[13] Both were associated with Antichrist in a monstrous alliance against true Christianity: Rome was the head of Antichrist and Mohammadanism was his body.[14] That this fantasy of an alliance between Rome and Mohammadanism completely contradicted a history of 400 years of the most deadly hostility did not matter. People could say what they wanted about 'Islam' because it was not a reality any more to people like Luther, but part of his inner emotional landscape: a symbol of horror and of monstrous evil. It could therefore easily be associated with other real enemies of the reformed Church who were in a malign conspiracy against the 'truth'. This is a tendency that has continued to the present day and 'Jews' have also been linked with absolute enemies in the conspiracy fantasies of the West. In Nazi Germany and in McCarthy's America Jews were associated with the 'Communists'. Similarly during the Iranian revolution, many Americans could explain this Muslim hostility only by seeing it as a 'plot' of the Soviet Union, even though Khomeini denounced the Soviets as well as the Americans and the Soviets were clearly just as disturbed by the revolution, for their own reasons, as the Americans.

After the Reformation, Christians in Europe often explained Islam in terms of the quarrel between Protestants and Catholics. The Shiite–Sunni division was frequently discussed in those terms; Shiites were seen to be more like Catholics, with their cult of holy figures and passion plays, while the severer Sunnis were held to be more like the Protestants.[15] This comparison could be very misleading, as I explained in Chapter 8, because it implied a theological division between Shiites and Sunnis which did not exist. The habit showed that Christians found it impossible to see Islam as a religion in its own right; it was an extension of the old medieval insistence on seeing the 'Mohammadans' as Christian heretics. Sometimes this distortion had ludicrous results, as when the seventeenth-century Catholic missionary M. Febvre wanted to describe Islam by presenting Muslims as 'Mohammadan Protestants', believing in justification by faith: 'they hope for the remission of all their sins, provided they believe in Mahomet.'[16] Just as absurd was the eighteenth-century Protestant travel writer L. Rauwolff, who saw his Muslims as 'Mohammadan Catholics', who believed in justification by works: 'they go after their own invented devotion to good works, alms, prayers, fasting, redeeming of captives etc., to make satisfaction to God.'[17] It is, of course, natural to seek to explain another culture in terms of one's own, but this Western habit of absorbing both Islam and Judaism and making them interior states of mind meant that it became impossible to see either clearly. Islam had become not a reality but an image, utterly drained of objective fact, yet reflexively associated with anything threatening and therefore with the 'other' side.

Luther was just as hostile to the Jews. He told the Jews in Germany that because he had reformed Christianity and made the scriptures central, they could now become Christians: they would now find their own scriptures venerated properly, free from Romish error. This was an insulting and arrogant invitation which showed that he was as blind to the Jews as an independent reality as he was to Muslims. He assumed that there was no difference between the Jewish and the Christian interpretation of what Christians significantly called the 'Old' Testament and completely ignored Jewish objection to the message of Christ.[18] When the Jews replied that they found an even closer approximation to their scriptures in the Talmud, Luther at once became an aggressive persecutor. In his pamphlet *On the Jews and their Lies* (1543) he looked forward to Hitler: Jews should be absolutely segregated from Christians, their houses must be demolished, they should all live under one roof and do forced labour. All synagogues should be systematically burned to the ground and the prayer books destroyed.[19] In 1537 Luther had already had all the Jews expelled from Lutheran cities as they had been from Catholic cities in the fifteenth century. Jews were also expelled from Calvinist cities, even though Calvin sometimes spoke positively of Jews. It is significant that the Lutherans used this apparent 'friendship' with Judaism to discredit their Calvinist rivals and called them 'Judaizers', associating them automatically with the 'other'.[20]

But in the seventeenth century an entirely different Protestant attitude towards the Jews appeared which would have very important consequences. In England some Protestants wanted to abolish the ritual and hierarchy of the Anglican Church and return to a simpler religion of direct intimacy with God, without the intervention of priests and ritual. They were called 'Puritans' by their Anglican and Catholic opponents, because of their concern for moral and religious purity. The Bible is always crucial in any extreme Protestant sect that refuses to conform to the established Church, because it is the Word of God, the chief way in which he has communicated with man, and people usually interpret it quite literally. The Puritans were particularly drawn to the stern ethics of the Old Testament and took St Paul very seriously when he wrote that Christians were the New Israel. Like the Crusaders before them, they insisted that they were God's new elect, the new chosen people. Unlike the Crusaders the Puritans felt not that they had to slaughter Jews, but that it was their duty that God's clearly expressed wishes for them in the Old Testament be carried out. They also applied to their own experience the lessons that God had given to the Jews in the days of the old Covenant. Christians had always done this, but the Puritans took the logical step of identifying with the Jews of the past and gave themselves a rather Jewish identity: they called their children Jewish names like Samuel, Amos, Sarah or Judith, for example. Further they believed that they were living in the Last Days and St Paul had said that before the Second Coming the Jews would be converted. The Jews would, therefore, not be Jews for very much longer.

During the seventeenth century it became increasingly dangerous to be a Puritan in England. They rejected the authority of bishops, so the establishment feared that this made them a political threat: soon they might also rebel against temporal authority. King James and Archbishop Laud became very hostile indeed, and James vowed that he would harry the Puritans from the land. It seemed to the Puritans that James and Archbishop Laud would shortly reintroduce Catholicism in England. In 1618, for example, James issued a *Declaration of Sports* which encouraged revels when planting and harvesting was over, instead of honouring the sabbath and enforcing church attendance. This shocked the Puritans, who saw such revels as Godless and many attacked the government angrily. Some were imprisoned and others were threatened with persecution. One of these was Thomas Shepard, who recorded a meeting with Laud in 1618 that gives some idea of the intensity of feeling. Laud:

> looked as though blood would have gushed out of his face and did shake as if he had been haunted with an ague fit, to my apprehension by reason of his extreme malice and secret venom. I desired him to excuse me. He fell then to threaten me and withal to bitter railing, calling me all to naught, saying, You prating coxcomb! Do you think all the learning is in your brain? He pronounced his sentence thus: I charge you that you neither preach, read, marry, bury, or exercise any ministerial function in any part of my diocese, for if you do, and I hear of it, I will be upon your back and follow you wherever you go, in any part of the Kingdom, and so everlastingly disenable you.[21]

There was naturally a good deal of debate among the Puritans about what they should do. Some Puritans had already fled the contamination of England and taken themselves off to Amsterdam where they formed a tight community, living according to their own ideals. But this seemed a cowardly solution to many: 'Shall we leave [God's] subjects and children,' asked the great Puritan preacher Richard Sibbes, 'for this or that fear? Let our condition be never so uncomfortable, he can make it comfortable.'[22] But Puritans were getting more and more angry and increasingly articulate. 'To suffer imprisonment and disgraces for good causes, this is a good work,' said John Preston in his sermons on *The Breast-Plate of Faith and Love*. But he also made it clear that Puritans should not just sit back and wait for deliverance from on high. They would have to take their destiny into their own hands and rebel against this oppression. 'Let us not say we must be moderate...we must be men of contention.'[23]

As so often in Christian history, this experience of trauma led most Puritans in England into a new holy war. They formed a fighting force called the New Model Army under Oliver Cromwell, which was also a spiritual way of life and a means of disciplining the self.[24] In this army the soldiers of God began to prepare their hearts for the reception of grace. Even though Cromwell would have condemned the Catholic Crusaders, it is clear that he and his new soldiers of God had a good deal in common with them. The Crusade had also originally been designed to create a new self and, ultimately, to fight the enemies of God. During the 1640s the army was strong enough to fight against the monarchy in the Civil War and the conduct of the army was again similar to the Crusades. There was much public reading of scripture and prayer; Cromwell was also very careful to listen attentively to the seers and prophets who believed themselves inspired by God with political or military messages, for Puritanism was an exalted faith, encouraging extreme visionary states not dissimilar to those of the medieval holy wars.[25]

But a minority felt that this was not the answer and instead of joining the army took a decision that would change the course of history and also have important consequences in the conflict in the Middle East today. As early as 1620 the first band of Puritans left England in the *Mayflower* and sailed to the New World; from that date more and more settlers joined them in the new settlement that they called the Plymouth Plantation. Every year Americans remember this crucial moment in their history at Thanksgiving and the story and experience of the Pilgrim Fathers has been crucial in shaping the American identity. The very fact that they called themselves 'Pilgrims' like the Crusaders and the early Zionist settlers shows how closely allied the Puritan migrations were to the spirit of other religious migrations that we have considered in this book. It also shows that a crusading enthusiasm is not only embedded deeply in the American identity and crucially formative in American history, but also that there is a natural American affinity with Zionism. Let us examine this more closely.

First, it is important to say that like the Zionists the Pilgrim Fathers were fleeing oppression in Europe. Familiarity with the story of the *Mayflower* can lead us to see this as a rather romantic episode, perhaps not dissimilar to the glamorous way in which some people see the Crusades. But the emigration was painful and dangerous. The voyage was long, perilous and acutely uncomfortable. Some people actually died on the long journey across the Atlantic and when they arrived many more died of disease and hunger. It was in its own way as traumatic as crusading. The country seemed inhospitable and the settlers spoke of it as 'a vast and empty chaos'.[26] They were more impressed by the desolation of the New World than by the beauties of which Americans are now so rightly proud. The whole experience was a struggle to achieve a new, independent identity in a new world, not at all dissimilar to the aims of the early Zionists. Like other émigrés that we have met in this book, the Pilgrim Fathers would have denied that they were *merely* fleeing persecution and would have stressed their positive hopes. They were very sensitive to the charge levelled against them by their English brethren that they were running away.[27] But the fact remains that had they not been persecuted by the English establishment none of them would have considered this drastic uprooting. John Winthrop, the Governor of the colony, wrote a list of reasons for 'the Plantation in New England' (1629) in which the second was this:

> All the other churches of Europe are brought to desolation, and our sins, for
> which the Lord begins already to frown upon us, do threaten us fearfully, and

who knows but that God hath provided this place to be a refuge for many whom he means to save out of the general calamity; and seeing the church hath no place to fly into but the wilderness, what better work can there be than to go before and provide tabernacles, and food for her, against she cometh thither.[28]

The corruption they had seen and the dangers they had endured in England had given them an apocalyptic sense of an impending catastrophe, not unlike that experienced by Herzl, who rightly sensed an imminent anti-semitic calamity. This sense of extremity and fear and desperate search for a refuge was as strongly felt by the New England settlers as all their more positive hopes for the country. America has prided itself on being a nation of refugees and for providing a haven for immigrants who have fled oppression and persecution in Europe. The giant Statue of Liberty in New York Harbour must have been a moving sight to all the persecuted, downtrodden Europeans who later made the dangerous and uncomfortable voyage over the Atlantic. America, like Israel later, was a country born out of suffering in Europe.

Yet there are closer and more positive similarities. Like the Crusaders, the Pilgrim Fathers and their followers turned spontaneously to the experience of the old chosen people, the Jews, when they were setting up their colony, and as was their wont they interpreted their struggle in the light of the ancient Jewish experience. Indeed they called their colony the 'English Canaan'[29] and gave their settlements in the American wilderness biblical names: Hebron, Salem, Bethlehem, Zion and Judaea. The Zionists too, secular as they were, turned back to the Bible in their colonising effort. In making a Christian presence an 'established fact' in the New World, the Americans also had to grapple with the problem of the native American Indians, whose land they proposed to take away. They came up with the same justification as the Zionists would make use of later when defending their claim against the Palestinians': America was an 'empty' country, a barren wilderness, which the natives were too primitive to develop properly. As early as 1622 Robert Cushman, the business agent of the colony, wrote of the Indian problem, significantly referring to the Old Testament.

[They] do but run over the grass, as do also the foxes and wild beasts. They are not industrious, neither have art, science, skill or faculty to use either the land or the commodities of it, but all spoils, rots and is marred for want of manuring, gathering, ordering, etc. As the ancient patriarchs therefore removed from straiter places into more roomy, where the land lay idle and waste, and none used it, though there dwelt inhabitants by them (as Genesis 13:6, 11, 12, and 34:21 and 41:20) so it is lawful now to take a land which none useth to make use of it.[30]

When they found that gentle persuasion was insufficient to allay Indian hostility, the Puritans turned their migration into a holy war, on the ancient Jewish paradigm in the early books of the Bible. Like the Crusaders and like the Zionists they resorted to extreme and ruthless methods in their holy war against the Pequot Indians during the 1640s. They naturally compared these enemies with the Amelecites and the Philistines 'that did confederate against Israel',[31] and massacred the Pequots with a truly Joshuan zeal. Yet ironically some eminent settlers like John Eliot, Thomas Thorowgood and Samuel Sewall took the opposite view: they believed that the Indians were of Jewish origin and that their conversion would be a step towards Christ's Second Coming.[32]

Puritans were generally convinced that they were living in the Last Days and many of the settlers saw their migration as a prelude to the Second Coming. In this they were obviously very much of the same mind as the early Crusaders, when they migrated to Jerusalem at the end of the eleventh century, and also of the early Labour Zionists, who confidently expected the socialist millennium and looked forward to creating a model society in Palestine, which would be a light unto the Gentiles. In 1654 the Puritan settler Edward Johnson published his *Wonder-Working Providence of Sion's Savior in New England*, a history of the colony, and expressed a common feeling among the Puritans, who were living in what they called the 'new' world for a very special reason:

> Know this is the place where the Lord will create a new heaven and new earth in, new churches, and a new commonwealth together. Verily if the Lord be pleased to open your eyes, you may see the beginning of the fight, and what success the armies of our Lord Jesus Christ have hitherto had.... Further know these are but the beginning of Christ's glorious reformation and restoration of his churches to a more glorious splendor than ever. He hath therefore caused the dazzling brightness of his presence to be contracted in the burning glass of these his people's zeal, from whence it begins to be left upon many parts of the world.[33]

In 1654 it seemed very unlikely that the struggling little colony would one day be the centre of Christianity, but today even though Johnson's fervent apocalyptic hopes have come to nothing, it is perhaps true that the leadership of the Christian world has passed from Europe to the pioneers in America.

When Johnson wrote his book it would have seemed to most Puritans that the first-fruits of the millennium had been manifested not in America but in England, for Cromwell had led his New Model Army to victory against the royalists in 1649, had beheaded King Charles I and established a Puritan republic in England with himself as 'Lord Protector'. He did not think that New England was important in the least and wrote of America as a 'poor, cold and useless'[34] place. But in Cromwell's Puritan England there were two events that showed the shape of things to come. In the heady days of his victory in 1649 Cromwell had received a petition from the Puritan colony that had been established in Amsterdam, headed by Anne and Ebenezer Cartright, urging him to hasten the Second Coming of Christ. In the Bible it was prophesied that the Jews would be scattered 'to the ends of the earth' (Deuteronomy 28:64; Daniel 12:17) but that prophecy had not been fulfilled for there had been no Jews in England (a country that Jews at that time called Kezer ha-Aretz: the end of the earth)[35] since King Edward I had expelled them from the country. Cromwell, the Cartrights urged, should hasten the coming redemption by bringing the Jews back to England. In the new Puritan republic the Jews would surely be converted to Christianity and this would also hasten the Second Coming of Christ. Secondly, the Cartrights asked:

> That this nation of England, with the inhabitants of the Netherlands, shall be the first and readiest to transport Israel's sons and daughters on their ships to the land promised to their forefathers Abraham, Isaac and Jacob for an everlasting inheritance.[36]

The Cartrights' petition shows how close the Puritans were in spirit to the Crusaders and to extreme religious Zionists today. Instead of waiting passively for the redemption, the Puritans believed that they should hasten it by fulfilling the prophecies themselves. Cromwell did nothing about this petition, probably because of the upheaval that came later that year when King Charles was executed. Although he was not personally interested in returning the Jews to Zion, it is significant that this Gentile Zionist initiative should have first manifested itself in England, which would one day produce the Balfour Declaration. But the first part of the petition *was* interesting to Cromwell, not for millennial but for purely practical, economic purposes. England had become impoverished during the Civil War and Cromwell knew how much the Jews had helped the economy of Holland. The following year saw the publication of *Spes Israeli* (The Hope of Israel), which was written by Manasseh ben Israel, a Jew living in Amsterdam. Manasseh called for the return of the Jews to England for exactly the same reason as the Cartrights: the fulfilment of prophecy to hasten the redemption, which Manasseh expected in 1666. British Puritans read the book with enthusiasm and when Manasseh eventually presented Cromwell with a petition, Cromwell was happy to open discussions with him. At first nothing came of these and Manasseh died in 1655, a disappointed man. But in 1656 some London Jews, who had been living *incognito* as Christians, declared their true Jewish identity and asked permission to build a synagogue. Cromwell was happy to agree, and gave the Jews in England full religious liberty and full British citizenship. After 1656 Jewish immigrants began to arrive in the Kezer ha'Aretz.[37]

The English Puritans' concern with the Jews during Cromwell's rule would prove to be characteristic of Protestant policy towards the Jewish people in that country. They were prepared to use the Jews for their own convenience but were not really very interested in the Jewish view of the matter. Cromwell wanted to use them for his own political ends and the Cartrights simply saw them as part of the plan of Christian redemption. This attitude is particularly evident in the Zionist project to return the Jews to their homeland. This might have been wonderful for Jews if at that time they had wanted to go to Palestine but in 1649 they would have had to be forcibly deported there against their will. In the seventeenth century the Jews believed that they would fulfil their vocation as God's elect in the diaspora and that they would not return to Eretz Yisrael until the Messiah came. This opinion was reinforced when in 1666 a Jew called Shabbtai Zvi caused an immense stir by claiming to be the Messiah, journeying to the East, only to capitulate to the Turkish authorities there and submit to Islam.[38] This scandal made religious Jews very suspicious indeed about any projects for initiating a return. But this did not in the least deter the Protestants in England from repeatedly calling for a Jewish return to Zion. They were brought up on a diet of Bible stories and came to see Palestine as a Jewish country. They also seemed to see Judaism as a subsection to Christianity, the higher religion, to whose interests the Jews must submit by divine decree. A non-Jewish Zionism became an established tradition among the British during the eighteenth century but however genial or even flattering to Jews this tradition sounded it was based on uncertain foundations. This myopic view would finally contribute to and even cause much of the tragedy in the Middle East today.

This is very clear in a volume of essays entitled *Two Journeys to Jerusalem* that was published by Nathaniel Crouch in 1704 and enjoyed a great popularity, going through several editions. The volume included several essays discussing Jewish affairs: there was an account of the present and past state of the Jewish nation; a report of the Manasseh ben Israel affair and an account of the Shabbtai Zvi fiasco.[39] But this surge of interest in Jewish matters was intrinsically connected with the matter of Palestine, as the title of the book shows, and the most popular section comprised the two travel diaries written in the Promised Land of the Jews. Crouch himself, using the pseudonym Robert Burton, had written one of these and it was from 'Burton' that the British people first heard that Palestine was a barren desert. He was struck by the contrast between the present state of the country and the biblical accounts of a thriving, populous society, when the land had flowed with milk and honey.[40] Burton instinctively saw Palestine as the land of the Bible and decided that its past fertility had been entirely due to the Israelites, who, he says, had terraced and fertilised the land and wasted none of it. He did not seem to recall that the land had been flowing with milk and honey *before* the Israelites had conquered it, as the Bible itself makes clear, nor did he understand that, like most Western travellers, he was only familiar with the country between Jaffa and Jerusalem, which had never been very fertile.

But there was one major objection to Burton's argument that was staring him in the face, but which he could not 'see'. Jerusalem is full of the architectural relics of civilisations that had been established in the country *after* the fall of Jewish Jerusalem in CE 70. The Romans, Byzantines, Arabs, Mamluks and Crusaders had all established societies there and some of these had been very prosperous. They had also left many imposing buildings and works of art behind them. Burton ignored all this and narrowed the entire history of the country down to the relatively short period of the Jewish occupation. In particular he failed to interpret the message of the Dome of the Rock, which dominates the Old City. This should have reminded him that Muslims had been established in the country for over a thousand years and had made their own unique contribution to its beauty. Burton could not 'see' Islam and could not take in the fact that Jerusalem was a holy city for Muslims too, any more than the Crusaders could. He differed from the Crusaders, who had always been convinced that Jerusalem belonged to them by right. He was not a particularly religious man, but he knew his Bible and this told him that the land was Jewish. The Muslim claim was simply not serious enough to be considered. In fact he called the Arabs 'inhabitants' of the land, as though they were simply living there temporarily, and decided that, if the prosperity of the country was entirely due to the industrious Jews, its decay had been caused by the 'want of culture and tillage among the barbarous Infidels . . . who by their continuous wars and ravages have made it almost desolate and like a desert'. It was now 'like a place forsaken by God.'[41] In Burton's confident and enlightened Western view, there were only two sides of the religious triangle; he could 'see' Judaism because he had read the Christian Bible, but he left Islam out of the picture and this would later prove a common but dangerous British oversight.

The attitude can also be seen in the writing of the Unitarian minister and chemist Joseph Priestley, who wrote in the latter part of the eighteenth century. Priestley urged the Jews to convert to Christianity because he saw Judaism and Christianity as complementary. This, of course, was not taking Judaism seriously, despite Priestley's flattering and sympathetic words, which are worth quoting because they probably express a point of view which many people in the Christian West would hold today. He urged the Jews to acknowledge Jesus as the Messiah and concluded with a prayer that:

> the God of Heaven, the God of Abraham, Isaac and Jacob whom we Christians as well as you worship, may be graciously pleased to put an end to your suffering, gathering you from all nations, resettle you in your own country, the land of Canaan, and make you most illustrious of all nations on the earth.[42]

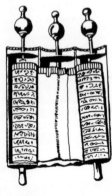

Priestley cannot seem to see that, although *he* graciously acknowledges the Jewish patriarchs, the Jews are not necessarily going to be able to acknowledge Jesus, because they had a completely different view of what a Jewish Messiah should be. *He* may see the Jewish scriptures he has in his Bible as essential to *his* Christianity, but he seems to have no understanding that Jews have many other holy writings that are closed books to him and that Judaism doesn't need Christianity as Christianity needs Judaism. Priestley is like the Puritan Cartrights in that he sees the conversion of the Jews as necessary to his religious fulfilment, but cannot see that Jews have an independent vision. He does at least acknowledge a relationship with one of the other religions in this tradition, which is an improvement on the

Crusaders' attitude. But when Priestley goes on to tell the Jews that once they have converted they will be able to go back to their own country, which is now a barren desert, waiting only for Jewish presence to burst into flower, he shows a total myopia about Islam.[43] Muslims also worship the God of Abraham, Isaac and Jacob and they also venerate Jesus as the Messiah, which is what Priestley urges the Jews to do. But for Priestley, Muslims don't exist; he did not realise that the Land of Israel was not deserted but had a largely Muslim population and that Jerusalem was one of their holy cities. Like Burton, he left Islam out of the picture and saw only two religions in the tradition of historical monotheism.

There had clearly been a great change, and this inability to register the existence of Islam marks a shift in the Western attitude. What had happened to the 'unspeakable' Turk and the monstrous Muslim, who threatened to crush Western society? By the end of the eighteenth century, the Christians were more confident; they were rising to ever-greater heights of sophistication and power; the British had already invaded the East again and in 1769 established themselves as the rulers of India. The Ottoman empire, on the other hand, was beginning its long process of decline and people thought that the Muslim problem was over. 'Mohammadanism' seemed a spent fire and no longer haunted the dreams of Europeans. But it is always dangerous to imagine that because *we* think something has gone away, or because *we* don't see it, it no longer exists. The Iranian revolution showed us that Islam had been alive and well all the time and this was a great shock to us. Other British Zionists of the eighteenth century also had this blind spot. In 1790 James Beere, the Rector of Sandbrook, sent a petition to William Pitt asking him to assist in bringing about the impending 'final restoration of the Jews to the Holy Land', which would hasten the Second Coming. It would also, Beere shrewdly pointed out, be of great benefit to the British. Once the Hebrews were settled in their ancient land they 'will stand in need of many manufactured articles, of the necessities of life . . . especially woollens and linens'.[44] The return of the Jews would, therefore, be extremely useful to British trade. In 1800 James Bicheno published *The Restoration of the Jews – The Crisis of the Nations*, which argued that not only should Britain help the Jews to return because it would hasten the millennium, but it would also guard her interests in the Middle East.[45] Again, neither Beere nor Bicheno had considered the fact that most Jews did not want to return to Palestine, but they were prepared to exploit them for political and economic reasons as well as forcing them into a pattern of Christian fulfilment. The existence of Islam and the Muslim inhabitants of Palestine was either ignored or not even considered. Already the British were looking greedily at the decaying Ottoman empire and preparing to exploit both Jews and Arabs for their own interests.

The eighteenth century is often called the Age of Reason. Thinkers like Voltaire and the *philosophes* believed that modern man no longer needed religion and should rise above the old irrational beliefs which had oppressed the people and kept them enthralled to superstition. There was a new search for liberty and freedom, especially in France, which culminated in the revolution of 1789 when the Goddess of Reason was enthroned as the deity of the liberated people. Some rationalists did not abandon religion but tried to make it reasonable. They rejected the idea of revelation, which had produced so many unnatural forms of belief, and created deism, a belief in a God whose existence could be demonstrated by reason alone; and they developed a rational moral code. In many ways the eighteenth century closely resembles our own. We also believe in freedom and strive for a reasonable, secular ideal. Many people thought, until recently, that religion was dead and would never be a force again in major world events. This was a very mistaken view. The eighteenth century shows us that it is not possible to batten religion and irrational emotion down completely. It seems impossible to replace strong emotional habits and opinions with cool reason and logic. These things will out, sometimes more passionately than before because of a period of repression. We seem not to be rational animals but to have strong emotional, religious needs. Even when we try to effect an objective appraisal of a situation or to view our 'enemies' dispassionately, by attempting to see two sides to a question, superstitions, prejudices and fantastic distortions still continue to colour our view. This certainly happened during the eighteenth-century Age of Reason.

It is important to say at the outset that in some ways the Europeans of the eighteenth century did acquire a broader religious and cultural outlook. Hitherto the view of the East had been dominated by Islam, but during the eighteenth century a far more venerable and mysterious Orient was discovered. In 1759 the French orientalist Abraham-Hyacinthe Anquetil-Duperon translated the *Avesta*, the Zoroastrian scriptures of ancient Persia, which had been the official religion before the Persians had converted to Islam. He followed this with a translation of the Indian Hindu *Upanishads*.[46] A new religious world had been opened up that was quite outside the Christian, Islamic or Hellenic traditions and was far more challenging to the Christian view than either of the two other religions of Abraham. Surely this would mean that there was no place for the old claustrophobic hostility towards Muslims and Jews? This new Orient led many Europeans to develop a strong 'love' of the East. Orientalists like Sir William Jones made the newly discovered world available to the general reader, and painters, composers and writers started to produce a new Orient. This was an exotic alternative to Europe, a place of mystery, luxury and sensuality. It was no more accurate than the old hostile image of 'Islam', and was a similar reflection of Europe, this time expressing different Western dreams of fulfilment that were unavailable at home. It was also proprietary and a way of taking spiritual possession of the fabulous East and making it a province of the Western imagination. Indeed it was accompanied by a new colonial longing. In 1767, after a struggle with the French, Britain became the political and commercial rulers of the subcontinent of India. The West was aggressively back in the East once more, for the first time since the Crusades. This inevitably brought back a possessive, acquisitive attitude to the image of the East, which was something to be controlled and mastered.[47] As Europeans hoped to colonise Islamic countries too, it was unlikely that there would be any more truly positive view of Islam, despite the popular legend of the exotic and attractive East. Indeed the creation of this new Eastern fantasy showed that people were still governed by emotion and still created quite unobjective fantasies when they approached other cultures.

The problem of coming to terms with alien cultures is always delicate and difficult and indeed one may question whether it is possible to understand another culture fully. Our very thoughts are shaped by language and by institutions that colour our attitudes very deeply and perhaps make it impossible to appreciate something quite different. It is certainly not helpful to have a long history of entrenched prejudice and hatred of another people and a habit of aggression, as Europe had for Muslims and Jews. During the Age of Reason people were genuinely struggling for a greater objectivity and this is demonstrated by George Sale's translation of the Koran, which was published in 1734. Sale was not perfect: he wrote an introduction in which he aired the old medieval prejudice: 'It is certainly one of the most convincing proofs that Mohammadanism was no other than a human invention, that it owed its progress and establishment almost entirely to the sword.'[48] He does follow this up by arguing that Mohammad's right to take up arms in self-defence 'may perhaps be allowed'.[49] But, despite this ingrained prejudice, Sale's actual translation was an enormous improvement on the old

biased and distorted medieval translations, on which people had relied hitherto. He used proper Muslim and Arabic commentators instead of prejudiced Christian sources, and if people criticise the translation today it is not because they consider it inaccurate, but because they find the style rather heavy.[50] Nevertheless giving people in Europe an accurate translation should have meant that people would have had no excuse for propagating the old fantasies about Islam as a depraved religion, particularly the scholars of the Enlightenment. The translation should have aroused a new interest. Yet this did not happen; I think for two reasons.

The first is that however technically accurate Sale's version of the Koran was, it suffered from one unavoidable defect: it was not in Arabic. Had he been able to achieve a livelier style, this insurmountable problem would still have remained. Muslims claim that the Koran is untranslatable, for the beauty of the Arabic is an essential part of its meaning. They point to this beauty as proof of its divine origin. Indeed the beauty of the Koran is one of the reasons for the spreading of the Arabic language from the Arabian peninsula throughout the Middle East and North Africa. When people in these countries converted to Islam they had to learn the Koran in Arabic and they then went on to change their language. That even the ordinary, uneducated people were inspired to make this linguistic change is a tribute to the extraordinary emotional and intellectual attraction of the sacred book of Islam. It is very striking to watch even unreligious Arabs listening to the Koran when it is broadcast on the radio, sung to a special chant. They are clearly enthralled and find it very difficult to express exactly why these words give them such pleasure. Perhaps the Koran is comparable to some of Shakespeare's songs or to certain well-known passages of the King James Bible in English. The language has an absolute beauty that is enhanced by emotional associations. Obviously nothing of this can come out in translation.

For a non-Arabic speaker, the Koran is not very accessible. It is always true that other people's holy books are difficult to penetrate; it is an indication of the great difficulty of truly understanding another culture. Anglicans who are loyal to the King James Bible would probably not be so moved by the Hebrew words, if they could read them, because beautiful as the English is, it has transformed the Hebrew into something very different and quintessentially English. Hebrew versions of the psalms, for example, are a lot less sonorous and mellifluous and more brutal and direct than a King James devotee might expect. To attach ourselves to the Jewish scriptures, we have had to translate them into another idiom and have turned them into something else. It is possible that some great stylist might be able to do something similar with the Koran, but then it would not be the Koran any more. Part of the difficulty is that Arabic has a different logic from European languages and words have a far wider and more complex range of meaning and association, which makes a translation an impoverishment. Without the beauty, the complexity and associative power of the Arabic, and English translation of the main 'sense' of the words, however careful and accurate, is bound to be a distortion. I myself have found that constant reading of the Koran in an English translation does familiarise one to a certain dynamic and beauty, but I am quite aware that this is probably entirely different from the experience of reading the Arabic original. Even though I am in the early stages of learning Arabic, I have to recognise that I shall probably never be proficient enough to appreciate the beauty and the complexity of the Koran as a native speaker does.

Therefore, though Sale's version was undoubtedly an important and essential contribution to Western knowledge of Islam, the Koran still remained a very difficult book for English people to read and understand. It was not likely to make people suddenly aware of the power of the book and the religion. But there was another reason why there was not a radical change in the understanding of Islam in the West during the Age of Reason which showed that, however reasonable we are, we are still profoundly emotional creatures. 'Mohammadanism' still had an aura of fearsome and threatening emotional associations for many Western people. Some could, as we have seen, forget all about it on the principle of 'out of sight, out of mind'. Other writers and scholars were still fascinated and appalled enough to want to write about the Prophet and his religion and when they did so they simply repeated all the old medieval attitudes and myths, as I shall show. Some were moved to vehement disgust; others were so used to seeing 'Mohammadanism' as the enemy of all things Western that they were incapable of a fresh appraisal, despite the possibility of more accurate knowledge. The power of what are called received ideas, or established and inherited prejudice, is very strong indeed and, however rational and objective people try to be, there are usually only a few people in each generation who are capable of rising above them and willing to do so. Even serious scholars in the Age of Reason found it impossible to view Islam as anything but a depraved version of Christianity.

This is clear at the very beginning of the period. In 1697 the *Bibliothèque orientale* of Barthelmy d'Herbelot was published posthumously. It remained an important and authoritative reference book in Europe and England until the beginning of the nineteenth century and was a major source of knowledge about the Orient. D'Herbelot seemed to have made a real attempt to break out of the old limited Christian scholarship; he had actually used Arabic, Turkish and Persian sources and presented his reader with a history of the world that took in the traditions of the non-Christian religions. He gave alternative accounts of the creation of the world, for example. There was a certain arrogance in his attempt to reduce the vast complexity of the East into a neat, alphabetical Western system, but it could be argued that we need such a scheme when we first approach an alien culture.[51] Yet despite this broader view and the use of sources that would certainly have contradicted his thesis, d'Herbelot's view of Islam remained quite unchanged from the medieval. Under the section 'M' we find 'Mohammad' described as 'the famous impostor' and 'founder of a heresy which has taken the name of religion, which we call Mohammadan. See entry under *Islam*.'[52] Although d'Herbelot was obviously aware of the real name of the religion, the important thing was that 'we' prefer to call it 'Mohammadan'. D'Herbelot also specifically compared this 'heresy' to other Christian heresies like Arianism.[53] It was a faithful repetition of the medieval view. Despite his massive researches d'Herbelot preferred to transmit the received opinion about Islam and so re-established it firmly in the minds of his readers. This was not due to perversity, but because he simply could not see 'Mohammadanism' in any other way. The consequences were serious, however. This confident Western intellectual had codified, defined and cut the Prophet down to size according to a Western scheme of things. Islam was presented as an eccentric deviation from mainstream Western thought, which had no power to challenge or threaten 'our' point of view.

In the same year the English orientalist Humphry Prideaux published *Mahomet: The True Nature of Imposture*. The title alone shows that he had unquestioningly accepted the old prejudice. Indeed he openly cited Ricoldo da Monte Croce as his major source, so he could have done nothing else. Yet Prideaux presented himself as an apostle of reason, and one might therefore have expected him to strive for a more objective view. He claimed that besides being a mere imitation of Christianity, Islam was an example of the hysteria and idiocy to which a religion can sink if it was not based firmly on the rock of reason, like Christianity.[54] Prideaux was doing in effect what the medievals did and had used 'Islam' as a foil against which to define himself, no matter how irrationally. The strength of received ideas is even more striking, however, in the *Vie de Mahomed* of Henri,

Comte de Boulainvilliers, which was published in Paris in 1730 and in London the following year and seems to have enjoyed a certain popularity. The Count also repeated all the medieval distortions as self-evident facts, but turned the whole tradition on its head. The medievals claimed that Mohammad had made up his religion in order to make himself conqueror of the world. The Count agreed that this was so but instead of seeing this as a reason to condemn Islam he saw it as admirable: unlike irrational Christianity, which was a revealed religion, Islam was a natural religion based on reason and Mohammad was a military hero, like Caesar and Alexander the Great.[55] The Count must have been one of the first people in Europe to speak positively about Islam but his 'Islam' is a complete travesty of the religion because it is based on the same old lies. Even when people see themselves as rational human beings and even when they are trying to break new ground, old received opinions have an authority that is far stronger than any of our more consciously sought opinions. They are so deeply ingrained that no amount of logic can reason them away, because they are not even questioned. It must be the case that many very sensible and thoughtful people still have mistaken views of 'Islam', which they have never thought to query, but which are so much a part of their intellectual equipment that hostility to 'Islam' is a part of the way they define themselves. This makes it very difficult for them to realise that their view of Islam has no connection with the reality, no matter how rational and critical they are about other things.

So entrenched was the old view that it appeared even when later eighteenth-century historians of Islam were trying to dispute European shibboleths. As early as 1708 Simon Ockley distressed many of his readers when he brought out the first volume of his *History of the Saracens*, because he did not reflexively present Islam as a religion of the sword but tried to see the seventh-century Islamic *jihad* from the Muslims' point of view.[56] Yet even though Ockley was striving for accuracy and was painstakingly meticulous in his research (volume two did not appear until ten years later) he was still subject to the ancient prejudice. Mohammad, he said, was 'a very subtle and crafty man, who put on the appearance only of those good qualities, while the principles of his soul were ambition and lust'.[57] It would be hard to find a more succinct summary of the medieval view. What is perhaps even more significant is that the introduction of the *Cambridge History of Islam* (1970) hails Ockley's work together with d'Herbelot's *Bibliothèque* as 'highly important' in broadening 'the new understanding of Islam'.[58] If Islamic scholars in our own day praise d'Herbelot and Ockley, who were not hesitant about denouncing 'Islam' as a depraved 'heresy',[59] it is no wonder that many of us lesser mortals are still so confused about the religion.

A more distinguished and influential historian of Islam also seemed to praise and understand the religion and yet at the same time repeated the old view. In his fiftieth chapter of the *Decline and Fall of the Roman Empire*, Edward Gibbon sonorously praised the 'lofty monotheism' of Islam, but also wrote that Mohammad was either a fraud or an enthusiast, a religious fanatic beyond reach of reason, who was able to convert the barbarous Arabs for most unworthy reasons:

> From all sides the roving Arabs were allured by the standard of religion and plunder; the apostle sanctioned the licence of embracing female captives as their wives and concubines; and the enjoyment of wealth and beauty was a feeble type of the joys of Paradise prepared for the valiant martyrs of the faith.[60]

Gibbon allowed that despite this unfortunate start Muslims did manage to attain to a certain nobility in their religion – sometimes, he felt, it was a little too stark in its lack of understanding of human failings (unlike Christianity, is the implied comparison).[61] But Gibbon really showed his colours when he dealt with the Koran, and his comments indicate the difficulties people had, even if they had access to an accurate translation. Gibbon began by referring to the Muslim belief that the beauty of the Koran shows that it came from God:

> This argument is most powerfully addressed to a devout Arabian whose mind is attuned to faith and rapture, whose ear is delighted by the music of sounds, and whose ignorance is incapable of comparing the productions of human genius. The harmony and copiousness of style will not reach, in a version, the European infidel; he will peruse with impatience the endless incoherent rhapsody of fable and precept and declamation, which seldom excites a sentiment or an idea, which sometimes crawls in the dust, and is sometimes lost in the clouds.[62]

This is self-congratulation indeed: 'we' are discerning, civilised and rational enough to see through the preposterous claim of the Prophet, but 'they' are incapable of any such insight, because they are childish barbarians. Writing at the end of the century, Gibbon had absorbed the Western self-confidence and sense of superiority that brought with it an arrogant blindness: because *he* cannot understand the Koran, he assumes that there is nothing in it and that the 'devout Arabian' does so because he is an inferior human being. It would seem from reading Gibbon's chapter that the old irrational terror of 'Mohammadanism' was dead, and that it had been replaced by a calm, slightly amused contempt for a religion that should not be taken too seriously.[63]

Reason, therefore, was proving inadequate as a means of acquiring a rational and balanced understanding of Islam and perhaps this should give us, in the enlightened twentieth century, food for thought about our own attitudes. The *philosophes* show most forcibly the inadequacy of reason alone in overcoming inherited prejudice. They proclaimed that all such prejudices and superstitions had to be surmounted, but they seem to have made two significant exceptions: prejudice against the Jews and prejudice against the Muslims. Voltaire, for example, found it quite acceptable to write in the *Dictionnaire philosophique* that the Jews were 'a totally ignorant nation, who for many years have combined contemptible miserliness and the most revolting superstition with a violent hatred of all those nations which have tolerated them'.[64] That the apostle of pure reason could write such dangerous nonsense is instructive. For centuries, Europeans had accustomed themselves to seeing the Jews as the murderous enemy of Christians and of every Western aspiration; this had meant that the Jews had suffered more than anybody in Europe from the Christian oppression and persecution that Voltaire denounced so passionately. Yet Voltaire never even questions this cruel prejudice but repeats it in all its essentials, leaving out only the lurid illustrations of it, like the blood libel. There is one great difference: Christians had always claimed that Jews were the enemies of religion. But as Voltaire believed that religion was a bad thing, he turned the old stereotype on its head and denounced the Jews *because* they were religious. He took it for granted that the Jews were against everything that decent Europeans stood for and so now that Europeans were becoming rational beings he accuses the Jews of being irrational.

This is also what he did with Islam. Voltaire wrote a tragedy on the life of Mohammad which he called *Fanaticism* (1742); it was another instance of the lofty assumption that if civilised Europeans did not understand Islam, this was due to a defect not in themselves but in the religion. Because Islam was nonsense, the religious enthusiasm of Muslims must be mindless frenzy. It is a solipsistic and deluded view of the world, which Voltaire derived from the medieval Catholics he despised so thoroughly. The only way in which he differed from the medieval critics of 'Mohammadanism' was that he found their fantasies insufficiently scurrilous, so he made up some new stories of his own.[65] It is true that, when Voltaire wanted to show how tolerant *he* was and how intolerant Chistianity was in his *Essai sur les moeurs*, he praised Islam for its toleration, so he was not as ignorant or deprived of sound information about Islam as might appear from his conclusion that Mohammad had been 'regarded as a great man even by those who knew he was an impostor and revered as a prophet by all the rest'.[66] It was not that Voltaire was deliberately acting in bad faith; he just could not see either Judaism or Islam differently, despite his enlightened rationalism. What one never thinks to question, one cannot logically refute.

But even in the calm, superior eighteenth century there were signs of the old irrational terror. Thus the celebrated French philosopher Baron Paul Henri Holbach wrote in his *L'Esprit du judaisme* (1770) that Moses had founded a blood-thirsty religion, which had corrupted Christian society and made the Jews 'the enemies of the human race. . . . The Jews have always displayed contempt for the clearest dictates of morality and the law of nations. . . . They were ordered to be cruel, inhuman, intolerant, thieves, traitors and betrayers of trust. All these are regarded as deeds pleasing to God.'[67] That one of the leaders of the Enlightenment should be able to produce such a distorted portrait, which had no basis in fact and could be refuted by a simple reading of large parts of the Bible, is symptomatic of a great fear. He had created a bogey that was as paranoid and hysterical as any of the medieval fantasies of the Catholics he so despised. Similarly a life of Mohammad that was published in England in 1799 seems scarcely sane. Mohammad was worse than Caligula, Domitian or Judas Iscariot.[68] 'Many millions of rational human beings', the author cried in anguish, 'are degraded to the rank of brutes by the consummate artifice and wickedness'[69] of the Prophet. The very idea that Muslims believe that their 'religious farrago' is a valid form of ritual and spiritual experience seems to drive the author into a state of frenzy.[70] These monstrous distortions reveal a deep dread lurking beneath the cool façade of society. There were some Europeans who were still haunted by the same inner demons as had plagued the medievals. Here again, reason was powerless to assuage or even touch a fear that existed far below the conscious and cerebral self, which can dismiss only trivial fears and worries. In our own enlightened century we have seen the horrifying results of such buried terror.

Yet one must give the French Enlightenment the credit it deserves. After the French revolution, the Jews were given legal emancipation and enjoyed the same protection and privileges as the Gentiles of France. It marked a great change in the fortunes of European Jews and was the first official sign of acceptance since the Crusades. It was a public acknowledgement, that Jews were normal human beings, equal to Gentiles and entitled to the same human rights. When Napoleon came to power, he showed that he had a respect for the Jewish nation and even tried to revive in Paris the Sanhedrin, the supreme religious court of the Jews in Jerusalem.[71] This was not a practical idea, as many Jews believed that only the Messiah could revive the Sanhedrin, but it showed that Napoleon was ready to concede the independence of religious Judaism and did not see it as an inferior branch of Christianity. Nonetheless, in 1807 Napoleon's Great Sanhedrin declared that the Jews were a religious group and not a nation and so must be accorded full citizenship. This principle was gradually accepted by the other leaders of Western Europe in the years that followed, and during the first part of the nineteenth century the secular and revolutionary ideals of the Enlightenment spread and the position of the Jews was greatly improved.[72] Even countries like Germany, which had a very long tradition of extreme anti-semitism, emancipated the Jews. European Jews themselves were affected by the new secularism and began to assimilate, seeing themselves as French or German rather than Jewish. It did seem the dawn of a new era and for this we must give full credit to the Age of Reason.

But if Napoleon pursued enlightened policies of toleration, he also shows us that the old dreams of the Crusaders were not dead, irrational though they were. Napoleon was an idealist, but he was also a practical man and he determined to use the new knowledge of the Orient to control and master it. This has also become an entrenched habit, as Edward W. Said has argued in his important book *Orientalism*.[73] Napoleon wanted to exploit Muslims and Jews for his own ends. In 1798 he made a bid for colonial power that captured the imagination of many Europeans because it revived old buried dreams, but it also showed the new cool sense of superiority that we have seen developed in Europeans during the Enlightenment.

Napoleon wanted to challenge the British empire in India by establishing his own empire in the Middle East, but he was also inspired by older European, crusading fantasies. Until the end of his life he saw the defeat of his Eastern expedition as the moment when his fate had been sealed.[74] Europe seemed too small for his talents, and Napoleon was convinced that his destiny lay in the East. It is possible to see Napoleon as being moved by a secular version of the Last Emperor myth, not unlike the dream of Frederick II.[75] Before the expedition, Napoleon founded the Institut d'Egypte and scores of orientalist scholars from the Institut sailed with him as advisers to the occupying forces. As soon as the fleet landed, Napoleon sent them off on what we should call a fact-finding mission and gave his officers strict orders to follow their instructions. But it is very clear that the orientalists had already given Napoleon excellent advice about how to approach a country of Muslims. From the first, he was at pains to explain to the Egyptians that 'nous sommes les vrais musulmans',[76] as he proclaimed to the people of Alexandria. He tried to convince them that he was fighting *for* Islam and, when he realised that his army was not large enough to conquer the whole of Egypt, he resorted to the tactics of Nur ad-Din and Saladin. He had the sixty sheikhs of the great madrassa el-Azhar in Cairo brought into his quarters with full military honours. He then earnestly praised the Prophet, the Koran and Islam and seemed quite able to hold his own. This piece of propaganda was as effective as it had been during the medieval *jihad*. Once the people had been satisfied by Napoleon's Islamic sympathies, they began to feel less hostile towards the French. Before he left Egypt, Napoleon insisted that his officers must be very careful not to offend Muslim sensibilities and impressed upon them the importance of following the advice of the orientalists and of winning over the religious leaders.[77] There are certain leaders in our own day who might have profited from this advice.

Naturally Napoleon was no Muslim at all, but he was perfectly prepared to exploit Muslim sympathies to achieve his own secular and imperialist ambitions.

He was also ready to exploit the Jews. In the spring of 1799 he called upon the Jews
of Asia and Africa to rise up and take possession of their ancient homeland. They
were the 'Rightful Heirs of Palestine':

> Israelites, unique nation, whom, in thousands of years, lust of conquest and
> tyranny were able to deprive of the ancestral lands only, but not of name and
> national existence!
>
> Attentive and impartial observers of the destinies of nations, even though not
> endowed with the gifts of seers like Isaiah and Joel, have also felt long since
> what these, with beautiful and uplifting faith, foretold when they saw the
> approaching destruction of their kingdom and fatherland: that the ransomed of
> the Lord shall return, and come with singing unto Zion, and the enjoyment of
> henceforth undisturbed possession of their heritage will send an everlasting joy
> upon their heads [Isaiah 35:10].
>
> Arise, then, with gladness ye exiled![78]

Even though Napoleon would later encourage his specially convened Sanhedrin to
declare, in the Jews' own interests, that Judaism was a faith not a nation, he was
earlier quite prepared to seek to revive a Jewish sense of nationhood if that suited
his own ambitions. His plan was to conquer Palestine from the Turks, establish
himself in Jerusalem, hand the country over to the Jews and remove his Eastern
capital to Damascus. Under France, the Jews would defend the country against all
comers. Nothing came of this grand scheme, because Napoleon was defeated a
month later by the British, who had joined forces with the Turks to prevent this
French penetration into the Middle East.[79] To further their own colonial ambitions
the British were now prepared to 'help' the Turks, until such time as they managed
to eject the Ottomans from the Middle East and establish colonies there.
Europeans were now ready to begin a full-scale invasion of the East once more and
to do this they would be ready to exploit the Arab or Turkish Muslims and the
Jews.

As we move ever closer to our own century, it should be clear in what direction
Europe was moving and how this would affect the modern crisis in the Middle
East. A rational man like Napoleon still cultivated crusading fantasies and, though
there had been a marked shift in the European attitude towards Muslims and Jews,
there was no permanent fundamental change. In Europe during the nineteenth
century, Jews were certainly acquiring a new dignity and were enjoying a toleration
that would hitherto have seemed unimaginable, but as we know only too well, this
would not last. During the nineteenth century the old crusading hostility surfaced
again and set Europe on the path that led ultimately to the gas chambers of
Auschwitz. The Jews were living in the midst of Europe; they were under people's
noses, whereas, ever since Europeans had purged their countries of Muslims, Islam
had increasingly become a distant threat. That meant that hatred of Arab and
Turkish Muslims did not reach the same crescendo of horror. Indeed, during the
eighteenth century, Europeans had acquired a confidence which enabled some of
them to look down on Muslims as primitives, others to ignore the existence of
Islam altogether and still others to use even the weapon of knowledge to exploit
and oppress them. The basic aggression that had been originally inspired by the
Crusades was still there.

The nineteenth century has useful and sometimes chilling lessons to teach us
about our own attitudes. In the first place, it marked the end of the Age of Reason
and indeed led to the vehement rejection of the cult of pure reason of the Romantic
movement. The Romantics, in the early years of the century, began a cult of feeling
and imagination. They also encouraged a revival of basic Christian beliefs, to
which they gave a new secular form. In particular the ideals of redemption and

salvation powerfully affected the imagination of many Europeans and this affected the colonialists, who, as I showed in Chapter 3, invaded the Middle East and North Africa during the nineteenth century and set up colonies there.[80] They tended to see themselves as saviours, redeeming the barbarous East from hopeless stagnation. The Crusaders had never exactly seen themselves as saviours of the Muslims; they had, if you like, a more honest attitude and were quite clear that liberation meant elimination or oppression. But the Crusaders *were* like the nineteenth-century colonialists in thinking that their control of the Middle East was of crucial importance to the future of the whole world, which one day the West hoped to conquer. In the next part of this chapter, I shall look at some of these romantic views of the Middle East and the Holy Land. Even secular Romantics were either imaginatively inspired by basic Christian themes or else expressed themselves in terms of old Christian habits, even when they professed a deep loathing of Christianity. This quasi-religious revival was succeeded by a revival of religion in earnest. Particularly in Victorian England, there was a new surge of religiosity that was highly emotional. It is a classic expression of the fact that religion cannot be suppressed. The nineteenth century shows us people who felt starved of feeling and a religious answer to the world, in rather the same way as many people feel today. Because of its long repression, the Victorian period, as is well known, was not a psychologically healthy period. There was, for example, a massive sexual repression and a terror of sexuality that reached new heights. Victorians were still obsessed with their inner demons.

As people looked towards the Middle East, we shall see that they all produced inadequate solutions, for one simple reason: they all failed to take into account the interests of all three religions and all three peoples. In France, a Catholic country, people tended to return to the classical crusading attitude of seeing Europeans as a chosen or privileged race, superior to both Arabs and Jews. Frenchmen often ignored or despised both peoples, fusing the two together in the old crusading way. Germany returned to the racial chauvinism and anti-semitism that crusading and crusading myths had fostered for centuries and threw off the new, unfamiliar rational toleration; Britain, a Protestant country, maintained the non-Jewish Zionism that had been the result of Protestant crusading. This took neither peoples seriously enough but was prepared to use the Jews to fulfil a religious dream and oppress the Arabs for their colonial ambitions. Nobody was able to see that an equitable solution meant respecting absolutely the inalienable rights of all three religions and all three peoples.

It is instructive to begin with the French Christian apologist François-René Chateaubriand, because when he wrote about Palestine he was consciously seeing himself in the traditions of crusading. He certainly saw Napoleon's Eastern expedition in this light. Napoleon, he wrote, was 'the last Frenchman who left his country to travel in the Holy Land, with the ideas, the goals and the sentiments of a pilgrim of former times'.[81] Chateaubriand could see that, although Napoleon clearly had many very different ideas from the Crusaders and pilgrims of the Middle Ages, he was like them in that he had sought his own dreams of Western fulfilment in the East and had seen his conquest of the Middle East and the Holy Land as an event of vital importance for the whole world. Chateaubriand, however, had a peculiarly Romantic view of crusading. He did not see the Crusades as cruel, violent, intolerant and traumatic episodes. In his Romantic view all the horror and oppression had been drained out of these medieval expeditions and they showed that Christianity was the religion that would save the whole world: 'the modern world owes all to [Christianity] from agriculture to the abstract sciences.'[82] It is certainly true that Christianity had been vitally important in the resurrection and creation of modern Europe, but this was not true of the 'modern world' in general.

Judaism and Islam had also been crucial to people living in other parts of the world, for example. Above all, Chateaubriand taught, Christianity was of all religions 'the most favourable to freedom'.[83] This was blatantly untrue, of course. Judaism and Islam had both been concerned, in their different ways, with equality and liberty, even though not all Muslims and Jews had lived up to these high ideals. Islam, in particular, could be called a revolutionary faith. There was a revolutionary strain in Christianity too that is marked in the New Testament and we have seen that the Crusades encouraged in the poor ideals of revolution and social justice. But sadly Christianity had been a very oppressive religion: it had persecuted and massacred Muslims and Jews, encouraged a rich establishment to oppress the poor and had persecuted other Christians who held different opinions about the faith, but Chateaubriand could not see this. For him the Crusades were a struggle between two ideologies: a revolutionary and a despotic faith. The Crusaders had tried to bring Christianity to the Holy Land, a cult which 'had caused to reawaken in modern people the genius of a sage antiquity, and had abolished base servitude'. But alas they had clashed with 'Islam': 'a cult that was civilization's enemy, systematically favourable to ignorance, to despotism and to slavery'.[84] The triumph of this barbaric religion meant that the East had been lost and must be redeemed.

Naturally when Chateaubriand visited the Holy Land, he applied this fantasy to the reality in front of him. The native inhabitants of Palestine seemed to him to be crying out for salvation: 'They have the air of soldiers without a leader, citizens without legislators, and a family without a father,'[85] he wrote in his best-seller *Journey from Paris to Jerusalem and from Jerusalem to Paris* (1810–11). The Palestinians were an example of 'civilized man fallen again into a savage state'. They would be unable to redeem themselves because they lacked the ideology. In the Koran there was 'neither a principle for civilization nor a mandate that can elevate character', and Islam 'preaches neither hatred of tyranny nor love of liberty'.[86] The Holy Land itself seemed to be yearning for an audience to understand its mysteries. 'God Himself has spoken from these shores,' Chateaubriand mused as he gazed at the Judaean desert, which he thought 'still seems struck dumb with terror, and one would say that it still has not been able to break the silence since it heard the voice of the eternal.'[87] The present inhabitants of the land were obviously incapable of listening to these sublime lessons and what the land and the people both needed was enlightened, freedom-loving Christianity. When Chateaubriand reached the Holy Sepulchre, the climax of his pilgrimage, he presented himself as a representative of God's new chosen people, who would crusade to save the East.

There were many other travellers in the Holy Land during the nineteenth century, who were essentially pilgrims, seeking their own fulfilment in a land that, as the Crusaders had before them, they regarded as belonging to them in some obscure but important way. When Alphonse de Lamartine began his journey to the East, he wrote that it was the fulfilment of a dream. It was 'a great event in my interior life',[88] and so he preferred his own visions to the reality. The real River Jordan was less important than the 'mysteries' that rose up in his soul when he gazed at it.[89] He actually says that the Holy Land looks best on the canvases of Poussin and Lorrain.[90] He is quite frank that his journey had become a spiritual quest that involved his memory, his heart and his soul far more than it exercised his eyes or his intellect. Naturally therefore he could not see 'real' Muslims but chose a perspective in which they were lazy, capricious, passionate and in every sense hopeless. The Orient was longing to be saved, for it was a place of 'nations without territory, *patrie*, rights, laws or security . . . waiting anxiously for the shelter'[91] of Western colonialism:

This sort of suzerainty thus defined, and consecrated as a European right, will consist principally in the right to occupy one or another territory, as well as the coasts, in order to found there either free cities or European colonies or commercial ports of call.[92]

In the Crusades mystical visions, which were just as fantastic, had also led to an aggressive war of occupation, and Lamartine and Chateaubriand had all the solipsism of their crusading ancestors. They too were convinced that the Holy Land belonged to them, never considering the Jewish claim and preferring their own vision of Muslims and the Holy Land to the reality. So did Gerard of Nerval, who made a pilgrimage to the East in 1842–3 and saw it as 'dead, dead, because man has killed it, and the Gods have fled'.[93]

As one might expect, the British visitors to the Holy Land were less given to exquisite musings, but they too preferred their own visions to the reality. When Lord Lindsey published his *Letters from Egypt, Edom and the Holy Land* he had a distorted Zionist vision: the decay of the land was due to 'the removal of the ancient inhabitants'[94] and would be redeemed by the 'return of her banished children and the application of industry commensurate with her agricultural capacities to burst once more into universal luxuriance and be all she was in the days of Solomon'.[95] There is the usual blindness to the Arab history of Palestine. In 1844 Eliot Warburton looked back to the Crusades for colonial inspiration and produced the usual solipsistic vision in his extremely popular book *The Crescent and the Cross*. Like a Crusader, Warburton felt that he was going home when he went East and wrote of 'a sort of patriotism for Palestine',[96] as though it were his own fatherland. As he wandered round the Holy Land, visiting places that had been familiar to him in the Bible since he was a small child, he reflected on Britain's duty to take possession of Egypt and Palestine, which were already hers by right. Thus she would secure her right of way to India and to this end there must be a new and more successful crusading effort: 'the interests of India may obtain what the Sepulchre of Christ has been denied.'[97] Wherever he went in the Middle East, Warburton was actually able to convince himself that people were expecting the British to come to save them and bring to them the prosperity and freedom that they had brought to the Indians of the subcontinent.[98]

If Western imperialists were turning, sometimes quite consciously, to crusading ideology to spur on their new colonial enterprise, so were the enemies of imperialism. In 1853 Karl Marx condemned British colonialism in India, and sympathised with the distress of the native Indians, who were being torn from their roots and seeing their way of life destroyed. Yet Marx also warned his reader not to idealise these Asian village communities, because:

> inoffensive though they may appear, [they] had always been the solid foundation of Oriental despotism. . . . they restrained the human mind within the smallest possible compass, making it the unresisting tool of superstition, enslaving it beneath the traditional rules, depriving it of all grandeur and historical energies.[99]

Although he hated religion, Marx reverted naturally to the Christian habit of seeing the oriental as the obverse image of his own ideal. He too felt that the East needed to be saved and decided that Britain was actually 'the unconscious tool of history'[100] because her repulsive policies would cause the people to rise up, shake off their inherent lethargy and cause a real social revolution. England was, therefore, effecting India's salvation. When he speaks of England's role in India, Marx seems to have a Jewish and messianic ideal of a double-edged salvation, which is a redemption and a destruction: 'England has to fulfil a double mission in

India: one destructive, the other regenerating,' he explained; 'the annihilation of the Asiatic society, and the laying of the material foundations of Western society in Asia'.[101] Only thus 'can mankind fulfil its destiny'.[102] Marx's view of the revolutionary struggle was really just as romantic and religious in tenor as Chateaubriand's and though he is passionately arguing for an equal society he still dreams like any Crusader of annihilating the people of the East in order to save the world.

Neither had Marx any love for the Jews, though he was Jewish himself. He saw the Jewish problem not as religious but as economic: 'Let us consider the real Jew,' he wrote in 1844. 'Not the *Sabbath Jew* . . . but the *everyday Jew*.' The real basis of this Judaism was '*Practical* need, *self-interest*. What is the worldly cult of the Jew? *Huckstering*. What is his worldly god? *Money*.'[103] Marx had taken the Western image of a Jew like Shylock as the whole of the reality. Jewish commercial ability had actually enabled many Jews to survive in anti-semitic Europe for centuries, for they were often protected by rulers like Oliver Cromwell who were ready to exploit their talent. But jealousy of Jewish success had led Gentiles to see it all as an international Jewish plot and was therefore an extension of the old Christian conspiracy theory. Marx firmly believed that the Jews had corrupted all mankind by making money the God of the world and infecting Christianity with this poison: the Jew-corrupted Christian had become a Shylock and 'is convinced he has no other destiny here below than to become richer than his neighbours', and 'the world is a stock exchange.'[104] In order 'to make the Jew impossible', therefore, the whole economic order had to be changed. Once that had happened, all 'religious consciousness would evaporate like some insipid vapour in the real, life-giving air of society.'[105] By getting rid of the money-Jew, the world would save itself: 'In emancipating itself from *hucksterism* and *money*, and thus from real and practical Judaism, our age would emancipate itself.'[106] In his book *A History of the Jews* Paul Johnson has argued that Marx's anti-semitism actually gave birth to his later militant socialism:

> His mature theory was a superstition, and the most dangerous kind of superstition, belief in a conspiracy of evil. But whereas originally it was based on the oldest form of conspiracy-theory, anti-Semitism, in the late 1840s and 1850s this was not so much abandoned as extended to embrace a world conspiracy-theory of the entire bourgeois class. Marx retained the original superstition that the making of money through trade and finance is essentially a parasitical and anti-social activity, but he now placed it on a basis not of race and religion, but of class.[107]

It is interesting that Johnson uses the word 'superstition' because it highlights one of the themes of this chapter. Even when we are struggling to get away from religion, we are still unable to free ourselves from irrational myths and hatreds. Crusading had nurtured a strong anti-semitism in Europe that was particularly virulent in Germany, and in the nineteenth century we discover in Marx an anti-semitic Jew. If Johnson is correct in his interesting analysis, it will mean that a secular form of a crusading superstition and hatred gave birth to revolutionary socialism.

But it is important to stress that anti-semitism was not confined to Germany; it also manifested itself in apparently liberated France during the 1840s in the work of the influential philologist Ernest Renan. Renan and Marx can be fruitfully considered together. Both rejected the religions they had been born to and yet both argued in terms of those religions. Indeed a very conscious rejection of religion often means a deeper obsession with it and that paradoxically religion continues to affect us powerfully. There is a difference in the anti-semitism of these two important men, however, because Marx isolated the Jews as his target, where Renan would broaden the scope of his hatred and contempt and in so doing would repeat an old crusading and Christian habit.

Both Renan and Marx were also finding new ways of reading history. Like Marxism, philology also offered a new secular interpretation of the past, which claimed to be scientific.[108] Instead of seeing language as a gift that God had given to man in the Garden of Eden, as the medievals had imagined, philologists saw language as a purely human invention. In place of the original sacred tongue, the idea of which had so fascinated Frederick II, the philologists posited an original Indo-European language which had been developed by the Aryan peoples of Asia and Europe and which gave birth to later Aryan languages. They believed that they could reconstruct this original language by applying their scientific rules but in fact they produced some new myths which were as potentially harmful as the old Christian myths. Renan turned to philology when he lost his Christian faith and later he would reinterpret the early Christian past in the new 'scientific' way, writing the lives of Jesus and St Paul and explaining them in human, natural terms instead of theologically. He wanted to show that religion had a purely natural basis, like language. These books were widely read and caused consternation. When Renan became a philologist he turned to the study of what he called the Semitic languages, which included Hebrew and Arabic, but this was not out of love for these tongues. He argued that Hebrew and Arabic were degraded forms, which had deviated from the Aryan tradition and had become irredeemably flawed. The languages could only be studied as an example of arrested development, because they lacked the progressive and developmental qualities that were inherent in 'our' linguistic systems. These Semitic languages could no more redeem themselves than could the Semites, the Jews and the Arabs, whom Renan said were 'une combinaison inférieure de la nature humaine'.[109]

> Therefore we refuse to allow that the Semitic languages have the capacity to regenerate themselves, even while recognising that they do not escape – any more than other products of human consciousness – the necessity of change or of successive modifications.[110]

It is important to say that from this nineteenth-century linguistic theory came the concept of the 'Semite' as diametrically opposed to the 'Aryan'; this dangerous myth gave scientific reasons to replace the old outmoded religious reasons why 'we' should continue to hate Arabs and Jews, and in Nazi Germany this would have disastrous and tragic consequences.

Renan's theory is an almost uncanny translation of the old religious prejudice into a 'modern' scientific form. In the 'Semite', the Jews and Arabs have been fused together just as Jews and Muslims had been seen as a common enemy of Christian Europe. The concept of the inferior Semitic languages makes Jews and Arabs once again a distorted mirror-image of the enlightened and progressive West because they cannot develop like 'us'. This led Renan to pass quite easily from a condemnation of the Semitic languages to a condemnation of the Semites themselves:

> One sees that in all things the Semitic race appears to us to be an incomplete race, by virtue of its simplicity. This race – if I dare use the analogy – is to the Indo-European family what a pencil sketch is to a painting; it lacks that variety, that amplitude, that abundance of life which is the condition of perfectibility. Like those individuals who possess so little fecundity that, after a gracious childhood, they attain only the most mediocre virility, the Semitic nations experienced their fullest flowering in their first age and have never been able to achieve true maturity.[111]

The old religious fantasies had been transformed into a racial myth and scientifically 'proved'.

Such dangerous theories of race inevitably became crucial in the second half of the nineteenth century, when, as I pointed out in Chapter 3, nationalism became a new enthusiasm and people started to define themselves anew, in national or racial terms. In Germany the cult of the *Volk* was perhaps most obviously seen in the operas of Richard Wagner, which would later have such a profound influence on Hitler and his followers in Nazi Germany. The pure, noble German race, the source of all goodness and beauty, was celebrated in a form that musically and dramatically made it larger than life. It is significant that in the main they seek to return to the German pagan past, before the Germans submitted to Christianity. The new sense of the German self despised the pacifism of Christian teachings, and wanted to recreate a more robust and martial past, though a little reflection could have taught them that Christianity had many fiercer lessons to teach them than the pacifist gospel of Christ. The Wagnerian cult of the noble Aryan race of Germans went hand in hand with a revival of anti-semitic mythology in Germany. As Wagner wrote in 1881:

> I regard the Jewish race as the born enemy of pure humanity and everything that is noble in it; it is certain that we Germans will go under before them, and perhaps I am the last German who knows how to stand up as an art-loving man against the Judaism that is already getting control of everything.[112]

It is a classic expression of the old Christian paranoia, with its horrified vision of giant and satanic plots. The Jews have also become larger than life and the enemy of all 'our' Aryan values.

Friedrich Nietzsche was also attacking Jews during the 1880s. He likewise hated Christianity and urged Germans to throw off its puling values and return to the pagan values of the Aryans: 'pride, severity, strength, hatred, revenge'. Christianity had corrupted the world and Christianity had derived from Judaism. As he wrote in *Antichrist*, in the gospels:

> One is among Jews – the first consideration to keep from losing the thread completely – Paul and Christ were little superlative Jews. . . . One would no more associate with the first Christians than one would with Polish Jews – they both do not smell good. . . . Pontius Pilate is the only figure in the New Testament who commands respect. To take a Jewish affair seriously – he does not persuade himself to do that. One Jew more or less – what does it matter?[113]

Like Marx and Wagner, Nietzsche saw the Jews as the corrupters of mankind; through Christianity they had poisoned the world. 'The Jews', he wrote in *Antichrist*, 'have made mankind so thoroughly false that even today the Christian can feel anti-Jewish without realizing that he is today the *ultimate, Jewish consequence*.'[114] Nietzsche had a mental breakdown, from which he never recovered, in 1889, the year that Adolf Hitler was born, and his ideas, which were widely disseminated in Germany, would be ready to hand when Hitler began to shape the Aryan identity once again.

But the Arab Semites were also being discussed during the 1880s. Expert orientalists, who were often making a scholarly study of Islam, began to produce an equally racist fantasy of the 'Arab mind'. Unlike the Jews, who were omnipresent in Europe and sometimes in powerful or influential positions, the Arabs were a distant, unthreatening reality. As Europe prepared to colonise the Middle East, it was consoling to hear these scholarly fables that presented the Arabs as a primitive people who need Western redemption. These myths were different from the musings of the French Romantics earlier in the century, because like Renan's linguistic theories they claimed to be objective, scientific studies. In 1881, for example, the orientalist William Robertson Smith toured the Hejaz in order to research the religion of Islam. The assumption was that nothing had changed since the time of Mohammad and that one could understand the first Muslims perfectly by studying modern Arabs in the peninsula. Robertson Smith concluded regretfully that the problem with Islam was that it was too Arab, and therefore constitutionally incapable of development:

> The prejudices of the Arab have their roots in a conservatism which lies deeper than his belief in Islam. It is, indeed, a great fault of the religion of the Prophet that it lends itself so easily to the prejudices of the race among whom it was first promulgated, and that it has taken under its protection so many barbarous and obsolete ideas, which even Mohammad must have seen to have no religious worth, but which he carried over into his system in order to facilitate the propagation of his reformed doctrines.[115]

It is an astonishingly arrogant assumption to claim to understand their religion better than the Muslims themselves. Smith concludes authoritatively that 'many of the prejudices which seem to us most distinctively Mohammedan [*sic*] have no basis in the Koran.' As Edward Said has pointed out in *Orientalism*, 'Smith's vision of the world is binary, as is evident in such passages as the following:

> The Arabian traveller is quite different from ourselves. The labour of moving from place to place is a mere nuisance to him, he has no enjoyment in effort [as "we" do], and grumbles at hunger or fatigue with all his might [as "we" do not]. You will never persuade the Oriental that, when you get off your camel, you can have any other wish than immediately to squat on a rug and take your rest (*isterih*), smoking and drinking. Moreover the Arab is little impressed by scenery [but "we" are].'[116]

The expert, therefore, is reverting to the long tradition of defining himself and his culture against Muslims of the Middle East. Robertson Smith finds that he can have absolutely no respect for 'the jejune, practical and . . . constitutionally irreligious Arabic mind',[117] without seeming to realise that this is just as fictional as the portrait he gives of 'us', who never cease striving purposefully onwards to ever greater heights of achievement.

Said goes on later in the same chapter to discuss the work of another famous and important turn-of-the-century orientalist, Duncan Black Macdonald, who was often sought out by colonialists for advice about how to manage the Orientals. Macdonald was firmly committed to the old medieval view that Islam is a Christian heresy, not an independent faith. In his *The Religious Attitude and Life in Islam* (1909) he gives what he sees as a self-evident definition of the oriental mind. He begins by saying that 'it is plain' that the conception of the Unseen is much more real to the 'Oriental' than to Western people: the 'large modifying elements which seem, from time to time, almost to upset the general law' do not upset this apprehension of the Unseen.[118] But 'the essential difference in the Oriental mind is not credulity as to unseen things, but inability to construct a system as to seen things.'[119] The Oriental has 'no sense of law' and therefore the implication is that he cannot fruitfully organise his existence in the way that Western people can. The oriental mind is so lawless indeed that 'it is evident that anything is possible to the Oriental.'[120]

> *Inability*, then, to see life steadily, and see it whole, to understand that a theory of life must cover all the facts, and *liability* to be stampeded by a single idea and blinded to everything else – therein, I believe, is the difference between the East and the West.[121]

At the turn of the twentieth century, scholars were 'proving' that the Arab Semite was, as Renan had said, a case of arrested development who needs to be taken in hand by the beneficent and progressive West. This theorising was just as blatantly racist as the definition of the Jewish Semites. Europeans were preparing to annihilate the Jews at home and to colonise the Arabs in the East.

But not all Europeans were willing to persecute the Jews. More and more, the British were turning to the Zionist solution as a means of colonising the primitive East. In 1838 Prime Minister Lord Palmerston had sent William Young to be the first Vice-Consul in the new Consulate in Jerusalem, with special instructions 'to afford protection to the Jews generally'.[122] The British wanted to make use of Jews instead of persecuting them. This latest Zionist initiative came from the great philanthropist Ashley, seventh Earl of Shaftesbury, who was the friend and stepfather-in-law of Palmerston and the mentor of William Young. An ardent evangelical, Lord Shaftesbury was possessed by the old millennial dream of converting the Jews and returning them to Zion to bring the Second Coming of Christ more quickly.[123] He had persuaded Palmerston to send Young to Jerusalem with a special mandate for the Jews, and was convinced that this was an important step towards their final return. As he wrote in his diary: 'What a wonderful event it is. The ancient city of the people of God is about to resume a place among the nations, and England is the first of the Gentile Kingdoms that ceases to tread her down.'[124] Yet this zeal for the Jews was not inspired by true concern for them as a separate people. In fact there was a residual anti-semitism in Shaftesbury, who would vote against Jewish emancipation in 1861.[125] As usual he simply saw the Jews as a tool for the Christian redemption. He also shared the blindness of most Zionists about a possible Palestinian problem because he could not 'see' the Arabs. It was Lord Shaftesbury who coined the slogan, which the Jewish Zionists would later adapt and make their own, that Palestine was 'a country without a nation for a nation without a country'.[126]

As usual, this Gentile Zionist initiative was combined with a practical and political British ambition. Lord Palmerston was a secular politician who had no dreams about the Second Coming but saw Young's mission as part of England's colonial policy in the Middle East. Russia and France were also looking covetously at the Middle East and were both courting minority groups within the Ottoman empire to act as a future power-base. France was claiming the protection of the Catholics and Russia the protection of the Orthodox Christians. Britain was now claiming to be the protector of the Jews.[127] Two years later, again under the influence of Lord Shaftesbury, Lord Palmerston wrote an extraordinary letter to John, Viscount Ponsonby, his Ambassador in Istanbul, telling him to work to return the Jews to Palestine:

> There exists at present among the Jews dispersed over Europe, a strong notion that the time is approaching when their nation is to return to Palestine. . . . Consequently their wish to go thither has become more keen, and their thoughts have been bent more intently than before upon the means of realizing that wish. It is well known that the Jews of Europe possess great wealth; and it is manifest that any country in which a considerable number of them might choose to settle would derive great benefit from the riches they would bring into it.[128]

There was as yet no such Jewish desire, but that was of no consequence to Palmerston and his remarks about Jewish wealth smack unpleasantly of anti-semitic prejudice. Almost exactly a week later on 17 August 1840 Lord Shaftesbury persuaded the editor of *The Times* to publish a Zionist leader. The article disclosed a plan 'to plant the Jewish people in the land of their fathers', which was now under 'serious political consideration'. It was hoped that the Turkish Sultan would consent to receive the Jews in Palestine and would assure them of law, justice and safety, which would be 'secured to them under the protection of a European power'.[129] The leader caused a great stir. 'The newspapers teem with documents about the Jews,' Lord Shaftesbury recorded in his diary ten days later. 'What a chaos of schemes and disputes is on the horizon. . . . What violence, what hatred, what combination, what discussion. What stir of every passion and every feeling in men's hearts.'[130]

Despite the commotion, nothing came of this scheme. Lord Palmerston went out of office later that year and William Young died an untimely death shortly afterwards. The Ottoman Sultan was predictably apathetic about the scheme. Yet the Zionist hope still did not die in England. In 1844 the Reverend A. Bradshaw published *A Tract for the Times, being a Plea for the Jews*, which urged the government to grant the Jews four million pounds to hasten their return to Palestine.[131] In the same year Dr Thomas Clarke wrote a frankly colonial treatise urging the Jewish return to Zion: *India and Palestine: Or the Restoration of the Jews Viewed in Relation to the Nearest Route to India.* The Jews, he argued, were people like us: 'a brave, independent and spiritual people, deeply imbued with the sentiment of nationality'. Once they were re-established in their own land, 'there is no power at all that could ever take it from them.'[132] Later a committee was convened in London to work for the Return to Zion. The inaugural address, delivered by the Reverend T. Tully Crybbace, called for a state that fulfilled the biblical promises, stretching 'from the Euphrates to the Nile and from the Mediterranean to the Desert'.[133] These religious Christian Zionists had committed the usual error of assuming, like Shaftesbury, that the land was empty. They had ignored the existence of the Arab population in their grand schemes and had concentrated on only two of the three peoples and three religions involved.

Perhaps the most revealing of these British Zionists was George Eliot, who published *Daniel Deronda* in 1879, and, despite herself, showed some of the complications inherent in non-Jewish Zionism. Deronda, the hero, is fortunate enough not to discover his Jewish blood until he is quite grown up and has received an impeccably Gentile education. Daniel, the perfect English gentleman, is therefore a Jew who is really one of 'us' and in a perfect position to carry out the useful Zionist project. Throughout the novel, Deronda is described in Christ-like terms: he is always rescuing and redeeming people from various ills from the very first pages of the novel, when his strong moral presence prevents the (Gentile) heroine Gwendolen Harleth from gambling away any more of her money; he later redeems the necklace she has lost at the table. Deronda rescues people from suicide, from blindness, from failing examinations and from despair. As saviour and redeemer, Deronda will be able to rescue the East. The Zionist project is most fully discussed in the novel by a Jew called Mordechai, whose disciple Daniel becomes. Mordechai is a political Zionist and his solution looks forward to that which would be preached by Theodor Herzl in 1895. The Jews, Mordechai argues, will 'redeem the soil from debauched and paupered conquerors'; the polity of the Jewish state will be 'grand, simple, just like the old' Jewish kingdom, which had once established 'more than the brightness of Western freedom amid the despotisms of the East' in biblical times:

> And the world will gain as Israel gains. For there will be a community in the van of the East which carries the culture and the sympathies of every great nation in its bosom; there will be a land set for a halting place of enmities, a neutral ground for the East as Belgium is for the West.[134]

East and West are diametrically opposed. The East, which is the home of Islam and the Arab Semites described by Renan, is despotic, debauched and impoverished. Such people are quite incapable of governing themselves and in Deronda they will find a redeemer. The novel is a powerful and classic summing up of attitudes that had been enshrined throughout the nineteenth century.

Yet Eliot is also as ambiguous about the Jews as non-Jewish Zionists in England had always been. This is clear in the fact that the chief Jewish hero, Deronda, is pre-eminently an Englishman. It is also clear in her treatment of the characters who had had a more thoroughly 'Jewish' upbringing. Mordechai, for example, is a person who cannot personally realise this imperialistic Zionism. He is suffering from an incurable disease, and although his nobility of soul is constantly praised, because of his illness he is physically rather repulsive. At the same time as the reader is asked to admire him, he or she is constantly repelled. Anti-Jewish sentiment, therefore, finds a validation. Throughout the novel, Mordechai is made to speak in an archaic biblical style. The implication is, therefore, that Judaism is a moribund, anachronistic faith that needs a healthy infusion from the West, which it will find in Deronda. There is also an ambivalence in the portrait of Mira, Mordechai's sister, who finally becomes Deronda's wife and sails with him to the East to fulfil the Zionist dream. Pathos is the overwhelming emotion that is associated with Mira, and Eliot indulges in a sentimentality in this portrait which in her mature work she does not usually allow herself with her Gentile heroines. It seems as though Eliot is fighting against an anti-semitic tendency in herself or in her reader when she struggles to present a 'good Jewess', and to make Mira sympathetic she resorts to methods that are more familiar to us in the work of Dickens. Mira's diminutive size and the weakness of her exquisite singing voice is stressed. The characters exclaim in wonder at her physical smallness. She is like Little Nell and Little Dorrit, characters in which Dickens makes female virtue small, vulnerable and, perhaps, cloying. It is also true that Mira has had a traumatic past with her father, a truly evil 'Jew' and the reader must ask himself whether she would have been as likely to have emerged from this as such a paragon. In rather the same way a reader will ask whether Oliver Twist could realistically have remained such a little angel after his time in the thrall of Fagin, another classically wicked Jew. Although Eliot seems to be asking us to take a more sympathetic view of Judaism she is really cutting it down to size. Mordechai and Mira are too weak and ineffective in their various ways to be taken very seriously. Even though both cling passionately to their faith, they both desperately need Deronda if they are to make a strong contribution to the history of the world. Judaism is still subservient to Western Christianity and the only Jew who can be a real force in the world is one who has been brought up in the traditions of Great Britain.

It seemed that if people wanted to create either a Jewish or an Arab hero, he had in some sense to be British. The 'Arab' equivalent of Daniel Deronda is perhaps T. E. Lawrence, who became Lawrence *of* Arabia during the Arab revolt of 1916. Dressed in Arab clothes, fighting at the head of the Bedouin, and – apparently – completely identified with the Arab people, Lawrence caught the imagination of Western people. The image of Lawrence as the romantic representative of the Arab world was further reinforced by David Lean's famous film starring Peter O'Toole. For centuries Western people had pushed the Muslim and Arab people away from them; when they wanted to argue with Muslims, the medieval scholars had created fictional representatives, who argued about 'Mohammadanism' entirely from a Christian and European perspective. Since the eighteenth century, people had also fantasised and identified with a romantic and exotic Orient, that bore little relation to reality but was an imaginary province of the Western view of the world. T. E. Lawrence can be seen as the epitome of this long habit of making up a Western Orient that people prefer to the real East. With the possible exception of

Anwar Sadat, there has been no other Arab who has caught the imagination of the Western world during the twentieth century as much as Lawrence, the fake Arab. The romantic view of his career often overlooks the fact that his intervention in the Arab revolt was part of a cynical British plot to control the course of the revolution and tether it firmly to British colonial plans for the Middle East. As 'our' representative in the barbarous East, Lawrence was exploiting Arab sympathies for a Western fulfilment. It is also true that although Lawrence had a romantic view of the 'Arab', he also had a fundamental contempt for the 'Arab mind', which comes across frequently in *The Seven Pillars of Wisdom*.[135] As in the case of *Daniel Deronda*, love and admiration of the Semite goes hand in hand with a strong anti-semitism.

The year after Lawrence joined the Arab revolt, Foreign Secretary Arthur Balfour issued the famous Balfour Declaration and finally brought to fruition a long tradition of non-Jewish Zionism in Britain. Balfour was a typical Zionist. He had a practical and political motive, because he hoped that the declaration would win international Jewish support for Britain during the First World War and he was conscious of the strategic importance of Palestine. But he was also inspired by the Christian Protestant tradition. He had been brought up in the Scottish Church and the biblical image of a Jewish Palestine affected him powerfully: he imagined that there would be a cultural renaissance in the new Israel that would be a light unto the Gentiles.[136] Like all Zionists he was completely indifferent to the claim of the Palestinian Arabs, who had long been regarded by the British as barbarous and unworthy caretakers. As he said with astonishing bluntness in his *Memorandum Respecting Syria, Palestine and Mesopotamia*:

> For in Palestine we do not propose even to go through the form of consulting the wishes of the present inhabitants of the country, though the American Commission has been going through the form of asking what they are. The Four Great Powers are committed to Zionism. And Zionism, be it right or wrong, good or bad, is rooted in age-long traditions, in present needs, in future hopes, of far profounder import than the desires and prejudices of the 700,000 Arabs who now inhabit that ancient land.[137]

Like a true Crusader, Balfour was convinced that 'our' view of the Holy Land put him above ordinary moral considerations. Zionism was by now so firmly established as self-evidently right that it was impossible for Balfour to see that the Arabs had any claim at all to the land they had inhabited for 1200 years.

Balfour was also a typical Zionist in an uneasy anti-semitism. In 1905 he had introduced the Aliens Bill in Parliament in order to limit Jewish immigration.[138] He may have wanted Jews to be in Palestine, but he did not want them in his own country, and these anti-semitic feelings disturbed him.[139] He was aware of the shameful tradition of persecution in Europe and may well have felt that the enthusiastic support he gave to Zionism in some way atoned for his instinctive anti-semitism.[140] It is significant that his strongest opponents in England were Jewish. Lord Montagu, one of the leaders of British Jewry, opposed Zionism from the beginning and he accused Balfour and his colleagues of promoting a Jewish homeland in Palestine simply to get the Jews out of England. During the discussions leading up to the Balfour Declaration, he submitted a memorandum stating that 'the policy of His Majesty's Government is anti-Semitic in result and will prove a rallying ground for anti-Semites in every country of the world.'[141] But his Gentile colleagues were as blind to Jewish objections as they were to Arab objections. As had always been the case, what mattered was what Europeans wanted in the Holy Land.

Balfour could rely on the support of a generation of Zionist politicians who

included Prime Minister David Lloyd George, Mark Sykes, Leopold Amery, Lord Milner, Lord Harlech, Robert Cecil and C. P. Scott. They could all see the political
advantages of the Zionist idea, but they were also compelled by the old Protestant *Crusaders in*
view of a strictly Jewish Palestine. Lloyd George, for example, had been brought up *the West*
by his uncle, who had been a preacher in a fundamentalist Welsh Baptist sect with
a tradition of interpreting the Bible quite literally. When Lloyd George listened to
Weizmann talking about Palestine he was naturally stirred and excited by these
very early associations: the places that Weizmann mentioned were more familiar
to him, he said, than places on the Western front.[142] He could only see Palestine in
Jewish terms, as he explained in a speech to the Jewish Historical Society in 1925:

> I was brought up in a school where I was taught far more about the history of the
> Jews than about the history of my own land. I could tell you all the kings of
> Israel. But I doubt whether I could have named half a dozen of the kings of
> England, and not more of the kings of Wales. . . . We were thoroughly imbued
> with the history of your race in the days of its greatest glory, when it founded
> that great literature which will echo to the very last days of this old world,
> influencing, moulding, fashioning human character, inspiring and sustaining
> human motive, for not only Jews, but Gentiles as well. We absorbed it and made
> it part of the best of the Gentile character.[143]

There could hardly be a clearer statement about the Western habit of interiorising
Judaism, absorbing it and making it part of the Christian, European self. A Jewish
Palestine was in an important way a British Protestant projection in the Middle
East. But Lloyd George was well known for making anti-semitic remarks, despite
his love of the Jewish scriptures.[144] Although British Zionism seemed to deny
crusading anti-semitism, there was really no fundamental change. Such Zionists,
in a convoluted way, still wanted Palestine for themselves and were still either
anti-semitic or blind to the real power and independent integrity of Judaism.

British Catholics responded differently. Mark Sykes, for example, who had had a
Catholic upbringing, confessed that he had a strong 'distaste for Jews' and at first
opposed the Zionist project for precisely this reason. He was, however, an ardent
nationalist and colonialist and one of the architects of the notorious 1916
Sykes–Picot agreement. When the full colonial implications of Zionism were
explained to him, he became an enthusiastic convert. He would now see the 'Jew'
as 'our' representative in the barbarous Middle East who was taking possession of
Palestine in 'our' name. He also saw Zionism as a solution to the Jewish problem.
Instead of a hybrid, assimilating Jew living disturbingly in the heart of Christian
Europe, there would be a new Hebrew nationalist in his own country, reassuringly
distant and distinct.[145] Zionists like Balfour and Sykes were still opposed to the
idea of absorbing and assimilating Jews into European society, in much the same
way as fifteenth-century Spanish Catholics had been. Zionism was a way of
deporting Jews without giving way to overt anti-semitism and banishing them
from Europe by offensive persecution. Gentile support for the State of Israel in the
West was from the beginning complex and neurotic, moulded not simply by
political and humanitarian reasons, but by millennial Protestant and biblical ideas,
crusading colonialism and crusading anti-semitism. Non-Jewish Zionists were in a
very real sense neo-Crusaders, even if they were no longer inspired by the old
passion for the Tomb of Christ.

This becomes very clear when we consider the Gentile Zionists' attitude to the
'Arabs'. Yet again the old prejudice came into play and because the Arabs really
were, quite understandably, opposed to the Zionist scheme, they were made into
the distorted enemy of true civilisation yet again. But this time they were
juxtaposed and measured against 'our' new representative, the 'Jew'. Richard *371*

Meinertzhagen, chief political officer for Palestine and Syria on General Allenby's staff, was deeply anti-semitic. He confessed in his diary that he was 'imbued with anti-Semitic feelings'.[146] He feared Jewish presence in his own country as a threat to the British identity; the Jews could, he thought, easily gain too much influence 'in professions, in trades, in universities and museums, in finance and as landowners'.[147] He was ready for a radical if not for a final solution. If the Jews became too powerful, he decided, 'then of course we shall have to act against them, but it will not take the form of a concentration camp.'[148] But the Zionist solution, which proposed a convenient way of getting rid of this threat, was attractive in other ways. Meinertzhagen felt a 'great sentimental attraction' to the idea of the persecuted Jews returning to their ancient land.[149] The old biblical vision was linked to the new colonial vision: 'Jewish brains and money' would redeem the barren wilderness that was Palestine.[150] A friendly Palestine was 'vital' for the future strategic security of the British government and Meinertzhagen was convinced that this would be impossible if it was in Arab hands.[151] As had long been a British habit, Meinertzhagen was ready to split his anti-semitism and make the 'Arab' the opposite of the 'Jew'. This mythical bifurcation appears constantly in his diary. 'Intelligence was a Jewish virtue,' he wrote antithetically, 'and intrigue was an Arab vice.'[152] The Jews were 'virile, brave, determined and intelligent' while the Arabs were 'decadent, stupid, dishonest and producing little beyond eccentrics influenced by the romance and silence of the desert'.[153] If the Jews took over in Palestine there would be 'progress' and the 'up-setting of modern government', but an Arab government would mean 'stagnation, immorality, rotten government, corrupt and dishonest society'.[154] These new fictional stereotypes now set the two old crusading enemies off against one another:

> The Palestine Arab will never reach the Jewish standard of ability in any sense. The Jew will always be on top and he means to be there. He looks forward to a Jewish state in Palestine with sovereign rights, a real National Home and not a sham Jewish–Arab confederation.[155] The Jew, however small his voice, however mild his manner, will in the end be heard and he will succeed. The Arab will trumpet and bluster, others in Europe and America will sing his praises if the local orchestra breaks down, but he will remain where he is and has for ever been, an inhabitant of the east, nurturing stagnant ideas and seeing no further than the narrow doctrines of Mohammed [*sic*].[156]

The old blind prejudice against 'Islam' had modulated into the new secular prejudice against the 'Arab', who was the obverse of everything 'we' stood for. But Meinertzhagen's ineradicable Jewish anti-semitism is also revealed in this paragraph, not least in his use of the reductive term the 'Jew'. Like the 'Arab', the 'Jew' is a monolithic fantasy created by 'us'. There is no such thing as *the* 'Jew' nor *the* 'Arab' and it is dangerous to suppose that there is. There are rather millions of Jewish and Arab individuals with an infinitely varied combination of talents, enthusiasms, hopes, fears, faults, neuroses, defects and ambitions. But since the time of the Crusades fantasies were created that had no reality outside European peoples' views of themselves. The 'Jew' that Meinertzhagen contemplated was simply a flattering portrait of 'us' in endless opposition to his and our equally fantastic enemy the 'Arab'. The antithesis is a rhetorical ploy that gives the conflict an elegant logical and literary but not objective reality.

It was because of the fantasy of the 'Jew' that six million Jews were exterminated by the Nazis in the ultimate secular Crusade. This has naturally given people a very healthy fear of Jewish anti-semitism and has led to an increased support for the State of Israel in the West. But it would, I fear, be unrealistic to think that there is no longer any Western anti-semitism. Gentile support for Zionism was from the start complex, neurotic and anti-semitic and this is still likely to be the case. When Western people support the 'Jew' against the 'Arab', they are usually guilty of much the same fictional antithesis as Meinertzhagen, who created his out of a complex of egotism and racial prejudice. There is little squeamishness about Arab anti-semitism, however, which seems to be the only socially acceptable form of racism left. Biased and fictional remarks are constantly bandied about in public and in private, and people would, quite properly, be shocked if the same remarks were directed against blacks or Jews. The Middle East conflict has enabled the West to give a new twist to the stereotype of the 'Arab': he is an anti-Jewish-Semite. Now that 'we' are very nervously and stridently against Jewish anti-semitism, the 'Arab' is seen to be essentially and absolutely smouldering with anti-semitic fantasies and obsessed with the annihilation of the State of Israel. This is an oversimplified view and takes no account of the wrong that has been done to many thousands of Arab people during the implementation of the Zionist project, but it is attractive to Western people and gives them a healthy glow of righteousness when they attack the 'Arab'. But it is also indicative of a moral crisis in Europe.

I have been arguing that literature can often give us a telling insight into current attitudes and prejudice, and this must surely be the case today. In 1987, Elie Weisel, the Israeli chronicler of the Holocaust, was awarded the Nobel Prize for Peace. At the time some of my more sceptical Israeli friends said that they found some comfort in the fact that he had not been awarded a Nobel Prize for Literature. But whatever the literary merits of Weisel's work, I think it is safe to say that it is most unlikely that an Arab or Iranian novelist who chronicled his own people's suffering today in the Palestinian refugee camps, in war-torn Beirut or under the former Shah's regime in Iran, would be given this coveted accolade. The easy retort is that the 'Arabs' have not produced any comparable literature and to this I am bound to reply that it is impossible for us to be sure of this unless we are Arabic speakers. A few Palestinian and Arab writers have been translated into English by specialist presses, but there is very little translation of Arab writers in the Western world. We are still seeing only two angles in this murderous triangle. It seems that Arab voices are not welcome here and this silence must inevitably distort our view of the conflict. Certainly no work of Arab fiction has been made into a blockbuster like Leon Uris' *Exodus* or *The Hajj*, which continue the old bifurcation between Arab and Jew. The Jews are all noble heroes and brave freedom fighters, and the Arabs are primitive, disreputable terrorists, possessed by an anti-semitism that is absolutely evil. The complexities of this agonising conflict have been completely ignored in these popular works, which can be found in almost any corner shop in Britain.[157] Another famous blockbuster was the star-studded film *Raid on Entebbe*, which celebrated the Israelis' gallant, audacious and illegal rescue of Jewish hostages in Idi Amin's Uganda. But, again, it is most unlikely that there would be such a popular film celebrating a plucky group of Arab terrorists, striving to rescue their people from persecution and oppression. If we are ever to find a solution, it seems essential that we do not continue the long British tradition of ignoring the people of the Islamic world in the interests` of propping up our own fragile identity.

This fragility is particularly clear in the popular literature about the Nazi Holocaust. We have been deeply shaken by it in Britain and in Europe and we must always remember this horrific example of where our crusading vision can lead us. In our literature and popular presentations of the Holocaust we are usually unable to conceive it adequately, and perhaps this failure is inevitable. The Holocaust was an event of such monstrous evil that it possibly cannot be encompassed in art, without undesirable distortion. We have tried to mourn the victims of the Nazis in sometimes lamentably distorted ways. Certainly the popular television series

The Holocaust which was screened in 1978 was a sentimental and feeble representation of the evil of the Nazis and the suffering of the Jews. But there are works that have attempted a more serious and mature treatment and I should like to consider some of these.

The first is *The Diary of Anne Frank*, which has become a classic that we give our children to read at home and in school. This brave and moving journal of a Jewish girl who lived for years in hiding in Amsterdam and eventually died in Belsen has repeatedly been filmed and televised. It is clearly valuable to us in many ways. Anne is a very sympathetic and normal adolescent girl and reading her diary will prevent Gentile children from thinking that Jews are abnormal, perverted people. I find myself asking, however, whether the book would have been as popular if the Frank family had been more Jewish in their lifestyle. If they had been devoutly religious Jews, studying Torah, praying with *tfillin*, singing *zemiros* round the table on Friday evenings, they may have been a little 'too Jewish' for popular taste. Because they are 'just like us', however, they are sympathetic. It might also be the case that our constant promotion of this tragic diary of a young, doomed Jewish girl means that we cannot quite bear to relinquish an image of the Jews as victims. Because of our overwhelming and unmanageable guilt about the Holocaust, we seem unable to progress beyond this view of the 'Jew' as vulnerable and suffering. This makes it disturbing for us to see the Israelis, the new Jews, behave as cruel aggressors and we are thrown off balance. While we must always remember Anne and the six million other Jewish victims, it is surely important to remember that history has moved on and that we must not condone immoral Israeli behaviour because of *our* acute distress about the Holocaust. Again, I ask whether a story of a Palestinian child who suffered the trauma of the disaster of 1948 and endured the misery of the refugee camps would be such a classic here. It is not that I am claiming that the Palestinian catastrophe equals the Holocaust in horror; I am saying that we have a double standard here. There was a public outcry when Vanessa Redgrave was invited to play a leading role in the television film *Playing for Time*. This rather sentimental film portrayed Jews in the orchestra of a concentration camp who were playing in order to stay alive. People vociferously objected that because Redgrave had declared sympathy with the PLO she was absolutely unfitted to take the role of a Jewish victim of the Holocaust. This is to equate Yasir Arafat with Hitler and the Palestinians with the Nazis and is a distortion. To understand and sympathise with the suffering of the Palestinian people and their struggle for survival should not disqualify anyone from sympathising with the victims of the Nazis. This is especially true now that we are becoming more and more aware that the Israelis have resorted to a violence that is equal to and even greater than any of the terrorist attacks of the PLO. Our guilt must not make us over-compensate by adopting a blinkered policy of double-think. Surely we must instead struggle to achieve the 'triple vision' that I have been trying to articulate.

In January 1987 I spent a cold and uncomfortable day – albeit a rewarding one – in a North London cinema watching Claude Lanzman's nine-hour documentary about the Holocaust, *Shoah*. This film tried to avoid any sentimental clichés or any sensational and emotive footage. Its aim was to record the monstrous facts, coldly and objectively, and to record the experiences of the survivors and the SS who perpetrated such atrocities. There were dubious elements in the film. One was the filming of a lengthy interview with an ex-SS officer, without his knowledge or consent. This was felt to be justifiable in the interests of recording a total view of the Nazi obscenity, but it must be dangerous to create an abnormal moral category in this way. Lanzman was scrupulous to avoid cheap sensationalism and even risked being dull: we were treated to lengthy technical discussions about the

exact distance from one spot in Auschwitz to another, besides watching the emotional and moving testimonies of the survivors. Later in the year the film was shown in its entirety on Channel 4 Television. The only question I have to ask is whether such an extended and epic depiction of Arab or Palestinian suffering would be accorded the same respect. Our interest in the Holocaust is obsessive, not surprisingly given the measure of our guilt. The Arab and Islamic world has for a long time not found a place on our emotional and mythical map, and it is unlikely that we would be as 'interested' in poring over this suffering or in evaluating our responsibility for it: our responsibility for this suffering and anger has been shelved for too long. We in Britain could shrug off our responsibility for the Holocaust and claim that, after all, we did at one time stand alone against Hitler's Germany. We have not done so and it may be that the Holocaust fills us with the 'dread' that we have noted throughout the story of the holy wars and that we are subliminally strongly conscious that anti-semitism in Europe is not a thing of the past. The absolute veto that prevented the play *Perdition* being performed in London in 1986, because it showed Zionists collaborating with the Nazis in order to expedite emigration to Palestine, tells us a lot. It seems as though we feel that we are only a step away from another outbreak of violent anti-semitism and that even the smallest thing could bring it on. We could not trust ourselves to see such a play because it threatened our fragile new relationship with the Jewish people. Yet we have seen that this kind of 'dread' can lead to violence and further persecution.

When we contemplate the Holocaust, it seems that we are moved by very complex and threatening emotions that we cannot handle rationally or objectively and which can even give rise to disturbed or unbalanced states of mind. This is also manifest in the literature on the subject. It sometimes seems that any novel which deals with the Holocaust has a chance of being a huge success, whatever its literary merit. One of the most striking examples of this must be D. M. Thomas' *The White Hotel*, which was published in 1981 to enormous critical acclaim, even though none of his other books have ever attained such notoriety and he was accused of plagiarising a climactic passage. The novel begins with two chapters describing the sexual fantasies of a young Jewish woman whom Sigmund Freud, no less, has diagnosed as an hysteric. The presence of Freud is meant to make us take these bizarre and peculiar sexual fantasies seriously. The climax of this unpleasant and obsessive sexual theme occurs towards the end, when a Nazi soldier rapes the heroine with his bayonet. Throughout the novel the heroine has telepathically experienced this future agony and this combines pain and sex in a way that is both unhealthy and frivolous, given the tragedy that Thomas is treating. The last chapter contains a typical vision of a non-Jewish Zionist. After her death at Babi-Yar, the woman finds herself transferred to Palestine with the other victims. The State of Israel is, therefore, depicted as paradise. Life in the 'camp' there is euphoric, joyful and loving, but in *this* heaven everyone still has their wounds. Even in the New Heaven and the New Earth of Israel, the Jews are still victims of the Holocaust, though on the last page there is a hint that some may recover as they work to rebuild the Jewish people. Finally, even though the *goyim* are not debarred from this Jewish paradise, there are no Arabs in this heavenly country. There could scarcely be a clearer articulation of the Zionist fantasy that one day there will be no Arab problem and no Arab presence in Eretz Yisrael, but there are Israelis who realise how dangerous this fantasy is and realise that it must not be endorsed. The continued popularity of the novel shows that many people in the West who have praised it as a masterpiece sense nothing strange in the fact that Thomas has completely left the Arabs off the map of the Holy Land and left it all to the Jews. It also shows that we are indulging feelings about the Holocaust that are sadistic, voyeuristic and prurient.

There are signs, however, that we may be attaining a more balanced view of the Holocaust. In 1983 Thomas Keneally won the prestigious Booker Prize for Fiction for his book *Schindler's Ark*. The book is a realistic and unsentimental portrait of a German officer in charge of a concentration camp who saved the lives of many of the Jews in his charge. At the time of writing, it is good to see the novels of the late Primo Levi very much in evidence in the bookstores. Again, there is a robust realism in the work of this survivor of the Holocaust.

We shall probably never succeed in coming fully to terms with our feelings about the Holocaust, and that is probably right. The fact of the Holocaust should never be accepted or taken for granted. But we must not allow ourselves to indulge in mawkish or voyeuristic fantasies that will only prolong our sick state of soul. Sober realism about the Holocaust instead of neurotic or disturbed hysteria is more likely to help us to view the Palestinian case objectively.

In Britain it is probably more difficult for us to come to terms with the 'Arabs' since they have ceased to be a distant reality and have arrived in Britain. It has been very disturbing and threatening for us to watch Park Lane and Earls Court become virtually Arab neighbourhoods. We have felt invaded, especially when we witness Arab oil wealth at a time when our own economy has been in trouble. The Arabs have replaced the Jews as the 'rich enemies'. This has also happened in America. At the time of the OPEC oil crisis in 1973 Edward Said recalls cartoons depicting an Arab standing beside a petrol pump:

> These Arabs, however, were clearly 'Semitic': their sharply hooked noses, the evil, mustachioed leer on their faces, were obvious reminders (to a largely non-Semitic population) that 'Semites' were at the bottom of all 'our' troubles, which in this case was principally a gasoline shortage. The transference of a popular anti-Semitic animus from a Jewish to an Arab target was made smoothly, since the figure was essentially the same.[158]

This is a precisely observed example of the frightening fact that the hatred we used to allow ourselves to feel about the Jews has been transferred *in toto* to the 'Arab'. As Arabs from the Gulf flocked into England, anti-semitic Arab jokes became common. There was talk of stewed goat being served at the Hilton and of camels being parked outside the Playboy Club. Arabs were 'buying up our stately homes'.[159] The jokes reveal a buried fear that the 'Arabs' wanted to control the world with their oil or were buying up the whole of impoverished England. It is an extension of the old conspiracy fantasy. But we must try to control this new phobia. If the story of the Holocaust has a lesson to teach us, it is surely the danger of this kind of racial stereotyping. It is particularly dangerous in this case now that the 'Arabs' are seen as the enemies of the Jews and the new anti-semites. Much of our new prejudice is a transference of unmanageable guilt. The 'Arab' is being made to carry a double load of hatred in Europe: besides bearing the traditional Western hatred of the 'Muslim', he is now having to take on our load of guilt for our Jewish anti-semitism.

But Europe is no longer the capital of the West nor the capital of Christianity. The leadership has passed to the United States and, though there has been some anti-semitic prejudice there, in general America has not hated the Jews and should have none of these problems. Quite the contrary; we have seen that the Pilgrim Fathers identified with Jews and thought of the New World as another Canaan. America has provided a refuge for thousands of Jews who fled persecution in Europe and has given them a good home. Today many American Jews maintain that America has replaced Muslim Spain, which the Jews lost in the year that Columbus discovered America. They argue either that New York is the new capital of the Jews or that, together with Israel, American Jews 'will create something new for themselves and the world', which will replace the Jewish New culture that was lost in Europe.[160] Americans can rightly be proud of this *Crusaders in* achievement. They have established a strong emotional bond and even an *the West* identification with a people whom Europeans have persecuted and massacred ever since the Crusades.

This American identification with the Jewish people was shown very early in the history of Zionism. The Balfour Declaration was most enthusiastically received. President Woodrow Wilson gave it unqualified support, even though it was against the spirit of his famous Fourteen Points, which condemned private agreements about territory and proclaimed the principle of the self-determination of peoples. Point 12 had even insisted that the non-Turkish nationalities of the Ottoman empire should be assured an unmolested opportunity of autonomous development. But Wilson, who had been brought up in the American Protestant tradition, was a natural Zionist.[161] The Jews were a special case. Many Congressmen thought so too. Senator Henry Cabot Lodge, for example, made a classic Zionist statement which he worded very strongly.

> It seems to me that it was entirely becoming and commendable that the Jewish people in all portions of the world should desire to have a national home for such members of their race as wished to return to the country which was the cradle of their race and where they lived and laboured for several thousand years. sic] . . . I never could accept in patience the thought that Jerusalem and Palestine should be under the control of the Mohammedans [sic] . . . that Jerusalem and Palestine, sacred to the Jews . . . a land profoundly holy to all the great Christian nations of the West, should remain permanently in the hands of the Turks, has seemed to me for many years one of the great blots on the face of civilization that ought to be erased.[162]

His identification with the Jews has made Jewish Palestine sacred to his own identity and blinded him to the claim of the 'Mohammedans'. He has a double but cannot achieve a triple vision, like so many Gentile Zionists before him. Non-Jewish Zionism is a form of Protestant crusading and Senator Lodge feels as great a sense of outrage at the thought of Muslim occupation of Jerusalem as any medieval Catholic Crusader. Americans have continued to feel strongly about Israel and this fervour has increased with the rise of a new wave of American Christian fundamentalism which is aggressively Zionist. Fundamentalists have become very powerful in America; Jerry Falwell's Moral Majority has had to be courted as a power bloc during presidential elections. They have given strong support to the Jewish lobby, though they do not feel the same sense of identification with the Jews as the more secular American Zionists. Like the Puritans, they believe that the Last Days are at hand and that the Jews will either have to be converted or suffer in hell. But they also passionately believe that the Jews must live in Israel to fulfil biblical prophecy. They have returned to a classical and extreme religious crusading.[163]

For those millions of Americans who are not fundamentalists, however, there is another reason for this identification with the Zionists, which I have already referred to. From the earliest days of Labour Zionism, Americans found themselves naturally identifying with the Jewish pioneers. In 1929 the Protestant minister John Haynes spontaneously made this connection when he met the *chalutzim* during a visit to Palestine:

> As I met and talked with these toilers on the land, I could think of nothing but the early English settlers who came to the bleak shores of Massachusetts, and there amid winter's cold in an untilled soil, among an unfriendly native

population, laid firm and sure the foundations of our American Republic. For this reason I was not surprised later, when I read Josiah Wedgewood's 'The Seventh Dominion', to find this distinguished Gentile Zionist of Britain speaking of these Jewish pioneers as 'the Pilgrim Fathers of Palestine.'[164]

Pioneering Zionism was praised in glowing terms during the Congressional debate at the time of the Balfour Declaration. Thomas J. Lane, Representative for Massachusetts (the home of the Pilgrim Fathers), spoke in words which at once recall the words of the Founding Fathers of America:

> To build the Kingdom of God, the Jews must not be dissipated among other nations. Always ineffective as minorities, as the Prophets preached, they must have their own nation – there to work and develop the ideal social order, as a model and example from which other nations may learn.[165]

He was a religious Zionist before most Jews were. In 1937 Senator Alben B. Barkley visited Palestine and proclaimed that there was a 'natural link' between the Jews and their land, which was responding and flowering at their hands. He sounds not dissimilar to Nachmanides in the twelfth century. At the same time Senator Bennet Champ Clark produced the old argument about the Jews making the desert bloom: 'Their coming converted a barren land into a literal Biblical land of "milk and honey".... A barren country, desolate and forsaken for centuries.'[166]

But there is another important aspect of this pioneering attachment, which President Jimmy Carter touched upon when he made his speach before the Knesset in 1979:

> Seven Presidents have believed and demonstrated that America's relationship with Israel is more than just a special relationship. It has been and it is a unique relationship. And it is a relationship which is indestructible, because it is rooted in the consciousness and the morals and the religion and the beliefs of the American people themselves....
>
> Israel and the United States were shaped by pioneers – my nation is also a nation of immigrants and refugees – by peoples gathered in both nations from many lands.[167]

Like the Jewish Zionists, the American settlers were not just pioneers but refugees who fled oppression in Europe. Both America and Israel are in this sense the creation of Europe. For Americans and Israelis the bond is strong because each recognises the other at a deep level. People who have suffered oppression have a strong bond and empathy that others, who have not suffered in this way, cannot understand. Yet this does not mean that either of these countries of refugees should be able to oppress other people and drive them into permanent exile.

A strong identification, such as America feels for Israel, means that objectivity can be very difficult. A threat to Israel could be seen as a threat to the identity of America itself and as a wound in her integrity. Certainly the United States sees Israel as her *alter ego* in the Middle East. On 3 October 1987 Congressman Gerry Skorski wrote an open letter to the editor of the *Jerusalem Post* defending the massive amount of aid given to Israel, which in his view is cheap at the price. In the past US aid to Israel was a 'feel good', sentimental item in the budget. Not any more:

> The Pentagon classifies Israel as a 'major non-Nato ally.' Our relationship is one of strategic cooperation that cannot be exaggerated.
>
> The American Sixth Fleet now makes regular port visits to Haifa. The US carrier-based aircraft practise on Israeli firing ranges in the Negev desert. Joint anti-submarine exercises have become a matter of routine. US and Israeli

military planners meet every few months, and US material is now being pre-positioned in Israel.

Israel aids us in our intelligence-gathering operations, and recently initiated special participation in the development of an Anti-Tactical Ballistic Missile system.[168]

Israel and America are, therefore, fighting a war together. I have no doubt that Congressman Skorski would describe all this as 'peace-keeping' but we have already seen in Chapter 9 that American peace-keeping can be extremely aggressive. All this joint military activity in the Middle East must make the Arab states feel that they are in a perpetual state of imminent war. When President Reagan bombed Tripoli in Libya in April 1986, killing seventy people, many of them civilians, this impression must have been reinforced. Reagan himself, however, with the cynicism that we have seen in Innocent III at the time of the Catharist Crusade, would have declared that he was keeping the peace, by protecting his people from the scourge of international terrorism. When the moderate Arab leaders like President Mubarak of Egypt and King Husain of Jordan heard that America had been selling arms to Iran, the arch-terrorist state in the Middle East since the hostage crisis, they naturally felt outraged and insulted. They had put themselves in danger in their own countries by trying to curb extremism and to support American policies and were naturally alarmed by the paradigm of the Islamic revolution, which was a potential threat to their own regimes. They must have seen the arms deal as a slap in the face, as, obviously, did President Saddam Husain of Iraq.[169] Yet, with typical double-think, this deal was seen by the Americans who negotiated it as a move towards peace with Iran, though really it was a bid for renewed American influence there. The idea for the arms deal seems to have come originally from Israel. The two countries were making war together to keep the peace.

Congressman Skorski summarised the values that America saw in Israel in his letter to the *Jerusalem Post*. Israel 'provides a model for democratic developments in an area of the world that is not very familiar with the concept of democracy. It aids us in deterring Soviet-backed radicalism in the Middle East. It helps us in our continuous battle against terrorism.'[170] America clearly sees herself reflected in Israel, but this glowing image is at variance with the facts. Israel is a country which has conducted an aggressive and illegal occupation for over twenty years and has brutally oppressed the population of the Occupied Territories. In the winter of 1987/8 (the time of writing) the world was shocked to see the cruelty with which Israeli soldiers fired upon and killed unarmed people who were throwing rocks. If this is a model democracy, it is understandable that the people of the Middle East don't think much of it. To call Israel a partner in a war against terrorism is to commit the old crime of not seeing all three sides of the problem. It is to deny that the violence inflicted on the Palestinian people since the earliest days of the Jewish state has also been terrorism. It is to distort the picture by making the Israelis angels and the Palestinians monsters. American identification with Israel and blindness to the Arab position follows the same blinkered pattern as has always infected non-Jewish Zionism. Its causes are less dark and convoluted than the European reluctance to see all sides of the question, but no less deep. When you feel such a strong sense of identification with a country as the Americans feel for Israel, that country's enemies become your own and threaten your own identity, causing a 'dread' that leads to violence.

We have seen that even during the worst days of the Palestinian uprising in the Occupied Territories, Secretary of State George Shultz could still say that Israel was a democracy, peacefully going about its own business. This was not a rational assessment of the situation and it bewildered the American journalists. Yet throughout our story we have been witnessing wars and battles that are fought for feelings that are so deeply entwined with a sense of self that logic and reason cease to function. The wars in the Middle East today are like the Crusades because they are increasingly becoming religious wars. They are also holy wars because they are fought on emotional issues that are felt to be sacred by all three of the participants. A purely rational solution is impossible in this climate of extreme emotion, because people are not just fighting for territory, for rights or for interests that can be tidily sorted out. These wars are the latest round in a conflict that began when the Christian West persecuted and massacred Jews and Muslims in the First Crusade. As far as the West is concerned the issues are not very different from those that dominated the Crusades and they are highly emotive. We must realise that we are not acting sagely and rationally if we denounce anti-semitism and make anti-semitic anti-Arab jokes or claim that Palestinians are terrorists and Israelis only victims of terrorism. To deny a people's identity, as many Western people have long denied the Arab and Islamic reality, is to erase them from our emotional map and thus to annihilate them. We have seen in our own century where such fantasies of annihilation can lead.

Epilogue: Triple Vision

There is a popular postcard on sale everywhere in Israel that never ceases to astonish me. It shows an 'artistic' shot of the Shepherds' Field outside Bethlehem and there are real live shepherds, watching their flocks there today, just as they did on the first Christmas night. They look very biblical shepherds, for they are wearing the traditional headdress that all Christians have seen in countless Nativity plays. These *keffiyehs* hide the men's faces, which is just as well because these are Arab shepherds of the West Bank, posing as first-century Jewish shepherds in the Christian story. There could scarcely be a more ironic and distorted expression of triple vision. It shows the confused and troubled bond that links Jews, Christians and Muslims together and completely ignores the frightening realities of the present conflict. The card is obviously designed for Christian pilgrims to send home to show their friends that everything in the Holy Land is 'just the same' as it was in the time of Christ. But, as we know, things are very different. In the first century the Jews were struggling against an unwanted occupation which resulted in a holy war that lost them their land. Today it is the Jews who are the brutal occupiers of Bethlehem and the other towns in the Occupied Territories and some of their methods would have shocked even the Romans. But Christian pilgrims do not want to see this and they buy the card as intended. The Holy Land is still a mythical land to many of them, who show a ready willingness to suspend their disbelief as they tour the country in their air-conditioned buses, insulated from the troubling contemporary realities. When they visit Kfar Kana in Galilee they look with reverence at the large water-jugs which Jesus is supposed to have used when he worked his first miracle and turned the water into wine at the wedding in Cana. There is a postcard of these too. If the pilgrims actually notice that Kfar Kana is an Arab town, they probably see the Arabs in their *keffiyehs* as merely providing local colour and ignore the complexity of their position as Arabs in the Jewish state.

Of course not all pilgrims swallow everything they are told so gullibly but the very fact that in the twentieth century the mythical reality of that small strip of land between Egypt and Syria is more real to thousands of Christian pilgrims than the political reality is an important reminder. The people who make these pilgrimages are educated men and women, who do not believe in Father Christmas but who are prepared to kiss the gold star in the Church of the Nativity in Bethlehem which marks the spot of Christ's birth. When they go to the Holy Sepulchre Church in Jerusalem, they want to pray at the slab of stone on which Jesus is said to have been laid after the Crucifixion and at the ornate tomb of Christ, whence Jesus rose from the dead. The physical connection with Jesus makes these places in some way 'holy' and people want to believe in their authenticity.

Religious faith is not an obsolete passion. Nor is it a delusion which people cannot help because they lack the brains or the education to disprove the articles of the creed. Faith is a deliberate act of will. People choose to believe what cannot be rationally proved one way or the other, because they need this larger mythical dimension in their lives. We are now in a position to see that religion is not something that we can get rid of once we have progressed to a more 'enlightened' state. The eighteenth-century Age of Reason gave way to a strong and funda-mentalist resurgence of Christianity in the nineteenth century. Similarly the secularism of the twentieth century has given way to a renewed religious passion. People need to tell themselves stories about the world and their life in it, so that they have a sense of meaning and purpose. It is very hard to live according to the bleak light of the atheistic or agnostic day, which has rationally disposed of religious faith. In Judaism, Christianity and Islam, which all insist that their myths are historically true, people have a religious geography which gives them a sense of their place in the world and a tangible connection with the unseen. So strong is this desire to believe in the holy place that the political reality under the pilgrim's nose inevitably fades from view.

Throughout this book we have seen that a devotion to the holy place can make people act in a violent and irrational way. I am reminded of the last occasion on which I filmed in the Holy Sepulchre Church during the production of the television series that accompanies this book. It was a dark, gusty evening and while the electricians and the cameramen were setting up the lights around the tomb of Christ, I was standing outside the church with some members of the Israeli crew. Opposite us was the small mosque which was built to commemorate the spot on which the Caliph Omar prayed when he conquered Jerusalem for Islam in 637. It will be remembered that he had been invited by the Greek patriarch to pray inside the Holy Sepulchre, but he declined so that the Christian holy place could be preserved intact. The mosque was lit brightly and in the surrounding darkness it looked far more dramatic than it does during the day. The only other lights were in the Holy Sepulchre: Christianity and Islam faced each other. Suddenly the conversation I was enjoying with the crew was shattered by the ear-splitting call of the muezzin, summoning the faithful to prayer. The call to prayer is a long and passionate-sounding chant and I found it particularly exhilarating that night. In the dark, with no modern buildings visible, we could have been back in Jerusalem at the time of Saladin.

But my Israeli colleagues had a very different reaction. My rational and kindly companions of a few minutes ago were transformed into crude boors, who made obscene gestures at the mosque, gave exaggerated imitations of the muezzin with distorted, angry faces, and jeered at the Arabic sounds. I had seen this before during the filming. Sometimes we had had to stop shooting and wait for several minutes until the call to prayer was over, and this seemed to reduce the Israeli crew to particular fury. As I watched them I could not but be reminded of the medieval decrees that forbade the muezzin to give the call to prayer in Europe because this strident reminder of the presence of Islam was too disturbing to be permitted. My Israeli friends seemed afflicted by the 'dread' that we have seen impelling people to irrational violence throughout our long story. I could see why it was disturbing for them. The muezzin in Israel today is far louder than he was in medieval times, because his voice is recorded and amplified to great – sometimes excessive – volume. It sometimes seems deliberately aggressive: a reminder to the Israelis that Islam and the Arabs are still a strong presence in their Jewish state and that they will not go away. When Israelis are woken at dawn by the muezzin, have their conversations interrupted or are forced to suspend their activities until the sometimes deafening call to prayer is over, they are being regularly reminded of a fact which many would prefer to forget. It is right that they have this incessant reminder. Problems will not disappear just because we don't want to look at them. The muezzin of the Mosque of Omar pierces the Holy Sepulchre Church too and interrupts the activities of its great Christian neighbour; I watched a passing Franciscan friar shaking his head impatiently at the sound as he left the church. It is important that Christians and Jews, who have a strong tendency to ignore the existence and rights of Islam and of Muslims, should be constantly forced to acknowledge their presence. But as I watched the Israelis mouthing their insults I thought how sad it was that the mosque that commemorates Omar's courteous act and his vision of a peaceful coexistence of the three religions in the Holy Land should seem to issue a war cry. If there really *is* a threatening and aggressive intention in the blaring muezzin in Israel today, we must remember that this Islamic anger is not inherent in the religion. It was inspired first by the Crusaders, who had butchered Muslims when they liberated the Holy Sepulchre in 1099, and later by the Zionists.

Once the last echoes of the muezzin faded away, my Israeli companions became recognisable human beings once more. The reason we were standing outside the church was that very soon we were going to be locked up in it for several hours and we wanted to enjoy the fresh air beforehand. Ever since the Ottoman time, the key to the church has been in the keeping of a Muslim. The Turks were driven to this measure, not because they wanted to control the Christians in Jerusalem but because the different Christian sects who had chapels in the huge complex of the Holy Sepulchre Church were in a constant state of war. One sect was continually locking the others out, and eventually the Turks decided that this intolerable state of affairs must cease: none of the Christian sects should have the key; instead a neutral Muslim would supervise the locking of the church. Because we wanted to have the church to ourselves while we were filming, we went inside at seven o'clock, when it was closed to the public. We watched the great doors swing to and heard the Muslim custodian turn the key in the lock. Until he came back at midnight there was no way to get out and we settled in.

Because of the terrible acrimony that still exists between the different Christian denominations, each sect has a time during the night when it has exclusive control of the Church, on a rota basis. We always preferred to film when the Greek Orthodox were having their turn, because they were far more tolerant than the Latins, who were represented by the Franciscans. In this respect things have not really changed much since the time of the Crusades, except that the Greeks now truly loathe the Latins, instead of merely despising them. There had already been a collision earlier in the evening, when a Franciscan had brusquely told our locations manager that the Greeks had had no right to give us permission to film: he was clearly very suspicious indeed about this production, which he sensed would be critical of the Catholic Church. Fortunately, after a sharp exchange, the Franciscan was worsted and he stomped away muttering and shaking his head. That the holiest shrine in the Christian world should be the scene of such bitter hostility between Eastern and Western Christians is an indication that the irrationality and hatreds of crusading are far from dead.

We finished filming at ten o'clock and then had two hours to wait before we were let out. I prowled round the vast church, which looked extremely sinister in the dim light. Indeed, though I am not usually sensitive to 'vibrations' of this kind, I always have a strong sense of evil in the Holy Sepulchre, probably because I am so conscious of the blood that has been shed for the sake of this building. Occasionally I came across the slumbering forms of the Israeli crew, who had chosen to sleep the last two hours away. They were obviously quite impervious to either the holiness or the evil of this Christian shrine. I thought how very shocked most of the pilgrims would have been to have seen these Jewish visitors to the Holy Sepulchre snoring loudly only a few feet away from the Holy Slab that they kissed so fervently. It might revive in them the old anti-semitic myth of the 'Jew' as the blasphemous enemy of religion.

Eventually at midnight I went upstairs to the Golgotha chapel, which overlooks the front doors, to get a good view of the unlocking. As soon as they heard the knocking on the door, the Israelis woke up and waited to be liberated by a Muslim from this Christian insanity. The sensible Greek Orthodox priest, who had been looking after us that night and who told me that he considered this ceremony a sacred duty, passed a ladder through a hole in the door that had been cut precisely for this purpose. The Muslim took it, placed it against the door on the outside, climbed up it to the lock (which is high up in the door) and with deep and grateful joy we heard the key turn. Slowly the great doors swung open and it was an immense relief to see the outside world again: the dark square, the starry sky with the crescent moon – and the Mosque of Omar opposite.

It seems extraordinary that such a ridiculous and cumbersome arrangement should still be necessary in the twentieth century. The fact that a group of well-educated, religious men cannot sit round a table and find some reasonable *modus vivendi* in the Holy Sepulchre shows the depth and power of this crusading hatred. A holy place inspires a frightening irrationality and intransigence, and if Christians, who all believe that this is the holiest place in the world, cannot find it in them to live together in peace, then there is little hope that Muslims and Jews will find a means of peaceful coexistence in the Holy City and the Holy Land. It is no use expecting a rational and logical solution. People are blinded by fierce religious vision, which locks them into old exclusive prejudice.

When President Jimmy Carter, Prime Minister Menachem Begin and President Anwar Sadat signed the Camp David treaty in 1979, many of us thought with relief that the Arab–Israeli problem might be solved. Now we realise how wrong we were. President Carter lost office because he could not force the Ayatollah Khomeini's regime to return the American hostages. President Anwar Sadat was assassinated by Muslim extremists in his own country, largely because of the Camp David treaty. Menachem Begin, a passionately religious man himself, was condemned by religious and secular Jews in Israel for handing back the Sinai peninsula to Egypt. The problem cannot be solved by ordinary territorial agreements. Too many deep religious emotions are involved and they make the idea of sharing a country impossible. We are not wholly rational beings. We are illogical, emotional creatures, clinging to myths that are fundamentally sacred to our identity. We can make compromises on all kinds of pragmatic matters, but once these beliefs are threatened we close our eyes entirely to reason and common sense; they no longer apply. We cannot even see facts that stare us in the face, nor can we see how illogically we are behaving.

What will happen in the future? It would be a mistake to make ordinary political predictions, because too many unpredictable emotional factors are involved. Israelis like Professor Y. Harkabi who insist that Israel is committing political suicide by refusing to give up the Occupied Territories reckon without the immensely strong passion that religious and secular Israelis feel for the West Bank, seeing it as central to their Jewish identity and essential for Jewish survival in the Middle East. Meanwhile, the Palestinians have reached a stage of such desperation that they have nothing to lose and are ready to brave the guns of the Israeli soldiers. This revolution has been helped by the new Jihad groups, which fuel Muslims with a determined energy to fight oppression and persecution to the death.

We must take this revival of religion in Israel and the Arab world seriously and see it in its own terms. It would be wrong to dismiss these religious passions as the fantasies of an eccentric minority that cannot long survive in our enlightened world. They are very old and well tried and have recurred throughout history when the conditions have been right. Similarly we must not try to explain this religious enthusiasm away in secular or Western ways. At the time of writing, people in this country often speculate about what will happen when the Ayatollah Khomeini dies, but they seem quite uninterested in very important things that he is doing while he is alive. It is now six weeks since the Ayatollah made the heretical declaration that his government is above the Koran and promoted himself from the status of imam to the status of a prophet, equal to Mohammad. Yet still this event, which could be a most important crisis in the history of Islam, has not been recorded in the ordinary daily press in this country. People try to explain away Khomeini's power by saying that he rules by charisma, as Western leaders have often done. People like St Bernard at the time of the Crusades or Hitler in our own century have had an almost hypnotic influence on the crowds they address. But this does not apply to Khomeini, who is simply not a charismatic man. He has no charm. He has long been well known to be a very distant man, who scarcely ever looked his students in the face when he was teaching them at Qum. He is frequently very rude and has often offended Iranians who seek to pay him compliments by his brusque rejection of their effusions. It is no use trying to imagine that once the much-loved Khomeini dies the Islamic Republic will fade away like a bad dream, as Nazism died with Hitler. We are now in a position to see that the ideas and passions of the Iranian revolution were far more powerful than the man who revived them. We must also recall that they were revived as a response to Western oppression.

When we look to the present and the future it is not enough to seek to understand the Jewish or the Muslim side of today's conflict. We also have to remember the role of the Christian West. Before the Crusades, Jews, Christians and Muslims had been able to live side by side in relative harmony. Since the Crusaders slaughtered Muslims and Jews in their medieval holy wars such coexistence has proved impossible. Western people have kept alive the old crusading attitudes to Muslims and Jews, and we have seen that a form of Protestant crusading produced the blinkered vision of non-Jewish Zionism, which completely ignored the presence of Islam and the Arabs in Palestine. In both Europe and the United States our attitude towards the Jews is not as rational and objective as we might like to think. It is as complex and as emotional as any of the religious passions in the Middle East that we are so swift to ridicule. We cannot see what is before our eyes, because we have mythologised our map of the Middle East and make a strong identification with this myth. The same is true in our attitude towards Islam, the Arabs and uncomfortable facts like the Iranian revolution. Our anti-semitic remarks about 'Ay-rabs' are so deeply rooted that people look genuinely astonished if you point out that this is blatantly racist. We cannot seem to *see* that it is inconsistent to deride the Arabs and piously condemn anti-semitic remarks against Jews. Even though we pride ourselves on our logic and objectivity, we cannot *see* that our position is totally illogical. We also seem blind about Islam. Our attitude is one of lofty superiority, very like Voltaire's. We think that because 'we' don't understand the religion it means that there is nothing in it; therefore modern Muslim movements are nothing more than mindless frenzy. It is still very common at dinner parties to hear people attacking an imaginary religion that they insist upon calling 'Islam'. People have actually said to me that they don't *need* to read the Koran and they don't *care* what Muslims believe. They just 'know' that Islam is a very bad religion. It would be hard to find a clearer example of irrational, ill-informed prejudice.

　　In early January 1988 the British junior minister David Mellors visited a Palestinian refugee camp in the Gaza Strip and caused a great stir by condemning Israel's behaviour in the Occupied Territories and the oppression of the Palestinians. This was all very well and good, but in seeing only Arabs and Jews, Mr Mellors had shown that he had only double, not triple, vision and had distorted the matter. Without the support of Britain it is most unlikely that there would have been a Jewish state in Palestine, so Britain also has a responsibility for those camps. Further, without the support of our ally, the United States, it is most unlikely that Israel would survive. These camps have been there for forty years. When a visitor drives past them it is obvious how bad conditions must be inside. Britain and America have both supported Israel and have thus colluded in this oppression of the Palestinians. Ever since the Crusades there have always been three participants in conflicts involving Christians, Muslims and Jews in the Middle East. We must remember our crusading past and recognise our own role in the troubles of today. We are deeply implicated and unless we examine our attitudes carefully and work to eradicate our inherited irrational prejudice we are continuing to fuel the problem.

In the summer of 1987 I noticed that the stationery in my Jerusalem hotel celebrated the anniversary of the Six Day War by printing on the envelopes that it was twenty years since Jerusalem, the city of peace, had been 'reunited'. The Israeli tourist board likes to present Jerusalem as a Holy City where Jews, Christians and Muslims live and worship together in peace. In fact the struggle is more deadly than it has ever been, since the time of the Crusades. It appears that Israel might have a nuclear bomb and experts have predicted that some of the Arab states could also acquire bombs within the next ten years.[1] Without a solution there is a fearful danger that the whole area could explode in a nuclear holocaust. Peace in the area is an urgent priority and the Christian West will bear as great a responsibility for this catastrophe as either the Jewish or the Islamic states. The prophets of Israel, the parent of the two younger faiths, proclaimed the necessity of creating a new heart and a new soul, which was far more important than external conformity. So too today. External political solutions are not enough. All *three* of the participants in the struggle must create a different attitude. We in the Christian West must try to make the painful migration from our old hatred and embark on the long journey to a new understanding and a new self.

Notes

CHAPTER ONE *In the Beginning there was the Holy War. Why?*

1 Robert the Monk, *Historia Iherosolimitana*, quoted by August C. Krey, *The First Crusade: The Accounts of Eye-Witnesses and Participants* (Princeton and London, 1921), p. 30. There are no exactly contemporary accounts of Urban's speech and these quotations come from works written shortly after the success of the Crusade and reflect a later view than Urban's, at a time when crusading ideology had developed.

2 Fulcher of Chartres, *A History of the Expedition to Jerusalem, 1095–1127*, trans. Frances Rita Ryan (Knoxville, 1969), p. 66.

3 Modern scholars give various figures. It is very difficult to assess the medieval accounts accurately. The chroniclers had no means of counting these vast hordes.

4 *Alexiad*, ed. and trans. B. Leib, 3 vols (Paris, 1937–45), x, v, 7; vol. II, p. 208.

5 These early stories were handed down in an oral tradition and first committed to writing in about the ninth century BCE.

6 The Sea of Reeds was obviously not the Red Sea but was probably a marshy part of the Nile Delta. As I shall have to refer to this event later, I shall continue to use the traditional name, Red Sea.

7 The giving of the Ten Commandments or the Decalogue to Moses is described in Exodus 20. The other commandments are found in Leviticus, Numbers and Deuteronomy and in other chapters of Exodus. These first five books of the Bible are therefore also called the Torah.

8 II Samuel 7, I Chronicles 17.

9 I Chronicles 22:5–10, an account written by the sixth century priestly tradition; abhorrence of spilt blood is a feature of the priestly writings for ritual as well as for humanistic reasons.

10 Solomon's kingdom extended into what is now the Negev, Jordan and Syria. It included cities that are today Damascus and Amman.

11 For the pagan elements in Solomon's Temple, see I Kings 7:15–22 and Chaim Potok, *Wanderings; A History of the Jews* (New York, 1978), pp. 157–8.

12 Deuteronomy 7:3. See p. 6 of this chapter.

13 See in particular I Kings 18:20–46, where Elijah slays the 450 prophets of Baal, the fertility god.

14 For the reform of Josiah see II Kings 22 and 23.

15 See for example Isaiah 1:11–20.

16 Jeremiah 31:31–7.

17 For Original Sin see Glossary.

18 See Exodus 19:6. God will make Israel a 'holy' people, which can also be translated 'set apart', or even 'who dwell alone'. The idea of separation is very important in Judaism, which celebrates the 'holiness' of things by separating them from one another.

19 Ezechiel 34:25. Tel Aviv is Hebrew for the Hill of Spring, and if this is translated the point of the prophecy is lost.

20 Isaiah 2:2–5, 11:6–16.

21 Zion was the name of the ancient citadel which King David had captured from the Jebusites when he conquered Jerusalem.

22 See Potok, *Wanderings*, pp. 213–14.

23 See Ezra 4:1–4, and Potok, *Wanderings*, p. 241.

24 The story of the Jewish Revolt is told by Josephus in *The Jewish War*, trans. G. A. Williamson (London, 1959); the story of Masada is pp. 352–70.

25 See for example Zachariah 12 and Daniel 7:9–14.

26 See Zachariah 9.

27 In the Acts of the Apostles 5:36–8 Rabbi Gamaliel gives an account of two of these Messiahs.

28 Mark 1:15. The Greek is stronger: 'The Kingdom of God has already arrived.'

29 It is traditionally believed that Jesus' mission lasted for two years, but a closer look at the gospels suggests a shorter ministry.

30 See the story of Zaccaeus (Luke 19:1–10), who was a sinner because he collaborated with the Romans by collecting the taxes, and cheating his own people.

31 Mark 11:10, Matthew 21:12, Luke 21:37.

32 The episode of the expulsion of the moneylenders could be a relic of an account of a much larger demonstration. After it the chief priests 'were afraid of him because the people were carried away by his teaching' (Mark 11:19). Mark then goes on to give an account of Jesus' teaching in the Temple, where he had spent some days (14:48).

33 Matthew 5:39, Mark 15:1–6.

34 See Hyam Maccoby, *Revolution in Judaea: Jesus and the Jewish Resistance* (London, 1973), pp. 151–205.

35 Acts of the Apostles 2:40, 5:27–42.

36 The dispute is toned down in the interests of presenting a picture of Church unity in Acts 15, which was written about fifty years after the event. Paul himself was writing only seven years later and his is a much harsher account (Galatians 2:1–14).

37 For the teaching of Paul, see Karen Armstrong, *The First Christian: St Paul's Impact on Christianity* (London, 1983), passim.

38 Galatians, passim, I Corinthians 10: 1–13, II Corinthians 5:1–10, Romans 4:18–25, 6:1–4, 9:1–11.

39 Revelation 19:19 and Daniel 11:31, 12:12, which people also applied to the Beast.

40 II Thessalonians 1:4–8.

41 This appears as early as the second century in I John 2:14–19.

42 See W. H. C. Frend, *Martyrdom and Persecution in the Early Church: A Study of a Conflict from the Maccabees to Donatus* (Oxford, 1965), passim.

43 Matthew 16:24, Luke 14:27.

44 Foundation Charter of King Edgar for New Minster, Winchester, quoted by R. W. Southern, *Western Society and the Church in the Middle Ages* (London, 1970), pp. 224–5.

45 For a discussion of Byzantine attitudes to war, see Zoé Oldenbourg, *The Crusades*, trans. Anne Carter (London, 1966), pp. 70–1.

46 See Jonathan Riley-Smith, *The First Crusade and the Idea of Crusading* (London, 1986), pp. 6, 17, 27, 133, 165.

47 See Maxime Rodinson, *Mohammed*, trans. Anne Carter, 2nd edn (London, 1981), pp. 1–36, for a study of pre-Islamic Arabia.

48 Genesis 16:7–16, 17:20, 21:15–21.

49 This tradition of the *hanifs* has been incorporated into the Koran: 2:126–30, 3:97, 14:38.

50 Rodinson, *Mohammed*, p. 71.

51 Muhammad Zafrulla Khan, *Islam: Its Meaning for Modern Man* (London, 1962, 1980), p. 25.

52 A *hadith* (tradition) of the seventh century Muslim Bukhari, quoted by Rodinson, *Mohammed*, p. 74. For *hadith*, see Glossary.

53 Khan, *Islam*, pp. 26–7. See also Koran 42:52–3.

54 For Bukhari's mid-seventh century account of how the Koran was collected and compiled, see Bernard Lewis, *Islam from the Prophet Mohammad to the Capture of Constantinople*, 2 vols, vol. II: Religion and Society (New York and London, 1976), pp. 1–2.

55 See Rodinson, *Mohammed*, pp. 84–9.

56 Koran 2:46, 145, 13:11, 53:39–40.

57 See Khan, *Islam*, pp. 42–4, for this early account of the battle.

58 Rodinson, *Mohammed*, p. 171.

59 Khan, *Islam*, p. 164.

60 Ibid., p. 158.

61 Koran 8:62–3, 16:95.

62 Rodinson, *Mohammed*, p. 171. Al-Furqan is also another name for the Koran (25:1).

63 Koran 17:1.

64 Rodinson, *Mohammed*, p. 286.

65 For a fuller discussion, see W. Montgomery Watt, 'Islam and the Holy War', in T. P. Murphy (ed.), *The Holy War* (Columbus, 1974); Bernard Lewis, *The Jews of Islam* (New York and London, 1982), pp. 17–45.

66 *The Decline and Fall of the Roman Empire*, ch. 52:16, quoted by Bernard Lewis, *The Muslim Discovery of Europe* (New York and London, 1982).

67 Lewis, *The Muslim Discovery*, p. 19.

68 Lewis, *The Jews of Islam*, pp. 25–45 and passim. Also *Semites and Anti-Semites: An Inquiry into Conflict and Prejudice* (London, 1986), pp. 117–40.

69 Steven Runciman, *A History of the Crusades*, 3 vols, vol. I (London, 1984 edn), p. 3.

1 Norman Daniel, *The Arabs and Medieval Europe* (London and Beirut, 1975), p. 24. Daniel is quoting original sources by Eulogio and Alvaro, the apologists of the martyr movement, quoted in J. P. Migne (ed.), *Patrologia Latina* (Paris, 1864–84), vols 115 and 221.

2 Perfectus was probably a translation of the Arab name al-Kamil (Perfect) and two of the martyrs were called Servus Dei, which must be a translation of Abdullah (Slave of Allah). See Daniel, *The Arabs*, p. 23.

3 Ibid., pp. 39–45.

4 Ibid., p. 46.

5 Ibid., p. 34.

6 Ibid., pp. 39–45.

7 Ibid., p. 34.

8 With a rather dubious prurience, see ibid., p. 28.

9 On the martyrs' cultural confusion, see ibid., pp. 33–6.

10 Ibid., p. 29.

11 For these radical monasteries, Roger Collins, *Early Medieval Spain: Unity in Diversity, 400–1000* (London, 1983), pp. 214–19.

12 R. W. Southern, *Western Society and the Church in the Middle Ages* (London, 1970), pp. 56–7, and 53–72 for a fuller description of the relative positions of the Eastern and Western Churches.

13 Ibid.

14 Eddius Stephanus, *Vita Wilfridi*, quoted in ibid., pp. 57–8.

15 Migne, *Patrologia Latina*, vol. 89, columns 520, 524, quoted in ibid., p. 59.

16 Einhard and Notger the Stammerer, *Two Lives of Charlemagne*, trans. Lewis Thorpe (London, 1969), pp. 131, 142, 148, 153.

17 Ibid., pp. 143–6.

18 Ibid., pp. 103, 124, 125.

19 Southern, *Western Society and the Church*, pp. 62–3.

20 *Two Lives of Charlemagne*, p. 81.

21 Ibid., p. 71.

22 Quoted by R. W. Southern, *The Making of the Middle Ages* (London, 1987 edn), p. 34.

23 Jonathan Riley-Smith, *The First Crusade and the Idea of Crusading* (London, 1986), p. 4.

24 See Southern, *Western Society and the Church*, pp. 27–35.

25 For these penitentials, see Karen Armstrong, *The Gospel According to Woman: Christianity's Creation of the Sex War in the West* (London, 1986), pp. 35–6.

26 P. A. Sigal, 'Et les marcheurs de Dieu prirent leurs armes', *L'Histoire*, 47 (1982), 60–1 and passim. For the pilgrimage see also Ronald C. Finucane, *Miracles and Pilgrims: Popular Beliefs in Medieval Europe* (London, 1977), passim.

27 See Peter Brown, *The Cult of the Saints: Its Rise and Function in Classical Antiquity* (London, 1982), passim.

28 Finucane, *Miracles and Pilgrims*, p. 26.

29 Southern, *Western Society and the Church*, pp. 30–1.

30 Barbara Tuchman, *Bible and Sword: How the British Came to Palestine* (London, 1982 edn), pp. 13–21.

31 Francesco Gabrieli, 'Islam in the Mediterranean World', in Joseph Schacht and C. E. Bosworth (eds), *The Legacy of Islam* (2nd edn, Oxford, 1979), p. 91.

32 Riley-Smith, *The First Crusade*, p. 21.

33 Geneviève Bresc-Bautier, 'L'an prochain au Saint-Sépulchre', *L'Histoire*, 47 (1982), 74–9.

34 Georges Duby, 'The Peace of God', in *The Chivalrous Society*, trans. C. Postera (London, 1977); and H. E. Cowdrey, 'The Peace of God and the Truce of God in the Eleventh Century', *Past and Present*, 46 (1970).

35 Quoted by Henri Focillon, *The Year 1000* (New York, Paris and London, 1952), p. 67.

36 Quoted by Finucane, *Miracles and Pilgrims*, pp. 114 and 115, which also gives a fuller account of this episode.

37 Quoted by Sigal, 'Et les marcheurs de Dieu sont prirent leurs armes', 60–1.

38 For the Sibylline prophecies, see Norman Cohn, *The Pursuit of the Millennium: Revolutionary Millenarianism and Mystical Anarchists of the Middle Ages* (London, 1970 edn), pp. 30–5.

39 Riley-Smith, *The First Crusade*, p. 5.

40 Ibid., pp. 5–8, 16–17.
41 *Gesta Tancredi*, quoted in ibid., p. 36.
42 Jonathan Riley-Smith, 'The First Crusade and St Peter', in B. Z. Kedar, H. E. Mayer and R. C. Smail (eds), *Outremer: Studies in the History of the Crusading Kingdom of Jerusalem, Presented to Joshua Prawer* (Jerusalem, 1982), pp. 45–8.
43 *The Song of Roland*, trans. Dorothy L. Sayers (London, 1957), stanza 260, p. 185.
44 Ibid., stanza 72, p. 87.
45 Ibid., stanza 87, p. 94.
46 Ibid., stanza 173, p. 141.
47 Riley-Smith, 'The First Crusade and St Peter', p. 45. Also *The First Crusade*, p. 25.
48 Riley-Smith, *The First Crusade*, pp. 17–22, for the Cluniac ideal of liberation.
49 Ibid., p. 18.
50 Ibid., p. 19.
51 Ibid.
52 Ibid., pp. 22–5.
53 Steven Runciman, *A History of the Crusades*, 3 vols, vol. I (London, 1984 edn), p. 108.
54 Riley-Smith, *The First Crusade*, pp. 48–9.
55 Quoted in Runciman, *A History of the Crusades*, vol. I, p. 113.
56 Jonathan Riley-Smith dissolves the legend of the 'Peasants' Crusade' and explains that these were proper armies not fanatical hordes in *The First Crusade*, pp. 51–2.
57 Régine Pernoud quotes the twelfth-century historian William of Tyre, who attributes the crusading initiative to Peter in *The Crusaders*, trans. Enid Grant (Edinburgh and London, 1963), p. 24.
58 'The Narrative of the Old Persecutions or Mainz Anonymous', in Shlomo Eidelberg (trans. and ed.), *The Jews and the Crusaders: The Hebrew Chronicles of the First and Second Crusades* (London, 1977), p. 99–100.
59 For the position of the Jews in Europe before the Crusades, see Paul Johnson, *A History of the Jews* (London, 1987), p. 205.
60 See 'Chronicle of Solomon bar Simson', in Eidelberg, *The Jews and the Crusaders*, p. 62.
61 Ibid., p. 28: 'he . . . concocted a tale that an apostle of the Crucified had come to him and made a sign on his flesh to inform him that when he arrived in Magna Graecia, he [Jesus] himself would appear and place the kingly crown on his head and Emicho would vanquish his foes.' Magna Graecia is Italy; Emich was claiming that he should be the new Holy Roman Emperor and saw the Crusade as an extension of his divine mission, according to the old myths.
62 Romans 11, passim.
63 'Chronicle of Rabbi Eliezer bar Nathan', in Eidelberg, *The Jews and the Crusaders*, p. 80, but see also in the 'Mainz Anonymous', p. 99, where exactly the same motive is given.
64 See Riley-Smith, *The First Crusade*, pp. 53–8 for the argument that the Church was embarrassed by the pogroms and for official Church teaching on the Jews. See also Conor Cruise O'Brien, *The Siege: The Saga of Israel and Zionism* (London, 1986), pp. 56–7, where he quotes the *Encyclopaedia Judaica*, which repeats official Church teaching to the time of Thomas Aquinas.

CHAPTER THREE *The Present Conflict: Jews and Arabs Seek a New Secular Identity*

1 The armies of Lebanon, Syria, Jordan, Iraq and Egypt.
2 The UN figures were 656,000 Palestinian refugees; Israel's figures range from 550,000 to 600,000; 750,000 is the figure quoted by people sympathetic to the Palestinian cause. In any event, there are now four million people who call themselves Palestinians today, and apart from the 700,000 living as a minority in Israel, the others are either in exile or living under the Israeli occupation in the Gaza Strip and the West Bank. This occupation will be discussed later in the chapter.
3 Forty-nine people died; 495 were injured (95 per cent seriously) and there

were many cases of rape and mutilation. There was massive devastation: 1500 homes and workshops were looted and destroyed and a fifth of the population rendered homeless. The violence had been inspired by semi-official anti-semitic propaganda (Conor Cruise O'Brien, *The Siege: The Saga of Israel and Zionism* (London, 1986), p. 96). That these figures look puny to us today after later persecutions of Jews shows only how accustomed we have become to such disasters.

4 For *Volk*-style anti-semitism, see Paul Johnson, *A History of the Jews* (London, 1987), pp. 392–4.

5 I will discuss these in Chapter 12, p. 365.

6 Quoted in Amos Elon, *The Israelis, Founders and Sons* (2nd edn, London, 1981), p. 70.

7 'We are duty bound to take courage, to rise; and to see to it that we do not remain for ever the foundling of the nations and their butt.' (*Autoemancipation*, quoted in O'Brien, *The Siege*, p. 46).

8 As Pinsker attended the meetings, he was slowly converted to the idea that the Jewish state must be in Palestine, because it was the 'instinctive' wish of the people (Elon, *The Israelis*, p. 71). This instinctive, sub-rational feeling for Palestine will be a key factor in our story, medieval and modern.

9 'The Road from Motol', quoted in O'Brien, *The Siege*, p. 46.

10 Quoted in Elon, *The Israelis*, p. 71.

11 Ibid.

12 Johnson, *A History of the Jews*, p. 38.

13 Ussiskin's words were: 'His greatest deficiency will be his greatest asset. He does not know the first thing about Jews. Therefore he believes that there are no internal obstacles to Zionism, only external ones. We should not open his eyes to the facts of life so that his faith remains potent.' Quoted in O'Brien, *The Siege*, p. 86. Ussiskin was an unusual Zionist at this time because he was an Orthodox Jew and knew only too well the opposition most religious Jews felt to Zionism, as I shall discuss later.

14 *A Jewish State* (London, 1986), p. 29.

15 *Protocols of the Fourth Zionist Congress* (London, 1900), quoted in Regina Sharif, *Non-Jewish Zionism: Its Roots in Western History* (London, 1983), p. 74.

16 Quoted in O'Brien, *The Siege*, p. 80.

17 Ibid., p. 78.

18 The young Zionist Vladimir Jabotinski was at the Congress and, though he was a great admirer of Herzl, he voted against even looking at an alternative to Palestine. 'I don't know why,' he said later, 'simply because this is one of those "simple" things which counterbalances thousands of arguments.' Quoted in O'Brien, *The Siege*, p. 102.

19 Ibid., p. 103.

20 Ibid., p. 75.

21 Elon, *The Israelis*, p. 76.

22 Weizmann shared Herzl's urgency and sense of impending disaster. He expressed it starkly: 'One fundamental fact – that we must have Palestine if we are not going to be exterminated.' Quoted in O'Brien, *The Siege*, p. 132.

23 Text provided by Walter Lacqueur and Barry Rubin (eds), *The Israel–Arab Reader: A Documentary History of the Middle East Conflict* (4th edn, London, 1984), p. 17.

24 O'Brien, *The Siege*, p. 130.

25 The population of Palestine in December 1918 was composed of 512,000 Muslim Arabs, 61,000 mostly Christian Arabs and 66,000 Jews. O'Brien, *The Siege*, p. 133.

26 See Elon, *The Israelis*, pp. 76–7.

27 Ibid., p. 81.

28 Schlomo Avineri, *The Makings of Modern Zionism* (London and New York, 1981), p. 200.

29 Elon, *The Israelis*, p. 105.

30 Ibid., p. 98.

31 Ibid., pp. 116, 133.

32 Ibid., p. 77.

33 Ibid., p. 112.

34 Quoted in Johnson, *A History of the Jews*, p. 403.

35 Quoted in Eliezer Schweid, *The Land of Israel: National Home or Land of Destiny*, trans. Deborah Greniman (New York, 1985), p. 148.

36 Ibid., p. 143.

37 Ibid., p. 158. Kaballistic terms in italics.

38 Ibid., p. 143.

39 Elon, *The Israelis*, p. 338.
40 Quoted in Michael Palumbo, *The Palestinian Catastrophe: The 1948 Expulsion of a People from their Homeland* (London, 1987), p. 8; and Johnson, *A History of the Jews*, p. 435.
41 Elon, *The Israelis*, p. 110.
42 Schweid, *The Land of Israel*, p. 139.
43 Ibid., p. 140.
44 Elon, *The Israelis*, p. 334.
45 See also Moshe Dayan in *Ha'Aretz*, 4 April 1969: 'You do not even know the names of these Arab villages, and I do not blame you, because these geography books do not exist; not only do the books not exist, the Arab villages are not there either.... There is no place in this country that did not have a former Arab population.' Both quoted in Edward W. Said, *The Question of Palestine* (London, 1980), p. 14. Unlike Shahak, however, Dayan is not in the least sad.
46 Elon, *The Israelis*, pp. 140–4.
47 Ibid., p. 134.
48 Johnson, *A History of the Jews*, p. 435.
49 O'Brien, *The Siege*, p. 120.
50 Ibid., p. 126.
51 Ben Gurion thought him a 'thoroughly Hitlerian type'.
52 'The Iron Wall: We and the Arabs', quoted in Lenni Brenner, *The Iron Wall: Zionist Revisionism from Jabotinski to Shamir* (London, 1984), p. 75.
53 Quoted in Said, *The Question of Palestine*, p. 13.
54 Quoted in Brenner, *The Iron Wall*, p. 77.
55 'The Iron Law', quoted in ibid.
56 Elon, *The Israelis*, p. 155.
57 Article in *Zo Hadareh*, 30 July 1975. Quoted in Said, *The Question of Palestine*, p. 104.
58 Johnson, *A History of the Jews*, pp. 337–9.
59 Palumbo, *The Palestinian Catastrophe*, p. 1.
60 Ibid., p. 2.
61 Ibid., p. 4.
62 Ibid., pp. 22–3.
63 Ibid., p. 4.
64 O'Brien, *The Siege*, p. 230.
65 Ibid.
66 Palumbo, *The Palestinian Catastrophe*, p. 32.
67 O'Brien, *The Siege*, p. 733.

68 Johnson, *A History of the Jews*, pp. 522–3, for Begin's life and policies.
69 Ibid., p. 522, for Lehi, Stern and Shamir.
70 Ibid., p. 523.
71 Ibid., p. 524.
72 An Arab eyewitness put the figure at only ninety-three killed, and another account says that only twenty-three were shot. Ibid., p. 525.
73 For an account of Meir Pa'il's testimony, see Palumbo, *The Palestinian Catastrophe*, pp. 47–57.
74 Johnson, *A History of the Jews*, p. 29.
75 Palumbo, *The Palestinian Catastrophe*, pp. 82–92.
76 In *The Palestinian Catastrophe*, Michael Palumbo has used this newly released information to re-evaluate the events of 1948. He does not always give the source for his quotations, however, which is a pity.
77 In *Palestinians: From Peasants to Revolutionaries* (London, 1979), Rosemary Sayigh has based her history on interviews with refugees in the camps of the Lebanon. For the flight from Palestine, see pp. 64–92.
78 Quoted in Johnson, *A History of the Jews*, p. 446.
79 Trans. Robert Mezey, *Poems from the Hebrew* (New York, 1923), quoted by Schweid, *The Land of Israel*, p. 203.
80 Ibid., p. 204.
81 Elon, *The Israelis*, p. 281.
82 Ibid., p. 280. Elon calls archaeology a 'popular movement. It is almost a national sport. Not a passive spectator sport, but the thrilling active pastime of many thousands of people.'
83 Sigmund Freud, 'A Disturbance of Memory on the Acropolis', *Character and Culture* (New York, 1963), p. 311, and Freud's *Letters* to his fiancée, December 1883 (London, 1980). See also Elon, *The Israelis*, p. 347.
84 Elon, *The Israelis*, p. 281.
85 See Schweid, *The Land of Israel*, pp. 205–8.
86 Quoted and translated by Elon, *The Israelis*, p. 277. Yizar's italics.
87 Oz, *My Michael*, trans. Nicholas de Lange (London, 1984 edn), p. 215.
88 Ibid., p. 219.
89 Ibid., pp. 219–20.
90 Ibid., pp. 223–4.

91 Ibid., p. 224.
92 Uri Avnery, *My Friend, the Enemy* (London, 1986), passim.
93 Ya'el Paz-Melamed, 'The Fateful Decision', *Ma'ariv Weekend Magazine*, 13 February, quoted in *Middle East International*, 20 March 1987, p. 18.
94 Peter Mansfield, *The Arabs* (3rd edn, London, 1985), pp. 254–5.
95 He shouted at his junior minister Anthony Nutting on one occasion: 'But what's all this nonsense about isolating Nasser, of "neutralising" him, as you call it? I want him destroyed, can't you understand?' Anthony Nutting, *No End of a Lesson* (London, 1967), p. 69, quoted in Mansfield, *The Arabs*, p. 250.
96 Elon, *The Israelis*, pp. 219–21.
97 See E. Sivan, *Modern Arab Historiography of the Crusades* (Tel Aviv, 1973), passim.
98 Bernard Lewis, *Semites and Anti-Semites: An Inquiry into Conflict and Prejudice* (London, 1986), pp. 191–2.
99 Y. Harkabi, *Arab Attitudes to Israel* (Jerusalem, 1972), pp. 229–37.
100 Edward Mortimer, *Faith and Power: The Politics of Islam* (London, 1982), p. 273.
101 'We Muslims possess a glorious revolution, proclaimed fourteen [sic] centuries ago, in order to restore to humanity its proper sentiment and dignity, and to give man his proper due.' Nasser speaking at a Friday sermon in the al-Azhar mosque in Cairo, quoted in ibid., p. 274.
102 Ibid., pp. 273–4.
103 A refugee in Nahr al-Bared camp speaking to Rosemary Sayigh, *Palestinians*, p. 85.
104 Ibid., p. 5.
105 O'Brien, *The Siege*, pp. 469–70.
106 Ibid., p. 470.
107 *Arabia Through the Looking Glass* (London, 1983 edn), p. 320.
108 *After the Last Sky* (London, 1986), p. 32.
109 Sayigh, *Palestinians*, pp. 10–11.
110 Ibid., p. 10.
111 Ibid., p. 12.
112 Ibid., pp. 10–11.
113 Translated and quoted in Khalid A. Sulaiman, *Palestine and Modern Arabic Poetry* (London, 1984), pp. 119–20.
114 Ibid., p. 121.
115 Ibid., p. 122.
116 Ibid., pp. 202–4.
117 Sayigh, *Palestinians*, p. 110.
118 Ibid., p. 111.
119 See Alain Gresh, *The PLO: The Struggle Within, Towards an Independent Palestinian State*, trans. A. M. Berrett (London, 1985), pp. 26–8; O'Brien, *The Siege*, pp. 472–3; Maxime Rodinson, *Israel and the Arabs*, trans. Michael Pern and Brian Pearce (2nd edn, London, 1982), pp. 144–5, 148, 185, 219–29.
120 For this Resolution, see Lacqueur and Rubin, *The Israel–Arab Reader*, pp. 365–6.
121 Quoted in Gresh, *The PLO*, p. 33.
122 Ibid.
123 For the text of the PLO Charter, see Lacqueur and Rubin, *The Israel–Arab Reader*, pp. 366–72.
124 Interview with the Algerian paper *Mondjahid* in late 1969, quoted in Gresh, *The PLO*, p. 30.
125 Article 20 of the PLO Charter.
126 In an interview with the *Sunday Times*, 15 June 1919.
127 For Black September, see O'Brien, *The Siege*, pp. 480–1; Rodinson, *Israel and the Arabs*, pp. 246–52.
128 Gresh, *The PLO*, passim; Rodinson, *Israel and the Arabs*, pp. 287–309.
129 Sayigh, *Palestinians*, p. 146.
130 Ibid., p. 166.
131 Ibid., p. 167.
132 Said, *The Question of Palestine*, p. 135; see also pp. 139–40.
133 See Gresh, *The PLO*, pp. 167ff.
134 Lacqueur and Rubin, *The Israel–Arab Reader*, p. 518.
135 Rodinson, *Israel and the Arabs*, p. 286.
136 Ibid.
137 Uri Avnery, *My Friend, the Enemy*, p. 334, for a discussion of this law and its implications. On the same page, Avnery records the remark of a Palestinian friend: 'The gap between the two sides remains unchanged. The more we become moderate, the more the Israelis become extreme.' Avnery comments, 'He was not wrong.'
138 Gresh, *The PLO*, pp. 184–5; Rodinson, *Israel and the Arabs*, pp. 287–9.
139 Daoud Kuttab, 'Why the People Rose', *Middle East International*, 316 (9 January 1988).
140 Ibid., p. 5.

CHAPTER FOUR *1096–1146: The Crusade Becomes a Holy War and Inspires a New* Jihad

1 Jonathan Riley-Smith, 'The First Crusade and St Peter', in B. Z. Kedar, H. E. Mayer and R. C. Smail (eds), *Outremer: Studies in the History of the Crusading Kingdom of Jerusalem* (Jerusalem, 1982), p. 46.

2 *Gesta Francorum, or The Deeds of the Franks and the Other Pilgrims to Jerusalem*, trans. Rosalind Hill (London, 1962), p. 37.

3 Ralph of Caen, *Vita Tancredi*, quoted in Jonathan Riley-Smith, *The First Crusade and the Idea of Crusading* (London, 1986).

4 Riley-Smith, *The First Crusade*, pp. 44–5.

5 Ibid., p. 112.

6 Walter Porges, 'The Clergy, the Poor and the Non-Combatants on the First Crusade', *Speculum*, 21 (1940), quotes Anna, who makes a clear distinction between the Eastern and Western views of war: 'For the rules concerning priests are not the same among the Latins as they are with us. For we are given the command by the canonical laws and teaching of the Gospels: Touch not, taste not, handle not! For thou art consecrated, whereas the Latin barbarian will simultaneously handle divine things and wear his shield in his left arm and hold his spear in his right hand, and at one and the same time, he communicates the body and blood of God and looks murderously and becomes a man of blood. . . . For this barbarian race is no less devoted to sacred things than it is to war.'

7 Steven Runciman, *A History of the Crusades*, 3 vols, (Cambridge, 1954, London, 1965), vol. I, p. 153.

8 *Gesta Francorum*, pp. 33–4.

9 Riley-Smith, *The First Crusade*, p. 85.

10 Porges, 'The Clergy, the Poor and the Non-Combatants', quotes Adhémar: 'Not one of you can be saved unless he honours the poor and relieves them. Just as you cannot be saved without them, so they cannot live without you.' It shows the conscious desire to return to the spirit of the First Christians in Jerusalem who lived as one and held all things in common. Acts 2:44–5.

11 The phrase is coined by Riley-Smith in *The First Crusade*, p. 2.

12 Ibid., p. 63.

13 Fulcher of Chartres, *A History of the Expedition to Jerusalem, 1095–1127*, trans. and ed. Frances Rita Ryan (Knoxville, 1969), p. 85.

14 Ibid., p. 86.

15 Ibid.

16 Raymund of Aguilers, quoted in August C. Krey, *The First Crusade: The Accounts of Eye-Witnesses and Participants* (Princeton and London, 1921), p. 116.

17 Riley-Smith, 'The First Crusade and St Peter', pp. 54–5.

18 *Gesta Francorum*, p. 27.

19 Ibid., p. 23.

20 Riley-Smith, *The First Crusade*, p. 100.

21 *The Expedition to Jerusalem*, p. 80.

22 *Gesta Francorum*, p. 22.

23 Runciman, *A History of the Crusades*, vol. I, p. 91.

24 Raymund of Aguilers, *Liber*, quoted in Krey, *The First Crusade*, p. 125.

25 Fulcher of Chartres, *The Expedition to Jerusalem*, p. 96.

26 Riley-Smith, *The First Crusade*, p. 91.

27 Riley-Smith, 'The First Crusade and St Peter', pp. 59–62, for the numerous religious titles they gave to themselves and their army.

28 Fulcher of Chartres, *The Expedition to Jerusalem*, p. 102.

29 *Gesta Francorum*, p. 39.

30 Ibid., p. 40.

31 Riley-Smith, *The First Crusade*, p. 115.

32 Ibid., p. 116.

33 Ibid., p. 117.

34 Ibid., pp. 117–18.

35 *The Expedition to Jerusalem*, p. 226.

36 Riley-Smith, *The First Crusade*, p. 112.

37 Ibid., p. 113.

38 Porges, 'The Poor, the Clergy and the Non-Combatants', p. 13. He suggests that the nucleus of this group may have been survivors from Peter the Hermit's Crusade, who afterwards recruited poor Crusaders into their ranks.

39 Ibid.
40 Quoted by Norman Cohn, *The Pursuit of the Millennium: Revolutionary Millenarians and Mystical Anarchists of the Middle Ages* (London, 1957, 1970), p. 66.
41 Ibid.
42 Ibid.
43 Ibid., p. 67.
44 Ibid.
45 See Runciman, *A History of the Crusades*, vol. I, pp. 241–6, 257, 258, 259, 260, 273, for a clear account of Peter's visionary career.
46 Fulcher of Chartres, *The Expedition to Jerusalem* devotes a whole chapter to these visions: pp. 100–1. One soldier who was actually climbing down the walls to safety on the other side saw his dead brother, a crusading martyr, who urged him to return.
47 For Stephen's vision, see *Gesta Francorum*, pp. 56–8.
48 Fulcher of Chartres says that when the Crusaders had conquered Antioch 'many of them had at once commingled with unlawful [pagan] women,' and they thought that Kerbuqa's arrival with his confederacy was God's punishment: *The Expedition to Jerusalem*.
49 Ralph of Caen, *Vita Tancredi*. He comments that Bohemund was 'no fool'. 'When did Pilate ever come to Antioch?' he asked. Quoted by Krey, *The First Crusade*, p. 33.
50 The verse from the Office that Christ had told Stephen should be sung daily by the Crusaders was Psalm 47:5:

> There was a rallying, once, of kings
>   advancing together along a
>   common front;
> they looked, they were amazed,
>   they panicked, they ran.

It was obviously a reference to Kerbuqa's confederacy and a prayer that this victory of the chosen people should be repeated.
51 *Gesta Francorum*, p. 59.
52 Ibid., p. 67.
53 'When our men saw the host of warriors on white horses they did not understand what was happening or who these men might be, until they realized that this was the succour sent by Christ and that the leaders were St George, St Mercury, and St Demetrius. (This is quite true, for many of our men saw it.)' (*Gesta Francorum*, p. 69.) An interesting insight into the visionary consciousness of these desperate men.
54 *The Expedition to Jerusalem*, p. 106.
55 Izz ad-Din ibn al-Athir, quoted and translated by Francesco Gabrieli (ed.), *Arab Historians of the Crusades*, translated from the Italian by E. J. Costello (London, 1984), p. 8.
56 *The Expedition to Jerusalem*, p. 117.
57 Raymund of Aguilers, *Liber*, quoted in Krey, *The First Crusade*, p. 199.
58 Riley-Smith, *The First Crusade*, p. 97.
59 Ibid., for this exalted mood of fervour, p. 98.
60 Zoé Oldenbourg, *The Crusades*, trans. Anne Carter (London, 1966), p. 132.
61 'We could achieve nothing, so that we were all astounded and very much afraid.' *Gesta Francorum*, p. 90. This incident was a severe check to their mounting confidence in their supernatural abilities, and perhaps this 'dread' contributed to the final atrocity.
62 *Gesta Francorum*, p. 91.
63 Ibid., p. 262.
64 Krey, *The First Crusade*, p. 261.
65 Ibid., p. 262.
66 Ibid.
67 Ibid.
68 Riley-Smith, *The First Crusade*, pp. 124–5.
69 Ibid., pp. 122–3.
70 Ibid., p. 122.
71 Ibid., p. 121.
72 Ibid.
73 Ibid.
74 In the account of Urban's speech that Guibert of Nogent wrote in his *Gesta Dei per Francos* (c.1104) he made Urban say that unless Christians were in Jerusalem Antichrist would not appear and the Last Days would be delayed. Quoted by Krey, *The First Crusade*, p. 38.
75 Riley-Smith, *The First Crusade*, pp. 120–34.
76 Ibid., p. 143. See also account of Urban's speech, p. 1 and p. 389, note 1, in this book.
77 Robert the Monk, 'Apart from the mystery of the healing cross, what

more marvellous deed has there been since the creation of the world than was done in modern times in the journey of our men to Jerusalem.' Ibid., p. 140.

78 Ibid., p. 141.
79 Ibid.
80 Ibid., p. 149.
81 R. W. Southern, *Western Society and the Church in the Middle Ages* (London, 1970), p. 225.
82 Riley-Smith, *The First Crusade*, p. 119.
83 Riley-Smith, *The Knights of St John in Jerusalem and Cyprus, 1050–1310* (London, 1967), p. 40.
84 Norman Daniel, *The Arabs and Medieval Europe* (London and Beirut, 1975), pp. 203–4.
85 Oldenbourg, *The Crusades*, p. 208.
86 Ibn al-Athir, in Gabrieli, *Arab Historians of the Crusades*, p. 11.
87 Amin Maalouf, *The Crusades Through Arab Eyes*, trans. Jon Rothschild (London, 1984 edn), pp. 2–3.
88 Ibid., p. 53.
89 Ibn al-Athir, in Gabrieli, *Arab Historians of the Crusades*, p. 11.
90 Maalouf, *The Crusades Through Arab Eyes*, p. 53.
91 Gabrieli, *Arab Historians of the Crusades*, p. 11.
92 Maalouf, *The Crusades Through Arab Eyes*, p. 82.
93 Ibid., p. 83.
94 Gabrieli, *Arab Historians of the Crusades*, p. 55.
95 Ibid., p. 54.
96 Ibid., pp. 54–5.
97 Maalouf, *The Crusades Through Arab Eyes*, p. 134.
98 Ibid., p. 137.
99 Gabrieli, *Arab Historians of the Crusades*, pp. 52–3.
100 Ibid., p. 53.
101 Maalouf, *The Crusades Through Arab Eyes*, p. 143.
102 Gabrieli, *Arab Historians of the Crusades*, pp. 70–1.
103 The word 'lay' comes from the Middle English *lawede*, which not only means 'uneducated' but also means 'lewd'!
104 Ibn al-Athir, in Gabrieli, *Arab Historians of the Crusades*, p. 65.
105 Maalouf, *The Crusades Through Arab Eyes*, p. 143.
106 Poem quoted by Ibn al-Athir, without source; Gabrieli, *Arab Historians of the Crusades*, p. 71.
107 From the 'Ode to Zion', trans. T. Carmi in *The Penguin Book of Hebrew Verse* (London, 1984 edn), p. 348.
108 Eliezer Schweid, *The Land of Israel: National Home or Land of Destiny*, trans. Deborah Greniman (New York, 1985), p. 59. Also pp. 47–60 for a fuller account of Halevi's theory of the holiness of the Land of Israel.
109 T. Carmi, *The Penguin Book of Hebrew Verse*, p. 335.
110 Quoted in Schweid, *The Land of Israel*, p. 67.

CHAPTER FIVE *1146–1148: St Bernard and the Most Religious Crusade*

1 Bernard of Clairvaux, Letter to the Duke and people of Bohemia, in Jonathan and Louise Riley-Smith, *The Crusades: Idea and Reality, 1095–1274* (London, 1981), p. 97.
2 Ibid.
3 Quoted in Henri Daniel-Rops, *Bernard of Clairvaux*, trans. Elizabeth Abbott (New York and London, 1964), p. 40. Source not given.
4 Quoted in Steven Runciman, *A History of the Crusades*, 3 vols (Cambridge, 1954, London, 1965), vol. II, p. 254.
5 Jonathan and Louise Riley-Smith, *The Crusades*, p. 97.
6 Ibid.
7 Letter to the Eastern Franks and to the Bavarians, ibid., p. 95.
8 Ibid., p. 97.
9 Ibid.
10 Ibid., p. 95.
11 R. W. Southern, *The Making of the Middle Ages* (Oxford, 1953, London, 1987), p. 158.
12 In England he was called 'Hearding' and in France 'Stephen' but never both together.
13 Daniel-Rops, *Bernard of Clairvaux*, p. 45.
14 R. W. Southern, *Western Society and the Church in the Middle Ages* (Lon-

don, 1970), pp. 258–65, for Cistercian colonising.

15 Ibid., pp. 257–8.

16 The knights had become a military aristocracy and formed what we might today call a 'class'; many young knights who felt the need for this new spiritual quest were recruited by Bernard.

17 Southern, *Western Society and the Church*, p. 257.

18 Ibid., p. 258.

19 This was still the generally accepted view, though Bernard's was probably the last generation to hold it. In the next chapter I shall show a new secular spirit at work in Europe.

20 Bernard of Clairvaux, Epistle 64, quoted in André Vauchez, 'Saint Bernard, un predicateur irrésistible', *L'Histoire*, 47 (1982), 28–9.

21 Ibid., p. 29.

22 Southern, *The Making of the Middle Ages*, p. 20.

23 *Gesta Regum*, quoted in ibid., p. 69.

24 Quoted in Stephen Howarth, *The Knights Templar* (London, 1982), p. 70. Source not given.

25 From *De Laude Novae Militiae* (In Praise of the New Chivalry), quoted in Zoé Oldenbourg, *The Crusades*, trans. Anne Carter (London, 1966), p. 289.

26 Ibid., quoted in Ernst Kantorowicz, *Frederick the Second, 1194–1250*, trans. E. O. Lorimer (London, 1931), p. 87.

27 Ibid., quoted in Jonathan and Louise Riley-Smith, *The Crusades*, p. 102. Bernard is alluding to a passage in St Paul's letter to the Romans 8:31–9, celebrating the love of Christ.

28 Ibid.

29 Vauchez, 'Saint Bernard, un predicateur irrésistible', 27–8.

30 Quoted in Watkin W. Williams, *St Bernard of Clairvaux* (Manchester, 1935), p. 290.

31 Quoted in Henry Adams, *Mont Saint-Michel and Chartres* (London, 1986 edn), p. 296.

32 Vauchez, 'Saint Bernard un predicateur irrésistible', p. 27.

33 Williams, *St Bernard of Clairvaux*, pp. 271–3.

34 Ibid., p. 273.

35 Jean Markale, *Aliénor d'Aquitaine* (Paris, 1983), p. 26.

36 Georges Duby, *The Knight, the Lady and the Priest: The Making of Modern Marriage in Medieval France*, trans. Barbara Bray (London, 1985 edn), p. 196.

37 Odo of Deuil, *De profectione Ludovici VII in orientem, The Journey of Louis VII to the East*, ed. and trans. Virginia G. Berry (New York, 1948), pp. 17, 19. (The English version is on pages marked with odd numbers only.)

38 Ibid., p. 29.

39 Ibid., p. 41, but the charge is levelled with great frequency throughout.

40 Ibid., p. 55.

41 Ibid., p. 129.

42 Ibid., p. 57.

43 Ibid., pp. 57, 59.

44 Duby, *The Knight, the Lady and the Priest*, pp. 190–8, for the part this incident played in the divorce proceedings between Louis and Eleanor.

45 Especially from Usama Ibn Mundiqh, whose comments are quoted and translated in Francesco Gabrieli (trans. and ed.), *Arab Historians of the Crusades*, trans. from the Italian by E. J. Costello (London, 1978, 1984), pp. 73–83. Usamah's basic view is that the Franks are unintelligent and barbaric, but that a few of them have improved and become more civilised by having settled for a long time in Muslim countries. The tone of his urbane comments is of mild bewilderment and even astonishment at the Franks' outrageously stupid behaviour and the reader has to sympathise!

46 *De Consideratione*; Jonathan and Louise Riley-Smith, *The Crusades*, pp. 61–2.

47 Giles Constable, 'The Second Crusade as seen by Contemporaries', *Traditio*, 9 (1953), 268.

48 Quoted in Adams, *Mont Saint-Michel and Chartres*, p. 101.

49 Ibid., p. 100. Adams comments: 'Such deep popular movements are always surprising and at Chartres the miracle seems to have occurred three times, coinciding more or less with the dates of the Crusades and taking the organization of a Crusade.' Perhaps this popular movement can be compared to the popular movement of archaeology in Israel today.

50 Eleanor brought courtly love enthusiasm to England and in the thirteenth century an English version of the Grail legend was written. See *The Quest of the Holy Grail*, trans. and ed. P. M. Matarasso (London, 1969). The Introduction touches on the biblical and Cistercian influences on the legend.

51 See also Southern, *The Making of the Middle Ages*, pp. 523–4.

52 Chrétien of Troyes, *Arthurian Romances*, trans. W. W. Comfort (London, 1975), p. 91.

53 See Norman Daniel, *The Arabs and Medieval Europe* (London and Beirut, 1975), ch. 10, 'Arabic Scientific Literature in Europe'.

54 Ibid., p. 273.

55 Ibid., pp. 269–72.

56 Dante Alighieri, *The Divine Comedy: Hell*, trans. Dorothy L. Sayers (London, 1949), canto IV, lines 112–51, pp. 44–5.

57 Southern, *The Making of the Middle Ages*, pp. 39–40.

58 Benjamin Kedar, *Crusade and Mission: European Approaches towards the Muslims* (Princeton, 1984), p. 72.

59 Ibid., p. 102.

60 Ibid., pp. 104–5.

61 Ibid., pp. 106–7.

62 Norman Daniel, *Islam and the West: The Making of an Image* (Edinburgh, 1960), p. 123.

63 Kedar, *Crusade and Mission*, p. 99.

64 Daniel, *Islam and the West*, p. 124.

65 Ibid.

66 In interview with Raphael Mergui and Philippe Simonnot, *Israel's Ayatollahs: Meir Kahane and the Far Right in Israel* (London, 1987 edn), p. 113. Eytan was severely censured in the Kahan Report of 1983 for his role in the massacre of Palestinians in the Sabra and Chatilla camps in the Lebanon on 17–18 September 1982.

67 See Karen Armstrong, *The Gospel According to Woman: Christianity's Creation of the Sex War in the West* (London, 1986), pp. 74–5, for Bernard in the context of the Christian tradition of misogyny.

68 See Abelard's account of their decision to get married in 'The Story of My Calamities' in *The Letters of Abelard and Heloise*, trans. and ed. Betty Radice (London, 1974), pp. 70–4.

69 See Roger Boase, *The Origin and Meaning of Courtly Love: A Critical Study of European Scholarship* (Manchester, 1977), passim.

70 Daniel, *Islam and the West*, p. 154.

71 Ibid., p. 145.

72 Paul Johnson, *A History of the Jews* (London, 1987), pp. 209–10.

73 Norman Cohn, *The Pursuit of the Millennium: Revolutionary Millenarians and Mystical Anarchists of the Middle Ages* (London, 1957, 1970), pp. 76–86.

74 Maalouf, *The Crusades Through Arab Eyes*, p. 151.

75 Ibid.

76 Ibid., pp. 152–3.

77 Bernard Lewis, *The Assassins* (London, 1967), passim.

78 Ibid., p. 5.

CHAPTER SIX   *1168–1192: A Religious* Jihad *and a Secular Crusade*

1 Amin Maalouf, *The Crusades Through Arab Eyes*, trans. Jon Rothschild (London, 1984), p. 159.

2 Ibid.

3 Ibid., p. 169.

4 Ibid.

5 Stanley Lane Poole, *Saladin and the Fall of Jerusalem* (London and New York, 1898), p. 99.

6 Francesco Gabrieli (trans. and ed.), *Arab Historians of the Crusades*, trans. from the Italian by E. J. Costello (London, 1978, 1984), pp. 87–96.

7 Ibid., pp. 89–90.

8 Poole, *Saladin*, p. 99.

9 Gabrieli, *Arab Historians of the Crusades*, p. 100.

10 Ibid., p. 98.

11 Maalouf, *The Crusades Through Arab Eyes*, p. 172.

12 Ibid., pp. 173–4.

13 Ibid., p. 174.

14 Ibid., pp. 182–3.

15 Baha ad-Din, in Gabrieli, *Arab Historians of the Crusades*, p. 106.

16 Ibid., p. 107.

17 Ibid., p. 106.
18 Ibid., p. 105.
19 Ibid., p. 111.
20 Ibid., p. 98.
21 William of Tyre, *A History of Deeds Done Beyond the Sea*, trans. E. A. Babcock and A. C. Krey, 2 vols (New York, 1943), vol. II, pp. 505–6.
22 The marvellous story of Kerak is told by Steven Runciman, *A History of the Crusades*, 3 vols (Cambridge, 1954, London, 1965), vol. II, pp. 440–2.
23 Poole, *Saladin*, p. 272.
24 Runciman, *A History of the Crusades*, vol. II, p. 453.
25 Ibid.
26 Ibn al-Athir in Gabrieli, *Arab Historians of the Crusades*, p. 119.
27 Ibid., p. 120.
28 Ibid.
29 Quoted in Marshall Whitfield Baldwin, *Raymund III of Tripolis and the Fall of Jerusalem* (Princeton, 1936), p. 113.
30 Runciman, *A History of the Crusades*, vol. II, p. 457.
31 Gabrieli, *Arab Historians of the Crusades*, pp. 131–2.
32 Maalouf, *The Crusades Through Arab Eyes*, pp. 192–3.
33 Ibid., p. 193, but also Gabrieli in *Arab Historians of the Crusades*, pp. 112, 124, 133–4.
34 Gabrieli, *Arab Historians of the Crusades*, pp. 138–9.
35 Muhammad Zafrulla Khan, *Islam: Its Meaning for Modern Man* (London, 1962, 1980), p. 182.
36 Gabrieli, *Arab Historians of the Crusades*, p. 140.
37 Ibid., p. 153 (pp. 151–3 for the whole sermon).
38 Maalouf, *The Crusades Through Arab Eyes*, p. 196.
39 Ibid., pp. 196–7.
40 Ibid., p. 196.
41 Ibn al-Athir in Gabrieli, *Arab Historians of the Crusades*, p. 141.
42 Ibid., pp. 141–2.
43 Ibid.
44 Ibid., pp. 142–4.
45 Maalouf, *The Crusades Through Arab Eyes*, p. 200.
46 Ibid., pp. 203–4.
47 Gabrieli, *Arab Historians of the Crusades*, p. 144.
48 Ibid., pp. 145–6.
49 One can see such an inscription on the Church of St Anne in Jerusalem, which was the Royal Chapel of the Crusader Kingdom but which was turned into a madrassa by Saladin.
50 Joshua Prawer, *The Latin Kingdom of Jerusalem: European Colonialism in the Middle Ages* (London, 1972), p. 244.
51 Gabrieli, *Arab Historians of the Crusades*, pp. 148–9.
52 Ibid., p. 101.
53 Ibid., p. 90.
54 Maalouf, *The Crusades Through Arab Eyes*, p. 205. See also Baha ad-Din, who also describes such a 'poster', depicting a Muslim knight trampling the tomb of Christ on which his horse is urinating. 'This picture was carried abroad to the markets and meeting places; priests carried it about, clothed in their habits, their heads covered, groaning "O the shame!" In this way they raised a huge army.' Gabrieli, *Arab Historians of the Crusades*, pp. 208–9.
55 Gabrieli, *Arab Historians of the Crusades*, p. 215.
56 Paul Johnson, *A History of the Jews* (London, 1987), pp. 210–11.
57 Gabrieli, *Arab Historians of the Crusades*, p. 213.
58 Ibid., p. 214.
59 Maalouf, *The Crusades Through Arab Eyes*, p. 213.
60 Gabrieli, *Arab Historians of the Crusades*, p. 226.
61 Ibid.
62 Ibid., pp. 226–7.
63 Runciman, *A History of the Crusades*, vol. III, p. 58.
64 Gabrieli, *Arab Historians of the Crusades*, pp. 225–6.
65 Ibid., p. 91.
66 Ibid., p. 92.
67 Ibid.
68 Runciman, *A History of the Crusades*, p. 68.
69 Ibid., p. 72.
70 Norman Daniel, *The Arabs and Medieval Europe* (London and Beirut, 1975), pp. 182–3.
71 See B. B. Broughton, *The Legends of Richard I, Coeur de Lion: A Study of Sources and Variations to the Year 1600* (The Hague and Paris, 1966), passim.

1 Conor Cruise O'Brien, *The Siege: The Saga of Israel and Zionism* (London, 1986), pp. 143–4.

2 Harold Fisch, *The Zionist Revolution: A New Perspective* (London and Tel Aviv, 1978), pp. 89–90.

3 Ibid., p. 87.

4 'The Right of Israel', text of an address given by Rabin, formerly Israeli chief of staff, on the occasion of receiving an honorary doctorate from Hebrew University, 28 June 1967 in Walter Lacqueur and Barry Rubin (eds), *The Israel–Arab Reader: A Documentary History of the Middle East Conflict* (4th edn, revised and updated, London, 1984), p. 231. Rabin went on to discuss the soldiers' 'burning faith in their righteousness', and claimed (not unlike the Crusaders) that they were 'carried forward by spiritual values, by deep spiritual resources, far more than by their weapons'. He concluded that for this spiritual strength 'they have no rational explanations, except in terms of a deep consciousness of the moral justice of their fight' (pp. 232–3). It is a masterly expression of the irrational, highly emotional holy-war mentality.

5 Fisch, *The Zionist Revolution*, p. 89.

6 *Israel: An Echo of Eternity* (New York, 1969), quoted in ibid., p. 21.

7 An abridged edition was translated in English by Henry Near (ed.), *The Seventh Day: Soldiers Talk About the Six Day War* (London, 1970).

8 Quoted by Amos Elon in *The Israelis: Founders and Sons* 2nd edn, London and Tel Aviv, 1981, 1983), p. 246.

9 Ibid., p. 263.

10 Ibid.

11 Ibid., pp. 263–4.

12 Translated by T. Carmi, *The Penguin Book of Hebrew Verse* (London, 1984 edn), p. 571; a prose translation which I have ventured to re-line, 'The Locking of the Gates' is the *Ne'ila*, the evening prayer which concludes the Day of Atonement (Yom Kippur):

Open the gates to us when the gates are being closed, for the day is about to set.
The day shall set, the sun shall go down and set – let us enter Your gates!
(Also translated by T. Carmi, ibid., p. 241.)

13 Oz quotes this in 'An Argument on Life and Death (A)', in *In the Land of Israel*, trans. Maurice Goldberg-Bartura (London, 1983; Flamingo edn).

14 A. Cohen, *Everyman's Talmud* (New York, 1975), p. 65. The story is that a pagan told Hillel that he would convert to Judaism on condition that he was taught the whole of the Torah while he stood on one foot. Rabbi Hillel said: 'What is hateful to yourself, do not to your fellow man. That is the whole of the Torah and the remainder is but commentary. Go, learn it' (Shabbath 31a). Rabbi Hillel was at the height of his powers some fifteen years before the birth of Christ.

15 *Progressive Israel*, 8 (1982), quoted in Don Peretz, 'The Semantics of Zionism, Anti-Zionism and Anti-Semitism', EAFOD AND AJAZ (eds), *Judaism or Zionism: What Difference for the Middle East?* (London, 1986), p. 78.

16 Ibid.

17 Ibid., p. 79.

18 Bernard Avishai, *The Tragedy of Zionism: Revolution and Democracy in the Land of Israel* (New York, 1985), p. 254. 'Ben Gurion reiterated these points in interviews and periodic public appearances at Sde Boker. Few took them seriously, one heard grumblings about his senility.' Ibid., p. 255.

19 'His resignation and subsequent defeat in the elections of 1964 were greeted by a large number of younger Israelis with relief and even a wistful joy. Ben Gurion's rejection by his own party has been compared to the tribal killing of the divine king described by Frazer in *The Golden Bough*.' Elon, *The Israelis*, p. 258.

20 Avishai, *The Tragedy of Zionism*, p. 244.

21 Ibid., p. 245.
22 Ibid.
23 Lacqueur and Rubin, *The Israel–Arab Reader*, p. 365.
24 Raphael Mergui and Philippe Simonnot, *Israel's Ayatollahs: Meir Kahane and the Far Right in Israel* (London, 1987), p. 218.
25 Avishai, *The Tragedy of Zionism*, pp. 252–3.
26 Harold Fisch discusses this in *The Zionist Revolution*, p. 73, calling it a 'religious element in Zionist thinking on the commands of history.... After the Six Day War there was a feeling that there was no way back. There could be no return to a state of territorial vulnerability.'
27 Ibid., p. 77.
28 Avishai, *The Tragedy of Zionism*, pp. 252–3.
29 O'Brien, *The Siege*, pp. 504–5.
30 Ibid., p. 408.
31 Ibid.
32 Quoted in Klaus Herman, 'Politics and the "Divine Promise"', EAFOD AND AJAZ, *Judaism or Zionism*, p. 36.
33 Avishai, *The Tragedy of Zionism*, p. 94.
34 Rabbi Kook: 'The secularists will realise in time that they are immersed and rooted in the life – land, language, history and customs – bathed in the radiant sanctity that comes from above.' Ibid., p. 94.
35 Fisch, *The Zionist Revolution*, p. 63.
36 Avishai, *The Tragedy of Zionism*, p. 97.
37 Eliezer Schweid, *The Land of Israel: National Home or Land of Destiny*, trans. Deborah Greniman (New York, 1985), p. 172. See also pp. 171–86 for a fuller discussion of Kook's ideas.
38 Ibid.
39 Mergui and Simonnot, *Israel's Ayatollahs*, p. 125.
40 Ibid., p. 123.
41 Ibid.
42 Ibid., pp. 124 and 128.
43 Ibid., p. 128.
44 Hanan Porat, one of the leading West Bank pioneers, has written, 'Working in a settlement is a spiritual uplift, an antidote to the materialism and permissiveness which have swept this country. That is why the leadership of this country has passed from the secular into the national religious camp.' Ibid., p. 126.
45 Oz, 'An Argument on Life and Death (B)', in *In the Land of Israel*, p. 132.
46 Ibid., p. 133.
47 A. B. Yehoshua, *The Lover*, trans. Philip Simpson (New York, 1985 edn), pp. 305, 318, 329, 343.
48 Lenni Brenner, *The Iron Wall: Zionist Revisionism from Jabotinski to Shamir* (London, 1984), pp. 152–4.
49 Mergui and Simonnot, *Israel's Ayatollahs*, p. 114.
50 Oz, 'The Finger of God?', in *In the Land of Israel*, p. 70. He is quoting the American Gush settler Bobby Brown, also known as David Bar-On, who had recently made the *aliyah* and who works as a social worker in Jerusalem.
51 Ibid. Oz quotes Dr Amiel Unger, another new American immigrant, who is a lecturer in political science at Bar Ilan University near Tel Aviv: 'The Arabs are a problem. Maybe the Arabs are a test which the Lord, Blessed be He, is putting us through. If we are strong and tenacious, that will be the beginning of redemption. All our difficulties are stirrings of the Messiah.' As I will show later, the Gush settlers believe that by colonising the Land of Israel, they will bring the Messiah and the redemption.
52 Oz, 'An Argument on Life and Death (A)', in *In the Land of Israel*, p. 117.
53 Mergui and Simonnot, *Israel's Ayatollahs*, p. 124.
54 Ibid., pp. 122–3. The authors comment: 'Why should he worry, since it is God who guides him in his mad race for the colonization of the West Bank?' (p. 233).
55 'An Argument on Life and Death (B)', in *In the Land of Israel*, p. 144.
56 'The Finger of God?', in *In the Land of Israel*, p. 60.
57 Ibid. He adds: 'Our eternal rights come from above!'
58 Mergui and Simonnot, *Israel's Ayatollahs*, p. 86.
59 Oz, 'The Finger of God?', in *In the Land of Israel*, p. 71.
60 See Harriet, the Gush settler in Tekoa, in conversation with Amos Oz: the aid 'should stop. Totally!' And the arms? 'Men win wars! Faith

wins! God Almighty wins!' Ibid., p. 60.

61 'An Argument on Life and Death (B)', in *In the Land of Israel*, p. 127.

62 'An Argument on Life and Death (A)', in *In the Land of Israel*, p. 122.

63 For the policies and leaders of Tehiya, see Megui and Simonnot, *Israel's Ayatollahs*, pp. 99–115.

64 *Woman of Violence: Memoirs of a Young Terrorist, 1943–1948* (London, 1966).

65 Megui and Simonnot, *Israel's Ayatollahs*, p. 114.

66 Ibid., p. 115.

67 Daoud Kuttab, 'Violent Deeds and Words', *Middle East International*, 313 (1987), pp. 12–13.

68 Quoted in Alan Schonfield's documentary, *Courage Along the Divide*, 1987).

69 For this strain in biblical and Halachic Judaism, see Israel Shahak, 'The Jewish Religion and its Attitude to Non-Jews', *Khamsin*, 9 (1981), 3–49.

70 Ibid., pp. 25–6.

71 Ibid., p. 26.

72 Colonel Rabbi A. Avidan (Zemel), 'Purity of weapons in the light of the Halakah'. Quoted by in ibid., p. 26.

73 Ibid., p. 37.

74 'Gush Emunim have quoted religious precepts which enjoin Jews to oppress Gentiles, as a justification of the attempted assassination of the Palestinian mayors.' Ibid., p. 41.

75 Liebowitz is quoted in Alan Schonfield's two films about Israel, *Courage Along the Divide* (1987) and *Shattered Dreams* (1987).

76 Megui and Simonnot, *Israel's Ayatollahs*, pp. 22–3.

77 Ibid., p. 23.

78 Ibid., p. 51.

79 Ibid., pp. 22, 50.

80 Petetz Kidron, 'The Uprising Tilts Israel to the Right', *Middle East International*, 316 (1987), pp. 3–4.

81 'For me the word Zionism means God's order that we live in Israel. And to have this state is a miracle from God.' Kahane to Mergui and Simonnot, *Israel's Ayatollahs*, p. 44.

82 Ibid., p. 46.

83 Ibid.

84 Ibid., p. 42.

85 Ibid., p. 47.

86 Ibid., p. 55.

87 Ibid.

88 Ibid., p. 42.

89 Ibid., p. 45.

90 Ibid., pp. 78–82.

91 Ibid., pp. 49–50.

92 From a speech recorded by Alan Schonfield in *Shattered Dreams*.

93 Mergui and Simonnot, *Israel's Ayatollahs*, p. 85.

94 Ya'el Paz-Melamed, 'The Fateful Decision', *Ma'ariv Weekend Magazine*, quoted in *Middle East International*, 20 March 1987, p. 18.

95 *Davar*, 2 October 1986, quoted in Akira Orr, 'Lessons from South Africa', *Middle East International*, 9 January 1987, pp. 17–18.

96 Mergui and Simonnot, *Israel's Ayatollahs*, p. 43.

97 Ibid., p. 31: 'Western democracy has to be ruled out. For me that's cut and dried: there's no question of setting up democracy in Israel, because democracy means equal rights for all, irrespective of racial or religious origins. Therefore democracy and Zionism cannot go together.'

98 Ibid., p. 44.

99 Ibid., p. 141.

100 'The Tender among you and very Delicate', in *In the Land of Israel*, pp. 94, 99.

101 Ibid., p. 88.

102 Ibid., p. 95.

103 Ibid., p. 96.

104 Ibid., p. 98.

105 *Jerusalem Post International*, 29 August 1987.

CHAPTER EIGHT   *1979: Iran and the New* Jihad – *Muslims Demand an Islamic Identity*

1 During the hostage crisis, when American Embassy personnel were imprisoned in their embassy in Tehran, the well-known American observer Richard Falk asked: 'Is it not a serious matter when our embassy is used to subvert the constitutional order of a country, as was done by the

US in staging the coup that brought the Shah back to power in 1953? Is it not also serious that embassy personnel evidently helped establish and train the SAVAK, the secret police that committed so many crimes against the people of Iran?' 'Iran: Human Rights and International Law', in D. H. Albert (ed.), *Tell the American People: Perspectives on the Iranian Revolution* (Philadelphia, 1980).

2 See p. 240ff.

3 This is a basic Islamic principle. To attribute any power or absolute authority to anything other than God is the sin of *shirk*, which can be roughly translated 'idolatry'. *Shirk* in the Koran is directly related to the word *zann* (conjecture, guess) which is frequently opposed to *'ilm* (knowledge). All knowledge comes from God and returns to him. A Muslim will *know* that God exists and that he is unique, because God has revealed this, but he will not create new doctrines about other matters that are not included in the Koran. People who do this 'invent falsehood in his name' (10:59). The Koran, for example, pours scorn on the Christian doctrine of the Incarnation, which teaches that God sired a son, and says to Christians: 'No evidence whatsoever have you for this [assertion]! Would you attribute unto God something which you cannot know? Say: "Verily they who attribute their own lying inventions to God will never attain a happy state"' (24:31). To persecute other people for what can only be guesses would, therefore, be unthinkable.

4 Amir Taheri, *The Spirit of Allah: Khomeini and the Islamic Revolution* (London, 1985).

5 For the origins of the Shiah–Sunna conflict, see Malise Ruthven, *Islam and the World* (London, 1984), pp. 91–100.

6 Asaf Hussain, *Islamic Iran: Revolution and Counter-Revolution* (London, 1985), p. 23.

7 Ibid., pp. 54–8.

8 Ibid., p. 55.

9 Ibid.

10 Ibid., p. 23, for Hussain's story.

11 Ibid., pp. 24–5.

12 W. Montgomery Watt, 'The Significance of the Early Stages of Imami Shi'ism', in Nikkie R. Keddie (ed.), *Religion and Politics in Iran: Shiism from Quietism to Revolution* (New Haven and London, 1983), passim.

13 Hussain, *Islamic Iran*, p. 26.

14 Taheri, *The Spirit of Allah*, p. 22.

15 Ibid., p. 39.

16 Ibid., p. 325.

17 For an inspiring and scholarly account of a mullah's education, see Roy Mottahedeh, *The Mantle of the Prophet: Religion and Politics in Iran* (London, 1985, 1987), passim.

18 Ruthven, *Islam and the World*, pp. 158–9.

19 Hussain, *Islamic Iran*, p. 27.

20 Ibid., pp. 28–9.

21 Mottahedeh, *The Mantle of the Prophet*, pp. 23–5, for an account of the shrine and the pilgrims' devotions. He shows that the shrine is an important part of the mullahs' religious experience in Qum and that the students pray there as a means of linking themselves to the past and to the roots of the faith.

22 Hussain, *Islamic Iran*, pp. 59–60.

23 Mottahedeh, *The Mantle of the Prophet*, pp. 296–9, 307–16.

24 Hussain, *Islamic Iran*, p. 19.

25 Ibid., p. 20.

26 Ibid., p. 116.

27 Ibid., pp. 11–13.

28 Ibid., p. 11.

29 Ibid., pp. 13–16.

30 Mottahedeh, *The Mantle of the Prophet*, pp. 233–8.

31 Hussain, *Islamic Iran*, pp. 87–8.

32 Ibid., pp. 60–5.

33 Ibid., pp. 88–9.

34 Ibid.

35 Ibid., pp. 47–50.

36 William O. Beeman, 'Images of the Great Satan: Representatives of the United States in the Iranian Revolution', in Keddie, *Religion and Politics in Iran*, pp. 206–11.

37 Shaul Bakhash, *The Reign of the Ayatollahs: Iran and the Islamic Revolution* (London, 1986), pp. 206–11.

38 Hussain, *Islamic Iran*, pp. 43–4.

39 Bakhash, *The Reign of the Ayatollahs*, pp. 27–35.

40 Hussain, *Islamic Iran*, p. 95.

41 Ibid., p. 75: Muslims, Khomeini

argued, 'have turned their faces towards the West and regard the West
as the goal of all their aspirations and
which have sold themselves and do
not know themselves, which have
lost their own celebrities and sources
of their pride, which have lost themselves and in whose place a Western
mind is situated: these have satans as
their leaders and have gone from
light into darkness. . . . The satan of
recent times, of our own times [the
United States] encouraged their West-
ernization . . . our universities were
Western, our economy was Western.
Our culture was Western too.'

42 Ibid, p. 70.
43 Ibid., p. 95.
44 Gregory Rose, '*Velayat-e Faqih* and
the Recovery of the Islamic Identity
in the Thought of Ayatollah
Khomeini', in Keddie, *Religion and
Politics in Iran*, p. 181.
45 Ruhollah al-Musawi al-Khomeini,
*Islam and Revolution: Writings and
Declarations*, quoted by Gregory
Rose in 'The Thought of Khomeini',
p. 166.
46 Ibid.
47 Rose, 'The Thought of Khomeini',
pp. 167–80.
48 Hussain, *Islamic Iran*, p. 72.
49 Ibid., p. 67. Constantly Khomeini
urged the people to rise up and save
themselves (ibid., p. 70) rather like
the Zionists.
50 Ibid., pp. 71–2.
51 Ibid., p. 94.
52 Ibid., p. 69.
53 Ibid., p. 74.
54 Ibid., p. 71: Muslims, Khomeini said,
'had no alternative but to work for
destroying the corrupt and corrupting
systems and to destroy the symbol of
treason and the unjust among the
rulers of the people. This is a duty
that all Muslims wherever they may
be are entrusted – a duty to create a
victorious and triumphant political
war.'
55 Rose, 'The Thought of Khomeini', p.
182.
56 Ibid., p. 183.
57 'The Day the Imam Returns', trans.
and quoted by Taheri, *The Spirit of
Allah*, pp. 227–8.
58 Shahrough Akhari, 'Shariati's Social
Thought', in Keddie, *Religion and
Politics in Iran*, p. 140.
59 Hussain, *Islamic Iran*, p. 80.
60 Shahrough Akhari, 'Shariati's Social
Thought', pp. 137–8.
61 Hussain, *Islamic Iran*, p. 79.
62 Ibid., pp. 79–80.
63 Ibid., p. 81.
64 Shahrough Akhari, 'Shariati's Social
Thought', p. 136.
65 Ibid., p. 133.
66 Hussain, p. 82: *hajj*, Shariati taught,
was a way of 'training oneself in
becoming a responsible rebel by becoming genuinely involved in the
problems of the people', and not 'by
becoming a monk and isolating oneself from the people' (ibid.).
67 Quoted in Ruthven, *Islam in the
World*, p. 42.
68 Hussain, *Islamic Iran*, p. 82.
69 Ruthven, *Islam and the World*, p. 45.
70 Akhari, 'Shariati's Social Thought',
pp. 140–1.
71 Rose, 'The Thought of Khomeini',
pp. 185–6.
72 At one important moment he 'saw
the light', an experience crucial in
Sufi mysticism, which changes the
initiate's view of the world and
effects a vision of his unity with all
created things in the sight of God. 'It
was not an isolated light, like that of
the moon or a spotlight. It was
everywhere; in fact it was everything. The pool glowed with light,
the garden beds glowed, the sky
glowed, the very walls and arches
around the courtyard were made of
light. . . . Then he discovered the
light was also inside of him, and
he could no longer judge his own distance from objects.' Mottahedeh, *The
Mantle of the Prophet*, p. 140. This is
similar to experiences Buddhist mystics have achieved; Buddhists would
claim that these are entirely *natural*
states and that the techniques that
induce them cause the mystic to
expand his natural powers and
perceptions.
73 Ibid., p. 143.
74 Ibid.
75 Ibid., p. 258.
76 Ibid., pp. 173–9.
77 Roy Mottahedeh quotes a Turkish
traveller who saw this spectacle in
Iran in 1640: 'Shouts and screams
of "Alas, Husain" mount from the

people to the heavens and all the spectators weep and wail. Hundreds of Husain's devotees beat and wound their heads, faces and their blood flows. The green grassy field becomes bloodied and looks like a field of poppies.' Ibid., pp. 174–5.

78 Ibid., p. 179.

79 Mary Hegland 'Two Images of Husain: Accommodation and Revolution in an Iranian Village', in Keddie, *Religion and Politics in Iran*, pp. 218–35 and passim.

80 Ibid., p. 229.

81 Ibid., p. 230.

82 Ibid.

83 Hussain, *Islamic Iran*, pp. 112–13.

84 Ibid., p. 124.

85 Ibid., pp. 124–5.

86 Ibid., p. 126.

87 Ibid., p. 110.

88 Ibid., p. 127.

89 The government figures were 200, the Opposition 4000 (ibid.).

90 Ibid.

91 Ibid., pp. 128–30.

92 Ibid., p. 174.

93 Edward W. Said, *Covering Islam: How the Media and the Experts Determine How We See the Rest of the World* (New York and London, 1981, 1985 edn used).

94 Ibid., xxv–xxvi, quoting a transcript of a television programme provided courtesy of Veronica Pollard, ABC, New York.

95 Beeman, 'Images of the Great Satan', passim.

96 Its slogan was 'Our movement is Husayni and our leader is Khomeini.' Hussain, *Islamic Iran*, p. 142.

97 Ibid., p. 143.

98 Ibid., pp. 147–9.

99 The *Kayhan International* newspaper considered him to be too Westernised and commented that people like him 'had lost their "selves" to the superficial and dazzling "self" of the West'. Ibid, p. 158.

100 Ibid.

101 Ibid., p. 159.

102 Ibid.

103 Ibid., p. 158.

104 Nikkie R. Keddie, 'Introduction' to his *Religion and Politics in Iran*, pp. 15–16.

105 Ibid., pp. 14–15.

106 Rose, 'The Thought of Khomeini', p. 184.

107 Ibid.

108 Ibid., p. 186

109 Speech delivered on the day of the Arafah, 1979, quoted in Rose, 'The Thought of Khomeini', p. 186.

110 Rose, 'The Thought of Khomeini', p. 186.

111 Bakhash, *The Reign of the Ayatollahs*, p. 234.

112 Ibid.

113 Ibid.

114 Michael Janson, 'Desecration of the Hajj', *Middle East International*, 306 (1987), 4. Janson also points out that the Ayatollahs have trebled the Iranian representation at the *hajj* from 50,000 to 155,000, making it the largest foreign contingent, in a bid to politicise the pilgrimage.

115 Ibid.

116 Ibid.

117 Godfrey Janson, 'Mecca: reaction and aftermath', *Middle East International*, 306 (1987).

118 Shaul Bakhash, *The Reign of the Ayatollahs*, pp. 234–5.

119 Ibid., p. 233.

120 Ibid., pp. 233, 235, 239.

121 Quoted by Eric Rouleau, *Le Monde*, 4 May 1981.

122 Quoted by Robin Wright, *Sacred Rage: The Crusade of Modern Islam* (London, 1986). Musawi continues: 'We have already said that if self-defence and if the stand against American, Israeli and French oppression constitute terrorism, then we are terrorists in that context. This path is easier than smoking a cigarette if it comes while fighting for the cause of God and while defending the oppressed.' He was clearly emphasising the reactionary, defensive nature of the bombings as an important part of their ideology.

123 Robin Wright, *Sacred Rage*, pp. 215–42.

124 Ibid., p. 226.

125 Ibid., p. 233.

126 Ibid., p. 237.

127 Daoud Kuttab, 'Fundamentalists on the March', *Middle East International*, 311 (1987), 8–10.

128 Quoted by Godfrey Janson, 'Khomeini's Heretical Delusions of Grandeur', *Middle East International*, 317 (1988), 18.

129 Ibid.

130 Ibid.

CHAPTER NINE *1981: The Death of President Anwar Sadat –*
Holy War and Peace

1 Desmond Meiring, *Fire of Islam* (London, 1982), pp. 5–8.

2 Ibid., p. 31.

3 Mohamed Heikal, *Autumn of Fury: The Assassination of Sadat* (London, 1983, 1986 edn used), pp. 17–19. He points out that Sadat preferred to forget this and presented his childhood as idyllic: a much loved child leading a simple village life in the village of Mit-Abu-el-Kom, where he had in fact spent his very earliest years with his grandmother. Heikal says he would have won much more sympathy if he had told the true story. Mohamed Heikal is probably the greatest journalist in the Arab world, was a close friend of Nasser, a member of his government and helped Sadat in the early years of his presidency. Even though he was eventually imprisoned by Sadat and publicly denounced by him, this is a fair and compassionate assessment of Anwar Sadat.

4 Ibid., p. 20. In his autobiography *In Search of an Identity* (London, 1978), Sadat preferred to dwell on his studious days at Mit-Abu-el-Kom: 'I see it so clearly that I have the impression of leaving it yesterday. I owe a great deal to the excellent teacher I had there, Sheikh Abdul-Hamid, recently deceased; it is he who inculcated in me my love of knowledge and spirit of true faith. I remember my lessons with emotion: I sat on the ground with my comrades, holding on my knees my small slate and rustic reed pen, which served me for writing.' Quoted by Meiring, *Fire of Islam*, p. 41. Given the mawkish tone of this work it seems more charitable to Sadat to rely on Mohamed Heikal. The over-simplistic and unselfcritical nature of the work does reveal an essential flaw in Sadat's mind, which contributed to his tragedy. He was not a bad man so much as a simple-minded one.

5 Heikal, *Autumn of Fury*, pp. 20–35. Sadat, he says, had become submissive as a child in his miserable home, but had retreated into a private world of fantasy that had a streak of violence.

6 He was at first not told about the Free Officers because of this opposition. Ibid., p. 35.

7 Ibid., p. 37.

8 Ibid., p. 40.

9 Ibid., p. 42. Nasser appointed him to the post when he was leaving to go to the Arab summit conference at Rabat and had heard of a CIA plot against his life. 'If anything did happen to him, said Nasser, Sadat would be all right for the interim period. People in the Socialist Union and the army would look after the real business and Sadat's job would be largely ceremonial.' (Heikal reporting his conversation with Nasser on the subject; ibid.).

10 Ibid., p. 70.

11 Ibid., p. 51.

12 Sadat on Nasser in *In Search for an Identity*: 'We had hoped for the arrival of a benevolent dictator, a just tyrant: when we had him, we understood that this system, however seductive it might appear from the outside, was built on sand; naturally then it would crumble in a short time. But the most annoying thing about this experience wasn't the complete ruin of our economy, nor our humiliating military position: it was the mountain of hate that had accumulated during this attempt to build a community founded on power. Because of the absence of human values in such a community, people only worried about their external success and tried to make the biggest material profit possible, legally or not, and even if this meant the destruction of our next-door neighbour.' (Quoted by Meiring, *Fire of Islam*, p. 74.) This is a classic example of projection: every word of it could apply to his own regime.

13 Caption under a photograph of Sadat and the Shah, opposite p. 157 of Heikal, *Autumn of Fury*.

14 Ibid., pp. 123–6.

15 Edward Mortimer, *Faith and Power: The Politics of Islam* (London, 1982), pp. 286–7.

16 Also the code name for the operation was Badr, the name of Mohammad's decisive battle against the Meccans, ibid., p. 289.

17 Ibid., p. 286.

18 Heikal, *Autumn of Fury*, pp. 73–4.

19 Ibid., pp. 94–6.

20 Ibid., pp. 82–5, 90.

21 Ibid., pp. 179–82.

22 Ibid., p. 179.

23 Gilles Kepel, *The Prophet and Pharaoh: Muslim Extremism in Egypt*, (trans. Jon Rothschild) (London, 1985), pp. 129–30.

24 Abraham Rabinovich, 'A Split in the Golden Path', *Jerusalem Post International*, 19 December 1987, pp. 113–14.

25 Karen Armstrong, *The Gospel According to Woman, Christianity's Creation of the Sex War in the West* (London, 1986), passim.

26 Blu Greenberg, *On Women and Judaism: A View from Tradition* (Philadelphia, 1981), pp. 107–8, though the author does quote other, more negative traditions also (ibid., pp. 114–15). She also suggests that in Spain, contact with Christianity produced new prohibitions (ibid., p. 116).

27 Ibid., pp. 117–18.

28 See Geoffrey Parrinder, *Sex in the World's Religions* (London, 1980), pp. 162 and 155–76 for an account of sexuality and Islam.

29 Ibid., pp. 160–1. Circumcision of either sex is not mentioned in the Koran, but it later became a law for all men because it was said to be founded on the customs of the Prophet and some authorities thought it also obligatory for women.

30 H. R. Hays, *The Dangerous Sex: The Myth of Feminine Evil* (London, 1966), see p. 57 but also passim for an account of Western misogyny. For a convenient summary see also D. S. Bailey, *The Man–Woman Relation in Christian Thought* (London, 1959).

31 I have discussed this more fully in *The Gospel According to Woman, Christianity's Creation of the Sex War in the West* (London, 1986), pp. 2–4.

32 Parrinder, *Sex in the World's Religions*, pp. 162–3. He also quotes the sixteenth-century Sheikh al-Nafzawi of Tunis, who opens his book *The Perfumed Garden for the Soul's Delectation*: 'Praise be to God, who has placed man's greatest pleasure in the natural parts of man to afford the greatest enjoyment to woman.' The famous *The Thousand and One Nights* is a clear instance of the Muslim appreciation of sex, which is equally pleasurable to men and women. Judaism is also enthusiastic about love and sex, as can be seen by the inclusion of The Song of Solomon in the Jewish scriptures. See Parrinder, *Sex in the World's Religions*, pp. 192–3; he quotes a rabbi saying: 'every man needs a woman and every woman needs a man and both of them need the Divine Presence' (p. 191).

33 See for example St Jerome: 'If we abstain from coitus we honour our wives but if we do not – well, what is the opposite of honour but insult' (*Adversus Jovinian*, 1, 7) quoted in Bailey, *The Man–Woman Relation in Christian Thought*, p. 44. Luther took the same prejudice into Protestantism. He saw marriage as a 'hospital for sick people' to which a man was driven by uncontrollable lust against his will, and that 'the greater part of married persons still live in adultery' because of their unruly imaginations. Ibid., p. 118.

34 Parrinder, *Sex in the World's Religions*, p. 184.

35 Greenberg, *On Women and Judaism*, passim.

36 Muhammad Zafrulla Khan, *Islam: Its Meaning for Modern Man* (London, 1962, 1980), p. 28.

37 Parrinder, *Sex in the World's Religions*, pp. 158–9.

38 Ibid., pp. 173–6.

39 For conditions in the universities, see Kepel, *The Prophet and Pharaoh*, pp. 135–8.

40 Ibid., pp. 142–6.

41 Kepel, *The Prophet and Pharaoh*, pp. 139–40.

42 Ibid., pp. 47–9, 62–3.

43 Ibid., pp. 37–59.

44 Ibid., p. 74.

45 Ibid., pp. 75–6.

46 Ibid., pp. 7–105 for an account of Shukri Mustafa and the Society of Muslims.

47 Ibid., p. 84.

48 Ibid., pp. 87–9.
49 Heikal, *Autumn of Fury*, p. 138.
50 Kepel, *The Prophet and Pharaoh*, pp. 94–5.
51 Ibid., p. 95.
52 Ibid., pp. 96–8.
53 Ibid., pp. 98–9.
54 Heikal, *Autumn of Fury*, p. 98.
55 He was giving an interview to a Lebanese journalist in his rest-house and suddenly noticed a column of smoke rising from the town. 'What's that?' he asked. 'Perhaps the rioting from Cairo has spread here,' the journalist replied. 'What riots?' asked the astonished Sadat. (Heikal, *Autumn of Fury*, p. 99.)
56 Conor Cruise O'Brien, *The Siege: The Saga of Israel and Zionism* (London, 1986), pp. 571–3.
57 Ibid., pp. 569–70.
58 Ibid., p. 573.
59 Heikal, *Autumn of Fury*, p. 105.
60 Arafat had been summoned to Egypt especially to hear an 'important' announcement and was furious about the peace initiative and the trick that had been played upon him. Ibid., p. 106.
61 O'Brien, *The Siege*, p. 575.
62 *The Battle for Peace* (New York and London, 1981), quoted in Meiring, *Fire of Islam*, pp. 88–9.
63 Abridged text of the speech in Walter Lacqueur and Barry Rubin (eds), *The Israel–Arab Reader: A Documentary History of the Middle East Conflict* (4th edn, revised and updated, London, 1984), p. 592.
64 Ibid., p. 598.
65 Ibid.
66 Ibid., pp. 594–5.
67 Ibid., p. 595: 'In the absence of a just solution of the Palestinian problem, there will never be that durable and just peace upon which the entire world insists.'
68 Ibid., p. 599.
69 Quoted in O'Brien, *The Siege*, p. 577.
70 Ibid., p. 588.
71 Heikal, *Autumn of Fury*, pp. 114–15.
72 Ibid., p. 116.
73 Ibid.
74 Ibid.
75 Menachem Begin, 'Autonomy Plan for the Occupied Territories' (28 December 1977), in Lacqueur and Rubin, *The Israel–Arab Reader*, p. 615.
76 O'Brien, *The Siege*, p. 583.
77 Ibid.
78 Ibid., pp. 583–6.
79 'Camp David Frameworks for Peace' (17 September 1978), in Lacqueur and Rubin, *The Israel–Arab Reader*, pp. 609–14.
80 For Begin's position, see O'Brien, *The Siege*, pp. 600–2.
81 Lacqueur and Rubin, *The Israel–Arab Reader*, p. 620.
82 Ibid., pp. 61–7.
83 Heikal, *Autumn of Fury*, pp. 106–7, 221–2.
84 Ibid., p. 183.
85 Ibid., pp. 182–3.
86 Ibid., pp. 184–5.
87 Kepel, *The Prophet and Pharaoh*, p. 112.
88 Ibid., pp. 112–13.
89 Ibid., pp. 117–18.
90 Ibid., p. 112.
91 Ibid., pp. 119–24.
92 Ibid., pp. 150–1.
93 Ibid., p. 251.
94 Ibid., pp. 172–90.
95 Ibid., pp. 194–204.
96 Ibid., p. 197.
97 Heikal, *Autumn of Fury*, p. 253.
98 Ibid., pp. 118–19.
99 Ibid., p. 250.
100 Ibid., p. 251.
101 Ibid.
102 Ibid., p. 252.
103 Ibid., pp. 256–64.
104 Ibid., p. 263.
105 Peter Kemp, 'Terrorists in Cairo', *Middle East International*, 302 (1987), 12.
106 Uri Avnery, *My Friend, the Enemy* (London, 1986), p. 292. Avnery considers that Satawi had an exceptionally clear vision of the situation in the Middle East and of the urgent need to find a peaceful solution and means to coexistence: 'Issam really is irreplaceable – a man of vision, who dared to speak up and say the things which needed to be said.' Ibid., p. 335.
107 Ibid., p. 334.
108 Ariel Sharon, 'Israel's Security' (15 December 1981), in Lacqueur and Rubin, *The Israel–Arab Reader*, pp. 355–69.
109 Heikal, *Autumn of Fury*, pp. 284–6.
110 Speech delivered on 1 May 1978, quoted in Regina Sharif, *Non-Jewish*

Zionism: Its Roots in Western History (London, 1985), p. 136.

111 O'Brien, *The Siege*, pp. 637–8, 639, 644–6.

112 Donald Neff, 'Diplomatic Isolation', *Middle East International*, 317 (1988), 8. After this book went to press, however, the United States produced the 'Schultz Plan' and tried to persuade Israel to attend an international conference.

CHAPTER TEN *1199–1221: Crusades Against Christians and a New Christian Peace*

1 Steven Runciman, *A History of the Crusades*, 3 vols (Cambridge, 1954, London, 1965), vol. III, p. 110.

2 Henry VI, who enters our story only through his brother and his son Frederick II, was more formidable than any ruler in Europe since Charlemagne. He had a high sense of the office of emperor and almost succeeded in establishing it on an hereditary basis. This led him to see the Byzantines as absolute enemies, as Charlemagne had. In 1197 he laid careful plans for a Crusade against Byzantium but died as he was amassing his armada, or he could well have succeeded in making himself master of Christendom. After his death, Philip and Otto the Welf were engaged in a dispute for the succession, and Philip clearly wanted to use the Crusade to further his imperial ambitions.

3 Runciman, *A History of the Crusades*, vol. III, p. 124.

4 He wrote an ecstatic letter to the Emperor Baldwin, giving him his approval without reserve. Ibid., p. 128.

5 Hymns were sung to celebrate the downfall of *Constantinopitana, civitas diu profana.* Ibid.

6 Ibid., pp. 128–9.

7 R. W. Southern, *The Making of the Middle Ages* (Oxford, 1953, London, 1987), p. 60. He speaks of the 'homely conceptions' of the Franks of Byzantium, who 'laid more stress on personal rights than on large, strategic designs'. They were 'baffled' by the Eastern empire and by dividing it up they produced a 'disjointed mechanism'.

8 Southern (ibid., p. 61) is doubtful that it did. Runciman is convinced that it was 'the Crusaders themselves who wilfully broke down the defence of Christendom and thus allowed the infidel to cross the Straits and penetrate into the heart of Europe'. *A History of the Crusades*, vol. III, p. 477.

9 As it is by Runciman, *A History of the Crusades*, vol. III, p. 474.

10 Jacques Madaule, *The Albigensian Crusade: An Historical Essay*, trans. Barbara Wall (London, 1967), p. 63.

11 Though the wave of missionaries arrived in France at about the time of the Second Crusade, there had been Cathars in Europe since the middle of the eleventh century and we hear of them dying for their faith. Zoé Oldenbourg, *Le Bûcher de Montségur* (Paris, 1959), p. 55.

12 When Bernard had preached the Second Crusade in 1146 he had found the churches empty and had been able to get very little support, but the Catharist missionaries attracted large audiences and enthusiastic converts. Ibid., p. 44, and Madaule, *The Albigensian Crusade*, p. 50.

13 Oldenbourg, *Le Bûcher de Montségur*, pp. 37–49, for a summary of Catharist belief.

14 Ibid., pp. 49–50.

15 Ibid., p. 54.

16 Zoé Oldenbourg (ibid.) discounts this as one of the distorted myths of the Catholics about the Cathars, who were against violence of any kind. They would not have approved of this suicide. It seems that this fantasy of the *endura* was a projection of a Christian disturbance about the body, for many ascetics starved themselves into emaciation for the love of Christ.

17 Ibid., p. 61.

18 Ibid., pp. 63–7.

19 Madaule, *The Albigensian Crusade*, p. 53. He points out that the Cathars were very different from some 'heretics' in the north, like the Hussites

and the Lutherans, who were very pugnacious and bellicose in their attitude to the Catholic Church. I shall touch on Lutheran aggression in Chapter 12.

20 Ibid., p. 52.

21 Oldenbourg, *Le Bûcher de Mont-ségur*, pp. 96–105.

22 Jonathan and Louise Riley-Smith, *The Crusades: Idea and Reality, 1095–1274* (London, 1981), pp. 78–80, for a text of the letter.

23 Ibid., pp. 78–9.

24 Innocent accuses the Cathars of 'abstaining from certain vices in order that men should think them pious' but in reality they are 'the worst of men', given over to 'many-sided deceit'. Ibid., p. 79.

25 Ibid., p. 80.

26 Ibid., pp. 80–5. The events are not related as a normal crime but as a battle between good and evil in the manner of the holy war. The followers of Raymund are 'attendants of Satan' (ibid., p. 81) and Peter is a martyr, who, like Christ and St Stephen, died 'lovingly' forgiving his enemies, saying '"May God forgive you because I forgive you," repeating over and over again this phrase, so full of love and forbearance' (ibid.). Innocent is slightly embarrassed that this holy martyr does not seem to be working any miracles but puts this down to the 'incredulity' of the southerners, who are blocking the south off from God (ibid., p. 82).

27 Ibid., p. 85.

28 Ibid., p. 83.

29 Ibid., p. 84.

30 Ibid., p. 85.

31 Ibid.

32 Madaule, *The Albigensian Crusade*, p. 65.

33 This is the popular legend. What probably happened is that the Catholics were urged to leave the town to save their lives, but refused to leave their fellow citizens and died fighting for their sakes. From the start this Crusade was a confrontation between north and south. Oldenbourg, *Le Bûcher de Montségur*, pp. 115–16.

34 Madaule, *The Albigensian Crusade*, p. 68.

35 Ibid., pp. 73–4.

36 After the battle of Baucaire in 1217, when Raymund defeated Simon and the Crusaders, the people of Toulouse greeted him ecstatically and cried that he had rescued their way of life from the northerners. Their courtly values, which 'were in their grave, have found again their life and their strength and their health-giving capacities; our children and our children's children will be enriched.' Quoted in Madaule, *The Albigensian Crusade*, p. 83.

37 Georges Duby, 'Les pauvres des campagnes dans l'Occident médiéval jusqu'au xiii siècle', *Revue d'Histoire de l'Église de France*, 52 (1966), 23–32.

38 Umberto Eco (trans. William Weaver) shows how far this connection between the poor, heresy and revolution had gone by the fourteenth century throughout *The Name of the Rose*, 1983.

39 Peter Raedts, 'La croisade des enfants a'-t-elle eu en lieu?' trans. Jacques Bacalu, *L'Histoire*, 47 (1982), 32. This important article has transformed our view of the so-called Children's Crusade and I repeat its findings here.

40 Ibid., p. 30.

41 Ibid., pp. 30–1.

42 Ibid., p. 32.

43 This later version of the Crusade is followed by Runciman, *A History of the Crusades*, vol. III, pp. 139–44.

44 Ibid., p. 141.

45 Raedts, 'La croisade des enfants', p. 35.

46 Ibid.

47 Ernst Kantorowicz, *Frederick the Second, 1194–1250*, trans. E. O. Lorimer (London, 1931), p. 3.

48 Ibid., p. 4.

49 He said that he had had a dream; a young bear had got on to his bed and grown larger and larger until it pushed him off. Ibid., p. 53.

50 Frederick said it was a sign from heaven 'against all probabilities of men'. Ibid.

51 God, he said, 'contrary to human knowledge, had miraculously preserved for the governance of the Roman Empire' by calling himself. Ibid., p. 55.

52 Ibid., p. 57.

53 Ibid., pp. 58–9.

54 Ibid., p. 61.

55 Ibid.

56 Ernst Kantorowicz romantically says that he looked less like an emperor 'than a fairy prince or an adventurer in tatters'. Ibid., p. 55.

57 He declared that it seemed to him 'both reasonable and seemly to follow the example of the Great and Holy Charles and my other ancestors' (ibid., p. 73). He had clearly absorbed his ancestor Barbarossa's view of the empire as a German institution and of Charlemagne as the ancestor of the Germans not of the Franks. This may be why he appeals to the German scholar Kantorowicz, who was writing in the early 1930s.

58 Ibid.

59 He had noticed that 'the 666 years allotted in Revelation to the Beast were nearly spent. It was indeed nearly six and a half centuries since the birth of Mahomet.' Runciman, *A History of the Crusades*, vol. III, p. 145. It was not only poets and the poor who had apocalyptic dreams. Please note that the Muslims are now figures of absolute evil.

60 Ibid., p. 146.

61 Amin Maalouf, *The Crusades Through Arab Eyes*, trans. Jon Roths-child (London, 1984), pp. 219–22.

62 Norman Daniel, *The Arabs and Medieval Europe* (London and Beirut, 1975), p. 206. Daniel says that in Vitry's view the Franks were 'deLatinised Latins, deEuropeanised colonists . . . cultural defectors' (ibid.).

63 Benjamin Z. Kedar, *Crusade and Mission: European Approaches Towards the Muslims* (New Jersey, 1984), p. 73.

64 Ibid., p. 120.

65 Ibid., p. 130.

66 Ibid., p. 123.

67 Quoted by Régine Pernoud, *The Crusaders*, trans. Enid Grant (Edinburgh and London, 1963), p. 221.

68 Ibid.

69 Runciman, *A History of the Crusades*, vol. II, p. 161.

70 Ibid., p. 167.

71 Maalouf, *The Crusades Through Arab Eyes*, p. 226.

72 Norman Daniel, *Islam and the West: The Making of an Image* (Edinburgh, 1960), p. 121.

73 Pernoud, *The Crusaders*, p. 221.

74 Ibid., pp. 222–3.

75 Kedar, *Crusade and Mission*, pp. 125–6.

76 Daniel, *Islam and the West*, p. 121.

CHAPTER ELEVEN *1220–1291: The End of the Crusades?*

1 Ernst Kantorowicz, *Frederick the Second, 1194–1250*, trans. E. O. Lorimer (London, 1931), p. 356.

2 Ibid., pp. 396–7.

3 Norman Daniel, *The Arabs and Medieval Europe* (London and Beirut, 1975), p. 161.

4 Ibid., pp. 254–8.

5 Ibid., p. 148.

6 Ibid., pp. 150–3.

7 Ibid., p. 154.

8 Francesco Gabrieli (trans. and ed.), *Arab Historians of the Crusades*, trans. from the Italian by E. J. Costello (London, 1978, 1984), pp. 277–8.

9 Daniel, *The Arabs and Medieval Europe*, pp. 154–5.

10 Ibid., p. 156.

11 Kantorowicz, *Frederick the Second*, p. 311.

12 Ibid.

13 Ibid., p. 358.

14 Ibid., pp. 310–11.

15 Ibid., p. 171.

16 Ibid., p. 168.

17 Ibid., pp. 88–90.

18 Ibid., pp. 93–5.

19 Steven Runciman, *A History of the Crusades*, 3 vols (Cambridge, 1954, London, 1965), vol. III, pp. 175–7.

20 Amin Maalouf, *The Crusades Through Arab Eyes*, trans. Jon Roths-child (London, 1984), pp. 226–7.

21 Kantorowicz, *Frederick the Second*, p. 176.

22 Maalouf, *The Crusades Through Arab Eyes*, p. 226.

23 Ibid.

24 Ibid., but Steven Runciman, using Western sources, says that Frederick was trying to 'hasten matters by a military display' and that al-Kamil was eventually forced to come to terms because of the deterioration in his own political position in the area.

25 Runciman, *A History of the Crusades*, vol. III, p. 187.

26 Daniel, *The Arabs and Medieval*

27 Maalouf, *The Crusades Through Arab Eyes*, p. 230.
28 Gabrieli, *Arab Historians of the Crusades*, p. 271.
29 Ibid., p. 273.
30 Ibid., p. 274.
31 Runciman, *A History of the Crusades*, vol. III, pp. 188–9.
32 Kantorowicz, *Frederick the Second*, p. 200.
33 Gabrieli, *Arab Historians of the Crusades*, p. 274.
34 Ibid., p. 275.
35 Ibid.
36 Ibid.
37 Runciman, *A History of the Crusades*, vol. III, p. 192.
38 Kantorowicz, *Frederick the Second*, p. 519.
39 Ibid., p. 253.
40 Norman Cohn, *The Pursuit of the Millennium: Revolutionary Millenarians and Mystical Anarchists of the Middle Ages* (London, 1957, 1970), pp. 113–19.
41 Kantorowicz, *Frederick the Second*, pp. 264–5.
42 Ibid., p. 414. But again, as with his relations with Muslims, it is important not to idealise this. Frederick made the Jews wear special clothing, as Pope Gregory did, but he would often take the side of the Jews against the Church, in order to further his own ends. Jews were just more people to exploit when it suited him. Ibid., p. 268.
43 Daniel, *The Arabs and Medieval Europe*, p. 158.
44 Ibid., p. 164.
45 Ibid., pp. 238–9.
46 Ibid., pp. 243–5.
47 Norman Daniel, *Islam and the West: The Making of an Image* (Edinburgh, 1960), pp. 79–108.
48 Ibid., pp. 135–40. In fact Mohammad's introduction of polygamy had nothing to do with sexual self-indulgence, but arose out of concern for Muslim women. During the wars with Mecca, many women were widowed and they and their children were left without protectors, so in order to provide for them Muslim men married the widows and took them under their protection. No one was allowed to have more than four wives, and the Koran is very strict indeed about fairness and equality. 'If you fear you will not be able to deal justly with them, then marry only one' (4:4). The man must make identical provision for each wife and spend the same period of time with each and must show no extra affection for any of them. Because of this stringency, modern Muslim apologists argue that polygamy was allowed only under special circumstances, like those which pertained in Medina during the Prophet's life. Because it is impossible for any man to treat more than one wife with the equity that the Koran demands, they quote it as being in favour of monogamy. Geoffrey Parrinder, *Sex in the World's Religions* (London, 1980), p. 516.
49 Daniel, *Islam and the West*, pp. 148–52.
50 Ibid., pp. 289–90.
51 Ibid., p. 84.
52 Arius did not believe that Jesus was God, conceived in the womb of Mary, but that he was promoted to special status during his lifetime.
53 Paul Johnson, *A History of the Jews* (London, 1987), p. 211.
54 Ibid., pp. 217–18.
55 Dom Gaspar Lefebvre OSB (ed.), *Saint Andrew Daily Missal, with Vespers for Sundays and Feasts* (Bruges, 1961), pp. 1423–4.
56 Ibid., p. 1421.
57 John of Joinville, *The Life of St Louis*, trans. René Hague and ed. Natalis de Wailly (London, 1955), pp. 37–8.
58 Michel Dillange, *The Sainte-Chapelle*, trans. Angela Moyon (Paris, 1985), p. 9.
59 John of Joinville, *The Life of St Louis*, pp. 29–32.
60 Ibid., p. 36.
61 Ibid., p. 209.
62 Ibid.
63 Ibid.
64 'He asked me whether I wished to be respected in this world and enjoy Paradise after my death. When I answered that I did, "Take care, then," he said, "not consciously to do or say anything which, if all the world were to know it, you could not acknowledge"' (ibid, p. 27). This is a typical example of Louis' simple morality. Joinville's refreshing hon-

esty is worth quoting. When St Louis asked him whether he would rather be a leper or commit a mortal sin, Joinville promptly replied (for 'I could never tell him a lie') 'that I would rather commit thirty mortal sins than become a leper' (ibid., p. 28) and when Louis asked him if he washed the feet of the poor, he was even more vehement: 'God forbid, sir! ... No, I will not wash the feet of those brutes.' Louis replied 'That was a poor answer', but could only explain the desirability of this practice by saying that 'you should not despise what God did as a lesson to us' (when Jesus washed the feet of his disciples at the Last Supper) (ibid., p. 29).

65 Ibid., p. 33.
66 Ibid., p. 34.
67 Ibid., p. 35.
68 Ibid., pp. 33–4.
69 Ibid., p. 35.
70 Ibid., pp. 35–6.
71 Ibid., p. 36.
72 Blanche of Castille, a formidable lady who acted as his regent when Louis was a minor, 'chose for him the company only of men of religion. Child though he was, she made him hear all the hours of the Office and listen to the sermons on feast days. He used to recall that his mother had sometimes told him that she would rather he had died than that he committed a mortal sin.' (Ibid., p. 41.) Reading this, one has to feel sorry for Louis.
73 Ibid., p. 51.
74 Maalouf, *The Crusades Through Arab Eyes*, pp. 236–7, and Runciman, *A History of the Crusades*, vol. III, p. 257. Frederick's letter of warning to the Sultan must have inspired Matthew Paris' accusation.
75 Pernoud, *The Crusaders*, pp. 247–8.
76 *The Life of St Louis*, p. 56.
77 Norman Daniel, *The Arabs and Medieval Europe*, p. 244, for a discussion of these conversion fantasies.
78 John of Joinville, *The Life of St Louis*, p. 57.
79 Ibid., p. 144.
80 Ibid., pp. 144–5.
81 Ibid., p. 64.
82 Ibid., pp. 77–8.
83 Ibid., pp. 96–7. Joinville describes the horrible disease graphically: 'The skin became covered with black and earth-covered spots, just like an old boot. . . . the flesh on our gums began to rot away.' Ibid., p. 97.
84 Ibid., p. 105.
85 Ibid., p. 196.
86 Ibid., p. 116.
87 Ibid.
88 Ibid., p. 113.
89 Ibid., p. 196.
90 Maalouf, *The Crusades Through Arab Eyes*, p. 44.
91 Ibid., pp. 246–7.
92 Ibid., p. 250.
93 Ibid., p. 251.
94 Mamluk buildings are much in evidence in Israel.
95 Gabrieli, *Arab Historians of the Crusades*, p. 303.
96 Ibid.
97 Ibid., p. 304.
98 John of Joinville, *The Life of St Louis*, p. 213.
99 Ibid., Joinville goes so far as to say that all those who encouraged Louis to take the Cross again had committed a mortal sin.
100 Quoted by Stephen Howarth, *The Knights Templar* (London, 1982), p. 223.
101 Maalouf, *The Crusades Through Arab Eyes*, pp. 250–4.
102 They had actually fought alongside the Mongols during a fresh attempted invasion in 1281.
103 Gabrieli, *Arab Historians of the Crusades*, p. 342.
104 Ibid.
105 Maalouf, *The Crusades Through Arab Eyes*, pp. 256–7.
106 Gabrieli, *Arab Historians of the Crusades*, pp. 344–50; and Daniel, *The Arabs and Medieval Europe*, pp. 208–9.
107 Gabrieli, *Arab Historians of the Crusades*, p. 349.
108 Ibid., p. 346.
109 'Thirteenth-century contemporary documents convey an impression that all the long-repressed yearning of the Jews for the Holy Land – kept alive by persecution, faith and daily prayer – suddenly found an outlet in a movement of return. Pilgrimage and migration acquired a new and particular character.' Joshua Prawer, *The Latin Kingdom of Jerusalem:*

European Colonialism in the Middle Ages (London, 1972), p. 244.

110 Ibid., p. 250.

111 Ibid.

112 Ibid., p. 248.

113 Ibid., p. 247.

114 Nachmanides quotes God's commandments to Joshua to slaughter the Canaanites and denies vehemently that this command was not confined to the original 'holy war' for the Promised Land: 'This is not so, for we were enjoined to destroy the nations if they make war upon us. But if they wish to make peace, we shall make peace with them and let them stay on, upon certain terms. But we shall not leave the land in their hands or those of any other nation at any time whatsoever!' Ibid., p. 248.

115 Ibid., p. 251.

116 Runciman, *A History of the Crusades*, vol. III, p. 467.

117 Norman Cohn, *Europe's Inner Demons* (London, 1975), passim, for an account of the Inquisitorial process.

118 Gregory IX followed this initiative by calling a *general* Inquisition against other heretics in 1233, Jacques Madaule, *The Albigensian Crusade: An Historical Essay*, trans. Barbara Wall (London, 1967), pp. 95–6.

CHAPTER TWELVE *1300 to the Present Day: New Crusaders in the West*

1 'His aim was to discover India, and realize the old Crusader dream of overcoming Islam in a giant pincer movement.' Friedrich Heer, *The Medieval World, 1100–1350*, trans. Janet Sondheimer (London, 1962), p. 318.

2 Paul Johnson, *A History of the Jews* (London, 1987), pp. 221–2.

3 Ibid., pp. 225–9.

4 Norman Daniel, *The Arabs and Medieval Europe* (London and Beirut, 1975), pp. 313–14.

5 Johnson, *A History of the Jews*, p. 228; and Daniel, *The Arabs and Medieval Europe*, p. 313.

6 Bernard Lewis, *Semites and Anti-Semites: An Inquiry into Conflict and Prejudice* (London, 1986), p. 83. He quotes Juan Escobar de Caro, a Spanish Inquisitor in 1628: 'By *converso* [convert] we commonly understand any person descended from Jews or Saracens, be it in the most distant degree. . . . Similarly a New Christian is thus designated not because he has recently been converted to the Christian faith, but rather because he is a descendant of those who first adopted the correct religion.'

7 Johnson, *A History of the Jews*, pp. 216–17.

8 'From Vienna and Linz in 1421, from Cologne in 1424, Augsburg in 1439, Bavaria in 1442 (and again in 1450) and from the crown cities of Moravia in 1454. They were thrown out of Perugia in 1485, Vicenza in 1486, Parma in 1488, Milan and Lucca in 1489 . . . and all Tuscany in 1494.' Ibid., pp. 230–1.

9 Edward W. Said, *Orientalism: Western Conceptions of the Orient* (London, 1978, 1985 edn used), p. 74.

10 Norman Cohn, *The Pursuit of the Millennium: Revolutionary Millenarians and Mystical Anarchists of the Middle Ages* (London, 1957, 1970), pp. 119–25.

11 In his pamphlet issued during the Peasants' War: 'Against the thievish, murderous gangs of the peasants' (1525). Ibid., p. 248.

12 Ibid., p. 80.

13 Daniel, *The Arabs and Medieval Europe*, p. 302. Like John Wycliff in the fourteenth century, Luther 'introduced the idea of Islam as an interior state which may be imputed to the enemies of true doctrine (however the writer may define it). In doing so they in effect admitted the interiorization of Islam as the "enemy" (undifferentiated) which it had been for so long in the European imagination.'

14 Norman Daniel, *Islam and the West: The Making of an Image* (Edinburgh, 1960), p. 280. The Zwinglian reformer Theodor Buchman, who was terrified of the Turkish menace, mounted a vigorous campaign

against Islam, seeing Mohammad as the head of Antichrist and Islam as his body. In doing so he circulated many of the old medieval myths that could otherwise have been forgotten. Ibid., pp. 280–1.

15 Ibid., p. 284.
16 Ibid.
17 Ibid., p. 285.
18 Johnson, *A History of the Jews*, p. 242.
19 Ibid.
20 Ibid., pp. 242–3.
21 Quoted in Alan Heimert and Andrew Delbanco (eds), *The Puritans in America: A Narrative Anthology* (Cambridge, Mass., 1985), p. 21.
22 Ibid., p. 19.
23 Ibid., pp. 19–20.
24 Ibid., p. 20.
25 Keith Thomas, *Religion and the Decline of Magic* (London, 1971, 1985 edn used), pp. 163–4. It was customary for prophets to lobby both Cromwell and King Charles with an account of their visions and messages from God. On at least six occasions the deliberations of Cromwell and his colleagues were interrupted by obscure prophets, who had fasted themselves into a state of trance. Cromwell always listened to them with respect, because this direct access to God was a central Puritan belief.
26 Robert Cushman, 'Reasons and Considerations Touching the Lawfulness of Running Out of England into Parts of America' (1622), in Heimert and Delbanco, *The Puritans in America*, p. 44.
27 For example Thomas Shepard, 'The Sound Believer' (*c.*1633). He argued that it was their zeal to preach the Word, *not* cowardice, that led them to emigrate to a place where they could preach without danger of imprisonment. Ibid., p. 33.
28 Ibid., p. 71.
29 Thus Thomas Morton in his open letter 'New English Canaan', ibid., pp. 49–50.
30 'Reasons and Considerations', ibid., pp. 43–4.
31 Quoted in Regina Sharif, *Non-Jewish Zionism: Its Roots in Western History* (London, 1985), p. 90. Source not given.

32 Heimert and Delbanco, *The Puritans in America*, p. 278.
33 Ibid., pp. 115–16. Johnson also imagines Christ summoning the Pilgrim Fathers into his army through his heralds-at-arms: 'Oh yes! oh yes! All you the people of Christ that are here oppressed, imprisoned and scurrilously derided, gather yourselves together, your wives and little ones, and answer to your several names as you shall be shipped for his service in the Western world, and more especially for planting the United Colonies of New England, where you are to attend the service of the King of Kings' (p. 114).
34 Ibid., p. 7.
35 Johnson, *A History of the Jews*, p. 276.
36 Sharif, *Non-Jewish Zionism*, p. 24.
37 Johnson, *A History of the Jews*, pp. 276–7.
38 Ibid., pp. 268–74.
39 Barbara W. Tuchman, *Bible and Sword: How the British Came to Palestine* (New York and London, 1957, 1982), p. 153.
40 Ibid., p. 154.
41 Ibid.
42 Quoted in Sharif, *Non-Jewish Zionism*, p. 37.
43 Ibid.
44 Ibid., p. 40.
45 Ibid.
46 Said, *Orientalism*, p. 77.
47 Edward W. Said, to whom I am deeply indebted in this chapter, points out that the new knowledge was used to control the Indian people. Warren Hastings decided that they should be ruled by their 'own' laws, but instead of consulting the Indians themselves, he preferred the Western views of Indian law of scholars and jurists like Sir William Jones. Ibid., p. 78.
48 Daniel, *Islam and the West*, p. 300.
49 Ibid.
50 Ibid.
51 Said, *Orientalism*, pp. 64–7.
52 Ibid., p. 66.
53 Ibid.
54 Daniel, *Islam and the West*, pp. 283, 288.
55 Ibid., pp. 288–9.
56 Said, *Orientalism*, pp. 75–6.
57 Daniel, *Islam and the West*, p. 297.

58 P. M. Holt, Introduction to *The Cambridge History of Islam*, ed. P. M. Holt, Anne K. S. Lambton and Bernard Lewis (Cambridge, 1970), p. xvi, quoted in Said, *Orientalism*, pp. 63–4.

59 Said, *Orientalism*, p. 76. This seems to have been a wise move. Newton's successor, William Whiston, was expelled from Cambridge because of his enthusiasm for Islam (ibid.), which clearly carried much the same stigma as violent Jewish anti-semitism does today.

60 Quoted in Daniel, *Islam and the West*, p. 291.

61 Edward Gibbon, *The Decline and Fall of the Roman Empire*, ed. Dero E. Saunders, abridged in one volume (London, 1980), p. 651.

62 Ibid., pp. 657–8.

63 This attitude is also discernible in Thomas Carlyle, who in his essay 'The Hero as Prophet' was the first person in the West to speak of Mohammad with true admiration. He could not abide the Koran, which he saw as 'a wearisome, confused jumble, crude, incondite; endless iterations, longwindedness, entanglement; most crude, incondite, insupportable stupidity in short.' *On Heroes and Hero Worship* (London, 1841), p. 63. He does not seem to see that some of these epithets could be applied to his own rather tangled and unstylish sentence. He simply assumes, with his superior Western understanding, that because he does not understand the Koran, it is mere stupidity. However admirable the Prophet, Islam is still not a serious challenge to 'us'.

64 Quoted in Johnson, *A History of the Jews*, p. 309.

65 Daniel, *Islam and the West*, p. 289.

66 Ibid., p. 290.

67 Quoted in Johnson, *A History of the Jews*, p. 309.

68 Daniel, *Islam and the West*, p. 287.

69 Ibid.

70 Ibid., p. 384.

71 Conor Cruise O'Brien, *The Siege: The Saga of Israel and Zionism* (London, 1986), p. 729.

72 Ibid.

73 Said, *Orientalism*, p. 87. The *Description de l'Égypte* produced by Napoleon's orientalists in twenty-three volumes (1809–28) 'became the master-type of all further efforts to bring the Orient closer to Europe, thereafter to absorb it entirely and – centrally important – to cancel, or at least subdue and reduce its strangeness and, in the case of Islam, its hostility. For the Islamic Orient could henceforth appear as a category denoting the Orientalists' power and not with the Islamic people as humans nor their history as history.'

74 His brother heard him mutter: 'J'ai manqué à ma future à St Jean d'Acre,' in the moment of victory at the battle of Austerlitz. Tuchman, *Bible and Sword*, p. 167.

75 Said, *Orientalism*, p. 80.

76 Ibid., p. 82.

77 Ibid.

78 Sharif, *Non-Jewish Zionism*, p. 50.

79 Tuchman, *Bible and Sword*, p. 166.

80 Said, *Orientalism*, pp. 114–15.

81 Ibid., p. 171.

82 Quoted in Margaret Drabble (ed.), *The Oxford Companion to English Literature* (Oxford, 1985), p. 176.

83 Ibid.

84 Said, *Orientalism*, p. 172.

85 Ibid.

86 Ibid., p. 171.

87 Ibid., p. 173.

88 Ibid., p. 177.

89 Ibid., p. 178.

90 Ibid.

91 Ibid., p. 179.

92 Ibid.

93 Ibid., p. 182.

94 Tuchman, *Bible and Sword*, p. 213.

95 Ibid.

96 Ibid., p. 212.

97 Ibid.

98 Ibid.

99 Karl Marx, *Surveys from Exile*, ed. David Fernbach (London, 1973), pp. 306–7. See also Said, *Orientalism*, pp. 153–7.

100 Marx, *Surveys from Exile*, p. 320.

101 Ibid.

102 Ibid., p. 307.

103 Karl Marx, two essays 'On the Jewish Question' (1844) quoted in Johnson, *A History of the Jews*, p. 351.

104 Ibid.

105 Ibid., p. 352.

106 Ibid.

107 Ibid.

108 See Said, *Orientalism*, pp. 132–41.

109 *Histoire générale et système comparé des langues sémitiques* in *Oeuvres complètes*, ed. Henriette Psichari (Paris, 1947–81), vol. 8, p. 147, quoted in Said, *Orientalism*, p. 142.

110 *Histoire générale*, pp. 531–2, quoted in Said, *Orientalism*, p. 143.

111 *Histoire générale*, p. 156, quoted in Said, *Orientalism*, p. 149.

112 *Religion and Art* (1881), quoted in Johnson, *A History of the Jews*, p. 394.

113 Quoted in O'Brien, *The Siege*, p. 58.

114 Ibid.

115 *Lectures and Essays*, ed. John Sutherland Black and George Chrystal (London, 1912), quoted in Said, *Orientalism*, p. 236.

116 Ibid., p. 237.

117 Ibid., pp. 236–7.

118 Ibid., pp. 276–7.

119 Ibid., p. 277.

120 Ibid.

121 Ibid.

122 Quoted in Sharif, *Non-Jewish Zionism*, p. 57. Young duly reported to the Foreign Office that there were 9690 Jews resident in Palestine and that their position was 'deplorable' (ibid.). An exaggerated assessment.

123 Tuchman, *Bible and Sword*, pp. 178–90.

124 Ibid., p. 191.

125 Sharif, *Non-Jewish Zionism*, p. 41.

126 Ibid., p. 42.

127 Colonel Patrick Campbell, the British Consul-General stationed in Egypt, told Young that he was exceeding his powers. The native Jews were still under the sole jurisdiction of the Ottoman empire: 'You have no more right to protect [them] than Austria or France would have to protect the Rayah Catholics, or Russia or Greece to protect Rayahs of the Greek religion.' Ibid., p. 57.

128 Tuchman, *Bible and Sword*, p. 175.

129 Ibid., p. 176.

130 Ibid.

131 Ibid., p. 214.

132 Ibid.

133 Ibid., pp. 114–15.

134 *Daniel Deronda* (Panther edn, London, 1970), p. 486.

135 See also a letter to V. W. Richards in 1918: the Arabs 'think for the moment, and endeavour to slip through life without turning corners or climbing hills. In part it is a mental and moral fatigue, a race trained out, and to avoid difficulties they have to jettison so much that *we* think honourable and grave.' Quoted in Said, *Orientalism*, p. 229.

136 O'Brien, *The Siege*, p. 29.

137 Sharif, *Non-Jewish Zionism*, p. 78.

138 O'Brien, *The Siege*, p. 27.

139 Ibid., pp. 28–9. He quotes his niece and biographer Blanche Dugdale: 'I remember in childhood imbibing from him the idea that Christian religion and civilization owes to Judaism an immeasurable debt, shamefully repaid' (ibid., p. 27). O'Brien also points out that Balfour had visited Cosima Wagner, Richard's widow, and admitted that he shared her anti-semitic views (ibid., p. 122).

140 Ibid., p. 28.

141 Ibid., p. 26. See also Claude Montefiore, who wrote a letter to the War Cabinet in October 1917 to try to avert the coming Balfour Declaration: 'It is very significant that anti-Semites are always very sympathetic to Zionism' (ibid. p. 27).

142 Sharif, *Non-Jewish Zionism*, p. 80.

143 Ibid., p. 79.

144 Ibid.

145 Ibid., pp. 3–4.

146 Richard Meinertzhagen, *Middle East Diary, 1917–1956* (London, 1960), p. 67.

147 Ibid., p. 183.

148 Ibid.

149 Ibid., p. 49.

150 Ibid.

151 'In fact, it is no exaggeration to say that, for the future, a strong, friendly Palestine is vital to the future strategic security of the British Commonwealth. It can never be strong and healthy under divided control, still less under any form of Arab government.' Ibid., p. 203.

152 Ibid., p. 81.

153 Ibid., p. 17.

154 Ibid., p. 12.

155 Ibid., p. 161.

156 Ibid., p. 167.

157 According to my 1985 edition, *Exodus* was first published in England in 1959 by Alan Wingate. Corgi edi-

tion was published in 1960 and went through twenty-eight impressions by 1966. It was reissued in 1966, reprinted in 1968 (twice), 1969; reissued in 1970, reprinted 1970; reprinted twice in 1971, reprinted in 1972, 1973, 1974, 1975, 1976 (twice), 1977, reprinted 1978, 1980 (twice), 1982, 1983; reissued 1984, reprinted 1986. *The Hajj* was first published in 1984.

158 Said, *Orientalism*, pp. 285–6.

159 Jonathan Raban, *Arabia Through the Looking Glass* (London, 1979, 1983), pp. 9–13.

160 Chaim Potok, *Wanderings, History of the Jews* (New York, 1978), p. 522, and Bernard Avishai, *The Tragedy of Zionism, Revolution and Democracy in the Land of Israel* (New York, 1985), pp. 358–9.

161 Sharif, *Non-Jewish Zionism*, pp. 93–7.

162 Ibid., p. 108.

163 David Turner and Robert Olson, 'Praise the Lord and Save Israel', *Middle East International*, 306, (1987), 15–16.

164 Sharif, *Non-Jewish Zionism*, p. 135.

165 Ibid., p. 110.

166 Ibid.

167 Ibid., p. 135.

168 *Jerusalem Post International*, 3 October 1987, p. 23.

169 Robert Fisk, 'Arabian faith betrayed: the consequences of Reagan's arms deal with Iran', *The Times*, 28 November 1986. He concludes:

The parameters of Reagan's world, in which the Afghan mujahedeen are 'freedom fighters' and the Palestine Fedayeen 'terrorists' is a familiar one in the Middle East. But the Arabs do not like to be lectured, especially by a nation which wishes to play the role of honest broker but which is totally committed to one side in the Arab–Israeli conflict: and the Reagan administration has done more moral lecturing than most of its predecessors.

'The association of things western with things good, of things anti-American with things bad, has long been a theme of American policy in the Middle East; the Soviets have an almost identical policy except that it operates in reverse. But Reagan was the first man to carry a crusade into the Middle East, and he did so at the very time when a far more fundamentalist crusader had begun in the area: one under which Reagan has become the delight of his enemies and the despair of his Arab friends.'

170 *Jerusalem Post International*, 3 October 1987, p. 23.

EPILOGUE: *Triple Vision*

1 Frank Barnaby, 'The Nuclear Arsenal in the Middle East', *Journal of Palestine Studies*, 17:1 (1987).

Glossary of Terms

Alem. *See* Ulema.

Aliyah (Hebrew: ascension, immigration). Originally the word was used to describe the ascent of the Temple Mount by Jewish pilgrims to Jerusalem, and thus by extension it meant 'pilgrimage'. The word has also acquired connotations of rising to a more exalted spiritual state and to a higher level of being. The Zionists chose to describe immigration into the Land of Israel as an *aliyah* and it is still used today to denote the act of emigrating from the diaspora (q.v.) and becoming a citizen of the State of Israel. The word 'Aliyah' is also used in Zionist history to describe the five great waves of Jewish immigration into Palestine before the Second World War. Thus:

First Aliyah: 1882–1903
Second Aliyah: 1904–14
Third Aliyah: 1919–23
Fourth Aliyah: 1924–8
Fifth Aliyah: 1929–39

These Aliyahs corresponded with new waves of anti-semitic persecution in Europe.

Amir (Arabic: one who commands). This came to describe either a military commander or a prince. In Turkish, the word became emir.

Antichrist This was a figure which haunted the imagination of European Christians. From certain prophecies in the New Testament, they evolved a belief in a figure who would rise to power at the end of time. His coming would herald the Last Days. He was the opposite of a Messiah, because he was the enemy of Christ and of all Christians. (*See* Messiah, Last Emperor, Hidden Imam.) Antichrist would deceive many people and attract a large following, but he would also persecute the faithful and fight God's champions. Eventually he would be crowned in Jerusalem (q.v.), and establish himself on the site of the Jewish Temple. He would appear to rule in triumph but eventually God would send down the Archangel Michael to fight him and Christians would flock to join the last terrible battle. Then the Second Coming of Christ would occur and an era of peace and glory would begin. It was generally believed that Antichrist would be an ordinary human being, though a person of absolute evil. The Protestant Reformers did not jettison the belief in Antichrist, but added fantasies of their own. Instead of seeing Antichrist as an individual, they tended to see him as a whole evil institution, like the Church of Rome or Islam.

Apocalypse (Greek: revelation). All three religions have developed an apocalyptic tradition, relating to the events that will occur at the end of time, when God's power and justice will be finally revealed. In each tradition the city of Jerusalem (q.v.) plays a crucial part. In Jewish apocalyptic writing, the Messiah will appear on the Mount of Olives to fight a terrible battle with the enemies of the Jewish people, after which he will reign triumphantly from Jerusalem and bring peace to the whole world. The Gentile nations will pay tribute to God's chosen people. (*See* Messiah, Redemption.) In Christianity, Antichrist will be crowned in the Temple, will fight the Christians there and a New Jerusalem will descend from heaven, ushering in a new world order, where suffering and injustice are no more. (*See* Antichrist, Last Emperor.) In Islam, God's Last Judgement will finally punish the evil-doers and Islam will triumph over the world. Mohammad will descend from heaven on to the Mount of Olives and lead the faithful into the city, walking on a giant sword that acts as a bridge, and the Prophet Jesus will descend from heaven into the Great Mosque of Damascus. All three traditions envisage a final world victory for the true religion. People still believe in these future events today in all three religions, and this naturally affects their attitude to the political status of Jerusalem.

Ark of the Covenant This was a portable shrine, which the ancient Israelites carried with them during their forty years' wandering in the Sinai peninsula. It contained the tablets of the Law and also localised the Presence of Yahweh (q.v.), which rested upon it in the form of a cloud.

Ashkenazi Originally a corruption of the German *allemagne*, it was used to describe the Jews of Germany, but later was extended to refer to the Jews of Eastern, Central and Western Europe, as opposed to the Sephardi (q.v.).

Atabeg (Turkish: literally prince–father). Originally an atabeg was a guardian appointed to act as a regent and protector to minor princes in the Seljuk clan; later atabegs became *de facto* rulers in their own right, even governors and founders of dynasties.

Ayatollah (Persian: Miraculous Sign of God). In Iran, it is a term used to describe those scholars of Islamic law who have attained a sufficient knowledge and authority to give rulings on matters of Islamic practice. This authority has not, until recently, extended to matters of belief or theological opinion. The faithful choose an ayatollah on whom they can model themselves and so feel confident that they are keeping the Holy Law of Islam. They consult him or his more learned followers about finer points or abstruse matters, to make sure that they are living a truly Muslim life. The also follow their ayatollah in political matters, because they trust that his knowledge of Islamic law will guide them to make a correct assessment of a given situation and show them how true Muslims should act, if they face oppression and persecution for example.

Ba'ath (Arabic: renaissance). This is the name given to the socialist party of President Hafiz Assad of Syria.

Benedictine This is a religious order that follows the Rule of St Benedict of Nursia. It became the dominant form of Western monasticism during the Dark Ages and was a major force in the Christianisation and recovery of European culture and power after the destruction of the Roman empire. The Cluniacs and the Cistercians were eleventh- and twelfth-century forms of Benedictine monasticism. Even though they differed from one another sharply, both would have argued that they were living according to the spirit of St Benedict and living lives of poverty, stability and celibacy, and both centred their lives on the singing of the Divine Office (a daily service of psalms and readings from scripture) which they called the *Opus Dei*, the work of God.

Betar (an acronym for the Hebrew *Brit Trumpeldor*: the Covenant of Trumpeldor). An activist and military youth movement of Revisionist Zionism (q.v.), founded by

Vladimir Jabotinski and Joseph Trumpeldor, a one-armed Jewish hero of the Russo-Japanese war.

of this covenant Abraham circumcised himself and all the male members of his household. At eight days old each Jewish male undergoes circumcision (*brit*) and enters into this covenant agreement between God and the descendants of Abraham, who are his chosen people. By this covenant, God promises that the Jews will be his people above all others, provided that they obey him and keep the Torah (q.v.), the Law of Moses. They must not worship any other God but him and must obey his commandments absolutely.

Dhimmi 'From the Arabic *Dhimma*, which was a pact between the Muslim state and in Europe the Jews and Christians living under Muslim rule, and in the Middle East and Asia the Hindus, Zoroastrians and Buddhists. They were afforded full religious liberty and were given military and civil protection, on condition that they respected the supremacy of Islam. The people who came under the *Dhimma* were known as *dhimmis* which by extension came to mean 'protected minorities'.

Diaspora This is the name given to the dispersal of the Jewish people throughout the world and to those Jews who live outside the Land of Israel.

Dinar (*Greek: denarion*). The unit of gold currency used by Muslims.

Dirham (from Greek: *drakme*). The unit of silver currency used by Muslims until the Mongol conquests.

Emir (Turkish). *See* Amir.

Fatah (Arabic: opening). Refers to the conquest of Mecca by Mohammad and to the Islamisation of any city or country. Yasir Arafat has called his party Fatah, even though it is a secular party. It seems that he wanted to reassure the religious Arab states of the Gulf that he would not adopt foreign ideologies like communism or socialism in his struggle to return the Palestinian people to their homeland. Fatah is the largest party in the Palestine Liberation Organisation (q.v.).

Faqih (Arabic). A Muslim jurisprudent, who is deemed capable and sufficiently knowledgeable to give a *fatwa* (q.v.).

Fatwa (Arabic). An opinion or a ruling given by an appropriate Islamic authority that interprets a point of Holy Law in a way which will be binding on those Muslims who accept him as their guide.

Fedayeen. *See Fida'i.*

Feudalism A defensive network of dependent loyalties that grew up in Europe during the Dark Ages. A man would bind himself to his Lord and both would mutually swear to be loyal to one another: the vassal (q.v.) promised to fight for his lord's rights and to protect his patrimony and honour, and in his turn the Lord promised to defend his vassal from a mutual enemy. In his turn, the lord would have a more powerful overlord, and so on. At the head of this feudal pyramid was the King.

Fida'i (Arabic plural: *fedayeen*). Literally 'one who sacrifices himself' and by extension a freedom fighter, who is prepared to risk his life for the sake of the people.

Fief This was the name given to the land owned as patrimony and which was at the heart of feudalism (q.v.). A vassal held his patrimony or fief from his lord who was duty-bound to come to his aid if it was attacked, just as the vassal was bound to fight for the fief of his lord.

Fundamentalism This word is generally applied to any extreme religious movement, but I think that this is misleading. When Christians use the term 'fundamentalism' they mean a movement that is going back to the fundamentals of the faith and to what they see as the spirit of the gospels. Such Christian movements tend to be very literal-minded and aggressive in their interpretation of the Bible. This aggressive literalness is certainly manifest in some extreme Jewish movements today. Christian fundamentalists tend to be backward-looking and to cast off what they see as later accretions of the faith, and this too could be true of some Jewish 'fundamentalists' in Israel. But it is not true of modern extreme Islamic groups and to use the word 'fundamentalist' of the Iranian revolution raises certain expectations in a Western environment that are not applicable.

Gospels These are four documents that were chosen by the Church to be authentic accounts of the life and teachings of Jesus Christ. The earliest, that attributed to St Mark, was written about CE 70, some fifty years after the death of Christ. The gospels of Matthew and Luke were written during the 80s and that of St John in about CE 100. The gospels reflect the teaching of St Paul, which was radically different from the teaching of the apostles, who had intended to remain fully observant Jews and saw Christianity as a Jewish sect.

Goyim (Hebrew, singular: *goy*). The name given by Jews to denote non-Jews or Gentiles.

Gush Emunim (Hebrew: the Bloc of the Faithful). A religious–political group formed in Israel in 1974 to Judaise the Occupied Territories by means of illegal settlement there and by encouraging Jews in the diaspora (q.v.) to emigrate to Israel and join them in Gaza or the West Bank.

Hadith (Arabic). A tradition handed down orally through a reliable train of sources relating a saying or deed of the Prophet Mohammad for the guidance of Muslims. These were gathered together during the ninth century. The whole corpus of the *hadith* is one of the major sources of Islamic law.

Haganah (Hebrew: defence). The Jewish Defence Force formed in Palestine to protect Zionist interests under the British Mandate, which became the base of the Israeli army after the State of Israel was established in 1948.

Hajj, hajji (Arabic: pilgrimage). The pilgrimage to Mecca, Arafat and Mina which was originally made by pagan Arabs to pagan shrines there in pre-Islamic Arabia. Mohammad reinterpreted these ancient pagan rites and made the *hajj* one of the five pillars of Islam, an obligatory practice for all Muslims. Every Muslim is required to make the pilgrimage to Mecca at least once in his or her lifetime if circumstances permit. A Muslim who has made the *hajj* is given the title *hajji*.

Hajji. *See Hajj.*

Halakah (Hebrew). The part of the Talmud (q.v.) concerned with legal matters, as opposed to the Haggadah, which comprises tales and folklore.

Hanif (Arabic: infidel). This was the derisive name given by the pagan Arabs in pre-Islamic Arabia to the Arabs who had become monotheists, worshipping only Allah, and who claimed that he was the God of the Jews and the Christians.

Herut (Hebrew: freedom). A political party founded in 1948 by Menachem Begin and the Irgun to perpetuate the ideals of Vladimir Jabotinski and the Revisionist Zionists (q.v.). Herut is the major party in the right-wing bloc that was formed later and which is called the Likud.

Hidden Imam In what is known as Twelver Shiism, the Hidden Imam is an Islamic Messiah figure. The Shiites would not accept the political authority of the caliphs (q.v.) but took as their leader (imam) the direct descendants of Ali, the cousin and son-in-law of the Prophet Mohammad. There were twelve of these imams and because they set up a rival dynasty they were often murdered by the caliphs of the Sunni tradition (q.v.). Eventually the Twelfth Imam went into hiding in 874 and died in 920. After that there were no more direct descendants of Ali and the Shiites claim that there can be no more legitimate authority in the absence of this Hidden Imam, who they say is in a state of 'occultation'. They believe that one day the Twelfth Imam will return and inaugurate a golden age.

Hijra (Arabic: migration). Often misspelt *hegira*. The migration of Mohammad from Mecca to Medina in 622. It has been used by later Muslims to describe a migration from the community in order to live a more truly Islamic life. Such a *hijra* is seen as a positive protest and a move for revolution and reform.

Holy, holiness This is a crucial term. When we use the word 'holy' today we usually refer to a state of spiritual purity, but the word has more concrete meanings in all three traditions.

(1) In Judaism, the notion of holiness is bound up with the notion of a physical separation: the holiness of things is celebrated by setting them apart from one another: sabbath from the rest of the week, milk from meat and Jews from Gentiles. The Holy Land is the place where the Jews must live as a holy or consecrated people, set apart (Exodus 19:6). Today radical religious Jews in Israel claim that the Jews must be a nation 'which dwells alone' and some even want to purge the land of Gentile presence.

(2) In medieval Christianity holiness was popularly conceived as a tangible power inherent in certain physical objects and was, therefore, intensely localised. Relics of the saints provided a physical link with heaven. The Holy Land was the most holy relic of all because it was saturated with this holy force by means of its physical connection with Jesus.

(3) In Islam there would be no such veneration of anything physical, because this would be considered idolatry. But the 'sanctuary' of Mecca is a consecrated area and, as in Judaism, this means that it is set apart. Certain things are forbidden (Arabic: *haram*), notably violence, and there must be no non-Muslims in Mecca and its environs.

House of Islam (translation of the Arabic: *Dar al-Islam*). This is the name given to Muslim territory in the Islamic Holy Law.

House of War (translation of the Arabic: *Dar al-Harb*). In the Islamic Holy Law this describes the non-Muslim world beyond the Islamic frontiers. In Islamic legal theory, there must be a perpetual state of war until all the world submits to the supremacy of Islam and the true religion. Until that time, the state of war may be suspended by truces, but cannot be ended by a permanent peace. In practice, Muslims abandoned this notion in the eighth century, accepted that Islam had reached its territorial limits and had normal trading and political connections with the non-Muslim countries.

Ijtihad (Arabic). Literally, like many Muslim terms, this means 'exerting oneself'. Later it came to mean 'individual reasoning' about the revelation of God to Mohammad. One who was expert enough to develop Islamic tradition by means of individual reasoning was called a *mujtahid* (q.v.) (one who exercises *ijtihad*). Many Muslims believe that only the great masters of early Islam had had the right to use *ijtihad* and that after the ninth century the gates of *ijtihad* had been closed. Muslim scholars could only reason by analogy when applying Islamic law to contemporary conditions. In Iran, however, another Muslim tradition *does* allow *mujtahids* of sufficient standing to exercise individual reasoning and to make a contribution to the Islamic tradition.

Imam (Arabic: leader). Generally the word is used to describe any leader of the Muslim community or a Muslim who leads the prayers in the mosque. In the Shiah (q.v.) the word was applied to the descendants of Ali, whom Shiites believed to be the only legitimate rulers of Muslims; Shiites also expect the Hidden Imam (q.v.) to return as an Islamic Messiah to inaugurate a golden age. Consequently the term 'imam' has much greater force and authority.

Indulgence This is a complex Catholic practice that was important during the Crusades. By performing certain actions, the popes granted Catholics a means of remitting the temporal punishment they must endure for their sins in this world and also in purgatory, where they purge themselves of their sins before getting into heaven. A pilgrimage to Jerusalem or Compostela or, later, a Crusade ensured that a Christian was absolved of all the punishment that was awaiting him, and if he died during it he would go straight to heaven.

Irgun The underground military and terrorist wing of the Revisionist Zionists (q.v.) which operated in Palestine and in Israel from 1931 to 1949, led by Menachem Begin, who became Prime Minister of Israel in 1977.

Islam The correct name for the religion of Muslims. It means submission to God and a Muslim is 'one who submits'.

Jerusalem This city is holy to all three religions:

(1) When King David conquered this Jebusite city in about 1000 BCE he wanted to make it the centre of his kingdom and of Judaism; to house the Presence of God, David's son Solomon built a temple, which was destroyed by the Babylonians in 589. But Jews continued to pray facing Jerusalem, wherever they happened to be, and the city became central to the Jewish identity.

(2) The city was holy to Christians because it was the scene of the death and resurrection of Christ and housed the holiest relic of all, the tomb of Christ (*see* Holy). Although Jerusalem was always venerated by the Greek Orthodox and by oriental Christians, the Western Christians had the most fanatical devotion to the Holy City because of their physical interpretation of holiness. Protestants abolished practices like pilgrimages to shrines and relics and would regard excessive devotion to Jerusalem, as expressed by the Crusaders, to be idolatry.

(3) In Islam, Jerusalem is holy because Muslims believe that in the early days of his prophetic period Mohammad travelled there by night in a mystical flight. He alighted on the Temple Mount and thence ascended to heaven where he spoke to Jesus and Moses. The vision expresses the connection between Islam and the two older religions, and the two mosques that commemorate this event are built on the site of the Jewish Temple, which is regarded by Muslims as the third holiest place in the Islamic world, after Mecca and Medina.

Jihad (Arabic: striving, effort). Usually used in this book to mean 'holy war' against unbelievers or against Christians, who oppressed and persecuted Muslims in their Crusades.

Ka'aba (Arabic). The most holy shrine in Islam. It is a small square building in the centre of the Great Mosque in Mecca, which Muslims believe to have been built by Abraham and his son Ishmael to the One God. From Ka'aba we get our word 'cube'.

Kaballah (Hebrew). The system of Jewish mysticism.

Kibbutz (from the Hebrew *kibbush*: conquest). A Jewish agricultural settlement where property is owned in common.

Koran (Arabic: recitation). The name given to the holy book of Islam, which Muslims believe was dictated to Mohammad by God himself. Mohammad, who could not write, was told to recite the words after the divine voice. These utterances were written down by those of his disciples who were literate, and were collected by his disciples by the middle of the seventh century. As the revelations came to Mohammad, he passed them on to the Muslims, who had to learn them by heart and place each new revelation in the place that the Prophet prescribed.

Labour Zionism This is the school of Zionists led by David Ben Gurion, who became the first Prime Minister of Israel in 1948. Labour held undisputed sway in Israel until 1977, when the right-wing Zionists led by Menachem Begin came into power. Labour Zionists were secular socialists, who originally believed that they would create a model, equal society in Palestine. They also believed that labour (*avodah*) on the land of Israel would save the Jews from the weakness they had acquired in the diaspora and that this labour would give the Jews a claim to Palestine. Hence they called their colonising effort the 'Conquest of Labour'.

Last Emperor This was the Emperor whose coming was predicted by the Sibylline prophets (q.v.) and who was eagerly expected by lay Christians in Europe during the Middle Ages. This Emperor was expected to unite the East and West, slaughter the enemies of Christ, march to Jerusalem to be crowned, inspire the coming of

Antichrist (q.v.) and so inaugurate the Last Days and the glorious era of the Second Coming of Christ. In effect this hoped-for Emperor was a Christian Messiah. (*See* Messiah and Hidden Imam.)

Lehi (Hebrew; an acronym for *Lohana Herut Israel*: Fighters for the Freedom of Israel). This was a terrorist, militant Zionist organisation that fought the British and the Arabs in Palestine before the establishment of the State of Israel. It was founded by Avraham Stern and was called the 'Stern Gang' by the British. Later it was led by Yitzhak Shamir, who became Prime Minister of Israel in 1986.

Madrassa (Arabic). A seminary or college of Islamic learning, which is often, though not always, attached to a mosque.

Mamluk (Arabic: literally 'owned'). The word was at first used to describe a white slave who had been trained to be a soldier. This was a way for slaves to acquire freedom and eminence in the Muslim world. Some Mamluks, who converted to Islam and won their freedom, even became military commanders and founded dynasties. The most famous of these Mamluk dynasties was that founded in Egypt in 1250 at the time of the Seventh Crusade, which eventually drove the Christians from the Crusader states. The Mamluk dynasty survived until 1517.

Marranos The name given to the Spanish Jews who converted to Christianity under pressure and whom many Spaniards believed were practising their old religion secretly.

Martyr (Greek: witness). In the early Church a martyr was seen as witnessing to Christ in a pagan world by dying for him. The Arabic *shaheed* (martyr) also has this connotation of witnessing to the truth and power of the faith. In all three religions of Judaism, Christianity and Islam, martyrs who voluntarily expose themselves to the dangers of death for the sake of their religion are venerated. In the holy wars of all three religions, people who die in the struggle are venerated as martyrs, even though they have met their deaths by fighting other people aggressively.

Messiah (Hebrew: anointed one). The Messiah foretold by the prophets was expected to deliver the Jewish people from their suffering and oppression at the hands of the Gentiles. He would also ensure the final triumph of the chosen people, establish them gloriously in Jerusalem and vanquish their foes. All the Gentile nations would be forced to pay tribute to the Jewish people and a golden age of cosmic peace and harmony would begin. It must be emphasised that there was no thought of the Messiah's being a divine being. St Paul taught his converts that Jesus had been the Messiah (Christ is simply a Greek translation of the Hebrew: *Messhiach*), and later Christians developed the belief that Jesus had been God and assumed that the Jews had expected him to be the Son of God. But in the Jewish scriptures the phrase 'Son of God' means a perfectly normal human being, who is very close to God. Such a man was King David, whom God had anointed as king. Many Jews believed that the Messiah would be a descendant of King David at the time of Christ. Today the Jews who are expecting the imminent advent of the Messiah and the redemption (q.v.) are not expecting a divine being to arrive, though some of them are expecting catastrophic and miraculous events to accompany him.

Mizrachi (abbreviation of Hebrew *Mercaz Ruhani*: spiritual centre). This was a religious Zionist movement whose members wanted to form a religious state in Israel, rebuild the Temple and rule according to the Torah (q.v.). They did not want a secular democracy run on modern lines.

Mohammadanism This is the name that Christians and Western people often incorrectly give to Islam. Similarly they call Muslims 'Mohammadans'. This habit is offensive to Muslims, because it implies that Mohammad is the equivalent of Christ in Christianity. Medieval Christians believed that Muslims thought that

Mohammad was pretending to be God, like Christ, but this idea would have been considered blasphemous by Mohammad, who never claimed to be anything other than a normal, albeit privileged human being. Further, the word 'Mohammadan' was originally always used in a pejorative sense in the polemic against Islam, which produced a very distorted image of the religion in the West. Consequently, it has the same offensive connotations for Muslims as Yid or Zhid has for Jews.

Monotheism The worship of only one God, the central tenet of Judaism, Christianity and Islam.

Moriscos The name given to the Spanish Muslims (Moors) who converted to Christianity and were believed to be practising their former religion in secret.

Mortal sin This is a Catholic concept. Catholics have traditionally believed that there are two types of sins committed by Christians: mortal and venial. A venial sin is a lesser sin, like telling a lie, and it can be forgiven by means of a prayer of contrition. A mortal sin is a major sin like murder or adultery. As its name suggests it causes the death of grace in the soul, because it severs a Christian from God absolutely and can only be forgiven by means of the sacrament of penance, when a Catholic confesses it to a priest and receives absolution from God. If a person dies with unconfessed mortal sin on his soul, he or she will go to hell for all eternity. To qualify as mortal, the sin must be a grave one and must be committed knowingly and deliberately and with a clear knowledge of the spiritual consequences.

Mufti (Arabic). An expert in Islamic law. Unlike the Qadi (q.v.) his status is usually private and voluntary rather than an official appointment. It is bestowed on a Muslim who is renowned for his scholarship and personal reputation. That is what was scandalous about the British promotion of Hajji al-Husseini during the Mandate.

Mujahid (Arabic, plural: *mujahideen*). A freedom fighter who takes part in a *jihad* or struggle for the liberation of his people from tyranny and persecution. Not to be confused with:

Mujtahid (Arabic, plural: *mujtahideen*). An Islamic scholar qualified to exercise *ijtihad* (q.v.) or independent judgement in all matters pertaining to Islamic practice. This means he can issue authoritative opinions on the basis of his knowledge of Islamic law and this can also be a political judgement. A *mujtahid* is not supposed to issue judgements relating to doctrine or theological belief, which is considered a private matter for each Muslim, provided, of course, that he acknowledges the two articles of the Muslim creed: There is only One God and Mohammad was his Prophet.

Mullah (Arabic). An Islamic preacher.

Munafiq (Arabic: hypocrite; plural: *munafiqeen*). In the Koran (q.v.) the word refers to people in Medina who had converted to Islam, but were not totally committed to the faith and worked to undermine Mohammad's political supremacy. It has since been applied to people who only pretend to believe in Islam, or who pay lip-service to Islam while denying essential principles like justice and equality. Hence too, by extension, the term can mean any bad ruler who denies Muslims human rights that are their due and who is cruel and oppressive.

Muslim calendar This is strictly lunar and each year consists of 354 days. The months do not therefore correspond to fixed seasons. The Muslim era began on the first day of the year in which Mohammad migrated from Mecca to Medina, in *our* year 622.

Oley (Hebrew: pilgrim; plural: *olim*). This is the word applied by Zionists to Jews who emigrated to the Land of Israel and it is still used of immigrants today. The word *olim* is a near mystic term supercharged with emotion, ancient faith and historical associations. Besides meaning 'those who ascend', referring to the ascension of the Temple Mount, it also means to rise above earthly desire to a nobler state of mind. Compare *Aliyah, Chalutz* (q.v.).

Original sin This is a doctrine peculiar to Christianity and is not part of either the Jewish or the Muslim faiths. It teaches that when Adam and Eve sinned in the Garden of Eden all their descendants were doomed to hell and perpetual estrangement from God. Furthermore, man had 'fallen' from a state of primeval innocence and was permanently impaired, spiritually and even physically. Fortunately God promised that he would send a redeemer, who was of course Jesus Christ. Jesus rescued men from this separation from God, provided that they entered into his death and resurrection by means of the sacrament of baptism. But even after baptism Christians feel the effects of Original Sin. They still get sick and die, which was not part of God's original intention, and, however hard they try, they still have a tendency to go on committing sins. The state of Original Sin, therefore, means a displacement from one's best self, an exile from God and a state of weakness and disability.

Orthodox (Greek: the right opinion). During the first five centuries of Christianity there were many disputes about doctrine, particularly about the very difficult question of how Jesus could have been both God and man. In the Greek world particularly, which had always loved debating this kind of philosophical nicety, the argument was very acrimonious and many teachers and their followers were branded as 'heretics', who believed a false doctrine, as opposed to the Christians who remained loyal to the teaching of the official Church, which alone had the 'right opinion'. The Greek Church today still calls itself the Orthodox Church, to distinguish it from those Churches which have abandoned the correct interpretation of the faith. In Judaism the term is used to distinguish those Jews who practise a strict and literal interpretation of the Torah (q.v.), as compared to Conservative or Reform Judaism (q.v.), which have both modified the law to meet modern conditions. It must be stressed, however, that Orthodox Jews distinguish themselves from the Conservative and Reform Jews solely in matters of practice and not, like the Christians, in matters of belief.

Palestine Liberation Organisation, the PLO This is the organisation led by Yasir Arafat to restore the Palestinian people to their homeland. It is an alliance of several parties, the largest of which is Arafat's Fatah. The PLO has a charter which declares that Judaism is not a nation but a religion and that the enemy of the Palestinians is not Judaism but Zionism. The PLO is a secular movement, which is working to establish an independent Palestinian secular state in which Jews, Christians and Muslims will all enjoy equal rights. Some extreme members of the PLO have formed terrorist groups.

Pentateuch (Greek). The first five books of the Bible (Genesis, Exodus, Leviticus, Numbers and Deuteronomy), which Jews also call the Torah (q.v.), because it contains the Law of Moses.

Pillars (translation of Arabic *rukn*). These are the five practices which every Muslim must perform. First he or she has to make profession of the Muslim faith, which is expressed in the simple proclamation: There is only One God and Mohammad was his Prophet. The other 'pillars' are prayer at the appointed times, almsgiving, fasting during the Muslim month of Ramadan (q.v.) and the *hajj* (q.v.), or the pilgrimage to Mecca. It will be clear that like Judaism Islam is a religion of practice rather than a religion of theological orthodoxy, like Christianity, which requires assent to many quite abstruse *doctrines* but does not have a codified law that is comparable to either the Torah or the *Sharia* (q.v.).

Pogrom (Russian: destruction). An organised massacre which is directed towards the annihilation of any one body or class of people, particularly Jewish communities.

Polytheism The worship of many gods.

Prophet (Latin: to speak on behalf of). We often use this word to mean a person who foretells the future. But in all three religions of Judaism, Christianity and Islam that is not a prophet's first task, though predicting future events may be one of his functions. A prophet is a person who speaks on behalf of God; God has communicated his will to him directly. He is an intermediary between God and man, who will correct, guide and lead a community to a closer approximation of God's will.

Qadi (Arabic). A judge who officially administers the *Sharia* (q.v.).

Rabbi (Hebrew: master). A Jewish religious teacher.

Ramadan (Arabic). During this month in the Muslim calendar (q.v.) Muslims fast, and keeping Ramadan is one of the five pillars of Islam (q.v.). It is equivalent to the Christian Lent, but with one crucial difference. In Lent, the emphasis is on suffering and penance. A Christian who fasts during the six weeks leading up to Easter is particularly mindful of the suffering of Christ on Good Friday and often wants to suffer 'with' him. But Ramadan is not meant to be a suffering experience. Muslims rise before dawn and eat a large meal that will get them through the day. After sundown they eat another large meal. Sometimes people put on weight during Ramadan! The point of the fast is not penance but a means of remembering God in a special way each year.

Redemption Christians call the death and resurrection of Christ their redemption because they believe that by this means he saved the world. When Jewish people speak of redemption, they usually refer to the coming of the Messiah (q.v.) and the dawning of a new era of peace and harmony, when God's chosen people will live in their land according to the Torah (q.v.), and the whole world will acknowledge the truth of Judaism, and be redeemed through this recognition.

Reform Judaism has modified the Law or Torah (q.v.) to meet modern conditions.

Revisionist Zionism This was an ideology propounded by Vladimir Jabotinski, which broke away from Labour Zionism (q.v.). Revisionists denied that peaceful colonising would be sufficient to obtain Palestine for the Jews and advocated a military struggle. Revisionists also tended towards an extreme nationalism and were affected by the racial chauvinism that had filled Europe at the end of the nineteenth century. Jabotinski believed that Jews could only fulfil themselves if they had a land of their own and kept their race pure by not mixing with other nations. Menachem Begin, who became Prime Minister in 1977, was an ardent disciple of Jabotinski; and President Yitzhak Shamir, who became Prime Minister in 1986, was also a Revisionist.

Rum (Arabic: Rome). Commonly used by Muslims in the crusading period to refer to Christian Byzantium, which was the Eastern part of the old Roman empire. It was also the name given to the territory in Anatolia and Asia Minor which the Seljuk Turks had conquered from Byzantium during the late eleventh century, and the Turkish Sultan was called the Sultan of Rum.

Sabra (Hebrew). The name given to Jewish Israelis who are born in the Land of Israel. Literally it is the name of an Israeli fruit, which is tough and prickly on the outside but soft and sweet inside, and this is meant to be an image of the Sabra personality.

Salvation This word has been used in this book to describe those events in which God's elect are rescued from an impending and apparently inevitable destruction by a sudden reversal of fortune that seems miraculous and can only be explained by positing divine intervention. This experience has befallen Jews, Christians and Muslims throughout the story of the holy wars.

Saracen (Greek *Sarakenoi* and Latin *Saracenus*: the people that dwells in tents). This was the word used by Greeks and Romans and by Greek and Latin Christians to describe the people of the Arabian peninsula, who lived in tents that were much the same as those still used by Bedouin today. The 'Saracens' never referred to themselves like this: they just called themselves 'Arabs', but in the Christian world the name stuck, long after the 'Saracens' had stopped living in tents. The word came to be used by Western people to describe all Muslim people, no matter what their ethnic origin, until relatively recently. Arabs, Berbers, Turks and Kurds were all called 'Saracens'.

Sephardi A Jewish tradition that originated in Spain. In Israel today the term is usually used to describe the Jews who came to Israel from the Arab countries after 1948. The Ashkenazi (q.v.) tended to look down on the Sephardi Jews and reduced them in effect to the status of second-class citizens, which the Sephardi bitterly resent.

Sheikh (Arabic: old man, elder). The word is used in a number of contexts. A sheikh can be a religious leader, a chief of a tribe or a man who has won respect and renown in the community.

Sharia (Arabic). The Holy Law of Islam, which was compiled and codified by the great Muslim jurists of the eighth and ninth centuries, who applied the principles of the Koran and the *hadith* (q.v.) to the smallest details of everyday life, and which was flexible enough to give a distinct identity to Muslims all over the Islamic empire. Where the West inherited Roman law as a secular legal system, Islam developed its own code of religious law, so that there is no equivalent of either the *Sharia* or the Torah (q.v.) in Christianity. The word *Sharia* means the road or way to a watering hole, which must always be followed. In a desert society such a path would be a literal life-line, and deviation from it was possibly dangerous.

Shiah (Arabic, *Shiah i-Ali*: the partisans of Ali). Originally this was a political movement of a minority of Muslims in the community, who believed that the Prophet Mohammad had wanted Ali ibn Talid, his cousin and son-in-law, to succeed him instead of Abu Bakr, the first Caliph. After the period of the four rightly guided caliphs (*see* Caliph), the descendants of Ali offered an alternative to the rule of the caliphs, who had ceased to govern according to Islamic principles. In claiming to be the Imam (leader) of the Muslims they were accepting a revolutionary responsibility. After Ali's line died out, most Shiites declared that the Twelfth and last Imam would return as a Messiah. (*See* Hidden Imam.) Shiites developed different devotions and religious practices from the Sunni Muslims (q.v.) but there is no difference in the essentials of the faith in the two traditions: Shiites and Sunnis all uphold the five pillars of Islam (q.v.).

Shtetl A small Jewish town or settlement in Russia and Eastern Europe.

Sibylline oracles Hellenistic Judaism produced books, preserved in Rome, which claimed to be the utterances of inspired prophetesses. Christian Sibylline texts began to appear in the fourth century and were believed by many Christians in Europe to be gospel truth. They foretold the coming of an emperor, who would unite the East and West, slaughter the enemies of God and be crowned in Jerusalem (q.v.). Antichrist (q.v.) would then appear, the Archangel Michael would destroy him and Christ would return in glory.

Sultan (Arabic: originally government). The Sultan wielded military and political authority over a group of Muslims, but theoretically he was subservient to the Caliph (q.v.).

Sunna, Sunni (Arabic, *Sunna*: the way). The Sunna is the way of the Prophet Mohammad and includes everything he said, did, caused, ordered or allowed to happen. A Sunni is a Muslim who follows this way. The word is, however, most commonly used to distinguish the majority of Muslims from the Shiite minority. *See* Shiah.

Suzerain A medieval feudal overlord. *See* Feudalism, Fief.

Talmud The body of Jewish civil, ceremonial and traditional law, which developed from the Torah (q.v.) and from the oral and written commentary upon it by the great rabbis.

Taqlid (Arabic: emulation). This Muslim practice teaches the faithful to emulate the *mujtahideen* in their observance of the Holy Law of Islam, because they are not equipped to do this themselves. They are not professionally intent on the study of the law and cannot appreciate all the complexities involved. There are Muslims who object to this and say that it is an unIslamic practice because it creates an elite. *See* Ayatollah, *Ijtihad, Mujtahid.*

Tfillin Small leather boxes containing words from the Torah (q.v.) which proclaim the essence of the Jewish faith: 'Hear, O Israel, the Lord is our God, the Lord is one.' In the Torah, Jews are commanded to bind these words to themselves, and during prayer a Jewish man will attach the *tfillin* to his arm and forehead with leather thongs (Deuteronomy 6:4–9).

Torah (Hebrew: the Law). The whole of the Torah comprises the 613 commandments that bind observant Jews. The commandments regulate the conduct of everyday life, yet they are felt not as a burden but as a privilege and a joy. Jews believe that the Torah enables people to live a rich and healthy life, because it is the expression of the will of God. On Simchat Torah, which celebrates the gift of the law to the Jewish people, Orthodox Jews dance joyfully, holding the Torah scrolls aloft. The Psalms in particular dwell on the precious gift of the Torah. There is no equivalent to the Torah in Christianity.

Ulema (Arabic, singular: *alem*). The learned men who devote their lives to the study of the Holy Law of Islam.

Umma (Arabic). The community of Islam.

Vassal In the feudal system, the term referred to one who held his land from his lord on condition that he remained faithful to his lord's interests. (*See* Fief.) A vassal was bound to his lord in a relationship that was as strong as his relationship with his kin.

Vizier (From the Arabic *wazir*: minister). Under the Shiite dynasty in Egypt, conquered by Saladin and Shirkuh, the Vizier was in charge of the administration of the realm, under the nominal authority of the Caliph (q.v.). When Saladin abolished the caliphate, the Vizier became the supreme power in Egypt.

Yahweh This is the name that God gives to himself in the Jewish scriptures. When Moses asks him for his name, God replies: '*Ehyeh esher ehyeh*: I am what I am' (Exodus 3:14). God is refusing to reveal his name because he can never be defined or summed up by man. On this principle, devout Jews never mention this name of God. In English versions of the Bible, Christians often translate Yahweh as 'Jehovah'.

Yeshiva An institute for Talmudic learning.

Yishuv The Jewish community in Palestine, before the creation of the State of Israel in 1948.

Yom Kippur The Jewish Day of Atonement.

Zion Zion was the name of the ancient citadel of the Jebusites in Jerusalem (q.v.), which King David conquered from them in about 1000 BCE. It is often used as a synonym for Jerusalem. The Zionists, who wanted to return the Jewish people to the land of their fathers, naturally looked back to the old religious dream of a Jewish return to Zion.

Zemiros Religious Hebrew songs sung at meals on feast days and on the sabbath.

Zoroastrianism The official religion of the Persians before they converted to Islam. It was a dualistic religion, in which a good spirit fought an evil spirit in a constant battle.

Bibliography

Abelard, Peter, with Heloise *The Letters of Abelard and Heloise*, ed. and trans. Betty Radice (London, 1974).

Adams, Henry, *Mont Saint-Michel and Chartres* (London, 1986 edn).

Akhari, Shahrough, 'Shariati's Social Thought', in Nikkie R. Keddie (ed.), *Religion and Politics in Iran: Shiism from Quietism to Revolution* (New Haven and London, 1983).

Arberry, A. J., *Sufism: An Account of the Mystics of Islam* (London, 1950).

Armstrong, Karen, *The First Christian, St Paul's Impact on Christianity* (London, 1983).

  The Gospel According to Women, Christianity's Creation of the Sex War in the West (London, 1986).

Auerbach, Erich, *Mimesis: The Representation of Reality in Western Literature* (New Jersey, 1953).

Avineri, Schlomo, *The Makings of Modern Zionism* (London and New York, 1981).

Avishai, Bernard, *The Tragedy of Zionism: Revolution and Democracy in the Land of Israel* (New York, 1985).

Avnery, Uri, *My Friend, the Enemy* (London, 1986).

Bailey, D. S., *The Man–Woman Relation in Christian Thought* (London, 1959).

Bakhash, Shaul, *The Reign of the Ayatollahs: Iran and the Islamic Revolution* (London, 1986).

Balard, Michel, 'Des châteaux forts en Palestine', *L'Histoire*, 47 (Paris, 1982).

Baldwin, Marshall Whithed, *Raymund III of Tripolis and the Fall of Jerusalem* (Princeton, 1936).

Barkun, Michael, *Disaster and the Millennium* (New Haven and London, 1974).

Beeman, William O., 'Images of the Great Satan: Representations of the United States in the Iranian Revolution', in Nikkie R. Keddie (ed.), *Religion and Politics in Iran: Shiism from Quietism to Revolution* (New Haven and London, 1983).

Bellow, Saul, *To Jerusalem and Back: A Personal Account* (London and New York, 1976).

Ben-Ami, Aharon, *Social Change in a Hostile Environment: The Crusaders' Kingdom of Jerusalem* (New Haven, 1969).

Bendt, Ingela, and Downing, James, *We Shall Return, Women of Palestine* (London, 1982).

Berque, Jacques, *Arab Rebirth: Pain and Ecstasy*, trans. Quinton Hoare (London, 1983).

Boase, Roger, *The Origin and Meaning of Courtly Love: A Critical Study of European Scholarship* (Manchester, 1977).

Brenner, Lenni, *The Iron Wall: Zionist Revisionism from Jabotinski to Shamir* (London, 1984).

Bresc-Bautier, Geneviève, 'L'An prochain au Saint-Sépulchre!', *L'Histoire*, 47 (Paris, 1982).

Broughton, B. B., *The Legends of Richard I, Coeur de Lion: A Study of Sources and Variations to the Year 1600* (The Hague and Paris, 1966).

Brown, Peter, *Religion and Society in the Age of St Augustine* (London, 1972).
   The Making of Late Antiquity (Cambridge, Mass., and London, 1978).
   The Cult of the Saints: Its Rise and Function in Classical Antiquity (London, 1982).

Buber, Martin, *On Zion: The History of an Idea* (London, 1973).

Burman, Edward, *The Assassins: Holy Killers of Islam* (London, 1987).

Burns, Robert Ignatius, SJ, *Islam Under the Crusaders: Colonial Survival in the Thirteenth-Century Kingdom of Valencia* (New Jersey, 1973).

Burr, G. L., 'The Year 1000 and the Antecedents of the Crusades', *American Historical Review*, 6 (1900).

Calkins, Robert G., *Monuments of Medieval Art* (Ithaca and London, 1979).

Carlyle, Thomas, *On Heroes and Hero-Worship* (London, 1841).

Chrétien of Troyes, *Arthurian Romances*, ed. and trans. W. W. Comfort (London, 1975).

Cobban, Helena, *The Making of Modern Lebanon* (London, 1985).

Cohen, A., *Everyman's Talmud* (New York, 1975).

Cohen, Geula, *Woman of Violence: Memoirs of a Young Terrorist, 1943–1948* (London, 1966).

Cohn, Norman, *The Pursuit of the Millennium: Revolutionary Millenarians and Mystical Anarchists of the Middle Ages* (London, 1957, 1970).
   Europe's Inner Demons (London, 1975).

Collins, Roger, *Early Medieval Spain: Unity in Diversity, 400–1000* (London, 1983).

Comnena, Anna, *Alexiad*, 3 vols, ed. and trans. B. Leib (Paris, 1937–45).

Constable, Giles, 'The Second Crusade as Seen by Contemporaries', *Traditio*, 9 (1953).

Contamine, Philippe, 'Une Guerre pour le Royaume des cieux', *L'Histoire*, 47 (Paris, 1982).

Cowdrey, H. E. J., 'Pope Urban's Preaching of the First Crusade', *History*, 55 (1970).
   'The Peace and the Truce of God in the Eleventh Century', *Past and Present*, 46 (1970).

Daniel, Norman, *Islam and the West: The Making of an Image* (Edinburgh, 1960).
   The Arabs and Medieval Europe (London and Beirut, 1975).

Daniel-Rops, Henri, *Bernard of Clairvaux*, trans. Elizabeth Abbot (New York and London, 1964).

Duby, Georges, 'Les Pauvres des campagnes dans l'Occident médiéval jusqu'au XIII siècle', *Revue d'Histoire de l'Église de France*, 52 (Paris, 1966).
   The Chivalrous Society, trans. C. Postan (London, 1977).
   The Knight, the Lady and the Priest: The Making of Modern Marriage in Medieval France, trans. Barbara Bray (London and New York, 1983, 1985).

Dufourcq, Charles-Emmanuel, 'L'Impossible Voyage en terre sainte', *L'Histoire*, 47 (Paris, 1982).

Duncalf, F., 'The Peasants Crusade', *American Historical Review*, 26 (1921).

EAFOD and AJAZ (eds), *Judaism or Zionism: What Difference for the Middle East?* (London, 1986).

Edbury, P. W. (ed.), *Crusade and Settlement* (London, 1985).

Eidelberg, Shlomo (trans. and ed.), *The Jews and the Crusaders: The Hebrew Chronicles of the First and Second Crusades* (Wisconsin and London, 1977).

Einard and Notger the Stammerer, *Two Lives of Charlemagne*, trans. and ed. Lewis Thorpe (London, 1969).

El-Asmar, Fouzi, *Through the Hebrew Looking Glass: Arab Stereotypes in Children's Literature* (London and Vermont, 1986).

Eliot, George, *Daniel Deronda* (London, Panther edn, 1970).

Elon, Amos, *The Israelis, Founders and Sons* (2nd edn, London and Tel Aviv, 1981, 1983).

Evans, G. R., *The Mind of Bernard of Clairvaux* (London, 1983).

Falk, Richard, 'Iran: Human Rights and International Law', in D. H. Albert (ed.), *Tell the American People: Perspectives on the Iranian Revolution* (Philadelphia, 1980).

Favier, Jean, 'Les Templiers, ou l'échec des banquiers de la croisade', *L'Histoire*, 47 (Paris, 1982).

Finucane, Ronald C., *Miracles and Pilgrims: Popular Beliefs in Medieval Europe* (London, 1977).

Fisch, Harold, *The Zionist Revolution: A New Perspective* (London and Tel Aviv, 1978).

Fleming, Gerald, *Hitler and the Final Solution* (Oxford and London, 1985, 1986).

Focillon, Henri, *The Year 100* (New York, Paris and London, 1952).

The Art of the West in the Middle Ages, 2 vols, 3rd edn, trans. Donald King (Oxford, 1980).

Frend, W. H. C., *Martyrdom and Persecution in the Early Church: A Study of a Conflict from the Maccabees to Donatus* (Oxford, 1965).

Freud, Sigmund, *Character and Culture* (New York, 1963)

Letters to his Fiancée, December 1883 (London, 1960).

Fulcher of Chartres, *A History of the Expedition to Jerusalem 1095–1127*, trans. and ed. Frances Rita Ryan (Knoxville, 1969).

Gabrieli, Francesco (trans. and ed.), *Arab Historians of the Crusades*, trans. from the Italian by E. J. Costello (London, 1978, 1984).

Muhammad and the Conquests of Islam, trans. Virginia Luling and Rosamund Linell (London, 1968).

'Islam in the Mediterranean World', in Joseph Schacht and C. E. Bosworth (eds), *The Legacy of Islam* (2nd edn, Oxford, 1979).

Gauvard, Claude, 'La Chase aux hérétiques', *L'Histoire*, 47 (Paris, 1982).

Geoffrey of Villehardouin and John of Joinville, *Chronicles of the Crusades*, trans. and ed. M. R. B. Shaw (London, 1963).

Gibbon, Edward, *The Decline and Fall of the Roman Empire*, abridged in one volume, ed. Dero E. Saunders (London, 1980).

Gilmour, David, *Lebanon: The Fractured Country* (London, 1983).

Gordon, A. D., *Selected Essays* (New York, 1938).

Greenberg, Blu, *On Women and Judaism: A View from Tradition* (Philadelphia, 1981).

Gresh, Alain, *The PLO: The Struggle Within, Towards an Independent Palestinian State*, trans. A. M. Berrett (London, 1985).

Grunberger, Richard, *A Social History of the Third Reich* (London, 1971).

Harkabi, Y., *Arab Attitudes to Israel* (Jerusalem, 1972).

Havighurst, Alfred. F. (ed.), *The Pirenne Thesis* (Boston, 1965).

Hays, H. R., *The Dangerous Sex: The Myth of Feminine Evil* (London, 1966).

Heer, Friedrich, *The Medieval World, 1100–1350*, trans. Janet Sondheimer (London, 1962).

Hegland, Mary, 'Two Images of Husain: Accommodation and Revolution in an

Iranian Village', in Nikkie R. Keddie (ed.), *Religion and Politics in Iran: Shiism from Quietism to Revolution* (London, 1983).

Heikal, Mohamed, *Autumn of Fury: The Assassination of Sadat* (London, 1983, 1986).

Heimert, Alan, and Delbanco, Andrew (eds), *The Puritans in America: A Narrative Anthology* (Cambridge, Mass., 1985).

Herrman, Klaus, 'Politics and the "Divine Promise"', in EAFOD and AJAZ (eds), *Judaism or Zionism: What Difference for the Middle East?* (London, 1986).

Herzl, Theodor, *The Jewish State* (London, 1896).

    The Complete Diaries of Theodor Herzl, ed. Raphael Patai (New York, 1960).

Hess, Moses, *Rome and Jerusalem* (New York, 1943).

Hill, Rosalind (trans. and ed.), *The Deeds of the Franks and the Other Pilgrims to Jerusalem* (London, 1962).

Holt, P. M. (ed.), *The Eastern Mediterranean Lands in the Period of the Crusades* (Oregon, 1977).

Howarth, Stephen, *The Knights Templar* (London, 1982).

Hussain, Asaf, *Islamic Iran: Revolution and Counter-Revolution* (London, 1985).

John of Joinville, *The Life of St Louis*, trans. René Hague, ed. Natalie de Wailly (London, 1955).

Johnson, Paul, *A History of the Jews* (London, 1987).

Josephus, *The Jewish War*, trans. G. A. Williamson (London, 1959).

Kantorowicz, Ernst, *Frederick the Second, 1194–1250*, trans. E. O. Lorimer (London, 1931).

Kaplan, Michel, 'Le Sac de Constantinople', *L'Histoire*, 47 (Paris, 1982).

Kedar, Benjamin Z., *Crusade and Mission: European Approaches Towards the Muslims* (New Jersey, 1984).

Kedar, B. Z., Mayer, H. E., and Smail, R. C. (eds), *Outremer: Studies in the History of the Crusading Kingdom of Jerusalem. Presented to Joshua Prawer* (Jerusalem, 1982).

Keddie, Nikkie R. (ed), *Religion and Politics in Iran: Shiism from Quietism to Revolution* (New Haven and London, 1983).

Keneally, Thomas, *Schindler's Ark* (London and New York, 1982).

Kepel, Gilles, *The Prophet and Pharaoh: Muslim Extremism in Egypt*, trans. Jon Rothschild (London, 1985).

Khan, Muhammad Zafrulla, *Islam: Its Meaning for Modern Man* (London, 1962, 1980).

Kobler, Franz, *The Vision was There* (London, 1956).

    Napoleon and the Jews (New York, 1976).

Krey, August C., *The First Crusade: The Accounts of Eye-Witnesses and Participants* (Princeton and London, 1921).

Lacqueur, Walter, *A History of Zionism* (New York, 1972).

Lacqueur, Walter, and Rubin, Barry (eds), *The Israel–Arab Reader: A Documentary History of the Middle East Conflict* (4th edn, revised and updated, London, 1984).

Lane-Poole, Stanley, *The Moors in Spain* (London and New York, 1890).

    Saladin and the Fall of Jerusalem (London and New York, 1898).

Lawrence, T. E., *Seven Pillars of Wisdom: A Triumph* (London, 1926, 1935).

    The Letters of T. E. Lawrence of Arabia, ed. David Garnett (London, 1964).

Lecler, J., *Tolerance and the Reformation* (London, 1960).

Leslie, S. Clement, *The Rift in Israel: Religious Authority and Secular Democracy* (London, 1971).

Lewis, Bernard, *The Assassins* (London, 1967).

    Islam from the Prophet Mohammad to the Capture of Constantinople, 2 vols, vol I: *Politics and War*, vol II: *Religion and Society* (New York and London, 1976).

The Muslim Discovery of Europe (New York and London, 1982).

The Jews of Islam (New York and London, 1982).

Semites and Anti-Semites: An Inquiry into Conflict and Prejudice (London, 1986).

Lyons, M. C., and Jackson, D. E. P., *Saladin: The Politics of the Holy War* (Cambridge, 1982).

Maalouf, Amin, *The Crusades Through Arab Eyes*, trans. Jon Rothschild (London, 1984).

Maccoby, Hyam, *Revolution in Judaea: Jesus and the Jewish Resistance* (London, 1973).

The Sacred Executioner: Human Sacrifice and the Legacy of Guilt (London, 1982).

Madaule, Jacques, *The Albigensian Crusade: An Historical Essay*, trans. Barbara Wall (London, 1967).

Mâle, Émile, *The Gothic Image: Religious Art in France of the Thirteenth Century*, trans. Dora Nussey (London and New York, 1913).

Mansfield, Peter, *The Arabs* (3rd edn, London, 1985).

Markale, Jean, *Aliénor d'Aquitaine* (Paris, 1983).

Marx, Karl, *Surveys from Exile*, ed. and trans. David Fernbach (London, 1973).

Meinertzhagen, Richard, *Middle East Diary: 1917–1956* (London, 1960).

Meiring, Desmond, *Fire of Islam* (London, 1982).

Mergui, Raphael, and Simonnot, Philippe, *Israel's Ayatollahs: Meir Kahane and the Far Right in Israel* (London, 1987).

Metzger, Jan, Orth, Martin, and Sterzing, Christine (eds), *This Land is Our Land: The West Bank Under Israeli Occupation*, trans. Dan and Judy Bryant, Janet Goodwin and Stefan Schaaf (London, 1983).

Micheau, Françoise, '"Jihad": L'Islam relève le défi', *L'Histoire*, 47 (Paris, 1982).

Migne, J. P., *Patrologia Latina*, 383 vols (Paris, 1864–84).

Mitchell, R. P., *The Society of the Muslim Brothers* (Oxford, 1969).

Morrisson, Cecile, 'La Grande Rupture avec l'Orient', *L'Histoire*, 47 (Paris, 1982).

Mortimer, Edward, *Faith and Power: The Politics of Islam* (London, 1982).

Mottahedeh, Roy, *The Mantle of the Prophet: Religion and Politics in Iran* (London and New York, 1985, and London, 1987).

Murphy, Thomas Patrick (ed.), *The Holy War* (Columbus, 1974).

Musurillo, Herbert (ed. and trans.), *The Acts of the Christian Martyrs* (Oxford, 1972).

Nasir, Sari J., *The Arabs and the English* (2nd edn, London, 1979).

Near, Henry (ed.), *The Seventh Day: Soldiers Talk about the Six Day War* (London, 1970).

Nicholson, R. A., *The Mystics of Islam* (London, 1914).

O'Brien, Conor Cruise, *The Siege: The Saga of Israel and Zionism* (London, 1986).

Odo of Deuil, *De Profectione Ludovici VII in orientem: The Journey of Louis VII to the East*, ed. and trans. Virginia G. Berry (New York, 1948).

Oldenbourg, Zoé, *Le Bûcher de Montségur* (Paris, 1959).

The Crusades, trans. Anne Carter (London, 1966).

Ovendale, Ritchie, *The Origins of the Arab–Israeli Wars* (New York and London, 1984).

Oz, Amos, *My Michael*, trans. Nicholas de Lange (London, 1972, 1984).

The Hill of Evil Counsel, trans. Nicholas de Lange (London, 1978).

Where the Jackals Howl, trans. Nicholas de Lange and Philip Simpson (London, 1980).

Bibliography

In the Land of Israel, trans. Maurice Goldberg-Bartura (London, 1983).

A Perfect Peace, trans. Hillel Halkin (London, 1985).

Palumbo, Michael, *The Palestinian Catastrophe: The 1948 Expulsion of a People from Their Homeland* (London, 1987).

Parisse, Michel, 'Godefroy de Bouillon, le croise exemplaire', *L'Histoire*, 47 (Paris, 1982).

'Les "Profits" de la guerre sainte', *L'Histoire*, 47 (Paris, 1982).

Parkes, J. W., *The Jew and the Medieval Community* (London, 1938).

Parrinder, Geoffrey, *Sex in the World's Religions* (London, 1980).

Pastoureau, Michel, 'La coquille et la croix: les emblèmes des croisés', *L'Histoire*, 47 (Paris, 1982).

Patlagean, Evelyne, 'Les Juifs, les "Infidèles" de l'Europe', *L'Histoire*, 47 (Paris, 1982).

Peretz, Don, 'The Semantics of Zionism, Anti-Zionism and Anti-Semitism', in EAFOD and AJAZ (eds), *Judaism or Zionism: What Difference for the Middle East?* (London, 1986).

Pernoud, Régine, *The Crusaders*, trans. Enid Grant (Edinburgh and London, 1963).

Pirenne, H., *Mohammad and Charlemagne*, trans. Bernard Miall (New York, 1939).

Porges, Walter, 'The Clergy, the Poor and the Non-Combatants on the First Crusade', *Speculum*, 21 (1946).

Potok, Chaim, *Wanderings: A History of the Jews* (New York, 1978).

Prawer, Joshua, *The Latin Kingdom of Jerusalem: European Colonialism in the Middle Ages* (London, 1972).

The World of the Crusades (London, 1972).

Raban, Jonathan, *Arabia Through the Looking Glass* (London, 1979, 1983).

Raedts, P., 'La Croisade des enfants a'-t-elle eu en lieu?', trans. Jacques Bacalu, *L'Histoire*, 47 (Paris, 1982).

'The Children's Crusade of 1212', *Journal of Medieval History*, 3 (1977).

Ranelagh, E. L., *The Past We Share: The Near-Eastern Ancestry of Western Folk Literature* (London, 1979).

Richard, Jean, 'Vie et mort des États croisés', *L'Histoire*, 47 (Paris, 1982).

'La Bataille de Hattin: Saladin défait l'Occident', *L'Histoire*, 47 (Paris, 1982).

Riley-Smith, Jonathan, *The Knights of St John in Jerusalem and Cyprus, 1050–1310* (London, 1967).

The Feudal Nobility and the Kingdom of Jerusalem, 1174–1277 (London, 1973).

What Were the Crusades? (London, 1977).

'Crusading as an Act of Love', *History*, 65 (1980).

'The First Crusade and St Peter', in B. Z. Kedar, H. E. Mayer and R. C. Smail (eds), *Outremer: Studies in the History of the Crusading Kingdom of Jerusalem. Presented to Joshua Prawer* (Jerusalem, 1982).

The First Crusade and the Idea of Crusading (London, 1986).

(With Louise Riley-Smith), *The Crusades: Idea and Reality, 1095–1274* (London, 1981).

Rodinson, Maxime, *Israel: A Colonial–Settler State?* (New York, 1973).

Mohammed, trans. Anne Carter (2nd edn, London, 1981).

Israel and the Arabs, trans. Michael Perl and Brian Pearce (2nd edn, London, 1982).

Cult, Ghetto and State: The Persistence of the Jewish Question (London, 1983).

Rose, Gregory, '*Velayat-e Faqih* and the Recovery of Islamic Identity in the Thought of Ayatollah Khomeini', in Nikkie R. Keddie (ed.), *Religion and Politics in Iran: Shiism from Quietism to Revolution* (New Haven and London, 1983).

Rothschild, Jon (ed. and trans.), *Forbidden Agendas: Intolerance and Defiance in the Middle East. From the Journal Khamsin* (London, 1984).

Runciman, Steven, *A History of the Crusades*, 3 vols (Cambridge, 1954, London, 1965).

  The Medieval Manichee: A Study of the Christian Dualist Heresy (Cambridge, 1960).

Russell, Frederick H., *The Just War in the Middle Ages* (Cambridge, 1979).

Ruthven, Malise, *Islam in the World* (London, 1984).

Said, Edward W., *Orientalism: Western Conceptions of the Orient* (New York and London, 1978, London, 1985).

  The Question of Palestine (London, 1980, 1981).

  Covering Islam: How the Media and the Experts Determine How We See the Rest of the World (New York and London, 1981).

  After the Last Sky (London, 1986).

Saunders, J. J., *A History of Medieval Islam* (London, 1965).

Sayigh, Rosemary, *Palestinians: From Peasants to Revolutionaries* (London, 1979).

Schacht, Joseph, and Bosworth, C. E. (eds), *The Legacy of Islam* (2nd edn, Oxford 1979).

Schiff, Ze'ev, and Ya'ari, Ehud, *Israel's Lebanon War*, trans. Ina Friedman (London, 1985).

Scholem, Gershom, *The Messianic Idea in Judaism, and Other Essays on Jewish Spirituality* (New York, 1971).

Schweid, Eliezer, *The Land of Israel: National Home or Land of Destiny*, trans. Deborah Greniman (New York, 1985).

Shahak, Israel, 'The Jewish Religion and its Attitude to Non-Jews', *Khamsin*, 8 and 9 (1981).

Shahar, Shulamith, *The Fourth Estate: A History of Women in the Middle Ages*, trans. Chaya Galai (New York and London, 1983).

Sharif, Regina, *Non-Jewish Zionism: Its Roots in Western History* (London, 1983).

Sick, Gary, *All Fall Down: America's Fateful Encounter with Iran* (New York and London, 1985).

Sigal, P. A., 'Et les Marcheurs de Dieu prirent les armes', *L'Histoire*, 47 (Paris, 1982).

Sivan, E., *Modern Arab Historiography of the Crusades* (Tel Aviv, 1973).

Southern, R. W., *The Making of the Middle Ages* (Oxford 1953, London, 1987).

  Western Views of Islam in the Middle Ages (Cambridge, Mass., 1962).

  Western Society and the Church in the Middle Ages (London, 1970).

Sulaiman, Khalid A., *Palestine and Modern Arab Poetry* (London, 1984).

Taheri, Amir, *The Spirit of Allah: Khomeini and the Islamic Revolution* (London, 1985, 1987).

Talbi, Mohamad, 'Saint Louis: voir Tunis et mourir', *L'Histoire*, 47 (Paris, 1982).

Thomas, D. M., *The White Hotel* (London and New York, 1981).

Thomas, Keith, *Religion and the Decline of Magic* (London, 1971).

Toland, *Adolf Hitler* (London and New York, 1976).

Tuchman, Barbara W., *Bible and Sword: How the British Came to Palestine* (New York and London, 1957, 1982).

al-Udhari, Abdullah (trans. and ed.), *Victims of a Map, A Bilingual Anthology of Arabic Poetry* (London, 1984).

Usama Ibn Mundiqh, *An Arab–Syrian Gentleman and Warrior in the Period of the Crusades*, trans. P. K. Hitti (New York, 1929).

Vauchez, André, 'Saint Bernard, un prédicateur irrésistible', *L'Histoire*, 47 (Paris, 1982).

Ward, Barbara, *Miracles and the Medieval Mind* (London, 1982).

Watt, W. Montgomery, *Muhammad at Mecca* (Oxford, 1953).
    Muhammad at Medina (Oxford, 1956).
    Muhammad: Prophet and Statesman (Oxford, 1961).
    A History of Islamic Spain (Edinburgh, 1965).
    The Influence of Islam on Medieval Europe (Edinburgh, 1972).
    'Islam and the Holy War', in Thomas Patrick Murphy (ed.), *The Holy War* (Columbus, 1974).
    'The Significance of the Early Stages of Imami Shiism', in Nikkie R. Keddie (ed.), *Religion and Politics in Iran: Shiism from Quietism to Revolution* (New Haven and London, 1983).
William, Archbishop of Tyre, *A History of Deeds Done Beyond the Sea*, 2 vols, trans. E. A. Babcock and A. C. Krey (New York, 1943).
Williams, Watkin W., *St Bernard of Clairvaux* (Manchester, 1935).
Wolff, Philippe, *The Awakening of Europe*, trans. Anne Carter (London, 1968).
Wood, Charles T., *The Age of Chivalry: Manners and Morals, 1000–1450* (London, 1970).
Wright, Robin, *Sacred Rage: The Crusade of Modern Islam* (London, 1986).
Yadin, Yigael, *Masada: Herod's Fortress and the Zealot's Last Stand*, trans. Moshe Pearlman (London, 1966).
Yehoshua, A. B., *The Lover*, trans. Philip Simpson (New York, 1977, London, 1985).
    A Late Divorce, trans. Hillel Halkin (New York and London, 1984, London, 1985).

Index

Picture Acknowledgements

Picture Story 1 (plates 1–8). The British Library: 1, 2, 3 below. *Daily Express:* 6 above. Mary Evans Picture Library: 6 below, 7 above left. The John Hillelson Agency/photo Marc Riboud: 4 above left. Kobal Collection: 7 below left, right. Private Collection: 8. The Royal Library (Kungliga biblioteket), Stockholm: 3 above. Frank Spooner Pictures/Gamma: 4 above right, below, 5. Zed Books Ltd, London. Detail of jacket artwork by Henry Iles for *Through the Hebrew Looking-Glass, Arab Stereotypes in Children's Literature*, 1986, by Fouzi El Asmar: 6 centre right.

Picture Story II (plates 1–16). Mohamed Amin/Camerapix: 4. ARXIU-MAS: 12 insert below left. BBC Hulton Picture Library: 6 below, 6–7. The British Library: 1, 6 above left. Musée de Dijon, Bibliotheque Municipal: 13 above. Sonia Halliday Photographs: 2 below right, 12 photo Jane Taylor. André Held: 2 below left. The John Hillelson Agency: 2 above photo Dr Georg Gerster; 5 above, 10–11 photos J.P. Laffont/Sygma; 13 below, 15 below, 14–15 photos W. Karel/Sygma; 14 insert above right photo Moshe Milner/Sygma. Impact Photos: 3 above photo Mark Cator. Network Photographers: 3 below left and right photos Barry Lewis; 16 photo Mike Abrahams. Popperfoto: 7 above left and right, 8 below left, 8–9. Zev Radovan: 5 below. Frank Spooner Pictures/Gamma: 4 insert above right, 9 above left, 15 above.

Picture Story III (plates 1–8). ARXIU-MAS: 1. Bridgeman Art Library: 2 below. The British Library: 2, 3 above left, below. Sonia Halliday Photographs: 8 photo Barrie Searle. Lauros-Giraudon: 3 above right. Network Photographers: 5 above left photo Mike Abrahams; 5 below right photo Bar Lewis. Prado Museum, Madrid: 4 photo Scala. Frank Spooner Pictures/Gamma: 6, 7.